FAITH FOR TODAY:
Pope John Paul II's
Catechetical Teaching

FAITH FOR TODAY:
Pope John Paul II's Catechetical Teaching

RICHARD M. HOGAN
and
JOHN M. LeVOIR

Doubleday

NEW YORK   LONDON   TORONTO   SYDNEY   AUCKLAND

Nihil obstat: David A. Dillon
                    Censor Librorum

Imprimatur: ✠ John R. Roach, D. D.
                    Archbishop of St. Paul and Minneapolis
                    February 22,1988
                    Feast of Peter, Apostle

The *nihil obstat* and *imprimatur* are official declarations that a book or pamphlet is free of doctrinal or moral error. No implication is contained therein that those who have granted the *nihil obstat* and *imprimatur* agree with the contents, opinions, or statements expressed.

Published by Doubleday, a division of
Bantam Doubleday Dell Publishing Group, Inc.,
666 Fifth Avenue, New York, New York 10103

Doubleday and the portrayal of an anchor with a dolphin
are trademarks of Doubleday, a division of
Bantam Doubleday Dell Publishing Group, Inc.

Library of Congress Cataloging-in-Publication Data

Hogan, Richard M.
    Faith for today : John Paul II's catechetical teaching / Richard
M. Hogan and John M. LeVoir. — 1st ed.
        p.   cm.
    Bibliography: p.
    Includes index.
    1. Catholic Church—Doctrines—History—20th century.
2. John Paul II, Pope, 1920-   . I. LeVoir, John M., 1946-   .
II. Title.
BX1751.2.H625 1988
230'.2—dc19   88-18808
                                                            CIP

BG

Contents

Chapter 4: The Incarnation

Chapter 5: The Church as the Person of Christ

Chapter 6: Revelation: Scripture and Tradition

Chapter 7: The Sacraments

Chapter 8: Grace

Chapter 9: Morality

Preface

The first words of the Acts of the Apostles, "In the first book," are very appropriate for this preface. In our first book, *Covenant of Love,* we demonstrated that John Paul II has developed a new theological synthesis. This new synthesis of faith and reason is founded on the philosophical basis of phenomenology. Phenomenology and the faith are linked together through the reference in Genesis to our creation in the image and likeness of God.

In this present work, we present the Catholic faith within the framework of the Pope's new theological synthesis. It might be said that *Covenant of Love* proved that there was a new synthesis and briefly described it. This work applies that synthesis to the corpus of the faith. We think the results are positive. Of course, it is possible to read this entire work without knowing or even referring to the new synthesis specifically. In other words, the new synthesis provides the outline and the method for the presentation of the faith. Much as the general reader enjoys the results of a scientific investigation without understanding the theories behind those results, so the general reader of this volume might read it with great profit without knowing the specifics of its underlying theological synthesis. We offer this work to all, experts and non-experts, as a way to come to a better understanding of the Catholic faith. It is our hope that the present volume is written in such a style that it will be accessible to everyone who wishes to read it.

We said in *Covenant of Love* that we had incurred a responsibility towards John Paul II because we had received the priceless gift of truth from him. It was true at the time *Covenant of Love* was written, and it is even more true now. In the past years, we have learned even more through the homilies, speeches, addresses, and writings of John Paul II. Having received such a precious gift, we have some obligation to make a response. Thus, we offer this book to the reading public, Catholic and non-Catholic alike.

It should be noted that certain points pertaining to the theology of the body and to the familial and worker *communions of persons* have been re-worked from their presentation in *Covenant of Love*. In this volume, these points are presented in parts of Chapters 2 and 3, and to a lesser extent in Chapter 9. In addition, some material in Chapter 5, "The Church as the Person of Christ," is similar to the discussion of the Church in *Covenant of Love*.

Traditionally, Catholic theology has begun with a consideration of God as one and triune. We have followed that tradition as has John Paul II in his current catechetical series delivered at the Wednesday audiences in Rome. In fact, the teaching on God and the Trinity (Chapter 1) determines the structure of the entire work. The consideration of creation (Chapter 2) and of God's providence after original sin (Chapter 3) shows forth God's power, which is usually attributed to the Father. The wisdom of God, attributed to God the Son, is evident in the chapters on Christ (Chapter 4), the Church (Chapter 5), the exercise of the prophetic office of the Church (Chapter 6), i.e., Scripture and Tradition, and in the study of the priestly office of the Church (Chapter 7), i.e., the sacraments. Under the rubric of grace (Chapter 8), we consider God's work of sanctification, which shows God's love and is attributed to the Holy Spirit. While the work on grace views our sanctification more from God's point of view, the study of our role in our own sanctification is emphasized in morality (Chapter 9). By commenting on each of the commandments, the ninth chapter might seem to return to the topic of revelation (i.e., seemingly more properly considered under the topic of God's wisdom). However, since the commandments suggest a norm for human behavior, i.e., they suggest how we can live as images of God, they are integral to our participation in our own sanctification.

Power, wisdom, and love are related to the triple offices of Christ: prophet, priest, and king. A prophet reveals truth, and clearly God as Truth or Wisdom is revealed through Christ's prophetic office. A priest loves. Obviously, God as Love is revealed through Christ's priestly office. In His kingly office, Christ reveals God as Power. The Church continues the mission of Christ and reveals Christ in its triple offices of prophet, priest, and king. We have devoted separate chapters to the Church's prophetic and priestly offices. However, the Church's kingly office is discussed within the Church chapter. A separate chapter on the kingly office of the Church was not attempted because it would become a treatise on Church law and social justice. Law treatises are better left to lawyers. Further, a treatise on social justice would have unduly extended this volume.

Of course, as images of God, we are individually invited to act as God acts. We are empowered to act as God acts, even after sin, through the triple offices of Christ which we share through our Baptism. These triple offices are the basis for our acts: acts of love (priestly), of devotion to truth (prophetic), of self-governance and of dominion over things, i.e., using things for the sake of people (kingly). Thus, these triple offices actually enable us to act with power, wisdom, and love, i.e., to act as God acts. Christ employed the triple offices to reveal God. We need the triple offices to act as images of God.

One further theme of the present volume should be mentioned: the lies of Satan. From the very moment of his own rejection of God, Satan has sought allies. In the garden of Eden, the devil told Eve three lies and she (and, later, Adam) believed him. The lies attacked God as Power, Wisdom (Truth), and Love. The third lie, promising Adam and Eve that they could be like God, knowing good and evil, attacked God as Power. The devil promised Adam and Eve that they could exercise the same power and authority that God does. In the first lie, the devil persuaded Adam and Eve that God had lied. Obviously, this first lie attacks God as Wisdom (Truth). In the second lie,

Satan invited Adam and Eve to be like gods. In this lie, the devil implies that he loves Adam and Eve, i.e., that he wants their self-fulfillment as images of God, and that God does not wish Adam and Eve to become more and more like Him. In other words, especially in this second lie (but also in each of the lies and in the reason for lying), the devil attacks God as Love. These lies of Satan were answered by Christ when the devil tempted Him in the desert. We are enabled to give the same responses Christ gave through the gift of God's grace, which is the source of our share in the triple offices of Christ.

At the beginning of each chapter, we have quoted a segment from the Nicene creed to indicate the doctrinal material discussed in that chapter. At the end of each chapter, we have included a few broad study questions that summarize the main points of the chapter. These can be used for individual reflection or for group discussion. The Scripture citations are all from the Revised Standard Version.

The authors owe the greatest debt to Pope John Paul II. In addition, there are many others who deserve mention. Particularly, we wish to thank Mrs. Mary Jo Smith, who encouraged us, read each chapter as we finished it, and contributed many valuable comments. We also want to thank all the authors who are writing for Image of God (a non-profit company that exists to write a new grade and high school catechism series founded on Pope John Paul II's theology). These men and women also read each chapter. In addition, Mr. Douglas G. Bushman read the entire manuscript and offered suggestions to us. We would like to express our gratitude to Monsignor David A. Dillon, who granted the *Nihil obstat;* and to the Most Reverend John R. Roach, Archbishop of St. Paul and Minneapolis, who gave us the *Imprimatur.* We want to acknowledge Mr. Herman Elsen and Mrs. Marilyn Zappia, who compiled the index. We also wish to mention Mr. James M. Smith, who helped us design the diagrams found in the volume. A note of thanks should go as well to the parishioners of both St. Raphael and St. Charles Borromeo parishes in Minneapolis. In a special way, it includes the members of the St. Raphael Inquiry classes of 1986 and 1987. We are grateful to our pastors, Monsignor Stanley J. Srnec and the Reverend Francis R. Kittock. We wish also to express our gratitude to our families, who have helped us in many intangible ways while this work was prepared, especially to our parents, Earl and Jeanne Hogan, and Marvin and Mary LeVoir, and to Monsignor Richard J. Schuler, and Paul W. LeVoir. Finally without our editor, Patricia Kossmann, this work would never have appeared.

As with *Covenant of Love,* let it be said that the authors of this volume submit *in all things* to the Holy Father. It is their intention to present *his* thought, not their own. With this hope, they place this book into your hands.

Richard M. Hogan
John M. LeVoir
December 1987

List of Abbreviations

I. Abbreviations for the works of John Paul II

CS   *Catechetical Series.* (A series of addresses given at the Wednesday papal audiences. As of the printing of this book, these addresses are still in progress. The addresses are cited in the notes by number, 1–112. The numbers are given in parentheses after the dates in the following list.) All addresses are found in *L'Osservatore Romano* (English Edition). Vol. 17, nos. 50–51, 52–53 [December 10 (1), 17 (2), 24 (3), 1984]. Vol. 18, nos. 2–3, 10–19, 21, 23, 24–32, 35–50, 51–52 [January 14 (4), 21 (5); March 11 (6), 18 (7), 25 (8); April 1 (9), 9 (10), 15 (11), 22 (12), 29 (13); May 6 (14), 13 (15), 27 (16); June 10 (17), 17 (18), 24 (19); July 1 (20), 8 (21), 15 (22), 22 (23), 29 (24); August 5 (25), 12 (26); September 2 (27), 9 (28), 16 (29), 23 (30), 30 (31); October 7 (32), 14 (33), 21 (34), 28 (35); November 4 (36), 11 (37), 18 (38), 25 (39); December 2 (40), 9 (41), 16 (42), 23–30 (43), 1985]. Vol. 19, nos. 2–3, 5, 10–11, 14–26, 28, 30–41, 44–46, 50, 51–52 [January 13 (44), 20 (45); February 3 (46); March 10 (47), 17 (48); April 7 (49), 14 (50), 21 (51), 28 (52); May 5 (53), 12 (54), 19 (55), 26 (56); June 2 (57), 9 (58), 16 (59), 23 (60), 30 (61); July 14 (62), 28 (63);

August 4 (64), 11 (65), 18 (66), 25 (67); September 1 (68), 8 (69), 15 (70), 22 (71), 29 (72); October 6 (73), 13 (74); November 3 (75), 10 (76), 17 (77); December 15 (78), 22–29 (79), 1986]. Vol. 20, nos. 2–3, 5–10, 12, 17–18, 20–23, 26–37, 40–45 [January 12 (80), 19 (81); February 2 (82), 9 (83), 16 (84), 23 (85); March 2 (86), 9 (87), 23 (88); April 27 (89); May 4 (90), 18 (91), 25 (92); June 1 (93), 8 (94), 29 (95); July 6 (96), 13 (97), 20 (98), 27 (99); August 3 (100), 10 (101), 17 (102), 24 (103), 31 (104); September 7 (105), 14 (106); October 5 (107), 12 (108), 19 (109), 26 (110); November 2 (111), 9 (112), 1987].

DM   *Dives in Misericordia, On the Mercy of God.* Boston: Saint Paul Editions, 1981.

DV   *Dominum et Vivificantem, The Lord and Giver of Life. L'Osservatore Romano* (English Edition). Vol. 19, no. 23 (June 9, 1986), pp. 1–16.

FC   *Familiaris Consortio, Apostolic Exhortation on the Family. L'Osservatore Romano* (English Edition). Vol. 14, nos. 51–52 (December 21–28, 1981), pp. 1–19.

LE   *Laborem Exercens, On Human Work. L'Osservatore Romano* (English Edition). Vol. 14, no. 38 (September 21, 1981), pp. 1–13.

LR   *Love and Responsibility.* Translated by H. T. Willetts. New York: Farrar Straus Giroux, 1981.

RH   *Redemptor Hominis, The Redeemer of Man. L'Osservatore Romano* (English Edition). Vol. 12, no. 12 (March 19, 1979), pp. 3–14.

RM   *Redemptoris Mater, The Mother of the Redeemer. L'Osservatore Romano* (English Edition). Vol. 20, no. 30 (March 30, 1987), pp. 1–15.

RP   *Reconciliatio et Paenitentia, Apostolic Exhortation on the Sacrament of Penance. L'Osservatore Romano* (English Edition). Vol. 17, no. 51 (December 17, 1984), pp. 1–15.

SC   *Sign of Contradiction.* Translated by Saint Paul Publications. New York: Seabury Press, 1979.

SD   *Salvifici Doloris, The Christian Meaning of Human Suffering. Origins.* Vol. 13, no. 37 (February 23, 1984), pp. 609, 611–24.

SR   *Sources of Renewal: The Implementation of Vatican II.* Translated by P. S. Falla. New York: Harper and Row, 1980.

WC   *The Way to Christ: Spiritual Exercises.* Translated by Leslie Wearne. San Francisco: Harper and Row, 1982.

II. Abbreviations for the works of the Second Vatican Council

(The works of the Second Vatican Council are all cited from *Documents of Vatican II.* Edited Austin P. Flannery. Grand Rapids, Mich.: William B. Eerdmans Publishing, 1975.)

DVe   *Dei Verbum, Dogmatic Constitution on Divine Revelation* (November 18, 1965), pp. 750–65.

GS   *Gaudium et Spes, Pastoral Constitution on the Church in the Modern World* (December 7, 1965), pp. 903–1001.

LG   *Lumen Gentium, Dogmatic Constitution on the Church* (November 21, 1964), pp. 350–432.

SCo   *Sacrosanctum Concilium, The Constitution on the Sacred Liturgy.* (December 4, 1963), pp. 1–40.

III. Abbreviations for other books and journals

COVENANT   Richard M. Hogan and John M. LeVoir. *Covenant of Love: Pope John Paul II on Sexuality, Marriage, and Family in the Modern World.* Garden City, N.Y.: Doubleday, 1985.

IRNFP   *International Review of Natural Family Planning.*

ND   *The Christian Faith in the Doctrinal Documents of the Catholic Church.* Edited J. Neuner and J. Dupuis. Westminster, Md.: Christian Classics Inc., 1975.

WONDER Richard M. Hogan. *The Wonder of Human Sexuality.* St. Paul: Leaflet Missal, 1985.

1

Man/Woman and God

We believe in one God, the Father, the Almighty. . . . We believe in one Lord, Jesus Christ, the only Son of God, eternally begotten of the Father, God from God, Light from Light, true God from true God, begotten, not made, one in Being with the Father. . . . We believe in the Holy Spirit . . . Who proceeds from the Father and the Son. With the Father and the Son He is worshiped and glorified.

A. The Human Person as an Image of God

The creation of the first man and woman was unique. First of all, it was only of Adam and Eve that God said, "Let Us make man in Our image, after Our likeness."[1] Second, in the creation of Adam and Eve, God used the singular ("man" rather than "men"), even though He had brought forth all the other living creatures in the plural. Only human beings are created as individuals, as unique images of God, who are reflections of God in their own, slightly different ways. The author of Psalm 139 meditated on the mystery of the creation of each individual human being when he wrote, "Thou knowest me right well; my frame was not hidden from Thee, when I was being made in secret, intricately wrought in the depths of the earth. Thy eyes beheld my unformed substance; in Thy book were written, every one of them, the days that were formed for me, when as yet there was none of them."[2] God creates every human being as a unique individual who fashions his own personal history and biography. This cannot be said of the plants and animals or of the inanimate things God created.

While the Scriptures reveal in the objective order the unique creation of each and every man and woman as an image of God, most people have subjective evidence of their own individuality. Most experience themselves as unique individuals. People experience themselves as persons, as beings capable of knowing and choosing. They are able to gaze inwardly at themselves as they think and choose. For example, in viewing one of the glories of nature (the Grand Canyon, an ocean, a mountain peak), people not only see the canyon, the ocean, or the mountain, they also "see" themselves, so to speak, as they view it. They experience themselves as individuals who are thinking about the ocean, the canyon, or the mountain, and they experience themselves as people who have chosen to view the ocean, the canyon, or the mountain. They realize that they are persons, beings endowed with the possibility of thinking and choosing. This self-awareness of one's own being leads most people to recognize that they are each unique, individual persons. Almost all of us come to realize that no one else has experienced the same things in quite the same way as we have. Of course, most of us also recognize that other human beings are persons and are capable of knowing themselves through their own self-awareness. Most, if not all of us, realize that others are unique in themselves because they have had their own individual experiences.

In addition to the discovery of one's own uniqueness and the uniqueness of all other human persons, most of us come to know that we are not the source or foundation for the things that exist in the world around us or for our own being. Gazing at an ocean, most people are drawn to the discovery that this vast body of water exists independently of them. With this realization, the question arises, "Where did it come from?" But immediately upon posing this question, we realize that we must ask the same question about ourselves. The second and much more profound question looms before each and every human being: "But where did *I* come from?"

Of course, the sciences provide theories concerning the origin of the oceans. But science can only probe the history of nature to a certain point. The origins of the world are shrouded in mystery. Questions unanswerable by the sciences arise, e.g., "What began it all?" and "Where and how was the earth made?" As John Paul has written, scientific research *"always leaves an opening for further questions* in an endless process which reveals in reality an immensity, a harmony, a finality which is not explainable in terms of causality or through scientific resources alone. To this is added the *irrepressible question of meaning*, of higher rationality."[3] Science leads us to the conclusion that the world has an origin and a cause outside of space and time. As the Pope put it, "This universe in constant movement postulates a cause which, in giving it being, has communicated to it this movement and continues to sustain it. Without such a supreme cause, the world and every movement in it would remain 'unexplained,' and 'inexplicable,' and our intelligence would not be satisfied."[4] In another passage, the Pope remarks, "How is it possible that the immense progress in the knowledge of the universe, . . . its laws and its happenings, its structures and its energies, does not lead everyone to recognize the first principle, without Whom the world cannot be explained?"[5]

But there still remains the profound question "Where did I come from?" The answer to this question is partially given in genealogies, but they, like the scientific answers, serve to raise more questions. Clearly, human beings have human parents, but where did the first ones come from?

Yet, even if we were to solve the origins of our first parents, there still remains a thorny issue regarding our existence. While parents may give children flesh and blood, where do the spiritual capacities of thought and free choice have their origin? These powers lie beyond corporeal existence. Where did they come from? In experiencing himself, the human person faces not only the problem of his physical existence, but also the question of the foundation of his spiritual powers. If human beings are not responsible for the existence of mere material creation, e.g., oceans, canyons, and mountains, how much more unlikely is it that they are responsible for their own existence, which is far more than mere materiality? If we did not create the material world, how could we possibly create the spiritual beings that we are? Even if the origins of the material world might be explained by causes within this world (which is, as we have seen, impossible), the existence of the faculties of thinking and choosing in every human person would still be a profound mystery, calling forth an answer that lies beyond the confines of this earthly, material world! Human existence points to a thinking and choosing being greater than any human being. Human existence points to God!

B. God: The Divine Nature

Human life suggests not only the existence of a living God, but also "who" and "what" God is. As John Paul has noted, "Seeing that man is created in the image and likeness of God, there is reason for speaking of God 'in the image and likeness' of man."[6] Person signifies "who" someone is. Nature signifies "what" someone is. Since human beings are living persons with a nature that includes the powers of thinking and freely choosing, God must be a living, personal being possessing the powers of thinking and freely choosing.[7]

This living, free, personal being (God) Who created the world and the first human persons must not only be the source of the existence of the world and everything in it (including human persons), but He must also be the foundation of His own being. For a moment, imagine that God is not the source of His own being. In that case, some other being created Him. We might call this second being, the creator of God, god-2. But, of course, the question immediately arises, "Who created god-2?" We could suggest that god-2 was created by god-3. Very soon, it becomes quite clear that we have the same problem we had before! There cannot be an unending series of beings who were created by others. There must be an origin point: a being Who created everything but Who Himself is not created. That being we call God. God is the uncaused cause, the origin point, Who Himself is the source of His own being. He is one, and not many. There can be no god-2 or god-3. There is only one God, and He created the world and everyone in it.

God has confirmed this judgment about Himself many times in the Scriptures. Most notably, He indicated that He is the Creator and the source of His own existence when He revealed His name to Moses. Moses was pasturing his flock near Mount Horeb and saw a burning bush that was not consumed by the fire. God spoke to Moses from the burning bush and asked him to undertake the mission to free the Israelites from the slavery imposed by their Egyptian masters. Moses knew the people would want to know the name of God. God told Moses, "I am Who I am" (Yahweh).[8] "According to the tradition of Israel, *the name expresses the essence.*"[9] This name, "I am Who I am," expresses being or existence. "He *Who is* [i.e., God] expresses the very *essence* of God, which is *self-existence.*"[10] "He Who creates—the Creator—possesses existence in Himself and from Himself *(ens a se)*. To be pertains to His substance: His essence is to be."[11] Thus, God Himself, in revealing His own name, told Moses, and through him all of us, that He (Yahweh) is the uncaused cause, the one being Who is the source of His own being. In revealing this, God also indicated, as John Paul noted in the quote above, that His essence—what God is in Himself—is to exist. Existence or being defines What God is. Of all the things and persons in the universe, only God's essence is to be (existence). In the simplest terms, God *is.*

Since God *is,* no divine attribute or activity exists that does not belong to His essence. Every perfection, every attribute, and every act of God is fully present and pertains to What God is, i.e., they pertain to God's essence. For example, God is not only beautiful, He is beauty. God not only loves, He is Love. God not only knows truth, He is Truth. In other words, God has no parts. God is perfectly simple. (In this context, simplicity means without parts or distinctions, e.g., body and soul, knowing and loving.)

In creating the world, God gives being to the world. However, He is Being itself. Thus, when He created the world, He shared Himself with the world. Love is precisely the gift of oneself. Creation thus reveals the uncaused cause as One Who loves. John Paul summarizes this point quite well when he writes, "To create means to give (especially to give existence). And he who gives, loves."[12] The book of Wisdom echoes the same thought in the passage "For Thou lovest all things that exist, and hast loathing for none of the things which Thou hast made, for Thou wouldst not have made anything if Thou hadst hated it."[13]

Pope Paul VI summarized the foregoing points when he said that God is *"He Who is,* as He Himself revealed to Moses; and He is *Love,* as the Apostle John teaches us; so that these two names, *Being and Love,* ineffably express the very divine reality of Him Who wished to make Himself known to us and Who, inhabiting inaccessible light, is in Himself above every name, above all things and above every created intelligence."[14]

God as the Creator, the uncaused cause, brought the world into existence out of nothing. The act of bringing things into existence out of nothing is an act of power, of power beyond our comprehension. God, then, is all-powerful, omnipotent. Only He, as the uncaused cause, has the capacity to give being to the things of this world: *"The Creator's omnipotence* is shown . . . in calling creatures into existence from nothingness."[15]

Further, it is clear that God has all perfections. As mentioned above,[16] God is the uncaused cause. No one and no thing acts upon Him. Rather, He is the cause of everything that has existed, does exist, and will exist. In order to give, the giver must possess what he wishes to give. Since God is the cause of all things in all their perfections, He must possess all these perfections. In addition, He must possess not only all the perfections that actually exist, but also all those that created beings might be able to attain. In a word, He must be perfect, lacking nothing. Further, if He were to lack something, He would not be the fullness of being. He would not be "I am."[17] Clearly, God is the most perfect, living, personal being: He possesses the greatest intellect and will; He is perfectly one; He is Being; He is perfectly simple; He is perfect Love; and He is almighty.

As the uncaused cause, God cannot change under the influence of an outside cause. For example, He cannot react to things that occur because, quite obviously, He is the cause of all things. He does not react, but rather acts. Created things do not act on Him. Rather, He acts on them. He cannot, therefore, "be taken by surprise" at what occurs. It is quite clear that if God were to react or to change because of some influence or cause outside of Himself, He would not be the uncaused cause. But He is the uncaused cause, and therefore He does not change in reaction to outside influences.

Still it might be conceivable that God could cause Himself to change. It could be argued that since we are like God, He is like us. Even the Pope writes that "Seeing that man is created in the image and likeness of God, there is reason for speaking of God 'in the image and likeness' of man."[18] We change our minds and our habits. We change our ways and repent of our sins. Can it be suggested that God changes in the same way? No!

It is important to notice that when we make changes, even if they be unfortunate changes, we perceive them as improvements. No one undertakes the difficult process of altering a long-standing practice unless he makes the judgment that the change will somehow improve his life, or the lives of family or friends. In a word, changes are made when there are benefits to be gained. But God is perfect already. He cannot change because He cannot improve himself. (Clearly, this does not mean that there is no reason for speaking of God " 'in the image and likeness of man.' . . . This anthropomorphism *does not obscure God's transcendence:* God is not reduced to human dimensions."[19] God is not like us in our imperfections, but rather in our perfections. We change to improve. God does not change because He is perfection. His perfection is an image of our perfections. In this sense, God is in the image of man.)

The perfection and changelessness of God imply that He is totally spiritual and immaterial, i.e., without a body. Inherent in created things is a certain corruptibility, a decline. Material things are "by their nature . . . contingent and passing, and therefore *corruptible.*"[20] If God, as God, were to possess a body, its corruptibility would be contrary to God's perfection and His changelessness. God in His divinity does not possess a body. He is totally spiritual and immaterial. (Of course, in this context, we are speaking of God in His divine nature. God the Son incarnate, i.e., Jesus Christ, possesses both a divine and a human nature. The human body pertains to human nature. Thus, Christ has a human body because He is a man. However, His divine nature is totally spiritual and immaterial.) "Spirituality signifies intellect and free will."[21] God's intelligence exists, as all intelligence does, to know the truth. Since everything in God is perfect, God knows all truths. In fact, He is Truth. Since a will exists to make free choices, it must be free. In fact, God must be perfect freedom. "God is *intelligence, will,* and *liberty* in an infinite degree just as He is also *all perfection* in an infinite degree."[22] A further implication of God's spirituality is that we cannot see Him with our bodily eyes.

Since God does not change, He stands, as it were, outside of time. Without change, there is no time because time is the measurement of the process of change. The basic units of time mark and measure the changing positions of the earth and of the heavenly bodies. The twenty-four hours of the day measure the earth's rotation on its axis. The year marks the orbit of the earth around the sun. The month measures the moon's orbit around the earth. Without these changes, the most basic units of time would cease to exist because there would be no changes for them to mark. Of course, the concept of divine timelessness is difficult to understand because it is totally outside of human experience. In a way, it is depicted in certain movies and television episodes. In some cases, the plot calls for all but one or two characters to be frozen in place. All change stops (except for the one or two characters). Almost invariably, the chronometers, the clocks, and other timepieces also stop. Change has ceased as has time! God is timeless because He is changeless. He is changeless because He is the uncaused cause.

Since God exists, as it were, outside of time, He is *"eternity it-self."*[23] Eternity is a " 'now,' a 'present' subsisting and unchanging."[24] Since God is timeless, God lives in the present and everything He creates is present to Him at the same time. In the same gaze God sees Adam and Eve, Abraham, Isaac, Jacob, Mary, all those living now, and all those living at the second coming. It is as though God sees all time and the whole world frozen on a movie screen. Nothing happens for God "before" or "after." Everything is in the present. God sees everything on the "screen" in one perpetual, everlasting "look." Therefore, there is no question of God's predestining us in the sense of determining beforehand whether we will be in heaven, purgatory, or hell. He sees all our decisions at once. There is not, and could never be, any question of a pre-determination that would interfere with our free will.[25]

Since God is changeless and immaterial, He does not have emotions. The English word "emotion" originated from the Latin *ex-movere*, which means "to move out of." "Emotion" denotes an inter-

nal reaction within a living body. Common human experience
teaches that emotion is a reaction to a stimulus originating from
either outside or inside oneself. This reaction is a change in oneself.
Since God is changeless, He cannot be subject to emotions. Further,
emotions involve a physical reaction in a living body. Since God in
the divine nature does not have a body, He cannot have emotions.
(Of course, God, as man, i.e., God the Son made man, feels emotions
in His humanity. He experiences emotions in His human nature. If
the incarnation had never occurred, God would not have experienced emotions because emotion denotes a change in a living body
and the divine nature does not possess a body and is incapable of any
change whatsoever.)

Although God in His divinity does not experience emotions, He
does love. In fact, as we have noted, God is Love. Since God loves
and He does not experience emotions, it is important to realize that
love is not an emotion. Love is the choice to give oneself to another.
It is a choice made in the will founded on the truth known by the
intellect. In human beings, will-choices are almost always accompa-
nied by emotions because the body is the expression of the person,
i.e., the expression of what is known by the mind and chosen by the
will.[26] But in God, there are no emotions, and therefore in Him love
is a purely spiritual act, an act of the will.

This truth does not imply that God loves with any less intensity.
As John Paul notes, "In the 'depths of God' there is a Father's love
that, faced with man's sin, in the language of the Bible reacts so
deeply as to say: 'I am sorry that I have made him.' "[27] As Cardinal
Ratzinger has written, "Christian piety must involve the senses,
which receive their order and unity from the heart. . . . It is clear
that such piety, centered in the heart, corresponds to the image of
the Christian God, Who has a heart."[28] In this context, "heart" con-
notes the seat of feelings. How can God have a "heart," if He does
not have emotions? He has a "heart" because He loves. He gives
Himself to the world, and most especially to those made in His
image and likeness. When love is given, it should be received. If it is
not received, it can be wounded. In a sense, God "feels" the wounds
of rejected love. Even human beings sense this spiritual suffering. For

example, when children reject the love of their parents as the prodigal son did in the parable,[29] there is emotional pain, but there is also a spiritual sense of pain and suffering. The parent "longs for" the child. The parent desires to help and to aid the child. The "heart" of God is the heart of a loving father. God "longs for" the children who have rejected Him. God wishes to aid and to help His children, as any human father would. This is not emotion, but it is spiritual love!

God "longs for" all of us and therefore He reaches down to us through creation, revelation, and sanctification.[30] We cannot reach up to Him because He dwells "in unapproachable light."[31] God is unapproachable because He is infinite, i.e., He is the fullness of being (Being itself). Further, as the uncaused cause, He is infinite because He is eternity. In addition, since He is every possible perfection imaginable, He is infinite: "God superlatively surpasses all that exists outside of Him."[32]

Since God is infinite, He is immeasurable, incomprehensible, and transcendent. He is immeasurable because His essence "exceeds all that could be thought in the human mind."[33] Further, immeasurability implies incomprehensibility, i.e., God remains a mystery to us: "God . . . remains for the human intellect a something which is at the same time *known and incomprehensible.*"[34] Even God's attributes are not completely comprehensible because, as mentioned above,[35] they pertain to God's essence. Finally, God's incomprehensibility implies His transcendence. He "exceeds all that exists in the created world [including the human mind] and all that could be thought in the human mind."[36] He is "completely transcendent in regard to the world. By His essence, by His divinity, He 'goes beyond' and infinitely 'surpasses' everything created."[37]

C. God: Three Persons in One Nature

There is no attribute, no mystery, no perfection in God that is more incomprehensible to us than the mystery of the three divine Persons in the one divine unity. Even living with God for all eternity in heaven, we will never fully understand this mystery. "The intellect, however, enlightened by faith, can *in a certain way* grasp and explain the meaning of the dogma. Thus, it can bring close to man the mystery of the inmost life of the triune God."[38] Therefore, it is possible for us to examine this mystery in some detail. The purpose of such examination is not to comprehend the Trinity—an impossible task. Rather, the purpose is to appreciate more and more the glory and wonder of God. Such an examination might be compared to the jeweler's study of a beautiful diamond. He looks at it from different angles not to comprehend it or even to understand it fully, but rather to appreciate its beauty.

However, at first glance, the study of the Trinity seems doomed to failure. God is not a diamond that can be held in one's hand. How is it possible to "gaze" on Him, to "examine" Him from different angles? Of course, that question has already been answered! If man is made in the image of God, then God is, in a certain sense, " 'in the image and likeness' of man."[39] Clearly, it should be possible for us to examine ourselves and, guided by the Gospel, come to some understanding of God. This procedure was followed at the beginning of the discussion on God's nature.[40] It should be possible to follow the same procedure in "gazing" on God as a trinity of Persons in the one Godhead.

In regard to the Trinity there are four distinct "angles" or "viewpoints" to consider. First, there is the mystery of the processions. The question asked is: Why are there three Persons? The second consideration involves the relationship among the three Persons. The question asked is: What distinguishes each Person from the other two? The third mystery involves the activity of the Trinity within itself. The question is: What do the three Persons do among Themselves? While the first three "viewpoints" consider the Trinity in itself or, better, within itself, the fourth area of examination studies the Trinity as it acts outside of itself, i.e., as it acts towards the created order, especially towards human beings. In this fourth area, the question asked is: Does one divine Person or do all three divine Persons act towards human beings?

1. THE PROCESSIONS

At the very beginning of this chapter,[41] the creation of human persons in God's own image was mentioned. Each one of us is a human person with the powers of thinking and choosing, i.e., with a mind and a will. However, as persons, we not only are capable of independent thought and free choice, we are also aware of the thoughts we think and the choices we make. Thus, when we are appreciating a wonder of nature like the Grand Canyon, we know the beauty we are seeing and we also know that we have chosen to look. We have an awareness of our own acts. This self-awareness or consciousness pertains to personhood. Consciousness contains the acts that we knowingly and freely choose. Of course, consciousness mirrors all these acts—those expressed in and through the body and those that remain internal. Our consciousness is a kind of inner image that we have of the acts we knowingly and freely choose. By viewing this inner image, we know ourselves.

Since God is, in a certain sense, a reflection of man,[42] it is evident that God is a personal being Who must have the personal faculties that we have. Clearly, He must have a consciousness of His own acts as each human person has a consciousness of his acts. In other words, there is no doubt that God is aware of His acts of thinking and choosing, and that His consciousness contains His acts of thinking and choosing. God's consciousness is a kind of inner image that He has of all His acts. Thus, through His consciousness God knows Himself.[43]

In a certain sense, God knows Himself "before" He knows anything else. His act of knowing Himself is logically prior to His knowing anything else. In this, God somewhat resembles human beings. Before we learn about the created world, we learn about ourselves. For example, as a child develops and grows, there are the wonderful discoveries of hands, fingers, feet, etc. As human persons, we come to know ourselves before we know the world around us. What is true for us is, in this case, especially true of God. All reality depends upon God. As the Creator, by knowing Himself He knew the world and everything in it "before" it was created. As Being itself, He possesses all the powers and potentialities that are in creation. Thus, God knew Himself and in knowing Himself, He knew creation. Clearly, His "first" act of knowing is the act of knowing Himself. There was nothing else to know!

Since God is perfect, He knows Himself perfectly. In other words, His consciousness contains an identical image of Himself. This image would not be identical to God Himself if it only existed in the mind of God and not in reality. God *is,* i.e., He exists. If His consciousness contains an identical image of Himself, it, too, must exist. This image does exist in reality and *is* the second Person of the blessed Trinity, God the Son. God the Son is begotten from the Father's consciousness of His act of knowing Himself. The second Person mirrors the Father. He is the identical image of the Father. He is the Father's self-concept.

A word in a language signifies a concept or an idea. In fact, it is almost impossible for anyone to think of anything without at the same time thinking of the word for that thing (or, at least, a mental picture of it). In God's act of knowing Himself, He generates a self-concept. This self-concept is signified by a word. Since the self-concept of the Father is perfect, it encompasses all concepts and, therefore, all words. Clearly, the divine self-concept is *the* Word, *par excellence.* St. John confirms this insight when he names Christ the "Word" of God (in Greek, *Logos).*[44] Pope John Paul compared the procession of the Son from the Father to the self-knowledge of human beings: "By analogy with the cognitive process of the human mind, whereby man, in knowing himself, produces an image of himself, an idea, a 'concept,' that is a 'conceived idea,' which from the Latin *verbum* (word) is frequently called the interior word, we *dare to think of the generation of the Son* or the eternal 'concept' and interior Word of God. God in knowing Himself begets the Word, the Son, Who is God just as the Father."[45]

When the Father "sees" the Son Who is the identical image of the Father, and the Son "sees" the Father Who is the Son's identical likeness, They choose one another, i.e., They love one another. The consciousness of the Father and of the Son contains an inner reflection and image of Their act of love. This image of the love between the Father and the Son is identical to Their love. Since the love of the Father and the Son is real, the identical image of that love in the consciousness of the Father and the Son must actually exist. The Holy Spirit *is* the Love of the Father and the Son. The Holy Spirit proceeds from the Father's and the Son's act of love. Pope John Paul offers a description of the procession of the Holy Spirit: "The Father, Who begets, *loves* the Son Who is begotten, and the Son loves the Father with a love which is identical with that of the Father. . . . At the same time, the Father and the Son are *not only* united by that mutual love as two Persons infinitely perfect, but Their mutual gratification, Their reciprocal Love, proceeds in Them and from Them as a Person: the Father and the Son 'spirate' the Spirit of Love consubstantial with Them."[46] The processions in the Trinity have their source in God's acts of knowing and willing.

The divine processions are not time-related. As mentioned above,[47] God exists outside of time. The processions within the Trinity exist outside of time. They always were, are, and will be. There never was a time when the Son did not exist. There never was a time when the Holy Spirit did not exist. If there were a time when the Son and the Holy Spirit did not exist, neither would be God.

2. THE RELATIONSHIPS

Although it is a fundamental tenet of the Christian faith that there are three Persons in one God, this teaching in no way compromises or diminishes the other equally firm teaching that there is only one God. But there seems to be a difficulty. Since there are three Persons in one God, then there must be distinctions among the Persons. Since there are distinctions, then it would seem that God is not a perfect, simple unity. He would not be one God, but three. However, this is impossible. The problem can be stated in two ways: How can there be three if there is only one? or, How can there be one if there are three? (The difficulty can be approached from either vantage point.)

One might think that a possible explanation of the problem lies in the distinction between person and nature. Nature signifies "what" someone is and person signifies "who" someone is:[48] "Thus, for example, when we speak of 'human nature,' we indicate what makes a man a man, with his essential components and his properties."[49] On the other hand, "A [human] person is he or she who exists as a concrete human being, as an individual possessing humanity, that is, human nature."[50] All human beings share the same humanity, the same human nature. In a sense, they are all one because they are all human, i.e., they have a common human nature. Thus, there is a oneness among all human persons even though every human person is a unique individual. In God, there is one divine nature, but three Persons. If it were possible to establish that God had one divine nature as all men share one human nature, the unity and trinity of God could be explained in the same way as the unity of human nature among the millions of human persons.

However, this distinction is not sufficient in itself because God's nature is not exactly like human nature. Human nature exists separately and distinctly in each and every human person. In God, the divine nature does not exist separately and distinctly in each of the divine Persons because the divine nature is perfect, unified (one), and simple. There are not three individualized, separate, concrete repetitions of the divine nature (in each divine Person) as there are an incalculable number of individualized, separate, concrete repetitions of human nature (in each human person). Thus, the problem that began this discussion remains: How can there be one in three or three in one?

"The reply, which our reason stammers, is based on the concept of 'relation.' The three divine Persons are distinguished among Themselves solely by the *relations* which They have with one another."[51] In everything but Their relationships, the three divine Persons are identical. Our reason "stammers," to use John Paul's phrase, because the relations among the three divine Persons are unlike any relations that human persons experience.

For example, sonship is a relationship. It is a vital relationship only when at least two human persons exist: a living son and at least one living parent. After both parents have died, the son, at least in a certain sense, ceases to be a son. The relationship no longer exists (at least not as it had before). Nevertheless, the human being who was a son does not cease to be a human person just because death has ended the relationship. All human beings are persons because God created them as persons. In other words, a human relationship does not constitute a human person as the divine relationships constitute the three divine Persons in the Trinity. Human relationships do not *make human beings "who" they are,* but the divine relationships do *make the divine Persons "Who" They are.*

In God, then, the divine relationships define the three divine Persons. The Father is Fatherhood itself. Fatherhood defines "Who" He is. The Son is Sonship itself, existing in its own right. Sonship defines "Who" the Son is. The Holy Spirit is Love itself. (Love is a relationship between at least two persons.)[52] He is Love, existing in its own right. Love defines "Who" the Holy Spirit is. In other words, the relations in God are "subsisting."[53] These relations distinguish the three Persons in God from one another. The Father is distinct from the Son precisely because He is Fatherhood and not Sonship. The Son is distinct from the Father because He is Sonship and not Fatherhood. The Holy Spirit is distinct from the Father and the Son because He is Love and not Fatherhood or Sonship.

Since there is a distinction of the divine Persons on the basis of the divine relationships, how is it possible to maintain the unity of God? A solution is suggested by analogy with human relationships. Every human person has a multitude of relationships. A man might be husband, father, brother, son, uncle, great-uncle, grandfather, and even great-grandfather. A woman might be wife, mother, sister, daughter, aunt, great-aunt, grandmother, and even great-grandmother. But the man is only one individual and the woman is only one individual. Both have a multitude of relationships, but both remain one in themselves. If many human relationships can exist within the unity of an individual human being, can that not also be posited of God? Of course it can. (It should be noted that the above analogy does not completely explain the mystery of the Trinity. No human analogy could ever explain the Trinity.) God is three Persons, i.e., three subsisting relations, in one, perfect, and simple Godhead (nature).

3. THE TRINITY AS A *COMMUNION OF PERSONS*

The three divine Persons are perfectly united with one another. Christ said, "All that the Father has is mine."[54] In another passage, Christ indicates the union between Himself and the Holy Spirit when He says that the Holy Spirit "will take what is mine and declare it to you."[55] The Holy Spirit has what is Christ's, and what is Christ's is the Father's. Consequently, there is a total union among the three Persons of the Trinity.

This union within the Holy Trinity exists through the personal choice of each divine Person to give Himself totally to the others. This total self-gift of each Person within the Trinity is founded on the perfect knowledge that each Person has of the other two. This is what divine love is: a personal choice, a will-act, made by each divine Person based on knowledge of the truth, to surrender Himself totally and completely to the other two Persons. The self-donation of each divine Person to the others unites all three in a *communion of Persons.* In effect, among the Persons of the Trinity, there is an attitude, a choice, to act as one. The divine *communion of Persons* is a total union. It is a reciprocal compenetration or mutual indwelling. "The Council of Florence expressed this trinitarian truth in the following words: 'Through this unity . . . the Father is completely in the Son, completely in the Holy Spirit; the Son is completely in the Father, completely in the Holy Spirit; the Holy Spirit is completely in the Father, completely in the Son.' "[56]

The human family, as a loving union of human persons existing in relationships with one another and basing its life on the truth, should reveal the mystery of the Trinity to us, although only partially and very inadequately. Since God is in a certain sense in the image of man,[57] it should not be surprising that human family life expresses, again very inadequately and only partially, some aspects of the triune God.

4. THE TRINITY AND THE CREATED ORDER

The love within the Trinity is perfect and complete. However, God chose to act outside of Himself in creation, revelation, and sanctification. We attribute creation to the Father, revelation to the Son, and sanctification to the Holy Spirit. The almighty power of God (associated more with the Father Who is Power) is most clearly present in creation, the bringing of things into existence from nothing. Since revelation is the unveiling of God's self-knowledge, i.e., wisdom, it is associated more with the Son Who is Wisdom. Sanctification, a sharing in God's own life, is only accomplished by God's loving self-gift of His own life, i.e., of Himself, to human beings. God's self-gift of love is associated more with the Holy Spirit Who is Love. Nevertheless, the power of God (associated with the Father) is shown in God's acts of revelation and sanctification. The wisdom (associated with the Son) is present in creation and in sanctification. The love of God (associated with the Holy Spirit) is present in creation and revelation. As John Paul writes, "Although the work of creation is attributed especially to God the Father—this we profess in the creeds of the faith ('I believe in God the Father Almighty, Creator of heaven and earth')—it is also a truth of faith that the Father, the Son, and the Holy Spirit are the *unique and indivisible* 'principle' of creation."[58] The revelation of God and the sanctification of man are, just as creation, the work of the entire Trinity, Father, Son, and Holy Spirit.

God reveals in creation His power (attributed to the Father). *"The Creator's omnipotence* is shown . . . in calling creatures into existence from nothingness."[59] God the Creator powerfully brings things into existence out of nothing. In the twentieth century, the sciences have offered us incredible feats of power and even majesty. The launch of the Saturn V rocket that sent the first men to the moon comes to mind, as do the truly wondrous miracles wrought daily in our hospitals. But even in this twentieth century, it is not possible to bring things into existence out of nothing. Further, creation is not only an act of God's power, it also reveals God's wisdom. When we see the work of an artist, we perceive the artist's knowledge of his craft. When we see the world, we see a reflection of the divine artist's knowledge. However, in God, all knowledge is included in His own self-knowledge, i.e., in His wisdom, because His self-knowledge is perfect.[60] God's revelation of His wisdom through His creative act is most obvious in the case of man, who is made in God's own image and likeness. When anyone sees another person, he sees an image of God. In a limited way, he sees God, i.e., he sees wisdom (divine self-knowledge). In addition, creation is an act of God's love: "To create means to give (especially to give existence). And he who gives, loves."[61] In creation, the Trinity—Power, Wisdom, and Love—act as one principle.

The work of revelation, the unveiling of God's wisdom, is accomplished most completely through Christ, God the Son (the Wisdom of God) made man. In and through the incarnation and the redemption, God's wisdom is revealed. As the Second Vatican Council taught, Christ is "both the mediator and the sum total of revelation."[62] Christ Himself said in response to Philip, who asked to see the Father, "Have I been with you so long, and yet you do not know Me, Philip? He who has seen Me has seen the Father; how can you say, 'Show us the Father'?"[63] God's wisdom is revealed in every act of Christ, but most especially in Christ's passion, death, and resurrection.[64] In the paschal mystery, Christ revealed God as One Who loves. Clearly, God knows Himself as One Who loves.[65] Thus, in revealing God as Love, Christ revealed the divine self-knowledge, i.e., wisdom. Further, Christ's life is not only the most complete manifestation of God's wisdom, it is also an act of divine power. The power of God can be seen in the union of the two natures in the one divine Person. The power of God is also obviously present in the miracles of Christ and in the resurrection. But the awesome power of God can most clearly be seen in the effect of the paschal mystery: death is conquered with death.[66] In addition, in Christ's revelation of God's wisdom, we see an act of God's love. The incarnation shows us the self-gift (love) of God. God "emptied Himself, taking the form of a servant, being born in the likeness of men."[67] He emptied Himself, i.e., He gave Himself: "And he who gives, loves."[68] God's stupendous love is also marvelously present on the cross: "Greater love has no man than this, that a man lay down his life for his friends."[69] The incarnation and the redemption were the work of the Trinity. In the incarnation and the redemption, the Trinity—Power, Wisdom, and Love—acts as one principle.

God carries on the work of sanctification by giving human beings His very own life (grace).[70] This self-gift of God is clearly identified with the Holy Spirit. Just as it is fitting for the Son, Who is the Wisdom of God, to reveal the truths about God to us, so it is fitting for the Holy Spirit, Who is Love, to sanctify us by giving us God's life. Love unites persons. In the Blessed Trinity, the Holy Spirit (Love) unites Father and Son. In the world, the Holy Spirit through His gift of divine love, i.e., divine life or grace, unites human beings in the union of all those who share God's grace.[71] Further, when God shares His life (grace) with human beings, it is not only an act of His love, it is also an act of His power. In giving Himself to us, God gives us new life. Just as God's gift of human life in His creative act is an act of power, the giving of His divine life is also an act of power. God's caring for those He has blessed with His grace is also an act of His power. He not only gives His divine life, He cares and nurtures that divine life in all those who share it. The awesome number of people who share God's own life indicate the scope and magnitude of His omnipotence exercised through the gift of His own life. In addition, God's sanctifying work reveals His wisdom. All those who share God's life have "put on Christ."[72] They are other "Christs" because they live God's own life. Christ, as the Wisdom of God, revealed divine wisdom. Other "Christs" reveal God's wisdom in a way similar to Christ. In the work of sanctification, the Trinity—Power, Wisdom, and Love—acts as one principle.

It is no wonder that before the mystery of the one, triune God, we stand almost speechless in awe, able only to mutter, "Glory to God in the highest."[73]

FOR REFLECTION

A. How does human self-questioning suggest the existence of God?

B. How are the divine attributes interrelated? For example, how are God's changelessness and His eternity related?

C. Discuss how creation is an expression of the power, wisdom, and love of God.

NOTES

1. See Gen. 1:26.

2. See Ps. 139:14–16.

3. See CS, no. 23.

4. See CS, no. 22.

5. See CS, no. 8.

6. See CS, no. 32.

7. The following paragraphs in this section discuss the divine nature. For a discussion of the Personhood in God, see below, C. God: Three Persons in One Nature, p. 12ff.

8. See Ex. 3:14. See also the entire account beginning in Ex. 3:2.

9. See CS, no. 25.

10. See CS, no. 25.

11. See CS, no. 26.

12. See CS, no. 47.

13. See Wis. 11:24.

14. See CS, no. 26. In this passage, John Paul quotes Pope Paul VI.

15. See CS, no. 47.

16. See Ex. 3:14. See also above, p. 6.

17. See Ex. 3:14.

18. See CS, no. 32.

19. See CS, no. 32.

20. See CS, no. 58.

21. See CS, no. 29.

22. See CS, no. 29.

23. See CS, no. 28.

24. See CS, no. 28.

25. See below, Chapter 8: "Grace," pp. 123–25, where the proper relationship between human freedom, on the one hand, and God's will and His grace, on the other, is considered.

26. See below, Chapter 2: "God's Love: Creation," pp. 37–41.

27. See DV, § 39.

28. See Josef Ratzinger, "The Paschal Mystery as Core and Foundation of Devotion to the Sacred Heart," p. 156, in *Towards a Civilization of Love* (Proceedings of the International Congress on the Heart of Jesus, 1981), English Edition by Ignatius Press (San Francisco: Ignatius Press, 1985), pp. 145–65.

29. See Lk. 15:11–32.

30. See below, pp. 17–20.

31. See 1 Tim. 6:16.

32. See CS, no. 29.

33. See CS, no. 27.

34. See CS, no. 27.

35. See above, p. 5.

36. See CS, no. 27.

37. See CS, no. 26.

38. See CS, no. 40.

39. See CS, no. 32. See also above, pp. 4, 6.

40. See above, p. 4ff.

41. See above, p. 1.

42. See above, pp. 4, 6, 10–11.

43. For a more complete discussion of consciousness, see below, Chapter 2: "God's Love: Creation," pp. 36–37.

44. See Jn. 1:1.

45. See CS, no. 37.

46. See CS, no. 39.

47. See above, pp. 8–9.

48. See above, p. 4.

49. See CS, no. 40.

50. See CS, no. 40.

51. See CS, no. 41.

52. Of course, we can love ourselves as well as God and others. We can love ourselves even though love is a union of two or more persons, because in loving ourselves we unite our wills with God Who loves us. See below, Chapter 8: "Grace," p. 219.

53. See CS, no. 41.

54. See Jn. 16:15.

55. See Jn. 16:14.

56. See CS, no. 41.

57. See above, pp. 4, 6, 11.

58. See CS, no. 47, not only for this quotation, but for the entire foregoing discussion.

59. See CS, no. 47.

60. See above, pp. 13–14.

61. See CS, no. 47.

62. See DVe, no. 2.

63. See Jn. 14:9.

64. For a more complete discussion of Christ and His work, see below, Chapter 4: "The Incarnation."

65. God has a perfect knowledge of Himself. Since He is Love, He knows Himself as Love. See above, pp. 13–14.

66. Cf. SC, p. 194.

67. See Phil. 2:7.

68. See CS, no. 47.

69. See Jn. 15:13.

70. See below, Chapter 8: "Grace."

71. See below, Chapter 8: "Grace," pp. 223–25.

72. See Gal. 3:27.

73. See the "Gloria," *The Roman Missal: The Sacramentary,* promulgated by Pope Paul VI on April 3, 1969, and translated by the International Commission on English in the Liturgy (New York: Catholic Book Publishing, 1974), p. 367.

— 2 —
God's Love: Creation

*[We believe in one God, the] Maker of heaven and earth, of all
that is seen and unseen. . . . Through Him all things were made.*

A. Angels

Power, wisdom, and love are shared perfectly and totally within
the mystery of the Holy Trinity.[1] God lacks absolutely nothing. In
other words, God does not need anyone or anything outside of Himself to fulfill Himself. It was not in any sense necessary for Him to
create anything. In fact, God is completely free of any and all necessities. If something were necessary in Him or for Him, there would
obviously be some cause outside of Himself responsible for the necessity. Since He is the uncaused cause, there can be no outside cause
acting upon Him. Therefore, there is no necessity in God or in any of
His actions.

Since there is no necessity in God or for God, His creative acts are
not necessary. Still, He does create angelic and human persons.
However, it is fairly clear that many of those God has created have
turned their backs on Him. He knew this would happen. Since He
does not "have to" create, one might well ask: Why does He bother?

God is Power, Wisdom, and Love. Human beings possessing these
attributes give them to others. Power is meaningless if it is not exercised. For example, what benefit does bodily strength have if it is
never used in work or in play? Wisdom is useless if it is not shared.
For instance, why would a scholar spend years studying if he never

intends to transmit his knowledge either in teaching or in writing? Love is a self-gift of one person to at least one other person.[2] Thus, how can one love without giving oneself to another? As human persons, we share our strength, our wisdom, and our love. God is like us. As Power, Wisdom, and Love, God seeks to share Himself. He does not create out of any necessity, but rather out of a burning desire to give His power, His wisdom, and His love to others.

The creation of persons out of nothing is a stupendous act of power. We, as powerful as we are with all our advanced technology, cannot create. We cannot call things, not to speak of persons, into being from nothing. In creating persons from nothing, God shared His power. However, the creation of persons also reveals God's wisdom (divine self-knowledge) because God makes Himself known in a unique way through persons who are made " 'in the image and likeness' of God."[3] Further, the creation of persons is an act of love because in creating persons, God shared existence. Since He is existence (Being) itself, God gave Himself when He gave existence to persons. In other words, He loved. Thus, the creation of persons was not only an act of power and wisdom, it was also an act of love.

In creating persons, God gives Himself to them, i.e., He loves them.[4] God's love establishes a value, i.e., a goodness, in those He creates. Without God's love, there would be no value or goodness outside of God because nothing outside of God would exist. Clearly, then, God's love is not a response to an already existing value because His love is the source of all value. However, the self-gift of created persons does not establish value in others as God's love does. Instead, the love of created persons is a response to the value they discover in others.

In creating human beings and angels, God establishes their value by creating them in His own image. As images of God, they are persons, i.e., they have the faculties of thinking and choosing, minds and wills. Unlike human persons, the angels are pure spirits. Obviously, as pure spirits, they do not have bodies[5] and therefore are more like God than are human beings. However, they still are not God because they are not the source of their own being. Rather, God created them.

The existence of angels is clearly indicated in the Old and New Testaments. "If one wishes to get rid of the angels, one must radically revise Sacred Scripture itself and with it the whole history of salvation."[6] Scripture mentions the thrones and dominions, principalities and powers.[7] These are groups of angels usually known as choirs. In addition, there are specific names of angels in the Bible, e.g., Raphael, Gabriel, and Michael.[8] Further, every time we recite the Nicene creed, we confess our belief in the existence of pure spirits. We say, "We believe in one God, the Father, the almighty, Maker of heaven and earth, of all that is seen and unseen."[9] In this context, "all that is seen and unseen" refers to all beings. Unseen beings clearly signify the pure spirits, the angels, who, unlike us, do not possess bodies.[10] Thus, revelation as contained in Scripture and found in Tradition, e.g., the creed, attests to the existence of angels.

The existence of created pure spirits fits the order of the universe. If we examine the world, we notice a gradation from very simple inanimate objects to the most developed animal. There is a definite progression from the world of things to the world of plants and from the world of plants to the animal world. Generally speaking, each world shares the functions of the previous world, e.g., plants are material, as are rocks; animals grow, as do plants. However, there are also gradations within each of these worlds. Within the world of things, there is a gradation from the simplest to the more complex. Among plants, there is very definitely a gradation from primitive organisms to highly evolved ones. As among the plants, there is a gradation in the animal world. There is the one-celled amoeba as well as the highly developed chimpanzee.

In some respects, man resembles an animal. He is a material being because he has a body that is not unlike the bodies of animals. However, as an image of God, man is a person, a spiritual being. Thus, within the sphere of material creation, man represents, as it were, *"the boundary* between the visible and invisible creation."[11] The pinnacle of earthly development is reached in man because all other earthly beings are material, but man is both material and spiritual. Above man is God Who is perfect spirit. It is reasonable to suggest a gradation in the spiritual world similar to the one that exists in the material world, i.e., the order in the universe suggests the existence of pure spirits, beings in between God and man.

In material creation, there are not only inanimate things, plants, and animals, but also gradations within these kingdoms. There is a progression that is apparent from the different stages of physical complexity and functions. Thus, the order in the universe not only suggests that created pure spirits, angels, exist, but that the angels are different from one another.

The angels differ from one another in their natures. (Nature is "what" a being is.)[12] There are no two angels with the same nature. On the other hand, in material creation, there can be many creatures with the same nature, e.g., horses. Each horse is in some way different from all other horses because the body of each horse expresses the nature of a horse differently. Still, each horse possesses the nature of a horse. This unity in diversity occurs because there is almost an infinite number of bodily (material) variations that all express the identical nature. However, since angels, as pure spirits, do not have bodies, they cannot be distinguished from one another through bodily characteristics as horses are. In other words, there cannot be a multitude of bodily variations that all express the same angelic nature. Therefore, there cannot be more than one angel with the same nature because if there were, the angels with the same nature would be indistinguishable from one another. Further, each angel must differ from every other angel according to the powers angels possess, i.e., the spiritual faculties of mind and will. Obviously, then, the spiritual differences among the angels determine each angel as a separate species, i.e., each angel has his own individual nature. In terms of material creation, comparing two angels would be like comparing two species of animals, e.g., chimpanzees with horses.[13]

It has been suggested that the differences among the angelic natures rest specifically in the power of their minds. The less powerful angels need more concepts to organize their knowledge. The more powerful angels are capable of understanding themselves, the world, and God (to a certain degree) with fewer concepts than the lesser angels. Of course, even the highest archangel never approaches the infinite perfection of God Who understands everything through a single and infinitely perfect concept: His own self-knowledge.[14]

The angels are made in God's own image to act as He acts, i.e., to love as He loves.[15] God loves Himself (and all other persons) on the basis of the truth. The angels are called to love God (and through Him themselves and all other persons) on the basis of the truth: "The angels are called from the beginning . . . to know the truth and to love the good which they know in the truth in a more full and perfect way than is possible to man."[16] With their more powerful intellects, they penetrate the truth more deeply and more accurately than man ever could. Knowing the truth more fully and more accurately, their love is irrevocable. They will never "change their minds."

Men and women can "change their minds" because we often make our choices based on incomplete knowledge or understanding.[17] When we gain further knowledge or understanding, we "change our minds." But it is not possible for an angel to change his mind because angels are created with all the knowledge they will ever have.[18] Thus, an angel does not acquire greater knowledge or a greater understanding as we do. Therefore, angels always make an informed choice. Consequently, once an angel has chosen, the choice cannot be changed.

Called to act as God acts, the angels were invited to love. First and foremost, they were called to love God. However, the angels were unable to love God unaided by God's help because God is infinitely superior even to the angels.[19] God enabled the angels to love Him, i.e., to do what they were called to do by their creation, by sharing His own life, grace, with them: "God offered the mystery of His divinity [to the angels], making them thus *partakers,* through grace, of His infinite glory."[20] In addition to their powerful intellects and wills (which they possess simply because God made them as pure spirits), God created the angels with grace "from the beginning"[21] to enable them to love Him.

Since the angels were (and, of course, the faithful angels still are) blessed with the powerful, grace-filled capacities of intellect and will, the question arises: How was it possible for the angels to reject God? It was possible because the angels possessed free wills: "By creating the pure spirits as free beings, God in His providence could not but foresee also *the possibility of the angels' sin.* "[22] However, God created them with freedom because He willed that they should imitate Him, i.e., that they should love: *"True love . . . is possible only on the basis of freedom."*[23] Providence was willing to risk the horrendous evil of sin in order that there would be true love.

Some angels, led by Satan, did reject God. They thus rejected Truth itself.[24] This angelic sin was probably the result of a "blindness"[25] caused by pride. The fallen angels did not accept that God knew what was good for them. They wanted to define what was in their own best interests. In other words, they themselves wanted to define truth, i.e., they claimed to " 'know good and evil' like God."[26] In making this claim to define truth, they rejected God, Who is Truth, and tried to make themselves gods. Satan and his followers wanted to be more perfect than they actually were, i.e., they wanted to be truth as God is Truth: "All this is summed up concisely in the words: 'I will not serve.' "[27] With this rejection of Truth, Satan and his followers became liars. (A liar is one who rejects truth.) Satan himself "became the cosmic 'liar and the father of lies.' "[28] In addition, he consigned himself to hell, that place of loveless, everlasting separation from God. Totally separated from God and deprived of grace, Satan will never be as he was before he sinned. Further, he will never be fulfilled. Milton aptly expresses Satan's rejection of God and its results when he has Satan say, "Better to reign in hell than serve in heav'n."[29]

It is important to notice that the sin of Satan and his devils was different from most of the sins human persons commit. Since the angels do not have bodies, their sin was a choice in their wills, uninfluenced by any bodily desires, to accept a false understanding of their own position as creatures *vis-à-vis* God. While we are capable of such sins of pure pride, most often our sins begin with the selfish seeking of bodily pleasure or the avoidance of pain. The desire for bodily self-gratification makes it difficult for us to express in and through our bodies the values we initially choose.[30] For example, at a party, we might have decided not to drink to the point of intoxication, but, as all too often happens, we "change our minds." The "change of our minds" probably occurs because our bodily desires influence our minds and wills.[31] We had chosen not to abuse ourselves by overindulging in alcohol, but the selfish pleasure of the moment entices us. This kind of sin does not occur in angels because they do not have bodily desires. But sins of pure pride do occur because the angels do have intellects and wills. Satan and his followers were guilty of a sin of pure pride. Satan and his followers seek to entice others, i.e., human beings to follow them in their rejection of God. Satan tempted Adam and Eve in the garden of Paradise. He and his followers continue to tempt human beings to reject God.[32] Thus, human persons are enticed not only by their bodily desires, but also by Satan and his followers.

The angels who did not oppose the Truth have a two-fold mission: "The Old Testament emphasizes especially *the special participation of the angels* in the celebration of the *glory* which the Creator receives . . . on the part of the created world."[33] In other words, the angels praise God in the " 'heavenly liturgy,' carried out in the name of all the universe, with which the earthly liturgy of the Church is incessantly joined."[34] The angels also *"take part,* in a way proper to themselves, in God's government of creation, as 'the mighty ones who do His word,' "[35] i.e., they do God's will in the world.

The angelic participation in worldly affairs is primarily directed towards people. The word "angel" signifies a messenger or a delegate: "The angels, spiritual creatures, have a function of mediation and of ministry in the relationships between God and man."[36] Two of the archangels mentioned by name in Scripture, Raphael and Gabriel, clearly acted as messengers, and made God's will known to the people to whom they were sent.[37] The third, Michael, protected the Jewish people.[38] The guardian angels assigned to each one of us not only guard and protect us from spiritual and, sometimes, bodily harm, but they also bring our prayers before almighty God.[39] The participation of the angels in worldly affairs extends to the incarnation and the work of salvation. They are found at the beginning of Christ's life, indeed at His birth. They assist Him after His fast of forty days. They are at the tomb after His resurrection. They speak to the Apostles after the ascension and they will be present at the second coming.[40]

Since the angels participate in the lives of all men and women, they were present "at the beginning of time."[41] Sometimes it is thought that the angels were created before man. This idea might be traceable to the curious theory, taught by both St. Augustine and St. Anselm, that human beings were created to replace in heaven the number of angels who sinned.[42] It would seem, then, that before God could create men and women, it would have been necessary for Him to "see" how many angels sinned. Of course, even if this theory were correct, it still would not follow that the angels were created before man. It must be remembered that God "sees" everything in an eternal "now."[43] He knows everything as events of the present that we view as events of the past, present, and future. Therefore, He creates man at the same moment (the eternal present) that He "sees" Satan and his followers sin. In fact, God created the angels and man simultaneously: "God at the beginning of time created from nothing *both creatures* together, the *spiritual* and the *corporeal*, that is, the angelic and the earthly."[44]

B. Human Beings and the World

From God's viewpoint, i.e., from the aspect of the eternal present, the angels and human beings were created at the same time. From God's perspective, all creation happens "at once." However, from the human viewpoint, it is possible to conceive of our creation as a progressive series of events, i.e., evolution. In other words, it is possible to place the theory of evolution within the context of the divine creative act. Guided by the creative hand of God, the human body with all its physical powers and properties could have evolved through the processes of gene mutation and natural selection. Such a gradual unfolding of God's creative act would in no way diminish His divine power, wisdom, and love demonstrated in and through creation. Certainly, God could (and even might) have created us without an evolutionary process. But if He willed the creation of the human body through an evolutionary process, the act of creation becomes an even greater mystery with an incomprehensible complexity. If the human body did evolve, God would have willed and foreseen every single gene mutation and natural selection process on the path from the very first, most simple animal species to the most complex animal and ultimately to the crowning glory of material creation: the human body. The human body is the greatest of God's material creations because it is the expression of a human person.[45] As we noted at the beginning of the last chapter,[46] when God created man, He said, "Let Us make man in Our image."[47] Among all the earthly beings God created, only man was created in the divine likeness, i.e., only men and women are persons and are reflections of the divine Persons.[48] Thus, among all earthly bodies, only human bodies are the expressions of persons.

Even if the body did evolve, there are human powers that did not. Thinking thoughts, i.e., the manipulation of abstract ideas, is a common human experience. Most of us realize that it is possible for us to abstract certain ideas from the world around us, e.g., the idea of "one" or "two" (all numbers are mathematical concepts abstracted from the world around us), the concept of God, the ideas of beauty, of truth, or of freedom. These concepts, taken from the world and once established, exist independent of any sensory (bodily) impressions. Since these ideas are immaterial, they must exist within us in an essentially immaterial power. We call this spiritual, immaterial, and non-corporeal power within us the mind.

Similarly, most human beings exercise free choice daily. They experience themselves as beings endowed with the power to choose. This power is not dependent essentially on the material world.[49] For example, it is possible for us to choose what thoughts we shall think. Since free choice is immaterial, it must exist within us in an essentially immaterial power. We call this spiritual, immaterial, and non-corporeal power within us the will.

The spiritual powers of mind and will are faculties of the soul. The soul is the principle of life.[50] Since plants, animals, and human beings are alive, they all have souls. As living things, they are radically different from non-living things. This difference cannot be adequately explained simply and solely by a variation in the arrangement of atoms or by a special combination of chemicals. Life is more than the proper ordering of chemical and physical properties. Life must have its foundation in a life-force, in a principle of life, i.e., in a soul. Therefore, all living beings have souls.

However, not all living beings have personal souls, souls that possess the capacities of thinking and choosing, souls that give life to persons. The soul of a plant is merely vegetative. It enables the living organism to do only the vegetative functions. A plant takes nourishment, grows, and gives off waste. An animal possesses a sensory soul that enables it to perform the vegetative functions (which a plant can do) as well as the functions of the senses. Most animals see, smell, taste, hear, and touch. They have a memory and an imagination, and can move. The personal soul, unique to man, has all the vegetative and sensory functions, and also the personal ones. A human person has a mind and a will, powers of the personal soul, that enable him to think and to choose.

As mentioned above,[51] the theory of evolution does not completely explain man's creation. Since the theory postulates a physical process, it cannot account for the existence of a spiritual, immaterial, and non-corporeal personal soul in each one of us. The souls of all human beings cannot have their origin in matter. They must have their origin in the spiritual realm, i.e., in God, Who alone is the Creator. Therefore, Christians may employ the theory of evolution to explain the origin of the human body, but not the origin of the human soul. Yet, there could never be a human person without a personal soul: "There are no difficulties in explaining the origin of man, in regard to the body, by means of the theory of evolution. . . . The human soul, however, on which man's humanity definitively depends, cannot emerge from matter, since it is of a spiritual nature."[52] Thus, if Christians choose to accept the theory of evolution, they still would believe that when a suitable body had evolved, God infused into that body a personal soul.[53] In other words, by giving man a personal soul, God gave him life and made him into the divine image and likeness (as distinct from all other bodied beings in the universe). Further, God's creation of personal souls continues today. Every time a human being is conceived, God creates a personal soul that gives life to a human body.

Created with personal souls, human beings are immortal, i.e., they do not cease to exist. Plants and animals cease to exist when they die, when their souls separate from their bodies. Since souls give life to bodies, when the souls of plants and animals separate from their bodies, their bodies cease to have life. Further, in this process, the souls of plants and animals also cease to be because they have no functions independent of their bodies. Unlike the plants and the animals, persons have the capabilities of thinking abstractly and choosing freely. They have the powers of mind and will. Since these two powers are spiritual, immaterial, and non-corporeal, they can function without the body. In fact, they survive even if the body does not. Therefore, human beings are immortal because they are persons, because they are created in the image and likeness of God. The gift of immortality does not come with grace. Nor is it some special, extraordinary gift of God added to His creative gift. The gift of immortality is given by the Creator when He creates each and every one of us. It comes with our creation in the image and likeness of God: "The life given to man in the act of creation is such as to transcend the mere corporeal dimension (that proper to animals). It reaches, beyond the material, *the dimension of the spirit,* wherein there is the essential foundation of that 'image of God,' which Gen. 1:27 sees in man."[54] Immortality is inherent in every human being.

God created us in His image and likeness as immortal persons. Since we are images of God, we should act as God acts, i.e., we should love as He loves.[55] God loves Himself (and all other persons) on the basis of the truth. We are called to love God (and through Him ourselves and all other persons) on the basis of the truth. Thus, God made us so that we can relate to Him and through Him to others on a personal level: "Indeed man, thanks to his spiritual nature and to his capacity for intellectual knowledge and freedom of choice and action, is, *from the very beginning, in a special relationship with God.*"[56] If we had not been created in the divine image, we would not have minds and wills. We could not love God on earth or in heaven because we would be incapable of knowing Him (the foundation of love) or choosing Him (the means of love).

"The truth about man created in the image of God does not merely determine man's place in the whole order of creation, but it already speaks even *of his link with the order of salvation in Christ.*"[57] In other words, in making us in His likeness, God made us for heaven, for salvation. By creation, we are linked to Christ, the way to heaven: "Christian thought has perceived in *man's 'likeness' to God* the foundation of man's call to participate in the interior life of God: *his opening on to the supernatural.*"[58] Thus, the revelation that man is created in the divine likeness "contains not only *all that is 'humanum' in him* [man], and therefore essential to his humanity, but potentially also *what is 'divinum,'* and therefore gratuitous. That is to say, it contains also what God—Father, Son, and Holy Spirit— had *de facto* foreseen for man as the *supernatural dimension* of his existence, without which man could not attain *all the fullness destined for him by the Creator.*"[59] By God's creative act, human persons are *"capax Dei"*[60] (fit for God). Making us in the divine likeness, God made us able to share the divine life, i.e., grace. As St. Thomas Aquinas taught, "the [human] soul is naturally capable of grace because it is made in the image of God."[61]

However, God did not only create us with the capacity for grace, but He also gives us the gift of His own life. Since God created man in the divine image and likeness, He created him to act as He acts, i.e., to love. Human persons cannot love as God loves without grace because lacking grace, we would not share His ability to love.[62] Common experience provides an analogy. At times, we want our pets to act as we act, e.g., we want them to celebrate a birthday party with us. They cannot because they do not share human life. To act as we act, our pets would have to share human life. In a similar way, if we are to act as God acts, we must share the divine life. Therefore, God blessed man not only with the capability of grace, but also with grace itself. As John Paul II writes, God made grace "to dwell from the beginning . . . in the creatures made 'in the likeness of God.'"[63] We, through grace, are at one and the same time human and divine. Unlike the animals who cannot simultaneously share animal life and human life, we can simultaneously share human life and divine life. (Of course, we are divine in a different way and in a different sense than we are human.) Through grace, we are capable of acting as God acts. We are capable of doing what God created us to do, i.e., of loving Him, and ourselves and others through Him.

In addition to grace, freedom is necessary for love: "God willed that there should be realized in the world *true love* which is *possible only on the basis of freedom.*"[64] Since God gave us both freedom and grace for love, grace does not destroy our freedom. Thus, even with grace, man "has the capacity to *accept God* and His holy will [love], but also the capacity *to oppose* it [sin]."[65] Clearly, God was willing to risk the horrendous evil of sin for the sake of love. In other words, it was more important to God that there be love in the world through freedom "than the fact that those beings [created as images of God] may abuse their freedom against the Creator."[66] This "risk" by God allows us to view dimly the incredible importance of love!

The horrendous evil of sin affects human beings far more than God. Through our freely chosen acts, we shape and subsequently come to know ourselves. We can freely choose to shape ourselves more and more like God or more and more unlike God. We can come to know ourselves as images of God or as mis-shapen images of God. For example, a Catholic who attends Mass on Sunday acts as God created him to act, i.e., to love God. However, such a Catholic is also aware that he is worshiping. In a sense, he watches himself as he attends Mass. His self-awareness of his own act remains with him even after Mass has ended. Clearly, then, his self-awareness, i.e., his consciousness, of his own acts "contains" every act that he has freely chosen. This consciousness is part of him. By freely choosing his acts, he "fills" his self-awareness, i.e., his consciousness. In other words, in worshiping he shapes his consciousness, and in the process he shapes himself. He shapes or determines himself as one who acts as God acts. He becomes more like God. Further, our self-awareness is also a source of our self-knowledge. In the example above, after the worshiping Catholic has shaped or determined himself as a worshiper, he knows himself as a worshiper. His consciousness "contains" the experience of attending Mass. Thus, through our freely chosen acts, we form our consciousness, we determine ourselves, and we can come to know ourselves through an examination of the experiential data found in our consciousness. As images of God, we are invited to shape ourselves more and more into God-like creatures through God-like acts. Further, we should come to know ourselves as images of God through our God-like actions "contained" in our consciousness.

However, it is possible for us to choose freely not to act as God acts. When we do not act like God, we are, in effect, trying to become something we are not. We are trying to shape ourselves into something other than images of God. In addition, acting contrary to the very beings we are fills our consciousness with a confusing array of experiential data. Thus, when we analyze this data to gain a knowledge of ourselves, we see an inadequate and marred image of God. The attempt to determine and, subsequently, to know ourselves as something other than images of God never completely succeeds. When we sin, i.e., when we act contrary to the very beings we are, we tarnish or wound ourselves. We try to do the impossible, i.e., we try to destroy our likeness to God: "Sin is . . . a suicidal act."[67]

For good or for ill, we become what we do. We can choose to become more God-like or less God-like. Since God creates all men and women in His image and likeness, He invites each one of us to holiness, to imitate Him. But this is an invitation, a call. God invites us to holiness, but He does not force it on us. He not only invites, He offers us the means: grace. But like the call or invitation, the means, God's grace, is never forced on us.

It is quite clear that every human person is a spiritual being. Our thoughts and our choices are spiritual, immaterial, and non-corporeal.[68] However, each one of us also has a body that is physical, material, and corporeal. Further, the body is not something added to each of us as an afterthought. Rather, our bodies are given to us to express our persons. As embodied persons, we are different from all material things and from all other personal beings. We differ from inanimate things, the plants, and the animals because we are persons (images of God). We differ from all the other persons in the universe (the three Persons in God[69] and the angels) because we have bodies.

We are unique. There are no other creatures comparable to human beings. There are no other enfleshed spirits or spiritualized bodies in the universe. Only human beings are persons with bodies. We are the only beings who can express personhood in a physical way.

However, human beings are not only called to express their own personhood through their bodies, they are also invited to manifest God. As images of God, we are called to act as God acts. In other words, we are called to love as God loves. Since we have bodies, we are called to express love in and through our bodies. When our bodies express love, they not only manifest human personhood, but they also become physical images of God, i.e., signs or sacraments of God: "The body also participates, in its own way, in the dignity of the 'image of God,' just as it participates in the dignity of the person."[70] As the expression of a human person and a physical image of God, the human body is a unique creation.

As enfleshed spirits or spiritualized bodies, human beings are unique. The first man, Adam, discovered the radical differences between himself and the rest of creation. Adam realized that, as an enfleshed person, he was unique. In the account of creation found in the second chapter of Genesis, God creates Adam first and then asks him to name the animals. (In the account found in the first chapter, Adam and Eve are created together.) In the process of naming the animals, Adam experiences an extreme loneliness as he discovers that no other human being exists. Since Adam was made in the image of God, he had a need to act as God acts, i.e., to love as God loves. Since his body was made to express his person, he longed, as we all do, to express love in and through his body. However, love is a mutual self-gift. Since Adam was alone, he could not receive the self-gift of another bodied person. Further, since he was alone, he could not give himself in and through his body to another bodied person. Adam experienced loneliness because there could not be a mutual exchange of love with another bodied person.[71] God permitted Adam to suffer loneliness so that through this experience he would discover that the bodies of the animals were different from his own body. Adam saw that no body other than his own could express a person. In and through his loneliness, Adam discovered himself as an enfleshed spirit, as a person whose body was created to express his person. He discovered that, as a spiritualized body, he was unique.

Living among as many people as we do today, it is almost impossible for us to experience the kind of loneliness Adam felt. However, just as Adam came to realize that he was unique because his body could express his person, so it is important for all of us to appreciate our own uniqueness as enfleshed spirits.

Our bodies are integral elements in our lives. This point seems obvious. We received our bodies as part of the gift of life. None of us bought them. They were given to us by God through the cooperation of our parents. Further, when a small part of the body is harmed, e.g., the heart, we (our persons) suffer and can die. Our bodies are part and parcel of human life. They are created to be the expressions of our persons. In other words, there is a fundamental unity in each of us. We are body and soul, but the two are united as one: *"Biblical tradition* stresses *especially the personal unity of man,* by using the term 'body' to designate the whole man. . . . But notwithstanding this, *the duality* of man is also present in biblical tradition."[72] The unity does not exclude the duality, and the duality does not destroy the unity. In this unity-duality, we confront one of the essential mysteries about man. It should not surprise us that man is a mystery. After all, we are images of the supreme mystery, God Himself.

However, there are many who are uncomfortable with the essential uniqueness and mystery of the unity and duality of man. Rather than acknowledging the mystery, they try to eliminate it.[73] One very common means of trying to remove the unity-duality mystery is to make the body a thing, almost a machine that a human person inhabits. In this view, the human person is perfectly one, i.e., he is pure spirit, and the body is not part of human life. Given this false opinion, the human body is merely a machine that is necessary here on earth.[74] (It is important to note that while this mechanized view separates the body from the person, it does not make the body something evil.)

Not only do many people seem to believe that their bodies are machines, they act accordingly. How often do people refer to the human heart as a ticker or a pump? It is not uncommon for people to speak of the inner workings of the body as a motor. For example, one often hears statements such as, "I have to get the old engine running this morning." Food is many times called fuel or gas as if the body were an engine. Treating the body as a machine has become sufficiently integrated into our culture that it is now expressed in dancing. For example, the interest in imitating machines in break dancing is very revealing. Through dance motions, break dancers imitate robots, airplanes, and helicopters. The artistic expression of a particular attitude in a culture testifies that the attitude is not only widely accepted, but that it is also almost a "given."

However, our bodies are not machines. If they were, when two people shook hands, hugged, or expressed their love for one another, it would not be two persons touching, but rather their two machines. Moreover, if our bodies were machines, then a surgeon operating would be nothing more than a technician working on a defective machine much like a computer serviceman repairing a malfunctioning computer. Clearly, our bodies are our flesh and blood. They are the means by which our persons are expressed. When we are in pain, most of us do not cry out, "I have damaged my machinery." Rather, we cry out, "My leg!" or "My arm!" When our bodies are hurt, we are hurt. Thus, the human body is not a machine. Rather, it is created to be the expression of a person.

The human body is the sum of its biological functions; at the same time, it is more than these. Through these apparently understandable functions, the mystery of personhood finds expression: "In the body and through the body, one touches the person itself, in its concrete reality."[75] In addition, since each one of us is also a unique, separate individual,[76] our bodies are unique and created to manifest the personal mystery of each individual. Thus, in themselves the biological functions of the body are intriguing. If they were not, they would not be suited to express the mystery of personhood and the personal mystery of each human being. In studying the human body properly, men and women can come to some understanding of these mysteries.[77]

God created not only the human body, but also other living bodies: the animals and the plants. Further, God made all the inanimate things. All these things were created for man: "Let us make man in our image, after our likeness; and let them have dominion over the fish of the sea, and over the birds of the air, and over the cattle, and over all the earth, and over every creeping thing that creeps upon the earth."[78] It is interesting to note that if evolution did occur, it would confirm that all animal life was created for man. In this case, the various species of animals would have existed, at least in part, so that the human body could evolve from them![9]

C. God's Two Mandates

Made in the image and likeness of God, human persons are called to do what God does. As noted above,[80] God loves. Clearly, human persons should love as God loves if they are to be true to the kind of beings they are.

God's love is most perfectly present within the mystery of the three Persons in one God. Each divine Person knows the other two and, on the basis of that knowledge, chooses to give Himself to the other two. This choice is total, i.e., it is permanent and limitless. It is permanent because the Trinity was, is, and always will be.[81] The love of each Person in the Trinity is limitless because each Person gives Himself completely, i.e., each Person gives His very Being, His very life, to the other two. Divine love is therefore identified with life.[82] In God, there are not two realities called love and life, but rather only one: love which is the same as life. It could also be put the other way: in God there is only one reality, life, which is the same as love. The love of God the Father is an example of the permanent and limitless character of divine love. God the Father's love of the Son and the Holy Spirit is an act of His will founded on a perfect knowledge of the truth about the value and dignity of the Son and the Holy Spirit. God the Father never ceases to love the Son and the Holy Spirit. He would never decide to stop loving the Son and the Holy Spirit. Nor would He ever decide to "leave" the Trinity. Further, the Father's love of the Son and the Holy Spirit is a total gift, a gift of His very Being. If human persons want to be true to their very selves as beings made in the image and likeness of God, they will love as God loves.[83]

As in the mystery of the Holy Trinity, human love must be founded on a knowledge of the truth about the value and dignity of the one to be loved. Almost intuitively, but certainly based on our own self-knowledge (gleaned from the experiential data found in our consciousness),[84] each human being knows that he is different from the animals. Adam discovered this wonderful mystery in naming the animals.[85] Each of us discovers it in growing up. Even a three-year-old knows that he is different from the animals. In other words, we know that we are unique, i.e., we know that we are enfleshed spirits with bodies created to be physical images of God. While some may not be able to express human uniqueness in the technical terms used here, still they know that human beings differ from other earthly creatures.

Knowing our own dignity and value is the foundation of our knowledge of others' dignity and value. We experience ourselves intimately, but we cannot know others nearly as well as we know ourselves. Still, we see that other human beings are like us in many respects. The obvious and only conclusion is that they too are persons. They too have a value, worth, and dignity because they are created in God's image and likeness. Adam came to this conclusion when he first saw Eve. Knowing his own value, Adam met Eve and realized that she was like him. In other words, he realized that she, too, was made in the image and likeness of God. At the sight of Eve, he cried out, "This at last is bone of my bones and flesh of my flesh."[86] In Eve, Adam recognized an image of himself. Adam perceived in Eve the dignity and value he had discovered in himself.

With the recognition of Eve's dignity, Adam had the knowledge necessary to love Eve in a God-like way: to give himself to her through a will-act that was total, i.e., permanent and limitless. He knew that Eve was to be loved. To use John Paul's words, Adam knew that a "person is a good towards which the only proper and adequate attitude is love. . . . This [personalistic] norm, in its negative aspect, states that the person is a kind of good which does not admit of use and cannot be treated as an object of use and as such the means to an end."[87] Human beings have a value far superior to the rest of God's earthly creation. The extraordinary worth and value of persons gives each of them a right to be treasured for their own sakes. To put it another way, persons call forth love from other persons. The very existence of persons is an invitation for others to love them. One might even say that the existence of persons demands love from other persons. All this was known by Adam and then by Eve.

Adam and Eve knew from their own experience that they were to love one another. God invited them to put this knowledge into practice when He said to both of them: "Be fruitful and multiply, and fill the earth and subdue it."[88] In this invitation, God asked our first parents to form a family and to work. Human beings demand love from one another. In inviting Adam and Eve to form a family and to work, God was inviting them to act together and to love each other. When people love each other, they form a *communion of persons*. Therefore, God asked our first parents to form two loving *communions of persons* (one familial communion and one worker communion) in imitation of the love in the trinitarian *communion of Persons*.[89]

The invitation to form the two human communions is, in a certain sense, logically included in the creation of human persons in God's image. Since we are like God, we should act like God, i.e., we should love. When we love, we form loving unions with other persons. When God invited us to enter these two communions, He not only confirmed His creative act, but He gave each of us an opportunity to become more and more like Him. As noted above,[90] every act a person does is "contained" in his consciousness. Every conscious act shapes us. Consequently, through our conscious acts, we can shape ourselves into more and more perfect images of God or into more and more imperfect images of God. Since we *are* images of God, we should always try to become more and more like Him through repeated God-like acts. Conversely, repeated ungodly acts shape us more and more into distorted images of God. The invitation to form the two communions of love, i.e., to imitate God by loving in the family and in the workplace, is an invitation to shape ourselves more and more into images of God. In other words, by acting as God acts, we become more and more what we already are: images of God.[91]

Of course, the familial communion is more fundamental. The familial communion mirrors the divine communion more profoundly than the communion of workers. The familial communion imitates the trinitarian communion more closely in the limitless self-gift. In the family, as in the Trinity, each member gives all that he or she *is*, while each person in the worker communion gives all that he or she *has*.

As mentioned above,[92] we can glean from our own experience that "the only proper and adequate attitude"[93] towards persons is love. In inviting us to "be fruitful and multiply,"[94] God asked us to put our experiential knowledge to good use by establishing a familial communión of persons. God asked us to give ourselves within the family through will-acts that are total (permanent and limitless).[95] Familial love is permanent because spouses give all the days of their lives to each other. Familial love is limitless because the spouses give all that they are[96] (including the possibility of life).[97] Thus, the gift of each person in the familial communion imitates the gift of the divine Persons in the trinitarian communion because spouses love one another permanently and limitlessly.

It is critically important to note the incredible blessing that God gives human beings in inviting them to participate in the familial *communion of persons*. In a family, each spouse should love as God loves and therefore fulfill himself or herself as an image of God. Further, in and through this love, each spouse wills what is best for the other, i.e., the other's self-fulfillment as an image of God. (If there are children, each child finds fulfillment by loving as God loves. In addition, each child wills the self-fulfillment of all the other family members.) Through the profound mystery of familial love, husbands and wives (and any children) become more and more like God. They fulfill themselves as images of God because they love as God loves.

In loving as God loves, spouses also fulfill themselves by giving life. The love of spouses procreates new life, the life of an enfleshed spirit destined to spend all eternity with God. In an incredible gift of God, spousal love gives life to potential saints! Of course, God could have chosen to bring new life into the world in a different way.

However, He wants to make it possible for spouses to fulfill themselves as images of God by loving as He loves. Therefore, He gives spouses this unimaginable blessing: He allows them to procreate new life. It is because of this incredible gift that the sacred author of Genesis prefaces the invitation to "be fruitful and multiply" with the phrase, "God blessed them."[98] Indeed, familial love is a blessing, an awesome one, because through this love spouses fulfill themselves. Unfortunately, the specter of sin and its effects came to overshadow the blessing of familial love. Sadly, sin marred familial love and, while not destroying it, made it less than what it could have been.[99]

As has been said,[100] Adam and Eve knew from their own experience that they should love each other. God not only invited Adam and Eve (and, through them, all of us) to put this knowledge into practice in the familial *communion of persons,* He also asked them to imitate His trinitarian love by loving in the worker communion. All human beings are invited to be members of the worker *communion of persons* because all are invited to work. The goods of the earth are given to everyone in common and therefore everyone together is to engage in the immense task of subduing the earth. Such a goal would be impossible without everyone's cooperation. Thus, through work, the entire human race is called to be joined together. This bond should be one of love because "the only proper and adequate attitude"[101] towards persons (fellow workers) is love.

The *communion of persons* in the workplace is established through a free choice, a will-act, of each worker to give himself to every other worker in a self-gift that is total (permanent and limitless). It is a gift of self similar to the gift of each Person to the other Persons in the Trinity. Each worker continues to give himself to all other workers, permanently, i.e., until death. Further, each worker pledges himself to give himself limitlessly, i.e., he gives all that he has—including his talents, skills, and property, if necessary, to produce goods or to render services—for the life of other persons.[102] Clearly, this activity does not give life in the same sense as the family gives life. The family renews itself with new members, but the worker communion does not procreate new members. Rather, it gives life outside of itself and indirectly through the use of things or by providing goods and services.

Through the tasks accomplished in working, we share in God's creative activity as well as in His dominion over the world. When we work, we fashion things from the created order that God has given to us. After we have made these things, we legitimately govern them. Through work, we do what God does. Therefore, through work, we become more and more like God. We fulfill ourselves as images of God. Work, then, is truly *for* man. It is a means for us to become more and more the beings we are, i.e., images of the Creator. We are not made for work, i.e., work does not take precedence over a person. Rather, God invited us to work so that we might become more and more like Him. As John Paul has written, "In the first place work is 'for man' and not man 'for work.' . . . In the final analysis it is always man who is the purpose of work."[103] If we work primarily to fulfill ourselves as images of God, then every worker should work first and foremost to shape himself more and more into an image of God. A worker should not work primarily for money, for fame, or for success, but rather to fulfill himself. Of course, it is only in working, in accomplishing some task together with co-workers, that one has the opportunity to become more God-like. Since workers are called to love one another, they are called to will what is best for each other. Thus, they are called to will the self-fulfillment of one another. Workers then will the specific task or job as the means to an end, i.e., as the means of fulfilling themselves and their co-workers. Further, as the worker comes to know more and more people, he or she realizes that everybody works. Therefore, each worker wills the self-fulfillment of all workers, i.e., the entire human race. In other words, in and through a specific task, e.g., building cars, a worker chooses to unite himself in love not only with those building cars with him, but with every other worker, i.e., every other human being. The task accomplished through work is not the primary goal or end product of work. The self-fulfillment of all workers is the most important goal of all work.

This view of work and the union of all workers points towards solutions to a number of problems. If all people work and will the self-fulfillment of every worker in and through work, then the struggle between labor and capital, or between unions and management, should lessen. Both union members and managers are workers. Further, if work is *for* man, and not man *for* work, then the struggle in so many "two-career" families should also disappear. It is not the job that is important; it is people. Families should not quarrel over whose job is more important. It is unthinkable to value a particular job over spouse and children! Finally, the union of all people in the worker *communion of persons* could and should be the basis for peace in the world. If everyone realizes each person's dignity and loves all other people, one would think that war would be inconceivable.

The two *communions of persons* (of the family and of workers) that God invites us to enter are each imitations of the union of the three Persons in God. Each member of the two human communions makes a choice founded on a knowledge of the value and dignity of each of the other members. Each member makes a choice to give himself totally to each of the other members. In other words, each member makes a permanent and limitless (including life) self-gift to the other members. By choosing to form these communions, human beings imitate the Trinity.

The invitations by God to enter into the familial *communions of persons* continue to be offered to us despite our rejection of God through original sin. As one of the nuptial blessings in the wedding ritual has it, marriage is "the one blessing that was not forfeited by original sin or washed away in the flood."[104] The *communion of persons* of all workers also was not forfeited. However, both these communions were almost destroyed by sin (because the human race was radically altered by sin), but they are restored in and through Christ.

FOR REFLECTION

A. How do angels differ from human beings?

B. Describe the human person.

C. Why do we live in families and why do we work?

NOTES

1. See above, Chapter 1: "Man/Woman and God," p. 18ff.
2. We can still love ourselves. See below, Chapter 8: "Grace," p. 219.
3. See CS, no. 65.
4. See above, Chapter 1: "Man/Woman and God," p. 18.
5. See CS, no. 65.
6. See CS, no. 62.
7. See Col. 1:16.
8. See Tob. 3:17, Lk. 1:26, and Rev. 12:7. See also CS, no. 65.
9. See the "Creed," *The Roman Missal: The Sacramentary,* promulgated by Pope Paul VI on April 3, 1969, and translated by the International Commission on English in the Liturgy (New York: Catholic Book Publishing, 1974), p. 370.
10. See CS, no. 62. See also CS, no. 65.
11. See CS, no. 62.
12. See above, Chapter 1: "Man/Woman and God," p. 3.
13. See Thomas Aquinas, *Summa Theologiae,* I, Q. 50, Art. 4, Resp. This same distinction is not applicable to the three Persons in God. In God there is a total unity in nature, and the three Persons are distinguished by the subsisting relations. We cannot posit differences among angels on the basis of subsisting relations because this is unique to the mystery of the Trinity. See above, Chapter 1: "Man/Woman and God," pp. 14–17.
14. See Aquinas, *Summa Theologiae,* I, Q. 55, Art. 3, Resp.
15. See above, Chapter 1: "Man/Woman and God," p. 17.
16. See CS, no. 63.
17. Some might suggest that we "change our minds" because of new and unforeseen circumstances. Of course, this is true. However, this also betrays

an incomplete knowledge or understanding, i.e., we did not know what possible circumstances could occur. The angels know all the possible circumstances regarding any decision they make.

18. Of course, when the faithful angels came to see God face to face, He revealed Himself more fully to them. This revelation confirmed their previous knowledge of Him and their choice for Him. However, the knowledge of God that they gained by seeing Him face to face was not essential for their choice. Therefore, it cannot be said that in choosing against God, Satan and his followers were deprived of any essential knowledge for their choice.

19. For a discussion of the need for grace if we and the angels are to love God and others as God does, see below, pp. 35–36.

20. See CS, no. 63.

21. See CS, no. 66.

22. See CS, no. 63.

23. See CS, no. 63.

24. See above, Chapter 1: "Man/Woman and God," p. 5.

25. See CS, no. 63.

26. See CS, no. 70.

27. See CS, no. 63.

28. See Jn. 8:44. See also CS, no. 66.

29. See John Milton, *Paradise Lost*, Bk. I, l. 263.

30. See below, Chapter 3: "Original Sin and the Providence of God," pp. 53–58.

31. This kind of "change of mind" is founded on new (false) knowledge. See above, p. 28. See also below, Chapter 3: "Original Sin and the Providence of God," pp. 53–54.

32. For Satan's temptation of Adam and Eve, see below, Chapter 3: "Original Sin and the Providence of God," pp. 57–63.

33. See CS, no. 64.

34. See CS, no. 65.

35. See CS, no. 64.

36. See CS, no. 64.

37. See Tob. 12:15. See also Lk. 1:26–38.

38. See Dan. 12:1.

39. See CS, no. 64.

40. See CS, no. 64.

41. See CS, no. 65.

42. The argument is rather interesting. Since God is all-knowing, He must know and intend an ideal number of persons, angelic or human, to share

heaven with Him. Since some of the angels chose not to share heaven with God, God created human beings to replace the fallen angels. See Jasper Hopkins, *A Companion to the Study of St. Anselm* (Minneapolis: University of Minnesota Press, 1972), p. 24.

43. See above, Chapter 1: "Man/Woman and God," pp. 8–9.

44. See CS, no. 65.

45. See below, pp. 37–41.

46. See above, Chapter 1: "Man/Woman and God," p. 1.

47. See Gen. 1:26.

48. See John Eccles and Daniel N. Robinson, *The Wonder of Being Human: Our Brain and Our Mind* (New York: Macmillan, 1984), for an excellent argument against the rationality of animals. Although the authors would not admit that a fetus or infant (before two or three) is a human being, they do argue successfully that man thinks (abstractly) and animals do not.

49. Some might object that most choices are bounded by the material world, e.g., in the morning I choose what suit (a material, concrete thing) I will wear. However, I can only choose to wear one of the suits that I own (or, at least, one of those that are available to me). The response to the objection is obvious: the potential choices may be governed by the material world in some cases, but the freedom to choose (as distinct from the choices available) is not essentially determined by the material world.

50. See Aquinas, *Summa Theologiae,* I, Q. 75, Art. 1, Resp.

51. See above, p. 32.

52. See CS, no. 51.

53. Christians also believe that there were only two first parents, i.e., Adam and Eve. God infused personal souls into only two bodies, i.e., into the bodies of Adam and Eve. God did not infuse personal souls into more than two bodies even if there were more than two that had evolved and were suited to human souls. Thus, we are all descendants of two first parents: Adam and Eve. See below, Chapter 3: "Original Sin and the Providence of God," pp. 56–57, for a further discussion of this point.

54. See CS, no. 51.

55. See above, Chapter 1: "Man/Woman and God," p. 17.

56. See CS, no. 52.

57. See CS, no. 50.

58. See CS, no. 52.

59. See CS, no. 52.

60. See CS, no. 52.

61. See Aquinas, *Summa Theologiae,* I IIae, Q. 113, Art. 10. The text reads: *"naturaliter anima est gratiae capax: eo enim ipso quod facta est ad imaginem Dei, capax est Dei per gratiam, ut Augustinus dicit."*

62. See below, Chapter 8: "Grace," p. 204.

63. See CS, no. 66.

64. See CS, no. 63.

65. See CS, no. 52.

66. See CS, no. 58.

67. See RP, no. 15.

68. See above, pp. 31–32.

69. Of course, our Lord Jesus Christ is God and He has a body. However, He has a body because He assumed human nature. It is as a man, in His human nature, that He has a body. As God, in the divine nature, He remains spiritual, immaterial, and non-corporeal. For a discussion of nature, see above, Chapter 1: "Man/Woman and God," pp. 4, 14–15. For a discussion of Christ's human nature, see below, Chapter 4: "The Incarnation," pp. 90–91.

70. See CS, no. 51.

71. Since God willed that we love Him, and since He created us to give and to receive love in and through our bodies, He must have willed from "the beginning" to allow us to love Him in and through our bodies and to receive love from Him in and through our bodies. Clearly, the incarnation is linked to our creation in the image and likeness of God. As we quoted above, "The truth about man created in the image of God . . . speaks even *of his link with . . . Christ."* See CS, no. 50. See also above, pp. 34–35. In addition, see below, Chapter 4: "The Incarnation," p. 83.

72. See CS, no. 51.

73. See below, Chapter 9: "Morality," pp. 250–51.

74. This view also appears to solve the mystery of the soul existing after death before the resurrection of the body. The problem can be briefly stated. If the human person is defined as body and soul, then how can a human person exist separated from the body? Of course, if the body is not part of human life, but only a machine inhabited by a human person, the difficulty does not exist.

75. See Karol Wojtyla (Pope John Paul II), "The Ethics of Genetic Manipulation," *Origins,* vol. 13, no. 23 (November 17, 1983), p. 388.

76. See above, Chapter 1: "Man/Woman and God," p. 1.

77. For further discussions of this theology of the body, see Richard M. Hogan, "A Theology of the Body: A Commentary on the Audiences of Pope John Paul II from September 5, 1979, to May 6, 1981," *Fidelity,* vol. 1, no. 1 (December 1981), pp. 10–15, 24–27. See also *Wonder,* pp. 5–34. In addition, see *Covenant,* pp. 9–35. See also Richard M. Hogan and John M. LeVoir, "Is NFP Good?," IRNFP, vol. 9, no. 3 (Fall 1985), pp. 220–46, especially pp. 231–39.

78. See Gen. 1:26.

79. See above, pp. 31–32.

80. See above, Chapter 1: "Man/Woman and God," pp. 5, 17.

81. See above, Chapter 1: "Man/Woman and God," pp. 4–5.

82. See above, Chapter 1: "Man/Woman and God," p. 5, where it is noted that God is Being and Love.

83. It was mentioned above that in a sense Adam could not love without receiving the gift of love from another bodied person, i.e., Eve. In addition, Adam could not love without Eve because his love would not have been life-giving. See above, pp. 38–39.

84. See above, pp. 36–37.

85. See above, pp. 38–39.

86. See Gen. 2:23.

87. See LR, p. 41.

88. See Gen. 1:28.

89. For a discussion of the trinitarian *communion of Persons,* see above, Chapter 1: "Man/Woman and God," p. 17.

90. See above, pp. 36–37.

91. It is this concept that allowed Pope John Paul II to ask families in *Familiaris Consortio, Apostolic Exhortation on the Family,* to "become what you are." See FC, no. 17.

92. See above, p. 42.

93. See LR, p. 41. See also above, p. 33.

94. See Gen. 1:28.

95. See above, p. 42.

96. See the previous paragraph.

97. Even those couples who are incapable of procreation love as God loves, provided their marital acts are "open to life."

98. See Gen. 1:28.

99. See below, Chapter 3: "Original Sin and the Providence of God," pp. 54–55.

100. See above, p. 42.

101. See LR, p. 41. See also above, p. 42.

102. With regard to the limitless characteristic of the self-gift, there is a distinction between the familial communion and the worker communion. See above, p. 44.

103. See LE, no. 6.

104. See *The Rites of the Catholic Church: Rite of Marriage,* promulgated by Pope Paul VI and translated by the International Commission on English in the Liturgy (New York: Pueblo Publishing Co., 1976), no. 33.

3

Original Sin and the Providence of God

He has spoken through the Prophets.

A. Original Sin

Human persons are incredible beings. We are called to love as God loves and to express love in and through our bodies. Love is a choice, i.e., a will-act (founded on the truth known by the mind) of at least two persons to give themselves to one another.[1] It is quite obvious, then, that it is absolutely necessary for the spiritual faculties of mind and will to "orchestrate" our various bodily capacities, e.g., emotions, so that we can express love in and through our bodies.

Often, this "orchestration" of the bodily powers does not succeed. St. Paul probably put it best when he wrote, "I do not understand my own actions. For I do not do what I want, but I do the very thing I hate."[2] If we have a favorite food, e.g., chocolate candy, we might decide not to eat more than a certain amount. Yet, in the end, almost to our own amazement, we often find that we have eaten more than we had planned. In this case, our bodies do not express the proper love of self. In our dealings with others, we sometimes make a firm resolution that we will not allow others to anger us. Yet we find ourselves becoming angry. In this case, our bodies do not express the proper love for others. Obviously, the choices we make in our wills founded on the truths we know are not always carried out. Rather, we alter and change them.

It is important to notice that in the two examples, our love was not expressed because our bodily desires influenced our spiritual powers (our minds and wills) that enable us to love. In both these cases, we did not choose to love. Rather, we acted unlovingly because we allowed our bodily desires unduly to influence our minds and wills. However, despite the powerful influence we sometimes permit our bodies to have over our minds and wills, the human body is not somehow separate from the human person. The body does not have a mind and a will of its own in opposition to, as it were, the "real" human person "inside." If we have eaten too much, *we* have decided to eat too much. If we have become angry, *we* have decided to become angry. In the examples above, our bodily desires have influenced our minds and wills, and we have "changed our minds." We have decided not to love. Therefore, we are still responsible for our own acts. Our bodies have not decided (nor can they decide) to do anything "on their own."

But God did not create our bodies to influence our minds and wills unduly! Rather, God intended our bodies to express our persons. God could hardly have created us as enfleshed spirits and expected our bodies to express our persons (and be reflections of His own acts) without making the spiritual powers in the human person primary. The bodily desires and emotions should not be as powerful as they are. They should not be able to influence our minds and wills as they do because with their influence it is almost impossible for our bodies to express our persons. For example, as images of God, we are called to love in and through the familial and worker *communions of persons* in imitation of the divine *communion of Persons.* Love is a choice (founded on the truth) of at least two persons to give themselves totally to one another. These choices should then be expressed in and through their bodies. However, if their bodies do not respond to their choices and even unduly influence their choices, it is impossible for them to express love in and through their bodies. In other words, it is impossible for them to love as human beings. We appear to be the most pathetic of creatures because it is almost impossible for us to do what we are created to do: to express God-like acts in and through our bodies. We all experience this lack of wholeness or integration. We know our situation, but we do not know how it came to be. The story of the creation and the fall in Genesis explains why we are the way we are.

When God created Adam and Eve, they were naked and they were not ashamed.[3] After sin, "they knew that they were naked; and they sewed fig leaves together and made themselves aprons."[4] Obviously, their experience of nakedness had changed as a result of sin. The Pope writes, "This passage . . . speaks of the mutual shame of the man and the woman as a symptom of the fall."[5] Shame exists when one holds a particular value system and, in spite of what is believed, acts contrary to it. Before sin, Adam and Eve were naked and were not ashamed because they acted according to what they believed. However, after sin, they were naked and they were ashamed because they were engaged in an activity contrary to their value system, i.e., they experienced lust.[6] They believed, as they had before sin, that each one of them was of incredible worth and value. They accepted the personalistic norm that "the only proper and adequate attitude"[7] towards other persons is love. However, after sin, their bodies no longer always responded properly to their choices to love one another. Instead, their bodily desires sometimes influenced their minds and wills to use each other as a source of pleasure. The tendency to use one another was contrary to their own value system and was the cause of their shame.

The change in Adam and Eve occurred because of sin. God had asked them not to eat the fruit from the tree of the knowledge of good and evil. In spite of God's wish, Adam and Eve did eat this fruit. They disobeyed God. They sinned. They acted contrary to God. However, since Adam and Eve were created to love God,[8] when they sinned, they did not do what they were created to do. Thus, in sinning, they not only offended God, they also hurt themselves. As John Paul has written, "Sin is not only 'against' God, it is at the same time 'against' man."[9]

When Adam and Eve sinned, they hurt themselves in three ways. First, they lost the gift of God's own life, grace, because God (Love) and sin (anti-love) cannot exist together.[10] Second, they wounded their own spiritual faculties. Original sin caused a *"darkening* of the *intellect's* capacity to know the truth, and . . . a *weakening of free will.*"[11] Third, the bodies of Adam and Eve were wounded. Without grace, they could not come to the glory of heaven. Further, without grace and with the damage Adam and Eve did to their own natural being by acting against it when they sinned, it was almost impossible for them to love God: "Human beings deprived of divine grace have thus inherited a common mortal nature, incapable of choosing what is good and inclined to covetousness."[12] In addition, their bodies no longer responded properly to their choices, and their bodily desires now had an undue influence on their minds and wills. The ultimate result of the damage they did to their own bodies was death. As John Paul has written, "As a consequence of original sin, the whole man, body and soul, has been thrown into confusion."[13] The sin of Adam and Eve was a catastrophe for them, a *"dreadful 'destructive force!'* "[14] Of course, by not loving God and hurting themselves, they made it almost impossible for them to love each other. Thus, sin is an alienation from God, from oneself, and from others.[15]

The sin of Adam and Eve was a catastrophe not only for them, but also for all their descendants. We are all conceived and born with the sin of Adam and Eve and its effects. Still, it hardly seems fair and just that we should suffer for the personal sin of Adam and Eve. The Pope acknowledges the problem when he writes that in "Adam's descendants [original sin] *has not the character of personal guilt.*"[16] This problem might be expressed with the question: If original sin is not our personal sin, why should we suffer its effects? The Pope answers the difficulty: "The first human being (man and woman) . . . [was the] founder of the human family."[17] For good or for ill, Adam and Eve were the representatives of the human race. They could have responded to God by acknowledging Him as Creator and giving Him thanks for what He had done. Instead, as our representatives, they chose not to thank Him and to reject Him. As a result, we, their descendants, live with their decision. Had they chosen the other path, we would have benefited. As it is, Adam's sin is inherited by all.[18] This inherited sin is transmitted to us through the natural generative process: "Adam's sin is transmitted to all his descendants *by generation and not merely by way of bad example.'"*[19] It is passed from father to son, from mother to daughter.

The Church's teaching on the transmission of original sin and its effects through the generative process is clearly opposed to any evolutionary theories that suggest that the human race descended from more than one set of parents (polygenism). Pope Paul VI called attention to this at a symposium of theologians and scientists: "It is evident that the explanations of original sin given by some modern authors will appear to you as irreconcilable with genuine Catholic teaching. Such authors, starting from the unproved premise of *polygenism*, deny, more or less clearly, that the sin from which such a mass of evils has derived in humanity, was, above all, the disobedience of Adam 'the first man.' "[20] But as St. Paul writes, "Sin came into the world through one man and death through sin, and so death spread to all men because all men sinned."[21] The truth in St. Paul's text is "that *Adam's sin* (the sin of our first parents) had consequences *for all mankind.'"*[22] Adam's sin has consequences for all of us because we inherit it. In us, original sin is a *"hereditary* sin"[23] that we receive from our parents together with the gift of life. Since the sin is Adam's sin and since we inherit it, we must all be descendants of Adam. There could not have been a multitude of first parents. Adam does not represent an entire group of persons, but is, indeed, the name of one single human person, the father of us all.

Still, one might well ask why this rejection of God's love was so devastating not only for Adam and Eve, but also for all their descendants. Why did God take this rejection as the definitive act of Adam and Eve? Could it not have been seen as one small slip among many positive, loving acts? Of course not. There were no other mature loving acts. According to the Genesis account of the first sin, the temptation of the devil was the first chance for them to choose to love God in a mature way.[24] The devil presented Adam and Eve with the first opportunity to make a mature choice for God. Prior to the devil's temptation, the love of our first parents for God was like that of small children for their parents. It never occurs to very young children not to respond to the love their parents show them. Similarly, with Adam and Eve, before the devil's temptation, it never occurred to them not to love God; e.g., it never occurred to Adam to ignore God's wish when God asked him to name the animals.[25] The devil presented another possibility, another alternative, to Adam and Eve. The devil gave our first parents the chance to love God maturely, i.e., to choose to love Him above all things even in the face of other attractive alternatives. Therefore, until the devil's temptation, Adam and Eve did not have an opportunity to love God in a mature way.[26] Clearly, an opportunity for Adam and Eve to love God maturely was of the utmost importance. Perhaps God permitted Satan to tempt Adam and Eve so that they could come to a mature love for Him. Thus, the devil's temptation gave Adam and Eve a chance to respond to God's incredible gifts. It was their first real opportunity to satisfy God's "longing" for His children to turn to Him.[27]

A further question comes to mind: Why is it that God asked Adam and Eve not to eat the fruit of a particular tree? At first, such a request seems trivial. However, "The tree 'of the knowledge of good and evil' denotes the first principle of human life to which is linked *a fundamental problem.* The tempter knows this very well, for he says: 'When you eat of it . . . you will be like God knowing good and evil.' *The tree therefore signifies the insurmountable limit* for man and for any creature, however perfect."[28] In taking the fruit, Adam and Eve tried to know good and evil as God knows them. In other words, they tried to define what was good for themselves instead of accepting God as the "source of the moral order."[29] In trying to know good and evil as God does, Adam and Eve claimed "to become an independent and exclusive source for deciding about good and evil."[30] The sin of our first parents was not so much the eating of the fruit of a particular tree, but the attempt to make themselves gods. In effect, they attempted to surpass the *"insurmountable limit"* for any creature.[31] The first sin, therefore, was a sin of pride.

In fact, the first sin could have been nothing but a sin of pride. Before sin, Adam and Eve perfectly expressed their thoughts and choices in and through their bodies. They could not be tempted (as their descendants are) by particularly luscious fruit or other delicious foods, or by any of the bodily desires or emotions. Since their spiritual faculties properly "orchestrated" their bodily powers, any temptation to sin had to be directed at their spiritual faculties. In fact, the serpent, the devil, did attack a spiritual faculty, the mind. The devil attacked Eve's self-concept as a creature when he suggested that she could be "like God, knowing good and evil."[32]

"Now the serpent was more subtle than any other wild creature that the Lord God had made."[33] Indeed, Satan was (and is) more clever than any earthly creature God had made because he is an angel.[34] His intelligence is clearly visible in the brilliant tempting of Eve. It was a tragic charade. The serpent seemed to be inviting Adam and Eve to become more like God. It appeared that he was inviting them to fulfill themselves as images of God. Apparently, the devil was asking them to do only what God had asked them to do when God invited them to love as He loves.[35] It seemed that he was inviting Adam and Eve to become what God had created them to be. The devil, the "cosmic 'liar,' "[36] took the truth about the creation of Adam and Eve in the image of God, falsified it, and used it against them. The wonder, glory, and uniqueness of Adam and Eve (and of all other human persons) are founded in their personhood, i.e., in their reflection of the divine. The devil used this spark of the divine, which is the glory of each human being, against Adam and Eve and their descendants. In a sense, he used the source of the value and dignity of every human being to tempt Adam and Eve to tarnish and almost to destroy their own human dignity. The source of human dignity became the means of humanity's downfall.

Nevertheless, Adam and Eve could have recognized the temptation for what it was because the devil lied three times. Adam and Eve should have recognized these lies as part of the serpent's ploy to lead them to sin. The serpent's first lie occurred when he claimed that God had lied.[37] It is impossible for God, as Truth itself,[38] to lie. Adam and Eve should have recognized the devil's claim that God had lied as an obvious falsehood and an enticement to sin. The devil also lied when he promised them that "you will be like God."[39] In his previous (false) claim that God had lied, the devil was claiming to know truth because only one who knows truth can recognize a lie. In claiming to know truth, the devil was claiming to know what God knows. In other words, the devil put himself in God's place.[40] With the true God, their Creator, perceived as a liar, Adam and Eve believed that the devil knew an alternate god, a true one. Unfortunately, Adam and Eve believed that they could fulfill themselves as images of God by becoming like this alternate god. However, in reality, the devil was cunningly presenting himself as the alternate god. Adam and Eve should have recognized this second lie as an enticement to sin. The devil lied a third time when he promised Adam and Eve that they could know good and evil like God.[41] However, in promising Adam and Eve that they could fulfill themselves by knowing good and evil like God, he was promising that they could be gods. Adam and Eve should have recognized this third lie as an enticement to sin. It is interesting to note that the devil's third lie contradicts his second lie. Through the second lie, the devil put himself in God's place. Through his third lie, he promised Adam and Eve that they could be gods. In other words, the devil, playing god, was promising Adam and Eve that they also could play god. However, the devil would never have allowed Adam and Eve to assume the same position he had taken for himself. The inner contradiction within the devil's temptation of Adam and Eve should have been a warning to Adam and Eve that the devil was lying. (See the diagram, "Temptations of Adam/Eve," on this page.)

TEMPTATIONS OF ADAM/EVE

1. God lied.
2. You will become like a god, i.e., like me.
3. You will be gods defining good and evil.

Adam and Eve would probably have realized the devil was lying to them if Satan had not suggested a plausible reason to doubt God and to believe him. What reason could the devil possibly have used to persuade Adam and Eve to reject God, their loving Creator? Succinctly, almost cryptically, the author of Genesis reveals Satan's rationale in the dialogue between Eve and the serpent: "The serpent said to the woman, 'You will not die. For God knows that when you eat of it your eyes will be opened, and you will be like God, knowing good and evil.' "[42] The devil's third lie contains the motive. Satan suggests that God had forbidden Adam and Eve to fulfill themselves by becoming more God-like by knowing good and evil. In other words, the devil suggests that God had forbidden what was good for Adam and Eve, i.e., their self-fulfillment as images of God. Why would God do such a thing? The obvious answer is that God did not want anyone, any creature, to be like Him, even though it is good for some of His creatures to be like Him, i.e., those made in His image and likeness. In this false view, God is a mean-spirited, jealous being, Who, as a tyrant, will strive to maintain His own unique position against anyone and anybody. The serpent's third lie clearly supplies the motive for rejecting God and accepting the plausibility of an alternate god. Once Adam and Eve believe that God is a jealous being Who cares only about maintaining His own position, they also logically conclude that when God claimed to love and care for them,[43] He was lying. Further, they begin to look for an alternate god and the devil presents them with one, i.e., himself. As the Pope writes, "God the Creator is placed in a state of suspicion, indeed of accusation, in the mind of the creature. For the first time in human history there appears the perverse 'genius of suspicion.' . . . [The devil shows] *God as an enemy* of His own creature, and in the first place as an enemy of man, *as a source of danger and threat to man.* In this way, *Satan* manages to sow in man's soul the seed of opposition to the One Who 'from the beginning' would be considered as man's enemy—and not as Father."[44] The words the serpent speaks to Adam and Eve "contain *all the assault of evil* that can arise in the free will of the creature in regard to Him Who, as Creator, is the source of all being and of all good."[45] "Man is challenged to become the adversary of God!"[46]

In sinning, Adam and Eve did not reject God as completely and totally as the angels did when they sinned.[47] First, the powerful, angelic intellects had comprehended God and themselves much more clearly than Adam and Eve had comprehended God and themselves. Consequently, it was simply not possible for Adam and Eve to reject God as completely as the angels had.[48] Second, since Adam and Eve were at first seeking to fulfill themselves, i.e., to become more like God, their sin was not a total rejection of God. Man "accepted the suggestion to avail himself of a created thing, [the fruit], *contrary to the prohibition of the Creator,* thinking that he also—man —could be 'like God, knowing good and evil.' "[49] At first, Adam and Eve did not recognize the devil's lies for what they were. At this point, Adam and Eve were willing their own self-fulfillment as images of God. However, later, Adam and Eve must have perceived that the devil had lied. Nevertheless, they accepted and acted on the lies. At that point, they sinned. Still, since the initial motive of Adam and Eve was their own self-fulfillment, their sin was not a total and complete rejection of God: "It does not seem that man had fully accepted the totality of negation and hatred of God contained in the words of the 'father of lies.' "[50] Third, Adam and Eve at first accepted the devil's lies as the truth; the angels would never have accepted lies as truth. Some angels did reject truth, but they recognized truth as truth and lies as lies.[51] Fourth, Adam and Eve had the "help" of Satan while Satan and his followers sinned on their own. Humanity was not brought to its tragic downfall by itself. Without the temptation of the serpent, Adam and Eve might never have sinned. It was only through the temptation of the devil that they opposed the Creator. In other words, God created human persons in His own image with such goodness that it took someone from the outside, an angel, to entice man to sin. For all these reasons, the sin of our first parents was not as complete and as total a rejection of God as the angelic sin was.

However, even though Adam and Eve did not reject God as totally as the fallen angels had, still, their sin was *"in a certain sense a reflection* and the consequence of the sin that had already occurred in the world of invisible beings."[52] As stated above,[53] Satan and his followers turned away from God because they wanted to be truth as God is Truth. The fallen angels were the first to seek to "know good and evil like God."[54] In the guise of a serpent, Satan suggested to Adam and Eve that they, creatures though they were, should fulfill themselves by knowing good and evil like God. However, Satan did not actually want Adam and Eve to be gods. He was actually seeking followers. He wanted Adam and Eve (and through them the entire human race) to join in the same rebellion he and his angelic followers had already begun: "Man, by yielding to the suggestion of the tempter, became the slave and accomplice of the rebellious spirits!"[55]

The sin of Adam and Eve *"in a certain sense* contains *the original 'model' of every sin* of which man is capable."[56] We oppose God everyday as Adam and Eve did! God gives us the commandments for our own good just as He had asked Adam and Eve not to eat of the fruit for their own good. When we act against the commandments, we deny that the commandments are good for us just as Adam and Eve denied that God's commandment was good for them. For example, when we steal, we believe that our own best interests are served not through avoiding this act, but by doing it. At least implicitly, there is a belief that God told us not to steal not for our own good, but rather to keep us as His slaves. In effect, we deny God's love for us. We implicitly claim that God has given us the commandments not to benefit us, but to benefit Himself. We reject God because we deny the truth of what He has told us. Therefore, we determine that we know better than God. In effect, we claim to know good and evil as God knows good and evil.

Since we have all inherited original sin, we are all affected by Satan's lies. We have a distorted view of who God is because we do not properly comprehend Him as a loving and caring Creator. As John Paul wrote while he was still Archbishop of Cracow, "But the truth about the God of the covenant, about the God Who creates out of love, Who in love offers humanity the covenant in Adam, Who for love's sake puts to man requirements which have direct bearing on the truth of man's creaturely being—this is the truth that is destroyed in what Satan says. And the destruction is total."[57] With this false view of God accepted, man loses sight of himself because as images of God, we do not know who we are unless we know who God is.

B. God's Providence

"We cannot conclude this catechesis [on original sin] without emphasizing again what we said at the beginning of the present cycle, namely, that original sin must *constantly be considered in reference to*

the mystery of the redemption carried out by Jesus Christ, the Son of
God, Who 'for us men and for our salvation became man.' "⁵⁸ Even
while telling Adam and Eve the effects of their action, God gives
them hope that He would conquer the evil they had brought upon
themselves. For God says to the serpent, "I will put enmity between
you and the woman, and between your seed and her seed; he shall
bruise your head, and you shall bruise his heel."⁵⁹ "Here are the first
rays of light to appear above the abyss, above the conflict between
good and evil."⁶⁰ In these words, God is promising a Redeemer,
Who, born of a woman, will crush the serpent, i.e., Satan: "The
mystery of iniquity is dispelled by the 'mystery of mercy.' "⁶¹ God
will overcome the evil that entered the world through the surrender
of our first parents to Satan's temptation. Thus, "from the moment
of the very first denial, Truth—the divine Truth—will always seek, in
ways known only to itself, to penetrate world history, to enter the
minds and hearts of men."⁶² God's infinite and unbounding love for
Adam and Eve and their descendants is quite clear from His promise
to overcome the evil they had brought on themselves. Even though
they had rejected God, God did not abandon them. After original
sin, "God has not abandoned the human race to the power of sin and
death. He wished to rescue and save it. He did so in His own way,
. . . according to a self-effacement [the cross] such as only a God of
love could display."⁶³

God's love for Adam and Eve and their descendants, even after
sin, is a continuation of the divine judgment made at the dawn of
history that God's creation of Adam and Eve was "very good."⁶⁴ In
other words, God's judgment on His own creative handiwork is not
altered by sin: "Divine providence implies the recognition that . . .
that evil which originally had no place, once committed by man and
permitted by God, is in the last analysis *subordinated* to the good."⁶⁵
God's creation cannot be overcome by evil. Even sin cannot ultimately thwart God's infinite love as expressed in the creation of the
human species. As a loving, infinite, almighty Father, God is able to
draw from sin *"the definitive good of the whole created cosmos."*⁶⁶ Of
course, it is true that sin is the cause of much evil, but it "cannot
block the construction of the kingdom of God."⁶⁷

However, if God loves Adam and Eve and their descendants enough to save them from evil, why does He allow them to do evil in the first place? Certainly God has the power to prevent sin. Instead of exercising this power, God chose to permit sin and then to deal with its horrendous consequences. Would it not have been easier for God to have prevented the original sin in the beginning? *"Originating within man, in his will,* sin, by its very essence, is always an act of the person *(actus personae),* a conscious and free act, in which *man's free will is expressed."*[68] As a conscious and free act, original sin was a choice. The only possible way for God to have prevented the sin of Adam and Eve would have been for Him to have eliminated their capacities of knowing and freely choosing. In other words, if God had wanted to prevent the original sin, He would either have had to create Adam and Eve without minds and free wills or He would have had to inhibit the functioning of these powers, at least at the time of temptation. Clearly, without the capacities for knowing and freely choosing, Adam and Eve would have been little better than the animals. They would not have been images of God, i.e., persons. If God had inhibited the powers of thinking and freely choosing, Adam and Eve would have been like robots operated by God.

When God created man and woman, He wanted neither another animal species nor robots. By creating Adam and Eve and their descendants as persons (in His own image), God willed that they should imitate Him by loving.[69] God willed that there be love in the world and since *"true love . . . is possible only on the basis of freedom,"*[70] God was willing to risk the horrendous evil of sin in order that true love would exist. Human love was more important to God than the possibility that human persons might misuse freedom, i.e., that they might sin.[71]

As God permitted the sin of Adam and Eve, so He permits their descendants to sin. For the most part, the people of the Old Testament sinned because they had a tendency towards sin, a lack of grace and a "spark of sin."[72] This "spark of sin" is a lack of integration, one of the effects of original sin. As God allowed Adam and Eve (and through them their descendants) to experience some of the effects of original sin, so He allows the descendants of Adam and Eve to experience some of the effects of their own personal sins. In other words, as God allowed Adam and Eve to suffer the *"destructive force"*[73] of original sin, so He allowed their descendants to suffer the self-inflicted wounds of their own sins. As a good parent, God taught the ancient Israelites to take responsibility for their actions by allowing them to experience the effects of their sinful actions.

Although God permitted the people of the Old Testament to sin and to experience some consequences of their sins, He saved them from some of their sins and, more often, from the effects of their sins.[74] Experiencing God's love for them, the people of the Old Testament were often grateful to God, i.e., they often loved Him more. In other words, God was drawing good from the evil of sin. He was allowing the Old Testament people to experience merciful love: *"The People of God of the old covenant* had drawn from their age-long history *a special experience of the mercy of God.* This experience was social and communal, as well as individual and interior."[75] Thus, God was gradually preparing them to receive the promised Redeemer, the ultimate expression of God's merciful love. Mercy "was *constantly re-evoked* . . . in the very history of Israel"[76] as a means of making straight the way of the Lord.[77]

Many of the events recorded in the Old Testament clearly demonstrate the tendency towards sin inherent in man after original sin. We see the effects of the lack of grace and the "spark of sin" within Adam and Eve immediately following their eating the fruit of the tree. When God asks if they have eaten the forbidden fruit, Adam replies, "The woman whom Thou gavest to be with me, she gave me fruit of the tree, and I ate."[78] While there is some truth in this statement (Eve *did* bring the fruit to Adam), the implication that Adam was forced by Eve to eat the fruit is a lie. Adam is unable to control his own fear of how God would respond to his sin. Fearful of God's wrath, Adam tries to deflect the evil from himself. He tries to pretend that he did not eat the fruit through his own free will. Of course, he was not forced by Eve. Rather, he made a free choice to accept Eve's offer of the fruit. His attempt to elude the responsibility for his evil act is a lie, a further sin. It stems from a lack of grace and his own inability to "orchestrate" his own passions ("spark of sin").

Taking a cue from Adam, Eve also refuses to take responsibility. She blames the serpent for her sin as though she had no part in it, as though the serpent had deprived her of her freedom.[79] Again, there is some truth in what she says, but, nevertheless, she had a choice to accept or not to accept the devil's lies. She freely chose to accept the lies, i.e., she sinned. She blamed the serpent, ducking responsibility, because she, like Adam, feared her sin's results. Lacking grace and integration, she lied. The effects of original sin afflicted her as well as Adam.

God's response to Adam and Eve is very interesting. First, He announces the effects of sin on the serpent. Thus, God acknowledges the greater responsibility of the devil in the sin of Adam and Eve. Second, He announces the effects of sin on Adam and Eve.[80] It is important to note that God is not punishing Adam and Eve. Rather, He is announcing what they have done to themselves. Original sin weakened Adam and Eve. They were no longer able to "orchestrate" their own bodily fears and desires, nor were they able to exercise the proper dominion over the world. The effect of sin mentioned by God to Eve ("I will greatly multiply your pain in childbearing")[81] indicates that her body is no longer integrated. Most of the effects announced to Adam show that man could no longer exercise a dominion over the things of the world.[82] Lacking this dominion, Adam and Eve were no longer in paradise because paradise was precisely the dominion of man over the elements. God had not thrown them out of paradise. Rather, their sin had wounded them and made paradise an impossibility! Third, "the Lord God made for Adam and for his wife garments of skins, and clothed them."[83] Adam and Eve needed clothes to hide themselves from each other because their sin caused them to feel shame. Further, they needed clothes to protect themselves from the elements because their sin caused them to lose their dominion over things. Even though their need for clothing was the direct result of their sin, God did not let them suffer the *full* effects of their sin. They had hurt themselves. They had brought the need for clothing on themselves, but He fulfills the need. He does not eliminate the sin or all of its effects, but He does overcome some of the effects. The clothing provided by God for Adam and Eve is a sign of

His continuing care for the human race. Might it be suggested that God's care of the physical necessities is a sign of His care of the spiritual necessities? It is also obvious that Adam and Eve would have been grateful for God's gift to them. God's love—divine mercy —saves our first parents from some effects of their sin and encourages them to respond to Him in love.

The well-known story of Cain and Abel also attests to the lack of grace and the "spark of sin." Cain was angry that God accepted the sacrifice of his brother, Abel, but found his own offering unacceptable.[84] In other words, Cain could not accept God's will. In this rejection of God's will, Cain's sin resembled the sin of his parents. Lacking grace and integration, Cain became uncontrollably jealous of Abel and he murdered him. God announced the effects of the sin to Cain: "You shall be a fugitive and a wanderer on the earth."[85] God was not punishing Cain, but rather telling him what the consequences of his own act were. Cain had claimed his brother's life. Clearly, his own act had made it impossible for him to continue to live with his own family. Further, Cain had claimed the power and wisdom to take care of life, and God told him that he would be responsible for his own life. God permitted Cain to sin and to suffer the effects of sin. Still, when Cain cried out to God, "Whoever finds me will slay me," God said, "Not so! If any one slays Cain, vengeance shall be taken on him sevenfold."[86] Cain begged God for His protection. In other words, Cain asked God to take care of him. Having rejected that divine care, Cain realized his need and begged God for His protection. Rather than withholding it, as one might think, God offered Cain His providential care. God placed a special mark of divine protection on Cain so that others would know that Cain's murder would be avenged by the Lord. God protected Cain from a very serious effect of his sin. Cain would have felt an affection for God because God protected Him. God drew good (i.e., the protection of Cain's life and Cain's gratitude to God) from the evil of Cain's sin. In other words, God loved Cain mercifully.

Following Cain's murder of Abel, man continued to sin, and "the Lord was sorry that He had made man on the earth."[87] God was sorry He had made man because He was saddened that His earthly images were suffering the self-inflicted wounds of sin.[88] The more they sinned, the more they harmed themselves. One effect of their sins was that men and women exercised less and less dominion over the world. Thus, the flood overwhelmed men and women, destroying them. However, "Noah found favor in the eyes of the Lord."[89] Still, God allowed everyone but Noah to experience an effect of sin: death through the flood. Noah must have been grateful to God, and Noah's love enabled God to invite Noah to unite with Him in a new bond of love, a covenant. This new covenant was the first between man and God since Adam and Eve broke the covenant of creation. Noah accepted God's offer of this new covenant, and through it he and his descendants came closer to God. Again God shows His mercy: He draws good (the sparing of Noah and the new covenant, which brings mankind closer to God) from the evil of sin.

Even from these few examples, the pattern is apparent. Man sins because of the lack of grace and the lack of integration (the "spark of sin"). The sins committed inflict wounds on the sinners, but God never allows all these effects to be felt by His earthly images. In other words, He permits some effects of sin to be felt and then spares the human race from the rest of them. Since man is at least partially spared, he is grateful to God and is drawn closer to Him. God is merciful, i.e., He draws good from the evil of sin. This is the pattern with Adam and Eve, Cain, and Noah.

The story of the Tower of Babel suggests the same pattern.[90] The people sought to build a city with a great tower. However, they forgot God. Thus, the sin of the people of Babel was similar to the sin of Adam and Eve. Both sins consist in the exclusion of God. However, "in the story of Babel, *the exclusion of God* is presented not so much under the aspect of opposition to Him as of forgetfulness and indifference towards Him, as if God were of no relevance in the sphere of man's joint projects."[91] In Babel, the lack of grace and the "spark of sin" led the people to forget God. By excluding God, they excluded love because God is Love. Lacking love for one another they could not sustain their union. They reaped the result of their sin: they eventually could not understand one another, and they scattered "over the face of all the earth."[92] In other words, the *com-*

munion of persons that existed among the people of Babel was broken apart. But for some, God established a new, loving *communion of persons.* In choosing Abraham to be a father of a new nation, God formed His own people, a new *communion of persons,* from among the scattered nations. Making a covenant with Abraham, God drew Abraham and his descendants into a unique, loving relationship with Him and with each other.[93] God permitted the people of Babel to sin and, as a result, to be scattered. However, from the scattered peoples, He formed a new people. Thus, He saved them from the full effect of their sin. The new People of God were drawn closer to Him through the new covenant. Thus, God drew good from evil. His mercy triumphed over sin.

God's mercy towards sinners is found on many pages of the Old Testament. However, three more instances deserve some attention: the incidents of the seraph serpents, David and Bathsheba, and the exile. During their long exodus from Egypt into the promised land, the Israelites complained to Moses, "Why have you brought us up out of Egypt to die in the wilderness?"[94] Their lack of grace and their lack of integration (the "spark of sin") led them to reject God's providential care for them. As Adam and Eve, the Israelites believed that God was not concerned about their welfare[95] and that His will, as expressed by Moses, would eventually ruin them. Therefore, they rejected God's will, i.e., they rejected His offer of providential love and trusted their own idea: to return to Egypt. In rejecting God's providential care, the Israelites immediately subjected themselves to all the hostile forces of nature. Presumably, God had been protecting them from all these. However, with their rejection of His care, they rejected His divine protection. Fiery serpents "bit the people, so that many people of Israel died."[96] God let His people experience the deadly effect of their own sin, but not completely. He told Moses, "Make a fiery [bronze] serpent, and set it on a pole; and every one who is bitten, when he sees it, shall live."[97] Those who gazed on the bronze serpent were cured. They must have been grateful to God for the restoration of their health. In other words, they were drawn closer to God. Again, in this incident, God's merciful love is apparent.

The deservedly famous story of David and Bathsheba is another revelation of human sin and God's merciful response to man. King David had sent Joab and the Israelite armies to fight the Ammonites, but David remained in Jerusalem. One of the Israelite soldiers fighting with Joab, Uriah, had a wife named Bathsheba. The king saw Bathsheba bathing on the roof of her home. David sent for her and "he lay with her" and she conceived a child.[98] Then David called Uriah back to Jerusalem in hopes that Uriah would stay with Bathsheba. David hoped that his sin might not be discovered. However, Uriah refused to stay in his own house. Frustrated because his plan to conceal his sin had failed, David sent Uriah back to Joab. In a letter, David ordered Joab to place Uriah in the forefront of the fighting and then to abandon him so that Uriah would be killed. After Joab had followed David's order, the king sent for Bathsheba and "brought her to his house, and she became his wife, and bore him a son. But the thing that David had done displeased the Lord."[99] The lack of grace and the "spark of sin," i.e., the lack of integration, made it almost impossible for David to overcome both his passion for Bathsheba and his frustration with Uriah.

Through Nathan the prophet, David learned the tragic effects of his sin. Realizing what he had done, David confessed, " 'I have sinned against the Lord.' And Nathan said to David, 'The Lord also has put away your sin; you shall not die.' "[100] In claiming a life, David had done what Cain did.[101] In effect, David had claimed the authority to take care of life. However, David confessed his sin, and, as with Cain, God did not withdraw His protective care from David. With God's providential care, David would not die as a result of his sin: "Nevertheless, . . . the child that is born to you shall die."[102] The death of the child was the direct result of David's sin. David and Bathsheba had committed adultery, i.e., they had acted against love.[103] Since love and life are one and the same,[104] an act against love is an act against life. Thus, the murder of Uriah by David, the adulterer, should not surprise us. Similarly, the death of the child should not surprise us. Acting against love, David and Bathsheba acted against life. Thus, they brought the death of their child on themselves.[105] Nathan's prophecy notwithstanding, David did penance for the child hoping that God's mercy would even spare him this effect of his sin. However, God allowed David to suffer the death of the child. Still, from this horrendous situation, there comes a happy ending. After the death of the child, "David comforted his wife, Bathsheba, . . . and she bore a son, and he called his name Solomon. And the Lord loved him."[106] Solomon was born in the context of a true, loving union between David and Bathsheba. David must have been grateful to the Lord for his new son. From the initial sinful union of David and Bathsheba comes one of the wisest kings the world has ever known, Solomon! It was Solomon who was to build the Lord's temple, which was to stand almost four hundred years until the Babylonian exile. God's mercy is again evident. He permitted David and Bathsheba to suffer the effect of their sin, but not completely. Through their sin, David and Bathsheba had lost a child, but God allowed David and Bathsheba to conceive another child. Both David and Bathsheba must have been grateful to God, and this gratitude must have drawn them closer to God. David and Bathsheba experienced the merciful love of God.

God's providential mercy is also revealed in the incident of the exile.[107] Weakened by their lack of grace and the "spark of sin," the ancient Israelites refused more and more to follow God's will as expressed through the prophets. Lacking confidence in the wisdom of God's prophetic words, they began to rely on their own insights. In other words, they tried to put themselves in God's place, knowing good and evil like God.[108] This sin was not unlike the sin of their forefathers in the desert when the fiery serpents bit the people.[109] God allowed them to try to care for themselves. The result was exile. Their sin, the rejection of God's providential care and their reliance on their own powers, directly caused a catastrophe: exile. However, God saved them from their painful exile when He heard their confession of sin and their cries for mercy. He permitted them to return to the promised land. He renewed the covenant He had made with them, drawing them closer to Him than they had been before the exile.[110] He draws good from evil, i.e., He shows mercy to them.

In the cases of David and the exile, there is an element not found in the previous instances: the confession of guilt. David and the exiles acknowledge their sins, and then God shows mercy. His mercy includes the forgiveness of their sins. Thus, God not only saves them from the effects of their sins, He actually forgives their sins. The recognition of their own guilt shows that David and, later, the exiled Jews have developed a sense of sin. This sense of sin, this sense of evil, testifies to a sense of God. Sin can only be perceived with a knowledge and a love of God because sin is *"exclusion of God, rupture with God, disobedience to God."*[111] If there is a sense of sin, there must be a sense of God. The confessions of David and the exiled Jews show that God had drawn the Jews, throughout their long history, closer to Him: *"To acknowledge one's sin . . . is the essential first step in returning to God."*[112]

At this point, one might well ask: Why? Why had God "worked" for so long to bring the people of the Old Testament closer to Him? From man's perspective, all the merciful acts of God throughout the Old Testament would seem to have been totally in vain because God apparently had allowed the human race to suffer original sin and its most terrible effect: the loss of grace. Without grace, the Old Testament people could not come to the ultimate closeness with God: heaven. Further, original sin caused a wounding of man's very nature. This damage, especially the lack of integration (the "spark of sin"), together with the lack of grace, made it almost impossible for human beings to act as images of God. In other words, after original sin, it was almost impossible for human beings to love God and through Him other persons.[113] The lack of a true, loving friendship with God on earth is clearly illustrated by the differences between the way Adam and Eve spoke to God before sin and the way they spoke to Him after sin. After sin, God asked Adam where he was, and Adam replied, "I was afraid, because I was naked; and I hid myself."[114] The Pope comments, "A very significant reply. Man in the beginning (in the state of original justice) spoke to the Creator with friendship and confidence, . . . but now he has lost the basis of that friendship."[115] Making it almost impossible to love God, original sin had nearly destroyed any possibility for man to come close to God. All God's merciful acts in the Old Testament could never bring man as close to God as he was created to be. They were doomed to failure because they never overcame the ultimate obstacles to man's closeness with God: original sin and its most damaging effects. Throughout the Old Testament, God seemed to be working only on the symptoms and not on the disease! (There was one exception: in making skins for Adam and Eve, God did overcome one of the effects of original sin.)[116] Why did God not work on the disease itself? From God's perspective, His merciful acts in the Old Testament did not make it entirely possible for Him to continue His initial judgment that the creation of man was "very good."[117] The judgment of divine providence about man rested on man's capability to act as an image of God. It was precisely this capacity that was almost destroyed through original sin. For the most part,[118] divine merciful acts in the Old Testament did not even touch original sin or its effects. Thus, from man's point of view as well as God's, it seems that the divine merciful acts in the Old Testament were not very effective. Why did God not extend His mercy towards the real problem: original sin and its most serious effects?

The answer is clear: God had to prepare the way for the Redeemer Who would forgive sin, heal the wounds of original sin, and restore grace. Beginning with creation, God continually offered His love to His people. There needed to be a human response to this divine love. However, Adam and Eve both rejected God's love. The people of the Old Testament, afflicted with the effects of original sin, were incapable of responding to God's love. Of course, God had the capability of responding to His own love, but God wished a human response. God found a solution: Jesus Christ, the God-man Who redeems all people. As God, Christ responds to the Father's love. As man, Christ offers the Father a human response. In offering man's response to the Father, Christ includes all people. God did not send His Son earlier because man was not yet ready to participate in Christ's response to the Father. God's divine mercy as expressed throughout the Old Testament revealed some aspects of merciful love. In this way, divine providence prepared the way for Christ, the ultimate revelation of God's mercy. Christ reveals merciful love "within the framework of the same perspective and on ground already prepared, as many pages of the Old Testament writings demonstrate."[119] Christ is the ultimate penetration of divine providence into the world, i.e., into the evil caused by the sins of all people.[120]

God's mercy as revealed in the God-man saves us from original sin and its worst effects. As in the case of the people of the Old Testament, we are grateful to God because He saved us from sin and its worst effects. However, in and through Christ, we, unlike the people of the Old Testament, are enabled to respond properly to God's expression of love. The Old Testament pattern of God's mercy is followed, but it is infinitely transcended.[121] The Church even refers to the first sin as a *felix culpa,* a happy fault, because God drew incalculable good from the evil of that first sin.[122]

Thus, God does not abandon us. He takes care of us! He provides for us! His providence extends to becoming one of us so that He can be our friend and we can be His friends. "God so loved the world that He gave His only Son."[123] His mercy is not in vain and His judgment that man is indeed "very good"[124] continues!

FOR REFLECTION

A. What are the effects of original sin on human beings?

B. Discuss the lies of Satan in the Garden of Eden and why Adam and Eve believed them.

C. Explain God's merciful love as expressed in the Old Testament.

NOTES

1. We can still love ourselves. See below, Chapter 8: "Grace," p. 219.

2. See Rom. 7:15.

3. See Gen. 2:25.

4. See Gen. 3:7.

5. See Karol Wojtyla (Pope John Paul II), "Real Significance of Original Nakedness" *(Theology of the Body,* series no. 27), *Blessed Are the Pure of Heart* (Boston: St. Paul Editions, 1981), p. 40.

6. See Richard M. Hogan, "A Theology of the Body: A Commentary on the Audiences of Pope John Paul II from September 5, 1979, to May 6, 1981," *Fidelity*, vol. 1, no. 1 (December 1981), pp. 14–15, 24.

7. See LR, p. 41. See also above, Chapter 2: "God's Love: Creation," pp. 42–43.

8. See above, Chapter 2: "God's Love: Creation," p. 34.

9. See CS, no. 77. See also above, Chapter 2: "God's Love: Creation," pp. 29–30, where the sin of Satan and the fallen angels is discussed.

10. For a discussion of God's gift of grace to Adam and Eve when He created them, see above, Chapter 2: "God's Love: Creation," pp. 35–36.

11. See CS, no. 74.

12. See Josef Ratzinger, *Instruction on Christian Freedom and Liberation*, *L'Osservatore Romano*, English Edition, vol. 19, no. 15 (April 14, 1986), § 38.

13. See CS, no. 74.

14. See CS, no. 77.

15. See CS, no. 77.

16. See CS, no. 73.

17. See CS, no. 70.

18. There are only two exceptions: our Lord Jesus Christ, Who is God and Who, therefore, could not have been tainted with sin; and Mary, the Mother of God, who was preserved from original sin and its effects. See below, Chapter 4: "The Incarnation," pp. 90, 104–06.

19. See CS, no. 73.

20. See CS, no. 73, where John Paul quotes Paul VI.

21. See Rom. 5:12.

22. See CS, no. 73.

23. See CS, no. 72.

24. See Gen. 1, 2, 3.

25. See Gen. 2:19.

26. This point reinforces the goodness of man. Man did not sin on his own. In fact, the thought of sin did not even occur to him. It had to be presented to him as a possibility by someone from the "outside." See below, p. 62.

27. See above, Chapter 1: "Man/Woman and God," pp. 9–10. See also below, n. 88.

28. See CS, no. 70.

29. See DV, no. 36.

30. See DV, no. 36.

31. See CS, no. 70.

32. See Gen. 3:5.

33. See Gen. 3:1.

34. See above, Chapter 2: "God's Love: Creation," pp. 27–28.

35. See above, Chapter 2: "God's Love: Creation," p. 34.

36. See CS, no. 66. See also above, Chapter 2: "God's Love: Creation," p. 29.

37. See Gen. 3:4.

38. See above, Chapter 1: "Man/Woman and God," p. 5.

39. See Gen. 3:5.

40. See above, Chapter 2: "God's Love: Creation," p. 29.

41. Cf. Gen. 3:5.

42. See Gen. 3:4–5.

43. See Gen. 1:26–31, 2:16, 18.

44. See DV, nos. 37–38.

45. See CS, no. 70.

46. See DV, no. 37.

47. For an account of the angelic sin, see above, Chapter 2: "God's Love: Creation," pp. 29–30.

48. Cf. DV, no. 37.

49. See CS, no. 70.

50. See Jn. 8:44. See also CS, no. 70. In addition, see above, Chapter 2: "God's Love: Creation," p. 29.

51. There is a difference between rejecting truth (what the angels did) and not recognizing truth (what Adam and Eve did at first). To reject truth, one has to recognize it for what it is. The angels recognized it and rejected it. At first, Adam and Eve did not recognize it and therefore could not reject it. See above, Chapter 2: "God's Love: Creation," pp. 29–30.

52. See CS, no. 70.

53. See above, Chapter 2: "God's Love: Creation," pp. 29–30.

54. See CS, no. 70. Cf. also Gen. 3:5.

55. See CS, no. 70.

56. See CS, no. 70.

57. See SC, p. 30.

58. See CS, no. 73.

59. See Gen. 3:15.

60. See SC, p. 47.

61. See CS, no. 79.

62. See SC, p. 48.

63. See CS, no. 79.

64. See Gen. 1:31.

65. See CS, no. 54.

66. See CS, no. 63.

67. See CS, no. 67.

68. See CS, no. 76.

69. See above, Chapter 2: "God's Love: Creation," p. 34.

70. See CS, no. 63.

71. God also created the angels as free beings so that they might love. Thus, with the angels as well as with man, God risked the horrendous evil of sin for the sake of love. See above, Chapter 2: "God's Love: Creation," pp. 27–30.

72. See CS, no. 74.

73. See CS, no. 77. See also above, p. 55.

74. For instances when God saved them from their sins, see below, pp. 67–73.

75. See DM, no. 4.

76. See CS, no. 79.

77. Cf. Is. 40:3. Cf. also Mk. 1:3.

78. See Gen. 3:12.

79. See Gen. 3:13.

80. See Gen. 3:14–19.

81. See Gen. 3:16. The author of Genesis blames God for this effect of original sin, but this seems to be an attempt to avoid taking responsibility for sin and its effects. Just as Adam and Eve had tried to blame the serpent, subsequent generations blamed God.

82. See Gen. 3:17–19. However, the prediction of death in 3:19 pertains to man's dominion over his body, i.e., to man's lack of integration, and not to man's lack of dominion over the things of the world.

83. See Gen. 3:21.

84. See Gen. 4:2–16.

85. See Gen. 4:12.

86. See Gen. 4:15.

87. See Gen. 6:6.

88. God, like any loving parent, was sorry because of what men and women had done to themselves through sin. (Sin causes the sinner suffering. See above, pp. 55, 65. See also above, Chapter 2: "God's Love: Creation," pp. 36–37.) As the Pope writes, "The concept of God as the necessarily most perfect being certainly excludes from God any pain deriving from deficien-

cies or wounds; but in the 'depths of God' there is a Father's love that, faced with man's sin, in the language of the Bible reacts so deeply as to say: 'I am sorry that I have made him.' " See DV, no. 39.

89. See Gen. 6:8.

90. See Gen. 11:1–9.

91. See RP, no. 14.

92. See Gen. 11:9.

93. See Gen. 17:4–8.

94. See Num. 21:5.

95. See above, pp. 60–61.

96. See Num. 21:6.

97. See Num. 21:8.

98. See 2 Sam. 11:4–5.

99. See 2 Sam. 11:27.

100. See 2 Sam. 12:13.

101. See above, pp. 68–69.

102. See 2 Sam. 12:14.

103. See below, Chapter 9: "Morality," p. 266. In addition, see *Covenant*, pp. 51–53.

104. See above, Chapter 1: "Man/Woman and God," p. 5, where it is mentioned that everything God is, e.g., life and love, is identified with His very essence. See also above, Chapter 2: "God's Love: Creation," p. 41. In addition, see below, Chapter 8: "Grace," p. 205.

105. In this case, the biblical account clearly and unmistakably connects the death of a particular child with a particular sin. While death is generally speaking the result of sin, we cannot and should not attribute a particular death to a particular sin. It is justified in this one case because the linkage is revealed in Scripture. Thus, it is impossible to attribute a death or a sickness of an illegitimate child to the sin of the parents.

106. See 2 Sam. 12:24.

107. See 2 Kings 25.

108. Cf. the sin of Adam and Eve. See above, p. 58.

109. See above, p. 70.

110. See Bar. 1:15–3:8. See also Neh. 9.

111. See RP, no. 14.

112. See RP, no. 13.

113. See above, Chapter 2: "God's Love: Creation," p. 34.

114. See Gen. 3:10.

115. See CS, no. 72.

116. See above, pp. 67–68.

117. See Gen. 1:31. See also above, p. 64.

118. Of course, as noted, there is one exception: in making clothes for Adam and Eve, God did overcome one of the effects of original sin.

119. See DM, no. 4.

120. See above, pp. 63–64.

121. Even the forgiveness of sins, as opposed to simply saving sinners from the effects of their sins, was present in God's merciful acts of the Old Testament. See above, pp. 66, 71.

122. See the "Exsultet, Easter Proclamation," *The Roman Missal: The Sacramentary,* promulgated by Pope Paul VI on April 3, 1969, and translated by the International Commission on English in the Liturgy (New York: Catholic Book Publishing, 1974), p. 184.

123. See Jn. 3:16.

124. See Gen. 1:31. See also above, pp. 64, 73.

———— 4 ————

The Incarnation

For us men and for our salvation He came down from heaven: by the power of the Holy Spirit He was born of the Virgin Mary, and became man. For our sake He was crucified under Pontius Pilate; He suffered, died, and was buried. On the third day He rose again . . . [and] He ascended into heaven and is seated at the right hand of the Father.

A. Why Did God Become Man?

Throughout the Old Testament, God gradually prepared His people for Christ.[1] God eliminated some of the effects of His people's sins (and sometimes He even forgave the sins), and the gratitude of the people to God drew them closer to Him. In other words, God drew good from evil. He loved the people of the Old Testament mercifully. However, God's promise of mercy was completely fulfilled only in the God-man, Jesus Christ. In and through Jesus Christ, God's merciful love drew good from the evil of original sin and its effects.[2]

In order to redeem us, God "emptied Himself, taking the form of a servant, being born in the likeness of men."[3] Through the redemption, Christ satisfied God's love for man, the love that was left unreturned by Adam and Eve when they sinned. Thus, through Christ, the friendship between God and man, put to death by original sin, was revived. As God, Christ was capable of responding to the divine love. In His humanity, Christ made a human response to the divine love, i.e., He committed His entire self to God. In other words, He acted as a priest.[4] As a priest (an office He possessed in His human nature),[5] Christ loved. Christ loved the Father and the Holy Spirit as all human beings should. In other words, Christ loved the Father and the Holy Spirit as Adam and Eve should have.

By returning God's love for man through the cross, Christ filled the spiritual space between God and man with love. In Christ's suffering, "sins are canceled out precisely because He alone as the only-begotten Son could take them upon Himself, accept them with that love for the Father which overcomes the evil of every sin; in a certain sense He annihilates this evil in the spiritual space of the relationship between God and humanity, and fills this space with good."[6] The love of God offered to us is the divine life, i.e., grace. This life overcomes original sin's most damaging effects to the human person.[7] Further, the grace of God allows us to live the very life of God here on earth and most gloriously in heaven. Thus, through Christ's cross, original sin and some of its effects were overcome. Therefore, on the cross, Christ loved us mercifully by eliminating original sin and its most serious effects, and by drawing us close to God, i.e., reviving the friendship between man and God. Through the God-man, the ancient model of God's mercy, established in the Old Testament, is renewed but infinitely surpassed. Through Christ, God's merciful love for us is extended even to original sin and its effects.

Further, through His passion and death, Christ not only loved us but He even loved His Father and the Holy Spirit mercifully. God, in the divine nature, was pained at man's rejection of His love.[8] "The Father allows the Son to suffer [and this] constitutes the Father's own passion and this is also the suffering of the Spirit."[9] Christ undid the rejection of God's love by Adam and Eve and thus relieved God's pain. In other words, He eliminated the effects of sin. Further, Christ, as God-(perfect)man,[10] made a perfect response to God's love[11] and thus drew us closer to God. Thus, not only did Christ ease the sufferings of God, He drew from the evil of sin a greater good, a perfect human response to God's love. By eliminating the effects of sin and drawing us close to God, Christ even loved the Father and the Holy Spirit mercifully.

However, Christ not only loved us, His Father, and the Holy Spirit mercifully, He also revealed who we are as human images of God. Even without original sin, all men and women, as images of God, need to know the God-man to know fully their identity, proper activity, and to know that they should love God through a mutual bodily exchange of love and love others by using things for the sake of people. (See the diagram "Reasons for the Incarnation" on page 84.) As images of God, we do not know ourselves unless we know God. Further, since we are made like God, we are called to act like Him. However, we cannot act like Him unless we know how He acts. In addition, since human persons are enfleshed spirits, they love in their unified totality, body and soul: "Love includes the human body, and the body is made a sharer in spiritual love."[12] It seemed even at the dawn of creation that human beings were called to love God in and through their bodies. However, only in Christ was man's suspicion about himself definitively confirmed.[13] Finally, Christ confirms that we are to love others by exercising a dominion over things for the sake of people.[14]

Although the angels are images of God, God did not need to become an angel for them to know their identity and proper activity. The angels are pure spirits as God is pure spirit. Thus, the angels are able to relate to God solely on the spiritual level. By relating to God as spirits to spirit, they experience their prototype according to their own nature, and thus they can know themselves as spirits. Human beings, however, are both spirit and body. In order for them to experience God and thus come to know themselves, they must see God as spirit and body. In other words, they need to see Him enfleshed. Knowing this, and loving humanity with an everlasting love, God gave Himself to us in a bodily form to allow us to know ourselves and our proper activity and to reveal that we are to love God through a mutual bodily exchange of love.

Does all this mean that God *had* to become man? No, God did not have to become man, but He freely chose to become man at the same moment that He freely chose to create man. In other words, God would have become man even without original sin. God's choice to create man was simultaneously a choice to become man, so great was His love for us.[15]

In a sense, God's act of creating man and woman in His image and likeness was not completed at the dawn of history. God's gift of life to human beings would only be completed in and through the incarnation. The God-man brought God's act of creation to completion by revealing man's identity, man's proper activity, which was to love God through a mutual, bodily exchange of love and to love others by using things for their benefit: "Creation is thus completed by the incarnation."[16] Viewing God's act of creation in history, one could conclude that God, leaving His creative act incomplete, had abandoned man. Nothing could be further from the truth. God willed the incarnation at the same time that He willed creation. God created man out of love and would never abandon him. Not even sin led God to abandon man.

REASONS FOR THE INCARNATION

To love us, the Father, and the Holy Spirit mercifully,
> by returning God's love
>> 1. which eased God's pain and, at the same time, eliminated sin and its most serious effects in us;
>> 2. which also drew us closer to God (revived the friendship between us and God).

To reveal human beings to themselves
> 1. by showing human beings their proper identity;
> 2. by showing human beings their proper activity;
> 3. by showing human beings how to love God in and through a human body and how to love others by using things for their benefit.

Clearly, if Christ were not God and man, then we would be the most pathetic of creatures. Not being able to experience God (our prototype) in human form, we would not be able to see who God is, to see how He acts, or to see the One we should love. Consequently, we would not know our identity, our proper activity, or the fact that we are to love God through a mutual bodily exchange of love and that we are to love others by using things for their benefit. Further, only the divine Son could definitively love us, His Father, and the Holy Spirit mercifully.[17] Thus, if Christ is not God and man, then original sin and its effects remain, and the friendship between God and man, broken by original sin, is not restored. With the same breath that we proclaim Christ's divinity, we must proclaim His humanity.

God the Son became man to love us, His Father, and the Holy Spirit mercifully. Obviously, in Christ we see an act of God's love. God the Son also became man to reveal Himself, i.e., the Wisdom of God. God's wisdom is revealed in every act of Christ. However, the divine wisdom is most especially manifested in Christ's passion, death, and resurrection.[18] Further, Christ's life is not only an act of divine love and the most complete manifestation of God's wisdom, it is also an act of divine power. The power of God can be seen in the union of the two natures in the one divine Person. The power of God is also obviously present in the miracles of Christ. In the incarnation and the redemption, the Trinity—Power, Wisdom, and Love—act as one principle.

B. Who Is Jesus Christ?

Obviously, a knowledge of Christ is vital to each of us if we are to live fully as images of God and if we are ever to recover in any way from sin and its effects. We are never able to leave the question of who Jesus Christ is unanswered. Our Lord Jesus Christ first put this question to His disciples, including the Apostles: "And Jesus went on with His disciples, to the villages of Caesarea Philippi; and on the way He asked His disciples, 'Who do men say that I am?' And they told Him, 'John the Baptist; and others say, Elijah; and others one of the prophets.' And He asked them, 'But who do you say that I am?' "[19] However, through His Apostles, Christ is addressing this same question to every man, woman, and child who has had the Gospel preached to them: "Each one of us must let himself be touched personally by the question: 'But who do you say that I am?' You who hear Me spoken of, answer Me. What do I really mean for you?"[20] This question "never ceases to be asked in one form or another"[21] because, for each of us, to seek the identity of Christ is to seek one's own identity; it is to seek one's own proper activity; it is to seek to know how to love God through our bodies and how to love others by using things for their benefit; and it is even to seek salvation. In Christ's question and its proper answer lies the entire mystery of humanity. Consequently, those who do not correctly answer the question of Christ "Who do you say that I am?" remain in a state of confusion.

Peter, the spokesman for the Apostles, correctly answered Christ's question when he said: "You are the Christ, the Son of the living God."[22] However, over the centuries since Christ, especially in the first centuries after His ascension, there were many incorrect responses to Christ's question. One of the earliest incorrect answers was offered by Arianism, named after its founder, Arius (256–336), a priest of Alexandria in Egypt. Arianism held that Christ is only human, i.e., that Christ is only a human person (HP), possessing a human nature (HN).[23] For Arius, Christ is not God. Rather, He is only a human being, albeit a human being very close to God. However, this is impossible. If Christ were only human, He could not have satisfied God's love rejected by Adam and Eve when they sinned.[24] Moreover, if Christ were only human He could not have revealed God to us. Therefore, He could not have revealed who we are as images of God. Arianism is a false answer to Christ's question: it was condemned by the Council of Nicaea in 325.[25]

Monophysitism (the opposite of Arianism) proposed that Christ is a divine Person (DP) united to the divine nature (DN) only, i.e., that He is God, but not man. The Monophysites acknowledged that the Apostles and other contemporaries of Christ believed they saw God the Son enfleshed, i.e., with a human body. However, the Monophysites claimed that the Apostles and others could not have actually seen God the Son with a true human body because, as the Monophysites taught, He does not possess a human nature. In the view of the Monophysites, Christ's apparent human body was merely a vision that God the Son allowed His contemporaries to see. For the Monophysites, Christ does not truly have a human nature, i.e., He is not man.

The Monophysite position is untenable. For the Monophysites, Christ really did not die. It is impossible for God, in the divine nature, to die. In other words, it is impossible for God in His divine nature to suffer the separation of soul and body because the divine nature is perfectly simple and one, i.e., it is not composed of divisible parts. Further, it is completely spiritual, i.e., it does not have a body.[26] If the Monophysites are correct, Christ could not have satisfied God's love through His death on the cross because He really did not die. Further, the Monophysite answer to Christ's question would also mean that Christ did not truly express His divine Person through a human body. For the Monophysites, what the Apostles thought they saw—Christ's human body—was only a vision. It was not real. Obviously, the Monophysites would argue that anything apparently expressed through Christ's apparent human body was also not real. Thus, the Monophysite answer, if true, would mean that Christ did not reveal God, i.e., it would mean that He did not reveal who we are as images of God. The Monophysite response to Christ's question "Who do you say that I am?" was rejected by the Council of Chalcedon in 451.[27]

A heresy even more complex than either Arianism or Monophysitism arose in the first half of the fifth century. Named after Nestorius (c. 451), a bishop of Constantinople, Nestorianism held that there are two persons in Christ as well as two natures. In other words, Christ is both a divine Person (DP) and a human person (HP). Each person is separately expressed through its corresponding nature. In other words, the divine Person is expressed through the divine nature, and the human person is expressed through the human nature. The two persons and their corresponding natures are united through their mutual agreement with one another.

There are some difficulties with the Nestorian answer to Christ's question because it denies the union of the divine and the human in one divine Person. First, God's love would not have been returned because God the Son, the second Person of the Trinity, would not have suffered and died on the cross. A divine Person united solely to the divine nature cannot die.[28] On the other hand, persons united to a human nature can undergo death. The Nestorian Christ is a divine Person united to the divine nature and a human person united to a human nature. Since a divine Person united only to the divine nature cannot die, according to the Nestorians it was only the human person of Christ who died on the cross. However, as mentioned above,[29] after sin only God is capable of returning God's love. Therefore, if the second Person of the Trinity did not offer Himself to the Father through death on the cross, we are not redeemed, i.e., we are still alienated from God. Second, according to the Nestorian answer, Christ's body would have expressed only His human person, not His divine Person. Thus, for the Nestorians, when the Apostles saw Christ's body, they would not have seen the second Person of the Trinity expressed, but rather the human person of Christ. For the Nestorians, Christ did not reveal God and therefore did not show us who we are as images of God. Third, if Christ were two separate persons, Mary would not be the Mother of God. A mother is the mother of a person, not merely of a nature. In the Nestorian view, Mary would have given human nature only to the human person because only the human person would have been united to the human nature. Thus, she would not be the mother of a divine Person. She would not be the Mother of God. However, Mary is *Theotokos,* which means Mother of God.[30] Mary is the Mother of God, i.e., the mother of Christ, because she gave Him, God the Son, His human nature. Nestorianism was condemned by the Council of Ephesus in 431[31] because it denied our redemption, the revelation of God through Christ's human body, and Mary's divine motherhood. Clearly, Nestorianism does not properly answer the question of Christ "Who do you say that I am?" (see the accompanying diagram).

Any answer to Christ's question, "Who do you say that I am?", must include the teaching of the Council of Chalcedon, which proclaimed that "one and the same Lord Jesus Christ, the only-begotten Son, must be acknowledged in two natures, without confusion or change, without division or separation."[32] In other words, in Christ there is one divine Person (DP), i.e., God the Son, Who unites in Himself a human nature (HN) and a divine nature (DN): " 'By the power of the Holy Spirit' the mystery of the 'hypostatic union' is brought about—that is, the union of the divine nature and the human nature, of the divinity and the humanity in the one Person of the Word-Son."[33] As man and God, Christ "fully reveals man to himself."[34] Christ reveals man's identity, proper activity, and God's bodily expression of His love. In addition, as God and man, Christ is our reconciliation with the Father, dissolving the alienation between God and man and reforging the link of love that joins the two together: "He it was, and He alone, Who satisfied the Father's eternal love."[35] "The central nucleus of the Christian faith is constituted by the twofold truth that Jesus Christ is Son of God and son of man (*the christological truth*), and that God the Father brought about the salvation of man in Him, His Son and Savior of the world (*the soteriological truth*)."[36]

WHO DO YOU SAY THAT I AM?

DP = Divine Person
DN = Divine Nature
HP = Human Person
HN = Human Nature

The Church's Description of Christ
DP + DN + HN   Chalcedon

The Heresies' Description of Christ		*Error*
HP + HN	Arianism	Christ is not God the Son
DP + DN	Monophysitism	Christ is not human
DP + DN + HP + HN	Nestorianism	Human and divine are not joined in one divine Person

---

Peter, with the help of the Father, was the first one to answer Christ's question correctly when he said to the man standing before him in the district of Caesarea Philippi, "You are the Christ, the Son of the living God."[37] In other words, Peter was affirming that Christ was both human and divine. On the other hand, Arianism, Monophysitism, and Nestorianism all provided wrong answers to the question of Christ. The content of Peter's answer must be repeated for each age in a language appropriate to that era so that all would come to know Christ. This service is rendered by Peter's successors. Therefore, every Pope since St. Peter has been responsible for answering correctly the question posed by Christ to the first Pope. The Popes have confirmed who Christ is, and thereby they have confirmed who we are. They do this as a service to humanity as Peter did it in service to the Apostles and to the early Church.

The Popes have always taught that God the Son assumed a perfect human nature. Christ's humanity is absolutely perfect because it is united to the second Person of the blessed Trinity.[38] The fact that Christ had a real human body hardly needs substantiation. St. John says it best when He writes in the prologue of his Gospel, "And the Word became flesh and dwelt among us, full of grace and truth; we have beheld His glory."[39] Christ's human body was without flaw. Nothing less would have been worthy of God. In and through His body (His "flesh"), Christ manifests His divine Person, e.g., "He [God the Son] worked with human hands."[40] Thus, when He worked with His hands, He manifested or expressed His divine Person in and through His body.

Since Christ was fully human, He also possessed the spiritual powers of a man, i.e., a human intellect and a human will: "He thought with a human mind. He acted with a human will, and with a human heart He loved."[41] How do we know that Christ had an intellect? Christ was known as a teacher. A teacher teaches what is unknown by using what is known. For example, a math teacher often teaches that $1 + 1 = 2$ by using some experiences familiar to the students: one apple plus one apple makes two apples. Further, the teacher almost always takes the familiar experience and manipulates it slightly so that it will convey the principle of the lesson. This manipulation of common human experiences as teaching tools is a function of a human intellect. Obviously, when Christ lived in Palestine, He constantly manipulated the common human experiences of the Jewish people and of their neighbors to teach God's revelation. The parables, e.g., the Sower, the Lost Sheep, the Lost Coin, and the Prodigal Son,[42] clearly reveal common experiences that become in the hands of *the* master teacher incredibly fruitful educational tools. Amazingly, not only have these parables proven effective for the people of the time of Christ, but they still convey to us the truths of God's revelation. Clearly, Christ, as *the* master teacher, had to have a human intellect. He Himself is a witness to His intellectual faculty. He told His disciples the evening before He died, "You call Me teacher and Lord; and you are right, for so I am."[43]

How do we know that Christ had a human will? Christ's agony in the garden of Gethsemane reveals His human will. Clearly, at that moment, there was a struggle within Christ. The outcome was never in doubt. However, "He expresses all the psychological truth of His human nature which shudders at the prospect of suffering and death."[44] In other words, within Christ there was a conflict. Christ was debating with Himself. Such a conflict or debate could not have existed if Christ were only God, i.e., if He only had a divine will. Such a conflict presumes a human nature with a human will. Knowing what He was about to suffer, Christ experienced an incredible fear. Fear, welling up within His humanity, caused His human will to debate with itself. The words are memorable: "Father, if Thou art willing, remove this cup from Me; nevertheless, not My will, but Thine, be done."[45] Thus, through His body, i.e., through the words He spoke, Jesus Christ, the second Person of the Trinity made man, reveals that He possesses the spiritual powers that we, as persons, possess, namely, the powers of human intellect and human will. These powers demonstrate that Christ possessed a human soul.[46] Therefore, His humanity was complete: body and soul.

Of course, as God the Son, Christ is also united to the divine nature. In other words, He has the divine intellect and the divine will. In time, God the Son, the second Person of the Trinity, assumed a human nature. However, there is no confusion of the divine and human natures in Christ. Each nature remains what it is in itself, but both are united in Jesus, true God and true man, the second Person of the Trinity. Even though there are two minds and two wills in Christ, there is only one Person. Every other person, divine, human, or angelic, possesses only one mind and one will. It is possible for God the Son (or for either one of the other two trinitarian Persons if either had become man) to possess two minds and two wills, and still be one Person because He is God. Only a divine Person is capable of expressing Himself, i.e., His Person, in and through more than one nature. Human and angelic persons are too weak (as compared with

God) to express themselves in and through more than one nature. Thus, to repeat the words of John Paul, " 'By the power of the Holy Spirit' the mystery of the 'hypostatic union' is brought about, that is, the union of the divine nature and the human nature, of the divinity and the humanity in the one Person of the Word-Son."[47]

One might well ask, "What kind of knowledge did the Person of Christ possess?" In His divine nature, Christ possesses the knowledge of God because He is God the Son. This is simple enough. However, in speaking of Christ's knowledge as a man, two extremes are to be avoided. One extreme holds that Christ possesses all divine knowledge in His human intellect. This is something that is not possible for a limited, human intellect. The other extreme holds that in His humanity while He was on earth, Christ did not see God as the saints see God in heaven, i.e., that Christ did not enjoy the beatific vision. In reality, Christ did experience the beatific vision. As a man, Christ must have possessed self-knowledge. Christ is the second Person of the blessed Trinity. In order for Christ's human intellect to possess self-knowledge, Christ's human intellect had to possess the most comprehensive knowledge of the second Person of the blessed Trinity as possible. Such knowledge of God is only possible for human intellects through the beatific vision, i.e., by seeing God face to face. Thus, Christ's human intellect must have enjoyed the beatific vision on earth.[48]

In addition, as a man, Christ did gain human experiential knowledge, i.e., "Jesus increased in wisdom and in stature, and in favor with God and man."[49] He learned carpentry from His human father, Joseph. His mother, Mary, must have taught Him to pray. He experienced everyday life, and He learned to use these experiences to teach the truths of the kingdom of God. Thus, the one divine Person of Christ possessed all knowledge proper to God (in His divine nature) and all knowledge proper to man (in His human nature). His human intellect was perfected.

As mentioned above,[50] the one divine Person of Christ not only possesses the divine intellect and a human intellect, but He also has the divine will and a human will. Just as it is Christ, i.e., the second Person of the blessed Trinity, Who possesses the knowledge known by both His divine and human intellects, so also when Christ chooses, either in His divine will or in His human will (or in both), it is God the Son Who chooses. Clearly, Christ exercised His divine will in union with the Father and the Holy Spirit. Further, Christ's divine will is exercised in perfect freedom because God is perfectly and absolutely free.[51] However, there seems to be a dilemma regarding the freedom of Christ's human will. When Satan tempted Christ in the desert, Satan presented the Lord with the possibility of sinning.[52] Obviously, this choice could only be presented to Christ's human will. Christ's divine will could not possibly choose something totally contrary to the divine nature.[53] It would seem that Christ, if He possesses true human freedom, must have had the choice to accept Satan's temptation or not to accept it. Yet, it is not possible for the second Person of the blessed Trinity to sin. In other words, it is not possible for God to act contrary to Himself. Christ could not sin. Does that mean He was not free in His human will? We are faced with a dilemma: either Christ possesses human freedom and can sin or He is not free and He cannot sin. In other words, we either accord to Him His human freedom and allow the possibility that God the Son could sin, i.e., we claim an impossibility, or we deny His humanity by denying His human freedom.[54]

The dilemma is a false one. The problem lies in the definition of freedom. God is perfectly free. Since He cannot sin, perfect freedom cannot include a choice to sin. We are free because we are images of God. However, we are not perfect images of God. On the other hand, Christ is perfect. He possesses perfect freedom. United to God the Son, His human nature is confirmed in freedom, i.e., His humanity is as free as humanity can possibly be. Possessing such God-like freedom, it is not possible for Him to act contrary to that freedom, i.e., to sin, but it is possible for us to sin because we do not possess perfect freedom.

Since humanity remains imperfect and, in a way, incomplete, without God's grace,[55] as the perfect man, Christ possesses the fullness of grace, i.e., God's life, in His human soul. Further, Christ always possesses God's life to the fullest possible extent because He has the beatific vision, which is the greatest of all graces. Grace,

God's life, includes the gifts of the Holy Spirit.[56] These infused gifts
are sometimes called the infused knowledge of Christ.[57]

Since Christ has two natures (divine and human), He could act
through either nature alone or through both natures. For example,
when Christ healed the sick, gave sight to the blind, and calmed the
sea, He did so through both His divine and human natures. However, when He ate, drank, slept, or died, He acted only in and
through His human nature. Further, Christ probably performed acts
only in His divine nature. Obviously, these remained hidden from
man because they were not expressed through the Lord's humanity.
Clearly, whether acting in one or both natures, every act of Christ is
the act of God the Son, the second Person of the Trinity. The more
we look at Christ, the more apparent it becomes that the union of
two natures in the one Person of Christ is a great mystery and cannot
be fully comprehended by the human mind.

C. How Does Christ Reveal Man to Himself?

As God, Christ reveals who we are as images of God. In revealing
who God is, He reveals our identity. Further, in revealing how God
acts, Christ reveals how we should act. Moreover, as the incarnate
God Who loves us in and through His body, He reveals that we are
to love Him (God) in and through our bodies and to love others by
using things for their benefit. Christ accomplishes this mission
through His human nature. In Christ, "human testimony becomes
the expression of the salvific mission of God" through Christ as
prophet, priest, and king.[58] (See the accompanying diagram,
"Christ's Triple Offices.")

CHRIST'S TRIPLE OFFICES

Christ reveals human beings to themselves
1. by showing human beings their proper identity (prophetic office);
2. by showing human beings their proper activity (priestly office);
3. by showing human beings that they are called to love God
   through a mutual bodily exchange of love and to love others by
   using things for their benefit (kingly office).

---

1. JESUS CHRIST AS PROPHET

In His human prophetic office, Christ teaches us truth, i.e., He reveals God Who is Truth.[59] Since we are images of God, we do not know ourselves unless we know God. Christ, by revealing God (Truth), reveals the truth about us, i.e., He reveals who we are. Even before the fall, man did not know himself as he should because God had not revealed Himself as fully as He would in Christ. However, through the temptation of the devil and the first sin, man had accepted lies about God and about himself. Thus, man rejected his knowledge about God and himself. Christ definitively reveals God, and therefore He teaches us who we are and overcomes the lies told by Satan.

Christ revealed God as Truth when He refused to accept the same three lies that had led to the fall of Adam and Eve. (See the diagram on page 97.) With Adam and Eve, the devil claimed God had lied. He then suggested that they could become like a god, i.e., himself. He promised that they could be gods defining good and evil for themselves.[60] Clearly, since the devil employed the same lies with Christ as he did with the first human beings, Adam and Eve, the temptations were directed at Christ as a human being. In responding to Satan, Christ expressed truth through His human prophetic office.

In the second temptation of Christ in the desert,[61] Satan employs the first lie he had told Adam and Eve, i.e., that God lied. Satan invites Christ to throw Himself off the roof of the temple. The devil quotes the scriptural promise that God would ask the angels to protect Christ from all injury. In other words, Satan gives Christ only two alternatives: jump off the roof or admit that God lied when He promised to ask the angels to protect You from all harm. Of course, it would be foolhardy for Christ or for anyone to jump off a roof. Christ refuses to jump, and Satan seems to have won his point, i.e., it seems that Christ admits that God lied. However, quoting Scripture Himself, Christ provides a third alternative to the two impossible choices the devil gives Him. Christ answers that no one should test the Lord God. In rejecting the implication that His decision not to jump off the roof is an admission that God lied, Christ rejects the devil's scenario. In other words, Christ solves the false (lie-filled) dilemma posed by Satan, the father of lies.

In Satan's third temptation of Christ,[62] we find the second lie the devil presented to Adam and Eve. The father of lies offers Christ everything imaginable if Christ would only prostrate Himself in adoration before the fallen angel. The third temptation of Christ is Satan's attempt to make himself into a god. With Adam and Eve, Satan promised them they could be like god. Since he had convinced them that the true God was a liar, the devil was inviting Adam and Eve to be like a god, i.e., to be like him. Similarly, Satan asks Christ to adore him. In other words, the devil asks Christ to treat him as a god. In quoting the commandment that adoration is for God alone, Christ firmly rejects Satan's suggestion that he is worthy of adoration, i.e., that he is a god.

In Satan's first temptation of Christ,[63] there is the third lie the devil suggested to Adam and Eve, i.e., that they could be gods defining good and evil for themselves. Satan taunts the Lord by inviting Him to turn stones into bread: "If You are the Son of God, command these stones to become loaves of bread."[64] The devil is asking Christ for proof that He is indeed God the Son. However, he is also suggesting that the Lord should exercise the divine power so that He could eat. In other words, the devil is asking Christ to perform a divine act for His own selfish reasons. This temptation is almost identical to Satan's invitation to Adam and Eve: define good and evil for yourselves according to your own selfish reasons. Christ's answer shows that He clearly understands the devil's ploy: "Man shall not live by bread alone, but by every word that proceeds from the mouth of God."[65] The Lord's response indicates that man cannot live by trying to be a god, i.e., by presuming to perform divine acts for selfish reasons. Rather, man's very existence depends on accepting God as Creator and Lord. In these three temptations, Christ witnesses to the truth, i.e., to Truth itself. He expresses Truth through His human prophetic office. He overcomes the lies of Satan by showing us Truth, i.e., by showing us God. In showing us God, He shows us who we are.

TEMPTATIONS OF ADAM/EVE AND OF CHRIST BY SATAN

Adam/Eve	Christ	Answer
1. God lied.	1. Angels will rescue you. (Second temptation)	1. God should not be tested because He does not lie.
2. You will become like a god, i.e., like me.	2. Fall down and worship me. (Third temptation)	2. You, Satan, are not God.
3. You will be gods defining good and evil.	3. Command these stones to turn into bread. (First temptation)	3. Man must accept God and not try to be god.

Christ also marvelously revealed the identity of God as Truth in His human testimony before Pilate. Facing a horrible death and the terrible cruelty of His executioners, Christ still truthfully answered Pilate's question: " 'So You are a king?' Jesus answered, 'You say that I am a king. For this I was born, and for this I have come into the world, to bear witness to the truth.' "[66] Clearly, Christ gave witness to truth before Pilate, i.e., He revealed Himself as Truth: "There is no doubt that truth emerged"[67] from that meeting between Christ and Pilate. Christ stands to lose His life, His reputation, everything the world holds dear. But at no other moment does He give such testimony to the truth. When He stands before the judgment seat of the Roman civil authority represented in the person of Pontius Pilate, Christ in His humanity shows us God as Truth, i.e., He reveals who man is as an image of God.

Christ's prophetic work of revealing God as Truth was not completed with the rejection of Satan's lies and His testimony before Pilate. Satan not only lied about the true God, he also led Adam and Eve to sin by suggesting that God was not a loving father. Satan told Eve that the fruit of the forbidden tree would make her like God. Satan implied that God had forbidden Adam and Eve to eat that fruit in order to protect Himself and His position from any competition. God, after the acceptance of the lie by Adam and Eve, is seen as someone jealous of His own power and authority, as one imposing unreasonable rules and demands.[68] Once this view of God was accepted, Adam and Eve could not possibly have trusted God. As long as there was the hint that God is not a loving, all-caring Father, humanity could not trust Him because men and women could not know the truth about Him. Christ's rejection of Satan's lies in the triple temptation in the desert and His testimony before Pilate were only two threads in the fabric of Christ's revelation of God as Truth.

Christ overcame the false view of God as a jealous tyrant with His every word and act. Of course, His very birth as the God-man showed that "God so loved the world that He gave His only Son."[69] A God Who "emptied Himself, taking the form of a servant, being born in the likeness of men"[70] is hardly a jealous, mean-spirited tyrant. However, Christ definitively and dramatically reverses the devil's false portrayal of God with His words from the cross: "Father, into Thy hands I commit My spirit!"[71] No greater words of love and trust were ever spoken by any man. Christ, suffering a horrifying death and the psychological weight of all the sins ever committed, at the moment of death, i.e., at the moment when most people are the most anxious, entrusts Himself to the Father. The words "Father, into Thy hands I commit My spirit" are directly linked to the mistrust of the Father found in the first sin. Christ, speaking for the entire human race, at the most extreme moment of His life, entrusts Himself to the Father. The God Whom Adam and Eve saw as a tyrant is revealed as a loving Father Who can be trusted with one's life even at the point of death. With His "last breath," Christ unmasks the lie that Adam and Eve had accepted at the beginning with their "first breath."

Still, when Christ says, "My God, My God, why hast Thou forsaken Me?"[72] He seems to doubt God's care for Him. How could He speak of God forsaking Him and then entrust Himself to God? Of course, these words did reflect the loneliness and abandonment Jesus felt on the cross. Nevertheless, even amidst His physical and psychological pain, Jesus did not relinquish His trust in the Father. The

words "My God, My God, why hast Thou forsaken Me?" are actually the first lines of Psalm 22.[73] While this psalm begins with a
seeming lack of trust in God's constant care, the second half of the
psalm is a ringing affirmation of God's constant aid to all people,
especially to those who are afflicted unjustly. Christ may have prayed
the entire psalm, but even if He did not, the quotation of the first line
of this hope-filled psalm was a testimony to Christ's continued hope
and trust in His Father.

In expressing Truth through His human prophetic office, Christ
revealed God as Truth and revealed man to himself. He overcame
the lies Satan had told Adam and Eve and showed that God was
truly a loving Father.

2. JESUS CHRIST AS PRIEST

As images of God, we not only need to know who God is, we also
need to know how God acts. Unless we know how God acts, we will
not know how we should act as images of God. Jesus Christ reveals
to us how God acts and how we should act by loving us, the Father,
and the Holy Spirit mercifully. He reveals merciful love to us. Love
is the only way for us: "Man cannot live without love. He remains a
being that is incomprehensible for himself, his life is senseless, if love
is not revealed to him, if he does not encounter love."[74] Our Lord
reveals divine merciful love in His acts of merciful love accomplished
through His human priestly office.[75] In loving mercifully, i.e., in loving the way God loves, Christ shows us how we should love God and
others.

Love, as mentioned above,[76] is a union of two or more persons.[77]
This loving union of persons is established through a will-act, a
choice, made by each person, to give himself or herself to the oth-
er(s). At first glance, it might not be obvious that Christ chose to
suffer. In other words, it could seem that the cross was not an act of
love. It could be argued that Christ's suffering was imposed on Him
by Pilate and the Roman soldiers.[78] However, Christ's sufferings
were not imposed on Him at all. Pontius Pilate and the Roman
soldiers did not force Christ to suffer. They did not take Christ's life

from Him. He freely laid it down.[79] He *willed* each stroke of the lash, each thorn on His head, and each labored breath on the cross. In perfect freedom, He willed His own death out of love. As Pope John Paul writes in his meditation on the third station of the Way of the Cross, "To be insulted is what He [Christ] wills. To stagger and fall under the weight of the cross is what He wills. He wills it all. To the end, down to the very last detail, He is true to His undertaking."[80] The same theme appears again in the meditation on the seventh station: "And He wills all this, He wills fulfillment of the prophecy . . . He falls in accordance with His own will."[81] Christ gives Himself, i.e., He loves. He freely chose to suffer and die at an incredible cost to Him!

In choosing to suffer, Christ united His will with His Father (and, of course, with the Holy Spirit, Who is always in perfect union with the Father and the Son), Who loves us without any limitation. Christ's self-gift (love) to the Father (and through Him to us) was especially evident in His passion and death. Even though the cross involved terrible and inhuman suffering, the Son, out of love, carried out the will of His Father. In Gethsemane, Christ makes the Father's will His own: "The words: 'My Father, if it be possible, let this cup pass from Me; nevertheless, not as I will, but as Thou wilt,' . . . have a manifold eloquence. They prove the truth of that love which the only-begotten Son gives to the Father."[82] In Christ, suffering was "linked to love"[83] for the Father. The totality of Christ's love for the Father is clear when from the cross He cried, "Into Thy hands I commit My spirit."[84] Christ entrusted His entire self at the moment of His death to His Father. No one could give more: "Greater love has no man than this, that a man lay down his life for his friends."[85] Christ laid down His life according to the Father's will.[86]

In and through His human priestly office, the crucified Lord loved His Father and us mercifully and manifested God's love. In His passion and death, Christ loves and reveals how to love, i.e., He reveals that love involves a total union of wills. Seeing the love of Christ, we know how we should love God and others. In other words, we know how we should act as images of God.

3. JESUS CHRIST AS KING

Christ revealed God not only through His offices of prophet and priest, but also through His kingly office. Christ's kingly office was the source of the Lord's bodily self-discipline. Since it was precisely in and through His physical body that Christ revealed God, kingly self-rule over His flesh and blood was absolutely essential to the Lord's mission. The primacy of the mind and will over bodily emotions is an absolute requirement if the body is to express the person. Thus, without kingly self-rule, the Lord's human body would not have been subject to the Lord's Person. Without this kingly self-rule, Christ's human body could not have expressed truth (known by the intellect) or love (chosen by the will). Christ's kingly office was the source of His bodily self-discipline, and it is through that self-discipline that God the Son revealed Himself in and through His human body.

If Christ had not possessed kingly self-rule,[87] He would probably not have resisted the temptations of the devil in the desert after His forty-day fast. Further, if Christ had lacked kingly self-rule, He might have succumbed to His natural and understandable fear (a bodily emotion) before Pilate. In addition, if Christ were not a king, it is unthinkable that He would have entrusted Himself to His Father at the moment of His death. He would have been overcome with pain, fear, frustration, and even anger. Thus, the Lord's kingly office enabled the prophetic office to function properly. Kingly self-rule enabled Christ to reveal truth in and through His body.[88]

Further, Christ's kingly office enabled Him to reveal God's merciful love in and through His human body. In other words, the Lord's priestly office needed kingly self-discipline for the adequate, bodily expression of merciful love. Since love is a choice, i.e., a will-act,[89] it cannot be expressed in and through a body unless the body is governed by the will. In other words, a lover must be "in charge" of his body before it can become an expression of his love. Christ's body became the means of expressing His love because Christ "possessed" it. Christ could give Himself in and through His body because His kingly self-rule governed His body and enabled it to become an expression of His love. If Christ were not a king, it would have been impossible for Christ to choose the painful bodily suffering of His passion and death. The Pope emphasizes the kingly self-discipline of Christ in his meditation on the tenth station of the Way of the Cross, "With every wound, every spasm of pain, every wrenched muscle, every trickle of blood, with all the exhaustion in its arms, all the bruises and lacerations on its back and shoulders, this unclothed body is carrying out the will of both Father and Son."[90] There is no greater manifestation of Christ's kingly self-discipline than in Christ's expression of God's merciful love for us in His passion and death.[91]

Most important, Christ's kingly office definitively revealed to us that we are called to love God in and through a mutual bodily exchange of love. As embodied persons, we are invited to express love through our bodies. It seemed from the beginning that we were even called to love God in a mutual bodily exchange of love.[92] In assuming our human nature, God took to Himself a human body. In and through His kingly office, Christ was able to express God's love through His body, e.g., His cross. Since love includes not just the giving of oneself, but also the receiving of the gift by another, a bodily expression of love clearly calls forth a bodily response from another, e.g., the woman who washed Christ's feet with her tears.[93] Christ's expression of love in and through His body definitively revealed that we are called to love God through a mutual bodily exchange of love.

Further, in His kingly office, Christ revealed that we are called to love others by using things for their benefit. As the Creator, God cares for the universe. Since God created every *thing* in the world *for* man,[94] God exercises a divine dominion over the things of the earth for our sake. Through His human kingly office, Christ governs created things on behalf of people. In this way, He reveals God's dominion over the things of the earth. In other words, He shows us divine providence.

There are many examples of Christ's expression of the divine authority over the things in the world. On one occasion, He and His disciples were in a boat, and a threatening storm arose. Since Christ had fallen asleep, the disciples awakened Him. He chided them for their lack of faith and rebuked the wind. In other words, He spoke to the wind with His human voice. The storm ended, and there was calm.[95] Christ calmed the storm to demonstrate His divine authority, i.e., to show the disciples that He, indeed, was God. However, He also calmed the winds to alleviate the fears of His disciples. On this occasion, Christ, through His human kingly office, showed us that God governs all things for the sake of people. He showed us divine providence.

The multiplication of the loaves and of the fish reveals a similar pattern. A very large crowd had followed Jesus into the desert, and He had taught them for most of the day. By the time evening came, the crowd was hungry, but there was no food available, except for five loaves and two fish that one boy had with him. Jesus told his disciples to have the people sit, and then, with His human hands, He blessed the bread and the fish, asking His disciples to distribute them to the people. They were able to feed five thousand people because Jesus had multiplied the loaves and the fish. They even gathered twelve baskets of scraps after everyone had eaten.[96] In and through His kingly office, Christ expressed the divine authority over the things of the earth for the sake of those who were with Him, i.e., He showed us divine providence.

Christ also expressed the divine dominion over the things of the earth in choosing ordinary goods (e.g., water, bread, and wine) to be the channels of God's grace. Water became the sign of Baptism when Christ, in His physical body, received Baptism at the hands of St. John the Baptist. At the moment of His Baptism, in and through His body, Christ expressed the divine authority over water, making it the means of Baptism. Through His Baptism, water was dedicated in a special way for the benefit of all men and women, i.e., it became the means of the first gift of God's grace to each of us. Similarly, at the Last Supper, through the words He spoke over the bread and the wine, Christ expressed the divine authority over these elements. With His words, He transformed bread and wine into His very self so that He could give Himself to each and every one of us. Thus, through His kingly office, Christ expressed the divine authority over water, bread, and wine and made them the means of incredible benefits for all men and women. God provides for us!

Christ accomplished His mission to the world through the joint exercise of His triple offices: he never exercised one without the other two. For example, on the cross, Christ revealed truth (prophetic office); He showed us merciful love (priestly office); He exercised kingly self-discipline (kingly office); and He expressed the divine authority over things (kingly office) by making the wood of the cross the means of salvation.

The mission of Christ to reveal man to himself was accomplished in and through His triple offices. Since it was as a man, in His human nature, that He was prophet, priest, and king, it is through His humanity that He revealed God to us and thus revealed who we are, how we should act, that we are to love God in a bodily way, and that we are to love others by using things for their benefit. Since Christ's human nature was given to Him through His mother, Mary, she participated in a unique way in His mission.

D. Who Is Mary?

Since Mary participates uniquely in the mission of Christ, it is impossible to understand her without knowing Christ. As Pope John Paul II writes in his encyclical letter on Mary, "only in the mystery of Christ is her [Mary's] mystery fully made clear."[97] Further, since Christ reveals man to himself, it is impossible to understand anyone, even Mary, without Christ. In other words, since we discover the mystery of ourselves through a study of Christ, it is certainly true that we will learn the mystery of Christ's mother through a study of her Son!

God the Son entered human history through Mary in order to redeem fallen humanity. In and through the sin of Adam and Eve, the entire human race fell victim to sin. Each human being born into the world is a victim of sin.[98] In human history, there have been two human beings who were spared from original sin and its effects. Both were conceived and born without original sin and thus without its effects. Conceived with grace, with minds and wills unaffected by sin, and lacking the "spark of sin,"[99] both chose to respond to God's love. In other words, both loved God and never sinned. Who were these two sinless human beings? One was Jesus Christ, and the other was His mother, Mary of Nazareth. Christ was always free from sin because He is a divine Person, i.e., He is God. God (Love) and sin (anti-love) cannot exist together, and so Christ was never infected by sin.

On the other hand, Mary is a human person and thus could have inherited the sin of our first parents. However, she did not because God blessed her with a special grace. If Mary was to accept God's unique and extraordinary invitation to love Him by becoming His mother, she needed to be as free as possible for a human being.[100] She would not enjoy this freedom if she suffered from original sin and its effects. Since Mary's loving response to God's invitation "was decisive, on the human level, for the accomplishment of the divine mystery [the incarnation],"[101] God preserved Mary from original sin and its effects. Standing, as it were, outside of time,[102] God knew from all eternity that Mary was inclined to respond to His love. He recognized the inclinations of her will. Thus, He gave her the means to fulfill what she wished to choose, i.e., He gave her an extraordinary grace.[103] This grace preserved her from original sin and its effects. Thus, through this grace, she was as free as a human could be because she was not enslaved by sin. Therefore, this extraordinary grace enabled Mary to respond to the divine invitation. Still, Mary did not earn or merit God's grace. God gave her His grace before she responded! He preserved her from original sin and its effects from the very first moment of her existence, that is, from the moment of her conception in the womb of her mother, St. Anne.[104] This special privilege given to Mary is called her Immaculate Conception.

The extraordinary gift of God's love to Mary is inconceivable without Christ. Love is the mutual gift of at least two persons to one another. God's offer of His love to Adam and Eve was left unsatisfied and unreturned by the sin of Adam and Eve. Thus, without the response to God's love given by Christ, it would have been almost impossible for any human being wounded by original sin to love

God. However, it is obvious that the people of the Old Testament loved God, at least to a certain extent, and He loved them.[105] They were able to love Him because Christ's response to the divine love on the cross is both in time and outside of it. Christ offered *the* human response to God's love. This response made it possible for all human beings, before or after Christ, to enter a loving relationship with God. Even the exceptional gift of grace (God's love) to Mary depended on the response given to the divine love by Christ. Thus, the Immaculate Conception was accomplished through the cross of Jesus Christ. In other words, Mary, like all other humans, was redeemed by Christ. The Immaculate Conception of Mary is a sublime event in which "Mary receives life [grace] from Him [God the Son] to Whom she herself, in the order of earthly generation, gave life as a mother."[106] She is the one who is "full of grace."[107]

Mary was chosen by God to be the Mother of God the Son. Yet God did not force her to be the mother of His Son. Mary had a choice. At the annunciation, the messenger said to Mary, "And behold, you will conceive in your womb and bear a Son, and you shall call His name Jesus. He will be great, and will be called the Son of the Most High."[108] Obviously, the Angel Gabriel was revealing God's will to Mary. What reply would she make to this will? As the Angel waited, was God to hear from Mary the same reply to His will that He heard from her mother, Eve? Despite the risk involved,[109] "the Father of mercies willed that the incarnation should be preceded by assent on the part of the predestined mother."[110] Then, in freedom and with the help of God's grace,[111] Mary spoke her glorious words of consent: "Behold, I am the handmaid of the Lord; let it be to me according to your word."[112] Through her free choice, Mary accepted God's will for her and "the mystery of the incarnation was accomplished."[113] Mary became the new Eve who, unlike the first Eve, responded to God's love and did not turn her back on the Father of mercies.

After Mary's loving response to God's invitation conveyed by Gabriel, Mary received an even greater gift of God's love than she had at her conception. Since God the Son "in Whom is concentrated all the 'glory of grace' "[114] entrusted Himself to her in her womb, He loved her. His love brought to her soul a new and even greater gift of God's grace. Further, her Son's love for her brought Mary, body and soul, to reign with Him forever in heaven. Mary, at the end of her life here on earth, was assumed body and soul into heaven.

The Holy Father tells us that "Mary uttered this fiat ["let it be to me"] in faith."[115] In other words, Mary was a woman of faith. Mary believed in God and thus at the annunciation she "entrusted herself to God without reserve and 'devoted herself totally as the handmaid of the Lord to the Person and work of her Son.' "[116] In fact, her consent to the angel is "the point of departure from which her whole 'journey toward God' begins, her whole pilgrimage of faith."[117] Since her faith in God made her totally devoted to her Son, her journey towards God advanced in union with Christ. In and through this union of mother and Son, Mary's identity is revealed as a unique participant in the mission of her Son. Since she was (and is) joined in an extraordinary and absolutely singular way in His work, she shared (and shares) in His offices of prophet, priest, and king.

In His human prophetic office, Christ reveals God as Truth. As a prophet, Mary also reveals God as Truth: "In contrast with the 'suspicion' which the 'father of lies' sowed in the heart of Eve, the first woman, Mary, whom tradition is wont to call the 'new Eve' and the true 'mother of the living,' boldly proclaims the undimmed truth about God,"[118] i.e., that God does not lie and is therefore trustworthy. Eve chose to believe that God lied and therefore was not to be trusted.[119] On the other hand, Mary entrusts herself totally to God without even fully understanding what He was asking of her. Mary reveals that God is to be believed and trusted. Her words of trust, "Let it be to me," are surpassed only by the words of her Son on the cross when He utters, "Father, into Thy hands I commit My spirit."[120]

In addition to her prophetic role, Mary shared in Christ's priestly activity. Christ, as priest, revealed God's merciful love. Christ showed us how to love God, ourselves, and others. Christ loved God and us in and through the total self-gift He made on the cross. However, standing at the foot of the cross was Christ's mother, Mary. Through her faith, Mary was "perfectly united with Christ in His self-emptying [self-giving]." At the foot of the cross we see "how completely she 'abandons herself to God' without reserve, 'offering the full assent of the intellect and the will' to Him."[121] Her Son's Calvary is "her own Calvary."[122] In her unimaginable suffering beneath the cross, she loves her Son mercifully. She wills her own participation in the cross for the forgiveness of sins and the elimination of sin's effects. In other words, she lends her sufferings to His and, if it were possible, wishes to substitute her own pains for His. Thus, she draws as close to her Son, i.e., to God, as is possible for a human being. She loves Him mercifully and reveals merciful love to a unique and extraordinary degree.

Mary shared in Christ's kingly office. Christ's kingly office was the source of His bodily self-discipline. Christ needed kingly self-rule so that His body could express His Person. Christ's kingly office complemented His prophetic and priestly offices by enabling Him to express truth and love in and through His body. Mary's kingly self-discipline allowed her to abandon herself "to the truth of the word of the living God."[123] This abandonment occurred primarily when she pronounced her "fiat" at the annunciation. Even though she was at first disturbed by the angel's extraordinary greeting and even though she could only guess at the full meaning of her divine motherhood, she nevertheless had the courage to say, "let it be to me according to your word."[124]

Since Mary governed herself, she was able to express through her body the choices she willed. Love is an act of the will. Love is a choice to give oneself to another. Since Mary "possessed" her body, she was able to express her loving choices through her body. For example, in her "fiat," "there is a complete harmony with the words of the Son . . . 'I have come to do Thy will, O God.' "[125] With her lips, Mary was able to speak her "let it be to me" (words of abandonment to God) because of her kingly self-rule. Mary's kingly self-governance also made it possible for her to live a life of virginity. Mary's virginity itself is a perpetual bodily sign of her complete choice for God. By virtue of her love for God, "Mary wished to be always and in all things 'given to God,' living in virginity."[126]

Through His kingly office, Christ reveals to us that we are to love

God in and through a mutual bodily exchange of love. As the Mother of God, Mary loved Christ in a bodily way more intimately than any other human being. It was through her that God the Son received His human nature. The God-man, Jesus Christ, "is of the flesh and blood of Mary." Mary is "the mother who conceives Jesus in her womb, gives Him birth, and nurses Him."[127] In meditating on Jesus, stripped of His clothes before He is crucified, John Paul encourages us to "think of the mother of Christ, because in her womb, before her eyes, and at her hands the body of the Son of God was adored [loved] to the full."[128] Through His redemptive death on the cross, Christ expressed in a bodily way His entirely special and exceptional love for His mother. Mary returned that love to her Son, in a bodily way, by performing the tasks of a mother beneath the cross. Thus, between Jesus Christ, the God-man, and His mother, there was a mutual bodily exchange of love because both mother and Son had kingly self-rule.

Through His human kingly office, Christ not only expressed His self-discipline, but He also expressed God's care for creation. The divine care for creation includes all things, but it primarily concerns humanity, for whom all material things were created. Thus, Christ expresses the divine providential care for creation by governing created things on behalf of people. Like her Son, Mary exercises kingship by using the things of the earth for the sake of persons. For example, at the wedding feast at Cana, "when the wine gave out, the mother of Jesus said to Him, 'They have no wine.' "[129] Even though Jesus' hour had not yet come, Mary said to the servants, "Do whatever He tells you."[130] "Then Jesus orders the servants to fill the stone jars with water, and the water becomes wine, better than the wine which has previously been served to the wedding guests."[131] This incident shows Mary's kingly appreciation for the created order, i.e., that things are always to be put at the service of persons. Truly, Mary is a king both in her self-governance and in her proper concern for the created order.

As noted above,[132] Christ exercised His prophetic, priestly, and kingly offices together. The same is true for Mary. For example, when she visited her kinswoman, Elizabeth, she proclaimed the truth about God (prophetic act), i.e., that God "has done great things."[133] Love motivated her to go to visit Elizabeth in the hill country (priestly act). Finally, since Elizabeth was pregnant with John the Baptist, Mary must have done things for her during the visitation (kingly acts).

A study of Christ reveals to us the mystery of Mary as the Mother of God and as a singular participant in Christ's offices of prophet, priest, and king.[134] By her Son, she was redeemed from the very first moment of her existence and is thus called "full of grace." Further, by acting as a prophet, priest, and king, she cooperates in a unique way in the mission of Christ. In other words, through Christ, she returns God's love (especially at the foot of the cross) and reveals to us who we are.

Christ is the most wondrous gift of God to humanity. In Christ, humanity returned the Father's love, the love left unsatisfied and unreturned through the sin of Adam and Eve. Restoring the proper friendship between humanity and God, Christ made it possible for all men and women to share the divine life, grace. With this restored gift of the divine life, we again have the possibility of coming to eternal life with God in heaven. However, even without original sin, all men and women, as images of God, need to know the God-man to know their identity, proper activity, and to know that they should love God through a mutual bodily exchange of love and others by using things for their benefit.[135] In and through His humanity, our Lord Jesus Christ showed us God. In showing us God, He showed us ourselves. Through Christ's prophetic office, we know our identity. Through the Lord's priestly office, Christ reveals merciful love, our proper activity. In His kingly office, the Lord reveals that we should love God through a mutual bodily exchange of love. In His kingly office, the Lord also reveals that God exercises a dominion over the things of the earth for the sake of persons. As the Mother of God, Mary gave Christ His humanity. Thus, in a way, Mary enabled Christ to be prophet, priest, and king because it was in and through His humanity that He expressed these offices. In turn, Christ enabled her to share in an extraordinary way in His mission and in His triple offices.

In and through Christ and Mary, those people who knew them could return God's love and know who they were and how they should act. God did not abandon the people of Palestine two thousand years ago. However, has He abandoned us today?

FOR REFLECTION

A. Why did God become man?

B. Describe the Person of Christ.

C. How does Christ reveal man to himself in His triple offices of prophet, priest, and king?

D. Did Mary have freedom?

NOTES

1. See above, Chapter 3: "Original Sin and the Providence of God," pp. 63–75.

2. Of course, when God made clothes for Adam and Eve to wear after the first sin, God's merciful love did extend to the effects of original sin. See above, Chapter 3: "Original Sin and the Providence of God," pp. 67–68. However, original sin and its most damaging effects, i.e., darkening of the mind, weakening of the will, lack of integration in the body, were overcome only in Christ.

3. See Phil. 2:7.

4. A priest is one who commits his entire self to God. See SR, p. 224.

5. For a discussion of nature, see above, Chapter 1: "Man/Woman and God," pp. 3, 15. See also below, pp. 90–91. Christ was a priest in His humanity. In Christ, "human testimony becomes the expression of the salvific mission of God" through "the threefold power of Christ as priest, prophet, and king." See SR, p. 219. See also *Covenant,* pp. 90–91.

6. See SD, no. 17.

7. See below, Chapter 8: "Grace," pp. 220–21.

8. See above, Chapter 1: "Man/Woman and God," pp. 9–10. See also above, Chapter 3: "Original Sin and the Providence of God," p. 68.

9. See Josef Ratzinger, "The Paschal Mystery as Core and Foundation of

Devotion to the Sacred Heart," p. 154, in *Towards a Civilization of Love* (Proceedings of the International Congress on the Heart of Jesus, 1981), English Edition by Ignatius Press (San Francisco: Ignatius Press, 1985), pp. 145–65.

10. See below, pp. 90–91.

11. See above, Chapter 3: "Original Sin and the Providence of God," p. 74.

12. See FC, no. 11.

13. See above, Chapter 2: "God's Love: Creation," n. 71.

14. Cf. Gen. 1:26.

15. St. Thomas Aquinas allows for this possibility. Answering the question "Would God have become man had man not sinned?," St. Thomas writes: "There are different opinions about this question. For some say that even if man had not sinned, the Son of Man would have become incarnate. Others assert the contrary, and seemingly our assent ought rather to be given to this opinion." Thomas holds this opinion because "the work of the incarnation was ordained by God as a remedy for sin; so that, had sin not existed, the incarnation would not have been." However, having stated his opinion, Thomas acknowledges that "the power of God is not limited to this; even had sin not existed, God could have become incarnate." See Thomas Aquinas, *Summa Theologiae,* III, Q. 1, Art. 3, Resp.

16. See DV, no. 52.

17. See RH, no. 9. See also above, Chapter 3: "Original Sin and the Providence of God," pp. 72–74.

18. See above, Chapter 1: "Man/Woman and God," p. 19.

19. See Mk. 8:27–28.

20. See CS, no. 80.

21. See SC, p. 107.

22. See Mt. 16:16.

23. Nature (essence) signifies "what" someone is. Person signifies "who" someone is. See Chapter 1: "Man/Woman and God," pp. 3, 15.

24. See above, Chapter 3: "Original Sin and the Providence of God," pp. 55–57, 73–75.

25. See ND, nos. 7–8.

26. See above, Chapter 1: "Man/Woman and God," pp. 7–8.

27. See ND, nos. 613–16.

28. See above, p. 87.

29. See above, Chapter 3: "Original Sin and the Providence of God," pp. 73–75.

30. See ND, no. 605.

31. See ND, no. 606/4.

32. See ND, no. 615.

33. See DV, no. 50.

34. See GS, no. 22.

35. See RH, no. 9.

36. See CS, no. 81.

37. See Mt. 16:16.

38. See GS, no. 22. Even the human nature of Adam and Eve before sin was not as perfect as Christ's. God could not have made our first parents with human nature as perfect as Christ's because Christ's human nature belongs to God Himself. In Christ, the divine Person determined the absolute perfection of His human nature.

39. See Jn. 1:14.

40. See RH, no. 8.

41. See RH, no. 8.

42. See Lk. 8:5–15, 15:3–7, 8–10, and 11–32.

43. See Jn. 13:13.

44. See SC, p. 70.

45. See Lk. 22:42.

46. See Chapter 2: "God's Love: Creation," pp. 32–33.

47. See DV, no. 50.

48. See Aquinas, *Summa Theologiae,* III, Q. 10, Art. 4, Resp.

49. See Lk. 2:52.

50. See above, p. 91.

51. See above, Chapter 1: "Man/Woman and God," pp. 3, 6.

52. See Mt. 4:1–11.

53. This does not limit divine freedom any more than the impossibility of God making a square circle limits the divine freedom.

54. The dilemma could also be stated with regard to Christ's passion and death. However, His suffering and death were not imposed on Him. For a discussion of this point, see below, pp. 99–101.

55. See above, Chapter 2: "God's Love: Creation," pp. 34–36.

56. See below, Chapter 8: "Grace," p. 223, for a list of these gifts.

57. See Aquinas, *Summa Theologiae,* III, Q. 11, Art. 1, Resp.

58. See SR, p. 219.

59. See above, Chapter 1: "Man/Woman and God," p. 5.

60. See above, Chapter 3: "Original Sin and the Providence of God," p. 59.

61. See Mt. 4:5–7.

62. See Mt. 4:8–10.

63. See Mt. 4:3–4.

64. See Mt. 4:3.

65. See Mt. 4:4.

66. See Jn. 18:37.

67. See SC, p. 120.

68. It is appropriate here again to quote the lines we quoted in Chapter 3: "The truth about the God of the covenant, about the God Who creates out of love, Who in love offers humanity the covenant in Adam, Who for love's sake puts to man requirements which have direct bearing on the truth of man's creaturely being [made in the image of God]—this is the truth that is destroyed in what Satan says." See SC, p. 30. See also above, Chapter 3: "Original Sin and the Providence of God," pp. 62–64.

69. See Jn. 3:16.

70. See Phil. 2:7.

71. See Lk. 23:46.

72. See Mt. 27:46.

73. See Ps. 22:1.

74. See RH, no. 10.

75. See above, pp. 81, 94.

76. See above, Chapter 1: "Man/Woman and God," pp. 16, 17. See also above, Chapter 2: God's Love: Creation," pp. 38, 40ff.

77. Still, we can love ourselves. See below, Chapter 8: "Grace," p. 219.

78. Of course, Christ's death was not imposed upon Him by His Father because He was perfectly free. See above, pp. 92–94.

79. See Jn. 10:18: "No one takes it [my life] from Me, but I lay it down of My own accord."

80. See SC, p. 187.

81. See SC, p. 190.

82. See SD, no. 18.

83. See SD, no. 18.

84. See Lk. 23:46.

85. See Jn. 15:13.

86. See Mk. 14:36. See also SC, pp. 187, 190, and 192.

87. Of course, it is an absolute impossibility that Christ, as the God-man, would have lacked the kingly office. However, the positing of a hypothetical lack of kingly self-rule demonstrates its positive importance to His mission.

88. See above, pp. 95–99.

89. See above, Chapter 1: "Man/Woman and God," pp. 16–17.

90. See SC, p. 192.

91. See above, pp. 99–101.

92. See above, Chapter 2: "God's Love: Creation," n. 71.

93. See Lk. 7:36–50.

94. See Gen. 1:28.

95. See Mt. 8:23–27.

96. See Mt. 14:15–21.

97. See RM, no. 4.

98. For a discussion on original sin, see above, Chapter 3: "Original Sin and the Providence of God," p. 55. For a discussion of how sin wounds humanity, see above, Chapter 2: "God's Love: Creation," pp. 36–37.

99. See above, Chapter 3: "Original Sin and the Providence of God," p. 65.

100. See above, Chapter 2: "God's Love: Creation," p. 35.

101. See RM, no. 13.

102. See above, Chapter 1: "Man/Woman and God," pp. 7–9.

103. A similar argument could apply to the people of the Old Testament, i.e., they would have been unable to love God at all without the benefit of His grace. He saw the inclinations of their wills and blessed them with the capability of responding to Him as they wished. Of course, the graces given to the people of the Old Testament were never as great as the graces given to Mary because only she was to be the Mother of God. For example, Noah, Abraham, Moses, and David loved God and must have been blessed with His grace. See above, Chapter 3: "Original Sin and the Providence of God," pp. 68–72.

104. See RM, no. 10.

105. See above, Chapter 3: "Original Sin and the Providence of God," p. 63ff.

106. See RM, no. 10.

107. Cf. the "Hail Mary."

108. See Lk. 1:31–32.

109. See Chapter 2: "God's Love: Creation," p. 35.

110. See LG, no. 56.

111. See above, pp. 104–06.

112. See Lk. 1:38.

113. See RM, no. 13.

114. See RM, no. 8.

115. See RM, no. 13.

116. See RM, no. 13.

117. See RM, no. 14.

118. See RM, no. 37.

119. See above, Chapter 3: "Original Sin and the Providence of God," pp. 60–62.

120. See Lk. 23:46. See also above, p. 100.

121. See RM, no. 18.

122. See SC, p. 188.

123. See RM, no. 14.

124. See Lk. 1:38.

125. See RM, no. 13.

126. See RM, no. 39.

127. See RM, no. 20.

128. See SC, p. 192.

129. See Jn. 2:3.

130. See Jn. 2:5.

131. See RM, no. 21.

132. See above, p. 103.

133. See Lk. 1:49.

134. See above, p. 104.

135. See above, pp. 82–85, 94–104.

—— **5** ——

The Church as the Person of Christ

We believe in one holy catholic and apostolic Church.

A. Who Is the Church?

As we have seen,[1] it is vital to come to know Christ. Yet, what of us who have lived after the Lord? How are we to come to know Christ? Just because we did not live when Christ lived, are we doomed to exist in utter confusion without ever knowing who we are and how we should act? Are we never to know that we are to love God through a mutual bodily exchange of love because we were not born in Palestine under Augustus Caesar? Are we never to know how to love others by using things for their benefit? Are we never to be restored to friendship with God? Are we never to experience heaven? We desperately need Christ, but He is in heaven. Is Macbeth right about us when Shakespeare has him say, "Life's but a walking shadow, a poor player that struts and frets his hour upon the stage and then is heard no more: it is a tale told by an idiot, full of sound and fury, signifying nothing"?[2] Without Christ, our lives would be as pathetic as Macbeth seems to paint them. Seemingly, Christ revealed "man to himself"[3] only for those who lived in Palestine while He was alive. Further, was it only these who had a chance to escape the incredible tragedy of human existence caused by the sin of our first parents?

Of course, this pessimistic view is not true. God wishes that every single one of us should know himself or herself and come eventually to the glories of heaven. God the Son died to reveal man to himself and to give us life. He became man that all might come to know and love by seeing Him. Christ did not leave us orphans when He ascended to heaven. Rather, He established the Church, which is His body.⁴ Thus, when we see the Church, we see Christ.

The Church carries on the mission of Christ today. Our need for Christ is satisfied by the Church, i.e., by Christ today. The rejection of the Church is tantamount to rejecting Christ. The abandonment of the Church is the abandonment of Christ. To ignore the Church is to ignore Christ. Rejecting, leaving, or ignoring the Church is a self-destructive, suicidal act because to function as an image of God, i.e., to be fully a human person, and to come to heaven, we need the Church. The Church is God's incredible gift to us because the Church continues the work of Christ.

This view of the Church rests firmly on the tradition that the Church is the body of Christ.⁵ A human body expresses a person. Christ's body expressed His divine Person. Thus, if it is true that the Church is the body of Christ, then it is also true that it is the person of Christ. The Church cannot be Christ's body without being His person. The Church has a body, a visible reality, which reveals its invisible reality, Christ. As John Paul has written, "Christ and the Church are one single mystical person."⁶

In teaching that the Church and Christ are one single mystical person, Pope John Paul is echoing the teaching of St. Paul. Paul affirmed that the Church is the person of Christ when he referred to the Church as the body of Christ.⁷ In 1 Corinthians, St. Paul writes in the famous passage about charity, "If I deliver my body to be burned, but have not love, I gain nothing."⁸ Obviously, Paul does not use "body" here to mean only an attribute or an appendage of a person. Rather, "body" refers to the whole person. Earlier in the same epistle the Apostle writes, "The body is not meant for immorality, but for the Lord, and the Lord for the body. And God raised the Lord and will also raise us up by His power."⁹ At first in this passage, St. Paul is speaking of the body, but then he switches to the personal pronoun "us." When our bodies are raised, it is we ("us," i.e., our persons) who are raised. The body, for Paul, refers not just to part of a person, but to the whole person: "It is obvious that here it is not just the body which is meant, but the whole 'I.' "[10] As John Paul teaches, "St. Paul often identifies the Church with Christ Himself"[11] when he calls the Church the body of Christ.

In another passage of 1 Corinthians, St. Paul identifies the Church with Christ. He is discussing the divisions in the church of Corinth, and he asks his readers, "Is Christ divided?"[12] Clearly, for St. Paul, when there are divisions in the Church, it is Christ Who is torn apart. It is not merely Christ's body that is torn apart, it is Christ Himself, His person. Thus, Paul identifies the Church with the person of Christ. In this approach, Paul is only following the Lord's own words. On the road to Damascus, Christ asked Paul, "Saul, Saul, why do you persecute me?" Paul answered, "Who are you, Lord?" Christ answered, "I am Jesus, Whom you are persecuting."[13] Of course, St. Paul was persecuting the Church, but Christ identified Himself with the Church. Since it is impossible to persecute a mere body (it is always a person who is persecuted), the only possible conclusion is that the Church is the person of Christ.

The fathers of the Church, following the lead of St. Paul, understood the Church as the person of Christ. St. Augustine often referred to the Church as the person of Christ.[14] As John Paul teaches, "This doctrine . . . is one of the teachings that mattered most to the bishop of Hippo, and one of the most fruitful themes of his ecclesiology."[15] St. Gregory the Great taught that "Christ and the Church are one person."[16] St. John Chrysostom and St. Gregory of Nyssa identified the Church with the person of Christ.[17] Thomas Aquinas accepted Augustine's formulation of the Church as the person of Christ, using the phrase *una persona.*[18] In another passage, St. Thomas refers to the head and members of the Church as one mystical person *(una persona mystica).*[19]

The recovery of this long-standing tradition of the Church's understanding of itself began with Pope Pius XII and the publication of his encyclical *The Mystical Body of Christ* (1943). In that letter, Pope Pius wrote that "the unbroken tradition of the fathers from the earliest times teaches that the divine Redeemer and the society which is

His body form but one mystical person."[20] It is the concept of the Church as the mystical person of Christ that is the underlying foundation of the entire second section of the encyclical.[21] *The Mystical Body of Christ* had a profound effect on ecclesiology, and it shaped the thoughts of the fathers of the Second Vatican Council.

The Second Vatican Council was primarily concerned with the Church. Two of its four constitutions considered the Church.[22] The Second Vatican Council began its work by presuming that the Church is the mystical person of Christ. The first question that the conciliar fathers posed for themselves was, "Church, what do you say of yourself?"[23] Of course, only a person can speak and have an understanding of himself. Therefore, the conciliar fathers, in expecting the Church to formulate an answer to their question, conceived the Church as a person. Undoubtedly, this rediscovery of the personhood of the Church (as taught in St. Paul, St. Augustine and other fathers, and St. Thomas Aquinas) can be traced to the impact and influence of Pius XII's encyclical *The Mystical Body of Christ.*

Although the Church is Christ, it is obviously impossible to identify the Church with the incarnate Christ. Further, although each member of the Church is another Christ,[24] each one is not united with the second Person of the Trinity, as though God the Son were incarnate again in each member of the Church. There are differences between the incarnate Christ and the mystical Christ. (See the diagram, "The Incarnate Christ and the Mystical Christ," on page 121 for a summary of the following points.) One difference between the Church and the incarnate Christ lies in the elements of the union. In the incarnation, two natures, divine and human, are united in one divine Person. In the Church, persons, human and divine, are joined in a union with one another. A second difference between the Church and the incarnate Christ lies in the mode of union. The union of the two natures in Christ is accomplished through the grace of the hypostatic union. However, the union in the Church is accomplished through sanctifying grace. Finally, the union of the Church is established through the work of God the Son, of God the Holy Spirit, and of human beings. On the other hand, the union of natures in the incarnate Christ is only the work of God the Son and God the

Holy Spirit. In order to note these differences between the incarnate Christ and the Church, the Church is called the mystical person of Christ. The Church is a mysterious union of persons (the Holy Spirit, Christ, and the baptized) who unite to form the mystical person of Christ.

THE INCARNATE CHRIST AND THE MYSTICAL CHRIST

Differences	Christ	Church
What is united?	Natures	Persons
How is the union accomplished?	Hypostatic grace	Sanctifying grace
Who unites?	God the Holy Spirit and God the Son	God the Holy Spirit, Jesus Christ, and the baptized
Result:	Incarnate Christ (Incarnation)	Mystical Christ (Church)

The union of persons in the Church, founded on the work of Christ and the Holy Spirit, is joined to the union of the three Persons in the Trinity. Each member of the Church is joined to all other members because each human member has received the very life of God in Baptism.[25] In other words, each human member has received the very life of the Trinity. This divine life is bestowed on the human members of the Church when they freely ask to be baptized. (Of course, infants cannot ask to be baptized. However, parents speak for their children and freely ask the Church to baptize them.) Thus, human membership in the Church is founded on a personal choice, a will-act by each member to commit himself to Christ. In other words, the baptized choose to give themselves to Christ. Of course, in giving themselves to Christ, they give themselves to all the other baptized who are other Christs.[26] Further, in and through Christ's self-gift to them, they receive the self-donation of all those joined to Christ. The mutual self-giving among the members of the Church, founded on their own choices and God's grace, mirrors the self-donation of each member of the Trinity to the other members. Since the union of the three Persons in God is a *communion of Persons*, the union of the members of the Church is also a *communion of persons*. Of course, since each human member of the Church is another Christ and Christ is the second Person of the Trinity, it is as though each human member is invited to participate in the Trinity. In a sense, the human members of the Church are grafted to Christ and therefore to the Trinity. The *communion of persons* of the Church transcends all other communions of human persons. (The existence of the Church does not eliminate the familial and worker communions willed by God at the dawn of creation.[27] However, for baptized members of the Church, the familial and worker communions become specifications of the *communion of persons* of the Church.)[28]

As a *communion of persons*, the Church is called the People of God. The Second Vatican Council taught that "the universal Church is seen to be 'a people brought into unity from the unity of the Father, the Son, and the Holy Spirit.' "[29] It might seem that the Church cannot be one mystical person, if many persons are members. Of course, two simple answers come to mind. First, the Church is Christ because each member has "put on Christ."[30] Second, it might be suggested that the Church is one as the Trinity is one God. Neither of these answers satisfies completely. The first answer still leaves the primary question of how it is possible for one (mystical) Christ to be formed from many Christs. The second is a bit deceptive because the Church is not one as the Trinity is one. In God, there are three Persons in a single divine nature. In the Church, there are many persons who each possess human nature. The Church as one mystical person with many members can be explained more satisfactorily by examining the corporate personality of the Old Testament Jews.

The Jews in the Old Testament, many though they were, were joined together as one corporate person. (This idea is not to be confused with a legal person, such as a modern corporation.) A corporate person has four characteristics. First, the corporate entity has a past, present, and future. Second, the group is a real entity that is actualized in its members. Third, the name of the group can be applied either to an individual member, the head of the group, or to the whole group. Finally, even when an individual is seemingly in the foreground, the corporate person remains intact. What is said of one can be said of the group.[31] As a union of persons forming one whole, a corporate person is a *communion of persons*.

There are three distinct levels of corporate personalities. The first is the grouping of all those who live and work in the same area *(communion of persons* in the workplace). The second is a union of people founded on a biological link (familial *communion of persons).*[32] The third, and the strongest, is the religious corporate personality, e.g., the Israelites after the covenant at Sinai with God.[33] By the power of God, the Israelites of old were formed into the People of God, a corporate person, i.e., a *communion of persons.*

As the direct heir of the Old Testament People of God, the Church is the new People of God, the new corporate personality, i.e., a *communion of persons* forming the one mystical person of Christ. As a corporate personality, the mystical Christ is identified with all its members, and each of its members is identified with it. The Church, as a whole, is Christ, i.e., His mystical person, and each member is Christ. Galatians confirms this point: "For as many of you as were baptized into Christ have put on Christ . . . for you are all one in Christ Jesus."[34]

B. The Acts of the Church

Since the Church is the mystical person of Christ, when it acts, it is Christ Who is acting. "The Church looks at the world through the very eyes of Christ," proclaimed Pope John Paul II on October 2, 1979, during his homily at Yankee Stadium in New York City.[35] Clearly, for John Paul, when the Church acts, it is Christ Who is acting. Further, these acts are expressed visibly through the Church's body, i.e., through its members who are both spirit and body. Thus, the Church, as Christ, acts in a visible way.

The acts of the Church have the same purpose as the acts of the incarnate Christ. Christ satisfied the Father's love, the love left unsatisfied by Adam and Eve. By satisfying the Father's love, Christ offered forgiveness for original sin and made it possible for the most damaging effects of sin to be overcome. Further, in returning the Father's love, Christ made it possible for all of us not only to be friends of God, but even to be His adopted children. Thus, Christ expressed God's merciful love. All this was accomplished by Christ's sacrifice on the cross. In our own time, the Church expresses Christ's merciful love. By celebrating the one sacrifice of Christ, the Church returns the Father's love. Further, the Church offers forgiveness for sin and makes it possible to overcome the most damaging effects of sin through the sacraments. In addition, the sacraments are the concrete expression of the friendship between man and God.

Moreover, there can be no doubt that the Church also continues Christ's mission of revealing man to himself.[36] The Second Vatican Council teaches that the "Church . . . opens to him [man] . . . the innermost truth about himself."[37] Of course, to reveal man to himself and "to open up the truth" to man about himself is the same thing.

Christ revealed man to himself through His triple offices of prophet, priest, and king. The Church as the mystical Christ carries on the mission of Christ through these very same offices. Christ revealed Truth, i.e., God,[38] through His prophetic office. In other words, through His prophetic office, Christ counteracted the lies of Satan, especially the devil's lies about God.[39] As the mystical Christ, the Church teaches the Truth, God Himself, through its prophetic office. In teaching Truth, the Church constantly strives against the lies of the father of lies. Christ revealed merciful love through His priestly office. The Church, as Christ, expresses the same merciful love in and through its priesthood, i.e., the priesthood of Christ. As a king, Christ orchestrated His own body so that it could be the means of revealing Truth and merciful love. In addition, through His kingly office, Christ revealed that we are called to love God through a mutual bodily exchange of love and that the divine dominion over creation is exercised for the sake of people. In other words, Christ revealed divine providence. As the mystical Christ, the Church exercises a self-discipline so that it can reveal Truth and merciful love, and so that it may call us to love God through a mutual bodily exchange of love. Further, the Church also reveals divine providence by placing all material resources at the service of people. In this way, the Church demonstrates that all the things, the plants, and the animals were created for, and are legitimately governed by, mankind.[40]

The Church, the corporate person of Christ, shares the Lord's triple offices of prophet, priest, and king. As a corporate person, what is said of the Church as a whole can also be said of each member.[41] Therefore, each member of the Church possesses Christ's offices of prophet, priest, and king. St. Paul confirms this participation of each member of the Church in Christ's triple offices when he writes that all the baptized "have put on Christ."[42] "However, the Lord also appointed certain men as ministers,"[43] i.e., He appointed and ordained the Apostles. As baptized members of the Church, all the ordained possess the offices of Christ in the same manner that all the baptized do. In addition, through their ordination, those men ordained as deacons, priests, and bishops also share in one or more of Christ's offices in a hierarchical manner. Deacons share in the hierarchical kingly office. However, if the deacon is not a priest or a bishop, he does not share in the hierarchical offices of priest and prophet. Unlike a deacon, an ordained priest shares in the hierarchical priestly office of Christ. Still, it should be noted that every priest is a deacon. Consequently, the priest also possesses the hierarchical kingly office as does a deacon. However, if the priest is not a bishop, he does not share in the hierarchical prophetic office. It is only a bishop who has the fullness of Christ's priesthood because he alone —as deacon, priest, and bishop—shares in the hierarchical kingly, priestly, and prophetic offices of Christ. (See the accompanying diagram, "Hierarchical Offices.")

		HIERARCHICAL OFFICES		
Hierarchical offices:		Kingly	Priestly	Prophetic
	Deacon	X		
The				
Ordained:	Priest	X	X	
	Bishop	X	X	X

The ordained exercise these hierarchical offices for the People of God. Even though the baptized are given the triple offices of Christ, these baptismal offices need to be activated so that they might come to full, visible expression. The Church, as mentioned above,[44] has a structure similar to the incarnate Christ. Just as the incarnate Christ gave expression to His divine Person through His human body, so the Church expresses the mystical Christ through outward, physical acts. Christ expressed Himself, i.e., He accomplished His mission, through His triple offices of prophet, priest, and king. Similarly, the Church expresses the mystical Christ through the same triple offices. Therefore, if the Church is to express Christ, all the aspects of Christ's triple offices must be present. Of course, as Christ, the Church possesses all the triple offices of Christ in all their fullness. However, as was mentioned,[45] the members of the Church possess the triple offices in different ways, i.e., baptismal and hierarchical. The ordained (those sharing some or all of Christ's offices in a hierarchical manner) are the catalysts who activate the triple offices of Christ in the baptized. In the incarnate Christ, there was no distinction between the hierarchical and baptismal manner of sharing in the triple offices of prophet, priest, and king. Christ simply possessed these offices in every possible way. However, in the Church, viewed under the aspect of its many members, there are distinctions between the hierarchical and baptismal ways of sharing in the triple offices.[46] The distinction might be clarified through a comparison to our own acts. When we wake in the morning, we often find it difficult to move from the relaxing comfort of our beds. We may choose to begin the morning, but it still takes an effort. That extra exertion of energy we make in the morning—after we have chosen to begin the day—is something like the activation that the baptized need from those who are ordained.

The deacon who is not also ordained a priest or a bishop activates only the kingly office of the baptized. The deacon's own baptismal kingly office is activated by other deacons. The deacon's baptismal priestly office is activated by a priest or a bishop, and his baptismal prophetic office is activated by a bishop. The hierarchical priest activates Christ's priestly office in the baptized. The ordained priest's baptismal priestly office is activated by other priests. (However, in celebrating the Eucharist, the ordained priest does activate his own baptismal priestly office.) Since all ordained priests are also deacons, the hierarchical priest also activates the kingly office in the baptized. The ordained priest's baptismal prophetic office is activated by the bishop. The bishop shares in all the offices of Christ in both a baptismal and a hierarchical manner. Only the bishop, when he is in union with the Pope, the successor of Peter, activates the baptismal prophetic office of the baptized. Thus, the bishop's own baptismal prophetic office is activated by the Pope and other bishops. However, since all bishops are also deacons and priests, they also activate the baptismal kingly and priestly offices of the baptized. Clearly, the hierarchical priesthood differs "essentially and not only in degree"[47] from the common priesthood of the faithful because it is the active catalyst for the common priesthood. (See the accompanying diagram, "Activation of the Baptismal Offices.")

ACTIVATION OF THE BAPTISMAL OFFICES

Baptismal offices:		Kingly	Priestly	Prophetic
	Deacon	X		
Activated	Priest	X	X	
by:	Bishop	X	X	X

Of course, the ordained exist for the baptized. Without the baptized, the ordained would have no one but themselves to activate. In this case, the exercise of the hierarchical offices would seem self-serving. The Church would not properly or fully imitate the self-giving aspect of Christ's triple offices. Similarly, the baptized would not function as they should without the ordained. There would be no one to activate them, i.e., to allow them to express the mystical Christ fully. Obviously, the Church expresses Christ fully only through the union of the baptized and the ordained.[48]

All the baptized "have put on Christ."[49] Therefore, all the baptized are in some sense other Christs and are joined to the mystical Christ. The fathers of the Second Vatican Council taught that the Church is "joined in many ways to the baptized who are honored by the name of Christian, but who do not however profess the Catholic faith in its entirety or have not preserved unity or communion under the successor of Peter."⁵⁰ The conciliar fathers make a distinction between those who are members of the Church and those who are "joined" to the Church. Since the baptized have all received the same sacrament, there cannot be a distinction among the baptized on the basis of Baptism. In other words, a baptized Lutheran, Baptist, or Methodist is another Christ, just as a Catholic is. Therefore, the distinction among the baptized must rest on something other than Baptism. The differences among the baptized must involve the activation of the baptized by the ordained. Christians who are not members of the Catholic Church are not activated by the ordained as Catholics are. Some do not embrace the teaching of the Holy Father and the bishops. In other words, their prophetic office is not properly activated. Some Christians do not have ordained priests and do not recognize the hierarchical priesthood of the Catholic Church. The baptismal priestly office of these Christians is not properly activated. Further, without ordained deacons or a recognition of ordained deacons, the kingly activation of the baptized is missing.

It is critical to note that all the baptized are Christians. All the baptized "have put on Christ."⁵¹ All the baptized express Christ outwardly. However, for those whose triple offices of prophet, priest, and king are not properly activated, the fullest expression of Christ fails. It is simply not possible for them to express fully the mystical Christ. It must be emphasized, as the conciliar fathers teach, that the lack of full outward expression of Christ does not mean that all outward expression of the mystical Christ is lacking. It is more a question of degree and fullness. As the fathers of the Second Vatican Council taught, "These Christians are indeed in some real way joined to us in the Holy Spirit for, by His gifts and graces, His sanctifying power is also active in them."⁵²

All the ordained have a mission to all the baptized. Pastors are in some sense responsible for all Christians within their jurisdiction. Thus, bishops, priests, and deacons are called upon to activate the triple offices of Christ in all the baptized under their care. The papal office serves all the baptized in the world. When Pope John Paul II travels around the world, he activates the prophetic, priestly, and kingly offices in all the baptized. Further, since bishops are to be witnesses of Christ, "they should not limit themselves to those who already acknowledge the Prince of Pastors, but should also devote their energies wholeheartedly to those who have strayed in any way from the path of truth."[53] Thus, bishops exercise their prophetic, priestly, and kingly offices for all the baptized. Similarly, priests and deacons are to exercise their share in Christ's offices for all the baptized. (Of course, deacons, priests, and bishops also have responsibility in some way to the non-baptized.)

Clearly, then, it is possible for baptized non-Catholics to be fully activated. However, if baptized non-Catholics are to be activated in the fullest sense, it is not only necessary that bishops, priests, and deacons be available to non-Catholics, but it is also necessary for the non-Catholics to accept the ministries of deacons, priests, and bishops. For example, the bishop may be teaching, but the baptized, if their prophetic offices are to be activated properly, must be listening. Not only does this willingness to receive the ministries of the ordained fail with some baptized non-Catholics, it also is lacking in some baptized Catholics.[54]

1. THE PROPHETIC OFFICE OF THE CHURCH

Christ exercised His prophetic office by revealing Truth, i.e., by revealing God to us.[55] He counteracted the lies the devil used to tempt Adam and Eve. In revealing God as a loving, gentle Father, Christ overcame the devil's false presentation of God as a mean-spirited tyrant. Of course, in revealing God, Christ also revealed who we are. As images of God, we do not know ourselves unless we know God. In revealing God by the teaching of the Truth through His prophetic office, Christ taught us who we are.

The Church, as the mystical Christ, exercises the prophetic office of Christ. As mentioned above,[56] the prophetic office of the mystical Christ exists among the members of the Church in two ways: hierarchical and baptismal. In classical terminology, the Pope and the bishops form the *magisterium* or teaching authority of the Church.

This teaching authority, the hierarchical prophetic office, activates the baptismal prophetic office. Clearly, the Pope and the bishops do not teach for their own sakes. The Pope and the bishops do not impose their teaching on the baptized. Rather, the *magisterium* exercises its share in the prophetic office of Christ on behalf of the baptized and the entire human race. The magisterial sharing in the prophetic office of Christ is always at the service of the baptized because it conveys, as Christ did, the truth about God and the truth about mankind. Through their baptismal share in Christ's prophetic office, the baptized are empowered to accept the teachings of the *magisterium*.

With regard to the hierarchical prophetic office of Christ, it is important to realize that the Pope and the bishops are guided in their teaching by the Holy Spirit. They do not teach their own personal theories; rather, the Holy Spirit, through the hierarchical prophetic office, aids the *magisterium* in teaching the unchangeable truth of the Gospel. Although it is true that the Gospel is expressed differently from age to age, it is always the same truth that is expressed.[57] Thus, the *magisterium* teaches the same truth as Christ taught. As St. Paul wrote, "But even if we, or an angel from heaven, should preach to you a Gospel contrary to that which we preached to you, let him be accursed."[58] Pope John Paul II has emphasized that the Pope and the bishops, through the guidance of the Holy Spirit, teach the same truth as Christ taught: "The Holy Spirit will be the counselor of the Apostles and the Church, always present in their midst—even though invisible—as the teacher of the same Good News that Christ proclaimed."[59]

Clearly, only bishops in union with the Pope teach in the official manner. Yet, what about priests, deacons, lay teachers, parents, and others who teach the faith? Even though these men and women are exercising their prophetic office, they are not teaching as the Pope and the bishops teach. Rather, when they teach what they have received from the Pope and the bishops, they exercise their baptismal prophetic office in a responsible manner. They are allowing themselves to be activated by the hierarchical prophetic office. However, if they presume to teach on their own authority without reference to the hierarchy or even in opposition to the hierarchy, they are acting irresponsibly and not teaching the truth of Christ. Of course, not everything the Pope or the bishops say and do can be taken to be official acts of the *magisterium.* They teach officially, exercising their hierarchical prophetic office, when they preach or give speeches and addresses. They also teach officially through the printed medium. However, there are numerous occasions when they do speak about the faith but are not teaching as shepherds of the Church, e.g., at a dinner party with friends.

Christ teaches through the *magisterium* of the Church. In other words, Christ teaches through the Pope and the bishops. Since Christ, God the Son, is Truth itself,[60] it is not possible for Him to err or to deceive. The Scriptures indicate this very point when they record that Christ "taught them as One Who had authority and not as their scribes."[61] The Church speaks with the voice of Christ. As Christ did not err, so the Church does not teach error. Thus, it is possible to rely on what the Church teaches.

However, in the years since the Second Vatican Council and especially since the Pope Paul VI's encyclical, *On Human Life,* there have been repeated attempts to claim that the Church can and does err when it teaches in the usual magisterial manner,[62] i.e., through papal encyclicals, sermons, addresses, and exhortations. (Bishops also teach in the usual magisterial manner in their own dioceses, provided their teaching is in union with papal teaching.) The proponents of this point of view (dissenters) seem to argue that the Church can claim to teach the truth only when it teaches in a special manner, which theologians call "infallible." The infallible manner of teaching is not often exercised.

The Church teaches in an infallible manner on faith and morals in both an extraordinary and an ordinary way. The extraordinary infallible teaching mode is exercised in two ways. First, when the Pope makes a solemn statement on faith or morals *ex cathedra,* i.e., from the chair (the chair of Peter—the chair that symbolizes the Pope as the successor of St. Peter, the first Bishop of Rome), he exercises the extraordinary *magisterium* and teaches infallibly. Second, the Church teaches infallibly in an extraordinary way when a matter of faith or morals is defined solemnly by the bishops gathered in a general council in union with the Holy Father. The Church also teaches infallibly in an ordinary way when the same point of faith or morals is taught and defined individually by bishops, even though dispersed around the world, who are in communion with one another and with the successor of St. Peter.[63] (See the accompanying diagram, "The Infallible *Magisterium.*")

THE INFALLIBLE *Magisterium*

Extraordinary

1. The Pope teaching a point of faith or morals from the chair.
2. A teaching on a point of faith or morals defined solemnly by a general council of bishops gathered in union with the Holy Father.

Ordinary

1. The same point of faith or morals taught and defined individually by bishops, even though dispersed around the world, who are in communion with one another and with the successor of St. Peter.

The suggestion of the dissenters that only teachings of the Church proclaimed in the infallible manner ought to be accepted and that other teachings of the Church are subject to error betrays a fundamental lack of faith in the Church as the mystical Christ. However, since the Church is Christ, it teaches with the voice of Christ.

Faced with the attacks of the dissenters on some teachings proclaimed in the usual magisterial manner, some of those loyal to the Church have attempted to defend these teachings by arguing that they are in fact taught in the infallible mode, e.g., the teaching against contraception.[64] The dissenters claim the right to question the Church's teaching against contraception. They argue that this teaching could be in error because it is taught in the usual magisterial manner. Theoretically, if the loyalists could show that the teaching against contraception is actually taught in the infallible mode, the primary argument of the dissenters would lose its force.

The dissenters ground their dissent in the judgment of their own individual consciences. In other words, the dissenters pit their own consciences (and those of the faithful) against the prophetic office of the Church.[65] While it is true that they plead freedom of conscience only for teachings proclaimed in the usual magisterial mode, still their argument of conscience can apply just as much to pronouncements given in the infallible mode. In other words, once a dissenter has rejected a teaching of the Church on the basis of freedom of conscience, he or she can reject any teaching of the Church on the same basis. Therefore, the loyalist argument cannot succeed because it does not address the heart of the dissenters' argument: freedom of conscience. Even if the loyalists could prove that a particular usual magisterial teaching was actually taught in an infallible mode, the loyalists would not win over the dissenters. The dissenters would not change their positions, but only the arguments that they use to justify their dissent. Dissent is a rejection of Church teaching, i.e., a rejection of the voice of Christ. It is hardly realistic to think that the dissenters would change their minds on a particular teaching just because the Church altered the manner it taught that point of faith or morals.

Further, in defending certain teachings as infallible, the loyalists are actually admitting the major premise of the dissenters, i.e., that pronouncements taught in the usual magisterial mode are not binding. This is precisely the point that cannot be granted. For this reason, it seems better not even to enter such a discussion. The situation is similar to a Catholic confronted by a fundamentalist who wishes to know where in the Scriptures a particular doctrine is found. The question itself is loaded because implicit in its formulation is the fundamentalist doctrine that revelation is found only in the Scriptures (not in Tradition).[66] If the Catholic discusses such a question, he has already granted a premise opposed to the teaching of the Church. The only prudent choice in this case is to change the context of the discussion, to ask a different question.

While some loyalists attempt to defend particular teachings by suggesting that they are actually taught in an infallible mode, other loyalists call on the Church to define some of its teachings in an extraordinary infallible manner through a solemn, papal *ex cathedra* statement.[67] Their point seems to be that it is useless to quarrel about whether or not a particular teaching is taught in an infallible manner. They urge the Church to end the argument by clearly defining a teaching in the extraordinary infallible mode. Of course, this does not escape any of the objections already mentioned. However, it does raise a further problem.

The Church has taught in the extraordinary infallible mode through a papal definition only those things that are clearly beyond human reason unaided by faith, e.g., the Immaculate Conception (Mary's freedom from original sin from the first moment of her existence).[68] If such an extraordinary mode of teaching were to be extended to those things that can be known by human reason, e.g., certain moral issues, there would be a danger that divine revelation would destroy all human knowledge not founded on revelation. Some of the proposed definitions would make what are rational principles rest not on reason, but on faith alone. The clear implication would be that only matters of faith (i.e., revelation) would carry any conviction. If this implication were accepted, revelation would destroy human rational investigations not founded on revelation. Further, it would threaten the very dignity of the human person. As an image of God, a human being is created to discover truth by collecting evidence and constructing persuasive proofs. If nothing could be known for certain except through faith, even the best natural evidence and the most persuasive rational proofs (not founded on revelation) would be fruitless because no evidence and no argument would ever carry any conviction. The glory of our creation as beings seeking truth through the use of our own natural, rational powers would be tarnished. Solemnly defining those things that can be known by human reason seems to compromise human reason.

2. THE PRIESTLY OFFICE OF THE CHURCH

Christ exercised His priesthood by revealing merciful love to us, i.e., by revealing to us how God acts. Christ revealed that God loves by drawing good from evil.[69] Christ showed us God's love in His every word and action. However, Christ expressed God's merciful love primarily in and through His sacrifice on the cross. Suffering for the sins of all of us, Christ drew good from evil. For us, Christ eliminated sin and the wounds of sin and brought us closer to God. For God the Father and God the Holy Spirit, the cross eliminated God's suffering occasioned by man's rejection of God's love and thus revived the friendship between man and God.

However, it would be possible to see the cross as an evil in itself. Such a view misses the mark because it fails to notice that Christ embraced the sufferings of His passion and death not for their own sake, but as a means to an end. He gave Himself totally, permitting the agony, to undo sin and its effects. To offer oneself to God and others is the proper activity of a priest. Thus, Christ, as priest, showed merciful love by offering Himself on the cross. In other words, Christ showed us how to love God and others. The Church, as the mystical Christ, shows merciful love in and through the exercise of Christ's priesthood.

First and foremost, the Church manifests the merciful love of God through the re-presentation of the sacrifice of the cross in the Eucharist. Through this marvelous sacrament, Christ is present again as He was on the cross. He does not die again. Rather, His sacrifice is made present under the appearances of bread and wine. However, the Eucharist is the same sacrifice offered by Christ two thousand years ago. All the other sacraments of the Church also reveal God's merciful love.[70] They are expressions of the sacrifice of Christ on the cross. Through the exercise of the priesthood of the Church, we come to know how we should act, i.e., that we are to love God and others mercifully.

As mentioned above,[71] the priestly office of Christ in the Church is shared in the baptismal manner by all members of the Church. It is shared in a hierarchical manner by those who are ordained as priests. The baptismal priestly office is expressed in many different ways, e.g., seeking the sacraments, praying. The hierarchical priestly office is expressed in the celebration of most of the sacraments. Both the baptismal and the hierarchical manners of sharing Christ's priestly office are necessary. The baptismal priestly office needs to be activated by the hierarchical priestly office. For example, it would be useless for the baptized to seek the Eucharist if there were no ordained priests to consecrate bread and wine. However, it is also true that the hierarchical priesthood would have little purpose without the baptismal. Who would the ordained activate?[72]

3. THE KINGLY OFFICE OF THE CHURCH

Christ exercised His kingly office by governing or ruling Himself. He "possessed" Himself, i.e., He was "in charge" of His body and its desires.[73] Christ's kingly self-rule enabled Him to reveal truth through His prophetic office and to reveal merciful love through His priestly office. Further, Christ's kingly office enabled Him to express God's love in and through His body. Since such an offer of love calls forth a bodily response from another, Christ's kingly office revealed that we are called to love God through a mutual bodily exchange of love and to love others by using things for their benefit.

The universal Church continues the Lord's kingly self-rule by maintaining an internal order. This internal order of the Church enables the Church to reveal truth and merciful love. In addition, through this internal order the Church expresses God's love in a bodily way. Since such an expression of love calls forth a response from another, the Church's kingly office reveals that we are called to love God in a bodily way. As Christ "orchestrated" His bodily passions, so the Church "orchestrates" its activities through its various offices. These offices maintain the internal order of the Church. The various offices and honorary positions within the structure of the Church are divided into three different categories: sacramental offices, jurisdictional offices, and honorary titles.

The sacramental offices are those of deacon, priest, and bishop. These can be received only through the sacrament of Holy Orders. As mentioned above,[74] each of these offices activates or brings into full expression one or more of the triple offices of the baptized. It is important to emphasize that there are only three sacramental offices in the Church. There is no office "higher than" or "above" bishop. The Pope holds the sacramental office of bishop. He is Pope because He is Bishop of Rome, the successor of St. Peter.

The jurisdictional offices within the Church are many and varied. It would be impossible to name them all here. (If such an attempt were to be made, the list would simply be a transcription of one of the sections of the Church's law code.)[75] However, it is useful to sketch at least the most common jurisdictional offices. Most Catholics, and even non-Catholics, know the priests of the local Catholic parish. The pastor of the parish is the one who has the primary responsibility for the care of the souls of the parish. He is appointed to his office by the bishop of the diocese where the parish is located. A pastor must be an ordained priest. If the parish is large, there will sometimes be associate pastors who hold the office of parochial vicar. They assist the pastor in his responsibilities as a shepherd of the people of that parish.

The office of ordinary is the one held by the Pope, diocesan bishops, and superiors of religious orders. Ordinaries are all those who serve in an executive capacity over the universal Church (the Pope), over a diocese, or over a religious community. Not all bishops are ordinaries. Some, similar to associate pastors in parishes, are auxiliary bishops. These men assist the ordinary (usually the diocesan bishop) in caring for the diocese entrusted to his care. Further, not all ordinaries are bishops. For example, heads of religious communities are usually not bishops. In addition, with the absence or death of a local bishop, the diocese is often administered by a priest who is not a bishop.

Cardinals hold the office of cardinal in the Church. Cardinals have the tasks of electing the Pope and of advising him on the governance of the universal Church when asked. In addition to the office of cardinal, most cardinals hold other offices in the Church (e.g., ordinary of a diocese). Of course, there are many more offices in the Church (e.g., vicar general, chancellor, moderator of the curia). All these serve to help the Church govern itself in order that the mystical Christ can be expressed outwardly.

As with the jurisdictional offices of the Church, there are many honorary titles for both clergy and lay people. The honorary titles that are most familiar include those of monsignor and archbishop. The title of monsignor does not add any new responsibilities, i.e., it is not a jurisdictional office. Further, a priest is not ordained a monsignor. In other words, a priest who is a monsignor does not hold a sacramental office different from any other priest. The title of archbishop is also an honorary one. It is most often given to those bishops who are ordinaries of large dioceses called metropolitans. Commonly, metropolitan dioceses are called archdioceses. (Actually, the term "archdiocese" came to be used because the ordinaries of metropolitan dioceses were normally archbishops. Thus, the honorary title held by most bishops of metropolitan dioceses was adapted and became the popular term designating a metropolitan diocese.) The ordinaries of metropolitan dioceses have certain limited, but actual, responsibilities in the non-metropolitan dioceses in their geographical area. In the United States, there is usually one metropolitan see in each state. The other dioceses in each state are grouped together under the one metropolitan. Nevertheless, one could be an archbishop and not be ordinary of an archdiocese. It is also possible to be bishop (i.e., the ordinary) of an archdiocese and not be an archbishop. The title of archbishop is an honorary one and is not necessarily connected with holding the office of ordinary in a metropolitan diocese.

In addition to governing itself through offices, the Church also governs itself through rites. For example, there are the various Eastern uniate rites, i.e., those in union with the Pope. In addition, there are many who do not recognize the Pope, e.g., Coptics, Nestorians, and the Eastern Orthodox groups. The relationship among these various groups, and between each group and the Church, can be understood only in light of their origins. (See the diagram, "Sketch of the Major Eastern Churches," on p. 141.)

When the Apostles went out from Jerusalem to preach the Gospel, they often organized the newly baptized Christians in each city they visited into a diocese. St. Paul's letters in the New Testament are, for the most part, letters of the Apostle to the churches, i.e., to the dioceses he had founded. Each of these churches developed their own customs and traditions. Four dioceses—Jerusalem, Antioch, Rome, and Alexandria—claimed to rest their traditions and customs on one of the Apostles. In 381 A.D., the capital of the Eastern Roman Empire, Constantinople (modern Istanbul), was given a status equivalent to that of Antioch and Alexandria. (Of course, Jerusalem could not exercise much influence after its fall in 70 A.D.)

Rome, as the diocese of St. Peter, always claimed a jurisdiction over all the other churches.[76] The Roman primacy was acknowledged by the other dioceses very early. (Of course, throughout time, there were challenges to this Roman primacy.) In the fourth century A.D., Arius, one of the priests of Alexandria, taught that Christ was not divine (the Arian heresy). However, after the Councils of Nicaea (325) and of Constantinople (381) taught that Christ is indeed divine, the church in Alexandria remained faithful. Antioch was tainted with the Nestorian heresy in the fifth century but remained faithful to the universal Church once the Council of Ephesus (431) condemned the Nestorian position as incompatible with the faith. There were some who refused to follow the diocese. These remained Nestorians, and there are still Nestorians today in the Near East. In the fifth century, Alexandria embraced the Monophysite position. However, when this teaching was condemned at the Council of Chalcedon in 451, Alexandria, in contrast to its previous acceptance of the Church's teaching on Arianism, did not accept the conciliar teaching and broke away from the universal Church. Alexandria and most of Egypt, remaining Monophysite, came to be called the Coptic church.[77] Some in the Near East also became Monophysites. After the Moslems conquered lands of the Mediterranean in the seventh and eighth centuries, the dioceses that had remained faithful to the universal Church in the Near East and Egypt no longer functioned. Still, there were some isolated Catholics in some areas. Thus, by the ninth century, there were some Catholics, some Nestorians, and some Monophysites in the Near East, as well as the Coptic church in Egypt.

By the time of Charlemagne (c. 800), of the five great dioceses (Jerusalem, Antioch, Rome, Alexandria, and Constantinople), only two were still functioning: Rome and Constantinople. Of course, with only two, a power struggle developed. There were many skirmishes and a few instances when the two dioceses did not recognize each other. (This type of division between two or more dioceses, as distinct from a difference in faith, is called a schism.) However, the definitive break (which was not recognized as a momentous schism at the time) came in 1054. Since 1054, Constantinople and Rome have not been in union with each other.

Those dioceses that joined Constantinople, i.e., most of the dioceses in the East that were traditionally linked to Constantinople and still functioning, together with those dioceses founded after 1054 from Constantinople, e.g., the dioceses in Russia, are called the Orthodox churches. It seems strange that these should be called orthodox because "orthodox" usually denotes a unity in practice and belief. However, the term "orthodox" was given to Constantinople and the other eastern dioceses when they remained united with Rome at the time the Monophysites in Egypt (the Coptics) did not accept the decrees of the Council of Chalcedon (451). Constantinople and the dioceses linked to it were still called orthodox in 1054, and they retain this name even today. Thus, contrary to their name, orthodox, the Orthodox churches are not in union with the Bishop of Rome, (the Pope).

However, this complicated history did not end in 1054. For a variety of reasons and at different times, sub-groups of the Orthodox, of the Monophysites, and of other groups broke from their traditional ties and approached Rome. These groups asked to be re-united under the Roman primacy. The Popes have always accepted these groups and, for the most part, have allowed them to retain their ancient customs and traditions. These sub-groups, re-united with Rome, are called uniates. The uniate churches have their own bishops, liturgical customs, and rich theological traditions. Catholics who attend Mass at a uniate church do, in fact, validly and lawfully fulfill their religious obligations. There are numerous uniate churches that exist around the world. These are incorporated within the structure of the universal Church through their bishops, who are in union with the Bishop of Rome. In the United States, these uniate churches are organized into dioceses that, as one might imagine, cover vast geographical areas. For example, one bishop, residing in an Eastern city, might serve thirty parishes in twenty states.

SKETCH OF THE MAJOR EASTERN CHURCHES

Jerusalem
   Conquered by Romans in 70 A.D.
Antioch (Syria)
   Nestorian heresy (c. 431 A.D.)
   Some pockets of Monophysites
   Conquered by Moslems in seventh century
Alexandria (Egypt)
   Arian heresy (c. 325 A.D.)
   Monophysite (c. 451 A.D.)
   Egyptian Monophysites broke from Rome and became Coptics (451 A.D.)
   Conquered by Moslems in seventh century
Constantinople
   Orthodox churches, as distinguished from the Coptics (the Egyptian Monophysites who broke from Rome c. 451 A.D.)
   Broke from Rome in 1054 A.D.
Uniates
   Sub-groups from some of the above groups that were re-united with the Roman Church

One further word about the non-uniate Eastern churches should be mentioned. While these churches do not recognize the Pope, their deacons, priests, and bishops are truly ordained. They truly witness marriages. They do celebrate Mass. They do confirm. They do anoint the sick. However, most leaders of the Reformation in sixteenth-century Europe did not recognize ordination as a sacrament of the Church. Since the sacraments of Penance, Eucharist, Confirmation, and Anointing of the Sick depend on ordination, most of the Protestant churches do not validly celebrate Mass, forgive sins, confirm, or anoint the sick. Thus, the non-uniate Eastern churches are much more closely tied to Rome than the Lutherans and other Protestant groups because the non-uniate churches have valid sacraments whereas, for the most part, the others do not.

The Church also governs itself through religious orders. Orders are groupings of men or women who undertake a common life and work. They usually live the counsels of the Lord (evangelical counsels), i.e., the life of poverty, chastity (virginity), and obedience to a superior. Some male religious orders have only ordained priests as members. Others have a mixture of ordained and non-ordained. Some have only non-ordained. These orders are integrated into the general structure of the Church because each has an ordinary, i.e., someone who is the superior of the order and serves the other members of the order in an executive capacity. These superiors are often elected by the membership of the order. Further, the religious orders are subject either to the Pope directly or to a local diocesan bishop. Most orders are pontifical, i.e., directly under the jurisdiction of the Pope. The way of life of each order must be approved either by the diocesan bishop, if the order is subject to the diocesan bishop, or by the Pope, if the order is pontifical. The Pope exercises his jurisdiction over the religious orders through one of the offices in the Vatican, the Congregation for Religious.

The Church also fulfills the second aspect of Christ's kingly office: using things for the sake of people. At almost every level of the Church's structure, there are endeavors to provide the necessities of life for all human beings. In this activity, the Church imitates Christ who exercised His kingly office in its second function by subordinating the things of creation to the needs of persons, e.g., by feeding the five thousand.[78] Internationally, there are numerous offices administered by the Church that attempt to provide food, clothing, and shelter for all people in need throughout the world. The charitable activities of each diocese are impossible to list. Further, almost every parish carries on a mission to the poor. In caring for those who are in need, the Church demonstrates that everything God has made (except persons) exist for people. The Church acts as Christ acted when it employs its material resources for the benefit of those in need or when it encourages those who possess material things in abundance to share with those who lack even the most basic necessities. Through the Church's exercise of the kingly office of Christ in this second respect, divine providence is revealed.

The kingly office in the Church is shared in the baptismal manner by all the members of the Church. It is shared in a hierarchical manner by all those who are ordained as deacons, i.e., bishops, priests, and deacons. The baptismal kingly office is expressed through a bodily self-discipline and through a care for those who are in need. The hierarchical kingly office is expressed through an exemplary virtuous life (thus encouraging others to lead similar lives) and by a leadership role in caring for those in need. Both the baptismal and hierarchical manners of sharing in Christ's kingly office are needed. The baptismal kingly office needs to be activated by the hierarchical kingly office. Of course, the hierarchical kingly office would have little purpose if there were not people sharing the baptismal kingly office who needed to be activated.

Of course, as the mystical Christ, the Church does not exercise one of the triple offices in isolation from the other two offices. For example, when the Church celebrates the sacraments, the Church is not only exercising Christ's priesthood, but it is also teaching the whole world about God and about mankind, i.e., it is exercising Christ's prophetic office. Further, in celebrating the sacraments according to certain norms and customs, the Church is also exercising Christ's kingship through its own self-governance. Finally, in using created things (e.g., water, bread and wine, oil) for the sake of persons in the sacraments, the Church reveals divine providence, i.e., it exercises Christ's kingly office in its second aspect. Thus, in every act, the Church exercises the three offices of Christ.

In continuing the mission of Christ, the Church is aided at every moment by Mary. Since Mary is the mother of Christ, she is the mother of the mystical Christ, the Church.[79] Just as Mary cooperated with Christ on earth, so from heaven she now cooperates with the Church. She never ceases to help the Church, and the Church never ceases to look to her for aid.

The Church, as the mystical person of Christ, loves everyone as Christ does. This mystical person exercises Christ's triple offices in order to reveal God. In revealing God, the Church, as Christ, teaches people who they are (prophetic office), shows them how they should act (priestly office), and reveals that they are called to love

God in and through a mutual bodily gift and to love each other by using things for the benefit of people (kingly office).

Still, many people claim that the Church seeks only to remain politically powerful. They would categorically deny that the Church has a genuine love for all people. This attitude should hardly surprise anyone. Since the Church is the mystical person of Christ, it suffers from the same attack of evil as God does. In the temptation of Adam and Eve, the devil presented God as a jealous, mean-spirited tyrant Who cared nothing about His creatures and Who would do anything to protect His own powers and privileges. No one would love such a being.[80] Some do not trust the Church as a loving, caring mystical person because they are heirs to the devil's lie. However, Satan is wrong. Adam and Eve were wrong. Christ loves us and wishes only the best for us. The Church, as Christ, loves us and wishes only the best for us.

FOR REFLECTION

A. List and discuss the differences between Christ and the Church as the mystical person of Christ.

B. Why do the baptismal *and* the hierarchical offices of Christ exist in the Church?

C. Do Catholics have a right to "faithful dissent" from the teaching of the Church?

D. How does the Church exercise Christ's priestly and kingly offices?

NOTES

1. See above, Chapter 4: "The Incarnation."
2. See William Shakespeare, *Macbeth,* Act V, Scene V.
3. See GS, no. 22.
4. See Eph. 5:23.

5. See Eph. 5:23.

6. See Karol Wojtyla (Pope John Paul II), *Augustinum Hipponensem, Apostolic Letter on St. Augustine, L'Osservatore Romano,* English Edition, vol. 19, no. 37 (September 15, 1986), p. 6. See also Karol Wojtyla (Pope John Paul II), "The Church, Mystery of Communion, Is a Sign of Unity Among All Peoples," *L'Osservatore Romano,* English Edition, vol. 19, no. 48 (December 1, 1986), p. 16. See also below, pp. 120–21, for a discussion of the meaning of "mystical."

7. See Eph. 5:23.

8. See 1 Cor. 13:3.

9. See 1 Cor. 6:13–14.

10. See Heribert Muehlen, *Una Mystica Persona: Die Kirche als das Mysterium der heilsgeschichtlichen Identität des Heiligen Geistes in Christus und den Christen: Eine Person in vielen Personen,* 3rd Edition (Paderborn: Ferdinand Schoeningh, 1968), p. 117. The original reads, *"Es ist offensichtlich, dass hier . . . nicht der blosse koerper gemeint ist . . . sondern das ganze 'Ich.'"*

11. See Wojtyla, "The Church, Mystery of Communion, Is a Sign of Unity Among All Peoples," p. 17.

12. See 1 Cor. 1:13.

13. See Acts 9:4–5.

14. See Muehlen, *Una Mystica Persona,* pp. 27–33.

15. See Wojtyla, *Augustinum Hipponensem, Apostolic Letter on St. Augustine,* p. 6.

16. See *Patrologiae Latinae,* edited J. P. Migne, vol. 76, col. 110.

17. See John C. Gruden, *The Mystical Christ: Introduction to the Study of the Supernatural Character of the Church* (St. Louis: B. Herder Book Co., 1936). Gruden notes that John Chrysostom wrote that all Christians are "one person in Christ" (p. 118). Further, he notes that St. Gregory of Nyssa wrote that the "whole body of Christ (i.e., the Church) will surrender to the life-giving strength of God. The surrendering of this body is called the submission of the Son Himself" (p. 116). In fact, Gruden's entire discussion of the mystical Christ in the writings of the fathers is still very worthwhile (pp. 103–33).

18. See Thomas Aquinas, *Summa Theologiae,* III, Q. 15, Art. 1, Ad. 1. See also Muehlen, *Una Mystica Persona,* p. 40.

19. See Aquinas, *Summa Theologiae,* III, Q. 48, Art. 2, Ad. 1. See also Muehlen, *Una Mystica Persona,* pp. 40–41.

20. See Pope Pius XII, *Mystici Corporis, The Mystical Body of Christ* (Washington: National Catholic Welfare Conference, 1943), no. 66.

21. See Muehlen, *Una Mystica Persona,* pp. 44–45.

22. The two constitutions treating the Church are LG and GS.

23. See SR, pp. 35–36.

24. See Gal. 3:27.

25. See below, Chapter 7: "The Sacraments," pp. 181–82. See also below, Chapter 8: "Grace," pp. 208–10.

26. See Gal. 3:27.

27. See above, Chapter 2: "God's Love: Creation," p. 40ff.

28. See *Covenant,* p. 104.

29. See LG, no. 4.

30. See Gal. 3:27.

31. See Muehlen, *Una Mystica Persona,* p. 77; and H. Wheeler Robinson, "The Hebrew Conception of Corporate Personality," *Beihefte zur Zeitschrift für die alttestamentliche Wissenschaft,* vol. 66 (1936), pp. 50–55.

32. See Chapter 2: "God's Love: Creation," pp. 42–45.

33. See Muehlen, *Una Mystica Persona,* pp. 81–84.

34. See Gal. 3:27–28. See also 1 Cor. 1:2, 1 Thess. 2:14, and 2 Thess. 1:1, where the members of the Church are "in Christ." For a discussion of the Church as the bride of Christ, see *Covenant,* pp. 101–2.

35. See Karol Wojtyla (Pope John Paul II), "Jesus Christ, Living Peace and Living Justice" (Homily of His Holiness at the Mass in Yankee Stadium on October 2, 1979), *The Pope in America* (St. Paul: The Wanderer Press, 1979), p. 25.

36. See GS, no. 22.

37. See GS, no. 41.

38. See above, Chapter 1 "Man/Woman and God," p. 5.

39. See above, Chapter 4: "The Incarnation," pp. 94–99.

40. For a discussion of Christ's exercise of His triple offices, see above, Chapter 4: "The Incarnation," pp. 94–104.

41. See above, pp. 122–23.

42. See Gal. 3:27.

43. *Presbyterorum Ordinis, Decree on the Ministry and Life of Priests* (December 7, 1965), § 2.

44. See above, p. 118.

45. See above, pp. 123–25.

46. Even though there are distinctions among the members, this does not contradict the claim that what is said of one can be said of the group, and vice versa. Membership in the corporate person unites individuals, but does not destroy their individuality. See above, pp. 122–23.

47. See LG, no. 10.

48. The activation of the baptismal offices by the hierarchical ones is an example of actual grace. See below, Chapter 8: "Grace," pp. 225–26.

49. See Gal. 3:27.

50. See LG, no. 15. See also SR, pp. 128–33.

51. See Gal. 3:27.

52. See LG, no. 15.

53. See *Christus Dominus, Decree on the Pastoral Office of Bishops in the Church* (October 28, 1965), § 11.

54. See below, pp. 131–34.

55. See above, Chapter 1: "Man/Woman and God," p. 5. See also above, Chapter 4: "The Incarnation," pp. 94–99.

56. See above, pp. 124–27.

57. See below, Chapter 6: "Revelation: Scripture and Tradition," pp. 149–50 and 171–72, for a discussion of this point.

58. See Gal. 1:8.

59. See DV, no. 4.

60. See above, Chapter 1: "Man/Woman and God," p. 5.

61. See Mt. 7:29. Cf. also Mk. 1:22 and Lk. 4:32.

62. See Charles E. Curran, *Faithful Dissent* (Kansas City: Sheed and Ward, 1986), for a fairly recent and accurate summary of the opinions and writings of the authors who would take this or a similar position.

63. See LG, no. 25. However, it should be noted that the episcopal conferences do not possess a teaching authority in themselves. As Cardinal Ratzinger has said, "No episcopal conference, as such, has a teaching mission; its documents have no weight of their own save that of the consent given to them by the individual bishops." See Josef Cardinal Ratzinger and Vittorio Messori, *The Ratzinger Report*, translated by Salvator Attanasio and Graham Harrison (San Francisco: Ignatius Press, 1985), p. 60.

64. See the article, John C. Ford and Germain Grisez, "Contraception and the Infallibility of the Ordinary Magisterium," *Theological Studies*, vol. 39, no. 2 (June 1978), pp. 258–312. In this article, the authors make a strong case that the teaching against contraception is proclaimed in the infallible mode. See also William Smith, "The Role of the Christian Family, Articles 28–35," pp. 79–80, in *Pope John Paul II and the Family*, edited Michael J. Wrenn (Chicago: Franciscan Herald Press, 1983), pp. 73–107. For a comment on this approach, see Richard M. Hogan and John M. LeVoir, "To Think with the Church: A Report on the International Congress of Moral Theology," IRNFP, vol. 10, no. 4 (Winter 1986), pp. 339–46.

65. Clearly, such an exercise of freedom destroys freedom because genuine freedom can be found only by seeking Truth, i.e., God, Who is found in the Church.

66. See below, Chapter 6: "Revelation: Scripture and Tradition," p. 166.

67. See Hogan and LeVoir, "To Think with the Church: A Report on the International Congress of Moral Theology," pp. 344–45.

68. See above, Chapter 4: "The Incarnation," pp. 104–6.

69. See above, Chapter 4: "The Incarnation," pp. 81, 98–101.

70. See below, Chapter 7: "The Sacraments."

71. See above, pp. 124–28.

72. See above, pp. 127–28.

73. See above, Chapter 4: "The Incarnation," pp. 100–2.

74. See above, pp. 126–30.

75. See *Code of Canon Law,* promulgated by Pope John Paul II on January 25, 1983, and translated by the Canon Law Society of America (Washington: Canon Law Society of America, 1983), § 368–572.

76. For example, Pope St. Clement I wrote a letter to the Corinthian church (c. 96).

77. For a discussion of the Arian, Nestorian, and Monophysite heresies, see above, Chapter 4: "The Incarnation," pp. 86–89.

78. See above, Chapter 4: "The Incarnation," pp. 102–4.

79. Pope Paul VI, *Marialis Cultus, Apostolic Exhortation on the Blessed Virgin Mary, L'Osservatore Romano,* English Edition, vol. 7, no. 14 (April 4, 1974), p. 1.

80. See above, Chapter 3: "Original Sin and the Providence of God," pp. 60–62.

6

Revelation: Scripture and Tradition[1]

In fulfillment of the Scriptures.

A. Introduction

Christ employed each one of His triple offices to reveal a different and important aspect of humanity. The Church carries on this work of Christ. Thus, a study of the Church's exercise of Christ's triple offices is essential if we are to know ourselves. In this chapter, the Church's prophetic office will be treated while in the next chapter, the Church's priestly office will be examined. (A brief examination of the Church's kingly office was undertaken in the previous chapter.[2] A detailed study of the kingly office of the Church is more properly done in books on canon law and social justice.)

Using the commonplace experiences of His own people in the parables, Christ revealed Truth (God)[3] in and through His prophetic office, i.e., He preached the Gospel. In other words, Christ taught us revelation (the content of His life) in a certain historical and cultural garb. As Christ, the Church never ceases to reflect on the Truth and to reveal it (content) in the Church's own words (garb). Tradition[4] is the Church's continuing and constant effort to reflect on the Gospel and to state it (content) anew for each age (garb): "Tradition transmits in its entirety the Word of God [content] which has been entrusted to the Apostles by Christ the Lord and the Holy Spirit. It [Tradition] transmits it [the Word of God] to the successors of the

Apostles so that, enlightened by the Spirit of Truth, they may faithfully preserve, expound, and spread it abroad by their preaching
[garb]."[5] Of course, since the content of Tradition is the Word of
God, the content never changes. However, the garb does. Each re-
statement of the Gospel becomes part of Tradition. The New Testament holds a particularly important place as the Church's first surviving, written statement of revelation (content) in a particular garb.[6]
In turn, both the New Testament and other statements contained in
Tradition have become the stimuli for ever new re-statements of the
Gospel of Jesus Christ. Of course, the Holy Spirit guided the Church
in the writing of the New Testament and continues to guide the
Church in its proclamation of revelation, i.e., in re-stating the Word
of God in new garb for each age. In addition, the same Holy Spirit
enables the Church to study revelation (development).[7]

Christ revealed Truth. He is *the* revelation of the Father. To reveal
is to make something known that was not previously known. For
example, if someone did not know that atoms existed, it would be a
revelation if someone were to teach him about the existence of atoms.
When Christ taught us the Truth (i.e., God), He revealed truths that
lie beyond the powers of reason. In other words, revelation includes
those things that God tells us about Himself that we could never
have known in any other way. For example, it would be impossible
for us to come to know the Trinity through our own powers. We
know about the three Persons in the one God because God Himself
chose to tell us about the Trinity. Of course, in telling us truths that
we could never come to know with our own reason, God also tells us
many other things, e.g., that He exists. If we did not suffer the effects
of original sin, i.e., if we did not suffer from a darkened intellect,[8] we
could come to know these truths easily through our own rational
powers. However, with the effects of original sin, it is very difficult to
come to know these truths. Thus, Christ taught us the truths that lie
beyond human reason and the other truths that we could have easily
known had we remained in the garden of Eden. Revelation includes
both sets of truths. Revelation is absolutely necessary if human beings are ever to come to know themselves. In revealing Himself, God

tells us about Himself. Yet, in telling us about Himself, He tells us about ourselves as His images.

Revelation can either be public or private. Public revelation includes those truths that God intends everyone to know for the sake of their salvation. The truths revealed in the inspired books, i.e., in the Old and New Testaments, and in other statements found in Tradition,[9] e.g., in the writings of the fathers of the Church, in the liturgical books, in the decrees of ecumenical councils, belong to public revelation. Private revelation includes the truths revealed by Mary, the angels, or even Christ Himself to individuals. For example, St. Bernadette of Lourdes experienced a private revelation from the blessed Virgin Mary through a vision. However, private revelation might also be much less dramatic, e.g., a new insight into a particular passage of Scripture. Private revelations are given to some so that they might build a firm relationship with the Lord and so that they might help others come close to God. Nevertheless, it is not necessary for anyone to believe a private revelation in order to be saved.

Authentic private revelation is always from God and not from other sources (e.g., the devil), and it can never contradict public revelation. The God-man Jesus Christ is the source of public revelation. Thus, if private revelation could contradict public revelation, then we would be presented with the impossible scenario of a god who could contradict himself. However, God cannot contradict Himself. Therefore, if private revelation is authentic, it must agree with public revelation. In fact, one of the tests of true and authentic private revelation is that it agrees with public revelation given by Christ. Thus, the Church, the mystical Christ, determines whether or not private revelation is authentic. Most visibly, the Church authenticates private revelation in cases of widely publicized events, e.g., the appearances of the blessed Virgin at Lourdes. The Church makes such judgments slowly and with meticulous care because it respects both public revelation and the possibility of God's revealing Himself privately.

Public revelation ended with the death of the last Apostle, i.e., with the death of St. John the Evangelist, c. 100. In other words, public revelation ended with the last person to have seen and to have heard the Lord. Why does God not continue to reveal Himself to us in a public way? The answer is simple enough. As the author of the letter to the Hebrews indicates, "In many and various ways God spoke of old to our fathers by the prophets; but in these last days He has spoken to us by a Son."[10] In other words, in the Old Testament, God revealed Himself primarily through the prophets, but in Christ God spoke to us about Himself. Most important, however, God showed Himself to us in and through Christ. As Christ responded to Philip, "He who has seen Me has seen the Father."[11] What more could God do? He told us about Himself, and He showed us Himself. Once we have both heard and seen, what more could be given to us? For example, if someone had never seen Michelangelo's frescoes in the Sistine Chapel, a physical description of what they depicted, of the colors used, etc., would help him know about them. However, after he has seen them, he has little or no use for detailed physical descriptions of the frescoes. (Of course, he might refer to critical commentaries. He would read these for further insights, but not in order to know the content of the frescoes.)

An interesting and curious problem sometimes arises regarding public revelation. St. Paul may have written a letter that has been lost. What if someday we find this lost letter? Would such a discovery not be an instance of public revelation in our own time? Of course, the answer is quite simple: "No!" This lost letter would still have been written before the death of St. John. The date of the discovery is not important. Rather, it is the date of authorship that is critical. However, if this letter ever did exist and if it ever were to be rediscovered, it would contain nothing not already found in public revelation. It is not possible that God would have allowed a truth revealed by Christ and necessary for our salvation to be lost for centuries.

It might seem that each one of us, acting independently of the Church, could discover the truth by examining public revelation. Thus, it would seem that we could know revelation without the Church. However, this is impossible. Christ is *the* revelation of God. Revelation does not exist without the revelation of the Person of the

Word. Thus, revelation is not to be found in any one "place." Rather, it can only be seen in Christ. Clearly, revelation is not just a matter of truths, but rather it is a matter of *the* Truth, i.e., God. Since the Church is Christ, the Church embodies revelation and is absolutely essential if we are to "find" revelation. Therefore, it would be impossible for anyone to examine the truths of God without the Church.[12]

It is important to note that without the Church neither the Scriptures nor Tradition (supposing, of course, that these could exist without the Church) could accurately transmit revelation. If the Church did not exist, the truths Christ revealed would no longer be known. The written texts of the Scriptures cannot guarantee the accurate transmission of the truths Christ revealed. To almost every verse in the Scriptures, there are hundreds of possible interpretations. Each age has contributed its own explanations for many passages. Which interpretations contain the truth that Christ wished to reveal? With so many interpretations given by various ages, even the written texts are no guarantee that the truth will be handed on intact from age to age. Even more obviously, Tradition without the Church cannot guarantee the transmission of God's Word. Imagine a story told in secret to one of thirty people who is asked to tell the same story privately to the second, and the second to the third, and so on. We all know the outcome. By the time the thirtieth person heard the story, it would be totally changed. Christ told us the truths about God, truths infinitely more important than any story. Without the Church, these truths, if passed down through the centuries from one person to another, would be totally changed. In effect, we would not have the revelation of Christ. The Church serves as the embodiment of Christ. Thus, it ensures that the revelation of Christ contained in Scripture and Tradition is taught to each age. We need the Church to know revelation.

Not only does the Church teach the truths of revelation for each age, it also studies them. The fruit of these studies is called development. As the Church examines the truths Christ revealed, it teaches them to the faithful, who come to a greater understanding and appreciation of them. The Church undertakes this study through its *magisterium*. Further, theologians, saints, and all the People of God, guided by the hierarchical prophetic office, i.e., the *magisterium,* also contribute their efforts towards the development of doctrine: "The People of God, guided by the sacred teaching authority . . . penetrates it [the faith] more deeply with right judgment and applies it more fully in daily life."[13] Thus, those who share the baptismal prophetic office should always study the faith, but they should also receive the teaching of those who share the hierarchical prophetic office. For example, if a theologian examines a revealed truth and discovers a new insight that contradicts official magisterial teaching, he should recognize that his insight is not a valid development.

The development of revealed truths explains how the Church can continue to discover and teach revealed truths not previously taught. The question is often asked: If public revelation ended with the death of the last Apostle, how is it possible for the Church to teach a "new" truth? It appears that the Church is contradicting itself. On the one hand, it claims revelation ended with the death of St. John the Evangelist; and, on the other, it claims to teach "new" revealed truths. This issue arose with the solemn teaching on the Immaculate Conception (defined in 1854), with the definition of papal infallibility (defined in 1870), and with Pope Pius XII's solemn pronouncement on the assumption of Mary (1950). However, these were not "new" truths when they were defined. They were always contained in the revelation of Christ, but they were not clearly seen. The Church's examination of revelation led to the discovery of these truths. Development might be compared to an artist's viewing Michelangelo's frescoes in the Sistine Chapel. Even though he has seen them (content), he can discover new insights through commentaries on the artist's work. Development is constantly occurring in the Church: it is proof of the Church's vibrant life. It should also be noted that development is a different phenomenon from the re-statement (garb) of known truths (content), i.e., Tradition.[14]

People often ask why Christ did not simply tell us in detail about everything He revealed. Why leave the examination and study of revelation to mere human intellects? We could have heard all the revealed truths explicitly from the lips of Christ Himself, and thus there would be little question regarding their validity. Christ chose

not to explain everything to us because He respected our dignity as
human beings. Christ desires that we make the truths of revelation
our own through study and examination. If He had handed everything to us, we might have received it, but we would never have
"owned" it. However, in studying revelation and in developing it, we
make it our own: we truly know it. Once we know it, we can come to
love it. Of course, if Christ's truths are to transform our lives, we
must love them. Christ wanted us to be interested in what He revealed, so He allowed us to participate in the process of unfolding
revealed truths. What an affirmation of human dignity! As images of
God, we are privileged in a certain sense to reveal God to ourselves!

Christ revealed God, on the foundation laid in the Old Testament.
As Christ Himself said, "Think not that I have come to abolish the
law and the prophets; I have come not to abolish them, but to fulfill
them."[15] The Church, in its constant re-statement and development
of the revelation of Christ, does not neglect the Old Testament. On
the contrary, the Old Testament is an important source for the understanding of what Christ revealed. Many references to the Old
Testament are found in the New Testament.[16] Further, the Old Testament continues to be vital today. Pope John Paul II presented a
detailed analysis of the Genesis story in an effort to understand more
fully Christ's attitude towards divorce and remarriage.[17] Clearly, the
Old Testament is critical to the revelation of Christ.

B. Scripture

As mentioned above,[18] revelation is embodied in the Church. The
Church constantly re-states the Gospel for each age. The first surviving, written statement of the Gospel by the Church is found in the
New Testament. However, since the revelation of Christ cannot be
understood without reference to the Old Testament, in studying the
New Testament, it is necessary to take the Old Testament into consideration. As the Second Vatican Council teaches, God "in His wisdom has so brought it about that the New [Testament] should be
hidden in the Old [Testament] and that the Old should be made
manifest in the New."[19]

Still, the Bible presents some difficulties. In some places, Scripture seems to contradict itself, e.g., the flood is said to have lasted forty days in one passage and one hundred and fifty days in another.[20] In other places, there seem to be impossible stories that could not have occurred, e.g., the book of Jonah. Of course, some of these difficulties are inherent in revelation because even with the gift of faith, we will never completely understand God's revelation. However, other difficulties can be resolved through a proper textual analysis. Thus, (1) it is important to study the various literary forms found among the books of the Bible; (2) it is useful to know how these books were transmitted to our own era, almost twenty centuries after Christ; and (3) since none of the books of the Bible was originally written in English, some consideration of the problems of translations would be helpful in understanding the Scriptures. (These three tools of textual analysis barely scratch the surface of the analytical methods scholars have used to enhance our understanding of the sacred books.) In addition, since the Scriptures are inspired by God, it is necessary to consider certain theological categories: inspiration, inerrancy, and the canon of Scripture. (The examination of the canon is a study of how and why certain books are included in the Scriptures and others are not.)

1. SCRIPTURE: TOOLS OF TEXTUAL ANALYSIS

A. STUDY OF LITERARY FORMS

Sacred Scripture is divided into two collections of books called Testaments. The Old Testament includes the inspired books written before the time of Christ. The New Testament includes the inspired books written after Christ. The Old Testament has forty-six books; the New Testament, twenty-seven.[21] Each human author (or final editor)[22] of a sacred book wrote (or edited) it as a unified whole. For example, St. Paul wrote each of his letters as a complete work.

When someone decides to write, he chooses a subject matter as well as a literary form appropriate for his subject matter. For example, a mother might decide to write her son about his father's promotion. In choosing the subject matter, she also chooses the literary form: a letter. In other words, the subject matter determines the form. Similarly, if an author decides to write a fictional mystery, he might choose to write either a short story or a novel.

Each of us recognizes some literary forms and their purposes. We recognize a business letter as a letter that conveys information. We do not read it as we would a legal brief. Similarly, we do not read the front page of the daily newspaper in the same way that we read the comics because the front page contains news and the comic strip is intended to entertain.

We easily switch back and forth among literary forms used commonly in our society because we are familiar with them and their purposes. However, in reading works from a different culture, we are unable to comprehend properly what the subject matter is if we do not recognize the literary forms and their purposes. Since the Bible was originally written in a completely different culture, an examination of the Bible's literary forms and their purposes is necessary for us to understand the subject matter found in the Scriptures.

In the New Testament, there are four Gospels: Matthew, Mark, Luke, and John. A Gospel is a literary form. This form is used for a factual account of the deeds and words of the Lord. Most of the other books of the New Testament are letters written by St. Paul (Romans, 1 and 2 Corinthians, Galatians, Ephesians, Philippians, Colossians, 1 and 2 Thessalonians, 1 and 2 Timothy, Titus, Philemon), St. James, St. Peter (1 and 2), St. John (1, 2, and 3), St. Jude, and one letter directed to the Hebrews. The Acts of the Apostles is a historical book. Of course, St. Luke wrote Acts in the historical form employed by the writers of his time. Thus, Acts is not written in the modern literary form that present-day historians use. Revelation, the last book of the New Testament, is apocalyptic, a kind of prophecy about the end of the world and the fulfillment of the kingdom of God. It is similar in form to the book of Daniel of the Old Testament.[23]

In the Old Testament, there are forty-six books with many literary forms: histories, law books, prophetic works, a prayer book, wisdom books, and even fictional works. The historical books include Genesis (although the first eleven chapters are a kind of prehistory), parts of Exodus, Joshua, Judges, the two books of Samuel, the two books of Kings, as well as 1 and 2 Chronicles, 1 and 2 Maccabees, Ezra, Nehemiah, Baruch, and Lamentations. The law books include parts of Exodus, Leviticus, Numbers, and Deuteronomy. The prophetic books include the four well-known prophets—Isaiah, Jeremiah, Ezekiel, and Daniel; and twelve minor prophets—Hosea, Joel, Amos, Obadiah, Micah, Nahum, Habakkuk, Zephaniah, Haggai, Zechariah, Malachi, and Jonah. The book of Psalms is a prayer book and is still used for that purpose today. The wisdom books include Job, Proverbs, Ecclesiastes, Canticle of Canticles, Wisdom, and Sirach. Tobit, Judith, Ruth, and Esther are stories that are at least in part fictional. For example, Esther may be a story constructed around a kernel of historical fact. Of course, these categorizations of the Old Testament books are somewhat flexible (e.g., the classification of Exodus among both the historical books and the law books). Further, the foregoing classifications do not exhaust what could be said about the literary form of each book. For example, Psalms is a prayer book, but it is a poetic prayer book. Lamentations is certainly a history, but it is a poetic work as well. Obviously, the literary forms used in the books of the Old Testament have different purposes. It should be clear that we would not read Psalms as we would Numbers or Isaiah. Just as we would not look for a factual, historical account in a novel, we should not read Ruth as a history book. In reading the sacred books, we need to keep the differing literary forms and their purposes in mind.

B. TRANSMISSION OF THE TEXTS

The material contained in the sacred books was transmitted in various ways. In many cases, an oral tradition preceded the written text. For some books, the oral tradition predated the written text by several centuries. For example, at least some of the material found in the first five books of the Old Testament (the Pentateuch) originated in the time of Moses. Although probably not recorded in writing until the time of David (c. 950 B.C.), this material was part of an important oral tradition.

Even after the oral tradition was written, later authors and editors sometimes added material and re-worked the text. For example, Isaiah seems to be the work of three different authors. Apparently, each author wrote in a different period from a different historical and cultural perspective. Of course, the last author or some other editor must have combined the work of each author into a coherent whole. Consequently, the book of Isaiah, as it exists in the Bible today, is probably the fruit of at least two authors and an author-editor, or three authors and an editor. When the work of the authors and editors was completed, the original text of the sacred books was finished. The transmission of the biblical books includes all the work involved in the formation of the original texts. Thus, it includes the oral tradition predating the written text and the work of all the sacred authors and editors.

After the original texts of the sacred books were finished, copyists played a part in their transmission. The original handwritten texts of the books of the Bible are lost. Instead, we have copies of copies. Copyists sometimes make mistakes. For example, a copyist might be copying a paragraph in which the same word is used twice. As he copies, his eye might skip from the first use of the word to the second use. Later, noticing his mistake, he might record the correction in the margin of the manuscript. On the other hand, a copyist might not notice his mistake. In this case, the text would not read correctly. Further, a copyist might make comments and other notes in the margins. In addition, copyists sometimes altered a particularly difficult original passage so that it would read more easily.

Clearly, two copyists (copyist A and copyist B) working independently from an original would make different mistakes, add different corrections, write different comments, and alter different texts. Further, a later copyist, working from copyist A's work, would make his own mistakes, add his own corrections and comments, and alter different texts. In addition, he would find it hard to distinguish between the corrections and the comments in the margins of copyist A's work. Thus, as he copies, he might add a comment of copyist A

to the text, thinking it was a correction. Further, if copyist A had
made a mistake that he did not correct, the later copyist, seeing a
difficulty in the text, might alter this passage so that it would read
better. Still, the later copy would reflect copyist A's work, i.e., there
would be a preponderance of similarities. Another later copyist,
working from copyist B's work, would follow the same procedure.
There would be differences between the work of the later copyist and
copyist B's work, but there would be more similarities than differences. However, there would probably be significant differences between the copies of A and the copies of B. Obviously, as more and
more copies were made and manuscripts were lost, it became more
and more difficult to know exactly what was in the original.

Clearly, after several generations of copies, there exist a great
many manuscripts. The most ancient manuscripts presumably have
the texts most closely resembling the originals because their texts
have been transmitted through fewer generations of copies. Thus,
scholars who attempt to reconstruct the original texts first identify
the oldest manuscripts, i.e., the ones used to make other existing
copies. Second, scholars compare the differing readings of the most
ancient manuscripts with one another. Thus, scholars reconstruct
the most likely original reading of a passage from among the variant
readings in the most ancient manuscripts. They are guided in their
work by a number of general rules. For example, since copyists
tended to alter difficult readings, scholars will often choose the most
difficult reading as the most accurate, i.e., the one closest to the
original.

Since the books of the Old Testament were most often written in
Hebrew, in reconstructing the original texts of these books, scholars
are attempting to establish the ancient Hebrew text. A few books of
the Old Testament were either written in Greek or exist only in
Greek. All the books of the New Testament were written in Greek.
Of course, scholars attempt to establish the authentic Greek text for
these books. In a few cases, translations of the Hebrew or of the
Greek texts can help. When a translation depends on a manuscript
now lost, the translation can help establish the text of the lost manuscript. However, scholars generally prefer to work from manuscripts

of the original language rather than from manuscripts of translations.

For the most part, the oldest complete existing Hebrew texts of the Old Testament books are found in the Masoretic manuscripts. They were created by a group of Jewish scholars called Masoretes working during the ninth and tenth centuries of the Christian era in Palestine. Still, these texts are almost nine hundred years removed from even the latest Old Testament Hebrew original texts. In addition, in the late 1940's and 1950's, there were Hebrew manuscripts of the Old Testament discovered in caves at Qumran. Qumran, near the Dead Sea, was occupied by a community of Jews from c. 135 B.C. to c. 68 A.D. This community may have been a religious establishment something like a Christian monastery. Of course, this community had a collection of the sacred texts. The scrolls of the sacred books found at Qumran, called the Dead Sea scrolls, are generally incomplete texts. However, they do provide a far more ancient witness for certain passages of the Old Testament than the much later Masoretic texts do.

The oldest existing complete copies of those sacred books that were originally written in Greek or that exist today only in Greek— Tobit, Judith, Sirach, Baruch, Wisdom, 1 and 2 Maccabees, and the entire New Testament—date from the fourth century. Since these books were written between 200 B.C. and 100 A.D., the fourth-century manuscripts are relatively close to the time of the originals, i.e., only about five centuries removed from the oldest originals.

The process of transmission accounts for many of the variant readings found in different editions of the Bible. Some editions of the Bible indicate an alternate reading to a particular passage in a footnote. Still, almost no point of doctrine is called into question by possible variant readings of a particular passage. Obviously, God, Who inspired the sacred authors,[24] also guided the transmission of the texts.

C. TRANSLATIONS

Translations of the original texts of the sacred books are called versions. The most important and ancient translation of the Hebrew Old Testament was the Greek Septuagint (second century before Christ). The Septuagint included seven sacred books not included in the Hebrew Old Testament: Tobit, Judith, Sirach, Baruch, Wisdom, and 1 and 2 Maccabees. Except for Sirach, these books exist only in Greek. Except for Wisdom and 2 Maccabees, they were probably written in Hebrew or Aramaic. In addition, the Greek Septuagint includes some additions to the original Hebrew texts of Esther and Daniel. The Septuagint, coupled with the New Testament books originally written in Greek, was the Bible of the early Christian Church.

As the message of the Gospel was accepted by more and more people, including some from the Western Latin-speaking half of the Roman Empire, there was a need for a Latin translation of the Scriptures. The earliest translations of the Old Testament into Latin were made from the Greek Septuagint. Thus, the first Latin versions of the Hebrew Old Testament books were Latin translations of the Greek translations of the original Hebrew. However, it is difficult to judge these old Latin versions because there is no complete text still in existence. There were also early Latin versions of the seven Old Testament books found in the Septuagint and not in the Hebrew Old Testament. These early Latin versions were, like the New Testament, translated from Greek.

St. Jerome (c. 340–419), at the bidding of Pope Damasus (366–384), began a new Latin translation of the Old Testament. Unlike the earlier Latin versions, Jerome's translations of the Hebrew Old Testament were made from the original Hebrew. St. Jerome did not regard the books included in the Septuagint but not in the Hebrew Old Testament (i.e., Tobit, Judith, Sirach, Baruch, Wisdom, 1 and 2 Maccabees) as inspired works.[25] Thus, he did not translate them. However, working from the Greek, St. Jerome did translate the additions to the books of Daniel and Esther found in the Septuagint. For the New Testament, Jerome re-worked the earlier Latin versions of the Gospels. The Church added the early Latin translations of the seven Old Testament Septuagint books (Tobit, Judith, Sirach, Baruch, Wisdom, 1 and 2 Maccabees) to Jerome's translations. In addition, new translations of the New Testament (except the Gospels, which Jerome had already done) were made. Together, all these Latin translations were called the Vulgate version of the Bible. Nevertheless, the Vulgate, the Latin Bible of the Church, is substantially the work of St. Jerome.

The English translations of the Bible are many and varied. Most often, teams of translators work from modern scholarly reconstructions of the original texts. Modern translators do not usually work from previous translations, e.g., the Vulgate. Most often, all the sacred books—including Tobit, Judith, Sirach, Baruch, Wisdom, and 1 and 2 Maccabees—and the additions to Daniel and Esther are printed in all the English translations. Since the non-Catholics do not regard these seven books and the additions to Daniel and Esther as inspired, the publication of these in both Catholic and non-Catholic translations represents genuine ecumenical progress.

2. SCRIPTURE: THEOLOGICAL CATEGORIES

A. INSPIRATION

The texts of Sacred Scripture are "inspired by God."[26] Thus, they were "written under the inspiration of the Holy Spirit . . . [and] have God as their author. . . . God chose certain men who, all the while He employed them in this task, made full use of their powers and faculties so that, though He acted in them and by them, it was as true authors they consigned to writing whatever He wanted written, and no more."[27] Clearly, God is the author of the Scriptures, but the human authors also fully participated in the writing of the texts.

Between God and the human authors of the sacred texts, there existed a profound *communion of persons* so that the latter's wills were conformed to the divine will. As they wrote what God wished them to write, they did not suspend or violate their own minds and wills. Rather, through their own thoughts and choices, they wrote down what God wished them to write. Their minds and wills were in communion with God's mind and will. Just as Christ did not suspend or violate His own human faculties when He did the Father's will, so the human authors of the sacred texts did not suspend or violate their human powers when they wrote their books.

The human authors of Sacred Scripture received a specific and extraordinary gift from God: "No prophecy ever came by the impulse of man, but men moved by the Holy Spirit spoke from God."[28] This movement of the Holy Spirit, i.e., the grace of inspiration, extended to the mind and the will of the author as well as to the other faculties necessary to the composition of the sacred text (e.g., memory). Most often, the grace of inspiration was probably not given through a miraculous event or a miraculous interior insight. If God had done this, the sacred authors surely would have been aware of it. However, generally, they do not seem to be aware of the grace of inspiration. Thus, the grace of inspiration was given to the authors in the midst of their own efforts. For example, ideas probably occurred to them as they did their research. Sometimes inspiration helped the authors plan the work necessary for their projected text. Of course, events, places, things, and people also served God as a means of inspiring the sacred authors.

Further, since writing a book engages an author's entire psychological outlook, God began to prepare the sacred authors for their tasks even in the womb. As God revealed to Jeremiah, "Before I formed you in the womb I knew you, and before you were born I consecrated you; I appointed you a prophet to the nations."[29] Thus, the graces flowed long before the sacred texts were actually written. Of course, this grace did not violate the freedom of the individual authors. Standing, as it were, outside of time, God knew for all eternity that the sacred authors were inclined to respond to His invitation to write the sacred texts. Therefore, He gave them the necessary means to fulfill what they were inclined to do. As the grace of the Immaculate Conception did not violate Mary's freedom, so the graces given to the sacred authors, beginning even before they were born, did not violate the freedom of the sacred authors.[30]

"All Scripture is inspired by God."[31] Thus, every word of Scripture, i.e., of the books accepted as part of the canon,[32] is inspired. It is not possible to claim that only certain passages or certain parts of a particular sacred book are inspired. Every word has God as its author and is therefore inspired by Him. As we have seen,[33] many books of the Bible have a complex origin. Sometimes there was a long oral tradition that was later written and even later re-shaped by an editor. In other cases, there were multiple authors. The entire process was guided by God. Every change and every nuance that contributed to the final form of each book (in the original language) were inspired.

Inspiration extends, however, only to the original texts of the Scriptures: translations are not inspired. Thus, when we read the Bible in English, we are not reading the inspired text, but rather a translation of the inspired text! The accuracy of the translation of Scripture does not depend on God, but on the skill of the translator. The Septuagint may be an exception: some believe that the Septuagint translation was inspired because in certain books and in certain passages, the translation was more than a translation (e.g., the additions to Daniel and Esther). In these passages, the Septuagint went beyond the Hebrew text and developed it. Without a doubt, the books present in the Septuagint, which are not present in the Hebrew Old Testament manuscripts (i.e., Tobit, Judith, Sirach, Baruch, Wisdom, 1 and 2 Maccabees), are inspired.

B. IMPLICATIONS OF INSPIRATION

Through inspiration, God is the author of the sacred texts. Since there is one author, the Bible forms a single, complete whole. While at first it may appear to be a random collection of different books by different authors, in reality, it is the unified work of one author: God. Thus, all the verses of a particular book of Scripture should be seen not only in the context of that particular book, but also in relationship to all the other books of Scripture. Further, all Scripture must be seen in light of the living Church because the Church is Christ[34] and is *the* interpreter of Scripture.[35] Clearly, it is improper to quote Scripture without reference to the entire Bible and outside the context of the Church. Fundamentalist Christians will often refer to a particular passage as a definitive challenge to Catholic teaching or practice. Sometimes they even demand from Catholics a biblical verse that upholds the Catholic belief or practice in question. However, a Catholic cannot even enter into such a discussion without compromising his beliefs in the completeness and unity of Sacred Scripture as well as his faith that the Church is *the* interpreter of Scripture. If a Catholic does try to quote a Scripture passage, he or she is following the flawed method of the challenger by quoting Scripture out of context and without reference to the Church. These are precisely the points that cannot be granted.[36]

However, it is not only fundamentalist groups that can lead us to ignore the unity of the Scriptures and to deny the Church's legitimate role as interpreter of the Scriptures: literary criticism can give an extremely fragmented view of the Bible and can convey the idea that literary critics are the only ones who can truly understand the sacred texts. For example, in an attempt to identify influences on the biblical authors, scholars have postulated two or more sources for the same verse of Scripture! Clearly, this kind of investigation results in extreme fragmentation. Further, having identified potential sources, scholars have tried to reconstruct a hypothetical Bible based on these sources. Thus, we no longer have *the* Bible, but we do have *a* bible of biblical sources as re-created by scholars: "The real Bible disappears for the sake and benefit of a reconstructed Bible. . . . We are being locked up in the glass house of an intellectual world which turns on its own axis, but which may not exist any more."[37] Scholars replace the Church as the legitimate interpreters of the Scriptures. In this false view, literary criticism becomes essential for an understanding of the Scriptures. However, it is inconceivable that the Scriptures can only be understood by an elite group of scholars who have spent years studying them. On the contrary, God, the author of Scripture, intended the Bible for all men and women. As a complete, unified whole that reveals its author (God Himself), the Bible can be understood by anyone who reads it with faith and under the guidance of the Church. Thus, while the tools of literary criticism are a great boon to the Church, they are not absolutely essential.

C. INERRANCY

Since God is the author of the Scriptures and God is Truth,[38] it would seem that there should be no errors in the Bible. However, there are some errors in the sacred texts. The errors fall into four categories: (1) biblical self-contradictions (e.g., the flood is said to have lasted forty days in one passage and one hundred and fifty days in another);[39] (2) errors in science (e.g., a firmament separating the waters of heaven from the waters of the earth);[40] (3) historical errors (e.g., there is no one called Darius the Mede known to history);[41] and (4) moral errors (e.g., the total destruction of a people is said to be the will of God).[42]

Of course, since inspiration pertains only to the original language of the sacred texts, one cannot question the truthfulness of a passage based on a translation. Further, all the possible variant readings must be checked to ascertain whether or not there is a possible reading that does not contain the error. In addition, it is important to study the particular literary form used and the intent of the human author before questioning the truthfulness of a passage. For example, we would not suggest that a fictional work, e.g., the book of Ruth, is in error because it records events that did not happen. Ruth uses a fictional form to reveal a truth about God and man.[43] The application of these interpretive tools reconciles some of the apparent errors. However, others still remain.

The problem is lessened when we realize that inerrancy, as a fruit of inspiration, pertains to the entire Bible as a whole. For example, as noted above,[44] certain passages seem to teach that taking innocent human life is not wrong, e.g., the killing of non-combatants in a captured city. Nevertheless, it is clear that the Bible as a whole teaches that killing innocent human beings is gravely wrong. Thus, the moral errors disappear.

Still, there remains a nagging problem. Inerrancy does not simply mean that the Bible is free from moral error. It also indicates that the Scriptures are free from other errors as well. Yet there seem to be non-moral (factual) errors in certain individual texts. The argument used for the moral errors does not solve the difficulty because without individual texts that are free from non-moral errors, the Bible as a whole cannot be free from these errors. The fathers of the Second Vatican Council developed a partial solution to the problem when they wrote that "the books of Scripture, firmly, faithfully, and without error, teach that truth which God, for the sake of our salvation, wished to see confided to the Sacred Scriptures."[45] In other words, the truths necessary to our salvation were protected from all possible error. For example, it is not necessary for our salvation to know that it was probably Cyrus and not Darius the Mede who received the neo-Babylonian power when he was sixty-two.[46] Similar comments could be made about the scientific errors and the self-contradictory errors.

Even when inerrancy is applied primarily to the whole of Scripture and to those things pertaining to our salvation, problems remain. Still, "if, however, we cannot discover explanations of all those things in Scripture which are made the subject of investigation, . . . we should leave things of that nature to God Who created us, being most properly assured that the Scriptures are indeed perfect since they have been spoken by the Word of God and His Spirit."[47]

D. CANON OF SCRIPTURE

The books the Church includes in the Bible are called the canonical books. Together, the forty-six books of the Old Testament and the twenty-seven of the New Testament comprise the canon of Scripture.[48] These are the books the Church considers to be inspired, i.e., that have God as their author and that contain revelation. The canonical books are distinguished from the non-canonical books, i.e., those that are not inspired. Obviously, in the broadest sense, everything written and not included in Scripture is a non-canonical book. However, non-canonical usually designates books that date (or appear to date) from the biblical period, but are not accepted by the

Church as inspired works. Often, the non-canonical books are called the Apocrypha.

However, there are some complications in the canon of the Old Testament. As we have seen,[49] there are seven books that were not included in the canon of the Hebrew Old Testament, but were included in the Septuagint (Greek Old Testament). These seven are Tobit, Judith, Sirach, Baruch, Wisdom, and 1 and 2 Maccabees. These seven books, together with the additions to the books of Daniel and Esther that were also included in the Septuagint, are called the deutero-canonical books. It was the canon of the Septuagint that the Christian Church adopted as its own. Thus, the Vulgate Old Testament included the deutero-canonical books.[50]

At the time of the Reformation, the reformers expressed doubts about the deutero-canonicals. Some regarded them as less important than the other books of the Old Testament canon. Others rejected them. Some Protestant Bibles included these books but printed them in a different place, e.g., between the Old and New Testaments or in an Appendix at the end. Other reform Bibles did not include them at all. The Council of Trent (1545–63) definitively settled the canon of the Old Testament by solemnly declaring that the deutero-canonicals are inspired.

In addition to the deutero-canonicals, there are works of both the Old and New Testament periods that neither Catholics nor Protestants accept as inspired. Both call these books apocryphal. However, Protestants usually include the deutero-canonical books among the Apocrypha. (For clarity, "deutero-canonical" will be used in the Catholic sense; "apocryphal" will designate those books that neither the Protestants nor the Catholics accept as inspired.) Apocryphal books of the Old Testament period include Enoch, 3 and 4 Maccabees, the Prayer of Manasseh, 1 and 2 Esdras (sometimes called 3 and 4 Esdras because the canonical books of Ezra and Nehemiah are sometimes called 1 and 2 Esdras respectively), the Apocalypse of Moses, the Testaments of the Twelve Patriarchs, the Letter of Aristeas, the Psalms of Solomon, the Sibylline oracles, and the Assumption of Moses. There are also some Old Testament apocryphal writings discovered at Qumran.[51] The New Testament also has some apocryphal writings, including several Gospels, e.g., the Gospels of Peter, Paul, and Thomas. Further, there are several apocryphal letters purported to have been written by St. Paul, e.g., those to Seneca and to the Laodiceans.

The foregoing discussion of the deutero-canonical and apocryphal books leaves the fundamental question of the canon unanswered. How is the canonicity or non-canonicity of a particular book decided? As mentioned above,[52] the Church decided which books belong in the canon of Scripture. How was this decision made? From one point of view, it could be said that it was through a solemn decree of the Council of Trent. However, the canon had been substantially recognized long before Trent, i.e., long before the reformers challenged the inclusion of the deutero-canonicals in the Bible.

Fundamentally, the Church determined the canon of Scripture by usage. If a book, either from the Old or New Testament, was used in the liturgy and cited by the Fathers, it came to be accepted. If it was not consistently and universally used, it did not reflect the faith of the Church and was not included. For the New Testament, apostolic origin was also important because revelation ended with the death of the last Apostle (St. John), c. 100 A.D.[53] Thus, books not written by an Apostle or someone closely associated with an Apostle (e.g., the Gospel of Mark, written under the influence of St. Peter) were not included in the canon of Scripture. These works did not contain revelation and therefore were not inspired books. (It is obvious that the second criterion for determining the canon, apostolic origin, is included in the first criterion, usage. Apostolic origin would have ensured that a work would have been preserved and used.)

The Church determined the canon of the Old Testament at the same time that it recognized its faith as stated in the inspired books of the New Testament. The inspired books of the Old Testament were a preparation for Christ. Thus, even though they were completed earlier than the books of the New Testament, they could not be recognized without Christ, i.e., without the definitive revelation given by the Lord. The canon of both the Old and New Testaments was not closed, i.e., it was not substantially determined, until about the end of the fourth century. Although all the inspired books were written by c. 100 A.D., it still took some time until the Church clearly recognized which books were inspired and which were not.

C. Tradition

The Church accepted the inspired books of the Old and New Testaments because the Church saw in these books the reflection of its own faith. In other words, the Church, preserving the revelation of Christ through Tradition, recognized the Word of God (revelation) in the inspired books.[54] As mentioned above,[55] Tradition is the Church's continuing and constant effort to reflect on the Gospel (content) and to state it anew for each age (garb). The New Testament is the first surviving written statement of the Gospel by the Church. Further, in the Old Testament, the Church recognized the preparation for the revelation of Christ. Once accepted, the inspired books became part of Tradition, as did each new statement of the Church's faith. In turn, Scripture and the other re-statements of the Gospel are the stimuli for ever new re-statements of the Gospel: "Sacred Tradition and Sacred Scripture, then, are bound closely together, and communicate one with the other. For both of them, flowing out from the same divine well-spring, come together in some fashion to form one thing, and move towards the same goal. Sacred Scripture is the speech of God as it is put down in writing under the breath of the Holy Spirit. And Tradition transmits in its entirety the Word of God which has been entrusted to the Apostles by Christ the Lord and the Holy Spirit."[56] (The Catholic belief that Tradition transmits the Word of God in its entirety differs from the classic Protestant view that only Scripture contains the revelation of Christ.)

Since revelation ended with the death of St. John (c. 100 A.D.) and Tradition transmits this revelation, it would appear that Tradition is complete. Nevertheless, Tradition is a vital and living reality that is constantly growing through re-statements of the Gospel. This seeming dilemma can be resolved through the distinction between content and garb. The content of Tradition (the Word of God) is fixed, but its garb (the way the Word of God is expressed) changes from age to age.[57]

The Second Vatican Council taught that the Apostles "handed on, by the spoken word of their preaching, by the example they gave, by the institutions they established, what they themselves had received. . . . The Apostles left bishops as their successors . . . [and] gave them 'their own position of teaching authority.' . . . Thus, the apostolic preaching [Tradition] which is expressed in a special way in the inspired books, was to be preserved in a continuous line of succession until the end of time."[58] Clearly, the apostolic preaching is still handed on from one generation to the next through the hierarchical prophetic office of the Church. The baptismal prophetic office is not inactive in the transmission of the Word of God. Through the baptismal prophetic office the baptized have a "sense of responsibility towards the gift of truth contained in revelation."[59]

In addition to Scripture, expressions of the Gospel, i.e., Tradition, are to be found in professions of faith promulgated by the *magisterium*, e.g., the Nicene creed (325 A.D.); in statements of ecumenical councils, e.g., in documents from the council of Ephesus (431 A.D.); in papal documents and addresses, e.g., the letter of Pope Clement I to the Corinthians (96 A.D.); in the writings of the ancient Fathers, e.g., the homilies of St. Augustine (354–430 A.D.); in statements of provincial, national, and diocesan councils, e.g., the councils of Toledo (c. 400–700); in episcopal documents and addresses, e.g., the sermons and writings of St. Charles Borromeo (1538–84 A.D.); in the liturgies of the Church as recorded in the ritual books of the Church, e.g., the Roman sacramentary of Pope Paul VI (the book used by priests in celebrating Mass today) or the Gelasian sacramentary (a book used for Mass by eighth-century priests); in the researches and studies of theologians faithful to the Church, e.g., St. Thomas Aquinas (1225–74 A.D.); and in the writings of the saints, e.g., St. Teresa of Ávila (1515–82 A.D.). However, there are many other sources for Tradition. In fact, it would be impossible to give an exhaustive list because the transmission of Tradition involves the entire life of the Church.[60] Further, the sources of Tradition listed above are not mutually exclusive. For example, an episcopal document might be the work of a theologian who is also a saint. Finally, the sources listed above are not equally important. Clearly, a profession of faith is more important than a theological treatise.

The non-scriptural statements of Tradition are more difficult to study and to examine than Scripture because they cannot be found in one place. In fact, the study of the non-scriptural statements of Tradition is a historical study because the first task is to discover the statements of the Gospel by those who "have gone before us marked with the sign of faith."[61] The historian also analyzes the statements of Tradition using the same interpretive tools he would apply to any other source from the same period and culture. As with the textual criticism of the Scripture scholar, the historian's interpretation of the statements of Tradition is never authoritative. Rather, the work of the historian should be put at the service of the Church, which, as the mystical Christ, is the definitive interpreter of the statements of Tradition. As Cardinal Ratzinger has written, "The question is . . . that of establishing the connections between the living fabric of Tradition, on the one hand, and the rational methods of re-establishing the past on the other hand."[62] The *magisterium* and history need to work together in discovering the meanings of Tradition.

Through the prophetic office of Christ, the Church knows and faithfully transmits divine revelation. The *magisterium,* i.e., the hierarchical prophetic office shared by the bishops and in a special way by the Pope, has the responsibility of teaching revelation to the baptized, who receive it with faith: "Tradition, Sacred Scripture, the *magisterium* of the Church, and the supernatural sense of the faith of the entire People of God form that vivifying process in which divine revelation is transmitted to the succeeding generations."[63] However, just as in Christ none of the triple offices of prophet, priest, and king function independently of the others, so in the Church, all three offices function together. Thus, we cannot understand the Church's prophetic office without a consideration of the Church's priestly office.[64]

FOR REFLECTION

A. What is revelation and where is it found?

B. Is the English-language Bible one book or is it composed of many inspired books?

C. What is Tradition and where can it be found?

D. Why is it that the Church continues to teach "new" truths of the faith even though public revelation no longer occurs?

NOTES

1. We have relied heavily on *The Jerome Biblical Commentary,* edited Raymond E. Brown et al. (Englewood Cliffs, N.J.: Prentice-Hall, 1968).

2. See above, Chapter 5: "The Church as the Person of Christ," pp. 136–42.

3. See above, Chapter 1: "Man/Woman and God," p. 5.

4. See below, pp. 171–73.

5. See DVe, no. 9. See also CS, no. 13.

6. Of course, there were earlier statements of the Gospel in preaching and perhaps even in writing. However, the New Testament represents the first written statement still in existence.

7. See below, pp. 153–55.

8. See above, Chapter 3: "Original Sin and the Providence of God," p. 55.

9. See below, pp. 172–73.

10. See Heb. 1:1–2.

11. See Jn. 14:9.

12. For a discussion of the relationship between Scripture and Tradition, see above, pp. 149–50.

13. See LG, no. 12. See also CS, no. 13.

14. See above, pp. 149–50.

15. See Mt. 5:17.

16. See, among many others, Mt. 1:1–17, 2:6, 18, 3:3, 4:15–16, 5:35, 38, 12:17–21, 13:14–15, 15:7–9, 21:4–5, 42, 22:43–44, 27:9–10; Mk. 7:6–7, 9:11–

13, 10:2–9, 12:28–37, 15:34; Lk. 4:17–27, 7:27, 20:17; Jn. 12:38–41, 19:24; and Heb. 1:5–13, 2:6–8, 12–13, 3:7–11, 5:5–6, 8:8–12, 10:5–9, 12:5–6.

17. See Karol Wojtyla (Pope John Paul II), *Theology of the Body* series, nos. 1–127, *Original Unity of Man and Woman, Blessed Are the Pure of Heart, The Theology of Marriage and Celibacy,* and *Reflections on* Humanae Vitae (Boston: St. Paul Editions, 1981, 1983, 1986, 1984).

18. See above, pp. 152–53.

19. See DVe, no. 16.

20. See Gen. 7:17, 24.

21. See CS, nos. 15, 16. See also below, pp. 157–58.

22. See below, p. 159.

23. See the next paragraph.

24. See below, pp. 163–65.

25. See below, pp. 168–70.

26. See 2 Tim. 3:16.

27. See DVe, no. 11.

28. See 2 Pet. 1:21.

29. See Jer. 1:5.

30. See above, Chapter 4: "The Incarnation," pp. 104–6.

31. See 2 Tim. 3:16.

32. See below, pp. 168–70.

33. See above, pp. 158–59.

34. See above, Chapter 5: "The Church as the Person of Christ."

35. See above, pp. 152–53, 156.

36. Of course, a Catholic entering such a discussion would also grant the point that only Sacred Scripture, and not Tradition, contains revelation. See above, Chapter 5: "The Church as the Person of Christ," p. 133.

37. See Josef Ratzinger, "Transmission of the Faith and the Sources of the Faith," translated by Michael J. Wrenn, *The Wanderer* (Supplement), vol. 117, no. 15 (April 12, 1984), p. 2.

38. See above, Chapter 1: "Man/Woman and God," p. 5.

39. See Gen. 7:17, 24.

40. See Gen. 1:6–8.

41. See Dan. 5:31.

42. See Josh. 11:14–15.

43. See above, pp. 157–58.

44. See above, p. 167.

45. See DVe, no. 11.

46. See Dan. 5:31.

47. See Irenaeus, *Adversos Haereses, Against Heresies*, bk. 2, chap. 28, no. 2, p. 399, in *The Ante-Nicene Fathers*, vol. 1, edited Alexander Roberts and James Donaldson (Grand Rapids, Mich.: William B. Eerdmans, 1979).

48. See above, pp. 157–58.

49. See above, pp. 162–63.

50. See above, p. 163.

51. See above, p. 161.

52. See above, p. 168.

53. See above, p. 151.

54. See DVe, no. 8.

55. See above, pp. 149–50.

56. See DVe, no. 9.

57. See above, pp. 149–50.

58. See DVe, nos. 7, 8.

59. See SR, p. 245. See also below, Chapter 8: "Grace," pp. 231–32.

60. See DVe, no. 7. See also above, pp. 149–50, 153, 171.

61. See "Eucharistic Prayer 1," *The Roman Missal: The Sacramentary*, promulgated by Pope Paul VI on April 3, 1969, and translated by the International Commission on English in the Liturgy (New York: Catholic Book Publishing, 1974), p. 546.

62. See Ratzinger, "Transmission of the Faith and the Sources of the Faith," p. 2.

63. See CS, no. 13.

64. A brief consideration of the Church's kingly office has been undertaken in the Church chapter. See above, Chapter 5: "The Church as the Person of Christ," pp. 136–42. A detailed study of the Church's kingly office is more appropriately done in books on canon law and social justice.

—— 7 ——
The Sacraments

We acknowledge one Baptism for the forgiveness of sins.

A. Introduction

The miracle of the incarnation occurred nearly two thousand years ago. Born of the Virgin Mary, God became truly human: "And the Word became flesh and dwelt among us."[1] What a phenomenon! God took on our humanity, body and soul. Christ communicated with the people of His age through His body. He spoke the truth with His mouth, He looked lovingly on people with His eyes, and He touched people with His hands. In and through His body, Christ loved us mercifully. Most clearly, the God-man loved us mercifully on the cross. Every act of Christ, but especially His sacrifice on the cross, also expressed His merciful love for the Father and the Holy Spirit. Thus, in His flesh and blood, Christ revealed merciful love.[2] Obviously, in and through His body, Christ also revealed God to us.

But how does Christ speak to us, look at us, and touch us today? How does Christ manifest to us, in a bodily way, our proper activity, i.e., merciful love? As was previously mentioned,[3] the Church is the mystical person of Christ. Just as Christ revealed love to us through His human priestly office,[4] so does the Church, the mystical Christ, show us merciful love through the exercise of its priestly office: "The liturgy [the public celebration of the sacraments which are given to the Church by Christ][5] . . . is rightly seen as an exercise of the priestly office of Jesus Christ."[6]

Not only did Christ give the Church the sacraments, He is present in the sacraments. Pope John Paul calls the sacraments personal encounters with Christ.[7] In other words, the sacraments are the "place" where we meet Christ person to Person. It has been said that it is "Christ's hands stretching through time and space, that continue to touch us by the sacraments."[8] Moreover, quoting St. Augustine, the Second Vatican Council reminds us of Christ's presence in the sacraments: "By His [Christ's] power He is present in the sacraments so that when anybody baptizes it is really Christ Himself Who baptizes."[9] Thus, when we participate in the celebration of the sacraments, we experience the gentle, loving touch of Christ, i.e., divine merciful love as expressed through the priesthood of the mystical Christ. By experiencing this merciful love of Christ, we learn how to act.

Some question that Christ acts through the minister of each sacrament. For example, one often hears the question: "Why must I confess my sins to a priest (a man) in the sacrament of Penance?" It seems clear that only God can forgive sins. How is it possible for a mere man, even though he is a priest, to forgive sins? The answer is straightforward: in the sacrament of Penance, Christ acts in and through the priest. When the priest listens, it is Christ Who listens. When the priest speaks the words of the Church to the penitent, he is speaking the words of Christ.[10] Further, Christ wishes to hear each repentant sinner and to speak to him or her. He does so through His ordained minister, the priest.[11] Thus, in the sacrament of Penance, it is "Christ saying, through the minister of the sacrament of Reconciliation: 'Your sins are forgiven;' 'Go, and do not sin again.' "[12] In and through the minister of each sacrament, Christ reveals merciful love to us.

There are seven sacraments: Baptism, Confirmation, the Eucharist, Penance, Matrimony, Holy Orders, and Anointing of the Sick. In the sacraments, Christ meets us under the "guise of signs perceptible by the senses."[13] In Baptism, water is used. Confirmation and Anointing of the Sick involve anointing with oil. Of course, most familiar are the simple elements used in the Eucharist, i.e., bread and wine. In the other three sacraments, Penance, Holy Orders, and Matrimony, the human body (as the expression of the human person) corresponds to the tangible, visible elements used in the other sacraments. In Penance, we confess our sins. In Holy Orders, the bishop imposes his hands on the candidate for orders. In Matrimony, the physical presence of the bride and the groom is the tangible, visible element of the sacrament. Further, each sacrament necessarily includes the words established in the rites and spoken by the minister of the sacrament.

Through the sacraments, sensible signs, Christ touches us. These signs, perceptible by our bodily senses, clearly touch the body. However, in touching the body, Christ touches our very persons because the human body is the expression of the human person.[14] Clearly, in touching our bodies, Christ also "touches" our souls. In the sacraments, the merciful love of Christ embraces the entire person, body and soul. No part of us is left unloved by Christ in the sacraments. Of course, Christ is able to embrace us, body and soul, because He is God incarnate.

Some cannot understand why Christ chooses to love us and God mercifully through sensible signs. The answer is clear: we would not understand merciful love in a human way if it were not revealed to us through the ordinary human means of communication, i.e., in and through our bodies. This is why God the Son became man in the first place! Further, this is why He established the Church as His mystical person with a body that expresses that mystical person. For us today, the sacraments are the physical expressions of Christ, i.e., of His mystical person, and they are essential for us. The sacraments do for us today what Christ's physical presence in Palestine two thousand years ago did for the people who saw Him. Without the incarnate Christ, the people would not have properly understood the revelation of merciful love. Similarly, without the sacraments, we would not properly understand Christ's revelation of merciful love. For example, the confession of sins and the hearing of the words of absolution given by the priest are essential for us. Speaking and listening are the ordinary ways of human communication. In the sacrament of Penance and in the other sacraments, we experience Christ's love in a human way (the only way that truly meets our own needs), and in experiencing it, we learn how to love. We would not learn how to love in a human way if we only silently confessed our sins privately at home. We would not be speaking to Christ (in the usual sense of speaking, i.e., orally, in the physical presence of another person),[15] and we would not be hearing Christ through our bodily ears. What repentant sinner would not want to be addressed by Christ Himself and to hear His words of merciful love? In the sacraments, Christ encounters the entire person, body and soul, because He wants to reveal merciful love to us. Thus, the seven sacraments, as perceptible signs, are essential to us if we are to learn how to love. Learning how to love is vital for us because without a knowledge of love, man "remains a being that is incomprehensible for himself, his life is senseless, if love is not revealed to him, if he does not encounter love."[16]

Since the signs of the sacraments differ from one another, Christ loves us and God mercifully in a specific way in each sacrament. Primarily, the Church manifests the merciful love of Christ through the re-presentation of the sacrifice of the cross in the sacrament of the Eucharist. Nevertheless, all the other sacraments of the Church also reveal Christ's merciful love. They manifest, in varied ways, the love shown by Christ on the cross. For example, Christ expresses His love for us and God differently through Holy Orders than He does through Matrimony. By observing how He loves us and God in each sacrament, we know how to love. Thus, a married couple will know how to love through the sacrament of Matrimony as will the priest through Holy Orders. In other words, Christ reveals to those celebrating the sacraments the merciful love they are to manifest in their particular stage or state in life.

Further, if we are to love Christ and others according to our particular state in life, Christ must give us the grace appropriate for our particular state in life.[17] He does! Life and love are one reality.[18] In loving in a specific way in each sacrament, Christ gives us grace appropriate to our particular state in life. We know how each sacrament confers grace by examining the specific sign of that sacrament.

In a word, the sacraments give us grace according to their signs, i.e., the sacraments cause what they signify. For example, in Baptism, the minister uses water and says, "I baptize." To baptize means to cleanse. Thus, the sign of Baptism indicates a cleansing. The grace given by this sacrament causes a cleansing of the soul from sin.

B. The Sacraments

1. BAPTISM

Baptism is Christ's initial expression of merciful love in the life of a Christian. The sacrament is celebrated by the Church according to the wish of Christ, Who said to the Apostles: "Go therefore and make disciples of all nations, baptizing them in the name of the Father and of the Son and of the Holy Spirit."[19] The sensible sign of the sacrament is constituted by both the water and the words and actions of the minister of the sacrament. (The minister of the sacrament is usually a priest or deacon. However, in case of emergency, any person can and should baptize.) Either water is poured over the forehead of the person to be baptized, or he or she is immersed bodily in water, as the minister of the sacrament says over him, "I baptize you in the name of the Father and of the Son and of the Holy Spirit." Usually, a person is baptized as an infant "within the first weeks after birth."[20]

Through Baptism, Christ loves us and God mercifully because each baptismal touch manifests the merciful love shown on the cross. Through sensible signs, Christ brings us with Him on a journey from the cross, through the grave, to the resurrection. As St. Paul writes: "Do you not know that all of us who have been baptized into Christ Jesus were baptized into His death? We were buried therefore with Him by Baptism into death, so that as Christ was raised from the dead by the glory of the Father, we too might walk in newness of life."[21] Christ acts in Baptism just as He acted on the cross: He cleanses us from sin (both original sin and personal sin, if any), and He restores the friendship between us and God. In this way, He expresses His merciful love for us and God.[22] In Baptism, Christ also unites us with other Christians.

By loving us and God in Baptism, Christ reveals the proper activity of those who are baptized. We are to love God and to love others, just as Christ loves God and others, i.e., we are to be priests in imitation of Christ. As Christ forgives original sin and heals some of the wounds caused by it, so we should forgive any faults or weaknesses we see in others that originate in the sin of Adam and Eve. In a sense, this attitude of forgiveness is a prerequisite for any act of love towards others. It is the first step towards loving as God loves. Thus, the grace given in Baptism might be compared with the gift of human life at conception.

The sign of Baptism is one of cleansing. Thus, the grace given in the sacrament of Baptism cleanses our souls from sin. With our souls cleansed from original sin and any personal sins, the spiritual space between us and God is filled with love and not evil.[23] Thus, we are able to love God and others.

2. CONFIRMATION

Adolescent (and, of course, adult) Christians need to know how to love in a more profound way than children. As adolescents and adults, we need a special sacrament that ratifies our Baptism and reveals a mature, Christian, merciful love.[24] Like Baptism, Confirmation is a sacrament of initiation into Christian love. The sacrament is celebrated by the Church according to the wish of Christ Who promised to send the Holy Spirit on His Apostles: "The Holy Spirit, Whom the Father will send in My name, . . . will teach you all things."[25] This promise was fulfilled on Pentecost. The sacrament itself is celebrated very simply: after laying his hands upon the heads of those to be confirmed, the bishop (the usual minister of the sacrament) anoints their foreheads with chrism (oil, symbolizing strength) in the form of a cross, as he says: "Be sealed with the gift of the Holy Spirit."[26]

Through Confirmation, Christ loves us and God mercifully. Through the words and actions of the bishop in the sacrament,

Christ touches us and bestows the Spirit on those receiving the sacrament. Since this bestowal of the Holy Spirit flows from Christ's sacrifice on the cross, it takes place in accord with the will of the Father (and, of course, in union with the will of the Holy Spirit). Thus, Christ's action in the sacrament is an act of love for the Father and the Spirit. In addition, since the gift of the Spirit is for our benefit, Confirmation is also an act of love of Christ for us. In Confirmation, Christ actually loves God mercifully because He eliminates God's suffering (from man's failure to return God's love) and, at the same time, draws us closer to God. In Confirmation, Christ loves us mercifully because He empowers us to return the love of God and obviously draws us closer to God because the Spirit is bestowed on us. Thus, Christ in Confirmation loves us and shows us that we are to love God and to love others in a merciful way as adult Christians.

By loving us and God in Confirmation, Christ reveals that we are to love as the Spirit loves us. The Spirit empties Himself even to the point of uniting Himself with sinful humanity. God the Son assumed a perfect humanity. In a sense, the self-emptying of the Spirit is an even greater humbling of God because the Spirit comes and makes His abode with sinners. The revelation of love in Confirmation extends beyond the revelation in Baptism. A child cannot give himself or herself as an adult. In Confirmation, we see how an adult should love. As the Rite of Confirmation states, we are to give our "lives completely in the service of all, as did Christ, Who came not to be served but to serve."[27]

The grace given in the sacrament of Confirmation empowers us because the sign of Confirmation is one of empowerment. Oil was used in the ancient world to strengthen muscles, and it is still used that way today (e.g., Ben-Gay). The words of the sacrament, "Be sealed," also denote strengthening. When we seal something, e.g., a window, we are usually attempting to enable (empower) it to hold something either in or out, or both! Thus, the sign of the sacrament of Confirmation is one of strengthening or empowering. The sacrament of Confirmation empowers us to love as adult Christians.

3. EUCHARIST

The Eucharist is also one of the three sacraments of Christian initiation (Baptism, Confirmation, and the Eucharist). In many ways, the Eucharist is the most mysterious of the sacraments because Jesus Christ Himself, true God and true man, is present in the Eucharist under the simple appearances of bread and wine. John Paul says that even the teaching of the *magisterium* "is incapable of grasping and translating into words what the Eucharist is in all its fullness."[28] According to the wish of Christ at the Last Supper, "Do this in remembrance of Me,"[29] the priest, using bread and wine, acts in the Person of Christ[30] and presents again the sacrifice of Christ on Calvary. The words spoken by the priest are the words of Christ at the Last Supper. Over the bread, the priest says, "This is My body." Over the wine, the words are, "This is My blood."[31] "Accordingly, in the Eucharist we touch in a way the very mystery of the body and blood of the Lord, as is attested by the very words used at its institution."[32] Can anyone ever completely fathom this great mystery?

Through the Eucharist, Christ loves us and God mercifully. The Eucharist is the "sacrament of love."[33] *"The Eucharist signifies this charity* [love of God and love of neighbor], and therefore recalls it [and] makes it present."[34] First of all, the celebration of the Eucharist, like Calvary, shows Christ's love for the Father (and, of course, for the Holy Spirit): "For by Christ's will there is in this sacrament (the Eucharist) a continual renewing of the mystery of the sacrifice of Himself that Christ offered to the Father [and to the Spirit] on the altar of the cross."[35] In other words, the merciful love shown by the Son towards God on Calvary is renewed in the Mass. Christ represents the act in which He perfectly returned to God the love Adam and Eve refused to return. In each Mass, Jesus Christ, the eternal Son, by giving Himself totally to God in and through His human priestly office, manifests how He eases the pain inflicted on God's "heart" by the sins of our first parents and their descendants.[36] Further, He also draws us closer to God.

In addition, the celebration of the Eucharist is an act of merciful love by Christ for humanity because in the Mass, Christ gives Himself to us in the same merciful way that He gave Himself to us on the cross, with the exception that the Mass is an unbloody sacrifice. Thus, in the Eucharist, we experience Christ's love for mankind[37] through the sensible sign of the Eucharist. In other words, the merciful love shown by Christ on the cross is revealed to us in a sacramental way in the liturgy of the word and the liturgy of the Eucharist, the two main divisions of the Mass.

By loving us and God in the Eucharist, Christ reveals how we should love. In the Eucharist, Christ continually offers Himself to us in Holy Communion. Speaking of the coming of Christ to us under the appearances of bread and wine, Pope John Paul says, "Today Christ is still courageous in His love; He still does not spare Himself and constantly gives Himself to mankind, to me."[38] As Christ constantly and repeatedly gives Himself in love to God and to us, so we should never tire of giving ourselves in love to each other.

The grace given in the Eucharist enables us to love constantly. Without Christ's help given in the Eucharist, we would tire of loving. The appearances of the Eucharist signify food. The Eucharist actually *is* spiritual food, Christ Himself, for us. As bodily food gives us bodily energy, so the eucharistic food renews God's love (grace), i.e., His life, in us. By energizing us with divine love, the Eucharist enables us to love God and others mercifully. In fact, the Eucharist is a Christian's life-giving food and drink. The Eucharist "has always been at the center of the life of Christ's disciples. It has the appearance of bread and wine, that is to say of food and drink; it is therefore as familiar to people, as closely linked to their life, as food and drink."[39]

Since the Eucharist is the greatest of the sacraments, it differs from the others in some important respects. As mentioned,[40] the Eucharist does not merely signify spiritual food and drink, but rather truly *is* spiritual food and drink, i.e., Christ. Therefore, the Eucharist does not merely cause what it stands for (as the other sacraments do), but rather *is* what it stands for. In other words, the appearances of bread and wine signify food and drink; and, after the consecration, the Eucharist actually *is* food and drink for the soul. In addition, the separate consecration of the bread (first) and the wine (second) signifies a separation of body and blood. Of course, at the moment of death on the cross, Christ's body and His blood were separated, as St. John testifies, "One of the soldiers pierced His side with a spear, and at once there came out blood and water."[41] Thus, the Eucharist at one and the same time signifies and *is* the re-presentation of Christ's sacrifice on the cross. The separate consecration of the bread and the wine signifies the death of Christ, and the Eucharist actually *is* the body and blood of Christ separated. So, just as Christ willed to die for our sins on Golgatha, so does He will that His sacrifice be really re-presented on our altars. Without Christ really giving Himself on the cross on Calvary, there would be no redemption. Without Christ really giving Himself in the Eucharist, we would not fully experience our redemption. Further, bread and wine remain and do not spoil easily. This quality of bread and wine in the Eucharist signifies that Christ is always with us. However, since in the Eucharist Christ is actually present under the appearances of bread and wine, the Eucharist signifies and actually *is* Christ remaining with us.

Of course, the Eucharist as spiritual food, as the re-presentation of Christ's sacrifice on the cross, and as Christ with us depends on the mystery of the real presence, i.e., on the mystery of Christ truly present under the appearances of bread and wine. How is it possible for the bread and wine to look like bread and wine and yet not be bread and wine? A lamp has the characteristics of a lamp, not of a desk. If we were to say a lamp was actually a desk, we would not know the language, or our perception would be somehow impaired, or we would be in need of psychiatric help. In other words, we judge things by their appearances. How can the Eucharist look like one thing and be something else?

Everything in the world is composed of an outer set of characteristics and an inner reality. Just as human beings have souls and bodies,[42] so all other beings and things in this world are composed of an inner and outer reality. Our senses touch only the outer reality. This outer reality is also what science studies. The inner reality is only known through the outer reality. Philosophy studies the inner realities of things, particularly the inner realities of persons. No human being can change the inner reality of anything. However, we can change outer realities, e.g., we can make things cold or hot. On the other hand, God, as the Creator, can always change the inner and outer realities of things. In the Eucharist, God changes the inner reality of bread and wine while leaving the externals of bread and wine (the outer realities). Whatever makes bread actually bread (the inner reality of bread) and wine actually wine (the inner reality of wine) is no longer present in the Eucharist after the consecration. Rather, Christ is present and He is present under the appearances (outer reality) of bread and wine. This, indeed, is a mystery of faith. In the Catholic theological tradition, it is called the mystery and miracle of transubstantiation. It is only accomplished through the power of God (the Creator) given through the sacrament of Holy Orders to priests.[43]

The miracle of transubstantiation does not depend on the faith of the one receiving the Holy Eucharist. Just as a lamp is a lamp, even if the one viewing it thinks it is a desk, so the Eucharist is always the body and blood of Christ even if the one receiving it or viewing it does not believe it. An individual's faith does not *make* the Eucharist be what it is. Rather, faith is a means of perceiving what the Eucharist is, as our eyes are a means of perceiving what a lamp is.[44]

Finally, as mentioned,[45] the Eucharist is a profound mystery that we can never completely grasp. As with the Trinity, it is necessary to examine this mystery from more than one point of view. One point of view emphasizes the work of redemption, i.e., Christ's death on the cross. From this vantage point, Christ is present under the appearances of bread as His body was on the cross and under the appearances of wine as His blood was at the moment He died, i.e., separated from His body. The other point of view emphasizes the Person of Christ as He is today. From this point of view, His blood, soul, and divinity are present together with His body; and His body, soul, and divinity are present with His blood. Thus, from this second point of view, Christ is fully present under the appearances of bread and also under the appearances of wine. This is why it is unnecessary for the faithful always to receive Holy Communion under both species.

4. PENANCE

The sacrament of Penance is similar to the Eucharist in that it is Christ's constant and renewed expression of merciful love towards us. As with the Eucharist, we are able to receive this sacrament often and repeatedly. However, the sacrament of Penance does not make Christ's sacrifice present again. It does apply in a direct way the sacrifice of Christ to personal sins committed after Baptism. The sacrament of Penance was given to the Church by Christ. On the evening of the first Easter, Christ gave the Church, His mystical person, His power to forgive sins. Standing in the midst of His disciples, the risen Christ "breathed on them, and said to them, 'Receive the Holy Spirit. If you forgive the sins of any, they are forgiven; if you retain the sins of any, they are retained.' "[46] From then onward, the Church has continued, in the sacrament of Penance, this priestly ministry of Christ. Within the sacrament, the priest acts in the Person of Christ to forgive the sins a Christian commits after Baptism. In other words, the Person of Christ is present in the person of the priest, i.e., "it is Christ . . . Who is present in the confessional."[47] The sensible sign of the sacrament is composed of the penitent's confession of sins and of the words of absolution, "I absolve you from your sins in the name of the Father, and of the Son, and of the Holy Spirit."[48] Finally, our turning away from sin is completed by the penance that is given to us by the priest in the sacrament. The penance "should be suited to the personal condition of each penitent" so that the penitent "may restore the order which he disturbed." Thus, through the penance we, in union with Christ, participate in a small way in returning God's love.[49] As the Rite states, "True conversion is completed by acts of penance or satisfaction for the sins committed."[50]

Through the sacrament of Penance, Christ loves God and us mercifully: "Jesus forgives sins by the power of His cross and resurrection."[51] In other words, Christ takes away sin. In the sacrament, Christ loves the Father and the Holy Spirit in a merciful way by uniting Himself with the penitent and returning to God the love that the penitent refused to return when he sinned. In this way, Christ undoes the offense given to God through sin. Further, by forgiving our sins, Christ draws us closer to God.

Christ also loves us in a merciful manner in the sacrament. Through our sins, we alienate ourselves from God, ourselves, and others.[52] However, in the sacrament of Penance, Christ unburdens us from our sins and reconciles us with God and other Christians: "Those who approach the sacrament of Penance obtain pardon from God's mercy for the offense committed against Him, and are, at the same time, reconciled with the Church which they have wounded by their sins."[53] In other words, in the confessional, Christ draws from the evil of sin the good of our forgiveness, and our reconciliation with God and others. Christ heals the painful wounds caused by sin and draws us closer to God, i.e., He loves us mercifully.[54]

By loving God and us in Penance, Christ reveals an aspect of merciful love that we should express. Since sin is an offense against God (as well against ourselves and others), it is surprising that God, the "One Who is principally offended by sin,"[55] still loves us. But He does! Even when we have turned away from Him, He does not turn away from us. Jesus Christ, the God-man, even though He is offended by our sins, still wishes to forgive them. As John the Baptist declared at the beginning of Christ's earthly ministry, "Behold, the Lamb of God, Who takes away the sin of the world!"[56] As the Scriptures reveal, this is precisely what Christ did[57] and continues to do. By loving even those who have offended Him, Christ reveals that we are to love others even when they offend us.

The grace given in the sacrament of Penance reconciles us with God, with ourselves, and with others. In other words, it cures the threefold alienation caused by sin.[58] The sacrament of Penance causes a reconciliation because the sign of the sacrament, the confession of sins, and the absolution given by the priest symbolize a reunion between two friends. If a non-Christian were to witness the sacrament of Penance, he or she might think that one friend (the penitent) had hurt the other (the priest) and is asking pardon. The second friend forgives the first, and the two are reconciled. Thus, the sign of the sacrament signifies a reconciliation, and the sacrament causes a reconciliation between the penitent and God. Since we are reconciled with God, we are at peace with ourselves because we are able to do what we are created to do: love. Further, since we are reconciled with God, we are reconciled with all those He loves, i.e., all others. Cured from the wounds of sin, we are empowered to extend a Christ-like love to all others, even to those who have hurt us. Christ's action in the sacrament of Penance might be compared to that of a doctor. Just as a disease or sickness impairs our activities, so sin makes it difficult, if not impossible, to love as we should. By forgiving sin, Christ not only shows us how to love, but also cures us from the disease of sin, which makes merciful (forgiving) love almost impossible.

Moreover, Christ wishes to meet us in the confessional. John Paul II teaches that Christ has a right to meet individually each repentant sinner in the sacrament of Penance and to love him mercifully. There is "a right on Christ's part with regard to every human being redeemed by Him: His right to meet each one of us in that key moment . . . of conversion and forgiveness."[59] Thus, priests may never absolve serious sins[60] without the penitent confessing those sins privately to a priest (unless the penitent is unable to confess his or her sins because of a physical or moral impossibility).[61] Clearly, general absolution, if practiced in ordinary circumstances and without the subsequent private confession of serious sins, denies Christ the right to meet with each and every one of us.[62] Further, such practices do not respect the integrity of the sign of the sacrament of Penance.

5. MATRIMONY

Each human being is created in the image and likeness of God, and thus each of us has the vocation to love as God loves. However, in creating us, God made us either male or female and asked us to "be fruitful and multiply."[63] Through this invitation God confirmed the experiences of our first parents and invited them (and through them, all of us) to form a familial *communion of persons.*[64] The familial *communion of persons* is a specification of the broader ecclesial (Church) *communion of persons.* As such, the familial *communion of persons* is an intensification of the baptismal love that two people should have for one another.[65] As the ecclesial *communion of persons* is founded on the sacrament of Baptism, so the familial *communion of persons* is established by the sacrament of Matrimony.

The sensible signs of the sacrament of marriage are the physical presence of the bride and the groom (if married by proxy, the physical presence of the proxy substitutes for the physical presence of the bride or the groom) and the vows that the bride and the groom say to one another. In Christian marriage, both the bride and the groom are baptized, i.e., each has "put on Christ."[66] Thus, as the bride and the groom stand in the presence of the Church's minister and two witnesses, and as they face one another and with their right hands joined, each is Christ for the other. In other words, they confer the sacrament on one another. The Church's representative, usually a priest or a deacon, is simply a witness to the sacrament. Further, even though there is no explicit scriptural reference concerning Christ's institution of the sacrament, it is based on the words and actions of Christ. Traditionally, Christ's attendance at the marriage feast at Cana[67] and His remarks to the Pharisees about marriage[68] have been taken as Christ's institution of the sacrament of Matrimony.

Through the sacrament of Matrimony, Christ loves us and God mercifully. The bride and the groom love each other in spite of all failings, faults, foibles, and shortcomings. The spouse forgives or patiently endures these problems. Further, they are drawn as close as two people can be. In other words, they love each other mercifully. However, since they are Christs for one another, in and through their mutual love, Christ loves each of them.

By loving us mercifully in the sacrament of Matrimony, Christ also loves God. In celebrating the sacrament, "man and woman accept the intimate community of life and love willed by God Himself." They are married "in order to live in complete fidelity to the plan of God, the Creator."[69] In other words, they accept the mandate of creation, "Be fruitful and multiply."[70] Thus, through the exchange of vows, the couple does exactly what Christ did in the agony in the garden, on the cross, and in every other one of His acts, i.e., the

couple accepts God's will. They say to the Father, "Father, we love
You and we accept Your plan for marriage and family life." Thus,
the Christian couple tries to avoid sin and to return God's love. In
other words, they love God mercifully.[71]

By loving us and God in Matrimony, Christ reveals how we are to
love one another. In marriage, a man and a woman commit themselves to love each other as Christ loves us. Christ's love for us is
total, i.e., permanent and limitless. Christ's love is permanent because there is never a moment when Christ does not love us. Christ's
final words in Matthew's Gospel reveal the everlasting character of
His love for us: "I am with you always."[72] In addition, the love of
Christ is without limit. There is nothing good that Christ does not do
for human beings. For example, when John the Baptist sent his disciples to Christ to ask Him, "Are You He Who is to come, or shall we
look for another?" Christ revealed the depth of His love for people in
His answer to them. Christ said, "Go and tell John what you have
seen and heard: the blind receive their sight, the lame walk, lepers
are cleansed, and the deaf hear, the dead are raised up, the poor have
the good news preached to them."[73] Of course, always at the forefront of Christ's total love for us stands the cross. In Matrimony,
spouses love each other totally, i.e., permanently and limitlessly.
During the celebration of the sacrament, the couple says to one another, "I promise to be true to you in good times and in bad, in
sickness and in health. I will love you and honor you all the days of
my life."[74] Obviously, the marriage vows promise permanence because spouses give all the days of their lives to one another. Just as
obvious is the limitless character of the marital self-gift, i.e., the
spouses promise one another that there will be no circumstances
(good times, bad times, sickness, or health) that will prevent them
from loving one another. In addition, by promising to give themselves to one another limitlessly, the couple promises to give to each
other all that they are, including the possibility of life, i.e., children.
So marital love involves a "totality, in which all the elements of the
person enter." Marital love "aims at a deeply personal unity, the
unity that, beyond union in one flesh, leads to forming one heart and

soul; it demands indissolubility and faithfulness in definitive mutual giving; and it is open to fertility."[75]

The grace given in the sacrament of Matrimony empowers husbands and wives to love each other as Christ loves us. By loving us in the sacrament of Matrimony, Christ empowers men and women to form a familial *communion of persons.* In other words, He enables marriage to be "the one blessing that was not forfeited by original sin or washed away in the flood."[76] Even wounded by sin, human beings are still called to imitate the trinitarian *communion of Persons* by forming a family. The sign of the sacrament signifies a union between husband and wife. Thus, the sacrament creates a union between the spouses in Christ: their two hearts are made one.

Marriage is a bodily reality. If one of the spouses dies, the surviving spouse may enter a new marriage. However, as long as both live, they are one, i.e., they are married and cannot validly enter a new marriage. (In the last decades, there have been large numbers of annulments granted by the Church. Annulments are not permissions granted to spouses to enter new marriages while their previous marriages still exist. Rather, annulments are declarations that presumed previous marriages were not in fact marriages because there were flaws or obstacles standing in the way of the marriage at the time the vows were said.)

6. HOLY ORDERS

In and through His humanity, Christ exercised the triple offices of prophet, priest, and king. All the baptized share these offices of Christ. However, the baptismal offices need to be activated by the hierarchical offices. A deacon activates the kingly office. A priest, most properly, activates the priestly office. A bishop, most properly, activates the prophetic office.[77] The hierarchical offices are conferred by a bishop on individual men through the sacrament of Holy Orders. A bishop is the minister of Holy Orders. Since all three orders —deacon, priest, and bishop—are ultimately directed towards the Eucharist, i.e., towards *the* self-gift to God of Christ the priest,[78] the sacrament of Holy Orders is an expression of Christ's priesthood, even in the ordination of deacons and bishops. A deacon's kingly service, i.e., His love, flows directly from Christ's love expressed in the Eucharist. As Christ expressed His love for everyone on the cross, so a deacon expresses love and encourages others to love through his kingly office. A bishop's prophetic teaching of the truth flows directly from Christ, the Truth, present in the Eucharist. Not only do the ministries of a deacon and a bishop flow from the Eucharist, they are also directed towards it. A deacon activates the kingly expression of love that prepares people to express their love for Christ in the Eucharist. The teaching of a bishop draws people to Christ present in the Eucharist.

The bishop, acting in the person of Christ, ordains a man a deacon, priest, or bishop through the imposition of hands on the head of the candidate and by the recitation of a prayer. For example, the prayer for the ordination of priests reads: "Almighty Father, grant to these servants of Yours the dignity of the priesthood. Renew within them the Spirit of holiness. As co-workers with the order of bishops may they be faithful to the ministry that they receive from You, Lord God, and be to others a model of right conduct."[79] The sacrament of Holy Orders itself was instituted by Christ at the Last Supper, the night before He died. With the words, "Do this in remembrance of Me,"[80] Christ gave the gift of Holy Orders to the Apostles. As Pope John Paul II wrote to the priests of the world on Holy Thursday of 1986, "Here we are again, about to celebrate Holy Thursday, the day on which Christ Jesus instituted the Eucharist and at the same time our ministerial priesthood [hierarchical offices]."[81] Through ordination, a man becomes another Christ and when the ordained man celebrates the sacraments, he acts "in the Person of Christ."[82] In other words, in the ordination ceremony, the one ordained is touched by Christ and made capable of acting in His Person. For example, in speaking of the connection between the ordained priest and the Eucharist, John Paul states that Christ "calls some and enables them [through ordination] to be ministers of His own sacramental sacrifice, the Eucharist."[83]

Through the hierarchical offices conferred by the sacrament of Holy Orders, Christ loves us and God mercifully. The bishop teaches us truth, which overcomes the lies of Satan and draws us close to Christ. The priest celebrates the Eucharist, which is the expression of Christ's merciful love today. The priest also forgives sins in the sacrament of Penance, another expression of merciful love. The deacon loves us mercifully by expressing love in and through his flesh and blood. He invites us to respond to Christ's love in the same way. Thus, the deacon enables us to love Christ in and through our bodies. This love leads us to renounce sin and draws us closer to God. Further, the deacon expresses merciful love by using things for people. This diaconal service overcomes one of the effects of sin, i.e., greed or selfishness, and draws us closer to God because we see that God, as the Creator, is the One Who provides for us.[84] By eliminating sin and its effects as well as drawing us closer to God through the sacrament of Holy Orders, Christ also loves God mercifully.[85]

Christ's expression of merciful love through the sacrament of Holy Orders is most clearly evident in the link between the priesthood and the Eucharist. Through the ministry of the ordained priest, *the* sacrament of Christ's merciful love, i.e., the Eucharist, is celebrated. In other words, without the priesthood, there would be no Eucharist, and without the Eucharist, it would not be possible for us to experience to the fullest Christ's merciful love for us and God. This is made clear in the following question asked of the candidate by the bishop: "Are you resolved to celebrate the mysteries of Christ [the most important of which is the Eucharist] faithfully and religiously as the Church has handed them down to us for the glory of God and the sanctification of Christ's people?"[86] According to the Second Vatican Council, "It is in the Eucharistic cult . . . that they [priests] exercise in a supreme degree their sacred functions . . . and in the sacrifice of the Mass they make present again and apply . . . the unique sacrifice . . . of Christ offering Himself once for all a spotless victim to the Father [and the Holy Spirit]."[87]

By loving us and God in the sacrament of Holy Orders, Christ reveals how we should love. Through the sacrament of Holy Orders, the Church, i.e., Christ, establishes the hierarchical offices that exist for the baptized. In other words, a deacon, priest, or bishop is a man who works for others. A deacon, priest, or bishop loves others permanently and limitlessly. An ordained man remains a deacon, priest, or bishop forever.[88] Further, he gives all that he has, i.e., Christ's offices conferred by ordination, to the baptized. As the sacrament of Matrimony is a confirmation of the mandate in Genesis to form a familial *communion of persons,* so the sacrament of Holy Orders confirms the mandate in Genesis to form a worker *communion of persons.* Through the sacrament of Holy Orders, Christ reveals that we all should strive to love all men and women in the worker *communion of persons.*

The grace given in the sacrament of Holy Orders transfers one of the hierarchical offices of Christ to those ordained. The imposition of hands and the prayers that are said signify a gift from the one imposing hands to the one who receives the imposition of hands. In the sacrament, the one ordained actually receives a gift: one of Christ's hierarchical offices. The imposition of hands commonly signifies a wish to give a certain capability or power. For example, a father might embrace a son or daughter about to drive the family car for the first time. If it were possible, the father might like to transfer all his driving skills to his child through his fatherly embrace. Such a transfer is not possible for a father. However, in the sacrament of Holy Orders, the sign causes what it signifies, and it actually transfers one of the hierarchical offices of Christ to the ordained. With "the blessing of the Holy Spirit and the grace and power of the priesthood,"[89] the ordained man will exercise his priesthood with the love that it requires.

7. ANOINTING OF THE SICK

One of the effects of original sin is the dis-integration of the human body.[90] In other words, due to original sin, we are subject to various maladies of the body, to the deterioration of the body with age, and to the ultimate bodily effect of original sin, death. These effects of sin can be very difficult to bear because of the suffering that usually accompanies them. In addition, along with the loss of bodily capacity can come a fear of death. Finally, temptation also can accompany the dis-integration of the body, i.e., we can sometimes feel that God has abandoned us to suffering and to fear. The effects of original sin on the body can be so intense that we feel as Christ felt on the cross, and we cry out, "My God, My God, why hast Thou forsaken Me?"[91] We ask ourselves, "Are we left abandoned at the time of sickness or old age?" In other words, we can doubt Christ's love. However, He does love us since He comes to be with us through the sacrament of Anointing of the Sick. As the Second Vatican Council points out, "As soon as anyone of the faithful begins to be in danger of death from sickness or old age, the fitting time for him to receive this sacrament has certainly already arrived."[92]

How is Christ present to those in danger of death? As John Paul II writes, "By means of the priest He [Christ] is present . . . at the sickbed to which the priest brings the oils of anointing."[93] Through His healing touch, Christ cured many, many people from their physical ailments.[94] In other words, Christ had a genuine compassion (love) for the sick and suffering. In the sacrament of Anointing of the Sick, Christ has given that same compassionate touch to those ordained as priests in the Church. Christ touches the sick and the aged in a sacramental way when the priest anoints them with the oil of the sick on their foreheads and on the palms of their hands while praying, "Through this holy anointing may the Lord in His love and mercy help you with the grace of the Holy Spirit. May the Lord Who frees you from sin save you and raise you up."[95] The minister of the sacrament of Anointing of the Sick is always a priest (or, obviously, a bishop). The sacrament given to us by Christ is revealed in the rite for Anointing of the Sick: "Through the Apostle James, He [Christ] has commanded us: 'Are there any who are sick among you? Let them send for the priests of the Church, and let the priests pray over them, anointing them with oil in the name of the Lord.' "[96] Further, when Christ sent the Apostles out two by two, they "anointed with oil many that were sick."[97] Clearly, this passage certainly implies the institution of the sacrament of Anointing of the Sick.

Christ loves us and God mercifully in the sacrament of Anointing of the Sick. In this sacrament, Christ mercifully loves the sick and the aged because in this sacrament He forgives their sins. Further, He draws them closer to God because He assures them that God has not abandoned them. Thus, through Anointing of the Sick, Christ loves the sick and the aged with a merciful love. In loving them mercifully, Christ also loves God mercifully.

By loving us and God in the sacrament of Anointing of the Sick, Christ reveals to those suffering from sickness and old age that in their sickness and pain they are to love others mercifully. In other words, through the sacrament of Anointing of the Sick, those who are ill are exhorted "to contribute to the good of the People of God by freely uniting themselves to the passion and death of Christ."[98] With St. Paul, the suffering person can say, "In my flesh I complete what is lacking in Christ's afflictions for the sake of His body, that is, the Church."[99] Christ reveals to the sick and the aged that just as He suffered for the sake of the redemption of mankind, so can they offer their suffering, through the power of the sacrament, for the same purpose. In other words, they can love others in the way that Christ loved on the cross, i.e., mercifully.

By offering His suffering and death to God, Christ satisfied God's love. In the sacrament of Anointing of the Sick, Christ reveals to the old and the ill that through their suffering and death (if death comes), they can love God as Christ did on the cross. In other words, the sacrament "is a sign of definitive conversion to the Lord and of total acceptance of suffering and death as a penance for sins. And in this is accomplished supreme reconciliation with the Father."[100]

The grace given in the sacrament of Anointing of the Sick heals or strengthens us because the sign of the sacrament signifies healing or strengthening. Oil was used in the ancient world for healing or strengthening.[101] When spoken to the sick, the words "help you" and "save you" clearly indicate a healing. The sign of the sacrament of Anointing of the Sick signifies a healing, and it actually causes a healing of the soul from the sickness of sin.[102] Sometimes it does cause a healing of the body.

C. Conclusion

In each sacrament, Christ acts as a priest through the sign of the sacrament. He loves God and us mercifully and reveals how we should love God and others. Further, since each sacrament is received for a particular need and often at different stages in life, each sacrament reveals merciful love in a different way according to the needs of the one receiving the sacrament. In addition, each sacrament causes what it signifies. (Of course, the Eucharist does not only cause what it signifies, but it *is* what it signifies.) In other words, each sacrament gives God's life, i.e., grace, to the person celebrating the sacrament, enabling the person to love in the same merciful way that Christ loves in the sacrament.

Finally, the sacraments are not magic. Magic names an effect that is produced with an insufficient cause. For example, we call it magic when a man opens a door simply by waving his hand from a distance. Apparently, the effect is produced without a sufficient cause. (Of course, the real cause, an electric switch or a person hiding near the door, is known only to the magician.) The sacraments might appear to be magic, i.e., they seem to produce effects—the bestowal of grace—with insufficient causes: words and material things (oil, water, bread and wine, etc.). However, they are not magic. The effects of the sacraments depend not simply on the signs of the sacraments, but on Christ Himself. Christ is God the Son, and He can and does "touch" the soul through the signs of the sacraments. As God, He is not an insufficient cause of the bestowal of grace, and He chooses to work through sensible signs.

FOR REFLECTION

A. Why did Christ give us the sacraments?

B. How is the Holy Eucharist different from the other sacraments?

C. How does Christ show merciful love to us and to God in each sacrament?

D. What does Christ reveal to us about ourselves in each sacrament?

NOTES

1. See Jn. 1:14.

2. See above, Chapter 4: "The Incarnation," pp. 81–83, 98–101.

3. See above, Chapter 5: "The Church as the Person of Christ," pp. 120–22.

4. See above, Chapter 4: "The Incarnation," pp. 98–101.

5. According to the teaching of the Council of Trent (1547), "If anyone says that the sacraments of the New Law were not all instituted by Jesus Christ Our Lord; or that there are more or fewer than seven, that is: Baptism, Confirmation, the Eucharist, Penance, Extreme Unction [Anointing of the Sick], Order, and Matrimony; . . . let him be anathema." See ND, no. 1311.

6. See SCo, no. 7.

7. See RH, no. 20.

8. See Charles Journet, *The Meaning of Grace,* translated by A. V. Littledale (New York: P. J. Kenedy & Sons, 1960), p. 99.

9. See SCo, no. 7.

10. See the previous paragraph. If in Baptism, Christ baptizes, then in Penance, Christ listens and forgives.

11. See above, Chapter 5: "The Church as the Person of Christ," pp. 124–28. The hearing of confession and the sacramental absolution of sins is a function of Christ's hierarchical priesthood.

12. See RH, no. 20.

13. See SCo, no. 7.

14. See above, Chapter 2: "God's Love: Creation," pp. 37–38.

15. Even on the phone, there is a physical presence.

16. See RH, no. 10.

17. See above, Chapter 2: "God's Love: Creation," pp. 33–35. See also below, Chapter 8: "Grace," pp. 235–36.

18. In God, life and love are one and the same because they belong to the divine essence. See above, Chapter 1: "Man/Woman and God," p. 5. See also above, Chapter 2: God's Love: Creation," p. 41. In addition, see below, Chapter 8: "Grace," pp. 235–36.

19. See Mt. 28:19.

20. See *The Rites of the Catholic Church, Rite of Christian Initiation: Baptism for Children,* promulgated by Pope Paul VI, and translated by the

International Commission on English in the Liturgy, vol. 1 (New York: Pueblo Publishing Co., 1976), no. 8.

21. See Rom. 6:3–4.

22. See above, Chapter 4: "The Incarnation," pp. 81–83, 98–101.

23. See above, Chapter 4: "The Incarnation," p. 82.

24. See RP, no. 27.

25. See Jn. 14:26.

26. See *The Rites of the Catholic Church,* vol. 1, *Rite of Christian Initiation: Confirmation,* no. 27.

27. See *The Rites of the Catholic Church,* vol. 1, *Rite of Christian Initiation: Confirmation,* no. 22.

28. See RH, no. 20.

29. See Lk. 22:19. See also "Eucharistic Prayer I," *The Roman Missal: The Sacramentary,* promulgated by Pope Paul VI on April 3, 1969, and translated by the International Commission on English in the Liturgy (New York: Catholic Book Publishing, 1974), p. 545.

30. See below, pp. 193–96.

31. See Mt. 26:26–28. See also "Eucharistic Prayer I," *The Roman Missal: The Sacramentary,* p. 545.

32. See RH, no. 20.

33. See RH, no. 20.

34. See Karol Wojtyla (Pope John Paul II), *Dominicae Cenae, On the Mystery and Worship of the Holy Eucharist* (Vatican: Vatican Polyglot Press, 1980), no. 5.

35. See RH, no. 20.

36. See Chapter 4: "The Incarnation," pp. 82–83, 98–101.

37. See Wojtyla, *Dominicae Cenae,* no. 5.

38. See WC, p. 72.

39. See Wojtyla, *Dominicae Cenae,* no. 7.

40. See the previous paragraph.

41. See Jn. 19:34.

42. See above, Chapter 2: "God's Love: Creation," pp. 31–34, 37–38.

43. See below, pp. 193–97.

44. See below, Chapter 8: "Grace," pp. 218–19, for a similar discussion.

45. See above, p. 184.

46. See Jn. 20:22–23.

47. See SC, p. 143.

48. See *The Rites of the Catholic Church,* vol. 1, *Rite of Penance,* no. 46.

49. See below, Chapter 8: "Grace," p. 210.

50. See *The Rites of the Catholic Church*, vol. 1, *Rite of Penance*, no. 6.

51. See SC, p. 141.

52. See CS, no. 77.

53. See LG, no. 11.

54. See "Penitential Rite," option C, iv, *The Roman Missal: The Sacramentary*, p. 364.

55. See RP, no. 31.

56. See Jn. 1:29.

57. See for example, Mt. 9:2; Mk. 2:5–6; Lk. 7:48; and Jn. 5:14.

58. See above, Chapter 3: "Original Sin and the Providence of God," p. 55.

59. See RH, no. 20.

60. For a discussion of serious or mortal sins, see below, Chapter 9: "Morality," pp. 253–54.

61. See *Code of Canon Law*, promulgated by Pope John Paul II on January 25, 1983, and translated by the Canon Law Society of America (Washington, D.C.: Canon Law Society of America, 1983), no. 960.

62. See *Code of Canon Law*, no. 961.

63. See Gen. 1:28.

64. See above, Chapter 2: "God's Love: Creation," pp. 40–45.

65. See *Covenant*, p. 104.

66. See Gal. 3:27.

67. See Jn. 2:1–11.

68. See Mk. 10:2–12.

69. See FC, no. 11.

70. See Gen. 1:28.

71. It may be surprising that we are called to love God mercifully. For a discussion of this point, see below, Chapter 8: "Grace," pp. 228–29.

72. See Mt. 28:20.

73. See Lk. 7:18–23.

74. See *The Rites of the Catholic Church*, vol. 1, *Rite of Marriage*, no. 25.

75. See FC, no. 13.

76. See *The Rites of the Church*, vol. 1, *Rite of Marriage*, no. 33.

77. See above, Chapter 5: "The Church as the Person of Christ," pp. 125–27.

78. See above, Chapter 4: "The Incarnation," pp. 81–83, 98–101.

79. See *The Rites of the Catholic Church*, vol. 2, *Ordination of Deacons, Priests, and Bishops: Ordination of Deacons and Priests*, no. 26.

80. See Lk. 22:19.

81. See Karol Wojtyla (Pope John Paul II), *Letter to All the Priests of the Church for Holy Thursday 1986* (Vatican: Vatican Polyglot Press, 1986), no. 1.

82. See LG, no. 10.

83. See Karol Wojtyla (Pope John Paul II), *Letter to All the Priests of the Church on the Occasion of Holy Thursday 1979* (Washington, D.C.: United States Catholic Conference, 1979), no. 4.

84. See above, Chapter 4: "The Incarnation," pp. 102–4.

85. See above, Chapter 4: "The Incarnation," pp. 81–83, 98–101.

86. See *The Rites of the Catholic Church*, vol. 2, *Ordination of Deacons, Priests, and Bishops: Ordination of a Priest*, no. 15.

87. See LG, no. 28.

88. Even those who have left active pastoral work remain forever deacons, priests, or bishops. If they have left active work with the permission of the Church, the Church usually asks them to continue their service in some way, e.g., the recitation of the divine office.

89. See *The Rites of the Catholic Church*, vol. 2, *Ordination of Deacons, Priests, and Bishops: Ordination of a Priest*, no. 19.

90. See Chapter 3: "Original Sin and the Providence of God," pp. 53–57.

91. See Mt. 27:46.

92. See SCo., no. 73.

93. See SC, pp. 143–44.

94. See for example, Mt. 8:1–4, 5–17, 15:29–31; Mk. 2:1–12, 10:46–52; Lk. 7:19–23; and Jn. 9:1–7.

95. See *The Rites of the Catholic Church*, vol. 1, *Rite of Anointing and Pastoral Care of the Sick*, no. 76.

96. See *Pastoral Care of the Sick*, promulgated by Pope Paul VI, and translated by the International Commission on English in the Liturgy (New York: Catholic Book Publishing, 1983), p. 90.

97. See Mk. 6:13.

98. See LG, no. 11.

99. See Col. 1:24.

100. See RP, no. 27.

101. See above, p. 183.

102. See above, pp. 189–90.

8

Grace

[We believe in] the Lord, the giver of life. . . . We look for the resurrection of the dead, and the life of the world to come.

A. Sanctification: An Act of Power, Wisdom, and Love

The sacraments give us God's grace. In other words, they sanctify us. The work of sanctification is attributed to the Holy Spirit and it is a demonstration of God's love, but it is also an act of divine power and wisdom.[1] This point seems obvious since the sacraments, the primary means of grace, flow from the cross, a manifestation of divine power, and are the expression of the priesthood of Christ (Who is Wisdom).[2] Thus, as in the creation and the redemption, all three members of the Trinity act as one principle in sanctifying us.

1. POWER

Made in God's image and likeness, man is created to do what God does, i.e., to love as God loves. Obviously, it would be impossible for any creature to love as the Creator loves without sharing in some way in the Creator's ability to love. In God, every activity belongs to His very essence. Thus, His loving activity pertains to His very being, i.e., His life. Clearly, if man is to love as God loves, it is necessary for him to share God's own life in some way. Therefore, "Christian thought has perceived in *man's 'likeness' to God* the foundation of man's call to participate in the interior life of God: *his opening on to the supernatural.*"[3] In His creative act, God made man fit for Himself, i.e., *"capax Dei."*[4] We are fit for God because we are capable of sharing the divine life, i.e., grace. In an incredible act of divine power, God made man capable of possessing human and divine life simultaneously. Such a capability would have been given in vain if God had not actually given us His own life. Since God does not do anything without purpose, He did not merely give man the capability for grace: He gave man grace as well. God made grace "to dwell from the beginning . . . in the creatures made 'in the likeness of God.' "[5] Of course, we possess human and divine life in different ways. Nevertheless, those blessed with God's grace neither cease to be human beings nor become God.

Even with grace, it is possible not to love God and others. Even with grace, we remain free.[6] When we choose not to love God and others, we reject Him, i.e., His very being (His life). Since grace is God's being (God's life) in us, when we reject God, we reject grace. Further, as there is no distinction in God between His being, i.e., His life, and His acts, e.g., His love, so there is no distinction between God's being (God's life) and love in us. It might be said that grace is God's life/love in us because it is His very being in us. Therefore, when we choose not to love God and others, we reject God's grace, i.e., His life/love.

When Adam and Eve sinned by believing the devil and mistrusting God, they chose not to love God.[7] In other words, they lost grace, the divine life/love. They also injured their own spiritual faculties and wounded their bodies: "Sin is not only 'against' God, it is at the same time 'against' man."[8] "Sin . . . is a suicidal act."[9] Since the choice of Adam and Eve to sin was their first opportunity to respond to God's love for humanity in a mature way, this sin hurt them and us more severely than any other sin. We are the heirs of Adam and Eve, and we inherit their sin and its effects.[10] We are born without God's grace. Further, our minds are darkened and our wills are weakened. In addition, our bodies are no longer integrated.[11] Wounded and without God's grace, it is almost impossible for us to love God, ourselves, or others. However, even the sin of Adam and

Eve, as self-destructive as it was for man and as much a rejection of God (Love itself) as it was, could not thwart God's power. God empowered man to return the divine love, and God healed man so that he could again love himself and others.[12]

2. WISDOM

After Adam and Eve, the rejected and unreturned divine love for human beings was satisfied only through Christ.[13] He trusted God and chose to love Him even as He drew His last breath.[14] With Christ's act of love on the cross, the "longing" God had for His children to turn to Him was satisfied.[15] In Christ, all humanity responded to God because He alone "satisfied the Father's eternal love."[16] In a certain sense, Christ "annihilates this evil [the evil of sin] in the spiritual space of the relationship between God and humanity, and fills this space with good [love]."[17] In other words, as the new Adam, Christ responded to God's love. As the first Adam acted for all his descendants, i.e., all human beings, so Christ, the new Adam, acts for the entire human race.[18] In other words, He made it possible for all of us to respond to God's love. In Christ, we can all love God because in Christ we are all able to receive God's grace. Christ wishes to bestow His grace, His eternal life, on all human beings. Since each one who accepts God's grace has "put on Christ,"[19] all these are other Christs. Christ, God the Son, is the Wisdom of God. Therefore, all those who are other Christs have, in a sense, "put on 'Wisdom.'" As Christ reveals wisdom, so should they.[20] Clearly, the gift of God's grace is not only an act of power,[21] it is also a revelation of divine wisdom.

As mentioned above,[22] God the Son would have probably become man even without original sin. He would have become man to reveal man's identity, proper activity, and that man was called to love God in and through a mutual bodily exchange of love, and that man was called to love others by using things for their benefit. In other words, even if humanity had remained in the garden of Eden, God would have come to reveal divine wisdom.

As it is, God the Son became man to satisfy God's love as well as to reveal man to himself.[23] However, through original sin, man's intellect, will, and body were wounded. Thus, it was not sufficient for Christ merely to reveal man to himself. With the darkening of the human intellect, human beings are almost incapable of understanding their identity as revealed by Christ. Similarly, with the weakening of the human will, it is almost impossible for human beings to act as God acts. Further, with the wounding of the body, it is almost impossible for men and women to love God through a mutual bodily exchange and others by using things for their benefit. Therefore, Christ not only satisfied God's love and revealed man to himself, He also gave man the ability to understand what He revealed, to act as God acts, to love God in and through the body, and to love others by exercising a proper dominion over things. In other words, Christ not only accomplished our salvation, He also overcame the wounding of human nature. Of course, we are never restored to the very *state* of our first parents before sin. We still suffer from the effects of original sin. However, Christ does give us the ability to know, to choose, and to act in and through the body and in the world, as images of God. He gives us grace, i.e., God's life. Even with grace, it is difficult for us to act as images of God in the fullest sense. However, without grace, it would be almost impossible for us to do so.[24]

Christ gives us help to overcome the effects of sin through the gift of the divine life, grace. For Adam and Eve, grace had one function: it gave them a share in the divine life. If they had not refused it, grace would have enabled them to live both a human and a divine life here on earth and in heaven. In other words, with grace, Adam and Eve would have been able to love God here on earth and in heaven. In us, grace has two functions. As in Adam and Eve, grace enables us to live a divine and a human life, and to love God here on earth and in heaven. However, in addition, grace makes it possible for us to overcome some of the effects of original sin. Grace makes it at least possible for man to understand himself, to act as an image of God should, and to love God in and through the body, as well as to love others through the proper use of things. In a word, the grace enables us to act as images of God, i.e., Wisdom, and thus we reveal wisdom to others. However, most especially, the gift of grace is an act of divine love because grace is the divine love in us.[25]

3. LOVE

Love is a self-gift of one person to at least one other person. Since the Holy Spirit is Love, He unites the Father and the Son in the Trinity.[26] As the Love of God unites the Persons of the Trinity, so the love of God in us, i.e., grace, unites human persons. In other words, as the Holy Spirit, Love, unites the Father and the Son, so He unites all those who share the very life of God, i.e., all those blessed with the divine life. Thus, the gift of God's love through grace has been appropriately attributed to the Holy Spirit.

Not only does the Holy Spirit (in union with the will of Christ and the wills of the baptized) unite all the baptized in the *communion of persons* of the Church,[27] but He also unites all those who share the divine life in another *communion of persons,* the communion of saints.[28] The communion of saints includes all the baptized on earth who possess the divine life. (Some of the baptized may have lost God's grace through a serious sin,[29] and these, unless the sin has been forgiven and grace restored, are not members of the communion of saints.) In addition, the communion of saints includes even the non-baptized who have been given God's grace.

Ordinarily, Baptism is the primary means of receiving God's grace. However, there are those who are not baptized. Still, they must be able to receive God's grace because Christ satisfied God's love in the name of all humanity. Since He, as the new Adam,[30] wishes to bestow the divine love, i.e., divine life, on every human being, all men and women must have an opportunity to receive God's love (grace). God *does* give everyone a chance. For example, if a non-baptized aborigine who has never heard of Christ comes to believe that there is an ultimate being, i.e., God, Who will reward the good and punish the evil, he has received God's grace. Looking at a waterfall or witnessing a powerful event of nature could prepare one to receive grace.

At some point in everyone's life, God gives a chance to receive His love, i.e., His grace. Even those who die before birth have an opportunity to embrace God's love. One theory holds that at the moment of death, or just before, God infuses an understanding of Himself into the mind of the child. Understanding something of God, the child wishes to give himself to God, i.e., to love God. At that moment, God infuses His divine grace, i.e., His love, to empower the child to love Him. It is necessary that there be a inclination in the will of the child towards love because God always and in every case respects our free will. Even at the Baptism of a child, there is a choice for God made by the parents and godparents in the name of the child.

An older view suggested that those who died without Baptism, even though they had no opportunity to receive it, went to a place called Limbo. Limbo was not heaven, but it was not hell either. The souls in Limbo were relatively happy, i.e., they were not suffering. However, the theory of Limbo does not seem to be a very satisfactory solution to the problem of salvation for the non-baptized. If there were souls in Limbo, they would endure great suffering because they would never be able to fulfill themselves as images of God, i.e., they would never be able to come to heaven. According to the theory, Limbo was also the place for the saints of the Old Testament until the sacrifice of Christ was offered. However, since God exists, as it were, outside of time, it was not necessary for the Old Testament saints to "wait" for Christ.[31]

Sometimes the following questions arise: If everyone has a chance to receive God's grace, why should I be baptized? Why should I strive to be a good member of the mystical Christ? Would it not be easier simply to take the chance when God offers it to me? Of course, the answer is that we should all accept Baptism. First, if we have an opportunity to be baptized (this implies not only the availability of Baptism, but also an inclination towards Baptism on the part of the individual), God *is* giving us our opportunity to receive His grace. We should take advantage of such an opportunity. Second, Baptism joins us to the mystical Christ, i.e., the Church. Through the Church, Christ offers us the fullness of revelation, His merciful love given through the other sacraments, and many, many chances to express our love for God in and through our bodies, and our love for others by using things for their benefit. In other words, by our active participation in the Church, we act more like Christ. We become more and more the images of God that we are. We come to love God more and more.

In addition to the baptized and all those on earth who share God's grace, the communion of saints includes all those who have died sharing the divine life. The souls in hell do not possess God's love. However, the saints in heaven and the souls in purgatory do. The souls in purgatory are those who have died with God's grace, but who did not completely return God's love while on earth. It may be that they died without asking forgiveness for some lesser unloving acts towards God (venial sins).[32] It is also possible that they did not completely satisfy the "suffering" of God caused by these sins and, perhaps, other sins.[33] In other words, after their sins, either they did not completely restore the relationship they did have with God before their sins by asking forgiveness, or they did not "complete what is lacking in Christ's afflictions"[34] for their sins by doing some acts of love or penance. (In satisfying God's love perfectly, Christ enabled all of us, even after personal sins, to do some loving acts towards God. After receiving forgiveness for sins, our own dignity requires us, united with Christ, to participate in satisfying God's love through loving acts. Thus, the priest in the sacrament of Penance asks us to say or to do a penance before he absolves us.[35] However, sometimes it does happen that at death there remain some acts of penance we should do. The souls in purgatory complete any penances left undone.) Purgatory gives souls the opportunity to love God mercifully because in union with Christ's cross, they compensate for their sins and the effects of their sins, and they draw closer to God in love. Those in purgatory are often called the "poor" souls because they cannot help themselves other than by suffering. However, the "poor" souls will all eventually come to the glory of heaven.

We know that purgatory exists because we pray for the dead and these prayers have a beneficial effect. The souls in hell are beyond help because they have completely rejected God's offer of love. They themselves do not wish to share heaven. Their attitude is that of the

devil.[36] The souls in heaven do not need our prayers. If prayers for
the dead have any effect at all, there must be some state other than
heaven or hell. In other words, there must be purgatory, where the
souls of the faithful departed are given an opportunity to perfect
their love for God and to compensate for their sins and the effects of
their sins. We can help them perfect their love for God through our
prayers. Of course, some would suggest that we should not pray for
the dead. They regard prayers for the dead as useless because they do
not recognize the existence of purgatory. They acknowledge only the
existence of heaven and hell. However, the Church's entire Tradition
testifies to the practice of offering beneficial prayers for the faithful
departed. As Scripture teaches, we should make "atonement for the
dead that they might be delivered from their sin."[37]

Those who share God's grace on earth—the souls in purgatory,
the saints and the angels in heaven—are all members of the communion of saints. Since all members of this communion share God's
love, they are united not only with God, but with one another. Loving God and one another, they all have given themselves to one
another. All are striving for the good of the others. In other words,
every member wants all the other members to fulfill themselves, i.e.,
to come to the glory of heaven. Therefore, all the members try to
help one another. Of course, the saints and the angels are fulfilled.
They can help the souls in purgatory and those on earth, but they are
not in need of any assistance themselves. The souls in purgatory and
those blessed with God's life on earth welcome the help of the saints
and the angels. The souls in purgatory can only offer their loving
suffering to God. Of course, through these sufferings, they perfect
their love for God and come closer to the full realization of that love
in heaven. Those blessed with God's grace on earth can help the
souls in purgatory and one another.

Whenever we act as God acts, i.e., when we express our love for
God and for others whom He loves, we strengthen our relationship
with God. In other words, as a loving gesture between a husband and
a wife reinforces and strengthens their love, so when we act as God
acts, our loving relationship with Him is intensified. Of course, if a
wife does some especially kind act for her husband, the husband will

often reciprocate in some way. So it is with God. He will never be outdone. When we return His love, i.e., when we love as He loves, He bestows His love in even greater abundance on us. In other words, the divine life in us is intensified and strengthened. We act as God acts when we celebrate any one of the seven sacraments. God established the sacraments as the primary source for His grace. The flow of grace to those celebrating the sacraments depends primarily on God's power and to a lesser extent on the person celebrating the particular sacrament. Of course, the bestowal of grace through the sacraments does depend on the individual's decision to celebrate that sacrament! In addition to celebrating the sacraments, we act as God acts when we give alms, pray, and fast[38] because through these acts we reject the devil's temptations as Christ did. In giving alms, we reject the devil's suggestion that God does not care about us. We acknowledge that we trust in Him and not in our own resources or in material wealth. By praying, we acknowledge God's position and reject the devil's suggestion that he should be adored.[39] By fasting, we show that we recognize that God defines good and evil, and not the bodily desires. (See the accompanying diagram, "Devil's Temptations, Christ's Answers, Our Responses.") Through such acts, our relationship with God is strengthened. However, the intensification of God's grace life in us through these acts depends much more on us than on God. In other words, these acts are not the same as the seven sacraments.[40] After we have expressed our love for God and others by celebrating the sacraments or in other ways, we can ask God to strengthen His love in others, i.e., the souls in purgatory or other people on earth. (Of course, the divine life cannot be intensified for the saints and the angels in heaven. Each already lives the divine life as fully as is possible for him or her.)

Through the bond of the communion of saints, the angels and the saints are united in love with us and with God. As our friends, they wish to help us. Further, since they are our friends, we are confident in seeking their help. We can ask them to ask God for a particular blessing or gift. Thus, when we pray to the saints and the angels, we are asking them to ask God for help on our behalf. We are not asking the saints or the angels themselves to give us what we wish. Since they are not God, they themselves could not give us what we request. Clearly, we do not pray to the angels and the saints as we would pray to God. When we pray to God, we ask Him for what we need. When we pray to the angels and the saints, we ask them to ask God. Thus, we do not make the angels and the saints into gods.

DEVIL'S TEMPTATIONS, CHRIST'S ANSWERS, OUR RESPONSES

Adam/Eve	*Christ*	*Christ's Answer*	*Our Acts*
1. God lied.	1. Angels will rescue you. (Second temptation)	1. God should not be tested because He does not lie.	1. Almsgiving.
2. You will become like a god, i.e., like me.	2. Fall down and worship me. (Third temptation)	2. You, Satan, are not God.	2. Prayer.
3. You will be gods defining good and evil.	3. Command these stones to turn into bread. (First temptation)	3. Man must accept God and not try to be god.	3. Fasting.

However, if we can go directly to God, why bother with the angels and the saints? First, when we pray to the angels and the saints, we honor God. As most of us are honored when a loved one is acknowledged for what he or she has accomplished, so God is honored when we acknowledge the position of His closest friends, the angels and the saints. (The angels and the saints are the closest friends of God because they are in heaven.) Second, as the closest friends of God, the angels and the saints wish to cooperate in His work. Since God wills the salvation of everyone, the angels and the saints wish to help all of us come to heaven. Of course, they also choose to help us come to heaven because they love us in the communion of saints. Third, since the communion of saints is a *communion of persons,* its work is accomplished through the cooperation of all members. In a certain sense, we should not think of ourselves as loners relating individually to God.[41] Rather, we should think of ourselves as joined with others in striving for the good of all. As in a business corporation, everyone working for the company should be striving for the common goal, so everyone in the communion of saints should be helping each other reach heaven. Those who are in heaven have a legitimate part in helping us come to the glory of heaven. They love us because they are images of God and because they share God's love. As long as we are not completely fulfilled, their love for us needs to be expressed in an active way. Their cooperation in the communion of saints is an activity that pertains to their very dignity as persons. We should permit them to love us, i.e., we should pray to them for help. Obviously, when we pray to them, we are also expressing our love for them. We are acting as members of the communion of saints.

Mary is *the* member of the communion of saints *par excellence*. Her love for God is unparalleled, except for Christ's. Since she loves God, she wishes to cooperate in the work of salvation. Thus, in an absolutely extraordinary way, Mary wishes to help us come to heaven. She began this work at the annunciation and continued it especially at the foot of the cross when she expressed her love for God by accepting the sufferings the Lord's passion and death entailed for her. She continues this work in heaven. The Lord confirmed His mother's unique participation in the redemption when He entrusted her to us as our mother. Through the Apostle John, Christ looks at each one of us from the cross and says, "Behold your mother!"[42] "This 'new motherhood of Mary,' generated by faith, is *the fruit of the 'new' love* which came to definitive maturity in her at the foot of the cross through her sharing in the redemptive love of her Son."[43] Beneath the cross, she became our mother in the order of grace.[44] Thus, she "places herself between her Son and mankind in the reality of their wants, needs, and sufferings. . . . [In other words, Mary] *acts as a mediatrix, not as an outsider, but in her position as mother.*"[45] Clearly, as our mother in the order of grace, Mary intercedes for us in a unique way. Since Christ entrusted us to His mother when He said to Mary, "Behold your Son,"[46] we can confidently approach her as our mother. When we pray to her, we

allow her to love us as a mother. We allow her to express her motherhood. Further, in asking her to intercede for us, we acknowledge her
unique position. In other words, we recognize her as the closest
human person to God. Since God loves her as His mother, He is
pleased that we honor her. Who would not be comforted by the care
of such a mother as Mary?

Since for God there is no time,[47] He constantly sees the sacrifice of
Christ and the acts of love that the saints undertook in union with
the sacrifice of Christ. With the cross of His Son before His eyes,
God is constantly bestowing His love (grace) on us. This love of God
is a response, as it were, to the sacrifice of Christ. As the mystical
Christ, i.e., as the one who continually satisfies God's love through a
constant re-presentation of the sacrifice of Christ, the Church can
ask God to bestow His love (grace) in a particular way. In encouraging individual prayers or devotions by attaching indulgences to them,
the Church asks God to bestow His love in a particular way. An
indulgence may be partial or full. A partial indulgence eliminates
some of the effects of personal sins. A full indulgence eliminates all
the effects of personal sins. However, an indulgence does not forgive
sins. It only eliminates some of the effects of sin.[48] Indulgences can be
gained for oneself or for other members of the communion of saints,
i.e., those who share the divine life on earth or those in purgatory.
(Obviously, before an indulgence can be gained, an individual must
be a member of the communion of saints, i.e., he or she must possess
God's grace.) It should be noted that an indulgence is not automatic.
It always depends on the relationship between the individual seeking
the indulgence and God, as well as the relationship between God and
the proposed recipient (if different from the one seeking the indulgence). Even though we cannot gain an indulgence for the people on
earth who do not possess God's life, we can always pray for them
that God would draw them close to Him.

The communion of saints depends for its existence on the sharing
of the divine life. As mentioned above,[49] the gift of the divine life is
an act of divine love. It is the self-gift of God that unites persons.
This self-gift of God, this love, is identified with the Holy Spirit. In
fact, when one considers the incredible number of people who share

God's grace and who are united with Him and with one another, the full reality of the divine love is unfathomable. One cannot help but consider how God can possibly share Himself with so many and be concerned about the needs of each and every person. Yet, the gift of divine love is not only immeasurable in terms of numbers, it is also in one way even a greater self-gift, a greater humbling, than the incarnation. God the Son assumed a perfect human nature.[50] However, the Holy Spirit unites Himself with sinful human beings, i.e., with imperfect human beings. (Of course, as mentioned above,[51] the Holy Spirit is not united to each of us as God the Son is united to His human nature.) Such are the "unsearchable riches"[52] of God's love for us. "This love is able to reach down to every prodigal son, to every human misery, and above all to every form of moral misery, to sin."[53]

B. The Structure of God's Life in Us

As mentioned above,[54] we are created to love as God loves, and it is almost impossible for us to love as God loves unless we share something of God's ability to love. In other words, if we are to act as God acts, we need to share in His life, the source of His acts. Grace is God's life in us.

In discussing God's grace in us, there are two extremes that we need to avoid. On the one hand, we cannot treat the gift of God's grace as an extraneous, exterior alteration of the human person. Grace is not like the clothes we wear. When we change clothes, we do not change our very being or existence. However, grace does change our very being. On the other hand, we cannot treat grace as part of human nature. While God created us with grace,[55] it remains something added to human nature. Grace is an extraordinary gift of God that is His own life. Grace, a share in the divine nature, is the divine life in us. God created human nature with an *"opening on to the supernatural."*[56] In other words, He created human nature with the possibility of sharing human and divine life simultaneously.[57] However, He did not give us His grace as part of our very being. Had He done that, the divine life would be part of our very existence. If grace were part of our nature, then, if we lost the divine life through sin, we would cease to be.

Grace is neither an insignificant exterior alteration nor part of our nature. Rather, grace is God's own life that is grafted onto our human life. The soul is the foundation of human life. The soul is the spiritual or invisible part of us. The human soul is the source, i.e., the principle, of human life.[58] The soul gives life to the human body. Without our souls, we would not exist. Our intellects and our wills are capacities of our souls. They are powers that we possess because we have human life, i.e., because we have human souls. These powers give us the capacities to think and to choose. Thus, there are three levels: the level of being, i.e., soul; the level of powers or capacities, i.e., intellect and will, as well as other powers of the soul;[59] and the level of acting, e.g., specific acts of thinking and choosing.

God's own life, grace, has the same structure in us as our own human life. As the human soul is the principle or source of human life in us, so grace is the principle or source of the divine life in us. If we share the divine life, we have certain divine powers or capacities, as the soul has human powers or capacities. As the powers of the soul enable us to act as human beings, so the powers of grace enable us to act as God acts.

Grace is at the deepest level of our existence: it is like the soul. In a sense, it makes us be God as the soul makes us human. However, we are not God as we are human. Further, we are not God as God is God. If we were God as we are human or as God is God, we would cease to exist if we lost the divine life. If we were to say that we are God as we are human or as God is God, we would fall into the extreme of making grace part and parcel of human nature.

Grace is grafted onto the soul in an almost unbreakable bond. Nothing but our own wills' embracing sin and rejecting grace can break the bond of grace with the soul. Even in sinning, the will must completely reject God's grace before the bond is totally broken.[60] The bond of grace to the soul is much closer than the union of the parts of the body with one another. We can lose an arm or a leg against our will, e.g., in an accident, but we cannot lose grace except through our own choices. In a way, the bonding of grace to the soul is much closer than the union of the soul and the body. Without any choice on our parts, we all are subject to death, i.e., our bodies separate from our souls.[61] However, grace is never separated from our souls except through our own choices. Still, grace is not human life. Rather, it exists in us through a union with our souls, the foundation of human life. Thus, the existence of a human soul is necessary for the existence of grace in us.

As human life has certain powers, so does God's life in us. The powers or capacities of the divine life in us are the very powers of God. We have these powers or capacities when grace is united to our souls. Traditionally, these powers are called the divine virtues. The divine virtues are many and varied. As grace is united to the soul, so the divine virtues are united to the capacities of the soul. The divine virtues give additional capacities to the powers of the soul. The key divine virtues are the three theological virtues—faith, hope, and charity—and the four cardinal (or moral) virtues—prudence, justice, fortitude, and temperance.

The powers of faith, hope, and charity are called theological because they confer on us capacities that are necessary if we are to have a relationship with God. Faith is the power by which we come to know and believe the truths revealed by God that lie beyond the powers of human reason, e.g., the existence of the Trinity.[62] Since faith gives us the power to know and to believe these revealed truths, it gives an additional power to the intellect. Without faith, we could not know and believe the truths about God that cannot be known by human reason alone.

It is critically important to realize that faith is the means of knowing and believing these revealed truths. Faith is not the cause of the existence of the truths. For example, faith does not cause the Trinity to exist. Rather, faith is the power of God that gives us the capacity to know and believe that the Trinity exists. There are those who would claim that it is by the faith of the believer that the eucharistic bread and wine are the body and blood of Christ. However, the faith of the believer is not the cause of the change of bread and wine into the body and blood of Christ. Rather, faith is the means by which the believer knows and believes that the eucharistic bread and wine are the body and blood of Christ.[63]

Hope is the desire for an attainable goal. We do not hope for the impossible, but for the possible. For example, most of us do not hope to journey to the moon, but we might hope to see Europe some day. The divine power of hope gives our wills the power to desire God, i.e., heaven, as an attainable goal. Lacking the power of hope, we would never hope for heaven because it would be viewed as an unattainable goal.

Charity is love. It gives our wills the capacity to choose God above all things. Through charity, we are empowered to follow Christ's example in loving God with all our hearts, with all our souls, with all our minds, and with all our strength.[64] Without the divine power of charity, we would not love God as He loves us because we would not share the divine ability to love.[65] Further, the divine virtue of charity enables us to love those God loves, i.e., images of God. In other words, through charity we are empowered to love ourselves, other human beings, and the angels. Thus, without the divine power of charity, we would not truly be able to love ourselves and others as images of God should.

Before original sin, Adam and Eve were blessed with the grace of God.[66] Thus, they enjoyed the divine powers of faith, hope, and charity. They also possessed the divine powers of prudence, justice, temperance, and fortitude that gave them the capacity to relate even the slightest human affair towards God. For example, the divine power of prudence gave Adam and Eve the capacity to judge worldly things as relatively unimportant when compared with God. Since before sin Adam and Eve also possessed the human virtues of prudence, justice, fortitude, and temperance, the divine moral virtues cooperated with the human moral virtues. Still, the divine moral virtues did not supply a lack in human nature as they do in us.[67] Human prudence gave Adam and Eve the power to make sound judgments. The human moral virtue of justice gave Adam and Eve the power to return what was legitimately owed to another. The human moral virtues of fortitude and temperance allowed Adam and Eve to "orchestrate" their bodily appetites in accord with what they knew in their minds and chose in their wills. Through sin, Adam and Eve lost grace, i.e., they lost the divine theological and moral virtues. Further, in sinning, they weakened and almost destroyed the human moral virtues in themselves and in their descendants.

All of us are the heirs of Adam and Eve. We inherit a humanity almost lacking the human moral virtues. We almost do not have the capacity for developing these virtues. Clearly, almost lacking these virtues, it is nearly impossible for us to act prudently, justly, courageously, and temperately. However, in redeeming us, Christ won for us God's grace, which not only enables us to return the divine love, but which also gives us the capacity to develop, at least partially, the human moral virtues. These human moral virtues, together with the divine moral virtues, help us to act, as images of God should. Divine prudence partially overcomes the darkening of our intellects. Divine justice substitutes in part for the clouding of our wills. Divine fortitude and temperance partially empower the mind and will to "orchestrate" the bodily passions. As in Adam and Eve, the divine moral virtues enable us to relate human affairs to God.

The operation of the theological virtues differs radically from that of the divine moral virtues. The theological powers were never intended to be joined to any human virtues. However, the divine moral powers were intended to cooperate with the developed human moral virtues. After sin, they assist us in developing the human moral virtues and in acting as images of God. However, even with the aid of the divine moral virtues, the human moral virtues will never exist in us as they did in Adam and Eve. The divine and human moral virtues will never be the source of our prudent, just, courageous, and temperate actions in the same way that they were the source of the similar actions of Adam and Eve before sin. In other words, it is now impossible for the divine moral virtues and the human moral virtues to cooperate in the same way as they did in Adam and Eve. The divine moral virtues are powers of grace that cannot completely restore powers of human nature. It is this distinction that leads the Pope to say that God's grace restores us to the possibility of acting as images of God, but not to the state of original innocence.[68]

The wounding of human nature through original sin is directly attributable to the devil's lies that Adam and Eve accepted.[69] Unfortunately, Adam and Eve believed the devil when Satan told them that God lied. With that lie accepted, it was very difficult for them to perceive truth, even the truth they could formerly have known through the natural powers of their intellects. In other words, man's intellect was darkened. The devil tried the same temptation on Christ when Satan asked Christ to throw Himself off the parapet and to trust in God's angels to save Him. Christ rejected that lie by insisting that one should never tempt God. Through the divine virtue of prudence, our intellects are given a new capacity. Together with the theological and the other divine moral virtues, divine prudence empowers us to make the same response as Christ made.

In accepting the devil's second lie that they could be like God, our first parents wounded their wills. Wishing to be gods, they selfishly strove to make themselves into something they were not. They loved themselves "to the point of contempt of God."[70] Thus, their wills were weakened so that they could no longer give God and others what was owed to them, i.e., love. Satan tempted Christ in exactly the same way when he suggested that the Lord could have all the kingdoms of the world if only Christ would worship the devil. Christ responded that all adoration and worship belongs to God. In other words, He rendered to God what was God's.[71] He loved God properly, and He did not love Himself to the point of contempt of God. Through the divine virtue of justice, our wills are empowered to return to others what is legitimately owed. Together with the theological and the other divine moral virtues, divine justice empowers us to make the same response Christ made.

In believing the devil's third lie that they could define good and evil, Adam and Eve wounded their bodies. In defining good and evil for themselves, they ate the forbidden fruit. They wounded their bodies because it was with their bodies that they ate. The bodies of Adam and Eve were no longer integrated, i.e., their bodies no longer always responded to their minds and wills. The devil tried the same ploy on Christ when he told the Lord to change some stones into bread. Christ answered that one should live on every word that comes from God. In other words, God alone defines good and evil.

Through the divine virtues of fortitude and temperance, the human person can again be integrated. Through the divine moral virtues of temperance and fortitude, together with the theological and other divine moral virtues, we are empowered to make the same response Christ made. (See the accompanying diagram.)

DEVIL'S TEMPTATIONS, CHRIST'S ANSWERS, VIRTUES, OUR RESPONSES

Adam/Eve	Christ	Christ's Answer	Virtues	Our Acts
1. God lied.	1. Angels will rescue you. (Second temptation)	1. God should not be tested because He does not lie.	1. Prudence (God cares) and the other virtues.	1. Almsgiving.
2. You will become like a god, i.e., like me.	2. Fall down and worship me. (Third temptation)	2. You, Satan, are not God.	2. Justice (rendering just debts) and the other virtues.	2. Prayer.
3. You will be gods defining good and evil	3. Command these stones to turn into bread. (First temptation)	3. Man must accept God and not try to be god.	3. Temperance and fortitude (integration) and the other virtues.	3. Fasting.

In addition to the theological and cardinal virtues, there are other moral divine powers that flow from grace, e.g., the virtue of religion. These other moral virtues, too numerous to mention, are included in the four divine cardinal virtues. For example, the virtue of religion is included in the cardinal virtue of justice because religion enables us to render to God what is legitimately owed Him, i.e., worship.

In addition to the theological and moral virtues, grace also confers on us the seven gifts of the Holy Spirit. These seven gifts are wisdom,

understanding, knowledge, counsel, piety, fortitude, and fear of the
Lord. Like the virtues, the gifts help us to believe in God, to love
Him and others, and to express in and through our bodies the truths
we know and the loving choices we make. Still, the gifts differ in at
least one important respect from the virtues. When we act solely on
the basis of the virtues, we usually are thinking about what we are
doing. Such acts take some effort. Through the gifts, we are enabled
to respond to God effortlessly. The gifts operate almost as reflex
actions to God's initiatives.

The difference between the virtues and gifts might be illustrated
through an example from our own experience. When we learn to
drive a car, we develop a capacity, a power. When we actually drive
a car, we are exercising our capability, our power of driving. Usually,
we need to pay attention to what we are doing. However, on occasions when we must make split-second judgments to avoid an accident, we react almost intuitively and automatically. In such a situation, our skill is not bypassed or ignored, but the use of the skill is
effortless, almost without thought. The gifts of the Holy Spirit enable
us to respond almost effortlessly to God's love, as though through
instinct.

C. Acting as Images of God

By sharing God's own life, i.e., grace, we are transformed. Grace
unites us with God Himself. Since we are created in God's image, we
have a certain likeness to God. However, this created likeness to God
is fulfilled and transcended through grace. For example, since we are
created in God's image, we possess freedom.[72] However, with the gift
of grace, this human freedom is taken up and infinitely increased.
With grace, we share not just human freedom, but, in a certain sense,
divine freedom. (Of course, among all human beings, only Christ was
totally free. Only He was confirmed in freedom.)[73] Grace and freedom are not opposed to each other. If grace were opposed to freedom
or freedom to grace, God would have given us both freedom and
grace in vain. In this case, neither would have any effect. However,
God does not act in vain. Grace enhances freedom; and, in a way,

freedom enables grace because without freedom we would not be persons, i.e., images of God, and thus we would not be able to share grace.

As images of God, we are created to love as God loves. However, both freedom and grace are necessary if we are to love as God loves.[74] Still, since we are able to love God almost solely through the promptings of grace and since God bestows His grace freely on whomever He chooses, it would seem that we are predetermined or even predestined to love God or not to love Him by God's own choice. In other words, it seems that God determines our love through His choice to give us His grace or not to give us His grace. In such a scenario, our own freedom seems to have nothing to do with any love for God we might have because the exercise of our own freedom depends on the gift of God's grace.

However, even the gift of God's grace does depend to a certain extent on the exercise of our freedom. God does not predetermine or predestine us. Even at the moment grace is given, our freedom is respected. Grace is not opposed to freedom. The proper relationship between grace and freedom at the moment God bestows His grace can be partially understood in light of God's eternity. God exists, as it were, in an eternal present. For God, everything happens at once, i.e., there is no "before" or "after" for Him. Therefore, God sees the inclinations in every human will not as a series of events happening in succession, but as if they were happening entirely in the present. He sees each and every loving inclination of each and every person towards Him. He blesses these with His grace, enabling them to choose what they are inclined to choose. Thus, the gift of God's grace is simultaneous with our inclinations to love Him.[75] Of course, even though we might resist God's grace, i.e., His love, at a particular moment in our lives, we always have opportunities to respond to His love (until death).

It is as though a man is trying to chop a tree down without any success. A neighbor sees him and brings a power saw to help. The neighbor and his power saw, together with the first man, successfully fell the tree. The inclinations of the first man's will were quite clear. However, these inclinations were almost in themselves insufficient.

The neighbor's help was almost necessary. Still, the neighbor's help was totally gratuitous. Further, the neighbor would have never offered the saw unless he thought the first man was inclined to use it to chop down the tree. Thus, the neighbor would not have offered his help and his tool to his other neighbors who were not trying to chop down their trees. Of course, the example limps. In reality, God is outside of time and in the example there is a "before" and "after." Second, the first man has already chosen to chop the tree down. He is not just inclined to do it, he is actually beginning the work. The inclinations in our wills towards the love of God are far more subtle. Still, God Who sees the heart, sees these inclinations.

Inclinations to love God occur among those who have never been blessed with God's grace and those who have received this gift, but have lost it. God will give His grace to those who have never possessed it, enabling them to follow their inclinations. Of course, while on earth, even for those blessed with God's grace, there will always be the possibility of sin.[76] Sin weakens or destroys our relationship with God, i.e., it weakens or destroys God's life (grace) in us.[77] However, even if we have rejected God and lost His grace through sin, He does not abandon us. First, having shared God's grace, we always retain the theological virtue of faith (except when we sin directly against this virtue, e.g., the sin of apostasy). This virtue enables us to know God, even if we have rejected Him. Second, as with those who have never shared God's life, God will respond to our inclinations. If we desire to love Him, He will give us His grace enabling us to love Him again.

It is necessary to note that even an intense relationship with God does not eliminate all difficulties. Although Christ possessed the most perfect human freedom and a perfect relationship with His Father, He still sweated blood when faced with accepting His passion and death. The love of God does not eliminate suffering. Rather, the proof of love is found in suffering. When we love others despite personal trials, we prove to ourselves and to them (even to God, in a sense) that we love them. In our fallen world, love almost necessarily involves some difficulties. Grace does not eliminate all the effects of sin. Thus, even with grace, it is difficult to love. The greatest saints, even Mary, have loved God intensely and yet have suffered much.

In addition to sanctifying grace—which transforms our very being and is grafted to our souls—there are actual graces. Actual graces are momentary inspirations or enlightenments that incline our minds and wills towards God. However, actual graces never interfere with the freedom of the human person. They are given to those who possess sanctifying grace and to those who do not. To those who respond to these actual graces, God bestows His sanctifying grace. Those who already possess sanctifying grace and who respond to the actual graces experience an intensification of their love for God. Those who do not possess sanctifying grace and who respond to actual graces receive the former for the first time. Actual graces differ from the gifts of the Holy Spirit because they concern specific acts, whereas the gifts perfect certain natural powers, e.g., mind. The activation of Christ's baptismal offices by the hierarchical offices is an example of actual graces.[78]

Of course, sanctifying grace, the theological and moral virtues, the gifts of the Holy Spirit, and actual graces are given to us so that we might be able to act as images of God, i.e., to act as God acts. In other words, sanctifying grace, as well as the virtues and the gifts which accompany it, enable us to imitate Christ, the God-man, Who, in His prophetic, priestly, and kingly offices, shows us our identity, our proper activity, that we are to love God in and through our bodies, and that we are to love people by using things for their benefit. Through sanctifying grace, we have "put on Christ,"[79] and we share in His offices of priest, prophet, and king. We share in Christ's priestly office primarily through the divine virtues of charity and justice. We share in His prophetic office primarily through the divine virtues of faith, hope, and prudence. We share in His kingly office primarily through the divine virtues of fortitude and temperance. Thus, we can love God and others (priestly office), know the truth (prophetic office), express what we know and choose in and through our bodies, and govern all creation for the sake of people (kingly office). In other words, the tendencies to act on the basis of the devil's three lies are overcome by the priestly, prophetic, and kingly acts that we do through the strength of Christ in us.[80] (See the accompanying diagram.)

DEVIL'S TEMPTATIONS, CHRIST'S ANSWERS, VIRTUES (WITH OFFICES OF CHRIST), OUR RESPONSES

Adam/Eve	Christ	Christ's Answer	Virtues	Our Acts
1. God lied.	1. Angels will rescue you. (Second temptation)	1. God should not be tested because He does not lie.	1. Prudence (God cares), faith, hope (prophetic office).	1. Almsgiving
2. You will become like a god, i.e., like me.	2. Fall down and worship me. (Third temptation)	2. You, Satan, are not God.	2. Justice, charity (priestly office).	2. Prayer.
3. You will be gods defining good and evil.	3. Command these stones to turn into bread. (First temptation)	3. Man must accept God and not try to be god.	3. Temperance, fortitude (kingly office).	3. Fasting.

Sanctifying grace, the divine virtues, the gifts of the Holy Spirit, and actual graces enable us to act as we should. However, sanctifying grace and the virtues are strengthened through our acts. As mentioned above,[81] when we act as God acts, God is pleased and our relationship with Him is intensified. This intensification of our relationship with God lends a greater vitality to God's life in us. The virtues, as powers of the grace life in us, are strengthened as God's grace in us becomes more and more vital. In an extraordinary way, the celebration of the sacraments strengthens the divine life and the divine virtues in us. Of course, other virtuous acts also strengthen the grace life in us.[82] Further, the human moral virtues in us are strengthened through acts. For example, when we act courageously, we develop a habit of acting courageously. In other words, the power (or virtue) of human fortitude is strengthened. Just as an athlete's muscles are strengthened through repeated use, so the human virtues develop through repeated acts. Of course, as mentioned above,[83] it is nearly impossible to develop the human moral virtues without the impetus given to their development by the divine moral virtues.

Since it is the priesthood of Christ that enables us to love God, the most proper act of an image of God, it is "participation in the priesthood of Christ which denotes the simplest and most complete attitude"[84] of any Christian: "There is thus good reason to consider participation in the priesthood of Christ and the attitude that derives therefrom, before turning to the prophetic and kingly aspects."[85]

1. ACTING AS CHRIST THE PRIEST

Christ the priest showed us God's love as mercy throughout His life, but especially when He died on the cross. The cross demonstrated the totality of the priestly self-gift of merciful love. Even at the moment of death, His thoughts were concentrated not on Himself, but on His Father. As He drew His last breath, He said, "Father, into Thy hands I commit My spirit."[86] Further, Christ gave Himself to us: "Greater love has no man than this, that a man lay down his life for his friends."[87]

In demonstrating His merciful love, Christ showed us how we should love Him! Through His cross, we are invited to love Christ as He loves us. We are invited to show a merciful, priestly self-gift to Christ. Who can gaze upon the crucified God-man, "pinned immobile in that terrible position,"[88] and not want to ease the pain? A real contemplation of the passion urges us to cry out, "Stop!" But, then, in the quiet of our contemplation, something dawns on us: the crucifixion takes place because of us! Our sins put Christ on the cross! With John Paul, we say to ourselves, "Look what you have done, in this man, to your God!"[89] We realize that we are invited to love Christ, i.e., God, mercifully. From the evil of the suffering of the God-man, we realize that we should seek to eliminate sin from our lives and thus draw closer to Christ. This is merciful love! As astonishing as it is, God *invites man to have 'mercy' on His only Son, the crucified one. . . .* Could man's dignity be more highly respected and ennobled, for, in obtaining mercy, he is in a sense the one who at the same time 'shows mercy.' "[90] Since each one of us is created in God's image, we are called to love as God loves. In the total revelation of that merciful love, i.e., in the bodily death of Christ on the cross, God invites us to love Him mercifully. Beginning with that moment, we are actually invited to love God in the same manner as the members of the Trinity love one another[91] and us!

Christ the priest not only showed us that we are to love God mercifully, He also showed us that we are to love one another as He loves us, i.e., mercifully. By dying on the cross, Christ loved us, His neighbors, with a merciful love. We suffer from the evil of sin and its effects. However, Christ crucified relieves that suffering by saving us from sin and its effects. He also draws us closer to God. We are called to imitate the merciful love of Christ by loving our neighbors as Christ loves us. We should forgive any injustices they may have committed against us. In this way, we forgive their trespasses against us, and we draw them closer to us in love. Through love, they are drawn closer to God. When we forgive injustices, we love as God loves, i.e., we love others mercifully.

Christ makes this point with the parable of the unforgiving servant.[92] A king is settling accounts with his servants. One owes the king an enormous sum and is unable to pay. The king forgives the debt. The forgiven servant then meets someone who owes him a much smaller sum, a mere fraction what he had owed to the king. The first servant refuses to forgive the debt of his fellow servant, and the first servant has the second one imprisoned. The king hears about the action of the first servant and delivers "him to the jailers."[93] The Lord concludes, "So also my heavenly Father will do to everyone of you, if you do not forgive your brother from your heart."[94] We should always forgive injustices done to us, as God forgives the sins we have committed against Him.

We are not only expected to forgive injustices, we should also try to relieve the suffering of our neighbors, as Christ did through His miracles. Since all suffering is caused by the sins of the world, when we relieve the suffering of others, we are lessening the effects of sin. Further, by showing others our charity, we show them God's love.

Often, they are drawn closer to God by means of our kindnesses. In other words, by assisting others in their difficulties, whatever they might be, we are acting as Christ did, i.e., we are loving mercifully.

Christ made it quite clear that He expects us to relieve suffering according to our abilities. In speaking about the judgment at the end of the world, He indicated that He considers every kindness towards another as a kindness towards Him: "Truly, I say to you, as you did it to one of the least of these my brethren, you did it to Me."[95] By the same token, He regards every lack of charity towards another as a lack of friendship towards Himself: "Truly, I say to you, as you did it not to one of the least of these, you did it not to Me."[96] Of course, this is an incredible affirmation of the union Christ feels with each and every human being. As John Paul II has written, "He Himself [Christ] is the One Who receives help when this is given to every suffering person without exception."[97]

Through God's gift of His grace, and activated by the hierarchical priestly office, those who share in the baptismal priestly office are able to love as God loves. Consequently, those who exercise their baptismal priesthood show merciful love to others, even to God. Further, by extending merciful love to others, they also love themselves mercifully because their God-like actions return God's love (i.e., their actions make up for sin) and draw them closer to God. The baptismal priestly office is exercised by loving God, self, and others through the "reception of the sacraments, prayer and thanksgiving, the witness of a holy life, abnegation, and active charity."[98] Thus, in the exercise of their priestly office, those who share God's grace fulfill the two great commandments: "You shall love the Lord your God with all your heart, and with all your soul, and with all your mind, and with all your strength, . . . [and] you shall love your neighbor as yourself."[99]

Of course, we can always choose not to exercise the baptismal priestly office. However, if we choose not to love God, others, and even ourselves as God loves, we fail to fulfill ourselves, i.e., we fail to act as images of God. Such choices are self-inflicted wounds.[100]

Still, we cannot love someone if we do not know him or her. Thus, if we are to love God, i.e., Truth,[101] we need to know truth. Similarly, if we are to love others and ourselves, i.e., images of Truth, we need to know the truth. Clearly, there is no love without the truth. Therefore, Christ's priestly office (enabling us to love) would have been given to us in vain if we did not also share in His prophetic office (enabling us to know truth).

2. ACTING AS CHRIST THE PROPHET

Christ revealed God to us. He revealed that God cares for us. He showed us that the devil lied when he portrayed God as a jealous tyrant.[102] Further, in showing us God, Christ showed us who we are, i.e., images of God. Thus, "the man who wishes to understand himself thoroughly . . . must . . . draw near to Christ."[103] Without Christ, no one would be comprehensible to himself or to those around him. The Church continues this work of Christ. Through the exercise of Christ's hierarchical prophetic office, the Church reveals God to us and shows us who we are.

Those on earth who share God's grace are able to accept these truths and make them their own because these people share in Christ's prophetic office in a baptismal way.[104] The baptismal prophetic office endows those who possess it with a "sense of responsibility towards the gift of truth contained in revelation."[105] In other words, through our baptismal share in Christ's prophetic office, we each have a care and concern for the truths revealed by God and taught by the Church. Thus, when the Church's *magisterium,* i.e., the hierarchical prophetic office, teaches, the baptismal prophetic office enables us to accept these truths as a precious gift. In addition, the baptismal prophetic office makes it possible for us to profess these truths through word and action so that others might come to accept the teachings of Christ.

Of course, even with sanctifying grace, every human being can choose to accept or reject the truth. We have the choice, as St. Peter and the Apostles had, to continue to walk with Christ or to leave Him. The Church does not impose its teachings on its members through coercive force. If we choose to reject the truth, we are almost unable to love God because God would remain for us the jealous, uncaring tyrant portrayed by the devil's lies. Who could love such a god? However, through the baptismal prophetic office it is possible for the baptized to know the truth about God. Knowing the truth, they are able to love Him. Of course, in knowing the truth about God, they know themselves and others. Thus, they are able to love God, themselves, and others. As Josef Cardinal Ratzinger wrote, paraphrasing both Pope Paul VI and Pope John Paul II, "The Christian is called to act according to the truth and thus to work for the establishment of . . . [a] 'civilization of love.' "[106]

3. ACTING AS CHRIST THE KING

Christ's kingly self-rule enabled the Lord to reveal Truth and merciful love in and through His human body.[107] As images of God, we are called to act as Christ acts. Just as kingly self-discipline was necessary for the Lord, so it is for us if we are to express love (priestly office) in accordance with the truth (prophetic office). Through the gift of sanctifying grace, we share Christ's baptismal kingly office. This gift enables us to overcome, at least partially, one of the effects of original sin on the body: the "constitutive break"[108] within us, i.e., the lack of integration. Activated by the hierarchical kingly office, the baptismal kingly office enables our bodies to express our persons. Thus, we are able to express love through our bodies. We are able to show our love for God in many ways. However, one way is to express our love for the mystical Christ by "orchestrating" our bodies in order to observe the policies of the Church as established in the Code of Canon Law, e.g., fasting. We are also able to show our love to other human beings, e.g., those in our families. Family members are able to give themselves unselfishly, not caring so much about what they receive, but rather about what is best for the other members of the family. We are also able to express a proper love for ourselves by taking care of ourselves. We are enabled to do those things, even the difficult ones, necessary for our own health, e.g., making a dental appointment or agreeing to an operation. Proper self-love is also expressed by using the things of this world to fulfill the necessities of our lives, e.g., food, lodging, clothing. In addition, kingly self-rule enables us to express truth in and through our bodies. Through kingly self-discipline, we are able to profess the truths we know courageously, even under the most difficult circumstances.

In His kingly office, Christ revealed that we are to love God through a mutual bodily exchange of love. By expressing love for God in and through our bodies, we respond to Christ's invitation. In addition, in His kingly office, the Lord governed created things for the sake of people. He showed us divine providence.[109] Activated by the hierarchical kingly office, we are called to exercise a dominion over creation for the sake of people. We were given the privilege of governing the created order at the dawn of creation.[110] This kingly activity, marred by original sin, is partially restored through our share in Christ's baptismal kingship. For example, in working, we will regard workers as more important than the means of production.[111] Further, we will be able to give of our material possessions for the sake of people, e.g., almsgiving. (Although almsgiving is a function of the prophetic office in that we express our trust in God, it is a function of the kingly office as well.)[112]

Of course, as with the priestly and prophetic offices, we can choose not to exercise the baptismal kingly office. If we choose not to exercise our baptismal share in Christ's kingly office, we will continue to suffer the full effects of original sin, i.e., we will remain dis-integrated.[113] We will be almost unable to respond to God's invitation to love Him through a mutual bodily exchange of love, and we will not love others by exercising a proper dominion over creation.

Through the triple offices of Christ, we are empowered to act as Christ acts. Just as every one of His acts is the fruit of all three of His offices, so our share in Christ's priestly, prophetic, and kingly offices empowers us to act as God acts. Christ's kingly office enabled Him to reveal God's power. The Lord's prophetic office empowered Him to reveal wisdom. Christ's priestly office enabled Him to reveal love. Our God-like acts are possible because we have "put on Christ,"[114] i.e., we share in His triple offices. We act as God acts through God's power (kingly office), God's wisdom (prophetic office), and God's love (priestly office). To use a metaphor, the seed of grace bears fruit in us. St. Paul lists the more prominent of these God-like acts, calling them the fruits of the Holy Spirit.[115] Other important God-like acts are the corporal and spiritual works of mercy.[116] The acts that Christ listed in the beatitudes are also the fruits of grace.[117]

D. Death, Judgment, Heaven, and Hell

Acting as God acts, we will love God and others here on earth. At death, the body and soul separate. Our bodies are buried in the ground, while our souls come before God. As we "stand" before God, each of us will have a consciousness of all our acts.[118] In other words, we will be able to see the sum total of all our earthly acts. Such a vision of ourselves is only possible after death because only then has our earthly pilgrimage ended. We will be in a position to judge for ourselves whether or not we have returned God's love and drawn sufficiently close to Him. If we have not, we will either want no part of heaven (because we will not love God) or we will want to make up for our lack of love. If we have no love of God in us, we will find ourselves in hell. As an angry man is miserable because of his anger, and yet wants to remain angry, so, lacking love, we will be miserable in hell, and yet we will be unwilling to love. Hell is a place of spiritual and bodily pain. The spiritual pain stems from the total and complete lack of love. Each and every person in hell is totally isolated and alone. Even the meager ability of fallen human nature to love will not be present. If we do love God, but have not as yet fully returned His love and drawn close to Him, we will go to purgatory. There is spiritual pain in purgatory, a kind of isolation, but the souls there do love God. The isolation occurs because they are, for a time, deprived of God. If we do love God and have returned His love, and drawn close to Him, we will come to our fulfillment as images of God: heaven.

When we come before God at death, God will confirm the judgment we make on ourselves. This is called the particular judgment. There is also the general judgment. At the general judgment at the end of the world, Christ will come again and judge all those who have not yet died. Those living on earth at the general judgment will go to either heaven or hell. Purgatory will not be necessary for any of those living because they will have returned God's love and drawn closer to Him through the sufferings accompanying the end of the world. Further, at the general judgment, Christ will again judge all those who have died. At the general judgment, all the souls still in purgatory will be invited to enter heaven and will be reunited with their bodies. In addition, for those already in heaven or in hell, the particular judgments already made will be confirmed. Finally, at the end of the world, the bodies of those in heaven and hell will be reunited with their souls. Our bodies will participate in the joys of heaven because our bodies will be perfectly integrated. On the other hand, the physical pains of hell have been described as the pains of fire.

In hell, we will not possess any of the divine virtues because we will totally lack God's grace, i.e., the foundation of the divine virtues. In heaven after the second coming, even though we will possess God's grace in abundance, we will not have the divine moral virtues in the same manner because our humanity will be even more perfect than it was before original sin. Further, we will not have the theological virtues of faith or hope. Faith will not be needed because we will not believe in God. Rather, we will see Him. Hope will not be needed because we will no longer hope for heaven. Instead, we will be in heaven. On the other hand, charity, the love of God, will remain because we will love God with an unimaginable intensity.

As images of God, we are all created to live with God forever in heaven. However, it is only possible for us to come to the joys of heaven by loving God and His images while we are on earth. In other words, to come to heaven we need to love mercifully, i.e., we need to return God's love and come closer to Him. We love God mercifully through our God-like acts. However, there are many possible ways to express love. Since each of us is created as a unique individual, we are also called with the help of God's grace to fashion our own personal history of God-like acts.[119] We are each called to a certain way of loving God, ourselves, and others, i.e., we are each called to a vocation, a path to heaven.

There are two fundamental vocations: married life and the celibate or virginal life.[120] In each of these vocations, we express merciful love for God, for ourselves, and for others because in each vocation we are called to exercise the triple offices of Christ. The two vocations complement one another. It is only when marriage is valued that celibacy and virginity are held in high esteem. Who would forgo marriage for the sake of the kingdom of God if marriage were meaningless or without value? Conversely, virgins and celibates testify to the great value of marriage. Thus, each vocation contributes to the other. We cannot enter or continue in either vocation without the help of God's grace. Both require the exercise of all the virtues, of the gifts of the Holy Spirit, the assistance of actual graces, and the activation of the baptismal offices by the hierarchical offices. However, God never imposes a vocation on us. We are always free in choosing a vocation and in living it out. Grace never destroys our freedom. Rather, grace enhances our freedom.[121]

Of course, if we fail to love, i.e., if we fail to use the human and divine gifts God has given us, we reject God. If this rejection is definitive and final, i.e., if we die having rejected God and not having regretted this rejection, we have consigned ourselves to the kingdom of Satan. However, while we are capable of a definitive rejection of God, we are also capable of rejecting Him in a much less definitive way. Still, how shall we know if we have rejected God? We know because God has revealed to us the ten commandments. If we are to come to fulfill ourselves as images of God, we need to know both what we should and should not do. We have just examined what we should do. The commandments confirm the positive actions we should undertake and illustrate the ways it is possible for us to reject God.

FOR REFLECTION

A. Why do Catholics pray to the saints, for the souls in purgatory, and for one another?

B. How are the virtues of prudence, justice, fortitude, and temperance related to the lies of Satan and the temptations of Christ?

C. How do we freely act as priests, prophets, and kings?

D. Does Christ punish people for their sins by sending them to hell?

NOTES

1. See above, Chapter 1: "Man/Woman and God," pp. 19–20.

2. See above, Chapter 4: "The Incarnation," pp. 81–83, 84–85, 98–101. See also above, Chapter 7: "The Sacraments," pp. 177–78.

3. See CS, no. 52.

4. See CS, no. 52.

5. See CS, no. 66. See also above, Chapter 2: "God's Love: Creation," pp. 33–35.

6. See below, pp. 223–25.

7. See above, Chapter 3: "Original Sin and the Providence of God," pp. 55, 57–58, 60–61.

8. See CS, no. 77. See also above, Chapter 3: "Original Sin and the Providence of God," p. 55.

9. See RP, no. 15.

10. See above, Chapter 3: "Original Sin and the Providence of God," pp. 56–57.

11. See above, Chapter 3: "Original Sin and the Providence of God," pp. 53–55.

12. Man can love himself even though love is a relationship of two or more persons. See below, p. 219.

13. See above, Chapter 3: "Original Sin and the Providence of God," p. 66ff; but particularly p. 74.

14. See above, Chapter 4: "The Incarnation," pp. 81–83, 97–101.

15. See above, Chapter 4: "The Incarnation," pp. 82–83.

16. See RH, no. 9.

17. See SD, no. 17.

18. See Rom. 5:12–21. See also RH, no. 8.

19. See Gal. 3:27.

20. See above, Chapter 4: "The Incarnation," pp. 84–85, 94–99. See also below, pp. 231–32.

21. See above, pp. 204–6. See also above, Chapter 1: "Man/Woman and God," pp. 19–20.

22. See Chapter 4: "The Incarnation," pp. 83–84.

23. See GS, no. 22. See also RH, no. 8.

24. Cf. Richard M. Hogan, "A Theology of the Body: A Commentary on the Audiences of Pope John Paul II from September 5, 1979, to May 6, 1981," *Fidelity*, vol. 1, no. 1, (December, 1981), p. 13.

25. See above, pp. 204–5.

26. See above, Chapter 1: "Man/Woman and God," pp. 13–15, 19–20.

27. See above, Chapter 5: "The Church as the Person of Christ," pp. 121–23.

28. This is the work of sanctification attributed to the Holy Spirit. However, in the work of sanctification, the Trinity acts as one principle. Of course, the Trinity acts in union with the wills of those who receive the divine life. See above, Chapter 5: "The Church as the Person of Christ," p. 121.

29. See Chapter 9: "Morality," pp. 253–54.

30. See above, p. 206.

31. See above, Chapter 1: "Man/Woman and God," pp. 7–9. For the divinity of Christ, see above, Chapter 4: "The Incarnation," pp. 81, 85–88, 91–93.

32. See below, Chapter 9: "Morality," pp. 253–54.

33. See above, Chapter 1: "Man/Woman and God," pp. 9–10. See also above, Chapter 3: "Original Sin and the Providence of God," n. 88. See also above p. 206.

34. See Col. 1:24.

35. See above, Chapter 7: "The Sacraments," p. 188.

36. See above, Chapter 2: "God's Love: Creation," p. 29.

37. See 2 Mac. 12:45.

38. See Mt. 6:1–18.

39. Sacramentals (e.g., holy water, rosaries, statues, incense) help us to pray.

40. See above, Chapter 7: "The Sacraments," pp. 177–81.

41. This point does not mean that we will not be judged individually by God. All of us can help each other love God. However, the help we receive strengthens or empowers us to act in the way we have already freely chosen. We will be judged on the acts we have freely chosen.

42. See Jn. 19:27.

43. See RM, no. 23. See also above, Chapter 4: "The Incarnation," p. 95.

44. See LG, nos. 61–62. See also RM, no. 38.

45. See RM, no. 21.

46. See Jn. 19:26.

47. See above, Chapter 1: "Man/Woman and God," pp. 7–9. See also above, p. 209.

48. Some may remember that partial indulgences were listed in terms of days or years. These days and years had nothing to do with the time spent in purgatory, as many thought. Rather, it was a way of measuring the bestowal of God's love. The days referred to the days of public penance sometimes performed by those who received the sacrament of Penance in the early Church. For example, a partial indulgence of three years would mean that the Church had asked God to look upon the one saying a particular prayer with the same mercy that He would look upon someone doing public penance for three years. Since public penance is, for the most part, no longer performed and since it is almost impossible to measure the intensity of God's love, Pope Paul VI simplified the classification of indulgences. They are now simply called partial and full.

49. See above, p. 205.

50. See above, Chapter 4: "The Incarnation," pp. 88–91.

51. See above, Chapter 5: "The Church as the Person of Christ," pp. 120–22.

52. See Eph. 3:8. See also RM, no. 46.

53. See DM, no. 6.

54. See above, p. 204.

55. See above, Chapter 2: "God's Love: Creation," p. 36. See also above, p. 205.

56. See CS, no. 52. See also above, Chapter 2: "God's Love: Creation," p. 35. Further, see above, p. 205.

57. Similarly, God created the angelic natures with the possibility of sharing angelic and divine life simultaneously. See CS, no. 66. See also above, Chapter 2: "God's Love: Creation," p. 36.

58. See above, Chapter 2: "God's Love: Creation," p. 32.

59. Other powers of the soul include the bodily capacities of digestion, movement, feelings (emotions), memory, etc. Although these exist in the body, they are powers of the soul because they pertain to human life.

60. See below, Chapter 9: "Morality," pp. 253–54.

61. We do not choose to be subject to death. However, given the reality of death in our lives, we may choose it over some greater evil, e.g., the martyrs choosing to die for Christ.

62. God reveals these truths in Christ, and these are transmitted to us through Scripture and Tradition as taught and interpreted by the Church. See above, Chapter 6: "Revelation: Scripture and Tradition," pp. 149–51.

63. For a similar discussion, see above, Chapter 7: "The Sacraments," p. 187.

64. Cf. Mt. 22:37; Mk. 12:30; and Lk. 10:27.

65. See above, pp. 204–5.

66. See above, pp. 204–5.

67. See the next paragraph.

68. See Hogan, "A Theology of the Body: A Commentary on the Audiences of Pope John Paul II from September 5, 1979, to May 6, 1981," p. 13.

69. For the following discussion of the devil's lies, see above, Chapter 3: "Original Sin and the Providence of God," pp. 58–61.

70. See CS, no. 75.

71. See Lk. 20:25.

72. See above, Chapter 2: "God's Love: Creation," p. 36.

73. See above, Chapter 4: "The Incarnation," pp. 92–93.

74. See CS, no. 63. See also above, Chapter 2: "God's Love: Creation," p. 36. Further, see above, pp. 204–5.

75. This is what happened when God blessed Mary with the extraordinary grace of the Immaculate Conception. See above, Chapter 4: "The Incarnation," pp. 104–5.

76. Except, of course, in the case of Jesus and Mary. See above, Chapter 4: "The Incarnation," p. 104.

77. See below, Chapter 9: "Morality," pp. 250, 253–54. See also above, pp. 204–5.

78. See above, Chapter 5: "The Church as the Person of Christ," n. 48.

79. See Gal. 3:27.

80. The triple offices in us differ in function from the triple offices in Christ. Christ employed the triple offices to reveal God. In us, the triple offices enable us to act as images of God.

81. See above, pp. 211–12.

82. See above, pp. 211–12.

83. See above, pp. 219–20.

84. See SR, p. 224.

85. See SR, p. 224.

86. See Lk. 23:46. See also above, Chapter 4: "The Incarnation," pp. 98–101.

87. See Jn. 15:13.

88. See SC, p. 193.

89. See SC, p. 186.

90. See DM, no. 8.

91. See above, p. 204.

92. See Mt. 18:23–35.

93. See Mt. 18:34.

94. See Mt. 18:35.

95. See Mt. 25:40.

96. See Mt. 25:45.

97. See SD, no. 30.

98. See LG, no. 10.

99. See Mk. 12:30–31.

100. See above, Chapter 2: "God's Love: Creation," pp. 36–37. See also above, Chapter 3: "Original Sin and the Providence of God," pp. 56–57. Further, see above, pp. 205–6.

101. See above, Chapter 1: "Man/Woman and God," p. 5.

102. See above, Chapter 3: "Original Sin and the Providence of God," pp. 60–62. See also above, Chapter 4: "The Incarnation," pp. 98–99.

103. See RH, no. 10.

104. Even if this grace has been given outside of Baptism, we still share in Christ's prophetic office in the same way as the baptized do. See above, Chapter 5: "The Church as the Person of Christ," pp. 124–29.

105. See SR, p. 245.

106. See Josef Ratzinger, *Instruction on Christian Freedom and Liberation, L'Osservatore Romano,* English Edition, vol. 19, no. 15 (April 14, 1986), no. 99.

107. See above, Chapter 4: "The Incarnation," pp. 101–3.

108. See Karol Wojtyla (Pope John Paul II), "A Fundamental Disquiet in All Human Existence" *(Theology of the Body* series, no. 28), *Blessed Are the Pure of Heart* (Boston: St. Paul Editions, 1981), p. 50.

109. See above, Chapter 4: "The Incarnation," pp. 102–4.

110. See Gen. 1:28.

111. See LE, no. 7.

112. See above, p. 212, and also above, diagram on p. 227, where almsgiving is related to the prophetic office. Further, see below, p. 233, where the point is made that all three offices operate together.

113. The kingly office enables us to express truth and love through our bodies. In other words, it restores the possibility of acting as integrated persons. There is a certain image of integration when someone is disciplining himself to do a difficult but unloving act, e.g., robbing a bank. Lacking a proper foundation, this "integration" usually turns the individual towards truth and love or disappears.

114. See Gal. 3:27.

115. The fruits are love, joy, peace, patience, kindness, goodness, faithfulness, gentleness, and self-control. See Gal. 5:22–23.

116. The corporal works of mercy are (1) feeding the hungry; (2) giving drink to the thirsty; (3) clothing the naked; (4) sheltering the homeless; (5)

visiting the sick; (6) visiting the imprisoned; and (7) burying the dead. Cf. Mt. 25:31–46. The spiritual works of mercy are (1) converting the sinner; (2) instructing the ignorant; (3) counseling the doubtful; (4) comforting the sorrowful; (5) bearing wrongs patiently; (6) forgiving injuries; and (7) praying for the living and the dead. These are traditional forms of Christian charity based on the teachings of Christ and the practice of the Church.

117. The beatitudes are (1) Blessed are the poor in spirit, for theirs is the kingdom of heaven. (2) Blessed are those who mourn, for they shall be comforted. (3) Blessed are the meek, for they shall inherit the earth. (4) Blessed are those who hunger and thirst for righteousness, for they shall be satisfied. (5) Blessed are the merciful, for they shall obtain mercy. (6) Blessed are the pure in heart, for they shall see God. (7) Blessed are the peacemakers, for they shall be called sons of God. (8) Blessed are those who are persecuted for righteousness' sake, for theirs is the kingdom of heaven. See Mt. 5:3–10.

118. See above, Chapter 2: "Original Sin and the Providence of God," pp. 36–38.

119. See above, Chapter 1: "Man/Woman and God," p. 1.

120. See FC, no. 11.

121. See above, pp. 223–25.

—— **9** ——
Morality

He will come again in glory to judge the living and the dead, and
His kingdom will have no end.

A. General Principles of Morality

Since we are made in the divine image and likeness, we should act as God acts, i.e., we should love as God loves. However, before we can even attempt to act as God acts, we need to know what God does and what He does not do. In the commandments, God has revealed how He acts and how He does not act. The commandments may seem challenging, but as images of God blessed with divine grace, we are capable of loving as God loves, i.e., we are capable of choosing to follow the commandments. However, it is also possible for us to choose not to act as God acts.

Since we are composed of body and soul, we are not simple beings as God is perfectly simple, i.e., without parts.[1] All God's acts are identified with His essence. However, every human act is the result of a highly complex process usually involving most, if not all, the powers of the human person, i.e., the powers of the mind, the will, and the body. Therefore, morality exists to study and to evaluate human acts in light of God's acts so that each of us may become more and more an image of God.[2]

Morality examines every human act by studying the act itself; its origins in the mind, the will, and the body; and its relationship to reality or truth. (See the accompanying diagram. A human act itself is studied by observing the deed, its circumstances, and its result. Simply stated, the deed is what was, is, or will be done. The circumstances include all the external factors that affect the act in any way. (External here is used as opposed to internal. The circumstances of the act do not include factors internal to the human actor. The internal condition of the actor is taken into consideration under the rubrics of knowledge, freedom, and conscience.)[3] The result is the actual outcome of the act. Every human act (i.e., a consciously chosen act) is defined by the deed, its circumstances, and its result.

ELEMENTS OF MORALITY

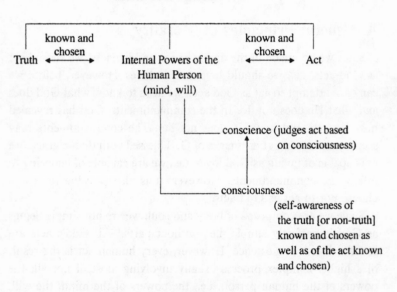

If someone is speeding on the freeway, he is breaking a civil law. However, this deed takes on a different character depending on its circumstances and its result. If someone is speeding because he wants to bring his wife to a hospital to deliver a baby, he probably would not receive a speeding ticket. The circumstances (pregnant wife in need of a hospital) and the result (bringing her to the hospital) change the character of the act. On the other hand, the same act under the same circumstances would change if the man were driving away from the hospital so that his wife would die in the birth process. Moralists examine human acts by studying the deeds, the circumstances, and the results.

As noted above,[4] studying the act itself does not take into account the internal dispositions of the actor. However, these are the most important aspects of morality because the study of morality should reveal how each of us can become more and more an image of God through God-like acts. As an image of God, each of us possesses a mind and a will. We can only become more and more like God by properly exercising our powers of thinking and choosing, i.e., by knowing the truth, and by loving God and other persons. (Similarly, we can only become less God-like if we know how we should act and still freely choose not to act like God.) Clearly, acts that do not engage our minds or our wills, i.e., acts that are not known or freely chosen, are not the objects of moral investigation. Thus, morality must separate the known and chosen acts from those that are not known and chosen.

Further, since to act as an image of God requires a knowledge of truth, a lack of knowledge of the truth will radically affect a particular act. Similarly, since acting as an image of God requires the use of free will, limitations on freedom will also affect human acts. Thus, an examination of what we know and choose (i.e., the truth we know and the freedom we have) is absolutely essential to the study of morality. In other words, morality must examine the internal dispositions of actors, i.e., of images of God.

There are innumerable acts occurring "in" us that we certainly do not choose, e.g., breathing, digestion. We may even lack specific knowledge about such acts. Acts occurring "in" us that we do not choose and sometimes do not even understand are sometimes called acts of a human, to distinguish them from consciously chosen acts, i.e., human acts. There are also innumerable acts occurring "to" us that we neither know nor choose prior to their occurrence, e.g., a car accident. Since these events that happen "in" us and "to" us do not involve our own minds and wills, they do not make us more God-like or less God-like. They are not the objects of moral investigation.

Although the distinction between human acts and acts of a human may seem obvious and unimportant, it is critical and assists in defining the scope of morality and thus the scope of human responsibility. For example, a sleep-walker is not responsible for his acts because he is asleep, i.e., he neither knows what he is doing nor does he choose any of his acts. In addition, people are not guilty of a moral transgression if an accident occurs. If someone were inadvertently to leave a car in neutral, parked on the downslope of a hill without the parking brake, morally he or she is not guilty or responsible for the damage the car, rolling down the hill, does to a second car parked farther down the hill. Even though the civil law does hold the owner of the first car responsible, there is no moral value attached to such an action because there was no known and chosen act.

As mentioned above,[5] in order to act as God acts, we need to know the truth. If we are ignorant of the truth, we cannot be expected to act in accordance with the truth! When we consider a particular course of action or even act on the basis of a falsehood we believe is true, we are not morally accountable for not acting on the basis of the truth. For example, many young people do not know that drunkenness is a sinful act. They do not know the truth about this act. How can they be expected to act on the basis of a truth they do not know? It would seem obvious that ignorance of the truth does alter the moral evaluation of the action.

However, there are different causes of ignorance. It is possible for someone not to know the truth about a particular act because he or she simply does not want to know the truth. For example, an individual might suspect that drunkenness or pre-marital sexual activity are acts not befitting an image of God. Still, such a person may dismiss his suspicions and never attempt to discover the truth because he or she wishes to drink excessively or to have pre-marital sex. This person does not want to know the truth because he or she does not want to know that drinking excessively or pre-marital sex is wrong. In this case, ignorance does not excuse the action. Rather, the unwillingness to investigate the truth shows a reluctance to come to know truth, i.e., to come to know God. In other words, ignorance is the fruit of one's own choice. This choice against truth itself is clearly a serious rejection of God Who is Truth.[6] In fact, the person who deliberately chooses not to know the truth often rejects God in a more profound way than the one who knows the truth and still chooses to act against it. At least in the second case, the person admits the truth even though he or she acts contrary to it.

In addition to the situation of someone suspecting the truth and not wanting to confirm his suspicions, it sometimes happens that those who are responsible for specialized knowledge actually are not aware of things they should know. For example, a surgeon who does not read the latest medical journals and is unaware of vital and life-saving developments within his own speciality is ignorant. However, this ignorance does not excuse his or her incompetent actions because it is his or her professional task to gain competence through the investigation of the truth. If he or she chooses not to learn what should be learned, he or she should change jobs. It might seem that such specialized knowledge is only required of professionals, but all of us have obligations to know certain truths. For example, those who drive cars can be held responsible for knowing the speed limits of the roads they drive. Similarly, those who drive boats can legitimately be expected to know the customs and rules of safe boating. Ignorance of such specialized knowledge does not excuse, but actually increases the gravity of any offense. If a policewoman stops a driver who is speeding, would the driver tell her that he did not know the speed limit? Almost everyone gives some other reason or makes no excuse at all. Ignorance, in this case, is even more serious than speeding.

If we are to act as God acts, we not only must know the truth, we also must freely choose our acts. Clearly, if our acts are not freely chosen, they are not God-like acts. Still, any particular act may not be chosen with complete freedom because internal factors, e.g., emotions, might limit our freedom. Our emotions can be stimulated either internally or externally. An external threat can cause an emotional reaction of extreme fear. This fear, in turn, influences our wills and limits our freedom. For example, if we are threatened with death unless we help in a robbery, many of us would help in the robbery. However, our participation in this act would not be what we would normally do. We would help in the robbery only under the threat of death, i.e., only out of fear. In this case, our freedom would be gravely impaired. The judgment made on our act of thievery in this case is completely different from that made on the act of thievery by someone who, without external threat, robs a bank. It is important to note that even in the case of grave external threat, we still retain our freedom. It is possible for us to refuse and to risk death.

Our emotions can also arise without any external agent attempting to stimulate them. In the case of a threat, the one threatening is attempting to arouse fear in us so that we would do whatever he or she wants. At other times, the things people say or do may be the occasion (not the direct cause) of an emotional reaction in us. However, in such cases, the people are not attempting to control us through our emotions. For example, at work, a man may become irritated at his employer even though the employer is not attempting to stimulate the emotion of anger. Anger is a very powerful emotion and can limit our freedom. If the employee reacts angrily with an outburst against his employer or fellow employees, it is probable that his actions were not completely free. It is important to notice that in this case, the employee reacted immediately to what irritated him.

However, it is possible to imagine an employee who is irritated by his employer, but who does not react immediately. Sometimes it happens that a person who is irritated nurses his anger. He consciously tries to become more and more angry by considering all the offenses he has suffered. He may think of ways to "get back" at the one who has offended him. Such a considered and studious build-up of anger is intended for revenge. Obviously, in this case, the emotion of anger is a means to an end, a means to carry out the plan to take revenge. The individual has consciously and freely chosen to become angry in order to accomplish the act he has planned. Clearly, consciously chosen anger does not limit one's freedom. Rather, the very emotion is the result of one's free choice. In evaluating the morality of an act, it is critical to distinguish between emotions and feelings that are aroused without the participation of our wills, and others that we have consciously chosen.

For an act to be a fully human act, the actor must have full knowledge of the act and choose it in complete freedom. In other words, if an act is to be fully human, the individual must know and choose the act in all of its aspects, i.e., the deed, its circumstances, and its result. It is possible and conceivable that a human being could know and freely choose an act that many would regard as seriously wrong. For example, it is possible for one person to murder another "in cold blood." The phrase, "in cold blood," indicates that the murderer is not in an emotional fever, i.e., that his freedom is not lessened by his emotions. While such a murder would in one sense be a fully human act, i.e., the murderer would undertake the act understanding and choosing it with full knowledge and complete freedom, most people would regard this as seriously wrong. On the other hand, there are acts that only a few people would regard as improper for a human being, while the majority would judge them to be either indifferent or even beneficial, e.g., dancing, smoking, or even contraception. (These three acts are quite different, and in no sense do the authors intend to suggest that they are of the same importance or nature.) Is majority opinion the norm to follow in choosing our behavior? The thoughts of the majority would seem inadequate. First, majority opinion fluctuates far too much to be a norm for human behavior. The majority in 1943 would not allow some things the majority in 1987 would allow. However, it cannot be that the same human acts are wrong in 1943, but right in 1987. Second, it is difficult to determine majority opinion. Are we supposed to take polls regularly? Third, it is necessary to define the group whose majority opinion would govern our behavior. Is it the majority of all parents? the majority of religious leaders? the majority of peer groups? Clearly, human behavior needs a clearer and firmer guide than majority opinion.

The firm and unchangeable guide for human behavior is God Himself, i.e., Truth. Since human beings are made in the image and likeness of God, they are not true to themselves, i.e., to their very humanity, unless they act as God acts. Thus, God is the ultimate norm. We should always measure our acts by the acts of God. Of course, without God's self-revelation in the Old Testament, but especially without *the* self-revelation of God, Jesus Christ, in the New Testament, it would be impossible for us to know how we should act. Before entering on a particular course of action, we should always ask ourselves: Would Jesus do this? If not, then we should not do it. If Christ would, then it is something we can or should do.

In the Old Testament, when God gave the ten commandments to Moses, God was giving him (and through him, all the Jews and the entire human race) a partial list of His acts as well as a longer list of the acts He does not do. In other words, God was saying to Moses: "These are some of My acts and the acts I do not do. Since you are My images, please do what I do because I want you to fulfill yourselves. Further, please do not do what I do not do because I do not want you to harm yourselves."

At times, we refer to the commandments as the law of God. However, this law differs radically from the civil laws, e.g., traffic rules, that govern many of the facets of our daily lives. Many civil laws can be changed according to the needs of the community, e.g., speed limits can be increased or decreased. Further, civil law is imposed on us by the community, i.e., by the government, under penalty of fines, imprisonment, etc. (Of course, it is always possible for us to choose not to follow civil law.) God's law differs from civil law in two ways. First, God's law is unchangeable because it refers to the way we are made. Every human being, whether born before or after the time of Christ, is made in the image and likeness of God. Therefore, every human being should act as God acts. Thus, God's law, i.e., the revelation of how He acts, is valid for people of all times and places. Second, God's law also differs from civil law because it is not imposed on us as civil law is. God does not impose penalties and punishments on us if we do not follow His law. Even the eternal suffering of hell is not a punishment imposed by God on those who sin. Rather, those in hell have freely chosen to reject the divine love. The souls in hell, like the devil and his angels, have consigned themselves to hell.[7] The other effects of sin are not punishments imposed by God.[8] Rather, they are the direct results of the sinful acts themselves.

The consequences of sin might be compared to an arsonist who burns himself while trying to start a fire. Normally, we would not say that his burns are a punishment. Rather, they are the direct consequences of his actions. Of course, if the arsonist is caught and convicted, the civil law will impose a punishment on him. The consequences of sin are like the arsonist's burns. Unlike the civil law which does impose additional punishments, e.g., imprisonment, on those who violate it, God does not impose additional punishments on the sinner. Sin "is a suicidal act."[9] Its first and most important consequences are suffered by the sinner himself.[10]

The divine laws reveal how God acts and therefore how human beings should act if they wish to be fully human. Since governments should promote the safety and welfare of their citizens, some provisions of divine law should be reflected in civil law. Even more clearly, a civil law should never contradict a divine precept. The divine law always promotes the welfare of human beings. A civil law that contradicts a divine law would not be promoting the welfare of those subject to it. Rather, such a law would cause untold harm to all those who lived by it.

God Himself, i.e., Truth, is the norm we should use for judging our own acts. We should strive to follow the norm because when we do, we are true to our very humanity, i.e., we act as God acts. If we fail to act as God acts, we harm ourselves.[11] We also hurt or wound God by rejecting His love.[12] Finally, in sinning, we often directly hurt other human beings, usually those who are very close to us, e.g., a spouse, our own children, parents, a brother or a sister, a close friend. Even when a sin does not injure another human being directly, it still hurts others indirectly because it weakens or destroys God's grace in us.[13] Since we are members of the Church and the Church draws its life from God's grace,[14] every sin harms the Church and its members. Further, every sin harms the relationship among all those who share God's grace, i.e., the relationship among the saints, the souls in purgatory, and those on earth who possess the divine life.[15] In addition, every sin affects even those who do not share the divine life because sin affects the relationship between the entire human family and God: "In other words, there is no sin, not even the most intimate and secret one, the most strictly individual one, that exclusively concerns the person committing it. With greater or lesser violence, with greater or lesser harm, every sin has repercussions on the entire ecclesial body and the whole human family."[16] The incidence of the Tower of Babel in Genesis illustrates the social aspect of sin.[17]

We need to apply the norm of divine behavior to our own acts. However, God's revelation of His own acts in the commandments is stated in general terms. On the other hand, our own acts are individual and specific. It is necessary, then, to relate the more general revelation of how God acts to our own specific acts. This task is performed by our consciences. Since judgments are made by our intellects and our consciences make judgments, the human conscience is a function of the human intellect. Our intellects make judgments by applying a standard norm to a particular thing, to an event, or to an act. The judgments of our consciences are made by applying the standard of divine behavior as revealed by God to our own acts, to our knowledge of them, and to our consent to them. Clearly, without the divine standard, no adequate judgment can be made. Through the self-awareness of our acts, our consciences know our acts. Further, human consciousness is aware of what we know, of what we choose. Supplied with the self-awareness of our acts, both those contemplated and those already in progress or completed, our consciences are able to compare our acts with the divine behavior. (See the diagram, "Elements of Morality," on p. 244.) Almost simultaneously, the conscience also evaluates the degree of knowledge and of freedom. With regard to a completed act or one in progress, the conscience evaluates the knowledge the actor has of the act and the degree of attention given to the act. If the individual did not pay much attention to the act or did not know the act was contrary to God's behavior, the evaluation of the act is different from what it otherwise would have been. Similarly, if the conscience judges that the will was unduly influenced by emotional or other factors so that the choice to engage in the act was not completely free, the judgment on the act is different. If the conscience is making a judgment about a contemplated act, usually the questions of knowledge and freedom do not play much of a role. Obviously, if the intellect is judging the act, it must have sufficient knowledge. Further, if the conscience is considering whether the person should engage in the act or not, the individual must possess the necessary freedom. However, it is not impossible that the questions of knowledge and of freedom would be factors even in the case of a contemplated act.

Therefore, on the basis of God's revelation of His own acts, and on the information provided by each individual's consciousness, the human conscience evaluates each human act (not acts of a human).[18] Further, the human conscience evaluates the knowledge the human actor has of a particular act, as well as the degree of freedom involved in the choice to undertake a particular act. (See the diagram, "Elements of Morality," on p. 244.) Clearly, the work of the conscience is very complex, but the judgments of our consciences can help us assess our strengths and weaknesses. Our consciences can show us the areas where we usually act as God acts, as well as other areas where we find it difficult to act as images of God.

Conscience can never change the reality that we are made in the image and likeness of God. By the same token, conscience does not determine the appropriate acts for human beings. Certain acts are good for us, and certain acts are harmful to us. They are either good or harmful because of the way God made us. God's revelation shows us how we should act as images of God. Our consciences apply the revelation of divine behavior, i.e., the way we should act, to specific and individual human acts. If our consciences could alter the way things are, we, in effect, would be on a par with the Creator. The Creator establishes the way things are; we do not. Certainly, our consciences do not establish reality!

We are always obligated to follow a certain conscience. Sometimes our consciences are unable to make a determination. We are not bound to follow an uncertain conscience. However, we should always seek certitude. Since a doubtful conscience can sometimes be attributed to a lack of knowledge, we are obligated to provide our consciences with the proper information so that they will not be doubtful or uncertain. Thus, as baptized Christians, we must exercise our baptismal prophetic office by accepting the revelation of God as taught by the hierarchical prophetic office.[19] On other occasions, a doubtful conscience results from an apparently insoluble conflict between two or more divine norms. Sometimes these apparent conflicts can be resolved by seeking advice from moralists.

We are also obligated to allow our consciences to function. In other words, we should not say, "I will not allow myself to consider whether or not God would do this particular act." For example, a businessman might remark that he is not concerned with morality, but only with profit. We should not suspend our consciences in this way. We should always allow them to function because they allow us to perceive beneficial acts so we can fulfill ourselves, as well as harmful (i.e., sinful) acts so that we can avoid them. If we do not allow our consciences to function, we can seriously harm ourselves or at least not fulfill ourselves as we might.

If we inform consciences properly and allow them to function, they will not only be able to judge whether or not an act is in accordance with divine behavior, they will also be able to recognize how close our God-like acts are to God and how much our un-God-like acts vary from divine behavior. Knowing how close our God-like actions are to divine behavior will help each of us know what we need to do to become more and more God-like. In other words, our consciences can help us fulfill ourselves as images of God.

Similarly, it is very important to know how un-God-like particular actions might be. We need to know how seriously we have harmed ourselves. In other words, we need to know whether a particular un-God-like act is a mortal or venial sin. A mortal sin destroys the life of God, i.e., grace, in us. A mortal sin is an act (1) directly contrary to the divine actions (2) that a person chooses in complete freedom (3) with full knowledge. Full knowledge implies that the person choosing the act realizes, at the moment the act is chosen, that it is directly contrary to the divine behavior. Thus, in some sense, every mortal sin directly contradicts love because God is Love.[20] A venial sin is a lesser sin and weakens, but does not destroy, the life of God in us. A venial sin is certainly an un-God-like act, but it is not a mortal sin because one, two, or three of the criteria for a mortal sin is (are) not present. A venial sin is an act not directly contrary to God's actions; and/or it may be an act not chosen with complete freedom; and/or it may be an act not chosen with full knowledge. For example, the act of speaking sharply to a wife is not as serious as the act of adultery. Further, the man who strikes a fellow worker in the heat of anger is not choosing the action in complete freedom. On the other hand, the worker who over a long period of time systematically embezzles funds from the company has probably chosen the act in complete freedom. The embezzlement is a much more serious sin than the striking of a fellow employee in anger because of the difference in the degree of freedom. Finally, the high school student who for the first time drinks to excess may well plead that he or she did not realize that drunkenness was an un-God-like act. However, a professor of moral theology who performs the same act cannot plead that he did so without knowledge that drunkenness was an un-God-like act. (These examples, of course, are over-simplified: no human act is as straightforward as presented here.)

One final note is critical: we should always accept the judgments of our consciences at the time an act is contemplated or actually committed. In other words, we cannot look back at past actions and judge that they were flawed because of new knowledge. For example, a teenager may decide to drink too much alcohol. At the time, he may not realize this is an un-God-like act. Later, he may discover that drunkenness is sinful. However, he cannot judge his past action on the basis of his new knowledge. The judgment about one's knowledge, freedom, and the nature of a particular act is made at the time the act is contemplated or actually committed. We cannot make moral judgments about past actions founded on knowledge not known at the time of the act.

B. Commandments

God gave Moses the ten commandments on Mount Sinai.[21] The first three commandments show us how God loves Himself and therefore how we should love God. The other seven commandments reveal what God does do and what God does not do towards us and others. Thus, they show us how we should love ourselves[22] and others. Through the ten commandments, God invites us, as His images, to act as He acts.

1. THE FIRST COMMANDMENT

The first commandment reads: "I am the Lord your God. . . . You shall have no other gods before me."[23] Through this commandment, God reveals that He recognizes Himself as the uncaused cause.[24] By inviting all human beings to worship only Him, God shows us that He knows Himself as the only being deserving of worship. In other words, He recognizes Himself as the Creator and therefore the only being to Whom worship is owed.

Since worship implies a knowledge of God and a choice to offer prayer, sacrifice, and adoration to God, the first commandment asks us to love God, i.e., to give ourselves to Him through an act of our wills founded on our knowledge of Him. In other words, this commandment invites us to enter a communion with God. (Of course, such a communion with God Who is transcendent[25] would be impossible without His grace.)[26] We are then invited to express this act of love through bodily acts, i.e., prayers, liturgies, and rituals. In these practices, we make use of the things God has created (e.g., candles, incense) as aids in our worship. We also employ works of human art (e.g., statues, vestments, music, painting) to give expression to our worship, i.e., our love, of God. The practice of asking the intercession of the saints does not violate the first commandment. As the Church constantly teaches, we should *worship* God alone. However, we are also called to *venerate*, or honor, the saints.[27]

Obviously, it is possible not to worship God through prayer, sacrifice, and adoration. Even if someone is offering worship to God externally, e.g., saying prayers, it is possible that the person is not paying proper attention to his prayers. Without an internal raising of the mind and heart to God, we do not worship God and we do not act as images of God. We also fail to worship God when we test God by challenging Him to work a miracle. A subtle manifestation of this failure to love God occurs when a person needlessly exposes himself to danger, trusting that God will protect him. Sacrilege, the violation of something or someone set aside for God and the worship of God, is a failure to love God. Of course, simony, the buying and selling of sacred things, e.g., a sacrament, is a failure to observe the first commandment.[28] Further, it is possible to give worship to someone or something other than God. We can invest things with powers appropriate only to God, e.g., sometimes people genuinely believe that someone gazing into a crystal ball can reveal their future to them. The same phenomenon occurs when people believe that external expressions of adoration are sufficient in themselves. Some would believe, for example, that lighting a votive candle automatically obtains whatever the person desires. In addition, we fail to worship God when we try to bargain with Him, i.e., when we only offer Him our worship or love on the condition that He answer our prayers positively. Finally, it is possible to put Satan in the place of God.

2. THE SECOND COMMANDMENT

The second commandment reads: "You shall not take the name of the Lord your God in vain."[29] A personal name designates the person. It stands for the person. The way we use a personal name indicates what we think of that person. Thus, the second commandment, by revealing that God regards His own name as holy and sacred, shows that God recognizes that He is holy, i.e., transcendent and perfect, deserving of adoration and reverence.[30] The second commandment invites all human beings to recognize the sacredness of the divine name because God Himself is all-perfect and all-transcendent.

The second commandment invites us to accept the divine transcendence. In other words, it invites us to come to know God and to choose, on the basis of that knowledge, to use our tongues to give praise to God. We praise God in His transcendence by praising His name because His name designates His personal being. In other words, the second commandment, as the first, invites us to love God as He loves Himself and to express that love through our bodily actions. The praise we give God, especially through words and songs, fulfills the second commandment.

Of course, the opposite is also true. When we misuse the divine name, we are not praising God. In a real sense, we are expressing our wish to misuse God or even to do violence to Him, if such a thing were possible. We misuse the divine name when we take a vow or an oath we do not mean. Blaspheming and cursing are also other ways of misusing the holy name of God. (Cursing things, plants, and animals is quite different from cursing people. The cursing of non-persons may be an act contrary to divine behavior, if it is an act of impatience or unjustified anger, acts that God does not do.)

3. THE THIRD COMMANDMENT

The third commandment reads: "Remember the sabbath day, to keep it holy."[31] Since holy means transcendent and God is the One Who is transcendent,[32] to keep something holy means to give it to God. In this commandment, God reveals His awareness that He is Lord of time. He recognizes that He, as the Creator, has legitimate dominion over time. He asks us to recognize the same reality by dedicating one day to Him. This dedication of one day symbolizes our recognition of His legitimate governance over all time. Clearly, it also gives us a chance to fulfill the first commandment by worshiping God.

We fulfill the third commandment by attending Mass on Sunday and by avoiding work. Sunday should indeed be a day of rest, i.e., difficult, tiring physical labor should be avoided. However, if cutting the grass is recreation for someone who works forty hours or more a week in an office, it would hardly seem against the third commandment for him to mow the lawn. On the other hand, unless it were absolutely necessary, such an executive should avoid going to the office on Sunday because he would be doing his usual work on the day set aside to do the work of God (Mass and other prayers) and to relax. Of course, those whose jobs are vital to society (e.g., policemen, firemen) may work on Sunday. Others may work at their normal jobs if they have no alternative other than to lose their jobs (e.g., sales personnel in shopping malls open on Sunday). Still, everything

must be done to keep Sunday as the Lord's day both by individuals
and by society.

4. THE FOURTH COMMANDMENT

The fourth commandment reads: "Honor your father and your
mother."[33] In this commandment and the six that follow it, God
reveals how He loves us and others. He invites us to love ourselves
and others the way He loves us and others. The fourth commandment reveals that God loves those who give life to new persons and/
or who care for them. Through the fourth commandment, God invites us to love those who gave us life as He loves them.

Quite simply, this commandment clearly invites all of us to do
what our parents ask while we are growing up. It also asks adult
children to "honor" their parents, i.e., to give respect to those who
gave them life and who raised them. As children mature and become
adults, they are no longer expected to do everything their parents
ask. However, adult children are asked to love their parents, i.e., to
give themselves to their parents by taking care of their physical and
spiritual needs. Children should love their parents even after the
parents have died. The love of children for deceased parents is expressed in many ways, but especially by praying for them.[34]

Since love is always a mutual relationship between at least two
persons and "honor" implies love, the fourth commandment
presumes that parents love their children. In other words, this commandment invites parents to care for their children by providing the
physical, educational, and spiritual necessities of life. If parents love
their children, they will never ask their children to do something that
is not God-like or that is harmful to them. Further, as their children
grow and become adults, loving parents will rejoice that their children are able to make decisions on their own and no longer expect
the parents to tell them what to do. With adult children, loving
parents will allow their children to make their own choices and to
take responsibility for these decisions. Thus, for example, loving
Catholic parents should not feel guilty if one or more of their adult
children do not practice the Catholic faith. Parents of adult children

have a role similar to *the* parent *par excellence,* God Himself. God is our loving parent Who reveals the truth to us and yet allows us to think and to choose for ourselves. Even when we sin, He does not interfere. He is a true parent, a parent Who allows His mature children to act on their own and to take responsibility for their actions even when He realizes the actions are harmful in some way.

5. THE FIFTH COMMANDMENT

The fifth commandment reads: "You shall not kill."[35] In this commandment, God reveals that He cares for all the persons He has created. In the words of Pope John Paul II, God reveals that when He gives life, "it is forever."[36] As noted above,[37] the gift of life and the gift of love cannot be separated. Clearly, God loves, i.e., cares for and protects, all the persons He has created. As the book of Wisdom reveals, "Thou [God] lovest all things that exist and hast loathing for none of the things which Thou hast made."[38] God's protective love shields created persons from true and lasting harm. Christ confirmed God's protective care revealed in the fifth commandment when He assured His disciples that they were worth more than the birds of the air[39] and when He promised them that not a hair on their heads would be harmed.[40] Through this commandment, God invites each of us to protect and to care for ourselves and for all other human beings.[41]

The fifth commandment invites us to care for ourselves and others especially by respecting and caring for the human body: our own bodies and the bodies of others. Since every human is immortal,[42] one's total destruction is impossible. Who would ask another to refrain from doing the impossible? It would be a meaningless request. The fifth commandment is not meaningless! Thus, "You shall not kill" cannot refer to the total destruction of the human person. Rather, the fifth commandment must ask us not to do something that we, in fact, could do. Human beings do die, i.e., their bodies cease to have life while their souls continue to live. Therefore, it is possible for us to inflict death, i.e., to take the life of the body. Obviously, the fifth commandment is an invitation to us not to impose death (the taking of the life of the body) on any innocent human being. Positively, the fifth commandment invites every human to respect and to care for all living human bodies.

The human body is the expression of the human person. Our bodies are part of the gift of life from God. Our bodies are not machines that we own and use. Rather, as life itself, they are a gift from God that we are invited to care for and to protect as God cares for and protects all our lives.[43] Clearly, "no man ever hates his own flesh, but nourishes it and cherishes it."[44] It is our own care and concern for our own flesh and blood that should help us realize that every other human body has the same dignity and value that our own bodies have.[45]

We should cherish our own bodies, but when we indulge the bodily desires to excess, we harm them. For example, if we eat or drink to excess, i.e., if we indulge in gluttony or drunkenness, we harm our bodies. Further, since when we eat or drink to excess we do not act as images of God, we also harm ourselves spiritually.

On other occasions, we may seek to satisfy our sexual desires. However, when sexual pleasure becomes a primary goal of our activity, we actually harm ourselves spiritually and sometimes physically. For example, in seeking sexual pleasure without responsibility, we may choose to have a tubal ligation (for women) or a vasectomy (for men). Such a medical procedure is an attempt to destroy a major, healthy, functioning bodily process, i.e., human fertility. Such an attempt is harmful to us because it is an attack on our own bodies, which are part of our very lives. An attack on a human body is an attack on a human person. What we do to our bodies, we do to our very persons. Further, tubal ligations and vasectomies harm us because when we choose to undergo these procedures, we are not acting as God acts. In choosing sterilization, we are not acting as images of God Who cares for and protects all living human bodies. In fact, sterilization procedures actually imply that God did not create the human body properly and does not really care for our bodies.[46] Similarly, many contraceptive devices are attacks on our bodies. Most contraceptives (e.g., the pill and barrier devices) clearly alter (and therefore harm, in the sense that the bodily process does not function as it should) a major, healthy, functioning part of the body.[47] Obviously, when we use contraceptives, we do not act as God acts because we do not care for our own bodies. We also suggest that God did not create us as He should have.

The use of drugs is also an attack on the body. The harm done to the body through drug dependency is clear to all. However, in addition, by using drugs, we harm ourselves spiritually because we fail to care for our bodies as God does, i.e., as images of God should.

Of course, the most devastating act against our own bodies and ourselves is suicide. In committing suicide, we obviously reject the invitation from God: "You shall not kill." Such an act, if accomplished, not only destroys our life on earth, it also is a spiritual attack on ourselves. Through suicide, we fail to act as God acts because we do not love ourselves as God loves us. (Many suicide victims lack either knowledge or complete freedom when they commit suicide and thus are not responsible for their acts.)

As mentioned above,[48] not only should we respect our own bodies, we should also respect other living human bodies because God loves and cares for all human beings (body and soul). We are invited to act charitably towards all. God invites us never to harm or to take innocent human life. For example, we are asked not to strike or molest others. The fifth commandment invites us not to rape or maim others. Further, the fifth commandment invites us never to kill an unborn child. Abortion is a heinous crime because it is the taking of an absolutely innocent life. Even when the physical health of the mother is somehow threatened by a pregnancy, it is always a terribly unloving act to take the life of an unborn child.[49] By the same token, the destruction of human embryos conceived in a test tube is a radical failure to love these little children.[50]

Further, euthanasia, the direct taking of an innocent human life in order to end suffering from illness or disease,[51] demonstrates an unwillingness to love as God loves. Clearly, we must do everything possible to alleviate and lessen the suffering from sickness. However, we may never directly take a life in order to end suffering. In effect, we are robbing the suffering person of an opportunity to share in the cross of Christ. Those who suffer have a chance to "repay the infinite price of the passion and death of Christ."⁵² To quote St. Paul, those who suffer can "complete what is lacking in Christ's afflictions."⁵³ In other words, God invites us through suffering to come close to Christ, i.e., to Himself. Is it an act of love to deprive someone of that opportunity?

In effect, euthanasia betrays a lack of confidence in the mercy of God. The person who commits euthanasia does not trust that God is strengthening the one who is suffering, even in the midst of pain. The individual who takes the life of a suffering person might be compared to St. Peter when he tried to persuade Christ to forgo His passion. Christ answered Peter sharply, "Get behind me, Satan. For you are not on the side of God, but of men."⁵⁴ In tempting Christ, St. Peter used Satan's argument because St. Peter was suggesting that God the Father would not watch over Christ in the midst of suffering. It is Satan's original lie first given in the garden of Eden: God does not care about you!⁵⁵

While the fifth commandment does ask us to love other people and to have a respect for their lives, it does not envision a totally pacifist stance. If someone attacks us, we have a right, even a duty, to defend ourselves. Self-defense is an expression of the proper respect we should have for our own lives. Thus, we may use adequate measures to defend ourselves and those who depend on us (spouses, children). By extension, a nation has a right to defend its citizens. Clearly, a nation may fight an aggressor. In such a war, soldiers may take the lives of the enemy soldiers. However, the war must be just, i.e., the nation fighting the war must be in the position of defending its citizenry against an aggressor or defending a friendly nation's people against an aggressor. In any event, the lives of non-combatants may never be taken or even threatened.⁵⁶

Positively, the fifth commandment invites us to care for our bodies and the bodies of others. However, we cannot care for the human body without a knowledge of it. Thus, it is the fifth commandment that asks us to develop a knowledge about ourselves and to apply that knowledge to benefit ourselves and others. Therefore, medical science and medical care fall under the fifth commandment. On occasion, difficulties arise in the application of medical knowledge to individual situations.

Sometimes doctors and others in the medical field will make a medical decision on a basis other than bodily health. For example, it is fairly common for Down's syndrome children to have a minor defect that makes it impossible for them to be nourished. (Of course, this condition is fatal if not repaired through routine surgery.) Some doctors suggest to the parents that the required surgery not be performed on these children. Clearly, the basis for such a recommendation is not the bodily health of the child because the child will die if the recommendation is followed. The recommendation is made on the basis of the assumed lack of "quality of life" for the Down's syndrome child. However, decisions about appropriate medical treatment must be made on the basis of bodily health, not on the basis of mental deficiencies or other conditions not related to bodily health. Still, doctors may legitimately decide not to treat a particular problem if the person is expected to die from another much more serious health problem (e.g., transfusions are not often given to patients who are dying of cancer). Yet every reasonable effort should be made to make patients comfortable.

It also happens that food and drink are sometimes not given intravenously to someone who is incapable of eating or drinking. However, since food and drink are not medicine, they should not be withheld even if the means of giving these is medical.

Competent patients and the guardian(s) of incompetent patients are sometimes faced with decisions on extraordinary medical procedures, e.g., heart transplants. We are never compelled to undergo a high-risk, expensive procedure with doubtful results that involves much discomfort or even bodily disfigurement. We *may* choose to undergo such treatment, but we are not obliged to submit to it.

There are some medical procedures that harm the body but also have beneficial bodily effects. Such procedures may be done if they conform to the principle of the double effect. The double-effect principle has four necessary conditions: (1) the act contemplated must be morally good or indifferent; (2) the acting person intends only the good effect and foresees, but does not intend, the evil; (3) the evil effect cannot be the means of achieving the good effect (the end does not justify the means); and (4) there must be proportionately grave reason for permitting the evil effect. Thus, applying the principle of the double effect, doctors may remove a cancerous uterus and do many other similar procedures.[57]

As noted above,[58] in inviting us to take care of ourselves, the fifth commandment also asks us to come to know ourselves. We know ourselves by studying our bodies, the expression of our persons. Each living, human body reveals a unique human person. The body fully expresses the person when it participates in the most proper (God-like) activity of the human being: love. The bodily expression of love occurs through our sexual powers. Thus, the study of our own sexual powers allows us to come to know ourselves. This study is undertaken by the teachers and students in the Natural Family Planning movement (NFP). NFP is far more than simply a natural method for spacing children. It should reveal the mysterious being of each human being who engages in the study of it![59]

6. THE SIXTH COMMANDMENT

The sixth commandment reads: "You shall not commit adultery."[60] In this commandment, God reveals that He does not treat people as things to be used. Rather, He reveals that He loves all people. In other words, God reveals that He observes the personalistic norm.[61] Not only does God love all created people, He also loves Himself as a personal being. Thus, this commandment reveals that we, as images of God, are called to love others as well as ourselves. Thus, we should not treat others or ourselves as things to be used, manipulated, or owned.

Since human beings are enfleshed spirits or spiritualized bodies,[62] loving them includes a love and respect for their bodies. Thus, love of self includes an appreciation of the body as the expression of the self, i.e., of the person. If we love ourselves as God loves Himself, we will not use or manipulate our own bodies. We will not treat them as things because to treat them as things is to treat ourselves as things. For example, prostitution and surrogate motherhood treat the body as something to be rented. We rent things, not people. Thus, those who engage in prostitution and surrogate motherhood treat themselves as things. They do not love themselves as images of God should.

While masturbation and homosexual acts do not involve the renting of our bodies, still, they are attempts to achieve sexual pleasure by stimulating the body. In other words, in these acts, we use our bodies to achieve sexual pleasure. The body becomes a kind of mechanism, almost like a drug, to achieve a certain "high." Clearly, such acts involve a use of our bodies. These acts are not God-like because through them we treat our bodies as things to be used. Through these acts, we do not love ourselves as we should.[63] (In the expression of love between husband and wife, the couple does not use their bodies because they are not primarily seeking a sexual "high." Rather, they seek to give themselves to each other. If a couple were to seek only sexual pleasure, they would indeed be using their bodies.)[64]

Not only are we called to love ourselves as God loves Himself, we are also called to love others as God loves them. We are called to give ourselves to others through a choice (will-act) that is permanent and without limit. In other words, we are called to form a *communion of persons* with others. First and foremost, we are invited to form a familial *communion of persons*.[65] Both pre-marital sex and adultery are acts that violate the familial *communion of persons*. In pre-marital sex, the couple tries to give themselves in and through their bodies without first choosing to give themselves to each other in and through their wills, i.e., they have not publicly exchanged the marriage vows.[66] Since love is primarily an act of the will, i.e., a choice to give oneself to another,[67] the pre-marital couple does not love each other. Since they are not loving each other, they are using each other. They are treating each other as things to be used. An adulterer also treats his spouse as a thing to be used because he does not love the spouse. The adulterer does not love his spouse because he takes back his supposedly (or initially intended) permanent and limitless self-donation and presumes to bestow this self-donation on someone else.

Since the adulterer does not love his spouse, the spouse is treated as a thing.[68]

As mentioned above,[69] contraception and sterilization within the family are violations of familial love as well as of the human body. These acts are the result of a refusal to give oneself fully. The husband and wife who contracept or sterilize themselves refuse to give their life-giving potential to one another. They limit their gift and thus they do not love.[70] In addition, since life is inseparable from love,[71] they do not love because they say "no" to life. They use each other. It is clear that parents who abort their child drastically limit their self-gift to each other and radically say "no" to life.[72] They do not love one another. Rather, they use one another. Thus, it is clear that abortion is a violation of familial love as well as an unspeakable crime against the child who is treated as a product that can be destroyed by its owners.[73]

We also fail to love others as God loves them through artificial fertilization (test-tube babies) and artificial insemination. When a couple attempts to give life outside the bodily expression of love, they are not loving each other. Life and love are inseparable.[74] The couple attempting artificial fertilization or artificial insemination reduces the gift of life to a biological event. By doing so, they make what should be a bodily gift of love a mere biological event. In other words, through artificial fertilization or artificial insemination, the couple denies that the human body is an expression of personal love.[75] For them, the body becomes a machine. They treat their bodies as things to be used. Further, the couple attempting artificial fertilization or artificial insemination also fails to love the child, who is treated only as a product, a thing. No child should ever be treated as a thing or a product. Rather, the child should be loved.[76]

7. THE SEVENTH COMMANDMENT

The seventh commandment reads: "You shall not steal."[77] In this commandment, God reveals that He has dominion over the things of the world and that He wishes that we, as His images, should have dominion over things. This commandment confirms the mandate in

Genesis, "Fill the earth and subdue it," because this commandment, as the mandate, invites us to have a dominion over the things of the world.[78] As God allows each of us to share in His governance over the world of things, so we should allow each other to have dominion over the things of the earth. In other words, we should not try to extend our dominion (ownership) over things that another person owns.

Since the seventh commandment reconfirms the mandate in Genesis to fill the earth and subdue it, this commandment also invites us to unite in a worker *communion of persons.*[79] In the worker *communion of persons,* every human being is united in love with all other human beings. This union of love assures each member, i.e., all human beings, that he or she will be treated with justice. (In the seventh commandment, the just rights and privileges that earthly images of God possess are symbolized by the right of private property.) Who would deprive a loved one of fundamental human rights? In other words, who would act unjustly towards someone they love? Justice is subsumed under love.[80]

8. THE EIGHTH COMMANDMENT

The eighth commandment reads: "You shall not bear false witness against your neighbor."[81] In this commandment, God reveals that He is Truth. Since God loves Himself, and He is Truth, He loves Truth. As images of God, we are images of Truth, and we should love ourselves and others as images of Truth. In other words, we should love truth. We do not love truth when we lie to ourselves or to others.

However, some truths, by their very nature, are to be known only by one or two people. When such truths are made more widely known, truth is violated because the exclusivity of the particular truth is violated. In effect, a lie is told: "This truth is for everyone." For example, in disclosing a secret entrusted to us, we violate truth because we violate the exclusivity of that truth. Similarly, we often lie when we reveal something that tarnishes another's reputation. The revelation of a failing in another is a lie when it leads to a lessening of their reputation. The failing is often taken to mean that the entire reputation of the one attacked is compromised by the failing (which is often not the case) or that the entire reputation of the one attacked is false because there are other hidden failings (which usually is not true). In effect, then, the revelation of the failing resulted in others believing a falsehood. Clearly, unless absolutely necessary, we should not reveal others' faults. (It may be necessary in certain circumstances to reveal a failing, e.g., in a courtroom, when it is necessary to defend oneself.)

It should be noted that the news media, entertainment industry, and advertising agencies bear an especially grave responsibility to reveal the truth because of their vast influence.

9. THE NINTH COMMANDMENT

The ninth commandment reads: "You shall not covet your neighbor's wife."[82] To covet means to desire possession of someone or something. In this commandment, God reveals that He does not wish to possess us. In other words, God gives us the freedom to love. The ninth commandment shows us that He does not want to force people to love Him. Through this commandment, God reveals that He does not wish to destroy human freedom (making it impossible to sin) just so all people would be with Him. In other words, God does not wish to make those who do not love Him into things so that He can possess them. A stunning example of God's respect for human freedom is found at the annunciation, where the Angel Gabriel waited for Mary's freely given response to his announcement.[83]

As images of God, we are called not to covet others, i.e., not even to think about them as things to be possessed. In other words, we are called to recognize human freedom in others. We should always recognize that people have the freedom to respond or not to respond to our offer of love. However, it is often tempting, at least in thought, not to grant human freedom to others. It is often much more enticing to imagine that we control others so that they will do what we want. As Christ said, "Everyone who looks at a woman lustfully has already committed adultery with her in his heart."[84] With these words, Christ asked us not to think of others as objects for our possession. Obviously, lustful thoughts would fall under the ninth commandment.

10. THE TENTH COMMANDMENT

The tenth commandment reads: "You shall not covet your neighbor's house . . . or his manservant, or his maidservant, or his ox, or anything that is your neighbor's."[85] To covet means to desire possession of someone or something. Thus, in this commandment, God reveals that He does not wish to possess all things. Rather, He is pleased that He gave us the right to possess the things of creation.[86]

As images of God, the tenth commandment asks us to respect, even in our thoughts, the right of all human beings to possess and to own the things of this world. Thus, this commandment, like the seventh commandment, confirms God's invitation in Genesis to form a worker *communion of persons.*[87] Therefore, it asks us to respect, even in our thoughts, all the rights of every earthly image of God. The seventh commandment refers to acts, whereas the tenth refers to thoughts. Just as we can fail to act as images of God when we attack the familial *communion of persons* in thought (by acting contrary to the ninth commandment), so we fail to act as images of God when we attack the worker *communion of persons* in thought (by acting contrary to the tenth commandment).

C. Conclusion

In each of the commandments, God reveals how He acts. Thus, He shows us how we should act. As images of God blessed with divine grace, we are empowered to act as He acts. When we fail to act as He acts, we sin. Usually, the failure to act as He acts can be traced to one of the seven capital sins: pride, covetousness, lust, anger, gluttony, envy, and sloth. These are called capital sins because it is from these sins that most other sins flow. Pride is the first capital sin because in some sense, every sin is a sin of pride. When we sin, we presume to "define good and evil," i.e., we presume to decide what is best for us and, at least implicitly, to reject God as a loving Father Who wants only what is best for us, His children.[88] The remaining six capital sins all refer to bodily desires and emotions. We are often inclined to sin because we fail to "orchestrate" our bodily desires and emotions as we should. In other words, we fail to exercise kingly self-control.[89]However, through grace and the triple offices of Christ (especially His kingly office) that we share through grace, it is always possible for us to act as Christ would act. It may not be easy, but it is possible. The alternative is suicide. Let us not destroy ourselves! Rather, let us act as images of God and fulfill ourselves in this life and most fully in the life to come!

FOR REFLECTION

A. What is a human act?

B. What are the elements of a moral decision?

C. How do the commandments reveal what God does and what we should do as images of God?

NOTES

1. See above, Chapter 1: "Man/Woman and God," p. 5.

2. See above, Chapter 2: "God's Love: Creation," pp. 36–37.

3. See below, pp. 244–48, 251–55.

4. See above, p. 244.

5. See above, p. 245.

6. See above, Chapter 1: "Man/Woman and God," p. 5.

7. See above, Chapter 2: "God's Love: Creation," p. 29.

8. The other effects of original sin include the wounding of our minds, wills, and bodies. See above, Chapter 3: "Original Sin and the Providence of God," p. 55. Other sins cause similar wounds. See above, Chapter 2: "God's Love: Creation," pp. 36–37.

9. See RP, no. 15. See also above, Chapter 2: "God's Love: Creation," pp.

36–37. In addition, see above, Chapter 3: "Original Sin and the Providence of God," p. 55.

10. See RP, no. 16.

11. See above, pp. 249–51.

12. See above, Chapter 1: "Man/Woman and God," pp. 9–10. See also above, Chapter 3: "Original Sin and the Providence of God," n. 88.

13. See above, Chapter 8: "Grace," pp. 209, 234–35.

14. See above, Chapter 5: "The Church as the Person of Christ," pp. 120–23. See also above, Chapter 8: "Grace," p. 208.

15. See above, Chapter 8: "Grace," pp. 208–16.

16. See RP, no. 16.

17. See Gen. 11:1–9. See also above, Chapter 3: "Original Sin and the Providence of God," pp. 69–71. For Pope John Paul's discussion of the Tower of Babel and its relationship to sin, see RP, no. 13–14.

18. See above, pp. 244–46.

19. For a discussion of dissent, see above, Chapter 5: "The Church as the Person of Christ," pp. 130–34.

20. See above, Chapter 1: "Man/Woman and God," p. 5.

21. See Ex. 20:2–17. See also Deut. 5:6–21.

22. We can love ourselves. See above, Chapter 8: "Grace," p. 219.

23. See Ex. 20:2–3. See also Deut. 5:6–7.

24. See above, Chapter 1: "Man/Woman and God," pp. 3–5.

25. See above, Chapter 1: "Man/Woman and God," p. 10.

26. See above, Chapter 2: "God's Love: Creation," pp. 33–36. See also above, Chapter 8: Grace, pp. 204–5.

27. See the discussion of the communion of saints above, Chapter 8: "Grace," pp. 210–16.

28. Simony does not occur when someone makes the usual offering for a Mass or a Baptism. These are not payments for the Mass or the sacrament. Rather, they are offered by the faithful to defray the expenses connected with the Mass or the Baptism and for the support of the priest or deacon. The priest or deacon would offer the Mass or celebrate the Baptism even if the offering were not made.

29. See Ex. 20:7. See also Deut. 5:11.

30. See above, Chapter 1: "Man/Woman and God," pp. 6, 10.

31. See Ex. 20:8. Cf. Deut. 5:12.

32. See above, Chapter 1: "Man/Woman and God," p. 10.

33. See Ex. 20:12. See also Deut. 5:16.

34. See above, Chapter 8: "Grace," pp. 210–11.

35. See Ex. 20:13. See also Deut. 5:17.

36. See Karol Wojtyla (Pope John Paul II), "Human Life Is the Gift of God" (Homily of His Holiness at the Mass at the Capitol Mall on October 7, 1979), *The Pope in America* (St. Paul: The Wanderer Press, 1979), p. 79.

37. See above, Chapter 2: "God's Love: Creation," p. 41. See also above, Chapter 8: "Grace," p. 205.

38. See Wis. 11:24.

39. See Mt. 6:26.

40. See Lk. 21:18.

41. The fifth commandment does not pertain to angels because angels, lacking a body, cannot die. Thus, they cannot be killed. See the next paragraph, below.

42. See above, Chapter 2: "God's Love: Creation," p. 34.

43. See above, Chapter 2: "God's Love: Creation," p. 37–41.

44. See Eph. 5:29.

45. For a similar argument, see above, Chapter 2: "God's Love: Creation," pp. 41–43.

46. Compare the temptations of Adam and Eve, and Christ by Satan. See above, Chapter 3: "Original Sin and the Providence of God," pp. 60–62. See also above, Chapter 4: "The Incarnation," pp. 94–99. The devil suggested at the very dawn of creation that God really did not care for us.

47. The acts contrary to the fifth commandment involve harming the human body. Sterilization and contraception do harm the body and fall under the fifth commandment. Misuses of the human body (e.g., prostitution, masturbation), as opposed to acts that harm it, fall under the sixth commandment. In other words, the acts contrary to Pope John Paul's theology of the body are divided between the fifth and sixth commandments. Further, sterilization and contraception also fall under the sixth commandment (which embodies John Paul's theology of the family) because they also attack familial love. See below, pp. 264–67. See also, *Covenant*, pp. 54–56. In addition, see *Wonder*, pp. 63–66. For the theology of the body and of the family, see Richard M. Hogan and John M. LeVoir, "Is NFP Good?," IRNFP, vol. 9, no. 3 (Fall 1985), pp. 220–46. See also Richard M. Hogan, "A Theology of the Body: A Commentary on the Audiences of Pope John Paul II from September 5, 1979, to May 6, 1981," *Fidelity*, vol. 1, no. 1 (December 1981), pp. 10–15, 24–27.

48. See above, p. 260.

49. See *Covenant*, pp. 53–54. See also *Wonder*, p. 66.

50. See Richard M. Hogan and John M. LeVoir, "Medical Ethics and the Human Body," no. 4, *Catholic Bulletin*, vol. 77, no. 18 (May 3, 1987), p. 6.

51. We are speaking here of the direct taking of a human life. Turning off a machine that is assisting someone to breathe or to perform some other

bodily function is not the direct taking of human life. Injecting someone with poison would be.

52. See SD, no. 21.

53. See Col. 1:24.

54. See Mk. 8:33.

55. See above, Chapter 3: "Original Sin and the Providence of God," pp. 60–62.

56. Clearly, nuclear power has changed the nature of war. Still, a nation has the right to defend itself and to possess the means to defend itself. Particular weapon systems cannot be immoral in themselves. Only the actions of men and women can be moral or immoral.

57. The double-effect principle is sometimes applied to the just-war question. See above, p. 263.

58. See above, p. 260.

59. See above, Chapter 2: "God's Love: Creation," p. 40, especially n. 77.

60. See Ex. 20:14. Cf. Deut. 5:18.

61. See above, Chapter 2: "God's Love: Creation," pp. 41–43.

62. See above, Chapter 2: "God's Love: Creation," pp. 37–8.

63. Since surrogate motherhood, prostitution, homosexual acts, and masturbation are primarily misuses of our bodies, they are considered under the theology of the body. However, they fall under the sixth commandment rather than the fifth because they do not harm the body, but rather involve a misuse of it. See above, pp. 259–65. Still, at least in a secondary sense, these acts also are attacks on familial love and are violations of the theology of the family. Thus, they could be considered below under the rubric of familial love. See below, pp. 265–67. For a further consideration of these acts, see *Covenant,* pp. 51–58. See also *Wonder,* pp. 60, 62, 66–68. For a discussion of the body as the expression of the person and, therefore, not something that we can rent for prostitution or for surrogate motherhood, see Hogan, "A Theology of the Body," p. 12. See also, Hogan and LeVoir, "Medical Ethics and the Human Body," no. 5, *Catholic Bulletin,* vol. 77, no. 19 (May 10, 1987), p. 6.

64. See Hogan and LeVoir, "Is NFP Good?," pp. 224–27.

65. See above, Chapter 2: "God's Love: Creation," pp. 41–45.

66. See *Covenant,* pp. 48–50. See also *Wonder,* pp. 62–63. In addition, see Hogan, "A Theology of the Body," p. 12.

67. See above, Chapter 1: "Man/Woman and God," p. 16.

68. See *Covenant,* pp. 43–44, 51–53. See also Hogan, "A Theology of the Body," pp. 12, 24.

69. See above, p. 261.

70. See *Covenant,* pp. 54–55. See also *Wonder,* pp. 63–66.

71. See above, Chapter 8: "Grace," p. 205. See also above, p. 259.

72. See *Covenant*, pp. 53–54. See also *Wonder*, p. 66.

73. See above, p. 261.

74. See above, pp. 259, 266.

75. For the body as the expression of personal acts, see above, Chapter 2: "God's Love: Creation," pp. 37–41. Since love is a personal act, it is expressed in and through the body.

76. Despite the impossibility of seeking children through artificial fertilization and artificial insemination, almost everyone, especially the Church, has profound sympathy for the infertile couple. There are other solutions to this terribly agonizing problem. For further discussions of these acts, see *Covenant*, pp. 54–56. See also Hogan and LeVoir, "Medical Ethics and the Human Body," nos. 5, 6, *Catholic Bulletin*, vol. 77, nos. 19, 20 (May 10, 17, 1987), pp. 6, 12.

77. See Ex. 20:15. Cf. Deut. 5:19.

78. See Gen. 1:28. See also above, Chapter 2: "God's Love: Creation," pp. 42, 44–47.

79. See above, Chapter 2: "God's Love: Creation," pp. 42, 44–47.

80. Cf. DM, no. 5.

81. See Ex. 20:16. Cf. also Deut. 5:20.

82. See Ex. 20:17. Cf. also Deut. 5:21.

83. See above, Chapter 4: "The Incarnation," p. 106.

84. See Mt. 5:28. See also a commentary in Hogan, "A Theology of the Body," p. 24.

85. See Ex. 20:17. Cf. Deut. 5:21.

86. This commandment reveals that God is not a tyrant who cares only for power and riches. It is a foreshadowing of Christ's rejection of Satan's view of God as an uncaring tyrant. See above, Chapter 3: "Original Sin and the Providence of God," pp. 60–62. See also above, Chapter 4: "The Incarnation," pp. 98–99.

87. See above, pp. 267–68.

88. See above, Chapter 3: "Original Sin and the Providence of God," pp. 58–62. This was the sin of Adam and Eve, and it is still with us as an inheritance of original sin.

89. See above, Chapter 3: "Original Sin and the Providence of God," pp. 53–55. In addition, see above, Chapter 8: "Grace," pp. 232–33.

Bibliography

I. The works of Karol Wojtyla (Pope John Paul II)

The Acting Person. Edited by Anna-Teresa Tymieniecka. Translated by Andrzej Potocki. Vol 10: *Analecta Husserliana: The Yearbook of Phenomenological Research.* Dordrecht, Holland: D. Reidel Publishing Company, 1979.

Augustinum Hipponensem, Apostolic Letter on St. Augustine. L'Osservatore Romano (English Edition). Vol. 19, no. 37 (September 15, 1986), pp. 3–10.

Catechetical Series (A series of addresses given at the Wednesday audiences). *L'Osservatore Romano* (English Edition). Vol. 17, nos. 50–51, 52–53 (December 10, 17, 24, 1984). Vol. 18, nos. 2–3, 10–19, 21, 23, 24–32, 35–50, 51–52 (January 14, 21; March 11, 18, 25; April 1, 9, 15, 22, 29; May 6, 13, 27; June 10, 17, 24; July 1, 8, 15, 22, 29; August 5, 12; September 2, 9, 16, 23, 30; October 7, 14, 21, 28; November 4, 11, 18, 25; December 2, 9, 16, 23–30, 1985). Vol. 19, nos. 2–3, 5, 10–11, 14–26, 28, 30–41, 44–46, 50, 51–52 (January 13, 20; February 3; March 10, 17; April 7, 14, 21, 28; May 5, 12, 19, 26; June 2, 9, 16, 23, 30; July 14, 28; August 4, 11, 18, 25; September 1, 8, 15, 22, 29; October 6, 13; November 3, 10, 17; December 15, 22–29, 1986). Vol. 20, nos. 2–3, 5–10, 12, 17–18, 20–23, 26–37, 40–45 (January 12, 19; February 2, 9, 16, 23; March 2, 9, 23; April 27; May 4, 18, 25;

June 1, 8, 29; July 6, 13, 20, 27; August 3, 10, 17, 24, 31; September 7, 14; October 5, 12, 19, 26; November 2, 9, 1987).

"The Church, Mystery of Communion, Is a Sign of Unity Among All Peoples." *L'Osservatore Romano* (English Edition). Vol. 19, no. 48 (December 1, 1986), pp. 16–17.

Dives in Misericordia, On the Mercy of God. Boston: Saint Paul Editions, 1981.

Dominicae Cenae, On the Mystery and Worship of the Holy Eucharist. Vatican: Vatican Polyglot Press, 1980.

Dominum et Vivificantem, The Lord and Giver of Life. L'Osservatore Romano (English Edition). Vol. 19, no. 23 (June 9, 1986), pp. 1–16.

"The Ethics of Genetic Manipulation." *Origins.* Vol. 13, no. 23 (November 17, 1983), pp. 385–89.

Familiaris Consortio, Apostolic Exhortation on the Family. L'Osservatore Romano (English Edition). Vol. 14, nos. 51–52 (December 21–28, 1981), pp. 1–19.

"Human Life Is the Gift of God" (Homily of His Holiness at the Mass at the Capitol Mall on October 7, 1979). *The Pope in America.* St. Paul: The Wanderer Press, 1979, pp. 79–80.

"Jesus Christ, Living Peace and Living Justice" (Homily of His Holiness at the Mass in Yankee Stadium on October 2, 1979). *The Pope in America.* St. Paul: The Wanderer Press, 1979, pp. 25–27.

Laborem Exercens, On Human Work. L'Osservatore Romano (English Edition). Vol. 14, no. 38 (September 21, 1981), pp. 1–13.

Letter to All the Priests of the Church on the Occasion of Holy Thursday 1979. Washington, D.C.: United States Catholic Conference, 1979.

Letter to All the Priests of the Church for Holy Thursday 1986. Vatican: Vatican Polyglot Press, 1986.

Love and Responsibility. Translated by H. T. Willetts. New York: Farrar Straus Giroux, 1981.

"Peace Through Truth and Justice" (Address of His Holiness to the United Nations on October 2, 1979). *The Pope in America.* St. Paul: The Wanderer Press, 1979, pp. 11–18.

Reconciliatio et Paenitentia, Apostolic Exhortation on the Sacrament of Penance. L'Osservatore Romano (English Edition). Vol. 17, no. 51 (December 17, 1984), pp. 1–15.

Redemptor Hominis, The Redeemer of Man. L'Osservatore Romano (English Edition). Vol. 12, no. 12 (March 19, 1979), pp. 3–14.

Redemptoris Mater, The Mother of the Redeemer. L'Osservatore Romano (English Edition). Vol. 20, no. 30 (March 30, 1987), pp. 1–15.

Salvifici Doloris, The Christian Meaning of Human Suffering. Origins. Vol. 13, no. 37 (February 23, 1984), pp. 609, 611–24.

Sign of Contradiction. Translated by Saint Paul Publications. New York: Seabury Press, 1979.

Sources of Renewal: The Implementation of Vatican II. Translated by P. S. Falla. New York: Harper and Row, 1980.

Theology of the Body, nos. 1–127. *Original Unity of Man and Woman, Blessed Are the Pure of Heart, The Theology of Marriage and Celibacy,* and *Reflections on* Humanae Vitae. Boston: St. Paul Editions, 1981, 1983, 1986, 1984.

The Way to Christ: Spiritual Exercises. Translated by Leslie Wearne. San Francisco: Harper and Row, 1982.

II. Works of the Second Vatican Council

(The works of the Second Vatican Council are all cited from *Documents of Vatican II.* Edited Austin P. Flannery. Grand Rapids, Mich.: William B. Eerdmans Publishing, 1975.)

Christus Dominius, Decree on the Pastoral Office of Bishops in the Church (October 28, 1965), pp. 564–90.

Dei Verbum, Dogmatic Constitution on Divine Revelation (November 18, 1965), pp. 750–65.

Gaudium et Spes, Pastoral Constitution on the Church in the Modern World (December 7, 1965), pp. 903–1001.

Lumen Gentium, Dogmatic Constitution on the Church (November 21, 1964), pp. 350–432.

Presbyterorum Ordinis, Decree on the Ministry and Life of Priests (December 7, 1965), pp. 863–902.

Sacrosanctum Concilium, The Constitution on the Sacred Liturgy (December 4, 1963), pp. 1–40.

III. Other Works

The Christian Faith in the Doctrinal Documents of the Catholic Church. Edited J. Neuner and J. Dupuis. Westminster, Md.: Christian Classics Inc., 1975.

Code of Canon Law. Promulgated by Pope John Paul II on January

25, 1983. Translated by the Canon Law Society of America. Washington, D.C.: Canon Law Society of America, 1983.

Eccles, John, and Daniel N. Robinson. *The Wonder of Being Human: Our Brain and Our Mind.* New York: Macmillan, 1984.

Ford, John C., and Germain Grisez. "Contraception and the Infallibility Authority of the Ordinary Magisterium." *Theological Studies.* Vol. 39, no. 2 (June 1978), pp. 258–312.

Gruden, John C. *The Mystical Christ: Introduction to the Study of the Supernatural Character of the Church.* St. Louis: B. Herder Book Co., 1936.

Hogan, Richard M. "A Commentary on 'Familiaris Consortio.'" *The Wanderer.* Vol. 115, no. 10 (March 11, 1982), supplement, pp. 1–3.

———. "A Theology of the Body: A Commentary on the Audiences of Pope John Paul II from September 5, 1979, to May 6, 1981." *Fidelity.* Vol. 1, no. 1 (December 1981), pp. 10–15, 24–27.

———. *The Wonder of Human Sexuality.* St. Paul: Leaflet Missal, 1985.

———, and John M. LeVoir. *Covenant of Love: Pope John Paul II on Sexuality, Marriage, and Family in the Modern World.* Garden City, N.Y.: Doubleday, 1985.

———, and John M. LeVoir. "Is NFP Good?" *International Review of Natural Family Planning.* Vol. 9, no. 3 (Fall 1985), pp. 220–46.

———, and John M. LeVoir. "Medical Ethics and the Human Body" (A Seven-Part Series on the Congregation for the Doctrine of the Faith Document, "Instruction on Respect for Human Life in Its Origin and on the Dignity of Procreation," issued February 22, 1987). *Catholic Bulletin.* Vol. 77, nos. 15, 16, 17, 18, 19, 20, 21 (April 12, 19, 26; May 3, 10, 17, 24, 1987), pp. 7, 6, 6, 6, 6, 12, 23.

———, and John M. LeVoir. "To Think with the Church: A Report on the International Congress of Moral Theology." *International Review of Natural Family Planning.* Vol. 10, no. 4 (Winter 1986), pp. 339–46.

Hopkins, Jasper. *A Companion to the Study of Saint Anselm.* Minneapolis: University of Minnesota Press, 1972.

Irenaeus. *Adversos Haereses, Against Heresies. The Ante-Nicene Fa-*

thers. Vol. 1. Edited Alexander Roberts and James Donaldson. Grand Rapids, Mich.: William B. Eerdmans, 1979.

The Jerome Biblical Commentary. Edited Raymond E. Brown et al. Englewood Cliffs, N.J.: Prentice-Hall, 1968.

Journet, Charles. *The Meaning of Grace.* Translated by A. V. Littledale. New York: P. J. Kenedy & Sons, 1960.

Krapiec, Mieczylaw. *I-Man.* Translated by Marie Lescoe et al. New Britain, Conn.: Mariel Publications, 1983.

Malinski, Mieczyslaw. Pope John Paul II: *The Life of Karol Wojtyla.* Translated by P. S. Falla. New York: Crossroad, 1981.

Muehlen, Heribert. *Una Mystica Persona: Die Kirche als das Mysterium der heilsgeschichtlichen Identität des Heiligen Geistes in Christus und den Christen: Eine Person in vielen Personen.* 3rd Edition. Paderborn: Ferdinand Schoeningh, 1968.

Pastoral Care of the Sick. Promulgated by Pope Paul VI. Translated by the International Commission on English in the Liturgy. New York: Catholic Book Publishing, 1983.

Patrologiae Latinae. Edited J. P. Migne. Vol. 76.

Paul VI, Pope. *Humanae Vitae, On Human Life.* Washington: United States Catholic Conference, 1968.

————. *Marialis Cultus, Apostolic Exhortation on the Blessed Virgin Mary. L'Osservatore Romano* (English Edition). Vol. 7, no. 14 (April 4, 1974), pp. 1–10.

Pius XII, Pope. *Mystici Corporis, The Mystical Body of Christ.* Washington, D.C.: National Catholic Welfare Conference, 1943.

Pope John Paul II and the Family. Edited Michael Wrenn. Chicago: Franciscan Herald Press, 1983.

Ratzinger, Josef. *Instruction on Christian Freedom and Liberation. L'Osservatore Romano* (English Edition). Vol. 19, no. 15 (April 14, 1986), pp. 1–9.

————. "The Paschal Mystery as Core and Foundation of Devotion to the Sacred Heart." *Towards a Civilization of Love* (Proceedings of the International Congress on the Heart of Jesus, 1981). English Edition. San Francisco: Ignatius Press, 1985, pp. 145–65.

————, and Vittorio Messori. *The Ratzinger Report.* Translated by Salvator Attanasio and Graham Harrison. San Francisco: Ignatius Press, 1985.

————. "Transmission of the Faith and the Sources of the Faith."

Translated by Michael J. Wrenn. *The Wanderer* (Supplement). Vol. 117, no. 15 (April 12, 1984).

The Rites of the Catholic Church. Promulgated by Pope Paul VI. Translated by the International Commission on English in the Liturgy. 2 vols. New York: Pueblo Publishing Co., 1976, 1980.

Robinson, H. Wheeler. "The Hebrew Conception of Corporate Personality." *Beihefte zur Zeitschrift für die alttestamentliche Wissenschaft.* Vol. 66 (1936), pp. 49–62.

The Roman Missal: The Sacramentary. Promulgated by Pope Paul VI on April 3, 1969. Translated by the International Commission on English in the Liturgy. New York: Catholic Book Publishing, 1974.

Seifert, Josef. "Karol Cardinal Wojtyla (Pope John Paul II) as Philosopher and the Cracow/Lublin School of Philosophy." *Aletheia.* Vol. 2 (1981), pp. 130–99.

Smith, William. "The Role of the Christian Family, Articles 28–35." *Pope John Paul II and the Family.* Edited Michael J. Wrenn. Chicago: Franciscan Herald Press, 1983, pp. 73–107.

Thomas Aquinas. *Summa Theologiae.*

Williams, George. *The Mind of John Paul II: Origins of His Thought and Action.* New York: Seabury Press, 1981.

Woznicki, Andrew. *A Christian Humanism: Karol Wojtyla's Existential Personalism.* New Britain, Conn.: Mariel Publications, 1980.

Index

ABOUT THE AUTHORS

Richard M. Hogan and John M. LeVoir are Roman Catholic priests of the Archdiocese of Minneapolis-St. Paul. Hogan holds a Ph.D. in medieval history from the University of Minnesota. He has traveled to Europe (Munich, Rome, and Seville). He has published a commentary on John Paul II's weekly addresses on "The Theology of the Body" (1979–80). John M. LeVoir holds an M.A. in theology from the St. Paul Seminary and has done graduate work in theology and philosophy at the University of Dallas. Before ordination, he worked as a C.P.A. He has traveled widely in Europe.

Hogan and LeVoir coauthored the highly acclaimed book *Covenant of Love*.

MENSURA

MASS, ZAHL, ZAHLENSYMBOLIK
IM MITTELALTER

MISCELLANEA MEDIAEVALIA

VERÖFFENTLICHUNGEN DES THOMAS-INSTITUTS
DER UNIVERSITÄT ZU KÖLN

HERAUSGEGEBEN VON ALBERT ZIMMERMANN

BAND 16/2

MENSURA. MASS, ZAHL, ZAHLENSYMBOLIK
IM MITTELALTER

WALTER DE GRUYTER · BERLIN · NEW YORK
1984

MENSURA
MASS, ZAHL, ZAHLENSYMBOLIK
IM MITTELALTER

2. Halbband

HERAUSGEGEBEN VON ALBERT ZIMMERMANN
FÜR DEN DRUCK BESORGT VON GUDRUN VUILLEMIN-DIEM

WALTER DE GRUYTER · BERLIN · NEW YORK
1984

CIP-Kurztitelaufnahme der Deutschen Bibliothek

Mensura — Mass, Zahl, Zahlensymbolik im Mittelalter / hrsg.
von Albert Zimmermann. Für d. Dr. besorgt von Gudrun Vuillemin-
Diem. — Berlin ; New York : de Gruyter
   (Miscellanea mediaevalia ; Bd. 16)
NE: Zimmermann, Albert [Hrsg.]; GT
Halbbd. 2. — (1984).
  ISBN 3-11-009770-2

INHALTSVERZEICHNIS

(2. Halbband)

INHALTSVERZEICHNIS

(1. Halbband, erschienen im August 1983)

ZEITMASS UND KOSMOS IM MITTELALTER

von Heribert M. Nobis (München)

Der Zusammenhang von Zeitmaß und Kosmos ist einer der ältesten Gedanken der abendländischen Philosophie. Schon das früheste naturphilosophische Fragment, der bekannte Ausspruch von Anaximander[1], enthält eine theoretische Andeutung auf einen solchen Zusammenhang, der in der Praxis sowohl in der babylonischen als auch in der ägyptischen Astronomie bereits unreflektiert vorausgesetzt ist[2].

Wir wissen heute, daß die astronomische Grundlegung der Zeitmessung und ihre Einbettung in eine mythologische Deutung des Kosmos mindestens auf das Jahr 2500 v. Chr., d. h. in sumerische Zeiten zurückgehen[3]. Trotz der Versuche einer Entmythologisierung der Natur bei den Vorsokratikern, findet sich im platonischen Timaeus immerhin noch ein letzter Rest, indem hier die Planeten als Götter bezeichnet werden[4]. Erst Aristoteles wendet den rationalen Begriff οὐσία für diese Astralgeister an und verweist den Bezug zwischen Planeten und Göttern ausschließlich in den Bereich der Mythologie[5].

Den Fixsternhimmel und seine tägliche Bewegung um den Polstern in der Nähe des Siebengestirnes stellte man sich als gewaltige Kugelschale vor, die im Bewußtsein der Spätantike den Kosmos gegen den Olympos abschloß, der im christlichen Glaubensverständnis eine Hierarchie von Sphären bildete[6], als deren unterste später die *natura universalis* galt, die

---

[1] Anaximandros, περὶ φύσεως, frgm. 1 (Diels).

[2] Die ägyptische Zeitbestimmung beruhte, ebenso wie die babylonische, auf der unmittelbaren Beobachtung der Himmelserscheinungen. Die jeweilige Position der Gestirne zu bestimmten Zeiten wurde von den Ägyptern in ein schachbrettartig aufgeteiltes Feld eingetragen und auf einen in der Mitte des unteren Randes sitzenden Menschen bezogen (Vgl. Anm. 35). Die Babylonier dagegen verwandten hierzu eine unserer Kontoführung ähnliche, abstrakte Tabellenmethode, die wahrscheinlich erst im Hellenismus Eingang in die griechische Astronomie fand.

[3] Dies hat Werner Papke eindrucksvoll in seiner Dissertation Die Keilschriftserie Mul. APIM. Dokument wissenschaftlicher Astronomie im dritten Jahrtausend (Diss. Tübingen 1978) nachgewiesen, nachdem bereits Kopff die Wege Enil's, Anu's und Ela's im Gilgamesch-Epos als drei Streifen an der Himmelssphäre erkannt hatte, die parallel zum Äquator verlaufen. Cf. Kopff ZA. 28,352.

[4] Plato, Timaios 40 BC.

[5] Aristoteles, Met. 1074 a 38—1074 a 9.

[6] Cf. die Miniatur des über den Sphären thronenden Christus in Cod. Paris. 3236.

auch *vicaria Dei* genannt wurde[7], weil sie die göttlichen Anordnungen an
den physischen Kosmos vermittelte[8], deren mittlere der Weltseele vorbehalten waren, während in den obersten Sphären jene Geistwesenheiten
herrschten, die bei Paulus als Engel, Erzengel, Mächte, Throne, Herr-
schaften, Gewalten, Cherubim und Seraphim beschrieben sind[9]. Zeit und
Zeitmaß im eigentlichen Sinne gab es nur im Kosmos oder *mundus* mit
seinem translunaren und sublunaren Bereich. In der Sphäre des Olympos,
des Empyreums, jenseits des Fixsternhimmels gab es jene äonischen
Abläufe, von denen z. B. die Rede im Tractatus De mensura angelorum des
Thomas-Schülers Aegidius Romanus ist[10]. Der κόσμος dagegen, im lateinischen Mittelalter mit *mundus* bezeichnet[11], wird in der Aristoteles
zugeschriebenen und im 12. Jahrhundert wieder entdeckten Schrift περὶ
κόσμου als Zusammenfügung (σύστημα) des Himmels, der Erde und der
in diesen eingeschlossenen Naturwesenheiten (φύσεις) bestimmt[12]. Man
verstand also unter κόσμος die Welt als Gesamtheit aller Körper unterhalb
des Fixsternhimmels: die *regio aetherica* mit den himmlischen Kugelschalen, an denen die Planeten, einschließlich Sonne und Mond befestigt
waren, und die *regio elementaris* mit den sublunaren Kugelschalen, die in
reiner Form und unvermischt als Feuerregion, Luft- und Wassermantel
die Erde wie Hüllen umgaben, und die miteinander vermischt Bestandteile
aller irdischen Körper waren[13]. Ihr Mehr oder Weniger bestimmte gleichzeitig das spezifische Gewicht der Körper zueinander und deren Eigenschaften wie Brennbarkeit, Löslichkeit, Dichte und anderes. Bei der
Umwandlung der Körper untereinander wurden diese Elemente, die man
sich in ihnen virtuell oder potentiell[14] anwesend dachte, nach dem Verschwinden der alten *forma substantialis* als *minima* aktuell, um instantan
− gleichsam in dessen *status nascendi* − im neu entstehenden Körper, als
seine Bestandteile in neuen Proportionen und unter einer neuen *forma
substantialis* einzugehen. Ursache für alle sublunaren Prozesse, gleichwohl ob sie nun in der Erde die Entstehung der Gesteine oder das
Wachstum von Kristallen und Metallen aus trockenem und feuchtem
Dunst[15] oder ob sie auf der Erde die Lebewesen betrafen, war die Bewe-

---

[7] Alanus de Insulis, De planctu naturae, Migne PL. CCX, 442 C.

[8] R. Fludd, Utriusque cosmi maioris scil. et minoris metaphysica, physica adque technica
historia, Frankfurt 1617; Praefatio 7 sq.

[9] Cf. Kol. 1. 16.

[10] Vgl. in diesem Band (1. Halbband) B. Faes de Mottoni, *Mensura* im Werk De Mensura
angelorum des Aegidius Romanus.

[11] Isidori Hispalensis Episcopi Ethymologiarum sive originum libri XX, ed. Lindsay, lib.
XIII, Oxford 1962, De mundo et partibus I, 2.

[12] Aristoteles, De mundo 2. 391 b 9 sq.

[13] Johannes de Sacrobosco, De Sphaera, Coloniae 1601, 6.

[14] A. Maier, Die Struktur der materiellen Substanz, in: An der Grenze von Scholastik und
Naturwissenschaft, 2. A., Roma 1952, 3.

[15] Aristoteles, Meteor. IV. 378 b 10 sqq.

gung der himmlischen Kugelschalen. Auch der Wechsel von Land und
Wasser, der sich in längeren Zeiträumen abspielte, und die meteorologi-
schen Erscheinungen, wozu außer Nordlichtern, Winden und Wetterwechsel, das Auftauchen von Kometen gezählt wurde[16], all das hatte seine
Ursachen in diesen translunaren Gestirnsbewegungen zu oberst im Fixsternhimmel, dessen tägliche Bewegung sich vermittlungsursächlich nach
unten d. h. zur Mitte des Weltalls hin fortpflanzte[17], in der die Erde
gleichsam als Gegenbild der riesigen Weltkugel ruhte.

Damit diese kosmische Urbewegung, die vom Fixsternhimmel ausging,
ungestört ihre Wirkung auch im sublunaren Bereich entfalten konnte,
postulierte Aristoteles rückrollende Sphären, auf denen sich keine Him-
melskörper befanden, und deren Zweck ausschließlich darin bestand, die
Eigenbewegung der jeweiligen Planetensphäre gegenüber der nächst nie-
deren aufzuheben, um nur die Urbewegung zu vermitteln. Alle Bewegung
kam also von oben und was als oben galt, wurde geradezu durch den
Ursprung der Bewegung definiert: *sursum est unde motus*[18]. Die Bewegung
der Fixsternsphäre war somit letzte physische Wirkursache sowohl für alle
Planetenbewegungen als auch für alle Bewegungen und Veränderungen
unterhalb des Mondes, bis in die Höhlungen der Erde hinein, wo man
neben großen Wasserspeichern unterirdische Flußläufe vermutete, wo sich
in Höhlen Gesteine und Salze aus Wasser bildeten[19] und wo in Erzlagern
aus Kupfer Silber und aus Silber Gold wurde[20]. Diese Wachstumsprozesse
der Metalle und vor allem des Goldes, die sich in sehr langen Zeiträumen
abspielten, versuchten die Alchemisten in Gefäßen nachzuahmen, die
den Formen der unterirdischen Höhlen nachgebildet waren und bei denen
sie sich der Elementarkräfte des Wassers als Lösungsmittel und des Feuers
als Bildungsmittel bedienten und sich gezwungen sahen, nach einem Stoff,
dem Stein der Wissenschaft (*lapis philosophorum*) zu suchen, der die natürlichen Vorgänge in ihrem Zeitablauf beschleunigte, indem er die Kräfte,
die man als *causae agentes* ansah, nämlich die kosmische Bewegung, die
vom obersten Fixsternhimmel über die Sphären vermittelt wurde, ver-
stärkte und auf diesen Prozeß lenkte[21].

Sowohl Plato als auch Aristoteles sahen die Bewegung der himmlischen
Kugelschalen mit ihren sichtbar ausgezeichneten Punkten als Planeten bzw.
Fixsterne, in deren Gegeneinander und Zueinander als Faktoren sich die

---

[16] Id. l. c. 5. 342 a 34−6. 344 a 4.

[17] H. Blumenberg, Die kopernikanische Wende, Frankfurt 1965, 16.

[18] Aristoteles, De coelo IV. 1. 308 a 21sqq.

[19] J. Holmyard−D. C. Mandeville, Avicennae De congelatione et conglutatione lapidum,
Paris 1927, 72−74.

[20] H. M. Nobis, Über die Bedeutung der geistigen Strömungen des Mittelalters für die
Entwicklung der Erdwissenschaften, in: Abhandlungen und Quellen zur Geschichte der Geo-
graphie und Kosmologie Bd. 3, Paderborn 1982, 28sq.; 32.

[21] T. Burckhardt, Alchemie. Sinn und Weltbild, Olten 1960.

Zeit konstituiert. Bei Plato ist dies ausdrücklich gesagt[22], bei Aristoteles in der Analyse und Definition von Zeit vorausgesetzt[23]. Im übrigen stimmen beide für das Mittelalter maßgebenden Denker in ihrer Definition von Zeit in wesentlichen Stücken überein: „Zeit ist die Zahl der Bewegung nach dem Früher und Später"[24] heißt es bei Aristoteles, „dasjenige, dem wir den Namen Zeit beigelegt haben, ist ein in Zahlen fortschreitendes unvergängliches Bild der in dem Einen verharrenden Unendlichkeit"[25], so formuliert es Plato.

Die platonische Zeitbestimmung beeinflußte insbesondere das frühmittelalterliche Denken, während die Definition von Aristoteles erst durch die Rezeption seiner Schriften im Hochmittelalter wieder ins Bewußtsein der Gelehrten trat[26]. Da jedoch der Timaios-Kommentar des Chalcidius ununterbrochen vom 5. bis zum 15. Jahrhundert die Naturphilosophie mitbestimmte, liefen vom 12. Jahrhundert ab beide Definitionen nebeneinander. Chalcidius führte die platonische Zeitlehre weiter und verknüpfte die Abbildlichkeit der Zeit gegenüber ihrem Urbild der Ewigkeit ausdrücklich mit dem Abbild-Urbildverhältnis des *mundus sensilis* und *mundus intelligibilis*. Wie der *mundus intelligibilis* durch das *Aevum* existiert, so existiert der *mundus sensilis* durch die Totalität der Zeit, und aus diesem Grunde entstand im gleichen Augenblick mit dem *mundus sensilis* das Aufeinander der Tage und Nächte als Elemente der Zeitenfolge, aus denen sich die Monate und Jahre als Zeitabschnitt konstituieren, die von unserer *ratio* durch Berechnung gegeneinander abgrenzbar sind[27].

Ein Zeugnis mittelalterlicher Sakralkunst, das ausgehend von diesem Zeitverständnis eine Beziehung von Zeitmaß und Kosmos in der Liturgie bildhaft zum Ausdruck bringt, ist das Altartuch von St. Kunibert in Köln, in das die Gebeine der Heiligen Ewaldi eingewickelt waren. Es stammt aus der Mitte des 9. Jahrh. und besteht aus zwei Seitenteilen und einem fast doppelt so langen Mittelteil, der ein gitterähnliches Labyrinth von unregelmäßiger Gestalt zeigt, das sich in ähnlicher Form auf unbeschriebenen Seiten von St. Gallener Handschriften findet, und das – wie Nyssen es beschreibt – „zur Anschauung bringt, wie ein vom Unendlichkeitsband umschlossenes Rechteck mittels eines solchen Labyrinthes den unermeßlichen Raum zeichenhaft hervortreten läßt"[28]. Noch bedeutsamer

[22] Plato, Timaios 38 C.

[23] Aristoteles, Phys. IV, 14. 223 b 21–23.

[24] Id., l. c. 219 b 1 sq.

[25] Plato, l. c. 37 DE.

[26] Cf. A. Maier, Die Vorläufer Galileis im 14. Jahrh. Studien zur Naturphilosophie der Spätscholastik, 2. A., Roma 1966.

[27] Chalcidius, Commentarium in Platonis Timaeum, ed. Waszink, 1962, 154, 10–20.

[28] W. Nyssen, Irdisch habe ich Dich gewollt. Beiträge zur Denk- und Bildform der christlichen Frühe, in: Occidens. Horizonte des Westens, hrsgg. v. W. Nyssen, Bd. VI, Trier 1982, 78: Die Ewaldi-Decke aus St. Kunibert, Köln.

sind die fast quadratischen gleich großen Seitenstücke, deren Thematik die Konstitution des *mundus sensilis* durch die Zeit ist. „Das eine Feld sucht die Architektur des Himmels durch die Beziehung von Sonne und Mond zum Zodiakus in ein Zeichen zu bringen, das andere Feld beschreibt einen thronenden Annus, der in einem doppelten Kreise von den Elementen und den Jahreszeiten sowie vom Zodiakus umgeben ist. Es beschreibt den größten irdischen Rhythmus des Lichtes und zugleich die dahinfließende Zeit"[29]. Wenn man sich vergegenwärtigt, daß Plato die Zeit als Bild der einen verharrenden Unendlichkeit bezeichnet, so ist hier das platonische Zeitverständnis in der Tat sinnenfällig wiedergegeben.

Die platonische Auffassung über die Planeten und Gestirne als Zeichen der Zeit schien den frühmittelalterlichen Christen und in Sonderheit den Mönchen so sehr mit der Aussage des Schöpfungsberichtes in Einklang zu stehen, daß sie u. a. diese Stellen als Beweis für ihre Lehre von den λόγοι σπερματικοί in den Schriften der antiken Philosophen betrachteten[30]. Dies erklärt, daß bis ins 14. Jahrh. hinein die Vorstellung bestand, Gott habe eigene engelhafte Intelligenzen eingesetzt, in deren inneren Schauakten die geometrisch intelligiblen äußeren Bewegungen der himmlischen Kugelschalen mit den Planeten, exemplarursächlich, d. h. durch Partizipation begründet sind[31]. Damit waren die Gebetszeiten der mittelalterlichen Christenheit, und besonders der Mönche, nicht nur durch den kosmischen Umschwung der unteren Himmel, wie man die translunaren Kugelschalen der *regio aetherica* auch nannte, bestimmt, sondern begründet in den inneren Schauakten reiner Geister und damit letztlich auf den Willen Gottes, die *voluntas Dei* zurückbezogen, durch die der ganze Kosmos ins Sein gesetzt worden war und ununterbrochen im Sein erhalten wurde.

Im Spätmittelalter ging das Bewußtsein eines Zusammenhanges von Zeitmaß und Kosmos dadurch verloren, daß man anstelle einer urbildhaften Teilhabe die Vorstellung einer instrumentalen Kausalität setzte und nach dem Ökonomieprinzip *entia non sunt multiplicanda praeter necessitatem* die Engel als Zwischenursachen der Planetenbewegung für überflüssig hielt[32]. Man bediente sich vielmehr einer spätantiken mechanischen Wurftheorie des Aristoteles-Kommentators Simplikios[33], um zu erklären, wie

---

[29] Id., l. c.

[30] Jeder von ihnen hat, soweit er Anteil hat an dem in Keimen ausgestreuten Logos (τοῦ σπερματικοῦ λόγου θείου) und für das Verwandte ein Auge hat, treffliche Aussprüche getan. Justinus, Apologia 2,13, Migne PG. VI, 441–70. Zit. n. Bibliothek der Kirchenväter: frühchristliche Apologeten und Märtyrerakten, Bd. I, Kempten–München 1913, 154.

[31] H. M. Nobis, Art. Gestirne, in: Lexikon der christlichen Ikonographie, hrsgg. v. E. Kirschbaum, Freiburg i. Br. 1970, Bd. II, 142.

[32] Buridani quaestiones subtilissimae super octo physicorum libros Aristotelis, c. 12, fol. 120.

[33] Simplikios in Aristotelis libros De coelo quattuor commentaria, ed. Diels, Berlin 1862, 263.

Gott – gleichsam als Werkmeister – unmittelbare Ursache für die Planetenbewegungen sein könne.

Ein frühes Beispiel für den Zusammenhang von Zeitmaß, Kosmos und
Liturgie findet sich in einem Traktat Gregors von Tours De cursu stellarum
ratio, der uns in einer Bamberger Handschrift aus dem 8. Jahrhundert
erhalten ist. Dieser Traktat ist eine Lehrschrift für Mönche bzw. für
die angehenden *vigilarii*, da der Untertitel lautet: *qualiter ab officium debet
observari* und er mit den Institutiones von Cassiodor zusammengebunden
ist[34].

Der Traktat beginnt mit einem Bericht von den bekannten sieben
Weltwundern als technischen Großleistungen des Menschen in der Antike
und leitet durch die Aufzählung von sieben Schöpfungs- oder Naturwun-
dern zum eigentlichen Thema über. Als solche Wunder der Natur werden
neben Geysiren und Vulkanen die Gezeiten, das Wachsen und Fruchten
und dessen Abhängigkeit vom Lauf der Sonne und ihrer Wärmestrahlung
sowie die Phasen des Mondes und die Figuren angesehen, in denen sich die
Fixsterne dem Anblick des Betrachters im Laufe der Jahreszeiten bieten,
und deren Kenntnis dazu dienen soll, das Lob Gottes in einem regelmäßigen Rhythmus zu singen und sich zur rechten Zeit in der Nacht
zum Gebet zu erheben.

Die Schrift betont ausdrücklich, daß sie weder mathematische Astronomie noch judiziarische Astrologie lehren will, sondern ausschließlich
diesem Zwecke dienen soll. Dazu reicht es nach Gregor aus, die ungefähre
Tageslänge in den einzelnen Monaten anzugeben, die den Sonnenauf- und
-untergängen entspricht, und zu wissen, daß der Mond im Sommer, wenn
die Nächte kürzer sind, die gleiche Bahn zieht wie die Sonne im Winter
und umgekehrt. Die Gestaltungen der Gestirnskonstellationen werden
dann in bezug auf die einzelnen Monate und bestimmte Stunden im einzelnen behandelt, und sind zeichnerisch so wiedergegeben, wie der Betrachter sie zu diesen Zeitpunkten am Himmel wahrnimmt.

Die Deutung der wiedergegebenen Konstellationen in dieser Handschrift
ergibt unter Berücksichtigung des antiken und mittelalterlichen Wissens-
standes der beobachtenden Astronomie, daß mit Sicherheit hier die Sternbilder der nördlichen Krone (*corona borealis*), der Leier (*Lyra*), des
Schwans (*Cygnus*), des Adlers (*Aquila*), der Pleiaden, des Orions, des
Großen Bären (*Ursus Maior*) sowie des Großen Hundsstern (*Canis Maior*),
mit mehr oder weniger großer Wahrscheinlichkeit die Sternbilder des
Delphins, der Hyaden, der Zwillinge (*Gemini*), des Bärenhüters (*Bootes*)
und eine gemischte Konstellation von Fuhrmann (*Auriga*) und Steinbock
(*Capricornus*) dargestellt sind. Daneben finden sich Angaben der Auf- und
Untergänge dieser Sterne, an deren Zeitpunkte in den einzelnen Monaten

---

[34] Cod. Bamb. Patr. 61 fol. 75 v–82 v.

genauere Regeln geknüpft werden, welche Gruppen von Psalmen bzw. Hymnen und welche Tageszeiten man zu beten hat.

Aus anderen Handschriften wissen wir, wie im Quadrivium, näherhin im Rahmen der Astronomie, die Klosterschüler in die Betrachtung des Sternenhimmels eingeübt wurden. Nach einer Methode, die bereits im Hellenismus, wahrscheinlich in Alexandria für diesen Zweck entwickelt wurde und die der Astronomie der Ägypter entspricht[35], ließ man sie die Sternbilder der verschiedenen Jahreszeiten, in einer Tabelle zusammengestellt, zeichnen, damit sie sich auf diese Weise dem Gedächtnis einprägten, so daß der Traktat De cursu stellarum eine Art Vademecum darstellt für diejenigen, denen später als Mönche die Aufgabe der *vigelarii* zufiel. Da sich eine entsprechende Zeichnung noch in einer Handschrift des 15. Jahrhunderts findet[36], kann man annehmen, daß diese Praxis bis ins Spätmittelalter hinein üblich war. Während diese Übungen der unmittelbaren Beobachtung des gestirnten Himmels mit bloßem Auge zum Zwecke der Bestimmung der Gebetsstunden diente, gab es nachweisbar seit dem 10. Jahrhundert auch solche mit Hilfe von Lehrmitteln wie Himmelsgloben, worüber wir aus den Klosternschulen von St. Gallen und der Reichenau Berichte haben. Auch wissen wir, daß die Mönche zur Beobachtung Sehrohre (ohne Linsen) benutzten, die man *fistulae* nannte[37].

Aber nicht nur zu qualitativen Bestimmungsübungen wurden Lehrmittel benutzt, sondern ebenso zu Übungen der quantitativen Ermittlung von Sternpositionen. Neben den verschiedenen Arten von Uhren, wie Kerzen-, Sand- und Wasseruhren, dienten hierzu vor allem Astrolabien. Das bekannteste Beispiel ist das Regensburger Lehrgerät für den Umgang mit einem Astrolab. Wir besitzen eine Steinplastik aus dem 11. Jahrhundert, die einen knienden Jüngling vor einem überdimensionalen Lehrgerät zeigt[38], der offenbar auf diese Weise die Höhe eines Sternes – etwa der Sonne – durch Anvisieren am hellen Tage bestimmen lernt, eine bekannte Methode, um die Tageszeit genau zu ermitteln, wenn man die Rückseite des Astrolabs zu entsprechenden Rechnungen benutzt, die ähnlich wie eine moderne Sternkarte den von einem bestimmten Horizont her, d. h. bei einer bestimmten Breite sichtbaren Sternenhimmel, wenn auch in Projektion,

---

[35] Im Grab von Ramses VII. in Luxor findet sich ein Bildnis, auf dem über einem sitzenden Mann jeweils für die 12 Stunden der Nacht Sterne angegeben sind, die in einer bestimmten Stunde über seinem linken oder rechten Ohr, über seiner Stirn oder über seiner linken oder rechten Schulter stehen sollten (nach einem Photo im Oriental Institute der University of Chicago).

[36] Clm. 14 583 St. Emmeran, 15. Jahrh.

[37] Vgl. S. Günther, Geschichte des mathematischen Unterrichtes im deutschen Mittelalter, Berlin 1878, 77.

[38] Die im Reallexikon der deutschen Kunstgeschichte, Stuttgart 1937, Bd. I, 1162 beschriebene steinerne Bildsäule des Regensburger Stadtmuseums stimmt genau mit einer Zeichnung im Clm. 14 689 fol. 1 r überein. Cf. E. Zinner Zeitschrift f. Instrumentenkunde 43 (1923) 278–282.

also nicht direkt, wiedergibt. Andererseits wissen wir, daß mindestens seit dem 10. Jahrhundert das Kloster St. Emmeran in Regensburg ein Zentrum astronomischer Forschung wurde und zwar in Zusammenhang mit dem Problem der richtigen Osterfestberechnung[39]. Bevor ich hierauf im Rahmen dieses Themas eingehe, sollen zunächst einige Bemerkungen über die allgemeine Zeitlehre und die Methode der Zeitmessung vorausgeschickt werden.

Die allgemeine Lehre von der Zeit wurde *Chronaca* genannt. Bei Isidor von Sevilla heißt es in seinen Ethymologiarum libri, jener großangelegten Enzyklopädie, die das Wissen seiner Epoche unter pädagogischen Gesichtspunkten darstellt unter diesem Titel von den Teilen der Zeit: *Tempora autem momentis, horis, diebus, mensibus, annis, lustris, saeculis, aetatibus dividuntur*[40]. Der Bezug zwischen Zeitmaß und Kosmos zeigt sich bei ihm vor allem in seinen Nominaldefinitionen von *momentum* als kleinstem Zeitteil und *dies*. Während die Ableitung von *dies* auf den im Mittelalter bekannten astrologischen Begriff der Tagesregenten hindeutet: *dies dicti a diis quorum nomina romani quibusdam sideribus sacraverunt*, heißt es *momentum est minimum atque angustium tempus a motu siderum dictum*[41], womit ein sachlicher Bezug zur Gestirnsbewegung und damit zwischen dem kleinsten Zeitmaß und dem Kosmos hergestellt ist.

An anderer Stelle spricht er von Zeitatomen, wenn es unter dem Titel De mundo et partibus; De atomis heißt: *In tempore vero sic intellegitur atomus: annum, verbi gratia, dividis in menses, menses in dies, dies in horas; adhuc partes horarum admittunt divisionem, quousque venias ad tantum temporis punctum, et quandam momenti stillam, et per nullam morulam produci possit, et ideo dividi iam non potest. Haec est atomus temporis*[42]. Das Zeitatom ist also für Isidor die letzte unteilbare Einheit, gleichsam der Tropfen eines *momentum*, der die Grenze seiner Teilbarkeit darstellt. Die Beziehung zum Kosmos unter dieser Rücksicht ist dadurch angedeutet, daß es bei ihm nicht nur für die Zeit, sondern auch für alle Körper eine Grenze der Teilbarkeit gibt, wozu er den Prozeß des Zerkleinerns und der schließlichen Pulverisierung eines Steines als Beispiel anführt.

Die Quelle, aus der Isidor unmittelbar die Vorstellung von Zeitatomen übernommen hat, dürfte Martianus Capella De nuptiis philologiae et Mercurii sein, bekanntlich eines der maßgebenden Lehrbücher des Frühmittelalters für die *artes liberales*. Martianus Capella schreibt nämlich über die Zeit: *Primum igitur tempus est, quod in morem atomi nec partes nec*

---

[39] Cf. Clm. 14689, fol. 85 r–87 v.

[40] Isidori Hispalensis Episcopi Ethymologiarum sive originum libri XX. ed. Lindsay, Oxford 1962, lib. V, XXIX. 1.

[41] Id., l. c. XXX. 5.

[42] Id., l. c. lib. XIII 2. 3–4.

momenta recisionis admittit, ut est in geometricis punctum, in arithmeticis monas, id est singularis quaedam ac se ipsa natura contenta . . . Atque hoc erit brevissimum tempus, quod insecabile memoravi[43]. Der griechische Musiktheoretiker Aristoxenes hatte die kleinste Maßeinheit des Taktes mit πρῶτος χρόνος bezeichnet, unter welchem er zwar keine unendlich kleine Zeit, jedoch ein letztes unteilbares Element des Rhythmus und der Metrik verstand, dessen absolute Größe zwar meßbar, aber nicht feststehend war, sondern von der ἀγωγή, dem Tempo, abhing, in der ein Musikstück dargeboten wird[44]. Aristides Quintilianus (ca. 3. Jahrhundert) hatte später dieses rhythmische Element als kürzeste Zeit in bezug auf die Wahrnehmung mit ἄτομος bezeichnet[45], wodurch sie aber immer noch eine relative Größe blieb, während bei Martianus Capella, der unmittelbar an Quintilian in dieser Hinsicht anknüpft, dieser als Ganzes zu fassende Taktteil eine absolut unteilbare Zeitgröße wurde. Bei Beda Venerabilis bekam das Element des Rhythmus als *atomus* dann den Charakter einer absoluten Größe, indem es bei ihm ein bestimmter Teil der Stunde ist. Diese teilte er folgendermaßen ein I *hora* = X *minuta* = XL *momenta* = xxiiDLX *atomi*. Nach unserer heutigen Rechnung entspräche demgemäß ein kürzester Zeitraum bei Beda einer Sechzehntel Sekunde, oder ca. drei Tertien (60 Tertien sind eine Sekunde)[46]. Beda teilt nun in der gleichen Weise wie die Tageszeit, auch die Bahn der Sonne durch den Zodiakus, den Tierkreis, ein. Er bemerkt in diesem Zusammenhang, daß namentlich die Astrologen, die bei ihm noch *mathematici* heißen, bis zum *atomus* kommen wollen, um den Augenblick der Geburt der Menschen mit möglichster Genauigkeit zu bestimmen. Er weist allerdings auch daraufhin, daß die Mehrzahl der Schriftsteller in der Bezeichnung des kürzesten Zeitraumes ungenau sind und diesen bisweilen *momentum, punctum* oder *atomus* nennen[47].

Diese Zeiteinteilung bis in Bruchteile von Sekunden hinein hatte demgemäß nur astronomische Bedeutung, da uns keine Instrumente aus dem Mittelalter bekannt sind, mit denen man die Zeit derart genau hätte messen können, wenn wir von einer primitiven Form des Metronoms absehen, das bereits im 9. Jahrhundert bei Abû'l Qâsim'Abbâs Ben Firnâs vorkommt, dessen Schwingdauer wir jedoch nicht kennen. Die Uhren, die das

---

[43] Martianus Capella, De nuptiis philologiae et Mercurii et de septem artibus libri IX, ed. Dick-Préaux, Lipsiae 1978, lib. IX § 971.

[44] Aristoxenos apud Porphyrios in Ptol. Harmon., ed. Düring, Göteborg 1932, 78, 15 sqq. Cf. H. Backes, Die Hochzeit Merkurs und der Philologie. Studien zu Notkers Martian-Übersetzung, Sigmaringen 1981.

[45] Aristeides περὶ μουσικῆς I, 14, ed. Jahn, Berlin 1882, 21.

[46] In diesem Zusammenhang ist darauf hinzuweisen, daß noch die Astronomen des 16. Jahrh., z. B. Copernicus, die Planetenörter, also ihre Breiten und Längen nicht nur nach Bogengraden, -minuten und -sekunden, sondern bis auf Tertien und Quartien hin genau zu bestimmen suchten, also auf astronomische Einheiten hin ihre Rechnungen abstellten, die den fast 13 Millionstenteil eines Bogens ausmachten.

[47] Beda Venerabilis, De temporum ratione, cap. III, Migne PL. XC, 304.

Frühmittelalter verwandte, waren — auch wenn sie bereits Mechanismen betrieben — durchgängig Wasseruhren. In einigen Fällen besitzen wir nämlich Nachrichten von sogenannten Astrarien, d. h. Planetenuhren, an denen die Bewegung von Sonne und Mond abgelesen werden konnten[48].

So wird in der Mitte des 6. Jahrhunderts eine Kunstuhr erwähnt, bei der die 12 Stunden, die mit den zwölf Arbeiten des Herkules verglichen wurden, von diesem mit einer Keule angeschlagen wurden[49]. Eine ähnliche Uhr mit Schlagwerk und mechanischen Figuren, die die Untertanen des Kalifen Harûn al Raschîd aus Bagdad 807 als Geschenk mitbrachten, existierte am Hof Karls des Großen[50], und eine dritte befand sich zu Verona, um 840 durch den Diakon Pacificius gebaut[51]. Auch der ehemalige Mönch von St. Emmeran in Regensburg und spätere Abt Wilhelm von Hirsau verfertigte ein Astrarium[52].

Während im Frühmittelalter all diese Uhren mit Wasser angetrieben wurden, findet sich bereits im 13. Jahrhundert ein Übergang zu einer mechanischen Antriebsweise, nämlich der Versuch einer Quecksilberuhr, deren Beschreibung sich in den Libros del saber de astronomia, dem astronomischen Werk Alphons X. von Kastilien findet, die dieser zu seinen astronomischen Beobachtungen benutzte[53]. Um so merkwürdiger erscheint es, daß in Frankreich noch zur gleichen Zeit am Hofe Ludwigs des Heiligen (1215—1270), sogar noch am Hofe Karls des Weisen (1364—1380) Kerzenuhren in Form von dicken und justierten d. h. geteilten Wachskerzen zur Zeitmessung in Gebrauch waren, die bereits Alfred der Große um 875 benutzte.

Augustinus hatte die technische Praxis der Antike, die Zeit nicht allein durch die Bewegung von Sonne, Mond und Sternen zu messen, unter Hinweis auf eine Töpferscheibe gerechtfertigt, indem er der Behauptung entgegentrat, die Bewegungen der Sonne, des Mondes und der Sterne seien identisch mit den Zeiten, und die Frage stellt: „Sollten nämlich nicht vielmehr die Bewegungen aller Körper die Zeit sein?"; wenn er als Beispiel die Bewegung eines Töpferrades bringt, das auch dann die Zeit noch messen kann, wenn alle Himmelslichter ruhen würden, hebt er den antiken Wesensuntrschied von κίνεσις κατὰ φύσιν und κίνεσις κατὰ τέχνην auf, indem dieser mindestens in bezug auf die Zeit keine Rolle mehr spielt. Er relativiert die Bedeutung der Gestirne und Lichter als Zeichen der Zeit, der Jahre und der Tage und behauptet, daß man mit ebenso gutem

[48] H. M. Nobis, Art. Astrarium, in: Lexikon des Mittelalters Bd. I, München—Zürich 1980, Sp. 1134—1135.
[49] Chronicon Gazaei, ed. Boissonade, Paris 1846.
[50] Eginhard, Annales francorum, in: Monumenta Germaniae scriptores I, 194.
[51] F. S. Maffei, Verona illustrata, Verona 1732, 20.
[52] Monumenta Germaniae scriptores XII, 211.
[53] Don Manuel Ricoy Sibonas, Libros del saber de astronomia del rey D. Alphonso X de Castilia. Madrid 1863—67, Bd. IV, 77—93.

Recht die Umlaufzeit jener hölzernen Rädchen einen Tag nennen darf und widerspricht der Meinung, dieser Umlauf sei gar keine Zeit[54].

Es ist bisher nicht untersucht, wieweit dieses Argument Augustins zu einem Motiv wurde, die Zeit durch Instrumente zu messen, die der Töpferscheibe aus hölzernen Rädchen nachgebildet waren. Sicher ist nur, daß in der gleichen Epoche, aus der die ersten Räderuhren bekannt sind, die Bezeichnung *machina mundi* für den Kosmos als Uhrwerk aufgefaßt wurde, und dieser damit in der Räderuhr ein technisches Gegenbild fand[55]. Bis dahin wurde die Welt eher als Organismus aufgefaßt, nachdem Chalcidius den platonischen Begriff σῶμα τοῦ κόσμου mit *machina mundi* wiedergegeben hatte[56]. Die Idee der *machina mundi*, der Weltmaschine, war es auch, die im 14. Jahrhundert der Herstellung jener astronomischen Kunstuhren zugrundelag, die nicht nur das Ablesen von Gezeiten erlaubten, wie das Astrarium Richards von Wallingford, des Abtes von St. Alban, sondern auch die Zeiten anzeigten, an denen man zur Ader lassen konnte, wie die ältere astronomische Uhr von Straßburg, die Jean Bournave 1352 gebaut hatte.

Hier war der Mensch als Mikrokosmos in den Makrokosmos einbezogen, da es zwischen ihm und dem Weltall nicht nur Ähnlichkeit, sondern darüber hinaus reale Abbildlichkeit gab. Noch in Galileis Schrifttum erscheint die Leber dem Jupiter und das Herz der Sonne zugeordnet. Nachdem Basilios den Menschen als Mikrokosmos bezeichnet hatte, in dem wir die große Weisheit des Schöpfers schauen[57], hatte Ambrosius diesen Gedanken dahin weitergeführt, daß der Mensch gleichsam summarisch das Universum verkörpere und die Schönheit der ganzen Schöpfung widerspiegele[58], ein Gedanke, den später Alanus de Insulis in seiner Schrift De planctu naturae aufnahm[59], und der somit die astromedizinischen Praktiken des Mittelalters naturphilosophisch und theologisch fundierte. Die Konstruktion von Planetenuhren war somit nicht nur ideengeschichtlich, sondern auch durch die praktischen Bedürfnisse der mittelalterlichen Gesellschaft motiviert, die zweien der *artes mechanicae* angehörten: der *medicina* und der *navigatio*.

Was die *navigatio* betraf, näherhin die Abhängigkeit des Einlaufens der Schiffe in die Häfen von den Gezeiten, hatte Beda Venerabilis bereits in seiner Schrift De temporum ratione, die 725 vollendet wurde, gegenüber Isidor von Sevilla eine klare Entscheidung in bezug auf die Gezeitentheorie

---

[54] Augustinus, Confessiones XI, 23, Migne PL. XXXII, 820.

[55] Cf. H. M. Nobis, Die Umwandlung der mittelalterlichen Naturvorstellung, ihre Ursachen und ihre wissenschaftsgeschichtlichen Folgen, in: Archiv f. Begriffsgeschichte, Bd. XIII, H. 1, 1969, 41 sq.

[56] Chalcidius, l. c.

[57] Cf. Basilius, Predigten, 2. Predigt 7, Migne PG. XXXI, 197–217.

[58] Ambrosius, Exaemeron VI, 10. 75, Migne PL. XIV, 123 sqq.

[59] Alanus de Insulis, l. c.

gefällt; *Aestus Oceani lunam sequitur*[60]. Er schließt sich also der bereits in der Antike ausgesprochenen Meinung an, daß sich die Gezeiten nach den Phasen des Mondes richten. Aufgrund der von Poseidonius überlieferten Theorie, daß die Flut durch die Anziehungskraft des Mondes verursacht wird, diskutiert Beda nun die Frage, wie Spring- und Nippfluten zustande-kommen.

Vor allem erkannte er, daß der Wind eine Flut beschleunigen und verzö-gern könne und sprach erstmals ein sehr wichtiges ozeanographisches Prinzip aus, das wir heute das Prinzip der Hafenzeiten nennen: es besagt, daß die Gezeiten hinter dem Mond in bestimmten Abständen zurück-bleiben, die ihrerseits wieder an den verschiedenen Orten derselben Küste verschieden sein können. Er forderte dann, daß für jeden Hafen beson-dere Gezeitentafeln aufgestellt werden müßten und zwar zunächst auf rein empirischer Grundlage[61]. Er versuchte aber auch bereits ein allge-meines Gesetz abzuleiten, indem er behauptete, daß die Gezeiten mittels eines 19-Jahreszyklus für jeden beliebigen Hafen vorausgesagt werden konnten[62].

Diese Theorie Bedas steht in engem Zusammenhang mit seiner Absicht, die Osterfestrechnung zu verbessern. Diese findet sich ebenfalls in seiner Schrift De temporum ratione, in der er neben der Behandlung allge-meiner Probleme der Zeitmessung und der dazu notwendigen Rechen-verfahren die Anweisung gibt, wie der 19-Jahreszyklus, der *cyclus lunaris*, der sich bereits bei dem Griechen Meton findet und eine Zahlenreihe von 19 Jahren darstellt, nach deren Ablauf sich dieselben Mondphasen wieder-holen, zu benutzen sei, um die Ostertafeln zu berechnen[63]. Zu bemerken ist, daß Beda im übrigen die Osterfestrechnung der Alexandriner über-nimmt und ihr durch seinen Einfluß Eingang in die mittelalterliche Kom-putistik verschaffte, wie er andererseits die Zeitrechnung von Exiguus Dionysius durch seine Schrift De sex aetatibus mundi in die Geschichts-schreibung des Mittelalters einführte.

Bekanntlich spielte die Frage, wie die Feier des Osterfestes zu einem bestimmten Termin und zwar für alle Christen an ein und demselben Tage gehalten werden könnte, bereits seit den frühesten Zeiten in der Kirche eine Rolle.

Nachdem bei den Christen anstelle des jüdischen Mondjahrkalenders immer mehr der julianische Sonnenjahrkalender gebräuchlich wurde, mußte das jüdische Osterdatum in das Datum des julianischen Kalenders um-gerechnet werden, was in der Folge Anlaß zu Streitigkeiten und Reformen

---

[60] Beda Venerabilis, De natura rerum Liber, cap. 39, Migne PL. XC, 458 A.

[61] Id., De temporum ratione, cap. XXIX, Migne PL. XC, 422 C−426 C.

[62] Wer die Computus-Schriften, die nach Beda entstanden, studiert, wird finden, daß der Lehre von der Berechnung des Osterfestes auf Bedas Anregung hin, nicht selten Gezeiten-tafeln folgen.

[63] Beda Venerabilis, l. c., cap. I, VI sqq.

gab. Darum bestimmte bereits Pius I. († 156) in der ersten Hälfte des zweiten Jahrhunderts, daß Ostern allgemein nur noch am Sonntag und nicht mehr am ersten Frühlingsvollmondtag ohne Rücksicht auf den einfallenden Wochentag gefeiert werde, und Papst Viktor I. († 201) bestätigte gegen Ende des 2. Jahrhunderts dieses Dekret seines Vorgängers. Endgültig wurde diese Frage dann bekanntlich auf dem Konzil von Nicaea 325 gelöst, indem man den ersten Sonntag nach dem ersten Frühlingsvollmond für die Feier des Osterfestes festlegte, wobei dem Patriarchen von Alexandrien die Feststellung des jeweiligen Datums und seine Weitergabe an den Patriarchen des Westens, den Bischof von Rom, oblag, der ihn seinerseits der ganzen Kirche mitzuteilen hatte[64].

Die Absicht der Konzilväter war zwar in erster Linie, daß die Christen das Osterfest an ein und demselben Tag feierten. Außerdem sollten das christliche Ostern und das jüdische Pascha nicht aufeinandertreffen. Andererseits zeigt die Tatsache, daß man den Ostertermin an das Frühlingsäquinoktium band, die Absicht, die Ostergrenzen, mit denen des Widdersternzeichens zusammenfallen zu lassen. Hierbei spielt zweifellos die altjüdische Tradition eine Rolle, nach der die Weltschöpfung im Frühlingsäquinoktium stattgefunden hat, aber auch die altchristliche Überzeugung von der kosmischen Bedeutung des Todes Christi. Dieser Überzeugung gibt Hippolyt von Rom († 250), dem wir auch den ältesten Osterkanon verdanken[65] in einer Osterpredigt Ausdruck, wenn er das Kreuz Christi den kosmischen Angelpunkt nennt, der die ganze Vielfalt der menschlichen Natur zur Einheit zusammenfaßt. Vom Sterben des Herrn heißt es dann: „Damals erschauderte vor soviel Geduld das All, wurden die Himmel bewegt, kamen die überirdischen Mächte ins Wanken, und die Throne und die Gesetze, als sie den obersten Feldherrn der großen Macht also hängend erblickten. Beinahe wären die Sterne vom Himmel gefallen, als sie den vor dem Morgenstern Geborenen so ausgestreckt sahen. Und das Feuer der Sonne erlosch für eine Weile, da es sah, wie sich das große Licht der Welt verfinsterte"[66]. Ein Nachklang dieser Gedanken Hippolyts fand sich im römischen Brevier und in den mittelalterlichen Sacrobosco-Kommentaren[67].

Während der Ostertermin sich im wesentlichen ergibt aus der Verflechtung des Sonnenzyklus von 28 Jahren, nach dessen Umlauf dieselben Wochentage wieder auf dasselbe Monatsdatum fallen, und dem Mondzyklus von 19 Jahren, nach deren Umlauf dieselben Mondphasen wieder

---

[64] Leo I., Epistola ad Imperatorem Marcianum, Migne PL. I, IV, 1056.

[65] Eusebius, Historia ecclesiae VI, 22, Migne PG. XX, 1073 B−1077 A; cf. E. Schwartz, Christliche und jüdische Ostertafeln, in: Göttinger Abhandlungen N. F. 8.6, Berlin 1905, 29−40, und H. Achelis, Das Christentum in den ersten drei Jahrhunderten, Leipzig 1925, Tafel 13.

[66] Hippolytus, De Pascha, Homilia 6, Migne PG. 59, 743−746.

[67] Sphaera Ioannis de Sacrobosco emendata, aucta et illustrata, Coloniae 1601.

auf dieselben Monatstage fallen, sowie dem Zyklus der Neumonde und Vollmonde, der 29½ Tage umfaßt, und diese Umläufe damit auch das Zeitmaß eines Jahres quantitativ bestimmen, gab es Rhythmen im Jahreslauf selbst, die diesen qualitativ unterteilten und die teilweise nur mit dem Sonnenlauf teilweise nur mit dem Mondphasenwechsel zusammenhingen.

In anderem Zusammenhang wurde bereits das Auf- und Abschwingen der Tageslängen zwischen den Jahrespunkten der Sommer- und Wintersonnenwende genannt, durch die das Jahr einen spezifischen Rhythmus für den mittelalterlichen Menschen bekam, der das Zeitmaß seines Tagesablaufes beeinflußte, während die beiden Äquinoktien zusammen mit den Solstitien die Jahreszeiten und damit die Folge der Arbeiten des Bauern bestimmten. Von den Mondphasen dagegen hing neben den Gezeiten auch der Wetterwechsel ab und diese Überzeugung schlug sich nicht nur in den Bauernregeln nieder, sondern auch in der Astrometeorologie[68], die entsprechend Judizien aufstellte − eine Verpflichtung, die im 15. und noch im 16. Jahrhundert an den Universitäten den Astronomen oblag − und deren Begründung im zu Anfang skizzierten Weltbild des Mittelalters gegeben war[69].

Ein Beispiel hierfür bilden die Kalendarien, die den Psalterien vorangestellt sind und deren Kalenderseiten einerseits durch das jeweilige Tierkreiszeichen, andererseits durch die entsprechende Monatsarbeit gekennzeichnet sind, die damit den Menschen in den Jahresablauf einordnen und sein Zeitmaß nicht nur quantitativ, sondern in ähnlicher Weise wie dies durch die kirchliche Festordnung geschieht, qualitativ an den Kosmos binden. So sind z. B. im Bohun-Psalter dem Februar die Fische und das Umgraben des Bodens, dem März der Widder und das Beschneiden der Bäume, dem Mai die Zwillinge und die Falkenjagd, dem September die Waage und die Weinlese und dem November der Schütze und das Schweineschlachten als jeweiliges Sternbild und als entsprechende Monatsarbeit zugeordnet[70].

Jedoch nicht nur der Rhythmus von Gebet und Arbeit in den Klöstern und nicht nur die Tätigkeiten der Bauern, sondern auch Handelsmessen und Märkte, Geld- und Zinswirtschaft hingen von dem Zeitmaß ab, das auf solche Weise − und hier insbesondere über den Festkalender − an den Kosmos gebunden war. So kam es, daß die Argumente, die im 16. Jahrhundert gegen die Einführung eines neuen Kalenders vorgebracht wurden, sich zu einem guten Teil darauf bezogen, daß durch Wegfallen von 10 Tagen finanzielle Schäden für die Loostage bei den Bauern und für die

---

[68] Lectio IV in II° nocturno diei 9 Octobris SS. Dionysii Episcopi Rurstici et Eleutherii Martyrum, in: Breviarium Romanum Ed. XIᵃ Pars autumnalis, Turonibus 1935.

[69] Cod. 608 Bibliothecae Jagiellonicae Cracoviensis, 259 sqq.

[70] Cod. Vindob. 1826, 1 v, 2 r, 3 r, 5 r, 6 r.

Zinstage bei den Handelsherren entstünden[71]. Hinzu trat, daß ein Teil der vom Nominalismus geprägten frühneuzeitlichen Theologen kein Verständnis mehr aufbrachte für die tiefe Symbolik, die noch Augustinus mit dem Pascha verband[72], noch gar für die kosmische Bedeutung des Todes Christi, von der Hippolyt überzeugt war.

In der gleichen Epoche hatte der Zeitgenosse Martin Luthers, der ermländische Domherr Nicolaus Copernicus, zur exakteren Bestimmung der natürlichen Jahreslänge – und dies paradoxerweise zum Zwecke der Reform des kirchlichen Kalenders, zu der er von Rom mitaufgefordert wurde[73] – sich entschlossen, die spätmittelalterliche und in Pariser Nominalistenkreisen entstandene Idee *quod coelum stet et terra movetur* wieder aufzugreifen[74] und zur Grundlage einer neuen Berechnungsmethode und entsprechender astronomischer Rechentafeln in seinem bekannten Werk De Revolutionibus zu machen[75].

Die sogenannten Prutenischen Tafeln, in denen nach copernicanischen Vorschriften und Werten die Ephemeriden der Planeten berechnet waren und die Erasmus Reinhold wenige Jahre später herausgab[76], wurden in der Tat von der Kalenderkommission Gregors XIII. berücksichtigt[77]. Auch wenn der für die Kalenderreform 1582 hauptverantwortliche Astronom und Mathematiker Christophorus Clavius ausdrücklich die Theorie, aufgrund der die Prutenischen Tafeln erstellt war, ablehnte, hatte diese unbeschadet dessen, daß sie seinerzeit noch unbeweisbar war[78], die antike und mittelalterliche Überzeugung von einem realen Zusammenhang zwischen Zeitmaß und Kosmos im Bewußtsein der Gelehrten endgültig zerstört[79].

---

[71] Bedenken, ob der Newe Bäpstliche Kalender eine Nothdurfft by der Christenheit seye und wie trewlich dieser Bapst Gregorius XIII. die Sachen damit meyne: ob der Bapst Macht habe, diesen Kalender der Christenheit auffzudringen. Ob auch fromme und rechte Christen schüldig seyn, denselben anzunehmen, Tubingae 1583.

[72] Augustinus, Epistolae ad Ianuarium, Lib. II epist. 55. IV, 6 sqq., Migne PL. XXXIII, 121, 207–208.

[73] P. von Middelenburg, Secundum compendium correctionis calendarii pro recta Pasche celebratione, Romae 1516, cart. A IIII v.

[74] Cod. N 764 Bibliothecae Trivultianae Mediolanensis, fol. 77–86.

[75] N. Copernicus, De Revolutionibus orbium coelestium, Norimbergae 1543 – Nicolaus-Copernicus-Gesamtausgabe im Auftrage der Kommission für die Copernicus-Gesamtausgabe, hrsgg. v. H. M. Nobis, Bd. II, De Revolutionibus – Kritischer Text besorgt v. H. M. Nobis und B. Sticker †, Hildesheim 1983.

[76] Prutenicae tabulae coelestium motuum. Authore Erasmo Reinholdo Salveldensi, Tubingae 1551.

[77] Cf. F. Kaltenbrunner, Die Polemik über die Gregorianische Kalenderreform, in: Sitzungsberichte d. Phil. Hist. Cl. d. Kaiserl. Akad. d. Wissensch. Bd. LXXXVII, Wien 1877, 496.

[78] Der endgültige Beweis konnte erst 1838 durch F. W. Bessels Messung einer Fixsternparallaxe erbracht werden.

[79] H. Blumenberg, Die kopernikanische Konsequenz für den Zeitbegriff, in: Colloquia copernicana I. Etudes sur l'audience de la théorie héliocentrique. Conférences du Symposium de l'UIHPS, Toruǹ 1973. Studia copernicana Bd. V, Wrocław etc. 1972, 57–77.

Wenige Jahrzehnte nach Erscheinung des Hauptwerkes von Copernicus
ersetzten vielmehr die Gegner der Gregorianischen Kalenderreform die
Verbindung von Zeitmaß und Kosmos endgültig durch eine neue: die-
jenige von Zeitmaß und Kapital[80].

---

[80] Vgl. M. Weber, Die protestantische Ethik und der Geist des Kapitalismus, in: Gesam-
melte Aufsätze zur Religionssoziologie, Bd. I, 4. A., Tübingen 1947, 17–205. F. Klemm,
Technik. Eine Geschichte ihrer Probleme, Freiburg/München 1954. Orbis academicus –
Problemgeschichte der Wissenschaft in Dokumenten und Darstellungen, Bd. II, 5, 188.

UN TRATTATO DI MISURA DEI MOTI CELESTI: IL DE MOTU OCTAVAE SPHAERAE DI PIETRO D'ABANO

di Graziella Federici Vescovini (Torino)

Come é quasi universalmente noto, nel Medioevo, la culla della matematica proveniente dall'antica sapienza indiana e greca, é stata la civiltà araba. I progressi della teoria dei numeri, positivi e negativi, i procedimenti di calcolo come l'algoritmo aritmetico, l'algebra e la trigonometria che permettono di risolvere complessi problemi astronomici ed ottici, arrivarono a uno stadio avanzato nel mondo arabo, particolarmente nei secoli IX−X e XI−XII[1]. Questa civiltà é stata anche il centro dello sviluppo di una disciplina tipicamente medievale e cioé l'astrologia: una funzione della matematica fu quella della redazione delle tavole dei transiti planetari per rendere possibile la previsione astrologica[2]. La scienza araba saldò così

---

[1] H. G. Zeuthen, Die Mathematik im Altertum und im Mittelalter, Berlin und Leipzig 1912, 80 B; in particolare G. Loria, Il miracolo arabo, in: Storia delle matematiche, Milano 1950, 187; M. Kline, Mathematics in Western Culture, Oxford 1953 (Milano 1979[2], 95−96); H. L. L. Busard, L'algèbre au moyen âge, Le liber mensurationum du Abu Bekr, in: Journal des Savants (1968) 65−132.

[2] I più famosi estensori di tavole astronomiche furono: al-Khwarizmi (al-Khwarizmi, abu Giafar Muhammad ibn Musa); cf. O. Neugebauer, the astronomical Tabels of al-Khwarizmi, Copenhague 1962 che dà la traduzione inglese del testo latino di Adelardo di Bath edito da H. Suter, Die astronomischen Tafeln des Muhammad ibn Musa al-Khawarizmi in der Bearbeitung des Maslama ibn Ahmad al Madjriti und der latein. Übersetzung des Adelard von Bath, Copenhague 1914; cf. J. J. Burckhardt, Die mittleren Bewegungen der Planeten im Tafel-Werk des Kwarizmi, in: Vierteljahrschrift. Naturforschungs-Gesellschaft Zürich 106 (1961) 213−231; E. Rybka, Mouvement des planètes dans l'astronomie des Peuples de l'Islam, in: Oriente e Occidente, Roma Accademia Nazionale dei Lincei 1971, 579−594. Altro estensore di tavole fu al-Battani (nato intorno al 929): cf. Al-Battani sive Albategni Opus astronomicorum latine versum, adnotationibus instructum a Carolo Alphonso Nallino, Pars prima, Mediolani Insubrum 1903 (= Pubblicazione del R. Osservatorio di Brera, Milano, 40, 1889−1903); Ibn Yunus (Alì ibn Abi Said Abderrahman ibn Ahmad ibn Yunus), morto intorno al 1009, autore delle tavole astronomiche hakamite perché dedicate al sovrano al-Hakim, pubblicate in estratto dal Caussin (= Notices et Extraits des manuscrits de la Bibliothèque Nationale, VII, 61−240); az-Zarqali (Ibrahim Abu-Ishak), noto come Azarchel o Azarchel, vissuto a Cordova intorno al 1029−1087, autore delle Tavole Toledane (cf. J. M. Millás-Vallicrosa, Estudios sobre Azarquiel, Madrid−Granada 1943−1950); quindi il gruppo di astronomi chiamati dal re Alfonso di Castiglia (1252−1284), estensori delle Tavole Alfonsine; su ciò cf. D. Romano, Le opere scientifiche di Alfonso X e l'intervento degli Ebrei, in: Oriente e Occidente cit., 700.

Tutti questi autori sono citati da Pietro d'Abano. Per le tavole al suo tempo cf. L. Thorndike, Astronomical Observation at Paris from 1312 to 1315, in: Isis 38 (1948) 200−205; dello stesso,

strettamente il calcolo matematico alla tecnica astrologica. Nel mondo medievale latino la parola matematica in quanto distinta da geometria, prese il significato di astrologia e i professori di astrologia furono chiamati matematici. Un esempio di ciò può essere rappresentato dal Mathematicus di Bernardo Silvestre, poemetto astrologico in cui si dibatte il problema morale della libertà in relazione al peso della previsione astrale. Il *mathematicus*, personaggio principale dell'opera, non é altri che l'astrologo[3]. I matematici dovevano avere conoscenze accurate dei dati delle stelle fisse (ossia dell'ottavo cielo) e dei pianeti, dovevano stabilire correlazioni esatte tra le loro posizioni in cielo e gli eventi terreni[4]. Il *mathematicus* (ossia l'astrologo-astronomo) era, quindi, uno scienziato che procedeva sulla base di rigorose dimonstrazioni scientifiche di carattere matematico[5] a redigere anche precise tavole astronomiche. Enrico di Gand nei suoi Quodlibeta[6] sembra consacrare definitivamente questa accezione del significato di *astrologus* come *mathematicus* che procede per dimostrazioni razionali che prescindono dai sensi, scrivendo: *intelligere autem est cognoscere aliquid ex alio per discursum rationis vel definitivum vel syllogisticum, qualiter*

Pre-copernican Astronomical Activity, in: Proceedings of the American Philosophical Society 94 (1950) 321−326. Sull'inserimento dell'insegnamento dell'astronomia-astrologia nelle Università medievali cf. R. Lemay, The Teaching of Astronomy in Medieval Universities, in: Manuscripta 20 (1976) 200−215 e il mio studio, Astrologia e scienza, Firenze 1979, passim; sui rapporti tra astronomia e astrologia cf. anche W. Petri, Tradition und Fortschritt in der Astronomie des Mittelalters, in: Oriente e Occidente cit., 633−41. Sulle tavole astronomiche in generale cf. E. Poulle, Les sources astronomiques (Textes, Tables, Instruments), Brepols, Turnbout-Belgium 1981.

[3] Mathematicus, ed. B. Hauréau, Paris 1895 (sotto il nome di Ildeberto di Lavardin anche in P. L. 171, 1365−80, ed. J. Bourasse); cf. P. Dronke, Bernardus Silvestris Cosmographia, Leiden 1978, 2. Anche Agostino aveva inteso per matematici gli astrologi e per questo invita a diffidarne: De civitate Dei, V, 3, 7 sgg., ed. B. Dombart−A. Kalb, Turnholti 1965, 131−135 (= Corpus christianorum, Series latina 47). La condanna religiosa di Agostino si affianca a quella politica dei legislatori romani del IV secolo del Codex Theodosianus IX, 16,1−12 De maleficis et mathematicis et ceteris similibus, dove i matematici sono identificati con gli astrologi: cf. H. Funke, Majestät und Magieprozesse bei Ammianus Marcellinus, in: Jahrbuch für Antike und Christentum 9 (1967) 30.

[4] *Partimur igitur omne(m) siderum stellarumque scientiam gemina specie in motum celestium ac motuum effectus. Prima quidem species mathematica universalis sapientia vocatur. Integram etenim perfectamque tradit scientiam quantitatis et habitudinis circulorum motuumque celestium in se eiusque primum, deinde ad alios tamen usque ad terrae globum* (Abu-Ma'shar ⟨Jafar ibn Muhammad al-Balkhi⟩, Introductorium maius in astronomiam octo continens libros partiales, Venetiis 1515, cap. 1, f. a2ᵛ).

[5] *Supernorum vero motuum quantitatis et qualitatis pars humanis sensibus patuit. Unde omnes scientiae primordium partem rationi tribus ex locis c o m p u t o p r o p o r t i o n e et m e n- s u r a argumentum necesse materia infert ubi qui huic sapientiae non concedant et sensu debiles et rationis alienos esse, consequens sit* (op. cit., l. c.). Anche Averroé aveva scritto: *Astrologia enim huius temporis nihil est in esse, sed est conveniens computationi non esse* (Metaphysica, XII, com. 45).

[6] Quodlibeta XII, q II, Parigi 1518, ff. 485ʳ−486ᵛ.

doctor astrologus intelligit per demonstrationem solem nunc eclipsari, quia oculis non vidit.

Tolomeo nel suo Liber quadripartiti aveva distinto l'astronomia in due parti, una teorica o quadriviale *qua novit homo quot sphaerae sunt in caelo et quot maneries motuum*, e una pratica *et haec est super stellarum iudiciis qua scire possunt virtutes earum et qualiter operant in rebus omnibus quae sunt infra sphaeram lunae*[7]. Nel mondo cristiano Isidoro di Siviglia prende posizione dei confronti di questa disciplina, dando una definizione che consacra l'astrologia come scienza matematica, separandola dall'astronomia naturale o fisica. Scrive infatti: *Astrologia vero partim naturalis, partim superstitiosa est; naturalis, dum exsequitur Solis et Lunae cursus vel stellarum certasque temporum stationes; superstitiosa vero est illa quam mathematici sequuntur*[8].

La matematica é il vero fondamento di questa scienza nel suo aspetto teorico, ma anche in quello pratico in quanto il carattere certo della previsione astrale si fonda sull'esattezza del calcolo matematico dell'astrologo[9]. Da ciò l'importanza della soluzione matematica di alcuni problemi astronomici come quello del computo del moto del firmamento o ottava sfera[10] da cui si faceva dipendere l'inizio del mondo e, quindi, degli eventi terreni.

Chi ha qualque consuetudine con le opere astronomiche medievali arabe e latine e con i problemi ivi dibattuti, non cessa di stupirsi dell'importanza che assume il quesito del moto dell'ottava sfera che é collegato anche con quello del numero delle sfere. Ancora agli inizi del XVI secolo Agostino Ricci (Augustinus Ricius) dedicherà un trattato sul moto dell'ottava sfera in cui sono riportate e ridiscusse tutte le più importanti tesi degli autori

---

[7] Liber quadripartiti translatus a Platone Tyburtino, Venetiis 1501, tract. I, 1, f. 4[r] e sgg.

[8] Isidori Hispalensis Etymologiarum sive Originum libri XX, ed. W. M. Lindsay, Oxonii 1911, 1, III, 27, 9–12; VIII, 9, 24–26.

[9] Pietro d'Abano difende l'astrologia-matematica come scienza certa e non *coniecturativa*, perché essa é matematica: *in scientia astrologiae non est ambiguitas; verum omnis certitudo est, cum sumat demonstrationes suas ex scientia numeri et mensura, idest arithmetica ac geometria, quae etiam investigat et considerat ea quae semper uno se habent modo* (Lucidator dubitabilium astronomiae, q I, ms. Parigi, Bibl. Nat. lat. 2598, f. 104ra; Roma, ms. Pal. lat. 1171, f. 324ra). L'attacco all'astrologia da parte di Oresme qualche tempo dopo é condotto, allora proprio dal versante del ragionamento matematico. Per questo Oresme cerca di dimostrare l'incommensurabilità dei moti celesti: *Posita aliqua incommensurabilitate ut prius, impossibile est arte praescire ad punctum locum aut tempus alicuius oppositionis, aut coniunctionis aut cuiuscumque alterius aspectus vel cuiusvis dispositionis praeteritae vel futurae* (Oresme, Ad pauca respicientes, 16 conc., ed. Grant, Madison–Milwaukee–London 1966, 420).

[10] Scrive ancora Oresme: *Sunt enim aliqui astrologi opinantes se ad punctum scire motus, aspectus, coniunctiones, oppositiones planetarum et corporum caelestium dispositiones credentes se esse sapientes et stulti facti sunt . . . Et de istorum numero fuerunt quidam qui propter motum octavae sperae in 36.000 annis mundum asserebant ad statum pristinum remeare; alii vero in 15.000 annis, sicut Plato completo peryodo seu anno maiori secundum antedictum. Ad hanc igitur fatuitatem eradicandam volo modice laborare* (op. cit., l. c., 382).

greci, arabi, ebraici e latini medievali, da lui riviste alla luce dei risultati degli scritti del Regiomontano, di Pico della Mirandola e di un sincretismo filosofico in cui fonde neoplatonismo e cabala[11]. Il problema del moto dell'ottava sfera é sempre stato di una rilevanza concettuale fondamentale e, in particolare nel Medioevo, per un complesso di aspetti filosofici, metafisico-teologici e fisici, matematico-astronomici. Ciò é dimostrato anche da una opera finora inedita di Pietro d'Abano (Petrus Aponensis, medico e astronomo padovano morto intorno al 1315), di cui abbiamo rintracciato alcune copie manoscritte[12] dedicate proprio al De motu octavae sphaerae, di cui intendiamo parlare in questo nostro contributo. Il problema del moto dell'ottava sfera é sviluppato da Pietro d'Abano anche nell'altra sua opera astronomica inedita, il Lucidator dubitabilium astronomiae, nella questione seconda (*an motus unus caeli communis sit vel*

---

[11] Augustini Ricii De motu octavae sphaerae, Imprimebat Simon Colinaeus, Parigi 1521. Nell'ultima parte si hanno riferimenti alla teoria degli sephiroth. La sua opera non é da confondersi con quella di Paolo Ricci, forse suo fratello; cf. F. Secret, Les kabbalistes chrétiens de la Renaissance, Paris 1964.

[12] *Incipit: Quoniam iuxta Ptolomeum rerum quippe causas rimaturo opus est primo caelestia contemplari.* Manoscritti: Arras 748 (688), sec. XV, ff. 60^r−65^v; Milano, Bibl. Ambrosiana, M 35 sup. sec. XV, ff. 18^r−26^r; Münich, codex lat. 28229, sec. XIV−XV, ff. 78^r−87^r; Oxford, Bodl. Canonici, Misc. lat. 190, sec. XV, ff. 79^r−84^r; Parigi, Bibl. Nat. lat. 2598, sec. XIV, ff. 122ra−125va; Parigi, Univ. 581, sec. XIV−XV, ff. 409^r−412^r; Utrecht, Bibliotheek van de Rijks-Universiteit, lat. 725, ff. 204^b−206^r (copia incompleta): in questa il trattato De motu octavae sphaerae di Pietro d'Abano é, non a caso, unito all'opera Almanach planetarum di Guglielmo di Saint-Cloud, con cui é stata confusa: quel Guglielmo di Saint-Cloud che, sembra, verso il 1290−92 ridiscute come Pietro d'Abano il movimento di accesso e recesso dei segni per sostisfuire come Pietro stesso una ipotesi di spiegazione di movimento precessionale; quindi calcola i nuovi valori numerici dello spostamento precessionale. In questa copia si legge infatti a f. 201^6 v: *Tractatus Petri de Padua de motu octavae sphaerae compositionequoque Almanach per vigenos quosque annos ac variis aliis astronomia concernendis* e l'incipit che segue immediatamente corrisponde con quello dell'Almanach di Guglielmo di Saint-Cloud: incipit: *Cum intentio mea sit componere Almanach planetarum ad . . . ex nunc vicelict anno Domini 1292 . . .* Pertanto il Tractatus di Pietro, che é anche incompleto, in realtà inizia dopo l'Almanach di Guglielmo e quindi non al f. 201^6 v, ma al f. 204$_b$, incipit: *Quoniam iuxta Ptolomeum* e si arresta al f. 205$_r$: *Explicit Tractatus de motu octavae spaherae ordinatus per magistrum Petrum Paduanum anno gratiae 1310.* Roma, Città del Vaticano, Pal. lat. 1377, sec. XIV, ff. 1ra−5ra; Pal. lat. 1171, sec. XIV, ff. 317va−320ra; Vat. Barb. lat. 256, sec. XV, ff. 103−114^v; Venezia, Museo Correr, Provenienza Cicogna 2289, sec. XV, ff. 111^r−125^r; Vienna, Nationalbibliothek, codex Vind. Palat. 5498, sec. XV, ff. 60^r−70^v. La copia di Oxford corrisponde con quella del Museo Correr; é stata redatta nel 1385 come risulta dalle tavole annesse in fine al testo di Pietro che deve aver composto la sua opera tra il 1303 e il 1310, anno di revisione di molti dei suoi scritti. Scrive, infatti, in tutte le copie da noi consultate: *usque ad praesentem annum 1310 gratiae quo ego Petrus Paduensis istud opus construxi.* Per una datazione degli scritti di Pietro d'Abano in particolare per il suo trattato De motu octavae sphaerae cf. anche L. Thorndike, Peter of Abano, in: a History of Magic and Experimental Science, II, New York 1974^4, 859; L. Norpoth, Zur Bio-Bibliographie und Wissenschaftslehre des Pietro d'Abano, Mediziners, Philosophen und Astronomen in Padua, Kyklos 3 (1930) 292−353. Cf. B. Nardi, Le dottrine filosofiche di Pietro d'Abano, in: Saggi sull'aristotelismo padovano, Firenze 1958, 19−74.

plures) e, in parte, nella terza (*an sphaerae sint novem, plures aut pau-ciores*)[13].

Il problema del moto dell'ottava sfera comprende un complesso di problemi che qui distingueremo per amore di chiarezza e che sono, invece, tutti presupposti negli scritti di Pietro d'Abano fino ad Agostino Ricci. Il più impegnativo era quello metafisico-ontologico che risale all'impostazione del discorso cosmologico di Aristotele del XII libro della Metaphysica: il moto é sostanziale, quindi, se si ammette una pluralità di moti come nel caso delle sfere celesti, si dovrà ammettere una pluralità di sostanze. E se le sostanze sono le sfere celesti, quante esse sono e si diversificano, altrettanti saranno i moti. Ma la natura del moto sostanziale è unica: può essere solo circolare o rettilinea e non si sa come estenderla ai moti misti. Il moto circolare non ha contrari e, così, tutti i moti delle sfere celesti dovranno essere semplici, unici, senza contrari, perfetti. Invece i moti sublunari costituiti dai quattro elementi, gravi e leggeri, saranno spiegati con la teoria dei luoghi naturali, in alto e in basso per contrari e, quindi, sarano imperfetti. Ma se tutto ciò che si muove nel mondo avviene per i luoghi naturali, qual'è il luogo dell'universo? Se il moto perfetto o circolare è quello che non ha contrari, si può veramente dire che il cielo si muove? Qual'è la causa agente del cielo? Secondo Aristotele il cielo é una sfera immensa, ma limitata che abbraccia il mondo intero; al di fuori di essa non c'è niente, né pieno né vuoto, l'ultima sfera essendo costituita da quella delle stelle fisse o firmamento: l'ottava[14].

Alcuni astronomi, interpretando il testo aristotelico che non era per niente chiaro, in senso stretto, arrivarono a non introdurre più di otto

---

[13] Si conoscono finora solo quattro manoscritti del Lucidator dubitabilium astronomiae, tra cui Parigi, Bibl. Nat. lat. 2598, ff. 99ra–121va; Città del Vaticano, Vat. lat. 1171, ff. 320ra–327[r]; incipit: *quoniam astrologicae considerationis ambiguitates.* Le *quaestiones* contenute nel Lucidator riguardanti: *an astrologia* ⟨*astronomia*⟩ *cum hiis quae ipsius extet scientia,* sono: *an astronomia sit scientia cum eius appenditiis; an motus unus caeli communis* ⟨*sit*⟩ *vel plures; an sphaerae sint novem plures aut pauciores; an sit ponere eccentricos et epiciclos; an planeta moveantur per se in eccentrico vel epiciclo; an Sol situetur supra lunam immediate vel planetarum medio; an Solis declinatio sit 24 graduum vel aliter; an Solis aux sit mobilis vel immobilis; an centrum eccentrici Solis distet a terra 2 gradibus et 23 primis sive ipsius aequatio; an Sol peragrat eccentricum eius in 365 diebus et 4 vel aliter.* Nel Lucidator Pietro fa un riferimento al suo trattato De motu octavae sphaerae scrivendo: *Sic quidem tota eius circulatio erit perfecta quasi annorum curriculo 36.000 in cuius quidem ostensione cum motu et latitudinis ab aequatore in septentrionem et ab inde in austrum, tractatum huic suscipiens specialem construxi ac sphaeram materialem nonam, octavam concludentem, denotantem huius motum evidentissime* (Lucidator, q II, Parigi, bibl. Nat. lat. 2598, f. 109rb). Torneremo sul Lucidator di cui abbiamo in preparazione l'edizione.

[14] Aristotele, De caelo II, 3, 286a 13–19; Averroè, Physica IV, com. 43, f. 142 G 8–H 4; com. 45, f. 144 A 11–C 15; com. 15, ff. 126 M 14–127 C 1; Sermo de substantia orbis, f. 4 F 11–K 2. Sulla teoria planetaria di Ibn Rushd cf. F. Carmody, The Planetary Theory of Ibn Rushd, in: Osiris 10 (1952) 556–86; cf. M. Cimino, L'astronomia araba e la sua dif-

sfere, negando la necessità dell'introduzione di una nona sfera, sulla base del ragionamento che le sfere esistono e si conoscono in base alla influenza che esercitano. Siccome la nona sfera non ha né astri, né pianeti, non agisce e se non agisce, non é[15]. A questa argomentazione che, in forma un pò diversa é riportata anche da Pietro d'Abano[16], si contrappone quella della maggioranza degli astronomi arabi e latini medievali, come é testimoniato anche dai diversi commenti del testo La sfera del Sacrobosco, per esempio quello di Roberto Anglico. La nona sfera é introdotta come primo mobile, ossia come causa prima di moto semplice dei moti delle altre otto sfere che, dall'osservazione delle apparenze dei moti, risultavano mosse da moti duplici o contrari. Siccome tutte le otto sfere si muovono di moti duplici – scrive Roberto Anglico – *igitur erit ponere aliquod corpus caeleste aliud ab istis octo, quod moveatur unico simplici motu tantum quare erit nona sphaera*[17]. Allo stesso modo la nona sfera era stata introdotta da alcuni astronomi arabi come Thebit ben Qurra e molti altri[18], per spiegare l'uniformità e la semplicità del moto celeste, la difformità essendo attribuita al moto dell'ottava: siccome l'ottava si muove *per accidens* in quanto si muove di moto contrario (quello della rivoluzione diurna e quello annuale di precessione degli equinozi), allora, bisogna presupporre una sfera che si muove *per se*, causa superiore dei moti inferiori: ossia la nona, il primo mobile.

Ma questa dottrine furono ulteriormente complicate dai filosofi e dai teologi cristiani perché la cosmologia naturale di Aristotele e di Tolomeo fu impiegata per spiegare la nozione teologico-religiosa dell'Empireo, ossia per risolvere il problema della collocazione astronomica del Paradiso. La questione del moto dell'ottava sfera era, quindi, da un lato collegata a

---

fusione, in: Oriente e Occidente cit., 662. Per il problema del luogo dell'universo mi sia permesso di rinviare al mio lavoro citato, Astrologia e scienza, 296–320.

[15] *Utrum debeamus ponere nonam sphaeram . . . argitur sic: ex quo orbis non habet influentiam nisi propter stellas quae sunt in eo, et in nono orbe non sit aliqua stella, quare non habebit influentiam et ita frustra esse, sed natura nihil facit frustra, quare non videtur quod sit nonum caelum* (Robertus Anglicus, in sphaeram, ed. Thorndike, Chicago 1949, 147). Roberto Anglico critica questa argomentazione contro la nona sfera che, era stata quasi universalmente introdotta nel X secolo per spiegare il moto diurno, mentre all'ottava si attribuiva il moto precessionale, concepito in modo diverso, come vedremo, da cui le discussioni.

[16] *Sciendum quod apud priores astrologos unus tantum motus communis ut qui octavi caeli, nondum enim sic tactum in nonum devenerunt orbem cum eum ob ipsius simplicitatem stellarumque carentiam non perciperent. Quae siquidem opinio, ut apparuit, tempore Aristotelis permansit vegetata* (Lucidator, q II, Parigi, Nat. lat. 2598, f. 107^{rb-va}).

[17] Robertus Anglicus, In sphaeram, ed. Thorndike, Chicago 1949, 148.

[18] The Commentary ascribed to Michel Scot, in: The spere of Sacrobosco and its Commentators, ed. Thorndike, Chicago 1949, 283–84. Sull'opera astronomica inedita di Michele Scoto Liber introductorius cf. P. Morpurgo, Il Liber introductorius di Michele Scoto, Roma, Accademia Nazionale dei Lincei 1979, 149–161 (= Rendiconti della Classe di scienze morali-storiche e filologiche, VIII, 34).

quella matematico-astronomica del numero delle sfere e dall'altro a quella teologico-religiosa della collocazione della sede dei beati[19].

Come sappiamo nel 1241 e, poi, ufficialmente nel 1244 il Vescovo di Parigi condannò come quarto errore[20], la tesi che le anime glorificate e la Beata Vergine non sono nel cielo Empireo con gli angeli, ma nel cielo acqueo o cristallino che é sopra il firmamento ossia sopra l'ottava sfera: in altre parole la tesi che esclude la collocazione del Paradiso dei beati nella decima sfera, sede separata di Dio. I teologi cristiani, infatti, come ricorda anche Michele Scoto, avevano sentito l'esigenza di porre una causa movente anteriore al primo mobile (ossia alla nona sfera), introducendo il cielo Empireo come decima, da non confondersi con il cristallino o nona sfera. In questa concezione teologica dei cieli, essi si popolano di intelligenze e di anime[21]. La visione meccanica dei moti celesti di Aristotele e di Tolomeo si fonde alla concezione animistica di ispirazione neoplatonica e orientale (come ha scritto il padre Chenu)[22], secondo la quale la sostanza dell'anima non é differente dalla sostanza del cielo sia esso costituito di fuoco, d'etere o di pura luce[23]. La discussione teologica del Paradiso investiva il problema della necessità o meno di una distinzione tra la sfera di Dio e la sfera dei beati e della Vergine. Così la visione gerarchica neoplatonica delle sfere tendeva a distinguere la decima dalla nona, la dimora di Dio e degli angeli da quella dei beati. Anche san Tommaso per distinguere la sostanza dell'Empireo da quella della sfera inferiore degli esseri sublunari scriverà: *illud caelum dicitur Empyreum idest igneum non ab ardore, sed a splendore*[24]. Tuttavia se l'Empireo é fatto coincidere con la decima sfera

---

[19] Cf. anche B. Nardi, La dottrina dell'Empireo nella sua genesi storica e nel pensiero dantesco, in: Saggi di filosofia dantesca, Milano 1930, 189−238. Cf. E. Gilson, A la recherche de l'Empyrée, in: Dante et les mythes, Paris 1965, 147−161 (= Revue des études italiennes, 11).

[20] *Quartus ⟨error⟩: quod animae glorificatae non sunt in caelo empireo cum angelis, nec corpora glorificata erunt ibi, sed in caelo aqueo vel cristallino quod supra firmamentum est, quod et de beata Virgine praesumitur*, in: H. Denifle−E. Chatelain, Chartularium Universitatis Parisiensis, I, Paris 1889, n. 128; per la datazione cf. V. Doucet, La date des condammations parisiennes dites de 1241. Faut-il corriger le Chartulaire de l'Université?, Louvain 1947, 184 (= Mélanges Auguste Pelzer).

[21] A. Wolfson, The Problem of the Souls of the Spheres from the Byzantine Commentaries on Aristotle through the Arabs and St. Thomas to Kepler, in: Studies in the History of Philosophy and Religion I, Cambridge 1973, 22−59; M. T. D'Alverny, Les pérégrinations de l'âme dans l'autre monde d'après un anonyme de la fin du XIIe siècle, in: AHDLMA 13 (1942) 239−299.

[22] M. D. Chenu, Le dernier avatar de la théologie orientale en Occident au XIIIe siècle, Louvain 1947, 165 e sgg. (= Mélanges Auguste Pelzer). Cf. dello stesso, Astrologia predicabilis, in AHDLMA 31 (1964) 62−65.

[23] Cf. anche J. Pepin, Théologie cosmique et théologie chrétienne, Paris 1964, 245.

[24] E prosegue: *Quod pro tanto dictum sit, ne aliquis opinetur Augustinum caelum Empyreum posuisse, sicut nunc ponitur a modernis* (San Tommaso, Summa theologica, 1 pars, q 66, art. 3).

e il cristallino con la nona e se la collocazione del Paradiso oscilla nelle discussioni teologiche tra la decima e la nona — come risulta dalla tesi condannata nel 1244 — l'assimilazione della nona sfera senza astri degli astronomi arabi come Thebit ben Qurra e gli altri, con il cielo cristallino dei padri della Chiesa, come la speculazione sul cielo Empireo, non sono ammesse dagli scienziati e dai matematici come Pietro d'Abano e molti altri, tra i quali, più tardi, Biagio Pelacani da Parma.

Scrive, infatti, Pietro d'Abano che l'affermazione di una decima sfera é fondata più sulla rivelazione che sulla ragione e l'esperienza; pertanto l'ammissione di una decima sfera *non est certa, potius phantastica et otiosa*[25].

Il problema astronomico-matematico dell'ottava sfera é precisamente delineato nel testo di Pietro d'Abano che stiamo esaminando, il Tractatus de motu octavae sphaerae. Questa opera costituisce un documento importante del tentativo di calcolare lo spostamento precessionale dell'ottava sfera, ossia del moto annuale di rivoluzione lenta della sfera delle stelle fisse o firmamento. Pietro d'Abano riporta tutte le cifre da lui conosciute e fa la cronistoria iniziando da Ipparco che aveva scoperto la precessione degli equinozi, e da Tolomeo che aveva accettato quei valori numerici di Ipparco senza considerare la differenza degli anni intercorsi tra lui e Ipparco; Pietro si sofferma anche a discutere le cifre date dal trattato di Thebit ben Qurra sul moto dell'ottava sfera e del suo seguace ar-Zarqali (Arzachen). Questi avevano introdotto nel Medioevo una teoria, detta di trepidazione o di accesso e recesso del moto dell'ottava sfera, per spiegare la variabilità dei punti equinoziali[26].

Thebit, astronomo arabo vissuto nel IX secolo, medita sulla discrepanza dei dati che riguarda la precessione degli equinozi scoperta da Ipparco nel 125 a. C. e ripresa poi da Tolomeo che applica un valore erroneo della costante di precessione. A causa del lento cambiamento della direzione dell'asse terrestre si manifesta un moto graduale della linea degli equinozi che Ipparco osservò, confrontando le sue determinazioni delle longitudini di determinate stelle, con quelle di Timocari, risalenti a circa 150 anni prima. Tolomeo, già come Ipparco, poi, aveva stabilito che questo spostamento doveva ammontare ad almeno un grado ogni cento anni[27], ma nell'opera successiva sugli spostamenti dei segni solstiziali ed equinoziali, egli dice di avere osservato che Spica si trova a 6 gradi dall'equinozio d'autunno, mentre Timocari aveva trovato che ai suoi tempi tale distanza era di 8 gradi. Ora questo astronomo aveva osservato Spica nel 294 e nel

---

[25] Lucidator, q III, Parigi, Bibl. nat. lat. 2598, f. 111rb; Vat. Pal. lat. 1171, f. 329va.

[26] Questa teoria di Thebit é stata studiata in particolare da B. R. Goldstein, On Theory of Trepidation According to Thabit B. Qurra and al-Zarqualli and its Implications for Omocentric Planetary Theory, in: Centaurus 10 (1965) 232−247; W. Hartner, Trepidation and Planetary Theories, in: Oriente e Occidente cit., 609−632.

[27] Tolomeo, Syntaxis, VII, 2, ed. Heiberg II, 15−16.

283 a. C.[28], mentre Ipparco la osservò nel 129 a. C., cosìcché la variazione ammonta a 45″ o 46″ all'anno. Tolomeo a sua volta, confrontando le longitudini di quattro stelle determinate da Timocari e da Ipparco con quelle trovate da Agrippa e Menelao nel 93 e nel 98 d. C., trovò una variazione annua di 36″, ovvero di un grado ogni cento ani e adottò questa cifra tonda. Teone di Alessandria accetta il valore tolemaico di un grado ogni cento anni, ma racconta anche che secondo alcune opinioni, taluni astronomi antichi avevano creduto che a partire da una certa epoca, i segni solstiziali si muovono di 8 gradi secondo l'ordine dei segni dopodiché ritornano indietro di uno stesso intervallo, dando origine all'idea ciclica del grande anno o filosoficamente parlando all'idea dell'eterno ritorno. Tolomeo, tuttavia, non era stato di questo parere, perché non fa intervenire questo moto nei suoi calcoli. In altre parole questi antichi astrologi, con i quali con concorda Tolomeo, ritenevano che la longitudine di una stella crescesse per 640 anni (di un grado ogni 80 anni) e che poi cominciasse subito a diminuire e lo facesse per altri 640 anni, dopo di che cominciasse nuovamente a crescere. Tali astrologi dovevano aver vissuto prima di Tolomeo (Teone li chiama *palaioi*[29]), ma dopo Ippparco, perché conoscevano la precessione e adottarono il suo valore di 45″ all'anno. Essi credevano, dunque, che la precessione fosse un fenomeno ciclico e avevano fissato nel 158 a. C., l'anno della inversione del moto. Tolomeo non aveva accettato questa teoria, perché per lui la precessione é semplicemente una lenta rotazione dell'ottava sfera da ovest ad est attorno ai poli dello zodiaco con un periodo di 36.000 anni. La precessione, dunque, avviene in una direzione sola. Thebit, invece, mostra di accettare la teoria ciclica riportata da Teone della precessione, introducendo però un elemento nuovo, ossia quello dell'oscillazione in avanti ed in indietro dell'inclinazione dell'eclittica (*trepidaxio fixarum*) e, quindi, riteneva che gli equinozi si spostano in avanti ed in indietro oscillando.

All'ottava sfera, pertanto, secondo la teoria di Thebit, é attribuito un triplice moto, di cui quello di trepidazione é il proprio e singolare. Il primo movimento é in longitudine da ovest ad est così come Tolomeo aveva spiegato la precessione; il secondo é in latitudine; il terzo é il moto diurno che é comunicato all'ottava sfera dalla nona, il primo mobile[30]. L'ottava

---

[28] Op. cit., VII, 3, 28–29.

[29] Pietro li chiama *priores*: *Quidam vero priores seu imaginum contructores, abnuentes motum praetactum octavae continuum, eam extimaverunt intercise moveri super duos circulos parvos imaginatos in capite Arietis et Librae, quorum circumferentiam octo ponebant partium, quem motum dixere accessus et recessus in 80 annis gradu uno ut curriculo 640 anorum, sic accessus existat, deinde totidemque recessio* (De motu octavae sphaerae, ms. Venezia, Museo Correr, Prov. Cicogna 2289 f. 116ʳ).

[30] In questo modo, ossia come moto triplice, é spiegato il modo dell'ottava sfera di Thebit e dei suoi seguaci, da Agostino Ricci, che lo critica e lo rifiuta nel suo De motu octavae sphaerae. La teoria di Thebit é esposta da Agostino come *opinio novissima*: *Sequaces omnes*

sfera é così dotata di un moto di rotazione estremamente lento intorno al suo asse, che era inclinato di 23 gradi, 35′ rispetto alla nona secondo i calcoli di Albategni (Albattani, sec. IX). Ora Thebit non solo corregge il valore di Albategni in 23 gradi, 33′, ma suppone anche che il semplice fenomeno della precessione sia variabile, immaginando nella nona sfera una eclittica fissa che interseca l'equatore in due punti, gli equinozi medi, formando con esso un angolo di 23 gradi 33′ 30″ e una eclittica mobile nell' ottava sfera, fissata, in due punti diametralmente opposti, a due piccoli cerchi, i cui centri si trovano negli equinozi medi e i cui raggi sono uguali a 4 gradi 18′ 43″. I punti tropici mobili del Cancro e del Capricorno non lasciano mai l'eclittica fissa, ma si muovono avanti ed indietro per un tratto pari a 8 gradi 37′ 26″, mentre i due punti sull'eclittica mobile, situati a 90 gradi dai punti tropici, si muovono sulla circonferenza di piccoli cerchi, cosicché l'eclittica mobile si alza e si abbassa rispetto a quella fissa, mentre i punti d'intersezione dell'equatore e dell'eclittica mobile vanno avanti ed indietro di 10 gradi 45′ in entrambi i modi. Questo moto appartiene all'ottava sfera ed é comune e tutte le stelle; perciò il sole raggiunge talvolta la sua massima declinazione nel Cancro, talvolta nei Gemelli. Thebit dice così che il mutamento di direzione e il valore del moto degli equinozi dai tempi di Tolomeo, quando era di 1 grado ogni cento anni é cresciuto, perché osservatori successivi hanno trovato che é di 1 grado ogni sessantasei anni. La teoria di Thebit fu accolta senza difficoltà da ar-Zarqali (Arzachel)[31], il quale pose il periodo di oscillazione di 10 gradi nei due sensi, uguale a 2000 anni musulmani o 1940 anni gregoriani, ossia di 1 grado ogni 97 anni, ovvero 37″ all'anno. Il moto ha luogo su un cerchio il cui raggio é lungo 10 gradi; all'epoca dell'Egira l'equinozio mobile si trovava a 40′ con precessione in aumento e nel 1080 d. C., a 7 gradi 25′. La diminuzione dell' inclinazione dell'eclittica, che gli astronomi di al-Mamum (dall'osservatorio eretto a Damasco nel 829) avevano trovato pari a 23 gradi 33′, favorì l'idea della trepidazione di Thebit[32] e il passo successivo nello sviluppo di questa teoria fu la combinazione di moto pregressivo ed oscillatorio.

---

novissimi, caelum stellatum triplici motu agitari: primo scilicet motu diurno a decimo orbe (duos enim supra octavo orbes locaverunt) procedente. Secundo motu tardissimo ex nona sphaera octavo illato, quem motum augium communem appellant, quo in quadraginta novem millibus annorum totus zodiacus, iuxta seriem signorum gyrum complet, ita quod in singulis annis 26 secunda et totidem unius gradus tertia peragrat. Tertio vero voluerint motu accessus et recessus quem motum proprium huius sphaerae esse affirmant (De motu octavae sphaerae, Parigi 1521, f. 22ʳ).

[31] Akakel vero constructor tabularum super Toletum cuius quidem nimis Thebit Core hunc motum amplectens, eum se fingit corrigere ponens praetactorum circumferentiam circulorum decem obtinere partes et 45 minutis cuius motum fore censuit in 66 annis et 4 mensibus parte illa, ita ut eorum alteruter perficiatur in 742 annis fere (Pietro d'Abano, De motu octavae sphaerae, ms. Venezia cit., f. 116ʳ).

[32] Il testo latino di Thebit De motu octavae sphaerae é stato edito da F. J. Carmody, Four Latin Tracts of Thabit b. Qurra, Berkeley 1942, ristampato in: The Astronomical Works of

Pietro d'Abano fa una storia della teoria che si ritroverà sviluppata e criticata anche da Agostino Ricci, medico del papa Paolo III, nel suo De motu octavae sphaerae. Ma già prima Alpetragio nel XII secolo[33] l'aveva criticata, prendendo l'avvio da Teone alessandrino che combinava il moto di un grado ogni cento anno con l'oscillazione. Al tempo del re Alfonso, i suoi astronomi si resero conto che gli equinozi si erano spostati all'indietro più di quanto non consentisse la teoria di Thebit. Agostino Ricci racconta che il re Alfonso aveva seguito la teoria di Thebit, quando si convinse della sua vanità, quattro anni dopo la composizione delle Tavole leggendo il libro delle stelle fisse di al-Sufi[34].

Già nel suo tempo la teoria di Thebit non era stata condivisa da Albategni[35] (Al-Battani) e ciò per più di un motivo di ordine filosofico e astronomico. La prima ragione per cui Albategni nega la teoria dell'oscillazione dell'ottava sfera é fondato sulla teoria di Aristotele della impossibilità del moto in due direzioni contrarie causata dall'oscillazione degli equinozi; la seconda ragione riposa sulla mancanza di evidenza ossia di osservazione astronomica, di una tale dottrina. Così Albategni sostiene che la precessione avviene in una sola direzione e adotta il valore di un grado ogni sessantesei anni[36] ovvero di 54″,5 all'anno e rifiuta il valore erroneo di Tolomeo dell'inclinazione dell'eclittica di 23 gradi 51′ 20″, per sostenere quello di 23 gradi 35′.

Thabit b. Qurra, Berkeley and Los Angeles 1960; si veda anche l'ed. di J. M. Millás-Vallicrosa, in: Al-Andalus 10 (1945) 98—108; cf. anche L. Gauthier, Une reforme du système astronomique de Ptolémée tentée par les philosophes arabes du XIIe siècle, in: Journal asiatique (1909), 486—520. Il De motu octavae sphaerae di Thebit é stato tradotto anche in inglese da O. Neugebauer, Thebit ben Qurra ‹On the Solar Year› and ‹the Motion of the Eigth Sphere›, in: Proceeding of the American Philosophical Society 106 (1962) 264—99. La teoria dell'accesso e recesso é conosciuta e esposta in modo superficiale da Campano da Novara: cf. Campanus of Novara, Theorica planetarum, ed. F. S. Benjamin jr—G. Toomer, Madison, 1971.

[33] *Non coincidit autem omnino Alpetragius cum his in quod ipsi motum appellant accessionis, hic recessionis et econtra. Non enim sensit octavam in nonae oppositum moveri, unde potius ab illius motu in consecutione retardat* (Pietro d'Abano, De motu octavae sphaerae, ms. Venezia cit., f. 116[rv]; ricordiamo che tutti i rimandi sono fatti da questo manoscritto). Per l'edizione latina del testo di Alpetragio De motibus caelorum, tradotto da Michele Scoto, cf. F. J. Carmody, Al-Bitruji de motibus caelorum, Berkeley and Los Angeles 1952; per l'edizione del testo arabo ed ebraico cf. B. R. Goldstein, Al-Bitruji (Alpetragio) On the Principles of Astronomy, New Haven and London 1971.

[34] *Eam enim Alphonsus paulo post revocabit opinionem* (Agostino Ricci, De motu octavae sphaerae, cit., f. 22[r]).

[35] Cf. lettera di Thebit a Hunain ibn Ishaq in: F. J. Carmody, The Astronomical Works of Thabit b. Qurra cit., 84—85.

[36] Così Pietro d'Abano: *conturbari autem hic contingit non modicum cum dictum sit Ptolomeum posuisse motum octavae sphaerae in 100 annis una parte, Albategni quidem 66, nonnulli vero in 70. . . . Unde Ptolomeus fundavit se super observationes Abrachis aut super eas quae Arsatilis et Timocaris non verificatas fortasse* (De motu octavae sphaerae, f. 116[r]).

Pietro d'Abano nel suo trattato del moto dell'ottava sfera, come ricorda anche Cusano nella sua opera di riforma del calendario, rifiuta la teoria della trepidazione dell'ottava sfera di Thebit: *Petrus etiam de Ebano in tractatu de octava sphaera opinionem accessus et recessus Thebith reprehendit*[37]. Pietro sostanzialmente aderisce alla teoria di Albategni dell'inclinazione in una direzione sola della precessione degli equinozi anche se non acetta i valori numerici da lui dati, che sono superati da quelli delle tavole redatte dagli astronomi ebraici ed arabi del re Alfonso[38]. Anzi l'opera di Pietro é notevole come documento dei diversi valori numerici riportati da lui della declinazione dell'eclittica e delle teorie diverse sostenute dagli astronomi greci, arabi e latini vissuti prima di lui, per spiegarla. Al moto dell'ottava sfera Pietro attribuisce, in realtà, solo un unico movimento, quello annuale, lento di precessione da occidente in oriente, in quanto quello veloce, diurno é causato dal primo mobile, la nona sfera, introdotta proprio a questo fine. Così dalla nona sfera dipende il moto diurno, dall'ottava quello annuale di precessione, anche se molti, incapaci di distinguere

---

[37] Nicola Cusano, Opera, Parigi 1514, II, f. 23^r; Basilea 1565, 1157.

[38] Sulle Tavole Alfonsine, in particolare le osservazioni di Agostino Ricci De motu octavae sphaerae, f. 22, f. 29 e sgg. che dice devono essere corrette con quelle di Giovanni Müller (Regiomontanus). Sulle diverse redazioni delle Tavole, in particolare sulla redazione delle Tavole Toledane, così chiamate perché calcolate a Toledo da Azarqel, e le Tavole di Al-Khawarizmi, commentate da Ahmad ibn al-Mutanna ibn Abd al-Karim, tradotte in ebraico nel 1160 dall'ebreo Abraham ibn Ezra (ben conosciuto da Pietro d'Abano), nonché sull'opera latina di Abraham ibn Ezra, Liber de rationibus tabularum, scritta tra il 1144 e il 1160, cf. E. Millàs-Vendrell, El comentario de ibn-Mutanna a las Tablas astronomicas de al-Jwarizmi, in: Oriente e Occidente cit., 759–773; per l'edizione del testo latino del Liber rationum tabularum di Abraham ibn Ezra cf. L. M. Millàs-Vallicrosa, El Libro de los Fundamentos de las Tablas Astronomicas, Madrid–Barcellona 1947; per l'ed. del testo ebraico cf. B. R. Goldstein, Ibn al-Mutanna's Commentary on the Astronomical Tables of al-Khwarizmi, New Haven and London 1967. Per il testo latino di commento di ibn al-Mutanna delle tavole di al-Khawarizmi di Abraham ibn Ezra, tradotto dall'arabo in latino da Ugo de Sanctalla, cf. C. H. Haskins, The Translations of Hugo Sanctallensis, in: Studies in the History of Medieval Science, Cambridge 1927, 67–81. Cf. anche J. Vernet, Las ‹Tabulae probatae›, in: Homenaje a Millàs-Vallicrosa, II, Barcellona 1956, 501–506. L'*Avenmucenne* citato da Ibn Ezra sarebbe dunque al-Mutanna autore delle tavole tradotte da Ibn Ezra e citato anche da Pietro d'Abano; cf. anche A. Birkenmajer, La Bibliothèque de Richard de Fournival, in: Etudes d'histoire des sciences et de la philosophie du moyen âge, Ossolineum 1970, 148 (= Studia Copernicana I). Pietro d'Abano cita Abramo ibn Ezra non solo nel De motu octavae sphaerae, ma anche a più riprese nel Lucidator, sia per le sue Tavole che per la sua opera astrologica che traduce in latino: cf. ms. Oxford, Bodl. Canonici Misc. 190, ff. 1–78^v, di cui anche l'edizione a stampa in Venezia 1505; per le indicazioni dei mss. di questa versione di Pietro d'Abano, cf. L. Thorndike–P. Kibre, A Catalogue of Incipits, Londra 1963 ad voces. Così Pietro cita ibn Ezra a proposito dell'ottava sfera: *Quidam vero consideratores posteriorum, ut Arzahel observator perspicacissimus, cum aliis Aegyptiorum et Johannes Hispalensis et Abraam Iudaeus, appellatus Avhenare, anno gratiae 142 intenderunt cum hiis quae observata hunc motum firmant in 70 annis parte una* (Lucidator, q II, ms. Parigi, Bibl. Nat. lat. 2598, f. 109vb). Per le tavole di Levi ben Gerson, altrettanto famose, cf. B. R. Goldstein, The Astronomical Tables of Levi ben Gerson, New Haven and London 1974.

i due moti- dice- li hanno attribuiti entrambi all'ottava[39]. Questo secondo moto lento, precessionale, é valido anche per spiegare la varietà e l'ineguaglianza dei moti dei pianeti, del sole e dalla luna, giacché *Solem vero lunamque et universaliter planetas conspicimus cum priori motu, diversos motus et inaequales habere*[40]. Pietro d'Abano parla delle tesi degli astronomi arabi più famosi per spiegare la precessione degli equinozi, partendo da Ipparco e Tolomeo fino ad Albategni e oltre. Di quest'ultimo scrive: *Albategni vero per 782 annorum confluxum post Ptolomeum reperit fixas in 66 annis circumvolvi una parte, velut per tres stellas observatas a Ptolomeo.* Quindi parla dei valori dati da Thebit, Azarquel, Albitrogi, Abram ibn Ezra (*cuius libros in linguam latinam ordinavi*)[41] e da Geber nel suo commento critico dell'Almagesto; passa poi all'esposizione della teoria del moto di trepidazione dell'ottava sfera di Thebit[42] che egli cita come Cusano, come moto di accesso e recesso dei segni[43]. Ma oltre questa spiegazione, prosegue, Pietro d'Abano si trova quella di Albategni (che nella realtà non sappiamo nemmeno se veramente conoscesse la teoria di Thebit) che é per una spiegazione diversa da quella della trepidazione. Pietro gli attribuisce quella della i n c u r t a z i o n e, ossia della perdita di movimento nel moto di rotazione dell'ottava sfera in una direzione sola, che dice Pietro — *invenitur in 20 gradiis eiusdem cum 15 minutis fere*[44]. Dopo aver riportato

---

[39] *Nosce quod motum diurnum fore simplicem et uniformen secundum unam dimensionem, puta longitudinem ab oriente in occidentem et hinc in orientem etc. 24 horarum spatio protensum continue. Motum autem orbis octavi cum his qui reliquorum pene commixti ex longitudine, latitudineque diagonali enim velut qui animalium etiam, est namque ab occidente in orientem atque ab austro in boream, ita et sit motus eius unus subiecto, ratione tamen diversus, quod aliqui nescientes distinguere duos motus praeter primum in sphaera posuerunt octava* (De motu octavae sphaerae, ms. Venezia, f. 115ʳ).

[40] Op. cit., f. 114ᵛ.

[41] Op. cit., f. 117ʳ.

[42] Op. cit., f. 114ᵛ.

[43] *Thebit Core indicat accessionis et recessionis motu inquiens: ‹cum Caput Arietis super 90 extiterit gradus in duobus partibus, ab aequatore septentrionis, videlicet et meridiei accessio est tunc tarda, cum autem illud appropinquant ut loco in quo circulus minor equinotialem secet, tunc velox erit accessio›. At quia motus accessus non potest etiam ad distantiam duo graduum, ut apparuit, extendi, falsatur et ipse modo quocumque confixe a tempore Abrachis tantummodo usque ad praesentem annum 1310 gratiae quo ego Petrus (Paduensis) id opus construxi* (De motu octavae sphaerae, ms. Venezia, f. 117ᵛ).

[44] *Penes autem Albategni modum hunc reliquosque praeceteris i n c u r t a n t e m invenitur in 20 gradiis eiusdem cum 15 minutis fere* (f. 118ʳ⁻ᵛ). Pietro d'Abano sembra intendere per *incurtatio* un ritardo nel moto o *retardatio*; per alcuni significati della terminologia astronomico-astrologica arabo-latina medievale (tra i quali non abbiamo trovato, tuttavia quello di questo termine) cf. O. Pedersen, Expositio nominum contentorum in Theorica planetarum, in: Classica et Mediaevalia 34 (1973) 584–594 (= Dissertationes 9); P. Kunitzsch, Mittelalterliche astronomisch-astrologische Glossare mit arabischen Fachausdrücken, München 1977, 4–58 (= Bayerische Akademie der Wissenschaften, Philosophisch-historische Klasse, Sitz. 1977, 5). Un piccolo dizionario tecnico in E. Poulle, Jean de Murs et les Tables Alphonsines, in: AHDLMA 47 (1981) 269–271. Cf. anche A. Le Boeuffle, les noms latins d'Astres et de Constellations, Paris Les belles lettres, 1977.

altri valori numerici, dice che queste sono le posizioni dell'accesso e del recesso che, però, non possono salvare le apparenze secondo Tolomeo e i moderni[45]. Nonostante le correzioni introdotte da Azarquel e da Avempace, afferma – le difficoltà che queste teorie hanno sollevato, hanno fatto introdurre fino a dieci sfere, proprio *propter hesitationem motus octavae*[46].

Le ultime parti del trattato sul moto dell'ottava sfera di Pietro sono dedicate espressamente ad esporre la misura del moto dell'ottava sfera. Egli si ripete più volte nella esposizione dei valori dati da Albategni che non condivide la dottrina del moto di oscillazione del suo collega Thebit e, seguendo Tolomeo e Ipparco (che Pietro chiama Abrachis) ritiene che il moto dell'ottava sfera sia *semper continuum et directum nunc decem partium et 30 minutorum fere*, ossia in una direzione sola, senza oscillazione. Infine affronta il problema filosofico, largamente svolto nel Lucidator dubitabilium astronomiae, di come possano inerire moti diversi, che hanno principio e fine, alla sfera che é circolare e perfetta, ossia senza principio né fine. La soluzione sarà quella tradizionale data anche da Averroè, fondata sulla distinzione tra moto sostanziale e moto per accidente, il primo del superiore, il secondo dell'inferiore, o anche sulla distinzione tra il moto della parte e quello del tutto. Le sfere che non hanno principio né fine, possono avere moti finiti con principio e fine, in quanto ciò che capita nell'inferiore come parte, non é del superiore, ed é per accidente[47]. Tutti i moti sono, allora, in diretta connessione tra di loro secondo la diretta connessione delle sfere per la quale si trasferisce la virtù del superiore nell'inferiore. Da tale trasmissione della virtù o influenza, conseguono tutte le vicende umane, il nascere della sapienza e della dottrina, il sorgere dei regni e degli imperi, delle religioni e delle credenze. Poi tutte le cose *incoeperunt permutari in contrarium*; così che *sapientia et virtus omnino foedatae, reges vilefacti, monarchia corrupta, fides et legalitas leves redditae . . . et velut Corpus coranicum redditum universum*[48]. E questo é avvenuto *propter etiam huius Capricorni depressionem*[49], ossia per il moto precessionale dell'ottava sfera[50]. Dalla variazione del moto

---

[45] *Ad haec per huius positionem accessus et recessus nequeunt apparentia salvari ut declarabitur. Non ergo motus accessus et recessus potest stare quicumque* (De motu octavae sphaerae, f. 118ʳ).

[46] Op. cit., f. 118ᵛ.

[47] *Accidit dubitari tum quia circulus rotundus carens principio omnifariam et fine, ratione namque eadem et principium et finem sit in omni assignare parte. . . . licet namque in se circulus cum sit perfectissma figurarum in modo careat et termino, ratione tamen alicuius accidentis ut dictum est, huius poterint eidem inesse* (De motu cit., f. 120ᵛ).

[48] Op. cit., f. 121ᵛ.

[49] Op. cit., f. 121ᵛ.

[50] *Ex cuius quidem tam grandi diversitate in orbe octavo cum hiis quae ipsius ac subiectis eidem omnibus relatione communi ut visum, permaxima causabitur in terrenis varietas* (Op. cit., f. 122ʳ).

dell'ottava sfera dipendono quindi i mutamenti nelle arti, nelle istitu-
zioni, nelle popolazioni e tutte le inversioni di tendenza. Non solo, Pietro
d'Abano riporta anche la leggenda di Fetonte per la quale dall'incendio delle
orbite planetarie sarebbero nati i continenti. Importante in questa prospet-
tiva di spiegazione dei mutamenti della storia é, dunque, stabilire l'origine
del mondo a partire dal moto dell'ottava sfera, quesito a cui si ricollega
quello di stabilire se il mondo (che secondo la Bibbia ha avuto un inizio)
si é originato quando esso era in corrispondenza a tutte le sfere in modo
diretto, oppure con la prima precessione, oppure prima della prima precessione e così all'infinito[51]. Se secondo l'insegnamento biblico, il mondo
ha avuto una origine e l'ha avuta con la prima precessione degli equinozi,
importante é la mensura esatta di questo spostamento che é legato con
tutte le variazioni oscillatorie o meno, dell'ottava sfera. Ma anche se si
sostiene con i filosofi che la *machina mundialis* non ha avuto né principio
né fine, non per questo la precisazione di questa misura é meno rilevante,
perché ogni variazione celeste ha la sua corrispondenza terrestre. Pietro
d'Abano sembra ritenere, tuttavia, in questo testo che é più ragionevole
supporre che il mondo, nella sua storia mondana, abbia avuto un inizio e,
pertanto riporta le date dell'*exordio mundis* della storia biblica riferite da
Beda, che coinciderebbero con l'inizio del moto dell'ottava sfera, sia esso
inteso come il momento in cui le sfere erano nella prima posizione in modo
diretto, oppure come il momento in cui erano nella prima precessione.
Infatti Pietro d'Abano, in questo testo non ci dà una risposta definitiva su
questo problema. Ma, sia che si accetti la teoria precessionale, come moto
particolare dell'ottava sfera, oppure quella oscillatoria di Thebit o quella
che é un misto di entrambe, le cifre che sono state date finora di variazione
di tale moto lungo i secoli, appaiono discordanti ed errate, per cui é diffi-
cile stabilire quella esatta. Questa constatazione é proprio la motivazione
che spinge Pietro d'Abano ad affermare che tale difficoltà non ostacola lo
studio e la considerazione del moto dell'ottava sfera in qualunque modo
esso sia posto (precessionale, oscillatorio o un misto di entrambi). Anzi
lo stimola e lo impone: *Haec est itaque dissonantia quae circa produc-*
tionem ac principium extat universi praesentem in nullo impediens consi-
derationem, quomodolibet enim ponatur motus etiam et diversitas[52].

---

[51] *Tunc namque videtur rationabilius incoasse, cum omnia ut praetactum sibique sphae-*
rarum corresponderit ex directe, aut revolutionem unam praetactarum praecessisse, vel ante
illam reliquam et aliam sicque deinceps per infinita temporis spatia (f. 123ʳ).

[52] Op. cit. f. 123ᵛ. Pietro d'Abano adombra qui quel complesso problema di filosofia
della storia che riguarda l'origine dei tempi e della storia umana. Ancora non é chiara la
distinzione tra storia e preistoria, né quella tra storia biblica e storia profana. Su ciò cf. Paolo
Rossi-Monti, I segni del tempo, Milano 1979, passim e gli studi di G. Ricuperati sulla storia
sacra e la storia profana nella storiografia dell'Illuminismo, in: Ruolo della storia e degli
storici nella civiltà, a cura di Giuseppe Butta, Messina-La grafica 1982, 274—386.

Così termina il testo di Pietro da Padova che é seguito da un elenco di tavole che stabiliscono l'inizio del mondo a partire dal moto dell'ottava sfera secondo la datazione biblica, fino all'anno 1310 (in un codice[53]), mentre in altri seguono le tavole aggiornate del moto dell'ottava sfera dal tempo di Tolomeo fino all'anno 1385[54]: il che fa supporre che siano state redatte non da Pietro, ma da un altro estensore, copista o meno, della sua opera. L'inizio delle tavole aggiunte al testo di Pietro é il seguente: *(T)ota est octava sphaera a tempore Ptolomei usque ad praesentem annum qui est a Christo 1385 imperfectus per gradus 16 minuta 39, secunda 7, qui gradi debent addi super loca stellarum fixarum tempore Ptolomei et sic haberetur vera earum loca tempore praescripto in nona sphaera*[55].

Per concludere il nostro studio desideriamo sottolineare come il trattato De motu octavae sphaerae di Pietro d'Abano presenti un notevole interesse per la storia del pensiero scientifico medievale, soprattutto da un punto di vista matematico: come esposizione, da un lato, delle diverse teorie astronomico-matematiche, greco-arabe, ebraiche e latine del Medioevo, per spiegare le variazioni che si erano avute lungo i secoli del moto precessionale degli equinozi (ossia degli spostamenti nel moto annuale di rotazione delle stelle fisse o ottava sfera); dall'altro, come documento dei diversi valori numerici di tali variazioni osservate dagli astronomi. M i s u r a r e questo movimento era divenuto un compito di rilievo che scaturiva da un punto di vista filosofico generale riguardante una particolare concezione cosmologica condivisa in quel tempo: ossia la dottrina filosofica che faceva derivare tutti gli altri moti, universali e particolari, le vicende umane e terrene, da questo moto dell'ottava sfera. Pietro d'Abano presenta la sua dottrina in modo critico, rifiutando quella, quasi universalmente accolta[56], di Thebit, detta di t r e p i d a z i o n e o di a c c e s s o e r e c e s s o (oscillazione) dei punti equinoziali, per accettare quella precessionale in una sola direzione.

Questo testo é stato finora immeritatamente ignorato, forse a causa della visione astrologica che sottintende, anche se Cusano sarà uno dei pochi che non mancheranno di ricordarlo. E'curioso, infatti, come Agostino Ricci, uno degli scienziati degli inizi del secolo XVI che dedica un

---

[53] De motu octavae sphaerae, ms. Pal. lat. 1377, f. 5ra. Ma il codice non riporta tutte le tavole, solo l'inizio.

[54] Ms. Venezia, Museo Correr, Provenienza Cicogna, 2289, f. 124[r] e Oxford, Canonici Bodl., Misc. 190, ff. 83vb–84rb. I due codici corrispondono anche se il veneziano deve essere stato copiato più tardi del canoniciano.

[55] Venezia, f. 124[r]; Oxford, f. 83rb.

[56] Anche Guglielmo di Saint-Cloud, tra il 1290 e il 1292 aveva sostenuto a Parigi una critica simile a quella di Pietro cercando di rivedere le tavole di Thebit e di Azarchel. Su ciò in particolare E. Littré, Guillaume de Saint-Cloud, Astronome, in: Histoire littéraire de la France, XXV, Parigi 1869, 70e E. Poulle ad vocem in: Dictionary of Scientific Biography, New York 1976, 389–390.

importante trattato allo stesso argomento, non lo ricordi mai a questo proposito, ma, invece per la teoria astrologica delle *imagines* che il Ricci rifiuta e, una seconda volta, per una frase del Conciliator differentiarum sul numero delle sfere, numero che non sarebbe stato ben conosciuto al tempo di Aristotele[57]. Il Ricci, in altre parole, ci fa intendere di conoscere bene le variazioni dei valori numerici dei mutamenti di declinazione dei punti equinoziali che erano stati presentati anche da Pietro d'Abano nel suo De motu, ma non degna di una menzione questo testo, forse per le predilezioni astrologiche di Pietro che il Ricci non condivide. Altrimenti detto, il De motu octavae sphaerae di Pietro d'Abano deve avere avuto una certa circolazione anche nei secoli successivi, fino al XVI secolo, come dimostrano le numerose copie manoscritte: ma con ogni probabilità, senza troppo clamore a causa della sua impostazione astrologica che i tempi moderni, a partire già da Oresme alla fine del secolo XIV stavano vivamente avversando. Questo testo costituisce, così, una espressione eloquente di un tentativo di riflessione critica della scienza della **misurae** di calcolo dell'astronomia greco-araba latina medievale.

---

[57] Agostino Ricci si riferisce al testo del Conciliator di Pietro d'Abano, differentia 99 (Venetiis Gabriele Tarvisiense 1476, carta q 3, colona an): *Etneque debet id Aristoteli in defectum reputari, quia illud quod comprehenditur per viam anathomicae est sicut res quae comprehenditur a numero motuum circulorum, neque illa erat completa scientia tempore Aristotelis.* Così scrive Pietro d'Abano. E Agostino cita: *notitia. sicut et numeri motuum circulorum, minime fuerit completa atque idem a Conciliatore, differentiis trigesima prima, trigesima quinta et nonagesima nona, confirmatur legitur* (Agostino Ricci, De motu octavae sphaerae, Parigi 1521, f. 10). L'altra citazione di Pietro da parte di Agostino Ricci é al f. 41: *Idem ex Petri Aponensis Imaginibus comprehenditur.*

MASS- UND ZAHLANGABEN BEI HILDEGARD VON BINGEN

von Elisabeth Gössmann (Tokyo)

> *Deus . . est enim spirituum ponderator, mulcens eos*
> *in suavitate blandimentorum et tranquillitatum,*
> *castigansque eos in tribulatione dolorum et mise-*
> *riarum, ut excutiantur ad rectam mensuram . . ita*
> *scilicet ut rationalitas hominis non plus elevetur in*
> *superiora nec plus deprimatur in inferiora quam*
> *iusto iudicio suo recompensat Deus . . . Nam ut*
> *plumbum iuste ponderat pecuniam, sic Deus aequa*
> *libra bonis et malis tale obstaculum opponit, quod*
> *nullo modo possunt effugere aequissimam normam*
> *iudicii eius.*
>
> Scivias III, 4

Die von Alois Dempf[1] neben Rupert von Deutz, Honorius Augustodunensis, Anselm von Havelberg, Gerhoh von Reichersberg und Otto von
Freising dem Geschichtssymbolismus beigezählte Äbtissin Hildegard von
Bingen (1098–1179) macht in ihrem so vielgestaltigen Werk reichen
Gebrauch von Maß- und Zahlangaben. Ihr natur- und heilkundliches
sowie ihr musikalisches Schaffen muß hier ausgeklammert werden, und
was ihre sogenannte Visionstrilogie betrifft, Scivias (1141–50), Liber vitae
meritorum (1158–63) und De operatione Dei (1163–73), so wäre es reiz-
voll, allen in den Visionsbeschreibungen bzw. den noch zu ihren Lebzeiten
oder bald danach entstandenen Miniaturen erkennbaren Proportionen und
geometrischen Figuren nachzugehen. Aber auch hier haben wir uns wieder
eine Beschränkung aufzuerlegen, indem wir nur jene Visionsreihen
betrachten, in denen Hildegard selbst eine Deutung ihrer Maß- und Zahlangaben gibt, die sie jedoch, dem Visionsstil entsprechend, als ihr durch
Audition zugekommen legitimiert. (Der auf dem Throne sitzt, sprach zu
mir . . .) Es bleiben also – neben der Konfrontation der Tugend des Maßes
mit dem Laster der Maßlosigkeit in ihrer Ethik[2] – die Visionen 2–10 des

---

[1] Vgl. A. Dempf, Sacrum Imperium. Geschichts- und Staatsphilosophie des Mittelalters
und der politischen Renaissance, München 1962³, 262–268.

[2] Obwohl alle Werke Hildegards an der Ethik interessiert sind, bezeichnet man insbesondere das mittlere Werk ihrer Visionstrilogie, Liber vitae meritorum, als ihre Ethik. Hier wird
im Gegeneinander der Laster und Tugenden (nach dem Vorbild der Psychomachia des
Prudentius) das Laster der Maßlosigkeit (*immoderatio*) in der Gestalt eines Wolfes beschrieben, der hockend auf Beute lauert. Die Tugend des Maßes (*discretio*) hält diesem Laster ent-

dritten Buches Scivias von der Stadt auf dem Berge und die Visionen der mikro-makrokosmischen Entsprechungen in der 2. bis 5. Schau von De operatione Dei. Die hier verzeichneten Zahl- und Maßangaben können nicht ohne ihre Beziehung zu den ebenfalls thematisierten Himmelsrichtungen verstanden werden, und dies ist das Verbindende zwischen den beiden Visionsreihen Hildegards. Denn nicht nur der Mensch, sondern auch der sakrale Bau erhält durch die allegorisch fixierte Bedeutung der Himmelsrichtungen einen mikrokosmischen Sinn[3].

Zuvor ist jedoch ein Blick auf die Hildegard-Forschung vonnöten, die sich seit langem darüber im klaren ist, daß Hildegard, die den Vulgatatext der Bibel und die lateinischen Kirchenväter kennt, die mit den bedeutendsten Persönlichkeiten ihrer Zeit über theologische Fragen korrespondiert hat und sogar lateinisch zu predigen verstand, ihre zahlreichen Bescheidenheitstopoi (simplex homo, mulier paupercula) dem Zeitbrauch und sicher auch der zeitgenössischen Überzeugung entsprechend benutzt, um ihre literarische Bildung zu relativieren und umso mehr als ungebildete, von Gott belehrte Prophetin zu gelten[4]. Daß Hildegard sich in der Tradition und im Geistesleben ihrer Zeit auskannte, steht heute in der Forschung fest. Auch ist sie nicht die einzige Frau, die mystische Auditionen und Visionen als ein – subjektiv echtes – Stilmittel benutzt, um ihre theologischen Überzeugungen sowie ihre Kritik an Staat und Kirche zu äußern, denn das Ansehen eines Magisters im Schul- und späteren Universitätssystem konnte die Frau im Mittelalter nicht gewinnen, und so stand ihr nur die – allerdings offiziell auf den Privatbereich beschränkte – Prophetengabe zu, um sich zu theologischen Fragen zu äußern[5]. Deshalb ist es auch nicht zu verwundern, wenn manches in Hildegards Visionsbeschreibungen und -deutungen große Ähnlichkeit hat mit dem, was die eingangs genannten Geschichtssymboliker im eigenen Namen schreiben.

---

gegen, daß jedes Ding einem Höheren zu dienen hat und daher sein Maß nicht überschreiten darf. Der Schwermut als Auflehnung gegen die von Gott zugemessenen Güter verwandt, ist Maßlosigkeit als ein Wuchern des Unmaßes in allen Beziehungen gedeutet. In dem dantesk anmutenden Teil dieses Werkes wird als Strafort der Seelen der Unmäßigen ein mit Schwefel durchmischtes Meer angegeben, das in gewaltigem Feuerbrand lodert. Auch das Laster der Mißgunst, durch eine unförmige Gestalt symbolisiert, die das menschliche Maß pervertiert, wird als der Maßlosigkeit verwandt bezeichnet, da der Mißgünstige sich an seinem Mitmenschen versündigt durch eine unziemliche Ausschreitung ohne jedes Maß. Vgl. die Übersetzung von H. Schipperges, Das Buch der Lebensverdienste, Salzburg 1972, 94. 113. 130. 152; ed. J. B. Pitra, Analecta Sacra VIII, Monte Cassino 1883, 68 s. 85 s. 99. 120 s.

[3] Vgl. B. Maurmann, Die Himmelsrichtungen im Weltbild des Mittelalters. Hildegard von Bingen, Honorius Augustodunensis und andere Autoren, München 1976, 130.

[4] Vgl. H. Grundmann, Die Frauen und die Literatur im Mittelalter, in: Archiv für Kulturgeschichte 26 (1936) 129–161, bes. 136.

[5] Vgl. E. Gössmann, Anthropologie und soziale Stellung der Frau nach Summen und Sentenzenkommentaren des 13. Jahrhunderts, in: Miscellanea Mediaevalia 12, Berlin 1979, 281–297.

Selbst wenn es bisher noch nicht gelungen ist, direkte literarische Vorbilder für Hildegards Architekturbeschreibungen und makro-mikrokosmische Entsprechungen zu finden, wenn also der Weg der historischen
Vermittlung noch nicht genau verfolgt werden konnte, so genügt es doch,
auf vergleichbares Gedankengut in ihrer Zeit, etwa in der Chartrenser
Schule[6], hinzuweisen, ohne zur Erklärung von Hildegards Allegorien auf
die Archetypenlehre von C. G. Jung zurückzugreifen[7]. Hildegard verfügt
in der Freiheit ihrer visionären Kombinationsgabe über das in ihrer Zeit voll
bewußte Traditionsgut an Symbolen, Allegorien und Metaphern, wenngleich sie in einem Bildrealismus lebte, der solche modernen Unterschei-
dungen transzendiert[8].

Hildegards Visionsreihe von dem auf Bergeshöhe gelegenen stadtartigen
Gebäudekomplex, angeregt durch die neutestamentliche Apokalypse (21,
12ff.) und auch durch die im Alten Testament beschriebenen Gebäude (vor
allem Ez. 40, 28ff.), unterscheidet sich von der im 12. Jahrhundert vorkommenden Architekturmetapher für die Bibel in den verschiedenen
Schriftsinnen, wobei etwa das Fundament den Literalsinn, die Wände den
allegorischen und tropologsichen, das Dach aber den anagogischen Sinn
bedeutet[9]. Nach Barbara Maurmann stellt bei Hildegard „die heilsgeschichtliche Konzeption des stadtartigen Gebäudekomplexes . . . eine ein-
malige Demonstration der Heilszeit von der Schöpfung und dem Sündenfall
bis zum Gericht als Phasen der Gerechtigkeit Gottes und eines entsprechenden sittlichen Postulats für die Verhaltensweise der Menschen gegenüber Gott dar"[10]. Dieser gegen Ende der Visionsreihe zunehmend eine
Transparenz für das Himmlische Jerusalem gewinnende Gebäudekomplex
ist jedoch nicht kubisch wie dieses, sondern seine Länge wird von Hildegard mit 100 Ellen, seine Breite mit 50 Ellen und seine Höhe ebenfalls mit
50 Ellen angegeben. Dafür gibt sie folgende allegorische Deutung:

Quod autem longitudo ipsius aedificii est centum cubitorum: hoc est quod dena-
rius numerus attenuatus erat in praevaricante homine et recuperatus est in Filio meo
per multiplicem denarium centenarii numeri multiplicium virtutum in salvatione
animarum, de quo denario per centenarium deinde ascendit millenarius numerus

---

   [6] Vgl. die von B. Maurmann (Anm. 3) aufgewiesenen zeitgenössischen Parallelen, bes. in
den Anmerkungen zu S. 34—73.
   [7] Einen entsprechenden Versuch macht die von dem Schweizer Th. Immoos in Tokyo
gegründete C. G. Jung-Gesellschaft. Es ist jedoch dazu zu bemerken, daß in der mittelalterlichen Bildwelt bestimmte Bedeutungen vorgegeben sind und nur die Kombination frei war.
So ist z. B. Schatten bei Hildegard nicht mit dem dunklen Bereich gleichzusetzen, den Jung
„Schatten" nennt, sondern von biblischen obumbratio-Vorstellungen abhängig.
   [8] Vgl. A. Führkötter, Hildegard von Bingen, in: J. Sudbrak J. Walsh (Ed.), Große Gestalten christlicher Spiritualität, Würzburg 1969, 135—151.
   [9] Vgl. H. J. Spitz, Die Metaphorik des geistigen Schriftsinns, München 1972, 205—218.
   [10] B. Maurmann (Anm. 3), 82f.

perfectus in omnibus virtutibus, ut pleniter evacuentur mille artes diaboli, cum qui-
bus seducit omnem cohortem amabilium omnium omnipotentis Dei[11].

Die Hundertzahl entsteht also aus dem durch den Sündenfall verlorenen
und durch die Erlösung in der Potenz wiedergewonnenen Zehner und kann
durch die Entfaltung der Tugendkräfte zur vollkommenen Zahl 1000 poten-
ziert werden, welche die entgegenstehende fatale Tausendzahl der *artes
diaboli* überwindet. 10 × 10 × 10 ist nach Hildegard die *mystica figura*,
in der Gott dem Menschengeschlecht von der Verzweiflung an der schuld-
haft ins Unheil gestürzten Geschichte abrät. Was es mit dem *denarius* auf
sich hat, erfährt man durch Hildegards Berufung auf das Gleichnis von der
Frau, die eine ihrer 10 Drachmen verlor (Luc. 15,8–10), so wie Gott von
den 10 ordines der zum Heil Bestimmten, den 9 Engelchören und dem
Menschengeschlecht, das letztere verloren hatte, um es wiederzufinden wie
die Frau ihre Drachme. Wie diese ihre Freundinnen, so läßt Hildegard in
ihrer poetischen Allegorese Gott die Tugendkräfte zusammenrufen: *Con-
gratulamini mihi laudabiliter et gaudenter et aedificate coelestem Jerusalem
viventibus lapidibus, quia hominem inveni, qui perierat deceptione diaboli*[12].

Die 50 Ellen Breite und 5 Ellen Höhe ihres Heilsgebäudes erklärt Hildegard ebenfalls mit Rücksicht auf die positive und negative Bedeutung der
zugrunde liegenden Fünfzahl:

*Hoc est quod omnis latitudo vitiorum hominum, qui in opere Dei aedificare
debuerunt, magis tamen concupiscentias suas sequentium quam opus Dei colen-
tium, in diffusis quinque vulneribus Filii mei, quae in cruce passus est, misericorditer
abstergitur et remittitur, ita quod vulnera manuum eius opera manuum inoboe-
dientiae Adae et Evae deleverunt, et quod vulnera pedum eius liberaverunt itinera
humani exilii, et quod vulnus lateris eius, de quo orta est Ecclesia, delevit culpam
Evae et Adae; quoniam de latere Adae Eva creata est . . .*

*Et altitudo eius est quinque cubitorum: quae est excellentia divinarum scientiarum
in Scripturis quae propter opus Dei sunt in quinque sensibus qui sunt in homine,
quos inspiravit Spiritus sanctus ad utilitatem hominum; quia homo cum quinque
sensibus suis respicit ad altitudinem divinitatis discernens unumquodque bonum scilicet et malum*[13].

Die anthropologische Auslegung auf den menschlichen Leib und die fünf
Sinne des Menschen, die in ihrer spirituellen Form der Gotteserkenntnis
dienen[14], wird noch unterstrichen durch die gleich anschließende Erklärung
der vier Außenwände des Gebäudekomplexes als Analogie zu dem aus den

[11] Scivias III, 2, PL 197, 585; ed. A. Führkötter, CC 43 A, 363 s.
[12] PL 197, 587; CC 43 A, 366. Für die Feministische Theologie wäre es interessant wahr-
zunehmen, daß Hildegard hier Gott durch eine Frau repräsentiert sein läßt.
[13] PL 197, 587; CC 43 A, 366 f.
[14] Zur mittelalterlichen Lehre von den *sensus spirituales* vgl. E. Gössmann, Metaphysik
und Heilsgeschichte. Eine theologische Untersuchung der Summa Halensis, München 1964,
33–36.

vier Elementen zusammengesetzten Menschenleib, ein deutlicher Hinweis
auf den mikrokosmischen Sinn der Architekturmetapher. Die durch Christi
Wunden gereinigten fünf Sinne des Menschen und ihre Spiritualisierung
durch die *inspiratio Spiritus sancti* bilden ein auch in anderen Zusammenhängen auftretendes Bedeutungsgefüge, so in Scivias I, 6, wo die 9
Engelchöre in konzentrischen Kreisen dargestellt sind und den mittleren
fünf Kreisen eben diese Bedeutung zugesprochen wird[15]. Eben weil
Hildegard, wie Heinrich Schipperges[16] hervorhebt, anders verfährt als
später Dante, der das pseudo-areopagitische Schema der Engelchöre auf
die ptolemäischen Sphären bezieht, kann man versucht sein, von einer
makrokosmischen Exponierung mikrokosmischer Verhältnisse bei ihr zu
sprechen.

Die Zahlen fünf und zehn in den Maßangaben von Hildegards Heilsgebäude weisen also in ihrer potenzierten bzw. multiplizierten Form auf
das heilsgeschichtliche Grundschema von *institutio, destitutio* und *restitutio*
als Überbietung des ursprünglich Gegebenen hin. Auch der aus ihrer
Heilkunde bekannte Gedanke der Heilung durch das entsprechende Ent-
gegengesetzte ist einbezogen[17].

Weitere Maß- und Zahlenangaben Hildegards beziehen sich auf die einzelnen Teile ihres allegorischen Gebäudekomplexes. So beschreibt sie den
an die von Osten nach Norden verlaufende Lichtmauer von außen ange-
bauten Turm des Ratschlusses Gottes, der die Heilsgeschichte in ihre Richtung gewiesen hat, als 4 Ellen breit und 7 Ellen hoch, wobei sie die Vierzahl
wieder mit den vier Elementen des Menschenleibes, die Siebenzahl aber
mit den Gaben des Hl. Geistes erklärt, der im Menschen die Tugenden zur
Entfaltung bringt. Die fünf Tugendgestalten, die an dem Turm wie Figuren
am Kirchengebäude sichtbar werden, die Liebe zum Himmlischen, die
Zucht (*disciplina*), die Scham (*verecundia*), die Barmherzigkeit und die
Überwindung (*victoria*), dienen der Verwirklichung der Gerechtigkeit. Sie
entsprechen dem in der Nord-Ost-Mauer verbildlichten, durch Noe und

---

[15] Übersetzung von Maura Böckeler, Wisse die Wege, Salzburg 1954, 141: „Die beiden Reihen schließen sich in Kranzesform um fünf andere Reihen. Das bedeutet, daß Leib
und Seele des Menschen die fünf Sinne, die durch die fünf Wunden meines Sohnes gereinigt
sind, mit starker Kraft zügeln und auf den geraden Weg der inneren Gebote leiten müssen."

[16] Vgl. H. Schipperges, Die Engel im Weltbild Hildegards von Bingen, in: H. Fromm
u. a. (Ed.), Verbum et Signum, München 1975, Bd. 2, 104f.

[17] Hildegard folgt dem spätantiken Grundsatz „Similia similibus", indem sie Ähnlichkeiten zwischen gewissen menschlichen Organen und den zu ihrer Heilung empfohlenen
Mitteln voraussetzt. Dies schließt die Verwendung des entgegengesetzt Entsprechenden ein,
indem für die physische wie geistliche Erschlaffung das Heil in der viriditas, der Grünkraft
der Kräuter der Erde wie der des Hl. Geistes gesucht wird. Vgl. die Kommentierungen der
Übersetzer von: Das Buch von dem inneren Wesen der verschiedenen Naturen in der Schöpfung (Physica), übers. v. P. Riethe, Salzburg 1959, und: Heilkunde (Causae et curae), übers.
v. H. Schipperges, Salzburg 1967.

Abraham begrenzten heilgeschichtlichen Stadium und werden wieder als Hilfe für die fünf Sinne des Menschen erklärt.

An der Nordecke des Gebäudes, die durch Abraham und Moses gekennzeichnet ist, und um eine Elle von ihr entfernt, beschreibt Hildegard die Säule des Wortes Gottes als Baukörper im Widerstand gegen Satan, die ein Dreieck zum Grundriß hat. Ihre nach Osten, Norden und Süden gerichteten Kanten stehen für das Gesetz, das Evangelium und die Väterlehre[18]. Furchtbar ist der Anblick der Säule deshalb, weil sie von so gewaltiger Größe und Höhe ist, daß ihre Maße nicht überschaut werden können. Als ein in die Transzendenz Gottes reichendes Symbol kann die Säule des Wortes Gottes von Hildegard nicht mehr mit Hilfe endlicher Maßangaben beschrieben werden.

Tantae est etiam magnitudinis ac altitudinis, ut mensuram eius nullo modo discernere possis: quia ipsum Verbum Filius scilicet Dei in magnitudine gloriae suae et in altitudine divinitatis suae omnes creaturas superexcellit in paterna maiestate, ita ut hoc nullus hominum in corruptibili carne ad perfectum possit considerare[19].

Dieser die Transzendenz Gottes versinnbildenden, weil durch kein menschliches Maß erfaßbaren Säule ist nur eine einzige Tugendgestalt zugeordnet, die scientia Dei, die der doppelten Bedeutung des Genitivs entsprechend, sowohl das Erkennen Gottes als auch die Gotteserkenntnis der vernunftbegabten Kreatur ausdrückt, deren Begrenztheit Hildegard bei der Erklärung der nicht meßbaren Höhe des Turmes betont hat.

Die dreifache Mauer, die vom Norden zum Westen des Gebäudekomplexes verläuft und die Zeit des alttestamentlichen Gesetzes repräsentiert, dient Hildegard zur Veranschaulichung ihrer Ständelehre. Sie sieht den Unterschied der Stände vorgegeben in der Unterscheidung zwischen dem *spirituale magisterium*, den *maiores* und *minores* weltlichen Standes zur Zeit des alttestamentlichen Gesetzes. Die innere höhere Mauer versinnbildet den geistlichen Stand und die beiden anderen niedrigeren die weltlichen Stände. Ihre Höhe von 3 Ellen wird von Hildegard auf die drei Gruppen des weltlichen Standes ihrer eigenen Zeit ausgelegt. Denn im Unterschied zum Alten Testament braucht sie eine Abstufung innerhalb der *maiores*, nämlich die zwischen Fürsten und Adeligen, denen das einfache Volk in Hörigkeit untergeben ist. In der einen Elle Abstand zwischen der inneren und der mittleren Mauer sieht sie die Überlegenheit der Würde des geistlichen Standes gegenüber der weltlichen Obrigkeit ausgedrückt. Dagegen wird der Abstand zwischen der äußeren und der mitt-

---

[18] Nach B. Maurmann, a. a. O. (Anm. 3) 92 f. wird die Zeit des Evangeliums als Vorstoß gegen den Norden, den Ursprung aller Ungerechtigkeit, der Nordkante zugewiesen, die Ostkante mit dem Gesetz kennzeichnet den Beginn der Heilszeit, und die Südkante im vollen Mittagslicht spielt auf die Wärme des Hl. Geistes an, die den in der Schrift Forschenden vonnöten ist.

[19] PL 197, 603; CC 43 A, 393 s.

leren Mauer nur mit der Handbreite eines Kindes angegeben, womit die Adeligen und das hörige Volk sehr nahe aneinandergerückt sind. Eine Mahnung Hildegards zur Einmütigkeit von Adel und Volk?

> *Inter exteriorem et . . . medium (sc. murum) est latitudo unius palmi quasi puerilis manus: quia est etiam inter inferiorem potestatem saecularis regiminis et inter subiectionem saecularis ministrationis extensio iustae considerationis, ita ut hae unanimi et simplici devotione puerilis innocentiae se invicem tangant in manu coniunctae operationis suae*[20].

Die Legitimierung der mittelalterlichen Ständegesellschaft als gottgegeben geschieht also nicht ohne Erinnerung an die Pflichten der Vorgesetzten gegenüber den Untergebenen, ebenso wie die überragende Höhe der den geistlichen Stand versinnbildenden inneren Mauer Hildegard nicht hindert, an dieser Stelle das Übel des Ämterkaufs und -verkaufs zu geißeln. Das Gemeinsame der in der dreifachen Mauer dargestellten Stände aber ist die Einheit im Glauben, in der Hildegard sowohl das alttestamentliche wie das christliche Volk verbunden sieht. Die diesem Gebäudeabschnitt zugeordneten Tugendgestalten führen als Vertreterinnen der vera iustitia vom Gesetz zum Evangelium[21].

Die Säule der wahren Dreieinigkeit, die wie die Säule des Wortes ein Dreieck als Fundament hat, beschließt an der Westecke von Hildegards allegorischem Gebäudekomplex die Phase des alttestamentlichen Gesetzes und drückt die neue Offenbarungsstufe des christlichen Glaubens aus. Wie zu erwarten, heißt es auch hier, sie sei von so überragenden Maßen, daß ihre Größe und Höhe der Seherin unzugänglich bleibt. Ihre scharfen Kanten sind am Boden von trockenem Stroh, abgeschnittenen Federchen und morschem Holz umgeben.

> *Quod tantae quantitatis est ut nec magnitudo nec altitudo ipsius intellectui tuo pateat: hoc est quod eadem Trinitas tam ineffabilis gloriae et potestatis est, quod nec in magnitudine maiestatis nec in altitudine divinitatis ullo circuitu aut praesumptione sapientiae humanae mentis determinari possit*[22].

Wieder äußert Hildegard hier eine Warnung vor der Vermessenheit des Menschen inbezug auf die Einschätzung seiner Gotteserkenntnis. Ihre bewußt auf die Meditation der Heilsgeschichte konzentrierte Mystik kennt

---

[20] PL 197, 633; CC 43 A, 448.

[21] Hildegard will jedoch nicht die Achtzahl besonders betonen, sondern ordnet die personifizierten Tugendkräfte in zwei Dreiergruppen und zwei einzeln stehende. Vgl. B. Maurmann, a. a. O. (Anm. 3) 96 f. Eine der letzteren ist die discretio, die Tugend des Maßes, eine besonders liebevoll ausgemalte Tugendallegorie, die sich als Mutter der Tugenden bezeichnet. An ihrer Brust bricht sich das Sonnenlicht, und auf ihrer rechten Schulter erscheint das Zeichen des Kreuzes, weil sie im Zeichen des Sohnes wandelt. Das fächerartige Holzgerät in ihrer Hand, aus dem drei Zweiglein mit einer Blüte sprießen, will besagen, daß durch diese Tugend die gläubigen Menschen in der Kraft der Trinität, wie Gott selbst, alle Werke in gerechter Berücksichtigung der kreatürlichen Verhältnisse abzuwägen wissen.

[22] PL 197, 644; CC 43 A, 464.

Grundriß des „Gebäudes des Heiles"

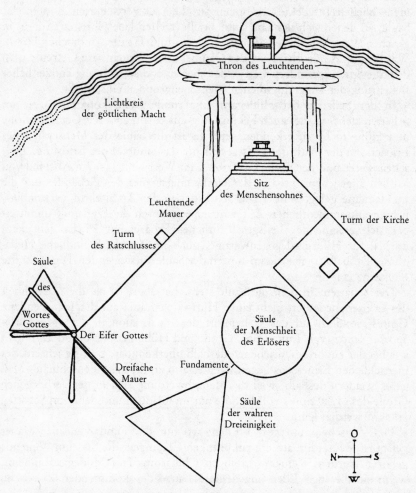

Stellung der personifizierten „Gotteskräfte" oder „Tugenden" im Gebäude

In und vor dem Turm des Ratschlusses: Liebe zum Himmlischen, Zucht, Schamhaftigkeit, Barmherzigkeit, Sieg – Geduld, Sehnsucht.

Vor der Säule des Wortes Gottes: Erkennen Gottes.

Bei der dreifachen Mauer: Enthaltsamkeit, Hochherzigkeit, Hingabe – Wahrheit, Friede, Heilszuversicht – Diskretion – Seelenrettung.

In der Säule der Menschheit des Erlösers: Demut, Liebe, Gottesfurcht, Gehorsam, Glaube, Hoffnung, Keuschheit – Gnade.

Vor dem Turm der Kirche: Weisheit – Gerechtigkeit, Stärke, Heiligkeit.

Vor dem Menschensohn: Beharrlichkeit, Himmlisches Begehren, Herzenszerknirschung – Vollkommenheit – Eintracht.

aus: Maura Böckeler, Hildegard von Bingen
(vgl. Anm. 15), 220.

nicht die Erfahrung einer Gotteserkenntnis, die der Begrenztheit des menschlichen Intellektes enthoben ist. Die schwertscharfen Kanten der Säule, an denen sich der Unglaube bricht, treffen laue Christen (Spreu) in gleicher Weise wie Juden (leichte Federn) und Heiden (morsches Holz). Was bis zum Ende bleibt, ist der Glaube, als das fruchtbare Getreide, von dem die Spreu gesondert wird[23], der aber auch die Hoffnung endzeitlicher Bekehrung der außerchristlichen Menschengruppen einschließt.

In der Südseite hat Hildegard eine runde Säule konzipiert, die im Schatten steht, so daß auch bei ihr, aber aus einem anderen Grund, Größe und Höhe nicht zu erkennen sind. Es ist die Säule der Menschheit des Erlösers, in der Stadt der Heilsgeschichte das Sinnbild der Erlösung. Zwischen dieser und der Säule der Trinität im Westwinkel ist ein Abstand von 3 Ellen angegeben, wo von der Umfassungsmauer des Gebäudes nur die Fundamente gelegt sind. „Die Statik der in der Architektur versinnbildlichten alttestamentlichen Zeit wird ersetzt durch die Dynamik unmittelbar sich ereignender heilsgeschichtlicher Progression"[24]. Es geht jetzt um die für Hildegard gegenwärtige, noch im Aufbau befindliche Heilsphase. Deshalb tragen die im Innern der Säule aufsteigenden Tugendkräfte Bausteine empor.

Der Schatten, in dem die Säule steht, hat aber, da sie die Menschheit des Erlösers bedeutet, nicht einen Hinweischarakter auf die Transzendenz Gottes, sondern auf das Geheimnis der Inkarnation in der *obumbratio Spiritus sancti* (vgl. Luk. 1,35). Größe und Höhe der Säule sind also nicht wie bei der zuvor beschriebenen deshalb unerkennbar, weil sie jenseits des menschlichen Ermessens liegen, weil es also an ihr kein menschliches Maß gäbe, sondern deshalb, weil die Menschwerdung sich in der verborgenen Größe des Mysteriums vollzog, die nur im Glauben und daher im Schatten erkannt werden kann.

Der Zwischenraum von 3 Ellen, wo nur das Fundament der Mauer gelegt ist, deutet hin auf die zukünftigen Gläubigen, die bis zum Weltende geboren werden. Keinem voreiligen Chiliasmus fällt Hildegard anheim, wenn sie die in 3 Ellen angedeutete Länge der kommenden Zeiten im

---

[23] Vgl. dazu B. Maurmann, a. a. O. (Anm. 3) 98: „Nutzlose Spreu und Getreidefrucht stehen für Unglauben und Glauben, die einer Scheidung bedürfen. Die Lokalisation der strohbedeckten Kante nach Südwesten ist vor dem Hintergrund der Windelehre der Causae et Curae nicht beliebig. Die Bedingung, die Hildegard in der Heilkunde an ein gemäßigtes Auftreten der Winde stellt, ist im Augenblick des Gerichts aufgehoben; denn dann sind sie als Strafaktion gegen die Sünder eingesetzt: Der Westwind verdorrt, was ihm nahekommt, der Südwind mäßigt nicht länger die Sonnenglut. Gegen die vermessenen Juden holt der Hieb der mit Federn bedeckten Nordkante aus. Wie die Pharisäer aus eigener Kraft in die Höhen des Himmels aufzusteigen beabsichtigen (644 D), fliegen sie vom Chorus getroffen wie haltlose Federn zu Boden. Von ebenso minderwertiger Qualität ist das morsche Holz an der Westkante der Säule. Es kennzeichnet die Irrlehre der Heiden zu der Zeit, da der Untergang (*occasus*) des Unglaubens schon durch den wahren Glauben besiegelt war."
[24] B. Maurmann, a. a. O. 99.

Geheimnis der Trinität beschlossen sein läßt. Die Mauer der Werke des Glaubens, noch ungebaut, ist vorausgeschaut im Wissen Gottes und daher im Fundament schon da.

Das letzte architektonische Einzelglied ist der quadratische Turm in der Südecke von Hildegards Heilsgebäude, dessen Breite sie mit 5 Ellen angibt, während auch hier die Höhe für sie, wieder aus einem anderen Grund, unabschätzbar ist. Die eine Elle Zwischenraum zur Säule der Menschwerdung weist ebenfalls den Mauerbau nur im Fundament auf. Trotz der unermeßlichen Höhe des Turmes ist sein Aufbau noch nicht vollendet, aber viele Arbeiter schaffen an ihm, und Scharen von Menschen erblickt Hildegard auf der in seinem Innern emporführenden Leiter, so wie sie noch viele Menschen aus der Welt in das Heilsgebäude eintreten sieht. Es gibt aber auch solche, die, des Gewandes entblößt, zur Welt zurückeilen. Dem Turm gegenüber, im Innern des Gebäudekomplexes, beschreibt Hildegard sieben weiße runde Marmorsäulen von 7 Ellen, auf deren Höhe die Gestalt der Weisheit sichtbar wird, während unten auf dem Pflaster im Innern des Gebäudes die allegorischen Gestalten der Gerechtigkeit, der Stärke und der Heiligkeit erscheinen.

Der Turm wird identifiziert als Turm der Kirche[25], der „neue Bau", entstanden nach der Menschwerdung des Sohnes. In der Deutung der Breite von 5 Ellen wiederholt sich die Auslegung auf die vom Heiligen Geist spiritualisierten fünf Sinne, in der der nicht abschätzbaren Höhe die Auslegung auf die Tiefe der göttlichen Weisheit (altus = hoch, tief), der die künftige Vollendung der Kirche anheimgegeben ist, und die eine Elle Zwischenraum des Turmes der Kirche zum Turm der Menschwerdung wird hier auf den einen wahren Gott ausgelegt, in dessen Wissen die Herrlichkeit der eschatologischen Kirche noch verborgen ist. Auch die sieben Brustwehren, die in der Höhe des Turmes erkennbar sind, denen die im Innern auf einer Leiter emporsteigenden Apostel und Apostelnachfolger entgegengehen, sind, wie nicht anders zu erwarten, die sieben Geistesgaben. Die in den Gebäudekomplex Eintretenden empfangen mit dem Lichtgewand den Glauben, die aus ihm Heraustretenden verlieren ihn. Solche, die räuberisch gegen den Turm der Kirche toben, sind die auch hier nicht vergessenen Ämterkäufer, deren Kennzeichen die Vermessenheit ist. Die sieben Säulen von 7 Ellen Höhe weisen in der Potenz auf die Siebenzahl der Gaben hin, die als eine Entfaltung der Macht Gottes im Irdischen die Kraft und Höhe des menschlichen Geistes zu überbieten helfen.

Die Mauer der Heilsgeschichte kehrt zurück zur Ostecke, von der sie ausgegangen ist, wo auf sieben Stufen der Sitz des Menschensohnes, des

---

[25] H. Liebeschütz, Das allegorische Weltbild der hl. Hildegard von Bingen, Leipzig 1930, 34. 51–55 weist auf Ähnlichkeiten zwischen Hildegards Versinnbildlichungen der Kirche (als Gestalt und als Turm) mit dem Hirten des Hermas hin und nimmt an, daß sie diese Schrift gekannt hat.

verus Oriens und *ortus iustitiae*, das Geschichtsende transparent werden läßt. Eine Lichtvision verwandelt die Stadt zum himmlischen Jerusalem, dessen nach dem geraden Maß der Gerechtigkeit behauene Bausteine, die Werke des Glaubens, den *aureus numerus* der eschatologischen Menschheit erstehen lassen[26].

Bei Hildegards Visionenreihe der makro-mikrokosmischen Entsprechungen in De operatione Dei ist zu bedenken, daß es sich für sie nicht wie für uns um eine symbolische Schau, auch nicht um Mythologie, sondern um Naturphilosophie und Naturkunde handelt, deren außerchristliche Herkunft[27] ihr in irgendeiner Form bekannt gewesen sein muß, was man aus ihrer eifrigen Bemühung erschließen kann, das Traditionsgut zu verchristlichen. Es handelt sich hier auch nicht wie bei der fiktionalen Stadt der Heilsgeschichte um Zahlenallegorien in Gestalt von Maßangaben, sondern um einander entsprechende Proportionen am Menschenleib und im Makrokosmos, aus denen praktische Nutzanwendungen ethischer Art abgeleitet werden (cf. Tafel I, Abb. 1).

Adelgundis Führkötter beschreibt die grundlegende Vision Hildegards vom kosmischen Menschen folgendermaßen: „In den zwei Urformen von Kreis und Kreuz erblickt die Seherin den Menschen, der mit weit ausgebreiteten Armen als Mikrokosmos dasteht und die Makrokosmos-Kreise durchdringt, die aber umfaßt, umspannt und getragen werden vom Schöpfergott"[28]. Dieses Letztere, daß das Weltenrad vor der Brust Gottes geschaut wird, ist das Unterscheidende zu antiken wie asiatischen Vorstel-

---

[26] Dieser Ausdruck steht allerdings nicht am Ende der Visionsreihe vom Heilsgebäude in Scivias, sondern an der entsprechenden Stelle im Liber de operatione Dei III, 10, 12, PL 197, 1015, wo Maß- und Zahlangaben im Vergleich zu Scivias eine verschwindende Rolle spielen. In Scivias ist der eschatologische Mensch als goldener Kreis eines Rades versinnbildet.

[27] Hans Liebeschütz, a. a. O. (Anm. 25) 59—118 macht verschiedentlich auf Hrabanus Maurus als möglichen Vermittler antiker Traditionen an Hildegard aufmerksam (benediktinische Tischlesung), auch darauf, daß das Weltbild der antiken Astrologie nicht erst durch die Übersetzungen im Toledo des 12. Jahrhunderts, sondern vereinzelt schon seit der Karolingerzeit bekannt war. Seit Isidor müsse man für das lateinische Mittelalter mit der Kenntnis der „Weltformel" der Verwandtschaft von Makro- und Mikrokosmos rechnen. Liebeschütz beruft sich auch auf R. Reizenstein, H. Schraeder, Studien zum antiken Synkretismus aus Iran und Griechenland, Leipzig—Berlin 1926 (und andere Werke), da Reizenstein für Hildegard und Honorius mit einer Beziehung zu den Adamsspekulationen des Henochbuches rechnet. (Erschaffung der Glieder Adams aus Teilen der Welt). Vgl. auch M. T. d'Alverny, Le Cosmos Symbolique du XIIe siècle, in: Arch. d'Hist. doctr. et litt. 18 (1953) 31—81; R. Allers, Microcosmus. From Anaximandros to Paracelsus, in: Traditio 2 (1944) 319—405; S. Braunfels, Vom Mikrokosmos zum Meter, in: S. Braunfels, G. Glowatski (u. a.) (Ed.), Der vermessene Mensch, München 1973, 43—74. H. Liebeschütz, Kosmologische Motive in der Bildungswelt der Frühscholastik, in: Bibliothek Warburg, Vorträge 1923/24, Leipzig 1926, 83—148. K. Werner, Die Kosmologie und Naturlehre des scholastischen Mittelalters mit specieller Beziehung auf Wilhelm v. Conches, Sitzungsber. der Akademie der Wiss. Wien, Phil.-Histor. Klasse 75 (1873) 309—403.

[28] A. Führkötter, Hildegard v. Bingen, Leben und Werk, in: A. Ph. Brück (Ed.) Hildegard v. Bingen, Festschrift zum 800. Todestag der Heiligen, Mainz 1979, 44.

lungen[29]. Dennoch hat man die Illustration von Hildegards Vision im Kodex von Lucca als „exact shape in which pagan cosmologies made their first re-appearance in the Middle Ages"[30] bezeichnet.

Hildegard läßt die Länge der inmitten des kosmischen Rades erscheinenden Menschengestalt gleich ihrer Breite mit ausgespannten Armen sein, und in dieser Proportion entspricht der Mensch dem Firmament (Kosmos).

Nam longitudo staturae hominis latitudoque ipsius, brachiis et manibus aequaliter a pectore extensis, aequales sunt, quemadmodum etiam firmamentum aequalem longitudinem et latitudinem habet, quia etiam per mensuram longitudinis et latitudinis hominis, quae in ipso aequales sunt, scientia boni et mali intelligitur, quae in utilitate bonum, in inutilitate vero malum scit.[31]

Die mikro-makrokosmische Gleichheit der Breite und Länge, Ausdruck einer Totalität, gilt bei Hildegard als Gewähr für das Wissen der Unterscheidung von Gut und Böse, ebenfalls einer Totalität, als Garantie also für die Leistungsfähigkeit des Menschen in seiner Welt. Diese Mitgift des Schöpfers, die *recta et distincta mensura*[32], ist dem Menschen zugemessen aus dem Urgrund der wahren Liebe, in deren Wissen der Weltenlauf ruht[33], die alle menschlichen Glieder *decenter distinguit, convenienterque iustae mensurae coaptat*[34]. Die Gleichheit der Proportionen des Menschenleibes und der kosmischen Proportionen bewußt zu machen, ist für Hildegard die Grundlage ihrer Ethik.

Die gegenseitige Durchdringung kosmischer Zonen wird zum Gleichbild dafür genommen, daß die *discretio* (Tugend des Maßes und der Unterscheidungskraft) die *bona opera in moderatione sua* in sich enthält[35]. Hildegard redet aber nicht einem astrologischen Determinismus das Wort, sondern spricht davon, daß die kosmischen Sphären sich gegenseitig moderieren und so den Einfluß auf die Erde mildern. Sie läßt negative kosmische Einwirkungen nur gemäß der strafenden Gerechtigkeit Gottes zu, *contritionen hominibus immoderatam in peccato moderationem non habentibus infligens*[36].

---

[29] Vgl. den Bericht über einen Vortrag von Th. Immoos in: The Asiatic Society of Japan, Bulletin No. 10, Dec. 1981, 3 über makro-mikrokosmische Entsprechungen (Kopf–Himmel; Füße–Erde; Augen–Sonne, Mond; Adern–Flüße; Haare–Sterne etc.) im Konfuzianismus und Taoismus.

[30] F. Saxl, Lectures 1, London 1957, 62. Beim ersten Anblick wirkt diese Illustration nach Saxl wie aus der Spätantike stammend.

[31] PL 197, 814. Gegenüber dem eiförmigen Universum in Scivias I, 3 gibt Hildegard ihm in ihrem Spätwerk Kreisform, woraus sich die gleiche Länge und Beite ergibt.

[32] PL 197, 789.

[33] Vgl. die Übersetzung von H. Schipperges, Hildegard v. Bingen, Welt und Mensch, Salzburg 1965, 59.

[34] PL 197, 789.

[35] PL 197, 758.

[36] PL 197, 809.

An Entsprechung der Maßverhältnisse der einzelnen Glieder oder
Abschnitte des Menschenleibes mit dem entsprechenden Kosmischen führt
Hildegard u. a. folgendes an:
Das Rùnd des menschlichen Kopfes spiegelt die Rundung des Firmamen-
tes,

*et in recta aequalique mensura eiusdem capitis recta et aequalis mensura firmamenti
demonstratur, quia idem caput rectam mensuram ubique habet, ut etiam firmamentum aequali mensura constitutum est, quatenus ex omni parte rectum cir-
cuitum habere possit, et ne ulla pars eius partem alteram iniusto modo excedat*[37].

Die Folge dieser Entsprechung für die Seele ist, daß sie *circumeunte ratio-
nalitate*, also die Kopf- und Kosmosform gleichsam nachzeichnend, *omne
opus hominis disponit et ordinat*[38]. Nichtsdestoweniger tragen Seele und
Leib einen gewaltigen Konflikt miteinander aus, dem Kreislauf von Gut
und Böse entsprechend[39], den Hildegard ebenfalls in der Rundung von
Kopf und Firmament ausgedrückt findet[40].
Die einzelnen Abschnitte des menschlichen Kopfes (Schädeloberfläche
bis Stirn, Augen bis Nasenspitze, Nase bis Kehle) setzt Hildegard in ihrem
untereinander gleichen Maß den äußeren drei Elemente gleich (wobei es
sich um fünf kosmische Kreise handelt): dem lichten mit dem dunklen
Feuer, dem reinen Äther mit Sonne und Mond, der wäßrigen mit der starken Luft.

*Et loca ista aequali mensura ab invicem discreta sunt, quemadmodum et densitas
superioris ignis cum nigro igne, densitas etiam puri aetheris, necnon densitas aquosi
aeris cum forti et albo lucidoque aere aequalis mensurae existunt*[41].

Die geistige Entsprechung zu diesem makro-mikrokosmisch gleichen
Maßverhältnis sieht Hildegard in den drei Seelenkräften *comprehensio,
intelligentia* und *motio*, die sich zu einer einzigen verbinden und gegenseitig moderieren, *ita ut si anima plus comprehenderet quam intelligere aut
movere posset, in iniusta mensura esset*[42]. Hildegard geht hier also durchaus eigene und nicht etwa nur augustinische Wege. Unter der *comprehensio*
ist so etwas wie ein körperliches Selbstbewußtsein zu verstehen, mit dem
die Seele den Leib erfaßt, *omnia scilicet in ipso recta mensura movens*, und
hier gebraucht Hildegard umgekehrt wie zuvor den architektonischen

---

[37] PL 197, 814.
[38] PL 197, 814.
[39] Vgl. dazu E. Gössmann, Zyklisches und lineares Geschichtsbewußtsein im Mittelalter,
erscheint voraussichtlich in den Akten des 7. Congrès International de Philosophie Médiévale,
Louvain-la-Neuve 1982.
[40] PL 197, 815.
[41] PL 197, 815.
[42] PL 197, 815s.

Mikrokosmos zur Erläuterung des menschlichen: *velut fabricator aedificium suum hominibus ad habitandum recte metitur*[43].

Hildegard nennt unter der gleichen kosmischen Analogie noch eine andere Maßgleichheit am menschlichen Kopf: vom Scheitel bis zu den beiden Augenbrauen, von dort bis zu beiden Ohren und rückwärts bis zum Anfang des Nackens. Diese *recta aequalisque mensura* entspricht für sie der Dreiheit der Seelenkräfte exspiratio – scientia – sensus[44]. Die Bezeichnung der ersten läßt deutlich den mikro-makrokosmischen Austausch erkennen: Der Mensch atmet zu seiner Stärkung die kosmischen Elemente ein und aus, wie die Sonne ihre Strahlen ausgießt und wieder an sich zieht[45]. So bedeutet die seelische *exspiratio* die Kraft, das menschliche Werk in Gang zu setzen, das mit Hilfe von *scientia* und *sensus* ausgeführt wird. Auch diese drei Kräfte moderieren sich gegenseitig:

> *Istae namque vires hoc modo aequales sunt, scilicet quoniam anima exspirando non plus facere incipit quam scientia comprehendere aut quam sensu sufferre possit, et sic unanimiter operantur, quia nulla istarum aliam excedit, quemadmodum et caput rectam mensuram habet*[46].

Die Maßgleichheiten zwischen Kopf, Schultern und Hals setzt Hildegard im Hinblick auf ihre moralische Deutung zum Kreis des schwarzen Feuers in Beziehung, das als Strafgericht Gottes einen Reinigungsprozeß auslöst, der aber von der Sphäre der starken weißen Klarluft gemäßigt wird.

> *Quod etiam ab aure ad alteram aurem, et ab auribus ad humeros, atque ab humeris ad finem gutturis una mensura . . existens, significat quod homo praecepta Dei auribus percipiens, humerisque suis illa fideliter imponens, et quasi gutture suo ea in se trahens, in omnibus aequalem et discretum modum habere debet*[47].

Erstaunen erweckend, weil heute bei gewandeltem Weltbild wohl am wenigsten nachvollziehbar, ist Hildegards Parallele zwischen sieben gleichmäßig voneinander entfernten Punkten an Schädel und Stirn des Menschen und den durch gleiche Zwischenräume am Firmament voneinander getrennten sieben Planeten, die sie kennt. Aber hier macht sich auch ihre Verchristlichungstendenz am deutlichsten bemerkbar.

> *A superiori etiam summitate vasis cerebri usque ad ultimam extremitatem frontis hominis, septem loca aequali mensura a se discernuntur, per quae septem planetae aequali spatio a se in firmamento distantes, signati sunt . . . Haec autem designant, quoniam anima in humano corpore ab incoeptione operum suorum*

---

[43] PL 197, 816.
[44] PL 197, 816.
[45] PL 197, 815.
[46] PL 197, 816.
[47] PL 197, 817.

usque ad finitionem eorum septem dona Sancti Spiritus aequali studio venerari debet[48].

Die makro-mikrokosmische Entsprechung in der Siebenzahl kann von Hildegard nicht vermerkt werden, ohne ihre Überhöhung in den sieben Gaben des Heiligen Geistes zu finden. Erst als christliche Interpretin sieht sie sich in der Lage, den wahren Sinn der Entsprechungen von Welt und Mensch zu erkennen und für ihre Mitmenschen zu deuten. Wie bei ihrem allegorischen Heilsgebäude, schafft sie auch hier durch die in der Kraft der sieben Geistesgaben den menschlichen Leib mit seinen fünf Sinnen bewegende Seele eine Verbindung zwischen der Fünf- und der Siebenzahl. Ob sie, die immer wieder die gegenseitige Einwirkung von Leib und Seele betont hat, unausgesprochen die Summe zieht und so in der vollkommenen Zwölfzahl das vollkommene Zusammenwirken von Leib und Seele besiegelt sein läßt?

Wie der Kopf den umgebenden kosmischen Sphären, so entsprechen nach Hildegard die übrigen Glieder des menschlichen Leibes der Erde als ihrem Zentrum. Sie wird nicht müde, Entsprechungen in den Maßverhältnissen von Menschenkörper und Erde zu entdecken, denn: *Ut autem nulla forma visibilis sine nomine est, sic nulla sine mensura est*[49]. Das gleiche Maß der Leibesabschnitte vom Scheitel bis zum Ende der Kehle, von da bis zum Nabel und von da bis zum *locus egestionis* sieht sie folgendermaßen kosmisch korrespondiert:

> *quemadmodum etiam a summitate firmamenti usque ad inferiorem partem nubium et ut ab eadem inferiori parte nubium usque ad summitatem terrae, et ut ab eadem summitate terrae usque ad infimum finem ipsius aequalis mensura existit.*[50]

In dieser Dreiteilung findet sie die Lebensphasen von Kindheit, Jugend und Alter abgebildet.

Ähnlich weist sie auf Maßgleichheiten hin von den Schultern bis zu beiden Ellenbogen und von da bis zur äußeren Spitze des Mittelfingers. Sie gibt diesen Maßgleichheiten eine moralisch-anagogische Deutung:

> *Mensura enim quae ab humeris usque ad flexuram utriusque brachii est, opera quae homo per elationem mentis operatur, significat, et mensura quae a flexura brachiorum usque ad finem medii digiti utriusque manus extenditur, demonstrat quod homo opera quae per elationem mentis operatus est, per poenitentiam deleat*[51].

Das gleiche Maß von einem Oberschenkel zum andern sowie vom Nabel bis zum *locus egestionis* setzt Hildegard zu queren Breite der Erde in Beziehung, die der Dichte ihrer Tiefe entspricht, und sieht in diesen

---

[48] PL 197, 819 s.
[49] PL 197, 831.
[50] PL 197, 843.
[51] PL 197, 844 s.

Maßgleichheiten den Mutwillen des Fleisches ausgedrückt, dem der Mensch manchmal zustimmt und manchmal widersteht, so wie die Dichte der Erde für sie hinweist auf die Begierlichkeit des Fleisches, die Länge und Breite aber auf die Selbstbeherrschung[52]. Die Maßgleichheit vom Oberschenkel zum Knie und vom Knie zum Fußknöchel bringt Hildegard – sachgemäß ohne Maßanalogie – mit dem Ozean in Beziehung, der die Erde umfaßt[53]. Die moralische Deutung der Körperpartie von den Schenkeln zum Knie auf die Leidenschaft der Lenden und die damit in Zusammenhang gebrachte Ursünde verwundert nicht, wenn man die zeitgenössische Erbsündenlehre kennt. Der Allegorikerin gelingt es sicher, mit dem Schmerz der Seele über die Sünde eine für ihre Zeit überzeugende Analogie herzustellen für das Maß vom Knie zum Knöchel, da dieser den Ort der Verbannung versinnbildet, in den Adam ausgesetzt wurde[54].

Die Füße, in ihrem Maß den Händen gleichend, versinnbilden für Hildegard die Flüsse, die sich über die ganze Erde verteilen, und die Maßgleichheit von Händen und Füßen deutet an, daß die Seele *aequali mensura sine omni defectu corpus possidet illudque eam aequali mensura sustinet*[55].

Dieser ohne Skrupel bis in alle Einzelheiten durchgeführte Aufweis der Entsprechungen in den Maßverhältnissen von Mensch und Kosmos findet seinen Schlüssel in folgendem Satz:

Homo itaque, per animam divinus et per terram terrenus, plenum opus Dei est; unde etiam terrena scit, et in speculo fidei coelestia cognoscit[56].

Nachprüfbares Wissen gibt es also nach Hildegard nur für das Irdische, aber es gibt ein solches Wissen, das der Mensch rudimentär in sich vorfindet und sich immer mehr vergegenwärtigen muß, um seinen Weg mit Sicherheit gehen zu können. Für das Himmlische dagegen, so sehr die makromikrokosmische Verhältnisgleichheit von diesem übergriffen ist, gibt es zeitlebens das speculum fidei, das in der Geschichtszeit speculum bleibt. Im Spiegel des Glaubens und seiner Sinnbilder läßt Hildegard Gott als den Erzgießer, den großen Künstler, erscheinen, der aus den vielen Einzelspiegeln, die sie in ihre visionären Fiktionen einbaut, in den Elementen von Kosmos und Heilsgeschichte erkannt werden kann.

Ut Deus magnum instrumentum firmamenti aequali mensura mensus est, sic etiam aequaliter mensus est hominem in parva et brevi statura sua, . . . eumque sic creavit, ut membrum membro coniunctum, rectam mensuram suam, rectumque pondus suum non excedat[57].

---

52 Vgl. die Übersetzung von H. Schipperges, a. a. (Anm. 33), 120.
53 PL 197, 869.
54 PL 197, 870.
55 PL 197, 871.
56 PL 197, 871.
57 PL 197, 876.

ZAHL-UND MASS IN DEN FIGURENGEDICHTEN DER ANTIKE UND DES FRÜHMITTELALTERS

Beobachtungen zur Entwicklung tektonischer Bauformen

von ULRICH ERNST (Wuppertal)

Betrachtet man das Panorama der poetischen Gattungen in der christlichen Spätantike und im Frühmittelalter unter kompositionstheoretischen Aspekten, so diagnostiziert man rasch, daß kein dichterisches Genos, die Bibelepik eingeschlossen[1], so sichtbar und substantiell durch Zahl und Maß geprägt ist wie das Figurengedicht, das dem jeweiligen Textproduzenten neben der präzisen Kalkulierung der Prosodie ein exaktes Messen und Zählen des sprachlichen Materials zum Zweck der typographischen Konstituierung einer sinnbildlichen *figura* abverlangt[2]. Die geheimnisvollen zahlhaften und zahlensymbolischen Baugesetze dieser Bild-Text-Kompositionen erschließen sich, wenn man auf die klassischen Muster der Gattung zurückblickt und die Evolution der poetischen Formensprache im Übergang von der Antike zum Mittelalter verfolgt.

Vielleicht unter dem Einfluß der synästhetischen Kunstauffassung des Simonides von Keos (um 500 v. Chr.), der die Malerei als ,,stumme Poesie" und die Poesie als ,,redende Malerei" definiert[3], und offensichtlich abhängig von der ästhetischen Doktrin des Pythagoreismus, in der die ontologisch fundierte Idee der Zahl eine dominierende Rolle spielt[4], haben die griechischen Dichter Simias von Rhodos, Dosiadas von Kreta und Theokrit im Zeitalter des Hellenismus erstmals poetische Gebilde textgraphisch nach den Konturen realer Gegenstände entworfen und eine

---

[1] Zur Tektonik der karolingischen Bibelepik verweise ich auf die grundlegenden Studien von J. Rathofer, Der Heliand, Theologischer Sinn als tektonische Form, Köln 1962, und W. Haubrichs, Ordo als Form, Strukturstudien zur Zahlenkomposition bei Otfrid von Weißenburg und in karolingischer Literatur, Tübingen 1969.

[2] Vgl. U. Ernst, Die Entwicklung der optischen Poesie in Antike, Mittelalter und Neuzeit, in: GRM 26 (1976), 379 ff.

[3] Plutarch, De gloria Atheniensium, III, in: Moralia 346 F–347 A, II, 2 (hg. von W. R. Paton / J. Wegehaupt / M. Pohlenz, Leipzig 1934), 125.

[4] Vgl. Philolaos, Fr. 11: ,,Man kann aber die Natur der Zahl und ihre Kraft nicht nur in der Welt der Götter wirksam sehen, sondern auch allenthalben in allen Werken und Reden der Menschen und im Bereich aller technischen Arbeiten und in der Musik" (übers. von W. Capelle, Die Vorsokratiker, Stuttgart [4]1953, 478).

Interferenz von verbaler Mitteilung und optischer Darstellung in streng zahlhaft strukturierter Komposition angestrebt[5].

I. Dosiadas von Kreta

Zu einer paradigmatischen Demonstration, in welcher Modalität die hellenistischen Technopägnien[6] in ihrer virtuosen Textorganisation durch zahlenästhetische und zahlensymbolische Prinzipien strukturell bestimmt sind, eignet sich vorzüglich ein Altargedicht (Text 1), das von der älteren Forschung in die Zeit Kaiser Hadrians datiert und einem L. Julius Vestinus zugesprochen wurde, für das aber inzwischen G. Wojaczek nach ausführlicher Diskussion der Verfasserproblematik mit überzeugenden Argumenten Dosiadas von Kreta als Autor namhaft gemacht hat[7].

Das dem Stilideal der *obscuritas*[8] verpflichtete, teilweise in einem forciert änigmatischen Stilduktus abgefaßte Gedicht[9] gliedert sich auf inhaltlicher Ebene in zwei gleichgroße Teile (v. 1—13; v. 14—26), von denen der erste in dreifacher Klimax ex negativo pointiert, der textgraphisch abgebildete Altar sei kein Altar für Blutopfer, er sei auch kein Altar für Rauchopfer und schließlich sei er überhaupt kein materieller Altar, während der zweite Teil der Inhaltsschicht den Altar als Musenaltar im symbolischen Sinn präsentiert, der, als Person vorgestellt, in unmittelbarer Apostrophe den Dichter, der aus der Pegasus-Quelle getrunken hat, auffordert, Opfer darzubringen.

Richtet man nach der Analyse der Aussagegliederung, die den verbreiteten Typus der bilateralen Disposition repräsentiert, das Augenmerk auf das tektonische Formgefüge des Figurengedichts, das auf keinen äußeren Altar, sondern — kryptisches Signum einer dichtungsautonomen Ästhetik — nur auf sich selbst als poetisches Kunstgebilde verweist, so liefert der Text selbst einen hermeneutischen Schlüssel zur Aufdeckung des zahlhaften

---

[5] U. Ernst, ibid., 379f.

[6] Das Wort Technopägnion, das eine Verbindung von Kunst und Spiel anzeigt, begegnet zuerst bei Ausonius, der es allerdings für Hexameter verwendet, die mit einem einsilbigen Wort anfangen und enden. Ausonius, Opuscula, hg. von R. Peiper, Stuttgart 1976, XII, I, 156: *libello Technopaegnii nomen dedi, ne aut ludum laboranti, aut artem crederes defuisse ludenti.* XII, II, ibid.: *Misi ad te Technopaegnion, inertis otii mei inutile opusculum. uersiculi sunt monosyllabis coepti et monosyllabis terminati.*

[7] G. Wojaczek, Daphnis, Untersuchungen zur griechischen Bukolik, Meisenheim am Glan 1969, 117ff.; Text nach H. Beckby (Hg.), Die griechischen Bukoliker, Meisenheim am Glan 1975, 570.

[8] M. Fuhrmann, Obscuritas, Das Problem der Dunkelheit in der rhetorischen und literarästhetischen Theorie der Antike, in: Immanente Ästhetik, Ästhetische Reflexion, Lyrik als Paradigma der Moderne, München 1966, 47ff. (= Poetik und Hermeneutik 2).

[9] Zur philologischen Texterschließung vgl. G. Wojaczek, ibid., 113ff., der auf Einflüsse der Orphiker und der Griphos-Literatur aufmerksam macht.

Ὀλός οὔ με λιβρός ἱρῶν
Λιβάδεσσιν οἷα κάλχη
Ὑποφοινίῃσι τέγγει·
Μαύλιες δ' ὕπερθε πέτρης Ναξίης θοούμεναι
Παμάτων φείδοντο Πανός· οὐ στροβίλῳ λιγνύι
Ἰξός εὐώδης μελαίνει τρεχνέων μεΝυσίων.

Ἐς γὰρ βωμὸν ὁρῇς με μήτε γλούρου
Πλίνθοις μήτ' Ἀλύβης παγέντα βώλοις,
Οὐδ' ὃν Κυνθογενὴς ἔτευξε φύτλη
Λαβόντε μηκάδων κέρα,
Λισσαῖσιν ἀμφὶ δειράσιν
Ὄσσαι νέμονται Κυνθίαις,
Ἰσόρροπος πέλοιτό μοι·
Σὺν οὐρανοῦ γὰρ ἐκγόνοις
Εἰνάς μ' ἔτευξε γηγενής,
Τάων ἀείζωον τέχνην
Ἔνευσε πάλμυς ἀφθίτων.
Σὺ δ', ὦ πιὼν κρήνηθεν, ἢν
Ἴνις κόλαψε Γοργόνος,
Θύοις τ' ἐπισπένδοις τ' ἐμοὶ
Ὑμηττιάδων πολὺ λαροτέρην
Σπονδὴν ἄδην. ἴθι δὴ θαρσέων
Ἐς ἐμὴν τεῦξιν· καθαρὸς γὰρ ἐγὼ
Ἰὸν ἱέντων τεράων, οἷα κέκευθ' ἐκεῖνος,
Ἀμφὶ Νέαις Θρηικίαις ὃν σχεδόθεν Μυρίνης
Σοί, Τριπάτωρ, πορφυρέου φὼρ ἀνέθηκε κριοῦ.

(Text 1; vgl. Abb. 1, Tafel II).

Formgefüges. Die Erwähnung der Neunzahl der Musen (Εἰνάς, v. 15)[10], die zusammen mit den älteren drei Musen (vgl. v. 14)[11] den Altar erbaut haben, signalisiert flagrant, daß die den Musen zugeordneten Symbolzahlen drei und neun die Aufbauzahlen der poetischen Architektur bilden.

In der Tat werden die Verse in den Rahmenpartien, welche die Altarstufen und die Altarplatte mit Untersatz und Altaraufsatz textgraphisch konturieren, im Sinne dieses Zahlenprogramms konsequent zu dreizeiligen

---

[10] Zur Neunzahl der Musen vgl. Homer, Odyssee, 24, v. 60; Hesiod, Theogonie, v. 75 ff.

[11] Zur archaischen Trias der Musen vgl. H. Usener, Dreiheit, Ein Versuch mythologischer Zahlenlehre, Hildesheim 1966 (Nachdruck der Ausgabe Bonn 1903), 10; R. Mehrlein, Drei, in: RAC 4 (1959), 272 f.

Strophen formiert. Entsprechend dem zentralen Aufbauprinzip der Polymetrie, der Kombination verschiedener Versmaße in einem Gedicht, das einen höchst rationalen Umgang mit dem Sprachmaterial erfordert, finden zudem 6 (2 × 3) Typen metrischer Organisation Verwendung, die sich gemäß der Lesestruktur in folgender vertikaler Verteilung abbilden:

1. drei anakreontische Zeilen (1—3);
2. drei trochäische Tetrameter (4—6);
3. drei Phalaikeen (7—9);
4. elf iambische Dimeter (10—20);
5. drei anapästische Dimeter (21—23);
6. drei choriambische Tetrameter (24—26).

Sprechen somit alle Indizien dafür, daß das Gedicht auf einem rational kalkulierten Zahlengrundriß errichtet ist, die Annahme eines sinnbildlichen Zusammenhangs zwischen numerischer Aufbaustruktur und expressis verbis erwähnter Neunzahl der Musen, denen die visuelle Textkomposition gewidmet ist, steht so lange auf unsicheren Füßen, wie die Gesamtverszahl des Gedichtes nicht in diesem Sinne prägnant zu deuten ist; denn die Zahl 26 scheint auf den ersten Blick tektonisch funktionslos und für die supponierte Enneadensymbolik[12] unergiebig. Hält man sich indes bewußt, daß zu den 26 horizontal verlaufenden Zeilen noch eine weitere vertikal zu lesende Zeile, nämlich ein Akrostichon, gleichsam eine zweite Textdimension, hinzukommt, so konstituiert sich als neue Gesamtverszahl die Zahl 27 (3 × 9), die im Rahmen des aufgezeigten Formprogramms symbolkräftig ist. Daß gerade das Akrostichon den — formal besonders ab- und hervorgehobenen — 27. Vers bildet, dürfte kein Zufall sein, da sich der Dichter gerade hier als Olympier, d. h. als Musenjünger, profiliert, wie der Appell des personifizierten Altars dokumentiert:

Ὀλύμπιε πολλοῖς ἔτεσι θύσειας
(Olympier, opfre noch viele Jahre lang)[13].

Betrachtet man, konzentriert ausschließlich auf das Textkorpus, den ersten Versblock (1—3) als tektonisch überschüssig, so ergibt sich eine wohlproportionierte, symmetrische Zentralkomposition, deren Mittelblock (10—20) von jeweils zwei gleichgroßen Flügeln, Außen- und Binnenflügeln (4—6, 24—26/7—9, 21—23), flankiert wird: Exakt im arithmetischen Mittelpunkt dieser präzise berechneten und exakt ausgemessenen Architektur — fast schon einer Schalenkomposition — steht der Hinweis auf die neun

---

[12] Vgl. W. H. Roscher, Die Sieben- und Neunzahl im Kultus und Mythus der Griechen, Leipzig 1904, 56/60 (Abh. der phil.-hist. Kl. d. kgl. sächs. Ges. d. Wiss. I).
[13] G. Wojaczek, ibid., 119 ff.

Musen (v. 15 = v. 12 der Zentralpartie[14]), der den Brennpunkt der gesamten poetischen Konzeption bildet.

Da der Leser bei einer solchen komplexen Zentralkomposition Räume durchmessen, hinter sich lassen und schrittweise zur Kernpartie vorstoßen muß, richtet sich der Blick abschließend auf den zentralen, von den beiden Binnenflügeln umlagerten Formblock: Dabei drängt sich die Beobachtung auf, daß die Nennung der neun Musen nicht nur den tektonischen Drehpunkt der zentrierten Komposition bildet, sondern, von oben wie von unten betrachtet, exakt im 9. Vers lokalisiert ist, womit sich der gesamte Strukturplan im Hinblick auf Aussagepotential und zahlensymbolisches Formprogramm als stimmig erweist.

Begreift man den tektonischen Baukörper des Gedichts in seiner mimetischen Dimension als Konterfei eines realen Kultaltars — Musenaltäre existieren zu dieser Zeit in Griechenland an verschiedenen Orten[15] —, so läßt sich konstatieren, daß Dosiadas ebenso wie in seinem zweiten Technopägnion, dem als Pendant entworfenen Iason-Altar, der Typus eines rechteckigen Altars mit Basis, ja mit Tendenz zum Stufenaltar, als Exemplum vorgeschwebt hat. Was den von Dosiadas in beiden Textbildern konstruierten Altaraufsatz anbelangt, so sind auf griechischen Vasen der Zeit mehrfach solche ἐπιβωμίδες zu erkennen, die als Unterlage für Opferholz dienten. Im Hinblick auf eine typologische Klassifikation der visuell angedeuteten Altarform ist daran zu erinnern, daß in der literarischen Tradition der Griechen streng differenziert wird zwischen der ἐσχάρα, dem niedrigen, stufenlosen Altar, der chthonischen Gottheiten errichtet wird, und dem — hier greifbaren — βωμός, der für himmlische Gottheiten reserviert ist[16].

Trotz solcher imitativer Realitätsbezüge der Textgraphik handelt es sich bei dem figurierten Poem erklärtermaßen nicht um ein objektbezogenes allokutives Bildgedicht[17]. Wenn der Leser des *carmen figuratum* anfangs zur genauen Betrachtung des Altars aufgefordert wird, dann aber rasch der dementierende Hinweis erfolgt, der vorliegende Altar sei überhaupt kein materieller Kultgegenstand, wird eines ersichtlich: Nicht einmal in der poetischen Fiktion geht es um die Inaugenscheinnahme (oder Deskription) eines realen oder als real vorgestellten Altars, sondern ausschließlich um die komplexe Rezeption eines symbolisch zu verstehenden literarischen Produkts durch simultane Betrachtung und sukzessive Lektüre. Die poetologische Thematik in ihrer mythischen Einbettung und ebenso auch die

---

[14] Möglicherweise signalisiert die Verszahl 12 die Gesamtzahl der drei älteren und neun jüngeren Musen.

[15] Vgl. W. F. Otto, Die Musen und der göttliche Ursprung des Singens und Sagens, Darmstadt ³1971, 56 und 64—67.

[16] Vgl. L. Ziehen, Altar I (griechisch-römisch), in: RAC 1 (1950), 317f.

[17] Zu diesem Typus vgl. G. Kranz, Das Bildgedicht, Theorie — Lexikon — Bibliographie, Bd. 1, Köln 1981, 236ff.

auf einen esoterischen Adressatenkreis zugeschnittene änigmatische Diktion legen dabei den Schluß nahe, daß der Musen-Altar von Dosiades anläßlich seiner Initiation in die kultische Sodalitas des koischen Dichterbundes verfaßt ist[18].

Das hellenistische Technopägnion, das sich bei Dosiadas als artistische Verbindung von zwei Textschichten und Leserichtungen (horizontale Verse, vertikales Akrostichon), verbaler und graphischer Zeichensprache, formalistischer Zahlenästhetik[19] und basaler, im polytheistischen Mythos verwurzelter Zahlensymbolik präsentiert, ist nicht ohne geschichtliche Wirkung geblieben, sondern hat intensiv auf die lateinische Dichtungstradition ausgestrahlt.

II. Publilius Optatianus Porfyrius

Eine produktive und innovatorische Rezeption des griechischen Technopägnions leistet Publilius Optatianus Porfyrius, der unter Konstantin dem Großen in Rom von 329 bis 333 die Stadtpräfektur bekleidete und, wie man aus der Tatsache, daß er von Konstantin in einem Brief mit *frater carissime* apostrophiert wird[20], schließen darf, zur unmittelbaren Umgebung des Kaisers gehörte. Dabei war sein Verhältnis zum Kaiser anfangs gespannt; denn er deutet mehrfach in seinen Gedichten an, er sei auf falsche Anschuldigungen hin von Konstantin mit dem Exil bestraft worden[21], wobei sich der genaue Ort seiner Verbannung bisher nicht lokalisieren läßt. Er beklagt nicht nur die schmerzliche Trennung von seinem Sohn[22], sondern beschwert sich auch über die drastische Beschränkung seiner ‚publizistischen' Möglichkeiten im Exil, kann er doch laut eigener Aussage seine Gedichte nicht in prunkvollen Purpurhandschriften mit silberner Schrift und goldenen Intexten schreiben lassen, sondern muß sich mit gewöhnlichem Pergament, schwarzer Tinte und Minium für die *versus intexti* begnügen[23], eine Form der Aufzeichnung, die ihm um so beklagenswerter

---

[18] G. Wojaczek, ibid., 126.

[19] Vgl. Aristoteles, Metaphysik, 1078a36: „Die hauptsächlichsten Formen aber des Schönen sind Ordnung und Ebenmaß und Bestimmtheit, was ja am meisten die mathematischen Wissenschaften zum Gegenstand ihrer Beweise haben" (übers. von H. Bonitz, Reinbek 1966, 295). Vgl. E. Grassi, Die Theorie des Schönen in der Antike, Köln 1962, 141.

[20] Epistula Constantini, Z. 7 (ich zitiere nach: Publilii Optatiani Porfyrii Carmina, Bd. 1: Textus, Bd. 2: Commentarium criticum et exegeticum, hg. von G. Polara, Rom 1973).

[21] Vgl. carm. II, v. 31f.: *Respice me falso de crimine, maxime rector, / exulis afflictum poena*. Vgl. M. Schanz, Geschichte der römischen Litteratur bis zum Gesetzgebungswerk des Kaisers Justinian, Bd. 4,1, München ²1914, 11.

[22] Vgl. carm. I, v. 15. Vgl. M. Schanz, ibid.

[23] Carm. I, v. 1—12:
Quae quondam sueras pulchro decorata libello
carmen in Augusti ferre Thalia manus,

erscheint, als seine Figurengedichte auf eine optimale visuelle Präsentation angewiesen sind, die dem eigenen poetischen Ingenium wie der hohen Würde des Kaisers einzig angemessen ist[24].

Um eine Aufhebung des Exils zu erreichen und das Wohlgefallen des Kaisers wiederzuerlangen, sendet er 325 anläßlich der Vicennalien dem Kaiser eine Kollektion von zwanzig panegyrischen Figurengedichten, die Konstantin tatsächlich dazu bewegt, ihn zu begnadigen[25] und mit ihm in Korrespondenz zu treten. Die Protektion des Kaisers veranlaßt ihn später dazu, eine noch größere Sammlung seiner Figurengedichte der Öffentlichkeit zugänglich zu machen, die weitere *carmina* (Nr. XXI−XXVII) enthält, dazu das Handschreiben Konstantins und ein älteres Dankschreiben des Dichters, in dem er sich für die freundliche Aufnahme seiner Figurengedichte bei dem Kaiser bedankt. Außer diesen Gedichten sind von Porfyrius noch einige Fragmente erhalten, die Fulgentius tradiert, und einige anacyclische Verse − Distichen, die rückwärts gelesen, wieder neue Distichen ergeben −, die im Codex Salmasianus überliefert sind, der vorwiegend Werke afrikanischer Dichter enthält, was die Vermutung genährt hat, Optatianus Porfyrius sei seiner Herkunft nach Afrikaner gewesen[26].

Porfyrius imitiert mit Textfiguren wie Altar und Syrinx einerseits die griechischen Umrißgedichte, allerdings unter Aufgabe des Prinzips der Polymetrie und der Griphos-Form, zum andern kreiert er den neuen Typus des Gittergedichts, bei dem sich aus einem kompakten Letterngrund horizontal verlaufender Hexameter gleicher Länge durch Rubrizierung figural zu lesende Verse herausheben, die wie in einen Teppich eingewebte Muster wirken. Während bei den griechischen Konturgedichten die *versus* die graphische *figura* konstituieren, fällt diese Funktion bei den Gittergedichten, die auf dem Prinzip der Buchstabenzählung basieren, den *versus intexti* zu, eine Bauform, die am 2. Gedicht des Konstantin dedizierten panegyrischen Zyklus exemplifiziert werden soll (Text 2).

---

ostro tota nitens, argento auroque coruscis
   scripta notis, picto limite dicta notans,
scriptoris bene compta manu meritoque renidens
   gratificum, domini visibus apta sacris,
pallida nunc, atro chartam suffusa colore,
   paupere vix minio carmina dissocians,
hinc trepido pede tecta petis venerabilis aulae,
   horrida quod nimium sit tua nunc facies.
Hos habitus vatis praesentia fata merentur;
   vix locus hoc saltem praebuit unde venis.

[24] ibid., v. 13 ff.
[25] Epistula Constantini, Z. 40−44: *Tu cum tibi videas operis tui gratiam, quam ex meis petiveras auribus, non perisse, et proventu praesentis temporis exultare debebis et non indebitam laudem ingenii exercitatione captare.*
[26] M. Schanz, ibid., 12 f.

```
SANCTETVIVATISCAESARMISEREREESERENVS
A VGVSTEOMNIPOTENS A LMOMORTALIACVNCTA A
N VMINELAETIFICANS N OBISADGAVDIANOME N
C ONSTANTINETVVMFE C VNDICARMINISEXHO C
T EDVCEDETMVSASNAM T RISTISCVRARECVSA T
E GREGIOS A CTVSIAMS E DENTCRI M INAPARCA E
T VNCMELI V SDOMINVM T EVOXSEC V RASONABIT T
V IRTVTVM R ECTORPOT V ITVIXPAN G EREVERS V
I STAMODO E TMAESTOS I CSALTIMD I CEREVAT I
V IXMIHIC A LLIOPEPA V ITANTICO N SCIANVT V
A DNVITAV S APRECEMV A TISQVEE D ICEREFATA A
T RISTIAS I GNATOPAR T ESVTLIMI T ECLAVDA T
I VREPARI C ARMENMED I ISVTCON S ONAINOMN I
S ITNOTAPRIMASVIET S ITPARSEXTIMATALI S
C EVMEDIAEPRIMISOC C VRRENSAPTIVSISTI C
A DLATERVMFINESETPA A RSQVAEDIVIDITORS A
E MEDIOCAPVTESSEQV E ATVERSVQVEREFERR E
SANCTETVIVATISCAE SARMISEREREESERENVS
A LMESALVSORBISROMA A EDECVSINCLITEFAM A
R EMELIORPIETATEPA R ENSADMARTIAVICTO R
M ITIORADVENIAMPERM M VLCENSASPERALEGV M
I VSTITIAAETERNAEV I RESETGLORIASAECL I
S PESDATA P LENABONI S ETFELIX C OPIAREBV S
E XIMIVMC O LVMENVET E RVMVIRT V TEFIDEQV E
R OMAEMAGN E PARENSAR R MISCIVIL I BVSVLTO R
E TSVMMILA V SGRATADE E IMENSCLA R ASVPERN E
R EBVSMISS A SALVSPER R TEPAXOP T IMEDVCTO R
E TBELLIS S ECVRAQVI E SSANCTA O MNIAPERT E
S OLISIVRA S VISFIDIS S SIMADEX T RAMARITI S
E TSOCIALE I VGVMPRAE E BETCONS O RTIAVITA E
R ESPICEMEFALSODEC R IMINEMAXIMERECTO R
E XVLISAFFLICTVMPO E NANAMCETERACAVSA E
N VNCOBIECTAMIHIVE N IAVENERABILENVME N
V INCEPIAETSOLITOS V PERANSFATALIANVT V
SANCTETVIVATISCAESARMISEREREESERENVS
```

(Text 2; vgl. Abb. 2, Tafel III).

Das Gedicht, das wohl nach Konstantins Sieg über Licinius (324) entstanden ist[27], repräsentiert den Typ des Gittergedichts in der geometrischen Form des *carmen quadratum*, das sich aus 35 Versen zu je 35 Buchstaben rekrutiert und an allen Seiten durch den Vers *Sancte, tui vatis, Caesar, miserere serenus* eingerahmt wird, der einen Gnadenappell des

---

[27] Vgl. v. 25 f.: *armis civilibus ultor / per te pax . . .*; vgl. E. Kluge, Studien zu Publilius Optatianus Porfyrius, in: Münchener Museum für Philologie des Mittelalters und der Renaissance 4 (1924), 337. Vgl. G. Polara (Hg.), ibid., Bd. 2, 29.

exilierten Dichters an den Kaiser fixiert. Da dieser Intext zudem im Innern des Quadrats eine vertikale und eine horizontale Mittelachse bildet, welche die Grundfläche wieder in 4 kleine Quadrate mit 18 Buchstaben Seitenlänge aufteilen, taucht er insgesamt sechsmal in verschiedenen tektonischen Positionen auf: je einmal als Akrostichon, Mesostichon und Telestichon, sodann dreimal als *versus intercalaris* (1, 18, 35). Im Codex Bernensis (Abb. 2, Tafel III) sind nicht nur die vertikalen *versus intexti* im strengen Sinn durch Rotfärbung visualisiert[28], sondern auch die *versus intercalares*, die, Bestandteil der Text- wie der Intextstruktur, somit weniger als lyrische Refrains denn als strukturbildende optische Letternbahnen zu interpretieren sind. Beiläufig bleibt darauf hinzuweisen, daß das virtuose Letternspiel des Intextmusters technisch dadurch ermöglicht wird, daß der hexametrische *versus intextus* mit dem Buchstaben S anfängt und aufhört, was dazu geführt hat, daß dieser Buchstabe alle Eck- und Schnittpunkte der Intextstraßen, insgesamt neunmal, ausfüllt.

Außer dem ersten Intext, der sechsmal in geometrischer Struktur begegnet, figuriert das Gedicht noch einen zweiten Intext, der aus 4 *columnae* zu je 8 Buchstaben im Zentrum der 4 kleinen Quadrate gebildet ist, wobei die lineare geometrische Strukturierung der Buchstabensäulen verbale Grenzen transzendiert, wie aus dem diskontinuierlichen Leseprozeß resultiert: Wenn man die Letternsäulen vertikal von oben nach unten liest und, jeweils von links nach rechts hinüberschwenkend, von der oberen zur unteren Hälfte des Gedichts fortschreitet, konstituiert sich folgender Hexameter: *Aurea sic mundo disponas saecula toto*, in dem der Dichter – im Unterschied zum ersten Intext, in dem er sein persönliches Heil erfleht – Konstantin als Wohltäter des ganzen Erdkreises, als Initiator einer eher mythisch-immanentistisch als christlich-eschatologisch verstandenen *aetas aurea* feiert.

Das gedankliche Skelett der poetischen Graphik, die sich in der Inhaltsschicht in vier Teile aufgliedern läßt, ist kompositorisch auf den zentralen *versus intercalaris* abgestimmt, wie das folgende Dispositionsschema erhellt:

I.   Eine elegische Klage des Dichters über die Verbannung, die ihn am poetischen Schaffen hindert (1–11);

II.   Eine Explikation der Intextstruktur des Gittergedichts (12–18), die eine Identität von Dichtung und Dichtungstheorie erkennen läßt;

III.   Ein enkomiastisch gehaltener Katalog der Tugenden des Kaisers (19–28), der, orientiert an den *res animi*, sich in den topischen Bahnen des antiken

---

[28] Im Codex Bernensis 212 (Abb. 2) sind dem Gedicht des Porfyrius oberhalb die Scholien vorangestellt.

genus demonstrativum bewegt[29] und die theologisch-christliche Herr-
scherpanegyrik eines Eusebius[30] noch nicht antizipiert;

IV. Eine an den Kaiser gerichtete Bitte des Dichters um Aufhebung der Verbannung (29—35), die die Dichtung einmal mehr als ein Stück der historisch übergreifenden Gattung der Exilliteratur ausweist.

Die Abschnitte I und II einerseits und III und IV andererseits werden
jeweils durch festen Kehrreim (*versus intercalaris*) eingerahmt, der somit
auf verbaler wie figuraler Ebene zäsurierende und disponierende Funktion
hat.

Wenngleich in dem Figurengedicht des Porfyrius, das unter einem dün-
nen christlichen Firnis seine formalen und geistigen Energien noch wesentlich aus der paganen Dichtungstradition bezieht, keine voll ausgebildete
christliche Allegoriestruktur zu erwarten ist — die intextuelle Zeichensprache erscheint bei ihm allenfalls durch die christliche Form des Mono-
gramms durchgreifend geprägt —, läßt sich doch eine potentielle christliche
Verweisungsrichtung des tektonischen Baugefüges nicht leugnen; denn das
in seiner poetischen Statik durch die Vierzahl bestimmte Formgerüst
(Quadratisches Textkorpus, quadratischer Intextrahmen, 4 Intextkolum-
nen, 4 Textquadranten) mit seinem zentralen Intextkreuz figuriert zu
ersichtlich als adäquates poetisches Signum für den als *homo quadratus et
perfectus* idealisierten Kaiser, der unter dem Siegeszeichen des Kreuzes[31]
das viergeteilte römische Imperium (Tetrarchie) und damit den *mundus
tetragonus* als Universalherrscher regiert.

Die *carmina figurata* des Porfyrius repräsentieren christliche Dichtung
indes nicht in reiner Form, sondern dokumentieren, stärker noch mit
antik-heidnischen Elementen durchsetzt als das unter gleichen Voraussetzungen entstehende christliche Bibelepos[32], einen religiösen Synkretismus, der vor dem Hintergrund der zu diesem Zeitpunkt noch keineswegs
abgeschlossenen Entwicklung des Christentums von einer bloß tolerierten

[29] Vgl. die Hinweise bei A. Georgi, Das lateinische und deutsche Preisgedicht des Mittelalters, Berlin 1966, 11 ff. Daß Porfyrius der klassischen römischen Dichtung noch zutiefst ver-
pflichtet ist, belegen auch die Quellenangaben in G. Polaras Ausgabe, ibid., Bd. 1, 10 f.

[30] Zur Tricennatsrede und Vita Constantini des Eusebius vgl. F. Bittner, Studien zum
Herrscherlob in der mittellateinischen Dichtung, Diss. Würzburg 1962, 26 f., und P. Hadot,
Fürstenspiegel, in: RAC 7 (1972), 614 f.

[31] Zur Kreuzvision Konstantins vor seiner Schlacht gegen Maxentius 312 n. Chr. und
zum Signum des Labarum (Monogramm Christi) vgl. J. Vogt, Constantinus der Große, in:
RAC 3 (1957), 318 ff. (mit reichen Quellenangaben). Vgl. speziell A. Alföldi, *Hoc signo victor
eris*, Beiträge zur Geschichte der Bekehrung Konstantins des Großen (1939), in: Konstantin
der Große, hg. von H. Kraft, Darmstadt 1974, 224 ff.

[32] D. Kartschoke, Bibeldichtung, Studien zur epischen Bibelparaphrase von Juvencus bis
Otfrid von Weißenburg, München 1975, 33, weist darauf hin, daß auch der erste lateinische
Bibelepiker Juvencus die Friedenszeit unter Konstantin preist.

religio licita zu einer unumschränkt herrschenden Staatsreligion im römischen Reich zu begreifen ist[33].

Die *carmina figurata* des spätantiken Hofdichters wurden für die mittelalterlichen Dichter vor allem durch die filigranartig artifizielle Struktur des Sprachgitters vorbildlich, zu der Porfyrius neben den Dichtungen Commodians vielleicht durch das Akrostichon im griechischen Musen-Altar des Dosiadas, vielleicht aber auch durch das bekannte Akrostichon der erythräischen Sibylle angeregt wurde, das Konstantin, der den Musen gegenüber aufgeschlossene Adressat und Mäzen derer akrostichischen Texturen, selbst in seiner ‚Oratio ad coetum sanctorum‘, einer 323 gehaltenen Karfreitagspredigt[34], als Zeugnis für eine geheime christliche Prophetie des Heidentums zitiert.

III. Venantius Fortunatus und Bonifatius

Der merowingische Dichter Venantius Fortunatus (*535/40−ca. 600), der aus Oberitalien stammt, im ‚byzantinischen‘ Ravenna Grammatik, Rhetorik und Metrik studierte, später zum Presbyter und 591 sogar zum Bischof von Poitiers geweiht wurde, vollendet die von Porfyrius begonnene Adaptation des von seiner Genese her paganen Figurengedichts an christliche Denk- und zahlenallegorische Bauformen, die fortan den poetischen Bild-Text-Kompositionen des Mittelalters ihren Stempel aufdrücken. Entstanden im Umfeld eines Monasteriums, bewegen sich seine drei visuellen Kreuzgedichte − zwei sind vollständig ausgeführt, ein weiteres ist Fragment geblieben[35] − nicht nur im Bannkreis patristischer Kreuzmeditation, sondern sind, Adressaten in Kloster und Weltklerus zugedacht, anschaulich-allegorischer Ausdruck einer teilweise enthusiastischen Kreuzverehrung, die frömmigkeitsgeschichtlich in engem Konnex mit dem christlichen Reliquienkult zu sehen ist, der ebenfalls auf sinnliche Zeichenhaftigkeit religiöser Glaubensinhalte drängt.

In der Tat gibt die Initialzündung zu seiner zeitweise intensiven Produktion von Kreuzgedichten − darunter so bekannte Dichtungen wie das Passionslied ‚Pange, lingua, gloriosi‘ und der Prozessionshymnus ‚Vexilla regis prodeunt‘[36] − im Jahr 569 die Schenkung einer großen Kreuzreliquie

---

[33] Eine wichtige Etappe auf dem Weg einer konsequenten christlichen Religionspolitik Konstantins ist gerade das Jahr 324, in dem das Gedicht vermutlich entstanden ist. Vgl. dazu J. Vogt, ibid., 338f.

[34] Die Verfasserschaft Konstantins ist allerdings in der Forschung umstritten. Vgl. J. Vogt, ibid., 365ff.

[35] Vollständig: carm. II, 4 (MGH AA, IV, 1, 30f.); carm. V, 6 (ibid., 116f.); torsohaft: carm. II, 5 (ibid., 32f.).

[36] A. H. 50,71ff., und A. H. 50,74f. Vgl. J. Szövérffy, Die Annalen der lateinischen Hymnendichtung, Bd. 1, Berlin 1964, 132ff.

durch den byzantinischen Kaiser Justin II. (565–578) und seine Gemahlin Sophia an das dem hl. Kreuz geweihte Kloster der Radegunde, der Witwe König Lothars I., zu der der merowingische Hofdichter in Poitiers seit 567 enge freundschaftliche Beziehungen unterhielt[37].

Das vorliegende visuelle Kreuzgedicht (carm. V, 6; Text 3), das Venantius dem Bischof Syagrius von Autun gewidmet hat, um die Freilassung eines Gefangenen zu erreichen, ordnet das heilsgeschichtliche Kreuzgeschehen in den Rahmen der patristischen Soteriologie ein, die durch starke Anklänge an die paulinische Apolytrosislehre und die patristische Idee des *sacrum commercium* im Sinne eines Loskaufs[38] spezifische Akzente enthält, was sich schon aus der inhaltlichen Gliederung ergibt:

I.   Schöpfung und Sündenfall
   a) v. 1–9: *Creatio* der Stammeltern des Menschengeschlechts und ihre Bestimmung zum paradiesischen Leben, bei dessen *descriptio* der Dichter auf den antiken Topos des *locus amoenus* zurückgreift.
   b) v. 10–18: Der Sündenfall, der auf die List des Teufels zurückgeführt wird, und seine Konsequenzen: Vertreibung aus dem Paradies, Schmerz und Tod.
II.   Menschwerdung Christi und Erlösung
   a) v. 19–25: Parusie des Gottessohns zum Zweck der Erlösung;
   b) v. 26–30: Befreiung der in der Hölle gefangenen Seelen aufgrund von Christi Kreuzestod und aktuelle Bitte um Lösung der Sündenfesseln[39].

Solche Distribution der Inhaltskomplexe ist wieder deutlich auf die Tektonik des Gedichts abgestimmt, dessen horizontale Mittelachse (v. 18) durch den Schnittpunkt der Balken des intextuellen Chi-Kreuzes und des zentralen Mesostichons im Buchstaben visualisiert wird.

Bis auf das Akrostichon (*Da Fortunato sacer haec pia vota Syagri*) und das Mesostichon (*Captivos laxans domini meditatio fies*), das einen Appell des Fortunatus an den Adressaten um Befreiung des Gefangenen in der Nachfolge des Erlösers Christus beinhaltet, akzentuiert das restliche Intextkontingent (Telestichon: *Christus se misit cum nos a morte revexit*; Chi-Kreuz: *Dulce dei munus quo merx te care coronet / Cara deo pietas animam*

[37] Vgl. J. Szövérffy, Weltliche Dichtungen des lateinischen Mittelalters, Bd. 1, Berlin 1970, 229 ff., der auch das Dankgedicht des Venantius Fortunatus an das byzantinische Herrscherpaar bespricht, in dem auf die Konstantinische Kreuzauffindungslegende Bezug genommen wird.

[38] Vgl. M. Herz, Sarcrum commercium, Eine begriffsgeschichtliche Studie zur Theologie der römischen Liturgiesprache, München 1958, 193 und 209 ff. Durch die Verbindung von Paradigma (Christi Erlösungswerk) und erbetener Nachahmung (Syagrius' Freilassung des Gefangenen) erinnert das Gedicht auch an germanischen Lösungszauber, wie er uns im ‚2. Merseburger Zauberspruch' entgegentritt.

[39] Vgl. H.-G. Müller, Hrabanus Maurus – De laudibus sanctae crucis –, Düsseldorf 1973, 125 f.

AVGVSTIDVNENSISOPVSTIBISOLVOSYAGRI

✠

```
DIVSAPEXADAMVTFECITDATSOMNIADONEC
AVVLSACOSTAPLASMATAESTEVANECINPAR
FELICESPARITERDIPLOIDELVCISOPERTI
ORECORVSCANTESINTERPIARVRAIVGALES
RIPAEIVCVNDAENARIGRATAAVRAREDIBAT
TVRISDELICIAESATVRABANTVBEREFLATV
VNAFOVENSAMBOSFLOROSASEDEVOLVPTAS
NOTABONISREGIOPASCEBATTEMPEBEATOS
ATCVMTAMMAGNOPOLLERENTMAIVSHONORE
TOTAHOMINVMMIREPAREBATTERRADVORVM
OCCVLTVSMENDAXMOXEXERITARMAVENENI
SERPENSELATVSZELATORLARVEVSHOSTIS
ATROXINNOCVOSEVINCENSFELLENOCENTI
CONLISITSVASVQVOSGRATIADIVABEARAT
ETHOMODETERRATVMDENVODECIDITILLVC
REPTANTISQ:DOLOEOOISEXCLVDITVRORTV
HACNATIMORIMVRDAMNATILEGEPARENTVM
ATDEVSEXCELLENSAIEETDELVMINELVMEN
ECAELISOLIODVMMVNERAPROVIDETVLTRO
CASTAECARNERVDIVIVAXINTROIITAGNVS
PRODIITINDESALVSMATVTINIVELVCERNA
INTACTAEPARTVLVXERVITEXCITAMVNDVM
APATREIVREDSHOMODEHINCCARNEVSALVO
VTNOSERIPERETVILISEDETRAHITAVCTOR
OREGISVENALECAPVTQVODDECRVCEFIXIT
TELOVOCEMANVMALFACTVSVERBEREFELLE
ACTVHACSOLVISCAPTIVOSSORTECREATOR
SEROVERADATAESTVITALISEMPTIOMORTE
YMNOSVNDEDEOLOQVORABSOLVENTEREATV
ATVOSAETERNAESVFFVLTILAVDECORONAE
GALLORVMRADIIVOBISQVOFVLGEATETNOX
RVMPITELORAIVGISETSVMITISARMADIEI
IPSAVELIBERTASVOSLIBERATATQ:BEABIT
```

(Text 3).

dat de nece solvi) das passionale Erlösungswerk Christi und seine Befreiung der Seelen aus der Hölle und Knechtschaft der Sünde.

In seinem Begleitschreiben an Syagrius bezieht Venantius die poetische Textur, die zwar einem Spinnengewebe ähnlich sehe, die aber eher mit der Kleidung des alttestamentlichen Priesters (Exod. 28; 39) zu vergleichen sei[40], gezielt auf den pragmatischen Zweck des Gedichts, indem er, ein Meister des Wortspiels, pointiert, er habe sich bewußt mit einer *catena*, die auf die formalen Zwänge und Schwierigkeiten der Textgraphik verweist, gefesselt, um die Befreiung des Gefangenen zu erwirken. In dieser Dedikationsepistel erklärt er auch – und das erscheint relevant zum Verständnis der hermaphroditischen, an bildender Kunst wie an herkömmlicher Poesie partizipierten Mischgattung –, er sei durch die ‚Ars poetica‘ (v. 9f.) des Horaz dazu ermutigt worden, *poesis* und *pictura*, Dichtung und Malerei, miteinander zu verbinden[41]. Malerischen Charakter gewinnt das Figurengedicht speziell durch das rubrizierte Malteserkreuz zwischen Überschrift und erstem Vers – gleichsam ein doppelter, verbaler und piktoraler *titulus* – und durch die kolorierten Intexte, für die ursprünglich Purpur vorgesehen war, für das aber als Ersatz Minium dienen mußte[42]. An dieser Stelle unterstreicht der Dichter erstmals einen von originär christlichem Formverständnis geprägten tektonischen Bauwillen, wenn er artikuliert, er habe in dem figurierten Kreuzgedicht bewußt im Hinblick auf die geometrische Abmessung des Textblocks eine Seitenlänge von 33 Buchstaben angestrebt, weil diese Zahl in Korrespondenz zu der Passionsthematik die Lebensjahre Christi, zugleich das Jahr seines Kreuzestodes, versinnbildlicht[43].

Während Fortunatus für das spirituelle Zahlenprogramm seines Gittergedichts, für das möglicherweise Porfyrius' ‚carmen XVIII‘ Pate stand[44], die Buchstabenzahl pro Vers und die Gesamtverszahl zugrundelegt, macht

---

[40] MGH, AA, IV, 1, 115: *Ne tamen causa nos oneret, quod velut aragnaea arte videmur picta fila miscere: quod vobis conpertum est in Moysi prophetae libris, polymitarius artifex vestes texuit sacerdotis.*

[41] Ibid., 114: *dum captivi solvere lora cupio, me catena constringo.* Ibid., 113. Vgl. Avitus, MGH, AA VI, 2, 202. D. Kartschoke, ibid., 70f.

[42] Ibid., 115: *unde, cum desit hic coccinum, res est texta de minio.* Purpur ist zum einen Farbsymbol für den König Christus, von dem es im Hymnus ‚Vexilla regis prodeunt‘ (Str. 4, v. 4) heißt: *Regnavit a ligno Deus* (vgl. Ps. 96, 10), symbolisiert aber zum andern als Farbe des Blutes auch die Passion Christi. In der Hs. G. (St. Gallen 196) tragen die Kreuzintexte grüne Farbe, die der Vorstellung vom Kreuzbaum korrespondiert. Vgl. die Anm. des Herausgebers F. Leo, MGH, AA, IV, 1, 30 und 116.

[43] Ibid., 114: . . . *cum pro captivo velim suggere, adtendens quae fuerint tempora redemptoris, quoto nos suae aetatis anno Christus absolverit, totidemque versiculis texerem carmen quot litteras . . . Habes igitur opus sic uno textu quadratum, ut sit legendo quinquifidum; et cum sint triginta tres tam versus quam litterae, ad similitudinem Christi carnalis aetatis, qua nos absolvit unus resurgens.* Klar beschreibt Fortunatus, ibid., 114f., die Position der Intexte: *duo per capita, duo ex obliquo, unus quoque per medium legitur in descensu.*

[44] Vgl. D. Schaller, Die karolingischen Figurengedichte des Cod. Bern. 212, in: Medium Aevum Vivum, Fs. für W. Bulst, Heidelberg 1960, 25.

Bonifatius, der in seiner Jugend als Scholaster im Kloster Nursling (bei Winchester) Grammatik und Metrik[45] dozierte und als Schüler Aldhelms akrostichische Rätselgedichte verfaßte, in einem vor seiner ersten Missionsreise entstandenen[46] Kreuzgedicht[47] die zahlensymbolische Verweiskraft metrischer Strukturen für das tektonische Baugefüge nutzbar (Text 4).

Sein figuriertes Intextgedicht, in dem das Prinzip der Buchstabenzählung nicht mehr streng beachtet ist, wird durch ein Akrostichon (*Vynfreth priscorum Duddo congesserat artem*) und ein Telestichon (*Viribus ille iugis iuvavit in arte magistrum*), in denen Autor und Adressat, Bonifatius und sein Schüler, der spätere Abt Duddus, genannt werden[48], an den vertikalen Seiten begrenzt. Beide Intextverse bilden zugleich die rechte und linke Seite einer rhombusförmigen *figura*, in deren Zentrum das *nomen sacrum* Iesus Xcristus in einer Kreuzfigur so plaziert ist, daß es von oben nach unten und von links nach rechts gelesen werden kann[49].

Im Widmungsbrief an Sigibert im Präkorpus seiner Grammatik, die das nur in einer Würzburger Hs. (Abb. 3, Tafel IV) erhaltene Kreuzgedicht[50] als Frontispiz in der zeichenhaften Funktion eines geistigen Wegweisers und zentralen Richtpunkts jedweder Wissenschaft zierte[51], weist Bonifatius

---

[45] Fragmente einer z. T. auf Isidors Etymologien fußenden Metrik sind überliefert im Vat. Pal. 1753 (9. Jh.), fol. 114r–116v.: *Incipiunt caesurae versuum Bonifacii, De metris* (hg. von A. Wilmanns, in: Rhein. Mus. 23, 1968, 403 ff.) und im Cod. Guelf. Weißenburg 86 (hg. von Th. Gaisford, Scriptores Latini rei metricae, Oxonii 1837, 577–585). Noch in Germanien wurden Bonifatius mehrfach Verse zur Verbesserung zugesandt. Bonifatii Epistulae, Willibaldi vita Bonifatii, hg. und übers. von R. Rau, Darmstadt 1968 (= Freiherr vom Stein-Gedächtnisausgabe Bd. IVb), 29 (Brief der Leobgyda), 104: *Istos autem subterscriptos versiculos conponere nitebar secundum poeticae traditionis disciplinam, non audacia confidens, sed gracilis ingenioli rudimenta exercitare cupiens et tuo auxilio indigens*; 103 (Brief Luls), 326: *Hos tibi versiculos, pater amande, subterscriptos correctionis causa direxi*. Vgl. H. Schüling, Die Handbibliothek des Bonifatius, in: Börsenbl. f. d. dt. Buchhandel, 17. Jg., Nr. 70 (1961), 1689.
[46] H. Schüling, ibid., 1688.
[47] Bonifatii Ars Grammatica, hg. von G. J. Gebauer / B. Löfstedt, CCL 133 B (1980), 4–6. Ältere Ausgabe: MGH, Poet. lat. I, 17.
[48] P. Lehmann, Ein neuentdecktes Werk eines angelsächsischen Grammatikers vorkarolingischer Zeit (1931/32)), in: P. L., Erforschung des Mittelalters, Bd. 4, Stuttgart 1961, 168, übersetzt: „Vynfreth hatte für Dudd die Lehren der Alten zusammengetragen, dieser half dem Lehrer mit nie nachlassender Mühe."
[49] Zu der hier greifbaren Tradition des Christusmonogramms als Bestandteil des Intextkorpus, die auf Optatianus Porfyrius zurückgeht, vgl. D. Forstner, Die Welt der Symbole, München ²1967, 44.
[50] M. p. th. f. 29, fol. 44r. (Universitätsbibliothek Würzburg).
[51] Entscheidender Nachweis von N. Fickermann, Der Widmungsbrief des hl. Bonifatius, Neues Archiv 50 (1935), 216. Vgl. die ausführliche Funktionsbestimmung des Bonifatius selbst; Bonifatii Epistulae, Willibaldi vita Bonifatii, ibid., 364: *Porro hoc est, quod per circulum ego intimis precordiorum penetralibus inplorans obsecro, ut quicquid per lata spatiosissimarum scripturarum arva scrutando lectitando lustrando inveneris sive in arte grammatica sive in metrica, in historiis aeternorum vel gentilium, sive in sacro eloquio novi vel veteris testamenti, semper memor sententiae apostoli: ‚Omnia probate, quod bonum est tenete' ad tutissimum*

Versibus en iuuenis durant et carmina cantu
Ymnos namque dei ymnica dicta uiri
Nisibus eximiis r e nouantis carmina lector
Fulmina namque pius frangere iudicii
Regmina temporibus torquebit torribus et sub
Excelsi fatu omnia saecla diu
Tuta tenent iusti pariter tum taenia sanctis
Hic dabitur regni aurea hacque pii
Per caeli campos stipabunt pace tribunal
Regnantes laudant limpida regna simul
In pia perpetuae ut dominentur gaudia uitae
Sordida in terris spernere gesta uiri
Cautum est ut numquam defleant supplicia cassu
Omnes gentiles Impia origo magog
Regmina ut perdant pariter sub tartara trusi
Vnus nempe deus saecula cuncta suis
Mirifico absoluens uitalia tradidit amni
Diues in arte sua omnia sancta gradu
Victor nam Iesus Xcristus sicque ordinat actu
Dapsilis in pastis uernis tua fata dicanda
Deuotis concede tibi cum laudibus id tu
Omnipotens genitor fac nostro in pectore poni
Casta suum resonans rectorem ut lingua cantet
O deus in solio iudex regnator olimpi
Numina namque tuum monstrant per saecula nomen
Gentibus in uastis caelebrant et gaudia mira
Edite in terris saluasti saecla redemptor
Spiritus aethralem tibi laudem splendidus aptet
Subiciens hominem et perlustrans limina terrae
Egregium regem gnatum praeconia faustum
Ruricolae iugiter dicant cum carmine clara
Almo quod feruens gremio signabat abisag
Totum quae radiens constat sapientia iusti
Architenens altor qui sidera clara gubernas
Rurigenae praesta ut certus solamina possit
Tradere per sacras scripturas grammate doctor
Excerptus prisco puerorum indaginis usu
Magna patri et proli cum flamine gratia dicam

(Text 4; vgl. Abb. 3, Tafel IV).

auf den zahlenallegorischen Charakter der Versstrukturen hin: Die Verse vom Anfang des Gedichts bis zur Kreuzfigur in der Mitte, genauer bis zum waagerechten Kreuzbalken, sind entsprechend dem Eidos der imperfekten Fünfzahl mit Pentametern durchsetzt und versinnbildlichen die Unvollkommenheit des Alten Testaments, in dem alles nach Erfüllung des Gesetzes durch den Erlöser Christus strebt, während die Verse vom waagerechten Kreuzbalken an gemäß der Idee der Vollkommenheit in Hexametern abgefaßt sind und den Anbruch des Neuen Testaments, die durch Christi Kreuzestod bewirkte Vollendung, signalisieren[52].

Auf die tektonische Komposition nimmt die zweiteilige Disposition der inhaltlichen Aussage Rücksicht, die das fraglos heilspädagogisch motivierte, vielleicht sogar missionarisch intendierte Programm des zentralen Intextbildes, der *figura crucis*, verbalisiert: Der erste Teil (v. 1–19) malt in eschatologischer Perspektivierung aus, wie Gott am Ende der Zeiten die Getauften belohnt und die Heiden bestraft, während sich der zweite Teil der Komposition (v. 20–38) – z. T. im Rückgriff auf das Mittel der Allegorie[53] – zu einem hymnischen Gebet an Gott als Schöpfer und Erlöser verdichtet, in dem sich auch das individuelle poetische Anliegen des Autors artikuliert[54].

Da Bonifatius der optischen Textpräsentation besondere Aufmerksamkeit widmete[55] und sich zudem eine Verwandtschaft zwischen Figuren-

---

catholicae fidei circulum sensus tui litteris occurrentibus dirigas et extra moenia huius circuli mentis inconstantia vagare non praesumas, ne forte vulnerantes te tulerint pallium tuum custodes murorum, et singula quaeque veteris ac novi testamenti decreta tunc te canonice intellexisse scias, cum in meditullio Christum crucifixum destruentem malignae cupiditatis aedificium et construentem benignae caritatis templum spiritalibus oculis contemplando contueri potueris.

[52] Ibid.: *Interea circulum quadrangulum in fronte huius laboris apposui in medio figuram sanctae crucis continentem JHS XPS et exprimentem, qui ludivaga sermonum serie duobus ambitus versibus, aliis in transversum currentibus socialis adiutorii utrimque sonantes in obviam offert litteras. Hunc autem circulum in scemate novi ac veteris instrumenti figurari non nescias. Nam prior pars circuli huius usque ad medium crucis quibusdam pentametris intersertis decurrens pingitur versibus, qui licet pedestri remigio tranent, non tamen heroici nec omnino perfecti decursu esse dinoscuntur: sic et intra terminos veteris testamenti universa quasi semiplena et inperfecta tendebant ad plenitudinem legis, id est ad Christum crucifixum. Post crucem autem supradictam in circulo heroici versus et perfecti decurrunt: ita et per gratiam Christi accepta remissione peccatorum ad integrum omnia renovata et perfecta sunt.*

[53] Laubmann, Mittheilungen aus Würzburger Handschriften (= Sb. d. Münch. Ak. d. Wiss., phil.-hist. Kl., 1, 1878), 16 f., weist darauf hin, daß die Deutung der Abisag, einer aus III Rg. 1, 3 f./4, 15 bekannten Dirne, als Allegorie der himmlischen Weisheit in v. 32 f. auf Hieronymus, Epistula 52 (CSEL 54, 415 ff.) zurückgeht.

[54] Vgl. besonders den Topos der Bescheidenheit und die Inspirationsbitte (v. 33–36) sowie die biographischen Äußerungen (36 ff.).

[55] Vgl. seine Bitte an die Äbtissin Eadburg, ihm die Briefe des hl. Petrus in Goldschrift zu schreiben, 35, ibid., 114: *Sic et adhuc deprecor, ut augeas quod cepisti, id est, ut mihi cum auro conscribas epistolas domini mei sancti Petri apostoli ad honorem et reverentiam sanctarum scripturarum ante oculos carnalium in predicando, et quia dicta eius, qui me in hoc iter direxit, maxime semper in presentia cupiam habere.*

gedichten und figuralen Schriftflächen zu dieser Zeit schwerlich leugnen läßt, erscheint der Hinweis auf zwei Handschriften aus der Handbibliothek des Bonifatius angebracht: auf den aus dem 8. Jahrhundert stammenden Ragyndrudiskodex (Cod. Bonif. 2), der mit trigonalen Schriftflächen operiert, und auf das, wie man schon im 9. Jahrhundert fälschlich glaubte, von Bonifatius selbst geschriebene Cadmug-Evangeliar (Cod. Bonif. 3), das als Schlußseite des Matthäusevangeliums ein textuelles Andreaskreuz mit geometrischer, rhombusförmiger Figur im Schnittpunkt zeigt[56].

Bonifatius hat mit seiner allegorisierenden Metrik vermutlich nicht nur die spirituelle Versästhetik Otfrids von Weißenburg inspiriert[57], er hat auch unmittelbar seinen engsten Mitarbeiter Lul, den späteren Erzbischof von Mainz, beeinflußt, der in einem nicht erhaltenen Gedicht an die angelsächsische Äbtissin Fufanna und die Nonne Erkenchind durch formale Disposition die Spannung von Vollkommenheit und Unvollkommenheit gezielt anzudeuten versucht. Wie Lul in einem Begleitbrief notiert, sind die durch ein strophisches, 37 Buchstaben umfassendes Akrostichon (*Esto Fufanna memor Domini regnantis in aede*) und ein parallel gebautes Telestichon (*Erkenchind esto memor Domini celorum in arce*) markierten vierzeiligen Versblöcke des insgesamt 148 Verse umfassenden Poems so angeordnet, daß die der Lehrerin gewidmeten Verse am Anfang stehen und höchst vollkommen konstruiert sind, während das der Schülerin zugeeignete Verskorpus an zweiter Stelle folgt und immerhin „nicht ungeschickt" geformt ist[58].

IV. Hrabanus Maurus

Nachdem die karolingischen Hofdichter Alkuin, Josephus Scottus und Theodulf von Orléans möglicherweise schon vor 790 eine Sammlung der Gedichte des Porfyrius, vermehrt um eigene Nachbildungen, Karl dem

---

[56] Cod. Bonif. 2, fol. 142 v (Stiftsbibliothek St. Gallen). Vgl. P. Lehmann, Figurale Schriftflächen (1924), in: P. L., Erforschung des Mittelalters, Bd. 3, Stuttgart 1960, 64; Cod. Bonif. 3, fol. 18 v. Für den Hinweis auf diese Seite danke ich Herrn Prof. Dr. J. Rathofer (Köln). Vgl. auch P. Lehmann, ibid., 63.

[57] Vgl. U. Ernst, Der Liber Evangeliorum Otfrids von Weißenburg, Literarästhetik und Verstechnik im Lichte der Tradition, Köln 1975, 431 f.

[58] Ibid., 372: *vobis dirigere versiculos metrice ratione conpositos diu fixum mente tenui, corde simul dulce habui, quia nullos legentium novi, quibus libentius mitterem, ubi pro certo scio nullam dirae fraudis suspicione mentem distinantis mordere nec dictantem hostili vituperatione lacerare, licet vitiosa pagina scabraque scedula repperiatur. . . . Hos namque versus iocistae more caraxatos repperietis, si dilingentur non dedignemini litterarum perscrutari capita, hoc est quaternis versibus ceteros in medio positos velut ambitu quodam cingentes. Illi autem quos tuo nomine proprie pretitulavi ceu spiritualis matris, a principio incipiunt regulariter ad finem usque decurrentes. Discipulae vero meae a calce tuorum inchoant non inoportune, quia discipula magistram sicut ancilla dominam suam sequi debeat:*

Großen – gleichsam als *novus Constantinus* – überreicht hatten[59], führt der Alkuin-Schüler Hrabanus Maurus mit seinem um 810 fertiggestellten Zyklus ‚De laudibus sanctae crucis‘[60] die Gattung zu einem Höhepunkt theologisch-tektonischer Formkunst.

Sind die griechischen Technopägnien mit Glossen überliefert, die sich in Worterklärungen erschöpfen (vgl. Abb. 1, Tafel II), beziehen sich die Scholien zu den Gittergedichten des Porfyrius auf die technische Anlage des Intextkorpus und haben Fortunatus und Bonifatius ihre allegorisierenden Selbstdeutungen Widmungsbriefen eingefügt, so baut Hraban die Ansätze der Tradition zu Selbstdeutungen systematisch aus, indem er jedem der 28 Kreuzgedichte eine *declaratio* beigibt, die, in den Hss. meist auf den Rectoseiten neben den Figurengedichten plaziert, nach der Texthermeneutik des mehrfachen Schriftsinns über Sinngehalt (*ratio figurae*), Anordnung (*expositio eius*) und die einbeschriebenen Verse der jeweiligen *figura* informiert[61].

Stärkeres Gewicht als bei seinen Vorgängern erlangt bei Hraban das Prinzip zahlensymbolischer Textkonstruktion, was an der ‚figura XVIII‘ (Text 5) exemplifiziert werden soll, die schon im Titulus ‚De mysterio quadragenarii numeri‘ diesen Aspekt programmatisch thematisiert[62]. Die Bedeutungstiefe der Zahl vierzig konkretisiert sich in der formalen Organisation des Gedichts durch eine *figura* von vier gleichseitigen Dreiecken, die in ihrem geometrischen Umriß aus je zehn Einzelbuchstaben zusammengesetzt sind, die, mit der Spitze nach innen gekehrt, sich zu einem Malteserkreuz fügen. Nach der poetologisch-theologischen *declaratio*, die das Geheimnis der Form dem Leser entschleiert, konstituieren die 4 Dekaden von Buchstaben die *figura crucis*, weil das durch den Dekalog repräsentierte Gesetz und die Majestät des viergestaltigen Evangeliums die Einheit des christlichen Glaubens und die Gemeinschaft der Liebe begründen. Die figural illustrierte Aufgliederung der Zahl 40 in die Faktoren 4 × 10 signalisiert, daß die Erfüllung des Gesetzes ohne das Viergespann der Evangelien nicht möglich war, ebenso wie das quaternarische Evangelium ohne die Vorstufe des Alten Testaments dem Autor nicht realisierbar erscheint. Neben der Aufschlüsselung der Zahl 40 in Faktoren geht Hraban bei seiner Deutung der *figura* von der Vierzahl der Dreiecke aus, wobei er proklamiert, daß – gemäß dem zentralen pythagoreischen Modell der Dreieckszahl, der Zehn über der Basis 4 (Tektraktys), – in den

---

Esto Fufanna memor Domini regnantis in aede;
ita de fine inchoant:
Erkenchind esto memor Domini celorum in arce.
[59] Vgl. D. Schaller, ibid., 47.
[60] Vgl. Die Facsimile-Ausgabe des Codex Vindobonensis 652 von K. Holter, Graz 1973, Kommentar, S. 9.
[61] Prologus, PL 107, 146 C. Vgl. H.-G. Müller, ibid., 120.
[62] PL 107, 219f.

```
P a n d e s a l u t a r e m d o m i n o v i n c e n t e t r i u m p h u m
L i n g u a f i g u r a m a n u s l a b i u m v o x s y l l a b a s e n s:
M a g n a c r u c i s d o m i n i q u e m g l o r i a p o s c i t v b i q;
S i d e r a c e l s a s u p e r e t q u o p e r t i n g i t a b y s s u s
L u x v b i p u r a m a n e t q u o t e t r a s i l e n t i a n o c t i s
P e r p e t u a e l a t i t a n t v b i n o x q; d i e s q; v i c i s s i m
S u c c e d u n t c e d u n t q; s i b i q u o t e m p o r e c u n c t u s
L a b i t u r o r b i s v b i v a r i a b i l i s i n d i t o r d o e s t
Q u a t t u o r i s t o v i n [C] i [R] e [v] i [x] s u f f i c i t a s t h a e c
P a g i n a d i g n a c r u c i p r a e c o n i a t r a m i t e d e n a s
H a s q u e q u a d r a g e n a s [S] [S] [A] [C] t o d e c a l l e m o n a d e s
A r t e l i g a r e s i m u l p l e n a s q u o q u e l u c e s e r e n a
M y s t i c a q' a s v i r t u s o [R] [A] t c o n s e c r a t h o n o r a t
T e m p o r i s i n s t a n t i s n u m e r u s h i c r i t e f i g u r ā
G e s t a t q u o t o t a c h r i s [T] o s u b p r i n c i p e s a n c t a
E c c l e s i a [R] a b i d o p i e f e r t c o n t r a r [I] a t e l a h i c
O p p o n e n s [h o] s t i b e l l a t r i x c o n s [c] i a p r e s t a n s
V i r t u t u m [E] t p u [G] n i s v i t i a s i b [I] l a u s e a c u n c t a
C u m f i d e i s c [u] t o d [o] m a t h a e c [R] i t u [a] s t a q; v e r b o
L o r i c ā l i [G] a t e [T] b e n e i u s t i t i [A] c i n [T] u i t a l m a m
A t q; s a l u t a r [I] s g a l e a m h a n c i n v e [R] t i c e g e s t a t
I p s a c r u c [I] s c l a r ā f a c i u n t i n s i g n [I] a f r o n t e m
F r o n t i s e t a d u e r s a e f [u] n d u n t f o r m o s a d e c o r ē
I n c r u c e s a l u a t o r s a e u u m n a m v i c e r a t h o s t e m
E i u s e t h o c n u m e r o s u [A] [d E] s e r t o a l m a t r a h e b a t
E x d a p i b u s c u n c t i s i e i u n i a s o b r i a c h r i s t u s
S t r i n x c r a t e r i p u i [T] [q E] [a R] t o d o f a u c e s u p e r b i
R a p t o r i s h o m i n e m q u e m c a s t r i m a r g i a t r a x i t
I n f a c i n u s d i r u m i [N] [m i] [t E] [m] s i m u l a t t u l i t i r a m
H u i c p h i l a r g i r i a l e u i s e t c e n o d o x i a t r u s i t
Q u e m a r e g n o d o m i n u s a e t e r n a r e d e m t i o i e s u s
S e d p r e s s i t h o s t e m p r a e d a m s a l u a u i t a b i p s o
D a p s i l i s a t q e h u m i l i s m i t i s e t s o b r i u s i p s e
C u i u s p u g n a s a l u s c u i u s v i c t o r i a s a n c t a e s t
C u i u s i n a r c e t h r o n u s a s p e c t: i n i n f i m a c u i u s
C r u x o u a t o r b i s h o n o r c r u x e s t e r e c t i o m u n d i
C r u x m i h i c a r m e n e r i t c r i s t i v i c t o r i a c l a r a
```

(Text 5; vgl. Abb. 4, Tafel V).

4 Triangeln [4 × (1 + 2 + 3 + 4)] die Fülle der Zehnzahl enthalten ist wie in den 4 Evangelien das Pleroma des Dekalogs[63]. Noch einer dritten Form der Faktorenzerlegung der Zahl 40 bedient sich Hraban, wenn er mit dem Blick auf die zwei Kreuzbalken den *numerus* in 2 × 20 aufteilt, wobei er auf die Präfiguration dieser Zahlenverhältnisse in den Maßen des Allerheiligsten des Salomonischen Tempels (*viginti cubitos in longitudine, et viginti cubitos in latitudine*; II Paralip. 3,8; vgl. Ezech. 41,4) hindeutet[64].

---

[63] Hraban, ibid., 221 ff.
[64] Ibid., 222 B/C.

Großen Raum nimmt die Beziehung der Vierzig auf die Idee der Bewährung in der Zeitlichkeit ein, die bei Hraban zugleich immer den Kampf gegen die Anfechtungen des Teufels und die Konkupiszenz des Fleisches impliziert. Er verweist hier in Form eines zahlensymbolischen Katalogs auf Christi 40tägiges Fasten in der Wüste (Mt. 4,2; Lc. 4,2), das als erster Sieg des Gottessohnes über den Teufel seinem zweiten auf Golgatha an die Seite gestellt wird, auf das präfigurative 40tägige Fasten des Moses (Exod. 34,28 / Deuter. 9,9) und des Elias (III Reg. 19,8), auf die 40stündige Grabesruhe des Gottessohnes und seine 40tägige Erscheinung nach der Auferstehung (Act. 1,3), auf Christi Geschlechtsregister (Mt 1,2ff.), die von Isaak im 40. Lebensjahr vollzogene Verbindung mit Rebecca (Gen. 25,20), die von Gott verhängte Bußzeit von 40 Jahren über Israel (Num. 14,33f.) und schließlich auf die Zählung der Stämme Israels (Num. 1,3ff.; 26,2ff.)[65].

Folgendes Fazit läßt sich ziehen: Die *declaratio* allegorisiert einmal mit der Methode der faktorenzerlegenden Zahlenexegese das im Gedicht intextuell und figural dargestellte Erlösungswerk Christi am Kreuz als Erfüllung des *lex vetus* des Alten Testaments, zum andern deutet sie das tektonisch konkretisierte Passionsgeschehen durch gezielte Reihung biblischer Belege zur Zahl 40 als Sieg Christi über den Satan, wobei das geometrisch und intextuell abgebildete Kreuz als Tropaion verstanden wird. Gerade die Vorstellung vom asketischen Leidenskampf, den Jesu vorbildhaft gegen den Teufel und alle seine Versuchungen geführt hat, hält als semantische Klammer in der *declaratio* die auf den ersten Blick disparat wirkenden Bibelbelege zum *sensus tropologicus* der Zahl 40 zusammen.

Signifikant für die zyklische Form der 28 Kreuzgedichte, die bei Porfyrius nur ansatzweise ausgebildet erscheint, ist die Technik der Verknüpfung von Gedichten, die Hraban in der *declaratio* zur ‚figura XIX‘ appliziert, die im Rückgriff auf die ‚figura XVIII‘ das Mysterium der Zahl 50 figuriert: Beide poetische Textfiguren in einen tektonischen Konnex rückkend, äußert der Autor hier, daß die Bewährung in der Zeitlichkeit auf die Belohnung im Jenseits hinführe wie der *numerus* 40 auf die 50[66].

Dabei ist die ‚figura XVIII‘ Bestandteil einer umfassenden zahlensymbolischen Komposition, weist Hraban doch selbst darauf hin, daß er bewußt 28 Figurengedichte zu einem Zyklus vereint hat, weil diese Zahl als *numerus perfectus* dem Kreuz als *consummatrix et perfectio rerum*[67]

[65] Ibid., 212B–222B. Vgl. B. Taeger, Zahlensymbolik bei Hraban, bei Hincmar – und im ‚Heliand‘?, München 1970, 28, 32f., 39, 72ff. Zur Deutung auf die 40-stündige Grabesruhe vgl. Honorius Augustodunensis, Elucidarium, PL 172, 1126B: *D. Quot horas fuit mortuus? – M. Quadraginta. – D. Quare? – M. Ut quatuor partes mundi, quae in decalago legis erant mortuae, vivificaret.* Vgl. H. Meyer, Die Zahlenallegorese im Mittelalter, München 1975, 160.

[66] Hraban, ibid., 225C.

[67] Hraban, ibid., 264C/D.

angemessen ist. Entsprechend den Divisoren dieser Zahl (*14, 7, 4, 2, 1*), die zusammengenommen wieder 28 ergeben, hat Hraban, wie B. Taeger nachweist[68], nach dem von ihm wieder streng observierten Prinzip der Buchstabenzählung das gesamte Werk intern strukturiert und *14* Gedichte mit Versen zu 37 Buchstaben (darunter auch die ‚figura VIII'), *7* mit Versen zu 35, *4* mit Versen zu 39, *2* mit Versen zu 36 und *1* mit Versen zu 31 Buchstaben gestaltet.

Nicht nur an der gruppenbildenden tektonischen Makrostruktur, sondern auch an der Disposition eines einzelnen Gedichts wird eindrucksvoll sichtbar, daß Hraban eine strenge Koordination von theologischem Sinn und tektonischer Form[69] anstrebt, wie sie Rathofer in ähnlicher Weise auch für das as. Heliandepos erwiesen hat, und — gerade im Medium von Zahl und Maß — Text und Intext, verbale und figürliche Strukturen kunstvoll verknüpft. So läßt sich die aus 40 Buchstaben bestehende kreuzförmige Intextstruktur keineswegs als bloßes formales Ornament verstehen, sondern sie korrespondiert entsprechend der Bedeutung der Zahl 40 mit der Inhaltsschicht des metrifizierten Trägergedichts, in der z. B. im Rahmen eines breit ausgeführten Antagonismus von Christus und Teufel auch das 40tägige Fasten Christi als asketischer Kampf dargestellt wird. Die Lesung des dem Malteserkreuz einbeschriebenen Intexts beginnt, jeweils horizontal von links nach rechts schreitend, oben am senkrechten Kreuzstamm, geht dann nach unten zum Kreuzfuß und setzt sich, jeweils vertikal verlaufend, am waagerechten Balken fort, wobei sie vom linken zum rechten Dreieck übergeht. Während in den Kreuzgedichten des Fortunatus und Bonifatius noch adressatenbezogene Bemerkungen im Intext auftauchen — das erinnert an die alte Funktion des Akrostichons als Sphragis — fügt sich bei Hraban der aus 40 Buchstaben bestehende Intextvers (*Crux sacra, tu aeterni es regis victoria Christi*) harmonisch zu Inhalt und theologischem Konzept des Gedichtes, was die Geschlossenheit, Kohärenz und Einheit der Komposition eindrucksvoll unterstreicht.

Hrabans artifizielles *carmen quadratum* zeigt, wie abschließend zu resümieren bleibt, eine komplizierte, aber in allen Elementen sorgfältig abgestimmte Zeichenstruktur, die, bis auf den Buchstaben zahlhaft geplant und flächenmäßig ausgemessen, den metrisch präzis kalkulierten Hexametertext, die aus 4 Dreiecken geometrisch exakt konstituierte Kreuzfigur und den der *figura crucis* minuziös einbeschriebenen Intext zu einem Formgefüge vereint, das in übergreifender Gestaltungsabsicht, alle Werk-

---

[68] B. Taeger, ibid., 55f.

[69] Der dem mittelalterlichen Kunstwerk adäquate Deutungsansatz J. Ratshofers, ibid., 424ff. ist gegen die forcierte Polemik B. Taegers, ibid., 9ff., in Schutz zu nehmen, der offensichtlich von modernen Kunstanschauungen, u. a. der Organismusvorstellung, ausgeht und es versäumt, die Leistung Hrabans vor dem Hintergrund der gattungsgeschichtlichen Entwicklung zu würdigen.

teile durchdringend, zahlensymbolisch komponiert ist und sich als komplexe Meditationsfigur präsentiert, in die der Rezipient – mit Hilfe der *declaratio* und der gegenüber dem diffizilen und hermetischen Verstext luziden Prosaversion[70] – lesend, schauend und sich geistig versenkend eindringen soll.

---

[70] Hraban, ibid., 265 A/B: *opus quod in laudem sanctae crucis metrico stylo condidi, in prosam vertere curavi, ut quia ob difficultatem ordinis et figurarum necessitatem obscura locutio minusque patens sensus videtur metro inesse, saltem in prosa lucidior fiat.*

Abb. 1. Der Kosmosmensch
Entnommen aus: Hildegard v. Bingen, Welt und Mensch, Das Buch „De operatione Dei"
aus dem Genter Kodex übersetzt und erläutert von Heinrich Schipperges, Salzburg 1965,
neben S. 48 (Otto-Müller-Verlag)

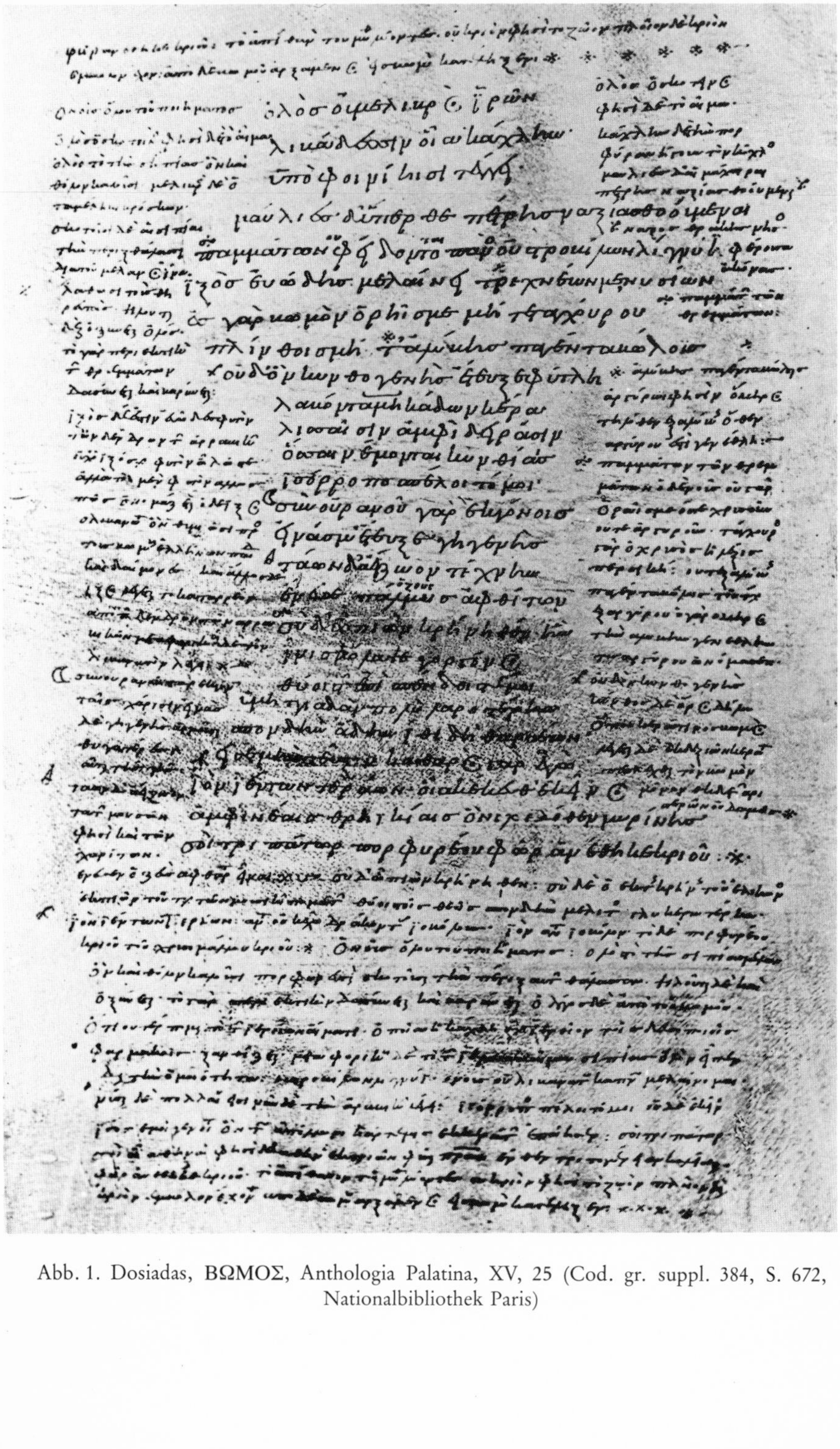

Abb. 1. Dosiadas, ΒΩΜΟΣ, Anthologia Palatina, XV, 25 (Cod. gr. suppl. 384, S. 672, Nationalbibliothek Paris)

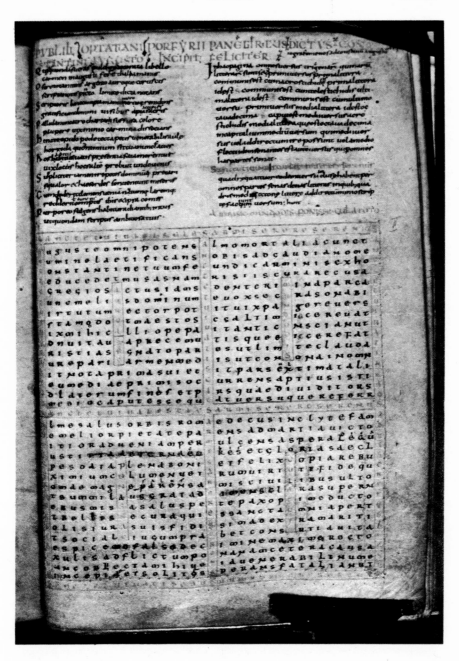

Abb. 2. Publilius Optatianus Porfyrius, Carmen II (Cod. Bern. 212, fol. 111 r., Burger-
bibliothek Bern)

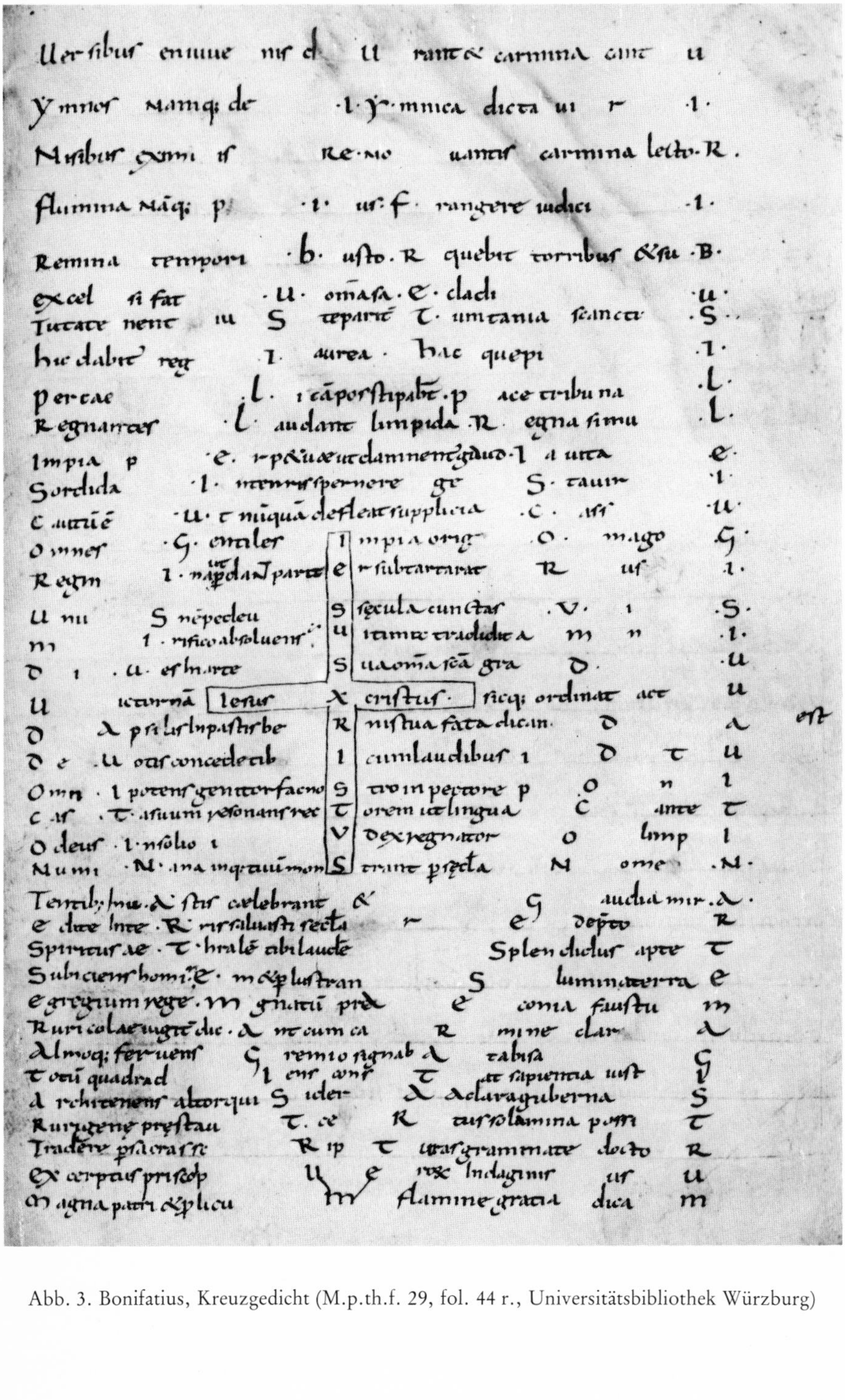

Abb. 3. Bonifatius, Kreuzgedicht (M.p.th.f. 29, fol. 44 r., Universitätsbibliothek Würzburg)

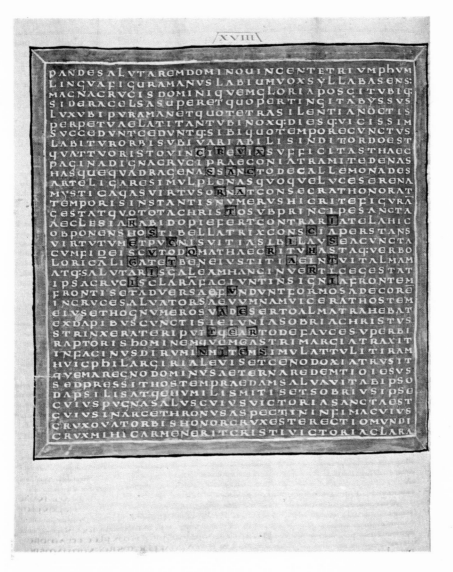

Abb. 4. Hrabanus Maurus, Figura XVIII (Cod. Reg. Lat. 124, fol. 25 v., Vatikanische Bibliothek Rom)

Abb. 1. Cod. Ept., fol. 1 v: Teil des 'Löwenvorhangs'

Abb. 3. Cod. Ept., fol. 3 r: Heinrich überreicht den Liber vitae der thronenden Madonna im Speyerer Dom

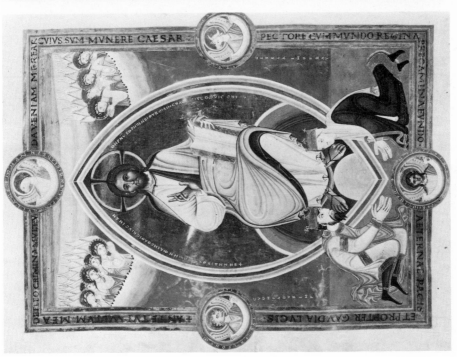

Abb. 2. Cod. Ept., fol. 2 v: Maiestas Domini mit Liber vitae

Abb. 5. Cod. Ept., fol. 15 v: Eine der Kanontafeln mit 7 Säulen

Abb. 4. Cod. Ept., fol. 3 v: Titulus zum Liber vitae

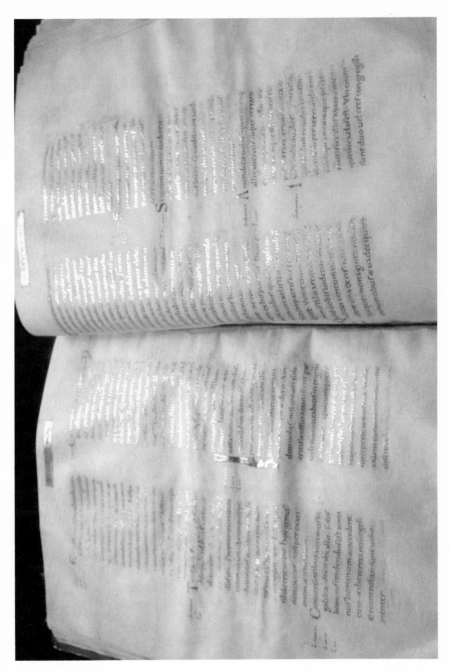

Abb. 6. Cod. Ept., Doppelseite des Evangelientextes (4 Kolumnen, 144 Zeilen) nach Matthäus

Abb. 8. Cod. Ept., fol. 38 r: Halbseitige Miniatur: Speisung der 5000
(Mt 14, 13–21)

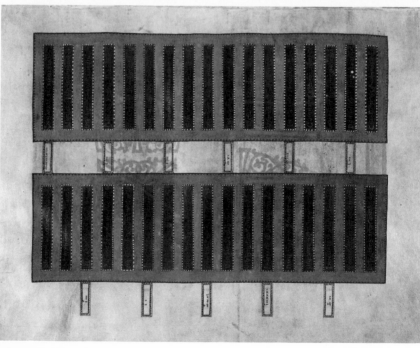

Abb. 7. Cod. Ept., fol. 162 v: Erste Seite des Perikopenverzeichnisses
mit 17er-Gliederung

Abb. 10. Cod. Ept., fol. 62 v: Markus-Initium; 4 Engel mit Lohnverheißungen der Apokalypse, 4 Märtyrermedaillons

Abb. 9. Cod. Ept., fol. 6 r: Initium der Ersten Vorrede. Im Rahmen
12 Papstbüsten

Abb. 2. A. Hirschvogel, Selbstbildnis, Kupferstich 1548

Abb. 1. G. Bellini (Umkreis), Bildnis eines Mannes, um 1500. London, Nat. Gal.

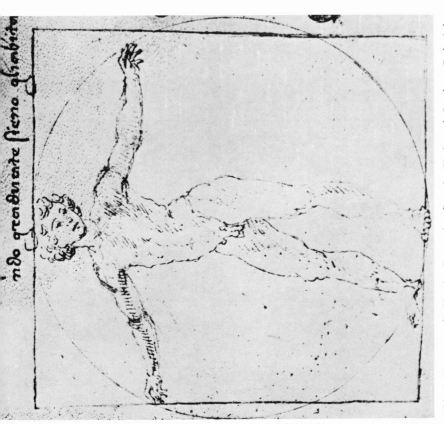

Abb. 4. Francesco di Giorgio, Proportionsfigur im Kreis und Quadrat, Cod. Ashburniano 361, fol. 5 r. Florenz, Bibliotheca Laurenziana

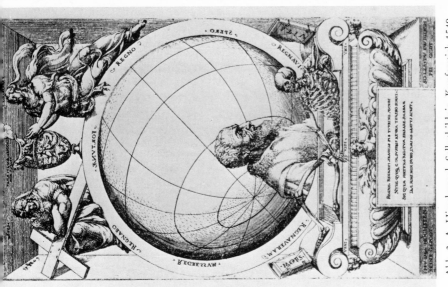

Abb. 3. A. Hirschvogel, Selbstbildnis, Kupferstich 1549

Abb. 5. Die Göttliche Providenzia, Holkham Bible, Ms. Add. 47680 fol. 2 r. London,
British Mus.

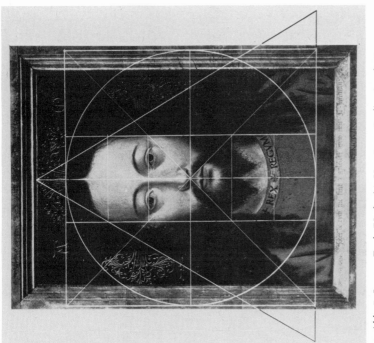

▲ Abb. 7. Jan van Eyck (Umkreis), Vera Icon, Berlin, Staatl. Mus.

▲ Abb. 6. A. Dürer, Selbstbildnis 1500. München, Alte Pinakothek

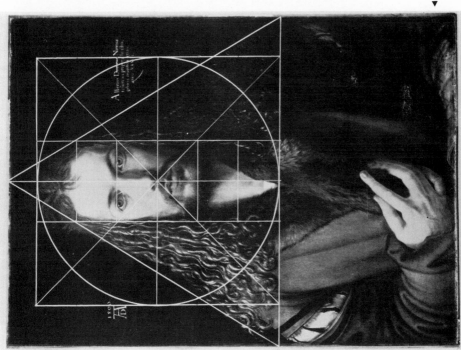

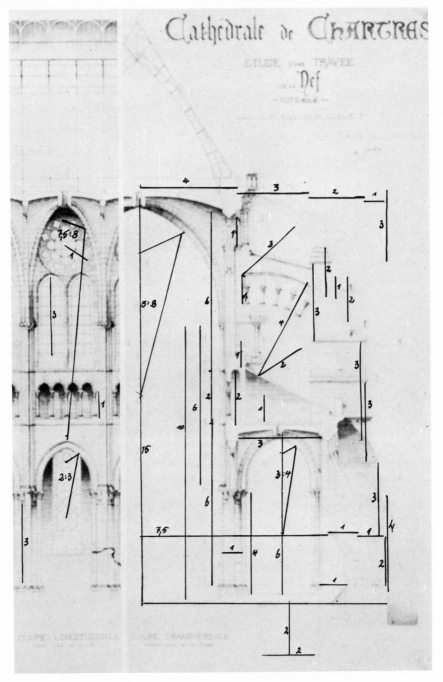

Abb. 1. Nef, Transversalschnitt durch die Kathedrale von Chartres (19. Jh.)

STRUCTURA CODICIS – ORDO SALUTIS
ZUM GOLDENEN EVANGELIENBUCH HEINRICHS III.

von Johannes Rathofer (Köln)

Die drei Grundthesen der hier vorgetragenen Überlegungen lauten:

Erstens: Das Goldene Evangelienbuch Heinrichs III. (Codex aureus Escorialensis[1]), das der König 1045/46 in Echternach als Weihegeschenk für den Speyerer Dom, die Grablege der Salier, herstellen ließ, ist in seinem äußeren Aufbau gemäß Sapientia 11,21 „nach Maß, Zahl (und Gewicht) geordnet".

Zweitens: Die verwendeten Maß-Zahlen sind durch die biblische und patristische Tradition als Bedeutungsträger bekannt und ausgewiesen.

Drittens: Die von solchen ‚be-deutenden' Zahlen bestimmte und gegliederte Ordnung des Codex ist ein Abbild des *ordo salutis*, d.h. der von den gleichen Zahlen geprägten Raum- und Zeitenordnung des Heils.

Als Codex, an dem die Bedeutung von Maß und Zahl für seine innere und äußere Gestalt-Ordnung aufgezeigt werden soll, wurde ein Evangeliar gewählt, weil es keine andere mittelalterliche Buchgattung gibt, in der bereits die Zahl als solche und ihre optische Erscheinung eine auch nur entfernt vergleichbare Rolle spielen. Nirgendwo ist ihr größere Aufmerksamkeit und Wertschätzung zuteil geworden. Es sei nur daran erinnert, daß alle Evangeliare in den sogenannten Kanontafeln die Sektionszahlen der vier Evangelien zu einer sozusagen abstrakten Zahlensynopse zusammenstellten und darüberhinaus den Evangelientext selbst fortlaufend marginal mit den Kapitel-, Kanon- und Sektionszahlen in Form von Konkordanzen ausstatteten. Neben den *litterae* seiner Texte enthielt damit ein Evangeliar jeweils rund 6.000 Zahlen mit insgesamt über 30.000 römischen Ziffern. Die Bedeutung, die man diesen *numeri* zusprach, geht bereits aus der Tatsache hervor, daß man sie nicht nur in einem Codex aureus, sondern gelegentlich selbst dann in reinem Golde schrieb, wenn der Evangelientext nur in schwarzer oder brauner Tinte aufgezeichnet war, wie dies z.B. beim –

---

[1] Escorial, Codex Vitrinas 17. Verf. dankt allen, die es ihm ermöglicht haben, die Handschrift selbst im Escorial einzusehen, wo sie seit 1566 ihre Heimat gefunden hat.

ebenfalls in Echternach hergestellten – Codex Caesarius Upsaliensis[2] der Fall ist.

Das Goldene Evangelienbuch Heinrichs III. wurde gewählt, weil es „an wahrhaft fürstlichem Prunk und Noblesse der Ausstattung, vom Umfang seines Programms und von der anspruchsvollen Gesamthaltung her" alles überragt, was an gleichzeitigen Handschriften überliefert ist[3]. Monumentalität des Werkes und Sorgfalt der künstlerischen Gestaltung, die Stellung des Auftraggebers und der Zweck der Handschrift lassen erwarten, daß dem Codex ein detaillierter Plan, ein klares geistiges Konzept zugrundeliegt.

I. Der Codex als Abbild des Kosmos

In seinem äußeren Aufbau und seiner Anlage entspricht das Goldene Evangelienbuch dem klassischen Typus des frühmittelalterlichen Evangeliars, das folgende 7-teilige Gliederung zeigt: 1. Die vier Allgemeinen Vorreden (*Novum opus, Sciendum etiam, Plures fuisse, Ammonius quidem*); 2. Die Kanontafeln; 3.-6. Die Texte der vier Evangelien (in der Reihenfolge: Mt–Mk–Lk–Jo) mit dem jeweils zugehörigen Argumentum und den Capitula; 7. Das Capitulare evangeliorum (Perikopenverzeichnis, Comes).

Allerdings hat die ornamentale, graphische und bildliche Hervorhebung und Markierung dieser sieben Hauptgliederungsstellen in dem aus exakt 3 × 7 Lagen bestehenden Codex hier ein sonst nirgendwo bekanntes Ausmaß erreicht. Dabei zeigt die geradezu verschwenderische Fülle der die einzelnen Kompositionsfugen kennzeichnenden Mittel ein Höchstmaß an Differenzierungs- und Nuancierungsfähigkeit, wie es dergestalt nur in einem großen Skriptorium auf dem Gipfel seiner Leistungskraft denkbar ist. So sind von den insgesamt 170 Blättern, deren imperiale Größe von 35 × 50 cm weder vorher noch nachher von einem Evangeliar erreicht wurde, allein 93 Seiten ganz und ausschließlich in schmückender und gliedernder Funktion eingesetzt. Weitere 54 Seiten zeigen halbseitigen Schmuck oder eine halbe Seite einnehmende Miniaturen.

Bereits die hier versammelte einzigartige Fülle von Figuren und Gestalten läßt das Evangelienbuch als ein Abbild des Universums einer- und der Heilsgeschichte andererseits erscheinen. In den Bildrahmen und auf den

---

[2] Uppsala, Univ.-Bibl., Cod. C 93. Vollständige farbige Faksimile-Ausgabe mit Kommentarband von C. Nordenfalk, Codex Caesareus Upsaliensis. An Echternach Gospel-Book of the Eleventh Century, Stockholm 1971.

[3] A. Boeckler, Das Goldene Evangelienbuch Heinrichs III., Berlin 1933, 10. Die bislang einzige Monographie gibt alle Schmuckelemente der Hs. sowie einige Schriftseiten in schwarz-weiß Abb. wieder. – Zwei originalgetreue Faksimile-Seiten (fol. 6 r u. 61 v) sowie die farbige Wiedergabe beider Einbanddeckel jetzt erstmals bei J. Rathofer, Das Goldene Evangelienbuch Kaiser Heinrichs III., München 1980. Zu fol. 6 r cf. Tafel XI, Abb. 9.

Purpur- und Goldgründen der Zierseiten und -tafeln finden sich z. B. über 100 Münzabbildungen, etwa ebensoviele Pflanzen und fast 200 Tiere. Daneben erscheinen zahlreiche Vertreter des Alten und Neuen Bundes, sowie die verschiedenen Amtsträger und Stände der Kirche. So begegnen dem Leser (außerhalb der 50 Miniaturen zum Evangelientext mit ihren rund 600 Figuren) 4 alttestamentliche Helden (wie David und Samson) und 4 Propheten; die 12 Apostel und 4 × 12 ihrer ersten Nachfolger auf dem Stuhle Petri; die 4 Evangelisten und ihre Symbole, 4 Bischöfe, 8 namentlich genannte Märtyrer und 16 Märtyrinnen der jungen Kirche; die Personifikationen der 4 Kardinaltugenden und der 8 Seligpreisungen; 8 Engel mit Tafeln, auf deren Goldgrund die Verheißungen des Lohnes für den Sieger stehen, gemäß den die Apokalypse eröffnenden Sendschreiben an die 7 Gemeinden. Die Antike ist mit Karyatiden und Atlanten vertreten, die Gegenwart präsentiert sich in den beiden salischen Herrscherpaaren, der Abbildung des Speyerer Domes usw.

Alle Stufen der Schöpfung sind in ihren Vertretern gegenwärtig. Sie reichen vom Anorganischen (Steine, Gebäude, Mineralien, Metalle, Farben), Pflanzlichen und Animalischen über den Menschen hinauf bis zu den reinen Geistwesen, ja bis zum unerschaffenen Schöpfer selbst, zu dem Logos, der mit seinem Wort alles ins Dasein und ins Leben rief.

Präsent wird auch die gesamte Geschichte des Heils: Der Alte Bund, die mit der Menschwerdung Gottes heraufgeführte ‚Wende‘ in der Mitte und Fülle der Zeiten und schließlich die vom Herrn auf dem Fundament der Apostel gegründete Kirche. Als ‚Jerusalem der Jetztzeit‘ ist sie unter der Leitung der Päpste und Bischöfe und nicht zuletzt der christlichen Herrscher Konstantin, Konstantius, Konrad und Heinrich, deren Porträts auf zahlreichen Münzmedaillons erscheinen, sowie kraft des Blutzeugnisses ihrer Märtyrer unterwegs zu den *caelestia regna*, zum Himmlischen Jerusalem.

II. Struktur als Bedeutungsträger

Die Fakten der teilweise singulären Ausstattung des Codex liegen zwar vor Augen, das hinter ihnen stehende Programm, sein Sinn und seine Bedeutung, erschließen sich weniger leicht. Was für die Kunst des Mittelalters im allgemeinen gilt, gilt im besonderen auch für das Evangelienbuch: Das Faszinierende dieser Kunst „hat einen Grund in ihrem Reichtum an Geheimnis . . . Was sie den Augen, den andern Sinnen bietet, hat den Reiz des lockenden Versprechens und hermetischen Verweigerns . . . Das den Sinnen Sichtbare ist ein Zeichen für Unsichtbares, das im Sichtbaren stumm sich ausspricht."[4] Am Leitfaden der Struktur des Codex, seiner planvoll

---

[4] F. Ohly, Probleme der mittelalterlichen Bedeutungsforschung und das Taubenbild des Hugo de Folieto, in: F. Ohly, Schriften zur mittelalterlichen Bedeutungsforschung, Darmstadt 1977, 32.

angelegten linearen Gliederung, wollen wir versuchen, die Intention von
Auftraggeber und Künstlern wenigstens in einigen Ansätzen zu erkennen.
Dabei sind wir in der seltenen und glücklichen Lage, daß unser Codex
diesem Versuch mit seinem eigenen deutenden Wort zu Hilfe kommt.

1. Die ‚Schlüssel‘-Funktion des Titulus

Die erste der beiden Widmungsinschriften, die Heinrich auf eigens ihnen
vorbehaltenen Seiten (fol. 3v—4r) den Dedikationsbildern folgen ließ, ist
ein Hymnus auf das Evangelienbuch, der entscheidende Akzente für das
zeitgenössische Verständnis gerade dieses Codex setzt und uns Nachgebo-
renen so als authentische Interpretationshilfe dienen kann. Die Verse lauten
(in einem ersten Übersetzungsversuch):

> Dies ist das Buch des Lebens,
> da es das Leben in sich enthält!
> Voll des himmlischen Taus
> ist es dem Munde des Christus entströmt
> hin auf alle die Völker,
> auf uns und all’ unsere Ahnen.
> Wie sehr müssen wir des Bösen entraten,
> damit wir die Güter des Geistes, die hier verborgenen, lieben!
> Wer diese Worte handelnd vollzieht,
> erlangen wird er himmlische Reiche![5]

Mit der Eingangszeile *Hic liber est vitae* ist der originale Titel unseres Evangeliars genannt und damit ein Rahmen abgesteckt, innerhalb dessen Anlage
und Ausstattung ihren Stellenwert und ihre Bedeutung erhalten, das künstlerische ‚Programm‘ also wenigstens in seinen Grundzügen ablesbar
werden könnte. Der Titel ‚Buch des Lebens‘ ist biblisches ‚Zitat‘ und der
Geheimen Offenbarung des Johannes entnommen, wo er insgesamt sechsmal (3,5; 13,8; 17,8; 20,12. 15; 21,27) begegnet (sonst nur noch: Philipper
4,3). Den Beweis hierfür liefert die Handschrift insofern selbst, als sie auf
der Initialseite des Markusevangeliums (fol. 63r) den ‚Engel der Gemeinde
in Sardes‘ abbildet, der auf goldener Tafel die Verheißung aus Apk 3,5 vor-
zeigt: *Et erit nomen eius in libro vitae.*

Wie schon die meines Wissens singuläre Darbietung der 7 (+1) Lohnverheißungen (Apk 2—3; 21,7), so weist auch der Gesamttitel des Evangelienbuches in besonderem Maße auf die Endzeit und die Apokalypse als
den Horizont hin, vor dem es gedeutet und verstanden werden will. Die für
die Titelwahl angeführte Begründung („da es das Leben in sich enthält“)

---

[5] *Hic liber est vitae / quia vitam continet in se. / caelesti rore / Chr(ist)i diffusus ab ore. /
omnes ad gentes / ad nos n(ost)rosque parentes. / ut mala vitemus / bona condita mentis
amem(us). / qui facit haec verba / capiet caelestia regna*; cf. Tafel VIII, Abb. 4.

verrät ebenfalls johanneisches Gedankengut; ist doch ‚Leben‘ der soterio-
logische Grundbegriff der Theologie des vierten Evangelisten, letztlich
identisch mit dem Leben in Person, mit Christus, der von sich gesagt hatte:
„Ich bin das Leben" (Jo 11,25; 14,6; vgl. 5,26). Im ‚Buch des Lebens‘ ist
das Leben, ist Christus ‚selbst‘ gegenwärtig; und als solches ist es zugleich
auch schon jenes Buch der Apokalypse, in das die ‚Namen‘ der Lebendigen
‚eingeschrieben‘ sind. Man wird zumindest die Frage aufwerfen dürfen,
was unter diesem Aspekt die Tatsache bedeutet, daß unserm Evangelienbuch konkret (und stellvertretend) soviele Namen ‚eingeschrieben‘ sind,
angefangen von David und Samson über die Apostel und Evangelisten, die
ersten Päpste und Märtyrer bis hin zu Kaiser Konstantin und den salischen
Herrscherpaaren, wobei Heinrich allein 65mal namentlich genannt wird.

Wir fragen, ob Vorstellungen und Aussagen der Apokalypse, wie sie im
originalen Titel des Evangelienbuches anklingen, möglicherweise auch die
structura codicis mitgeprägt haben.

2. Der programmatische Bucheingang

Wie immer der ursprüngliche Einband des Escorialensis − bei einer Neu-
bindung im 17. Jahrhundert erhielt er einen zeitgenössischen Lederein-
band − beschaffen gewesen sein mag: außerhalb des liturgischen Gebrauchs
verschloß er das Evangelienbuch[6]. Aus dem römischen Meßordo (I n. 11)
wissen wir, daß das Evangeliar nach der Verlesung des Evangeliums wieder
in eine Kassette gelegt, versiegelt und an seinen Verwahrungsort zurückge-
bracht wurde[7]. Wer, wie in unserm Fall, bereits bei der Titelgebung seinen
Blick auf das Urbild des Buches, wie es in der Apokalypse geschildert wird,
gerichtet hatte, mochte angesichts des geschlossenen oder gar versiegelten
Evangeliars an das ‚Buch mit den sieben Siegeln‘ denken, von dem es Apk
5,3−5 heißt: „Aber niemand im Himmel, auf der Erde und unter der Erde
konnte das Buch öffnen und es lesen. Da weinte ich sehr . . . Da sagte einer
von den Ältesten zu mir: Weine nicht! Gesiegt hat *der Löwe* aus dem
Stamm Juda, der Sproß aus der Wurzel Davids; er *kann das Buch . . .
öffnen.*" Bei der Öffnung des ersten Siegels ruft dann „das erste der vier
Lebewesen (das einem *Löwen* glich: Apk 4,7) wie mit Donnerstimme" dem
Seher zu: „Komm (und sieh)!" (Apk 6,1).

Diese Vision der Geheimen Offenbarung scheint auf das Konzept des
Bucheingangs eingewirkt zu haben. Schlägt man den Codex auf, so stößt
man nach dem Umwenden des ersten Blattes auf einen ‚Vorhang‘, ein
Purpur-Seitenpaar (fol. 1v−2r), das einen goldgewebten byzantinischen
Seidenstoff imitiert, der nicht weniger als 82 gegenständige *Löwen* zeigt.

---

[6] A. Boeckler, l. c., Abb. 1 und J. Rathofer, l. c., der den 1934 gefertigten Einband zeigt.
[7] J. A. Jungmann, Missarum sollemnia, Wien 1952, Bd. I, 575.

Die Vielzahl der brüllenden Löwen könnte die Gewalt der *vox tonitrui*, der Donnerstimme des löwengleichen ‚Lebewesens‘, verbildlichen und zugleich der Universalität seiner Aufforderung „Komm (und sieh)!“ Ausdruck geben. Das Bild des Löwen ist indes auch (wie das entsprechende der vier ‚Lebewesen‘) darüber hinaus Symbol für den ‚Löwen aus dem Stamme Juda‘, für den ‚Sproß Davids‘. In diesen mehrfachen Bedeutungskontext hinein paßt die Tatsache, daß in unserm Codex David selbst (wie auch die drei übrigen alttestamentlichen Helden) eine große quadratische Tafel hält, in die ein Löwe eingezeichnet ist: Präfiguration des wahren ‚Löwen aus dem Stamme Juda‘, der in seiner Auferstehung den Tod überwunden hat[8].

Es kann kein Zufall sein, daß diese vier Vertreter des Alten Bundes mit ihren Löwentafeln die Initium-Seite des Markusevangeliums (fol. 62r) schmücken, d. h. parallel zum Bild des Evangelisten und zu seinem Symbol, dem löwengleichen ‚Lebewesen‘ (fol. 61v), stehen, während die beiden folgenden Seiten in ihren Rahmen die acht Engel mit den Lohnverheißungen der Apokalypse und acht Märtyrer abbilden, die als solche – unter dem ‚Altar des Lammes‘, Apk 9,6f. – in der Geheimen Offenbarung an zentraler Stelle ebenfalls erwähnt werden.

Die einzelnen Elemente der *structura codicis* stützen und interpretieren sich gegenseitig. Wer den *Liber vitae* aufschlägt, wird daran erinnert, daß im Grunde nur einer, nämlich der Löwe aus Juda, das Buch zu öffnen vermag. Gleichzeitig wird ihm durch die *figurae leonum* vervielfacht das „Komm und sieh!“ des ersten Lebewesens der Apokalypse zugesprochen. Wer den Löwenvorhang hebt, wird nicht mehr ‚in Bild und Gleichnis‘, in *figura leonis* nur, sondern ‚von Angesicht zu Angesicht‘ den schauen, der ‚gesiegt hat‘. Und tatsächlich folgt auf der nächsten Seite (fol. 2v) die Maiestas Dei, der vor leuchtendem Goldgrund in der Mandorla thronende Christus, das geöffnete, mit der Innenseite dem Betrachter zugekehrte ‚Lebensbuch‘ in der linken Hand und auf dem linken Knie. Wie in Kapitel 6 der Apokalypse umgeben ihn die ‚vier Lebewesen‘ (in Form der Evangelistensymbole), huldigen ihm die (neun Chöre der) Engel, fallen nieder und beten ihn an: Konrad und Gisela – an Stelle der 24 Ältesten, wie diese goldene Kronen auf dem Haupt[9]. Zwar zeigt das Buch keine Inschrift – im Gegensatz etwa zum Epternacensis[10] –, doch beweist seine optische Iden-

---

[8] Dieser figurale Bezug wird besonders deutlich auf einem Bild des Evangelisten Markus, wo im Arkadenbogen sein Symbol, der Löwe, parallel zum auferstehenden Christus abgebildet und durch den Titulus: *Ecce leo fortis transit discrimina mortis* entsprechend gedeutet wird. Evangeliar Heinrichs II., Bayer. Staatsbibl., Clm 4454, fol. 86v; cf. Farbtafel V, in: Treasures of the Bavarian State Library. An exhibition of manuscripts, München 1970.

[9] cf. Tafel VII, Abb. 2 u. 3; cf. A. Boeckler, l. c., Abb. 6 u. 7.

[10] Fol. 2v: *Gaudete, quoniam nomina vestra scripta sunt in libro vitae*; cf. Faksimile-Ausgabe mit Kommentarband von R. Kahsnitz, Das Goldene Evangelienbuch von Echternach. Codex Aureus Epternacensis Hs 156142 aus dem Germanischen Nationalmuseum Nürnberg. Frankfurt 1982.

tität mit dem ebenfalls geöffneten Goldenen Evangeliar, das Heinrich auf dem nebenstehenden Dedikationsbild der Himmelskönigin als Patronin des Speyerer Doms überreicht, daß es den gleichen Titel haben muß: *Liber vitae*; den Titel, der als solcher ausdrücklich erst in den Widmungsversen auf der folgenden Seite (fol. 3 v) genannt wird, womit sich der hermeneutische Zirkel vorerst schließt. Wir sagen ‚vorerst‘, weil auch noch im zweiten Widmungsgedicht (fol. 4 r) die Terminologie der Apokalypse beibehalten wird, wenn Heinrich sagt, er bringe dem König aller (Könige)" (Apk 17,14; 19,16) das *diadema librorum* dar. Das Wort *diadema* kennt von den biblischen Schriften nur die Apokalypse: 12,3; 13,1; 19,12.

3. Typologischer Sinn des Löwenvorhangs

Bevor wir den Gang durch das Goldene Evangelienbuch fortsetzen, der sich schon jetzt als eine Art Initiationsweg darstellt, auf dem dem Leser zugleich die Mittel zum Weiterschreiten angeboten werden (fol. 3 r: die 4 Kardinaltugenden; fol. 3 v–4 r: die für die 8 Seligpreisungen vorausgesetzten Grundhaltungen; fol. 4 v–6 r: die bleibende Verbindung mit dem in den Päpsten fortlebenden Petrusamt), wollen wir noch einmal zu dem ‚Vorhang‘ im Eingang des Buches zurückkehren. Die Deutung seiner figürlichen Gestaltung (Löwen) ergab sich nicht zuletzt aus seiner Stellung vor dem Maiestasbild und seiner Funktion als Introitus in das ‚Heilige Buch‘. Jeder Versuch einer Sinnerschließung ohne Berücksichtigung der den Vorhangseiten zugemessenen Position im Gliederungsgefüge wäre willkürlich und ließe keinen Rückschluß auf ein der Handschrift zugrunde liegendes ‚Programm‘ zu. Daß ein solches Programm immer nur spezifisch sein kann, zeigt z. B. die Tatsache, daß die Purpurseiten vor dem Maiestasbild des Epternacensis keinerlei Muster aufweisen, während sein berühmter ‚Löwenvorhang‘ die Bildfolge des Lukasevangeliums eröffnet (fol. 75 v–76 r), sich also erst jenseits der Mitte des Codex findet. Er erforderte deshalb eine völlig andere Interpretation[11].

Zusätzlich und paradigmatisch wollen wir nun noch kurz die einzelnen Gliederungselemente, ihre Anordnung und Zahl, betrachten, von denen der erste ‚Vorhang‘ des Escorialensis bestimmt wird. Vielleicht läßt sich so über die allgemeine ‚Vorhang‘-Funktion hinaus seine spezielle Bedeutung

---

[11] Man weicht diesem Problem aus, wenn man bei der Dokumentation der Ausstattung des Epternacensis durch 40 Farbtafeln, die an sich der codexgemäßen Anordnung folgen, die Handschrift selbst mit eben diesem Löwenvorhang beginnen läßt. Durch den (willkürlichen) Positionswechsel wird ihm ein anderer Sinn beigelegt als der, der ihm nach dem Ordo des Codex zukommt; cf. R. Kahsnitz, U. Mende u. E. Rücker, Das Goldene Evangelienbuch von Echternach. Eine Prunkhandschrift des 11. Jahrhunderts (Katalog der Ausstellung vom 10. 7. bis 29. 8. 1982 im Germanischen Nationalmuseum Nürnberg), Frankfurt 1982, Tafel 3.

erschließen. Dabei gehen wir von den wichtigsten und ins Auge fallenden Zahlen und Zahlenverhältnissen aus. Die 82 Löwen sind über die Doppelseite hinweg in 11 Reihen angeordnet und zwar so, daß die 6 ungradzahligen Reihen je sieben und die 5 gradzeiligen je acht Löwen aufweisen. Diese horizontalen Reihen sind in sich durch jeweils 4 gleich breite – ebenfalls horizontal verlaufende – Farbstreifen unterteilt, die sich nur im Ton (dunkel – hell) der Purpurfärbung unterscheiden und regelmäßig alternieren[12].

Die genannten Zahlen stehen in auffälliger Parallelität zu den Maßangaben, die Moses auf dem Berge Sinai von Gott erhält, und nach denen er das äußere Zelt über der Bundeslade, dem „Allerheiligsten" des Alten Testaments, anfertigen soll. Gemäß Exodus 26,7f. muß Moses „für das Zelt über der Wohnstätte (Gottes)" 11 Zeltbahnen aus Ziegenhaar herstellen, von denen jede 4 Ellen breit (und dreißig Ellen lang) sein soll. Vers 9 heißt es: „Füge 5 von den Zeltbahnen zu einem Stück zusammen; dann füge auch die (übrigen) 6 Zeltbahnen zu einem Stück zusammen." Die rein zahlenmäßige Analogie ist so frappierend, daß sich die Vermutung aufdrängt, die Anfangsseiten des Escorialensis sollten das Außenzelt der Bundeslade symbolisieren. Die Farben dieser beiden Schmuckseiten und ihrer Randleisten würden dann die Farben des Vorhangs am Eingang zum Bundeszelt oder gar des ‚inneren' Vorhangs spiegeln, der als „Scheidewand zwischen dem Heiligen und dem Allerheiligsten" diente und aus „blauem und rotem Purpur und aus Karmesin und gezwirntem Byssus" herzustellen war (Ex 26,31. 36). Bis auf den weißen Byssus, der vielleicht bewußt und im Sinne der Steigerung durch das Gold der Löwen und Rosetten ersetzt wurde, zeigen die Ränder der Vorhangseiten nämlich die gleichen Farben wie die Vorhänge des alttestamentlichen *tabernaculum dei* (Lev 26,11), das als eschatologisches *tabernaculum dei cum hominibus*, als „Zelt Gottes unter den Menschen", im Himmlischen Jerusalem einst seine endgültige Erfüllung finden wird (Apk 21,3).

Wenn die (5 + 6 =) 11 Längsreihen mit ihren insgesamt (11 × 4 =) 44 Streifen den bewußt gewählten ‚Grundriß' der Eingangsseiten unseres Evangelienbuches bilden, dann würden sie im Medium der Zahl auf die äußere Hülle, nämlich die (5 + 6 =) 11 Zeltbahnen, des Bundeszeltes mit einer Gesamtbreite von (11 × 4 =) 44 Ellen verweisen und im Medium der Farbe den Vorhang vor dem „Allerheiligsten" symbolisieren. Mit andern Worten: schon die erste Doppelseite zielte darauf ab, das vorliegende Evangelienbuch in einen typologischen Zusammenhang mit der Stiftshütte zu bringen, die von Ex 28,43 an *tabernaculum testimonii*, Offenbarungszelt, genannt wird, weil sie in der Bundeslade die *duae tabulae testimonii* mit den *verba foederis decem*, also die beiden Tafeln mit den ‚Zehn Bundesworten', dem Dekalog, birgt (Ex 34,28f.).

---

[12] A. Boeckler, l. c., Abb. 4 und 5; cf. Tafel VI, Abb. 1.

Am Eingang des neutestamentlichen *Liber vitae* würde dergestalt dem Leser bedeutet, daß er — mit dem Durchschreiten des ‚Löwenvorhangs‘ — jetzt in das wahre Offenbarungszelt eintritt, das in seinem Zentrum die Worte des Lebens enthält, in denen sich das ‚Zehnwort‘ des Alten Bundes erfüllt hat. Mit den beiden ersten Vorhangseiten legte die *structura codicis* ihre Funktion fest, dem Leser eine Raumvorstellung zu vermitteln, die ihre endgültige Gestalt in dem ‚Zelt Gottes unter den Menschen‘, wie es die Geheime Offenbarung schildert, gefunden hat.

4. Die Kanontafeln

Diesem Ziel dienen in besonders eindrucksvoller Weise auch die Kanontafeln des Goldenen Evangelienbuches (fol 11v–17r). Ihre 12er-Folge repräsentiert zahlenmäßig den sehr häufig begegnenden Typus der sogenannten ‚kleineren lateinischen Kanonreihe‘, während die sogenannte ‚größere‘ sich über 16 Seiten erstreckt. Für eine eigene Deutung, die über das hinausginge, was vom Typus allgemein gilt, scheint hier kein Raum zu sein. Die ihrer künstlerischen Gestaltung zugrundeliegenden architektonischen Vorstellungen werden entweder auf die griechische Tempelfront (Gebälk- und Dreiecksgiebeltypus) oder auf die mehrgeschossigen Aquädukte der Römer (Bogentypus) zurückgeführt. Entsprechend ließe sich die Kanonfolge ganz unspezifisch interpretieren als Aquädukt, über den „dem Leser das Evangelium Jesu Christi als Quell des Lebens zufließt“. Sie ließe sich auch mit den Propyläen vergleichen, die gleichsam erst einmal mit den Augen abgeschritten werden, „um alsdann zum Heiligtum zu gelangen, in dem das Wort Gottes bewahrt wird“. Im Falle der 12er Reihe könnte man auch eine Analogie zum römischen Staatskalender des Jahres 356 sehen und demgemäß die Kanonfolge als eine „kalendarische Ankündigung der neuen Friedensära“ deuten, „die durch das Evangelium Christi verheißen ist“[13].

Dennoch zeigen unsere Kanontafeln Eigenschaften und Elemente, die entweder völlig singulär sind oder doch zumindest relativ selten anderwärts begegnen. Schon ein kurzer Blick auf das Grundschema ihres Aufbaus und ihrer Ausstattung kann dies verdeutlichen.

Die monumentalen Architekturgebilde sind jeweils paarig, also auf einer Doppelseite, angeordnet[14]. In eine große Säulenarkade mit Rundbogen ist stets eine vier- (= achtmal) bzw. dreiteilige (= viermal) kleinere Arkade eingefügt, deren äußere Öffnungen durch Giebel und deren innere Öffnungen durch Rundbogen abgeschlossen sind. Die so entstandenen vier

---

[13] Alle Zitate nach A. v. Euw (und J. M. Plotzek), die Handschriften der Sammlung Ludwig, Bd. I, Köln 1979, 142.

[14] A. Boeckler, l. c., Abb. 20–31; cf. Tafel VIII, Abb. 5.

bzw. drei langgestreckten Interkolumnien pro Seite — insgesamt sind es 44! — sind ganz mit Gold ausgelegt. Nur in ihrer Mitte bleibt jeweils eine schmale, gerahmte Tafel ausgespart, auf deren Pergamentgrund mit Goldtinte die Sektionsziffern eingetragen sind: auf den zusammen 44 vertikalen Streifen insgesamt 1.348 römische Zahlen. Da die äußere Arkade auf eigenen Säulen ruht, zählen acht der Kanontafeln 7 und vier Tafeln 6 Säulen, d. h. jeweils zwei Säulen mehr als alle anderen mir bekannten Handschriften dieser Zeit.

In dem halbkreisförmigen Feld (Lünette) des Hauptbogens, der — auffällig genug — in seinem Scheitel ein großes Medaillon mit dem Brustbild eines Apostels zeigt, tragen zwei bis vier (Menschen- oder Tier-) Figuren eine breite Tafel mit dem Titel des Kanons in goldenen Kapital-Buchstaben. Die Seitenzwickel außerhalb des Hauptbogens sind zusätzlich rechtwinklig gerahmt, mit dreiviertelrunden Ausbuchtungen an den oberen Ecken. Auf strahlendem Goldgrund zeigen sie gegenständige Vögel oder geflügelte Drachen.

Diese zweifellos großartigsten Dokumente der Darstellung einer imaginären Architektur in einer mittelalterlichen Handschrift, die ganz aus edlem Gestein und lauterem Gold errichtet zu sein scheint, bilden das einheitlichste und zugleich stärkste Gliederungselement des Evangeliars. Die Spezifika dieser 12 Architekturgebilde geben den Hinweis auf ihre Deutung. Die meines Wissens einzigartige rechtwinklige Einfassung des Hauptbogens scheint die Arkade wie in eine Mauer einzubinden, so daß die Arkade nach Aussehen und Funktion eher an ein offenes Tor erinnert, das den Blick auf spiegelnde Goldflächen (auch diese sind in Kanontafeln ganz ungewöhnlich!) freigibt. Die 12 Apostel (meist mit ihren Namen) im Scheitel der 12 Hauptbogen stellen eine weitere, nur selten vorkommende Eigenart unserer Kanontafeln dar. In dieser konkreten Gestalt, Ausschmückung und Zahl aber evozieren sie die Vorstellung von den 12 Toren des Himmlischen Jerusalem nach Apk 21: „Die Stadt hat eine große und hohe Mauer mit 12 Toren . . . Die Mauer der Stadt hat 12 Grundsteine; auf ihnen stehen die 12 Namen der 12 Apostel . . . Die Mauer ist 144 Ellen hoch . . ., und die Stadt ist aus reinem Gold . . . (Auch) die Straße der Stadt ist aus reinem Gold, wie aus klarem Glas . . . Ihre Tore werden den ganzen Tag nicht geschlossen . . . Nur die, die im Lebensbuch des Lammes eingetragen sind, werden eingelassen."

Daß die 12 Apostel auf unsern Tafeln nicht die Grundsteine sondern die Schlußsteine der Torbogen bilden, hat nichts Auffälliges, ist doch in der mittelalterlichen Kirchenarchitektur der ‚Grund'- oder ‚Eckstein' Christus ebenfalls zum ‚Schlußstein' geworden, „welcher die Wände von beiden Seiten eint"[15]. Die 44 Interkolumnien (zum Vergleich: der Epternacensis

---

[15] Suger von St. Denis, nach G. Bandmann, Mittelalterliche Architektur als Bedeutungsträger, Berlin [5]1978, 73.

zählt auf seinen zehn Tafeln 36, der Upsaliensis auf zwölf Tafeln 43 Interkolumnien) des Escorialensis nehmen die Zahl der Streifen des Löwenvorhangs und damit die Gesamtbreite des äußeren Bundeszeltes – gemessen
nach Ellen – wieder auf und setzen sie in typologische Relation zu
der 144 Ellen hohen Mauer der heiligen Stadt, des neuen ‚Zeltes Gottes
unter den Menschen‘. Sie übersteigt die alttestamentliche Maßzahl genau
um 100, d. h. um die ‚Zahl des ewigen Lebens‘ (vgl. Mt 19,29). Damit
wird ein Grundgesetz typologischen Denkens dokumentiert und wirksam:
der Typus (Bundeszelt) bleibt im Antitypus (Himmelsstadt) gegenwärtig,
„er geht nicht unter, er geht ein in die Gestalt seiner Erfüllung als eine
Zeugnisspur des gottgedachten Planes der Erlösung"[16].

Den stärksten und eindeutigsten Hinweis auf eine Selbstinterpretation
der (auf 7 Blätter verteilten) Kanontafeln unseres Codex in Richtung auf
die Himmelsstadt liefert die schon erwähnte Besonderheit der Säulen-
doppelung an den Außenseiten der Arkaden. Danach zählen acht der
zwölf Tafeln jeweils 7 Säulen (fol 11v–12r; 14v–17r). Neben Genesis
2,2 (Gottes Ruhen am 7. Tag) wird von der allegorischen Exegese am häu-
figsten die Zahl 7 in Prov 9,1 behandelt: „Die Weisheit hat ihr Haus
gebaut, hat ihre 7 Säulen behauen". Dieses ‚Haus der Weisheit‘ wird zumeist
als Vorausbedeutung der Kirche verstanden. In diesem Kontext präfigu-
rieren die 7 Säulen die 7 Gemeinden der Apokalypse, die ihrerseits die
Universalität und Vollkommenheit der mit Hilfe der 7-fachen Gnadengabe
des Heiligen Geistes aus ‚lebendigen Steinen‘ auferbauten Ecclesia bedeuten. Dabei ist die Sieben zugleich Zeichen der Dauer und Beständigkeit, das
auf die Ewigkeit, das *aeternum tempus*, hinweist, wie etwa Cassiodor,
Gregor der Große, Beda und Hrabanus Maurus betonen[17]. Das heißt: die
Kirche der Jetztzeit, die im alttestamentlichen Haus der Weisheit mit
seinen 7 Säulen vorausbedeutet war, ist nun ihrerseits und gleichzeitig ein
Vor-Bild seiner endhaften Vollendung im Himmlischen Jerusalem. Wenn
die 7 Säulen genau 8mal vorkommen, dann kann man hierin eine Verstär-
kung des Gedankens an die ewige Vollendung der Ecclesia in der *octava
aetas* erblicken[18], mit der das „ewige Heute" anbricht[19], der achte Tag,
„der keinen Abend kennt" (Augustinus) und der die Seinsweise des
Neuen Jerusalem bestimmt: *nox enim non erit illic* (Apk 21,25; 22,5).

---

[16] F. Ohly, Synagoge und Ecclesia. Typologisches in mittelalterlicher Dichtung, in: l. c.,
312.

[17] H. Meyer–R. Suntrup, Zum Lexikon der Zahlenbedeutungen im Mittelalter. Einführung in die Methode und Probeartikel: Die Zahl 7, in: Frühmittelalterliche Studien, Bd. 11,
Berlin 1977, 19. 29. 47f.

[18] Hrabanus Maurus, In Mattheum, PL 107, 1097 Df.; weitere Belege: J. Rathofer, Der
Heliand, Köln–Graz 1962, 307ff.

[19] Ambrosius, Epistola 44, PL 16, 1136, nach D. Forstner, Die Welt der christlichen
Symbole, Innsbruck-Wien-München ³1977, 54.

Zur Stützung unserer Interpretation der Sieben-Säulen-Arkaden sei darauf hingewiesen, daß Heinrich selbst in seinem zweiten Widmungsgedicht (fol. 4r, also exakt auf der 7. Seite des Codex) ausdrücklich die ‚Weisheit' den Grund dafür angeben läßt, daß er das ‚Diadem der Bücher' ganz in Gold hat schreiben lassen. Die *sapientia* nämlich habe gesagt: „Alles wird vergehn, meine Worte aber werden niemals vergehn"[20]. Auf fol. 63r wird darüberhinaus expressis verbis die Verheißung an eine der 7 Gemeinden zitiert: „Wer siegt, den werde ich zu einer Säule im Tempel meines Gottes machen (und er wird immer darin bleiben. Und ich werde auf ihn den Namen der Stadt meines Gottes, des neuen Jerusalem . . . schreiben)" (Apk 3,12)[21].

5. Die Textseiten der Evangelien

Trifft unsere bisherige Deutung der *figura codicis* zu, dann muß der vom Leser zu durchlaufende Weg bis zum Evangelienbeginn von der gleichen Maßzahl der ‚Verhüllung' geprägt sein, die den Löwenvorhang (44 Streifen in Analogie zu dem 44 Ellen breiten Bundeszelt) und die Kanontafeln charakterisierte (44 Interkolumnien mit dem in die Sektionsziffern hineinversiegelten Gotteswort). Und in der Tat steht der Leser nach exakt 44 Seiten (fol. 1–22v) erstmals unmittelbar vor dem ‚Allerheiligsten', vor dem ‚Geviert' der Evangelien, in denen sich die ‚Zehn Worte' des Alten Bundes erfüllt haben, und das seinerseits wiederum gesteigert in das ‚Buch des Lebens' der Himmelsstadt eingeht. Nur im Vorübergehen erwähnend, daß die vier Evangelien im einzelnen und untereinander durch den massierten Einsatz von Schmuckseiten klar voneinander abgegrenzt sind, wenden wir uns der Maß-Gestalt der ‚Worte des Lebens' selbst zu.

Der fortlaufende Text der Herrenworte, das wahrhaft ‚goldene' Zentrum des Evangelienbuches, das mit fol. 23r (also auf der 45. Seite) beginnt, bietet zunächst ein Bild klassischer Einfachheit. Rechnet man die monumentale Anfangsinitiale ab, so beginnt die *scriptio continua* stets auf einer gradzahligen Seite. Der Leser hat also immer ein prinzipiell gleichartiges Seitenpaar vor Augen. Nach dem generellen Aufbauschema ist jede Einzelseite für zwei Schriftkolumnen zu je 36 Zeilen eingerichtet[22], d. h. sie enthält insgesamt 72 Zeilen, eine Zahl, die an die 72 Jünger erinnern mag, die Jesus „zu zweit (also in 36 Paaren) voraus in alle Städte (in omnem *civitatem*) und Ortschaften sandte, in die er selbst gehen wollte" (Lk 10,1). Mit-

---

[20] *Quoniam Sapientia dixit: Omnia transibunt, numquam mea verba peribunt* (cf. Lk 21,33).

[21] Fol. 63r: *Qui vicerit, faciam illum columnam in templo Dei mei.*

[22] A. Boeckler, l. c., Abb. 118/124; cf. Tafel IX, Abb. 6.

gemeint sein könnte auch der sich in dieser Zahl dokumentierende universale Anspruch des Evangeliums, das sich während der Weltzeit an alle 72 Völker und Sprachen richtet[23].

Entsprechend hat die reguläre Doppelseite mit ihren (4 × 36 oder 12 × 12 =) 144 Zeilen als codexspezifische Zeilenzahl die Grundmeßzahl der *civitas* Dei, der Gottesstadt, deren Mauer 144 Ellen hoch ist und deren Grundfläche 144 Millionen Quadratstadien (12.000 × 12.000) beträgt (Apk 21,16f.). Ihre 144 Tausend Bewohner (Apk 7,4) symbolisieren die Gesamtzahl der Heiligen, die ‚Erstlingsgabe für Gott und das Lamm‘ (Apk 14,4), denen „eine große Schar aus allen Nationen und Stämmen, Völkern und Sprachen" folgt, „die niemand zählen konnte" (Apk 7,9).

Die vier Goldbänder des heiligen Textes, die als Kolumnen auf jeder Doppelseite aufschimmern und die der Leser 144 mal mit den Augen ‚durchwandern‘ muß, bedeuten dann die Straße im Innern des Neuen Jerusalem, die „aus reinem Gold" ist, und auf der „die Völker wandeln werden": et *ambulabunt gentes per lumen eius* (Apk 21,21. 24).

Soll das vierfach-eine Evangelium mit der ‚viereckig angelegten Himmelsstadt‘, der *civitas in quadro posita* (Apk 21,16) und ihren Maßzahlen wirklich strukturell korrespondieren, dann müßte auch der Raum, den die vier Evangelien im Codex insgesamt einnehmen, zahlenmäßig greifbare Entsprechungen zeigen. Erst wenn der Grundriß der Doppelseite und der Grundriß des gesamten Evangelientextes die gleiche Ordnung, die gleichen Maße aufweisen, scheidet der Zufall als Erklärung für das Gliederungsschema der Textseiten aus.

6. Die Raumzahl der vier Evangelien

Wir fragen deshalb nach dem Raum, den die Evangelien mit ihren Vorstücken im einzelnen und insgesamt in der *structura codicis* einnehmen. Dabei zählen wir jedesmal vom ersten Incipit des Argumentum bis zum Explicit des Einzelevangeliums, legen also das oben aufgezeigte Gliederungsschema des Typus frühmittelalterlicher Evangeliare zugrunde.

Danach umfaßt Matthäus (fol. 17v−56r) 78, Markus (fol. 56v−85r) 58, Lukas (fol. 85v−128r) 86 und Johannes (fol. 128v−161r) genau 66 Seiten. Zusammen sind dies 288 Seiten oder 144 ‚Blätter‘. Ordnet man nun die Evangelien in Form einer Kreuzfigur an, wobei die Stellung derjenigen der Evangelistensymbole im Maiestasbild des goldenen Evangelienbuches entsprechen muß (Jo: oben, Mt: unten; Mk: links, Lk: rechts) so beträgt die vertikale wie die horizontale Summe der Seiten (66 + 78 bzw. 58 + 86) jeweils exakt 144. Das Gleiche gilt, wenn man innerhalb der durch das

---

[23] cf. A. Borst, Der Turmbau zu Babel. Geschichte der Meinungen über Ursprung und Vielfalt der Sprachen und Völker, Bd. II/2, Stuttgart 1959, 625.

Strukturgesetz des Buches bedingten linearen Abfolge jeweils die beiden äußeren mit den beiden inneren Evangelien zusammenfaßt, also ihre chiastische Stellung gemäß der Rangordnung der Autoren (Apostel (Mt) – Apostelschüler (Mk) – Apostelschüler (Lk) – Apostel (Jo)) berücksichtigt.

Schemata

Raummaß der Evangelien   Raummaß der Civitas Dei

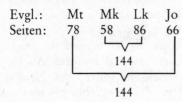

144   144 Ellen hohe Mauer

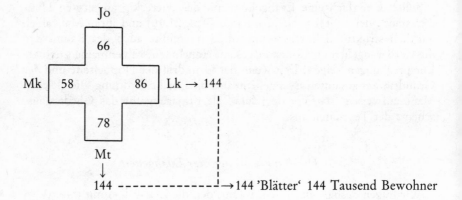

144 ------------------→144 'Blätter' 144 Tausend Bewohner

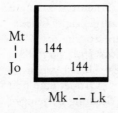

Mk -- Lk   144 Millionen Quadratstadi
                                               Grundfläche

Der auf einen Blick überschaubaren Mikrostruktur einer Doppelseite des heiligen Textes entspricht also genau die nicht ohne weiteres erkennbare Makrostruktur der Ordnung der vier Evangelien. Wie für jede Doppelseite die Folge verso-recto konstitutiv ist, so gilt die gleiche Folge auch für jedes einzelne Evangelium und die Begrenzung ihres Gesamtvolumens (fol. 17v–161r). Den 144 Zeilen in 4 Kolumnen korrespondieren als größere Maßeinheiten die 144 ‚Blätter‘ der 4 Evangelien, die im Medium der Zahl somit in jedem ihrer simultan sichtbaren Teile (= Doppelseite) ganz gegenwärtig sind. Die einzelne Zeile der Goldschrift signifiziert den ‚goldenen Meßstab‘ der Apokalypse, der 144 mal aneinandergelegt die Höhe der Mauer nach Ellen ergibt. Gleichzeitig gliedern die Goldzeilen die ‚viereckig angelegte‘ Doppelseite in 144 Flächeneinheiten, aus denen auch die *civitas in quadro posita*, die Grundfläche der heiligen Stadt besteht, die sich nach ebensoviel Millionen Quadratstadien bemißt. Dem Größenunterschied der beiden Maßeinheiten Elle und Stadie korrespondiert die maßstäbliche Differenz zwischen Zeile und ‚Blatt‘, einzelner Doppelseite und Summe aller Doppelseiten, Einzelspalte und Einzelevangelium. Die Bedeutungsidentität von Mikro- und Makrostruktur und deren Teilmengen wird durch die Identität des jeweiligen Zahlenfaktors garantiert: zwei zusammengehörige Seiten zählen 144 Zeilen, zwei zusammengehörige Evangelien 144 Seiten; vier Kolumnen mit 144 Zeilen entsprechen den vier Einzelevangelien mit insgesamt 144 ‚Blättern‘.

Daß die von uns aus der *structura codicis* überprüfbar abgelesenen Zahlen und Zahlenverhältnisse für das Evangelienbuch Heinrichs spezifisch sind, zeigt ein vergleichender Blick auf den Epternacensis. Zwar ist dessen Text ebenfalls ganz in Gold und zweispaltig geschrieben, doch sind damit die strukturellen Parallelen bereits erschöpft. Die jeweils 39 Zeilen ergeben für die Doppelseite 156 Zeilen. Eine zahlhafte Entsprechung im Bereich der Makrostruktur ist aber nicht zu erkennen, da hier Mt (14v–48v) 69, Mk (49r–72r) 47, Lk (72v–107r) 70 und Jo (107v–135r) 56, insgesamt also 242 Seiten bzw. 121 ‚Blätter‘ zählen. Entsprechend ergibt die chiastische Zusammenfassung der ‚äußeren‘ (125 Seiten) und ‚inneren‘ (117 Seiten) Evangelien weder untereinander noch gar mit der Zeilensumme der Doppelseite eine Identität der Maßeinheit[24].

Welch exakter Planungswille dagegen bei der Konzipierung unseres Codex am Werk war, ergibt sich aus einer weiteren, ebenso frappierenden Tatsache. Vergleicht man die Anzahl der Kapitel der nach ihrer Dignität zusammengehörigen Evangelien mit der Anzahl der für ihren Text benötigten Seiten (Anfangsinitiale bis Explicit), so findet man folgende Relationen: Mt und Jo verteilen (81 + 35 =) 116 Kapitel auf (67 + 53 =) 120 Seiten (23r–56r; 135r–161r), während die 120 Kapitel (= 47 + 73) des Mk und Lk 116 Seiten (= 45 + 71) einnehmen (63r–85r; 93r–128r). Die jeweilige Viererdifferenz der unterschiedlichen Summeneinheiten gleicht sich aus, die Addition der Teilsummen ergibt jeweils die gemeinsame Kennzahl 236.

---

[24] cf. die gleichen Zahlenangaben bei R. Kahsnitz (wie Anm. 11), 107.

7. Zum Miniaturenzyklus der Evangelien

Wie die *civitas in quadro posita*, die als Quadrat (und Kubus) angelegte Himmelsstadt, ganz von der Maßzahl 12 und derem Quadrat bestimmt ist, so ist auch die *quadrata aequalitas sancta*, die heilige Gradheit der Vierzahl der Evangelien[25], nach ihrer Mikro- und Makrostruktur im codicologischen Aufbau des Goldenen Evangelienbuches von der *forma* dieser Zahl geprägt, die schon das Maß gebildet hatte für den Grund, auf dem der ‚Bau‘ des Alten und die Kirche des Neuen Bundes errichtet waren (12 Stämme der Söhne Israels; 12 Apostel).

Man kann sich unschwer die Schwierigkeiten vorstellen, die bei der Planung des Codex zu bewältigen waren, um seine ‚Architektur‘, seine Raummaße, so nach dieser Zahl auszurichten, daß sie auch materialiter als konstitutives Gliederungsmerkmal in Erscheinung trat. Was für die reinen Schriftseiten und ihr Liniensystem relativ einfach sein mochte, mußte sich im Hinblick auf die großräumige Gestaltung der vier Evangelienbücher insgesamt als eine höchst anspruchsvolle Aufgabe erweisen. Die zahlreichen Schmuck- und Prunkseiten, doppelten und einfachen Zierkolumnen, die jeweils Anfang und Ende der drei Teile eines jeden Evangeliums (Argumentum, Kapitelverzeichnis, Text) signalisieren, mußten nach Anzahl und Größe sorgfältig ausgezählt und verteilt werden, um die zweimal (12² =) 144 Seiten für (Mt + Jo) einer- und (Mk + Lk) andererseits und damit die Gesamtzahl von (12² =) 144 ‚Blättern‘ zu erreichen.

Besondere Aufmerksamkeit erforderten bei dieser Verteilungsaufgabe die 50 Miniaturen, die den biblischen Text begleiten. Während der ähnlich umfangreiche Zyklus des Epternacensis auf 16 Seiten zusammengefaßt ist, von denen jeweils vier geschlossen einem der Evangelistenbilder vorangestellt und in drei horizontale Zonen untergliedert sind, wobei jeder der vier selbständigen Illustrationsteile einen Abschnitt des Jesuslebens thematisiert (Mt = Jugend, Mk = Wunder, Lk = Gleichnisse, Jo = Passion bis Geistsendung), folgt unser Codex dem sog. anatolischen System. Er nimmt also keine Rücksicht auf das die vier Evangelien übergreifende Zeitgerüst, sondern ordnet die Miniaturen unmittelbar in den zugehörigen Text ein, läßt also z. B. auf das letzte Bild des Markusevangeliums, die Himmelfahrt, als erstes Bild bei Lukas die Verkündigung an Zacharias und Maria als Doppelszene folgen.

Bei einem derartigen Vorgehen mußte die Verteilung der 7 ganz- und 43 halbseitigen Bilder in erheblichem Maße mitbestimmend für den Gesamtseitenumfang eines Evangeliums sein. Von den 50 Miniaturen finden sich 17 bei Mt, 11 bei Mk, 13 bei Lk und 9 bei Jo, wo zudem noch zwei Szenen, die bereits bei Mt verbildlicht sind (‚Speisung der 5000‘ und

---

[25] Terminus nach Otfrid von Weißenburg, Liber evangeliorum, Ad Liutbertum; cf. J. Rathofer, Zum Bauplan von Otfrids ‚Evangelienbuch‘, in: ZfdA 94 (1965) 36 ff.

‚Abendmahl'), wiederholt werden. Diese ungleichmäßige und scheinbar wahllose Streuung veranlaßte A. Boeckler zu der Festellung, daß „bei der bildlichen Illustration ein bestimmtes gliederndes Prinzip nicht zu erkennen" sei, zumal hier „sogar ohne Rücksicht auf Wiederholungen" vorgegangen werde[26].

Dem wird man zunächst entgegenhalten dürfen, daß bei einer anderen Aufteilung die offensichtlich beabsichtigte Gesamtseitenzahl der chiastisch einander zugeordneten Evangelien ebensowenig hätte erreicht werden können wie die chiastische Proportion zwischen deren Kapitelzahlen und den Seitenzahlen der entsprechenden biblischen Texte. Doch scheint auch sonst nicht bloße Willkür zu walten. So verteilen sich die 7 großen Bilder über die Einzelevangelien nach folgendem Zahlenschlüssel: 1–2–3–1, d. h. die ‚äußeren' Evangelien umschließen mit je einem Großbild die insgeamt fünf ganzseitigen Miniaturen der ‚inneren' Evangelien, so daß sich in der linearen Abfolge zahlenmäßig die Anordnung der 7 Säulen auf den acht Kanontafeln wiederholt, wo 2 Säulen der ‚äußeren' die 5 Säulen der ‚inneren' Arkade umrahmen. Selbst die Tatsache, daß sich diese Säulen in Ausstattung und Farbgebung spiegelsymmetrisch paarweise genau entsprechen, während die mittlere (also vierte) stets von allen unterschieden ist, scheint sich im Miniaturenprogramm zu spiegeln. Denn ausgerechnet das vierte Großbild (Lk: Der barmherzige Samariter, fol. 109r) hebt sich von allen übrigen ab durch seine um sechs beschriebene Zeilen verminderte Größe und durch die eigenwillige Aufgliederung des Hintergrunds der Mittelzone durch neun breite horizontale Goldstreifen.

Doch wenden wir uns der Gesamtzahl der Bilder des Heils zu, die in die ‚Goldstraße' des *Liber vitae* eingefügt sind. Ihre Verteilung auf die Apostel bzw. Apostelschüler unter den Evangelisten ergibt die Teilsummen (17 + 9 =) 26 bzw. (11 + 13 =) 24. Da bei Jo zwei Motive des Mt wiederholt sind, haben beide Gruppen je 24 eigenständige Szenen verbildlicht, wären also gegenseitig in der Meßzahl 2 × 12 austariert. Und bei der Auflistung der Motive wird man – mit A. Boeckler – in der Tat Abendmahl und Brotvermehrung auch „jeweils nur einmal" zählen, unter diesem Aspekt also der 48 vor der Zahl 50 den Vorzug geben. Gewiß wäre damit erneut eine Symmetrie gewonnen, doch kann im Rahmen unserer Fragestellung diese Lösung nicht befriedigen. Denn gerade das meines Wissens einzigartige Faktum einer doppelten Motivwiederholung im Ausstattungsprogramm eines Evangeliars scheint nachdrücklich darauf hinzuweisen, daß man unbedingt eben diese Zahl 50 erreichen wollte.

Zu welchem Zweck indes? Wie die Sieben, die als eigenständige Teilmenge der Bildersumme insgesamt ja besonders hervorgehoben ist, so ist auch die Zahl 50 nach Auffassung der Väter die Zahl des Hl. Geistes, durch den der ‚Bau der Kirche' errichtet wird. Gilt doch der 50. Tag nach der

---

[26] A. Boeckler, l. c., 16; cf. Tafel X, Abb. 8.

Auferstehung Christi, also das erste Pfingstfest mit der Herabkunft des Hl. Geistes, als die eigentliche Geburtsstunde der Weltkirche. Gerade bei Johannes aber weist Jesus in seinen Abschiedsreden während des Mahles immer wieder auf eben diese Sendung des ‚Beistandes‘ hin (14,16. 26; 15,26; 16,7–14). Unser Codex räumt diesem Faktum soviel Bedeutung ein, daß er es in einer eigenen Kapitelüberschrift festhält: *Ubi dicit: Cum venerit Paraclytus* (fol. 131 r, cap. 30). Das letzte Mahl Jesu aber und die dabei verheißene Ausgießung des Geistes sind räumlich eng miteinander verbunden. Wie beide im gleichen Saale (*cenaculum:* Mk 14,5; Lk 22,12 und Apg 2,13) stattfinden, so steht das Abendmahl als 50. Bild am gleichen arithmetischen Ort wie das Pfingstfest (pentekoste = der 50. Tag nach Ostern). Als letztes Bild im Heilsbilderzyklus des Goldenen Evangelienbuches steht das Abendmahl auch funktional an derselben Stelle, an der im Epternacensis das Pfingstereignis bildlich vergegenwärtigt wird, das ja die Evangelien selbst bekanntlich nicht mehr berichten!

Wie stark im Sinne der Vorausbedeutung die Speisung der 5000 und das Abendmahl aufeinander bezogen sind, braucht hier nicht im einzelnen erörtert zu werden. Besonders das 6. Kapitel des Johannesevangeliums zeigt den Zusammenhang zwischen dem vergänglichen Manna in der Wüste und dem neuen ‚Brot des Lebens‘ auf, das sich im Speisungswunder Jesu – wenn auch noch verhüllt im ‚Zeichen‘ – offenbart. Der typologische Bezug scheint sich auch in der *structura codicis* und ihrer zahlhaften Form zu spiegeln. Das ‚Zeichen‘, die Brotvermehrung, wird bei Mt im 10., bei Jo im 5. Bild dargestellt. Das Produkt der beiden Zahlen, die allegorisch stets auf das Alte Testament (10 Gebote, 5 Bücher Mose) hinweisen, ergibt den Stellenwert des Abendmahlsbildes: 10 × 5 = 50.

Damit dürften weder die Tatsache der Motivverdoppelung als solche noch die Wahl der Motive, die im Escorialensis wiederholt werden, rein zufälliger Natur sein. Beides muß vielmehr in Verbindung mit der betonten Endstellung des Abendmahles in der 50er-Reihe der Miniaturen des Heils gesehen werden. Wie in der Zahl 50 die Erfüllung der Geistverheißung gleichsam vorweggenommen ist, so ist in der Schlußstellung des Abendmahls im Bilderzyklus überhaupt auf dessen ‚endgültige‘ Form in der Himmelsstadt verwiesen, wo der Herr von neuem im Reiche seines Vaters mit den Seinen zu Tische sitzen wird (vgl. Mt 26,29; Mk 14,25; Lk 22,30). Diese Deutung wird durch den Codex selbst nahegelegt. Die beiden Abendmahlsbilder nehmen in der Miniaturenfolge ihres Evangeliums jeweils die 16. bzw. 9. Stelle ein. Es erstaunt beinahe nicht mehr, daß das Produkt dieser beiden Ordnungszahlen (16 × 9 =) 144 ergibt, die Grundmaßzahl der Heiligen Stadt und ihrer Bewohner, und daß zwischen dem ersten (fol. 52 r) und dem zweiten Abendmahlsbild (fol. 153 r) genau 100 Blätter liegen, also jene Zahl ausmachen, die das ewige Leben ‚bedeutet‘. In die gleiche Richtung weist die Tatsache, daß die Handschrift in ihrem Schmuckprogramm (fol. 62 v) ausdrücklich auch die beiden

Lohnverheißungen an die Gemeinden zu Ephesus und Pergamon zitiert, in denen der himmlische Mahlgedanke eine entscheidende Rolle spielt: „Dem Sieger werde ich zu essen geben vom Baume des Lebens, der im Paradiese meines Gottes steht"; und: „Dem Sieger werde ich vom verborgenen Manna geben" (Apk 2,7 u. 17)[27].

Bis dahin ist die Kirche, gestärkt durch das ‚Brot des Lebens', das sie in der täglich ‚wiederholten' Feier des Abendmahls bricht, und in der Kraft des pfingstlichen Geistes, der sich in den 50 Bildern des Heils bekundet, die im ‚Buche des Lebens' aufgezeichnet sind, unterwegs zum ‚Hochzeitsmahl des Lammes' (Apk 19,9), in dem das historische und das liturgische Abendmahl „seine Erfüllung im Reiche Gottes findet" (Lk 22,16).

8. Das Perikopenverzeichnis

Dieses Unterwegssein der Kirche auf ihre Vollendung hin findet seinen lebendigsten Ausdruck in der Feier des Kirchenjahres, das immer aufs neue die gesamte Heilszeit erinnernd oder vorwegnehmend in Wort und Sakrament liturgisch vergegenwärtigt. Die Ordnung des Jahreskreises ist im Perikopenverzeichnis nach der Festfolge des Kalenders (Beginn: Weihnachten) festgelegt. Als siebter und letzter Teil beschließt es das Evangelienbuch. Dieses zum Auffinden des jeweiligen Tages-Evangeliums ‚unbedingt notwendige' Capitulare ermöglicht allererst eine Verwendbarkeit des Evangeliars in der Liturgie. Während der Epternacensis kein Perikopenverzeichnis (mehr?[28]) besitzt, umfaßt es in unserer Handschrift insgesamt 19 Seiten, von denen die beiden ersten als Incipit- und Initialseite gestaltet sind. Die restlichen 17 Seiten zeigen alle das gleiche Ausstattungsschema: In zwei grüngrundige Kolumnen sind jeweils genau 17 horizontal verlaufende Purpurfelder eingelegt, auf denen in Goldschrift der jeweilige Festtag sowie Anfangs- und Schlußworte der zu verlesenden Perikope stehn. Jede der 17 Seiten zählt also 2 × 17 Purpurfelder mit ebensovielen Schriftzeilen[29]. Das Ausstattungsschema endet auf der letzten Seite der Handschrift, also mit Blatt 170v, obwohl der Text der Perikopenliste schon auf Blatt 170r schließt. Diese 17 letzten Seiten des Codex gehören zu den 17 Blättern, die auf die letzte der 50 Miniaturen, das Abendmahlsbild (fol. 153r), folgen. Demnach scheint die Bauform des Comes, in dem sich die gesamte Heilszeit sozusagen im Zeitenmikrokosmos des liturgischen Jahres verdichtet, ähnlich von der 17 als Maßzahl bestimmt zu sein, wie der von

---

[27] Wortlaut der Hs.: *Vincenti dabo edere de ligno vitae, quod est in paradiso Dei mei. — Vincenti dabo manna abscondita et in calculo nome(n) novum.* Cf. A. Boeckler, l. c., 22; cf. Tafel XI, Abb. 10.

[28] Hierzu zuletzt R. Kahsnitz, Kommentarband (wie Anm. 10), 124 und 126.

[29] A. Boeckler, l. c., Abb. 157 und 158. cf. Tafel X, Abb. 7.

den Evangelien benötigte Raum von der Zahl 12 und ihrem Vielfachen geprägt wird.

Da die 12 unbezweifelbar eine Affinität zum Raum (,Gottesstadt') aufwies, fragen wir, ob der Zahl 17 möglicherweise eine besondere Kongruenz zur Zeit (als Heilszeit) zugesprochen werden kann. Ihre Symbolwertigkeit kommt in der Väterexegese besonders gern bei der Deutung der 153 Fische zur Sprache, die Petrus nach dem wunderbaren Fischfang im See von Tiberias ans Land zieht (Jo 21,11). Einer der beliebtesten Erklärungsversuche dieser mystischen Zahl geht auf Augustinus zurück. Nach ihm bedeutet die Zahl 153 die unendlich große Fülle der Gläubigen aus allen Völkern und Zeiten, die durch die ,Menschenfischer' für das Gottesreich gewonnen werden, und zwar deshalb, weil 153 die Dreieckszahl von 17 oder ,17 zum Dreieck aufsteigend' sei. Diese Sprechweise besagt, daß 153 sich als Summe ergibt, wenn aus Punkten ein gleichseitiges Dreieck mit einer Seitenlänge von 17 Elementen gebildet und ausgefüllt wird. Anders ausgedrückt: Die Addition der Zahlen von 1 bis 17 ergibt 153. Unter solcher Hinsicht ist jede Dreieckszahl in ihrer Grundzahl oder Basis bereits enthalten und sind beide in ihrer Bedeutung austauschbar.

Die Bedeutung von 17 aber ergibt sich aus der Zerlegung in Einer und Zehner, wobei die 10 auf den Dekalog bezogen wird, der als pars pro toto für den Alten Bund, die Zeit des Gesetzes (*lex*), steht, während die 7 die siebenfache Gnade des Hl. Geistes, also die Zeit des Neuen Bundes (*gratia*), signifiziert. Die beiden Teilsummen, aus denen sich die Grundzahl 17 zusammensetzt, die ihrerseits 153 als Dreieckszahl in sich enthält, zeigen nach Augustinus an, daß das Gebot (= 10) nicht ohne die Gnade (= 7) erfüllt werden kann; denn das Gesetz befiehlt zwar, aber erst die Gnade des Geistes ist es, die hilft, wie er in einem prägnanten Wortspiel formuliert: *lex iubet, gratia iuvat*[30]. Wegen der Bedeutungsidentität von Grund- und Dreieckszahl steht 153 nach dieser Auslegung für die *turba magna, quam dinumerare nemo poterat* (Apk 7,9), für die unzählige Menge aller derer, die durch Gesetz und Gnade gerettet und geheiligt werden.

Möglicherweise bekommt unter diesem Aspekt die Wiederholung von Speisungswunder und Abendmahl im Bilderzyklus der Handschrift ihren eigentlichen Sinn, zumal letzteres ausgerechnet auf fol. 153 plaziert wurde, dem ebenso ausgerechnet noch 17 Blätter bis zum ,Ende' des Codex folgen, das durch die 17 Seiten des Perikopenverzeichnisses mit der 17er-Teilung der Kolumnen in augenfälliger Weise strukturiert wird. Sollte die arithmetische Stellung des letzten Bildes mittels der Zahlensymbolik deutlich machen, daß sich im Abendmahl erfüllt, was Jo 6,49ff. geschrieben steht: „Eure Väter haben in der Wüste das Manna gegessen und sind

---

[30] Ausführlich und mit reichem Belegmaterial hierzu: U. Schwab, Lex et gratia. Der literarische Exkurs Gottfrieds von Straßburg und Hartmanns Gregorius, Messina 1967, 22ff.

gestorben (10 = *lex*) . . . Ich bin das lebendige Brot, das vom Himmel herabgekommen ist. Wer von diesem Brot ißt, wird in Ewigkeit leben" (7 = *gratia*)? Die Wiederholung des Abendmahls jedenfalls ist die Konstante im Ablauf des liturgischen Jahres, in dem alle Stadien der Heilszeit feiernd vergegenwärtigt werden. *Lex* und *gratia*, Gesetz und Gnade, Alter und Neuer Bund, Verheißung und Erfüllung, *umbra* und *imago*: in der 17 als Strukturzahl des Perikopenverzeichnisses findet der Zeitenmakrokosmos der Heilsgeschichte seine mikrokosmische und maß-gerechte Entsprechung.

9. *Gesamtmaß des Codex*

Trifft unsere Deutung der *structura* des Comes evangeliorum zu, dann fällt von der in diesem siebenten und letzten Teil des Codex vorherrschenden Maßzahl 17 möglicherweise auch Licht auf die materialiter am deutlichsten greifbare Maßzahl, die den Grundriß und ,Bau' des ganzen Buches bestimmt, insofern es aus genau 170 Blättern besteht. Es liegt nahe, die Zahl 170 als Produkt der Multiplikation der jeweiligen Teilsummen von 17, nämlich 10 und 7, mit 10 aufzufassen. Der Multiplikator 10 wäre dann im Sinne der Väter als „Zahl der vollkommenen Seligkeit"[31], als der „Lohn eines Denars" (Augustinus[32]), zu deuten. Mit der Gesamtzahl seiner Blätter wiese so der *Liber vitae* in seiner Grundgestalt auf die „eschatologisch-anagogische Dimension der Heilsgeschichte als Verheißung der Zukunft" in der Himmelsstadt hin[33]. Das Goldene Evangelienbuch, das nach seinem im Titulus niedergelegten Selbstverständnis *ex ore Christi diffusus (est)*, signifiziert bereits in seiner *forma numerosa*, daß sein ,Autor' der Erfüller der Zeiten ist. *Lex* (10) und *gratia* (7), die Heilsgeschichte des Alten und Neuen Bundes, kommen in ihm zur Vollendung: (10 + 7) × 10 = 170. *Mensura* und *numerus* des Codex bezeugen das „Grundwort aller Typologie"[34], das Mt 5,17 überliefert: „Denkt nicht, ich sei gekommen, das Gesetz und die Propheten aufzuheben. Ich bin nicht gekommen, um aufzuheben, sondern zu erfüllen". In diesem Zusammenhang verdient Beachtung, daß ausgerechnet das Matthäus-Evangelium 17 Bilder des Heils aufweist und sich das Incipit seines Argumentums, d. h. der Beginn der vier Evangelien überhaupt, auf fol. 17 v befindet.

Wenn das Gesamtmaß des *Liber vitae* vom Zehnfachen der Zahl 17 bestimmt ist, dann schlägt sich in ihm jener typologische Dreischritt nieder, nach dem das Mittelalter den *ordo* der Heilszeit in alttestamentliche Vergangenheit, neutestamentliche Gegenwart und eschatologisch-jenseitige

---

[31] D. Forstner, l. c., 58.
[32] Sermo 252,10, PL 38, 1177; Enn. in Psalm. 110, PL 37, 1463.
[33] F. Ohly, Die Kathedrale als Zeitenraum. Zum Dom von Siena, in: F. Ohly, l. c., 192.
[34] F. Ohly, Synagoge und Ecclesia, in: F. Ohly, l. c., 318.

Zukunft teilte. In der mathematischen Formel $(10 + 7) \times 10$ wäre zugleich das Element der Steigerung ausgedrückt und bewahrt, das Anfang, Mitte und Ende der Zeiten als typologisch aufeinander bezogen bestimmt, d. h. ihre Aufeinanderfolge als Weg vom „Schatten übers Bild zur Wahrheit, vom Erbe durch Erfüllung und Vollendung zur Verklärung" deutet. In der Sprechweise des Ambrosius: *umbra praecessit, secuta est imago, erit veritas; umbra in lege, imago in evangelio, veritas in caelestibus*[35].

Daß diese Denkform über den Zeitenordo des Heils nicht willkürlich über die zahlhafte *structura codicis* in das Goldene Evangelienbuch hineininterpretiert wird, zeigt dessen erster Titulus. In etwas anderer, z. T. johanneischer Terminologie ist von den gleichen drei Zeiten die Rede: *parentes nostri* (vgl. Jo 6,31: *patres nostri* und *patres vestri*: Jo 6,49. 59) — *nos* — *caelestia regna*. Analog dazu verwendet der Text die drei entsprechenden Tempora in seinen Verben: *diffusus (est)* — *amemus* — *capiet*.

III. Ergebnis

Der Versuch, im nachmessenden Durchschreiten des Codex seine äußere und innere Struktur zu erfassen, scheint unsere eingangs aufgestellten Thesen zu bestätigen. Die *forma* des Evangelienbuches ist offenbar weitgehend von ‚be-deutenden' Zahlen geprägt. Ermöglichungsgrund hierfür war das Wort aus der ‚Weisheit Salomonis': *Omnia (in) mensura et numero . . . disposuisti*. Dieses biblische Wort hatte die Zahl als formbildenden Faktor des göttlichen Schöpfungs- und Heilswerkes geheiligt und ihm „metaphysische Dignität" verliehen[36]. Die arithmetische *dispositio* Gottes wurde zum Maßstab auch für das künstlerische Schaffen des Menschen. Wer dem so ‚disponierenden' *rex cunctorum* gar den *Liber vitae*, der *ex ore Christi* hervorgegangen war, als *diadema librorum* überreichen *(ferre)* wollte, mußte sein von Menschenhänden gemachtes Werk nach den gleichen göttlichen Ordnungsgesetzen gestalten. Das Evangelienbuch, das dem Titulus gemäß *vitam continet in se*, konnte nur dann die seinem Offenbarungsinhalt ‚angemessene' Gestalt haben, wenn es von jener *forma numerorum* durchwaltet wurde, die dem *ordo salutis* selbst innewohnte.

Daß Heinrich III. grundsätzlich eine *adaequatio* der äußeren an die innere Gestalt seines Evangeliars anstrebte, geht zumindest für ein signifikantes Strukturelement expresse aus dem zweiten Titulus (fol. 4r) hervor. Der König hat die *verba vitae* in Gold aufgezeichnet, *quoniam Sapientia dixit: Omnia transibunt, numquam mea verba peribunt*. Er beruft sich für sein Vorgehn also auf Lk 21,33: *Caelum et terra transibunt, verba autem mea non transibunt*. Es fällt auf, daß er in diesem Begründungszusammen-

---

[35] F. Ohly (wie Anm. 34), 324.

[36] E. R. Curtius, Europäische Literatur und lateinisches Mittelalter, München ³1961, 494.

hang für Christus den Würdenamen *Sapientia* wählt. Um den Sinn der von der *Sapientia* verkündeten Worte zu erfassen und diesem Sinn eine adäquate und ,be-deutende' Ausdrucksgestalt zu verleihen, bedarf es von Seiten des Auftraggebers und Herstellers (*auro scripsit!*) des Evangelienbuches allerdings ebenfalls der Weisheit. Es kann daher nicht überraschen, wenn der *Heinricus Caesar* gerade in seiner Eigenschaft als königlicher Dedikator des *Liber vitae* im gleichen Titulus als derjenige gerühmt wird, der alle übrigen Menschen an Fähigkeiten und Tugenden überragt (*cui non virtutibus est par*) und an Weisheit übertrifft (*quo non sapientior ullus*)[37].

Gewiß ist damit ausdrücklich noch immer kein Hinweis auf *mensura* und *numerus* und ihre den Welten- und Heilsordo konstituierende Funktion gemäß Sapientia 11,21 gegeben. Doch wußte das Mittelalter um den unauflösbaren Zusammenhang von Weisheit und Zahl, den bereits Augustinus gültig formuliert hatte: „Nicht umsonst ist in den Heiligen Schriften die Zahl mit der Weisheit verbunden, denn es heißt dort: ,Ich ging umher und beugte mein Herz, um zu erkennen, zu betrachten und zu erforschen die Weisheit und die Zahl': *ut scirem et considerarem et quaererem sapientiam et numerum* (Ecl 7,26)"[38]. Weisheit und Zahl und ihre Verbundenheit liegen nicht offen vor jedermanns Blick auf der Hand. Sie erschließen sich nur intensivem Bemühen, für das die Ecclesiastes-Stelle gewissermaßen die methodischen Schritte gleich mit nennt, deren erster und wichtigster das Umhergehn und Durchwandern (*lustrare*) in der Form der Suche (*quaerere*) ist. Auch der Raum- und Zeitenmikrokosmos des Goldenen Evangelienbuches Heinrichs III., in dem sich der zahlhaft bestimmte *ordo salutis* widerspiegelt, will und kann nur *deambulando* und *lustrando* mit dem Geist und allen Sinnen wahrgenommen werden. „Erst das nachschaffende Auge der Erkenntnis weiß ein jedes Ding an seinem Ort"[39].

---

[37] Der gesamte Titulus lautet: *Heinricus Caesar / cui non virtutibus est par / qui rex sit functus / quo non sapientior ullus. / Regi cunctorum / fert hoc diadema librorum. / auro quod scripsit / quoniam Sapientia dixit: / ˊOmnia transibunt / numquam mea verba peribunt.* cf. A. Boeckler, l. c., Abb. 9 und p. 18.

[38] Augustinus, De libero arbitrio II, 24.

[39] F. Ohly, Die Kathedrale als Zeitenraum, l. c. 267. – Es kann kein Zufall sein, daß ganze Passagen dieser grundlegenden Untersuchung Ohlys zur Kathedrale – mutatis mutandis – auch in die Deutung der *structura codicis* des Goldenen Evangelienbuches übernommen werden könnten. Heinrich III. ließ den Codex als *donum* für den damals größten europäischen Dom herstellen, der als Grablege, als ,Zeitengedächtnis', der Salier errichtet wurde. Der Raum des Domes und der immer neu zu öffnende ,Raum' des Buches, der mit Händen, Augen und Stimme im Laufe des Kirchenjahres zu durchmessen und zu durchwandern war, waren gleichermaßen „Ort des liturgischen Gedächtnisses der Zeiten" (Ohly, ibd.,). Auch vom Evangelienbuch gilt, was Ohly zusammenfassend von der Kathedrale (in Klammern jeweils von mir die Alternative hinzugefügt) sagt: „Die Konzeption der Kathedrale (bzw. des Evangelienbuches, Vf.) als Zeitenraum hat ihre Analogie in dem Verständnis der Liturgie als Zeitengedächtnis. Der Raum des Gottesdienstes (bzw. des Gotteswortes, Vf.) und der Gottesdienst, in dem sein Sinn erfüllt ist, harmonieren in der Vergegenwärtigung der Zeiten" (ibd.).

ZUM FORMALEN AUFBAU DER ERZÄHLENDEN WERKE WOLFRAMS VON ESCHENBACH

von Walter Röll (Trier)

Mit Selbstverständlichkeit geht der heutige Leser, wenn er einen Roman aufschlägt, davon aus, daß dieser in Prosa abgefaßt ist. Seit langem ist durch Absätze und in Kapitel gegliederte Prosa das normale Medium des Erzählens. Das war bekanntlich nicht immer so. Im Hochmittelalter etwa, von dem hier die Rede sein soll, wurden Erzählwerke in deutscher Sprache normalerweise in vierhebigen Reimpaarversen verfaßt; nur wenige Dichtungen sind in Strophen geschrieben und ein Roman, der ,Lanzelot‘, in Prosa. Durch Initialen gekennzeichnete Absätze gliedern das Verskontinuum äußerlich, Kapitelanfängen vergleichbare Einschnitte wurden in den meisten Fällen äußerlich nicht gemacht. Semantische Gliederungssignale waren selbstverständlich vorhanden, doch sollen sie hier nur am Rande erwähnt werden. Die Gliederung durch Initialen, deren Sinnbezug wir oft nicht sehen (falls er vorhanden war), ist zudem im allgemeinen uneinheitlich überliefert und nur teilweise noch für das Original rekonstruierbar. Will man den Aufbau eines Erzähltexts dieser Art analysieren, kann die Interpretation des Inhalts zumeist nur wenig durch Hinweise auf die überlieferte Form unterstützt werden; die Überlieferung der Form läßt den Interpreten oft im Stich oder läßt zumindest unterschiedliche Deutungen zu[1].

In den letzten Jahrzehnten ist oftmals versucht worden, nachzuweisen, daß mittelalterliche Dichter bei der Abfassung ihrer Werke Symbolzahlen oder Zahlenproportionen verwandt haben. Die meisten Versuche sind in irgendeiner Weise durch zuvor nicht allgemein anerkannte Annahmen belastet, die den oft beeindruckenden Rechenergebnissen vorausliegen — durch die Annahme zuvor nicht vermuteter Überlieferungsfehler, durch die Annahme von Erzähleinschnitten an Stellen, wo man sie zuvor nicht gesehen hat, durch die Annahme weitreichender arithmetischer Fähigkeiten

[1] Die folgende Darstellung versucht, dem interdisziplinären Charakter des Bandes dadurch Rechnung zu tragen, daß für den Gang der Dinge Wesentliches auch dann vorgetragen wird, wenn es dem Fachmann vertraut sein dürfte. Bei der zugleich geforderten Kürze ist dies vermutlich nicht immer gelungen. Danken möchte ich auch an dieser Stelle Kurt Gärtner und Christoph Gerhardt für ihre Hilfe, sowie Norbert Rehm für seine fachmännische Bestätigung der Richtigkeit meiner Statistik-Ansätze.

der Autoren usw., aber auch durch die Wahllosigkeit des Rückgriffs auf Elemente aus ganz unterschiedlichen Traditionen im Zahlendenken des Mittelalters. Eine kritische Durcharbeitung dieses letzten Bereichs und eine höchst willkommene tragfähige Basis für alle weiteren Arbeiten nicht nur germanistisch-philologischer Provenienz hat 1973 Ernst Hellgardt gelegt[2]. 1975 stellte Heinz Meyer außerdem einen Katalog von Forderungen auf, die erfüllt sein müssen, wenn ein Rückgriff auf die Zahlenallegorese in der Literatur nachgewiesen werden soll[3].

Ziel des vorliegenden Versuchs ist es, die Verwendung von Zahlenproportionen für Werke eines der großen, wenn nicht des größten deutschen Epikers des Mittelalters am ‚Willehalm‘ methodisch hieb- und stichfest nachzuweisen und damit sowohl diejenigen, die symbolischen Zahlengebrauch durch gelehrte Dichter für wahrscheinlich, Zahlenproportionen in der volkssprachlichen Dichtung des hohen Mittelalters hingegen für unwahrscheinlich halten[4], wie diejenigen zu überzeugen, die dergleichen Unternehmungen grundsätzlich für albern oder doch für wenig fruchtbar halten[5]. Hellgardt etwa, um einen hervorragenden Kenner zu zitieren, hat sich recht dezidiert geäußert. Es müsse „unbedingt eine eindeutige, feste Grundlage in der Überlieferung gegeben sein. Weder bei den von Lachmann behandelten Denkmälern noch bei der weitaus größten Zahl der später mit zahlenkompositorischen Kriterien bearbeiteten Texte ist das mit zureichender Sicherheit nachgewiesen"[6]. Wenig später schrieb er: „Von diesen Grundsätzen her bin ich nach wie vor jeder von der Forschung vermeintlich aufgedeckten literarischen Zahlenkomposition gegenüber skeptisch, sei sie nun als rein ästhetisch oder als zahlenallegorisch-bedeutungsträchtig aufgefaßt. Einfache Zahlenkompositionen halte ich für möglich; je komplizierter die Unterstellungen werden, um so geringer wird die Plau-

---

[2] E. Hellgardt, Zum Problem symbolbestimmter und formalästhetischer Zahlenkomposi-. tion in mittelalterlicher Literatur. Mit Studien zum Quadrivium und zur Vorgeschichte des mittelalterlichen Zahlendenkens, München 1973 (= Münchener Texte u. Unters. 45).

[3] H. Meyer, Die Zahlenallegorese im Mittelalter. Methode und Gebrauch, München 1975, 18 f. (= Münstersche Mittelalter-Schriften 25). Für die Frage, ob die Autoren Kompositionszahlen und Proportionen verwandt haben, um die es hier im weiteren geht, ist dieser Katalog allerdings unergiebig.

[4] Als Beispiel sei folgendes zitiert: „Man lasse von derart undichterischen arithmetischen Manipulationen, damit der Blick auf echte, bedeutungshaltige Zahlensymbolik des Mittelalters nicht vernebelt wird": Friedrich Ohly, Wolframs Gebet an den Heiligen Geist im Eingang des ‚Willehalm‘, ZfdA 91 (1961/62) 2 Anm. 9, wiederabgedr. in: Heinz Rupp (Hg.), Wolfram von Eschenbach, Darmstadt 1966, 457 Anm. 9 (= WdF 57).

[5] „Ästhetische Analyse, die etwa Symmetrien aufzeigt und den Kunstcharakter des ‚Willehalm‘ post festum demonstriert, steht angesichts dieses Stoffes und der Konkretheit seiner Gestalt leicht albern da": Karl Bertau, Deutsche Literatur im europäischen Mittelalter, Bd. 2, München 1973, 1160.

[6] Hellgardt, Problem (Anm. 2) S. 267.

sibilität"[7]. Der Versuch eines Nachweises muß es angesichts dieser Skepsis Hellgardts schwer haben — und das ist gut so.

Mit dem Nachweis der Verwendung von Zahlenproportionen soll zugleich gezeigt werden, daß dies in bescheidenem Maße offene Fragen zu beantworten ermöglicht und für anderes neue, in der Überlieferung verankerte Argumente liefert. Dabei ist mir nicht zuletzt wichtig, herauszuarbeiten, daß sich Wolfram von Eschenbach von seinen Zeitgenossen in der Formgebung seiner epischen Großwerke unterscheidet, daß diese Unterschiede alle einer und derselben Wurzel entsprungen sind und daß sich Wolframs gliedernde Durcharbeitung großer Stoffmassen auf diese Weise als subjektiv notwendig und als konsequent begreifen läßt. Auf eine Auseinandersetzung mit der einschlägigen Forschung[8], die zu stets neuem Abschweifen von meinem Ziel zwingen würde, verzichte ich weitgehend; hierzu zwingt schon der begrenzte Raum, der zur Verfügung steht.

Wolfram von Eschenbach hat zwei große epische Texte verfaßt, den ‚Parzival‘ (‚P.‘), dessen erster Teil vor 1204 in Franken entstand, und den ‚Willehalm‘ (‚Wh.‘), um 1217(?) in Thüringen begonnen, die Bearbeitung einer altfranzösischen Chanson de geste ‚Aliscans‘. Im Mittelpunkt der folgenden Ausführungen steht aus methodischen Gründen der ‚Wh.‘, dessen Inhalt zunächst kurz vorgestellt sei. Es handelt sich um eine Episode aus den Heidenkämpfen der Karolingerzeit. Willehalm von Oransche in Südfrankreich ist der Schwager des französischen Königs Loys. Er hat von einem Heidenzug Arabel, die verheiratete Tochter des obersten Heidenkönigs Terramer, mitgebracht und, nach ihrer Taufe auf den Namen Gyburc, geheiratet. Nach langer Zeit kommt Terramer mit einem Heer von zuvor unbekannter Größe an die französische Mittelmeerküste, um Arabel/Gyburc zurückzugewinnen und sich an Willehalm und allen Christen zu rächen. In einer ersten Schlacht wird Willehalms kleines Christenheer nach heroischem Kampf bis zum letzten Mann erschlagen — nur Willehalm entkommt. Sein geliebter, blutjunger Neffe Vivianz stirbt in seinen Armen. Während Gyburc nun mit einer kleinen Besatzung die Burg verteidigt, begibt sich Willehalm zu König Loys nach Munleun (Laon),

---

[7] E. Hellgardt, Victorinisch-zisterziensische Zahlenallegorese. Bemerkungen zu Theorie und Praxis der mittelalterlichen Zahlendeutung, in: Beiträge 98 (Tüb. 1976) 331—350, hier 333 (zu Meyers Anm. 3 genanntem Buch).

[8] Dies sind insbesondere: Richard Kienast, Zur Tektonik von Wolframs ‚Willehalm‘, in: Studien zur deutschen Philologie des Mittelalters, Fs. Fr. Panzer, hg. v. R. Kienast, Heidelberg 1950, 96—115, wiederabgedr. in: Rupp, Wolfram (Anm. 4) S. 427—454. Bernd Schirok, Der Aufbau von Wolframs ‚Parzival‘. Untersuchungen zur Handschriftengliederung, zur Handlungsführung und Erzähltechnik sowie zur Zahlenkomposition, Diss. Freiburg/Br. 1972. Uwe Pörksen und Bernd Schirok, Der Bauplan von Wolframs ‚Willehalm‘, Berlin 1976 (= Philol. Studien u. Quellen 83). Antje Mißfeldt, Die Abschnittsgliederung und ihre Funktion in mhd. Epik. Erzähltechnische Untersuchungen zum ‚König Rother‘, Vorauer und Straßburger ‚Alexander‘, ‚Herzog Ernst‘ (B) und zu Wolframs ‚Willehalm‘ unter Einbeziehung afrz. Laissentechnik, Göppingen 1978 (= GAG 236).

um Hilfe zu holen. Nach manchen Schwierigkeiten stellt ein großer Teil der Vasallen des Königs Truppen-Kontingente, und Willehalm kehrt mit diesen nach Oransche zurück. Umfangreiche Vorbereitungen werden geschildert, dann beginnt eine zweite Schlacht gegen die Heiden, die zunächst lange hin und her tobt; schließlich gelingt in einem Meer von Blut der Sieg über die Heidenheere. Man ist sich in der Forschung nicht darüber einig, ob Wolfram dieses Werk vollendet hat oder nicht. Das erhaltene Ende hat verwundert: Willehalm verabschiedet Matribleiz, einen heidnischen Anführer, und gestattet ihm, die Leichen der gefallenen heidnischen Adligen mitzunehmen. Man rechnet auch mit der Möglichkeit, daß dies nicht das von Wolfram ursprünglich geplante Ende ist, aber auch nicht einfach die Stelle, an der der Autor die Arbeit abbrach, sondern ein Ende, das Wolfram schrieb, als er sah, daß er zur geplanten Ausführung des Rests nicht mehr kommen würde (Notdach-Hypothese).

Die Handlung des ,Wh.' ist nicht nur übersichtlich gegliedert, die Gliederung ist zugleich ungewöhnlich komplex. Wolfram erzählt in Abschnitten zu dreißig Versen[9]. Diese durch Initialen gekennzeichneten Abschnitte sind nicht eigentlich Erzähleinheiten, Sinneinheiten. Das soll nicht heißen, daß es nicht in sehr vielen Fällen syntaktisch-semantisch Einheiten sind — aber es sind nicht notwendigerweise und nicht regelmäßig solche Einheiten, das Merkmal Sinneinschnitt ist nicht konstitutiv. Neun große Handlungseinheiten hat der erste Herausgeber, Karl Lachmann, im ,Wh.' voneinander abgesetzt, und man ist ihm darin allgemein gefolgt[10]. Wie Christoph Gerhardt gezeigt hat[11], wird Wolfram sich hierin an die Aventurengliederung des ,Nibelungenliedes' angelehnt haben — man sollte nicht von Büchern sprechen, wie es üblich ist. Oberhalb der Aventiuren gibt es offensichtlich eine weitere Strukturebene, die der Aventiurenkomplexe. Im ,Wh.' sind diese schon anhand des sehr einfachen Zeit- und des Handlungsschemas voneinander abgrenzbar. Joachim Bumke, der den Forschungsstand zu Wolfram in einer anerkannten Darstellung zusammengefaßt hat, konstatierte[12]: „Die stärksten Einschnitte liegen nach Buch II und Buch IV; sie heben die Munleun-Episode aus dem Handlungsraum der Provence heraus. Bereits in ,Aliscans' ist diese Dreiteilung: erste Schlacht — Mont-

---

[9] Der Abschnitt 57 des ,Wh.' hat — wohl irrtümlich — nur 28 Verse, der Abschnitt 257 des ,P.' 32 Verse; zum letzteren s. Bonath (Anm. 14) S. 67.

[10] Bumke (Anm. 12) meint jetzt in einem die Problemstellung stark verkürzenden Absatz: „Man kann kaum davon ausgehen, daß die Einteilung in neun Großabschnitte den Intentionen des Dichters entspricht" (1981[5], 117).

[11] Chr. Gerhardt, Die Bild- und „aventiure"-Überschriften in der Handschrift V (cod. Vind. 2670) von Wolframs ,Willehalm', in: Studi medievali 3[a] s. 12 (1971) 964—85.

[12] J. Bumke, Wolfram von Eschenbach, Stuttgart 1964, 5. vollst. neu bearb. Aufl. 1981. Ich zitiere an dieser Stelle die Darstellung von 1964 (S. 83), da sie hier prägnanter ist. Bumke hat sie inzwischen ersetzt, diesen Standpunkt aber, soweit ich sehe, in der Neubearbeitung durchaus beibehalten. Vgl. auch z. B. Pörksen-Schirok (Anm. 8) S. 35 u. ö.

laon – zweite Schlacht, die Grundlage des Aufbaus. Die übrigen Grenzen haben weniger Gewicht". Außerdem stehen „die beiden Schlachten . . . bis in die Einzelkämpfe hinein in antithetischer Beziehung zueinander" (S. 85). An einem Einschnitt vor der zweiten Schlacht wird man nicht gut zweifeln können, zumal dies dem von Bumke zu Recht herausgehobenen „symmetrischen Raumschema (Schlachtfeld – Orange – Munleun – Orange – Schlachtfeld)" entspricht. Im Zusammenhang mit der Annahme, daß für Wolfram zunächst jeweils zwei ‚Bücher' zusammengehörten, sieht man diesen Einschnitt normalerweise hinter der VI. Aventiure, also vor dem Aufbruch der Heere nach Alischanz. Genausogut kann der Einschnitt aber dort liegen, wo die Vorbereitungen für die Schlacht abgeschlossen sind, und in der Tat lese ich den Anfang der Aventiure VIII als einen solchen Einsatz: die Schlacht beginnt „genau nach dem Plan, der im VII. Buch angelegt ist"[13]. Die erfolgte Ankunft auf Alischanz und der Beginn der (Schlacht)Handlung auf Alischanz scheinen mir das Gliederungskriterium zu sein.

Lachmanns Gliederung des Texts auf der Aventiuren-Ebene beruhte auf der kritischen Auseinandersetzung mit den beiden vollständigen Textzeugen, die eine Großgliederung aufweisen, der St. Galler Handschrift 857 (G) aus der Mitte (?) des 13. Jahrhunderts[14] und der Wiener Handschrift ÖNB Cod. 2670 (V) von 1320[15]. Der Handschrift G erkannte Lachmann „den ersten platz unter allen mittelhochdeutschen (zu) die ich gesehn habe"[16]. In ihr finden sich große mit Gold und Farbe ausgeführte Initialen und „gemahlte erste zeilen der bücher" (Lachmann), in V große Schmuckinitialen und rot geschriebene Aventiure-Ankündigungen. Die 13 goldenen Initialen in G werden von V fast ausnahmslos[17] bestätigt, wie Werner Schröder dargelegt hat; außerdem bezeugt V einen weiteren Einschnitt gegen Ende des Texts, über den in G hinweggegangen ist. Schröder meinte, die Überlieferung erlaube nicht, diese Gliederung durch goldene Initialen „bereits auf den Archetypus oder gar auf den Dichter selbst zurückzuführen", sie stünden „zweifellos im Dienste einer Gliederung der Erzählung, die bei dem von Wolfram unfertig hinterlassenen Werk noch nicht überall endgültig festgelegt zu sein scheint"[18]. Andererseits teilt er Lach-

---

[13] Pörksen-Schirok (Anm. 8) S. 42.

[14] Zur Datierung der St. Galler Hs. s. den Überblick bei Gesa Bonath, Untersuchungen zur Überlieferung des Parzival Wolframs von Eschenbach, 2 Bd.e Lübeck und Hamburg 1970/71, hier II, 11 Anm. 2 (= Germanische Studien 238f.).

[15] Dies die Siglen der neuen Ausgabe: Wolfram von Eschenbach, Willehalm, hg. v. W. Schröder, Berlin 1978. Lachmann (Anm. 16) hatte sie K und m genannt. Einzelheiten zur Gliederung der beiden Hss. s. bei W. Schröder, Zur Bucheinteilung in Wolframs ‚Willehalm', in: Dvjs 43 (1969) 385–404. Dort auch farbige Faksimiles aus den Hss.

[16] K. Lachmann (Hg.), Wolfram von Eschenbach, Berlin 1833, Vorrede S. XXXV.

[17] Nur fehlt der dritte Anfang infolge Blattverlust. Der achte Anfang ist nur durch Aventiure-Ankündigung, nicht aber durch Initiale gekennzeichnet.

[18] Schröder Dvjs 43 (1969) 402 und Ausgabe (Anm. 15) S. XXIII.

manns Haltung gegenüber den großen Initialen. Lachmann hatte acht seiner Buchanfänge auf Großinitialen gegründet und nur den Anfang von Buch VI statt bei 278,1 schon bei 269,1 festgesetzt. Die übrigen vier Großinitialen von G unterteilen bei ihm die Bücher II−V jeweils und sind durch den Druck hervorgehoben. Lachmann hielt die Gliederung durch diese goldenen Initialen in G also für sinnvoll und ging offenbar davon aus, daß sie gut auf den Dichter zurückgehen könne. Gerhardt hat denn auch bei seinen ‚Wh.'-Studien betont, „dass keinerlei Grund bestehe, von ihr (sc. Handlungsgliederung) abzuweichen, zumal man ohne konjekturale Eingriffe auskommt"[19]. Lachmann schien allerdings eine Reihe von Großgliederungszeichen offenbar höherrangig als andere. Mit beidem dürfte er Recht haben − damit, daß sie auf den Dichter zurückgehen, wie damit, daß sie unterschiedlichen Rang haben −, wenn der Befund auch wohl etwas anders zu verstehen ist, als er dachte.

Die von mir bisher zusammengestellten Gliederungsebenen: Dreißiger, durch goldene Initialen gekennzeichnete Abschnitte, Aventiuren/Bücher, durch Schauplatzwechsel usw. sich ergebende Aventiurenkomplexe stellen eine Gliederungshierarchie dar, wie sie in keinem Werk eines deutschsprachigen Zeitgenossen zu finden ist. Dies ist ein Befund, der als solcher bereits Beachtung verdient. Sieht man sich aber den Umfang der einzelnen Teile des ‚Wh.' im Verhältnis zueinander an, so werden zwei weitere Eigenheiten des Aufbaus sichtbar.

Auf der obersten Ebene sind vier Erzähleinheiten gegeben. Die erste ist durch goldene Initialen dreigeteilt: in die erste Schlacht, Vivianz' Tod und Willehalms Abschied von Oransche, die zweite mit dem Weg nach Munleun und Willehalms Aufenthalt dort ist viergeteilt. Der Teil mit den Vorbereitungen für die zweite Schlacht − also einschließlich Aventiure VIII − hat ebenfalls vier Einheiten und bis zum Ende sind es dann wiederum drei. Die 14 Abschnitte sind in den Proportionen 3:4:4:3 auf vier Erzähleinheiten der obersten Ebene verteilt, und diesem harmonischen Verhältnis 3:4 werden wir gleich noch einmal begegnen.

Die zweite Gliederung nach harmonischen Proportionen ist im Versumfang einzelner Teile zueinander gegeben. Beginnen wir am Anfang. Der erste Hauptteil des ‚Wh.' endet mit Willehalms Aufbruch von Oransche und besteht aus 105 Dreißigern. In ihm wechselt der Schauplatz einmal, vom Schlachtfeld zur Burg. Dies ist nach Vivianz' Tod, nach dem 70. Dreißiger; Wolfram teilte diesen ersten Hauptteil also 70:35, d. h. wie 2:1[20].

[19] Chr. Gerhardt, Zur Überlieferungsgeschichte des ‚Willehalm' Wolframs von Eschenbach, in: Studi medievali 3ª s. 11 (1970) 379 Anm. 22.

[20] Lachmann hatte nicht den Schauplatz-Wechsel, sondern das Ende der Schlacht als den wichtigeren Einschnitt angesehen, genau wie im vierten Hauptteil, s. Anm. 21. Sein Buch II beginnt daher mit 58,1. Wie Gerhardt (Anm. 19) 379 Anm. 22 richtig angemerkt hat,

Hauptteile	Initial-abschnitte	'Bücher'/Aventiuren	Dreißiger	Anzahl d. Dreißiger	Inhalt	Anzahl d. Dreißiger	Proportion
A	1	I	1–57	57	Prolog. 1. Schlacht	70	2
	2	II	58–70	13	Vivianz' Tod		
	3		71–105	35	Willeh. in Oransche	35	1
B	4	III	106–125	20	Wh.s Ritt nach Munleun		
	5		126–161	36	Zusammenstoß mit König Loys		
	6	IV	162–184	23	Versöhnung mit Loys		
	7		185–214	30	Rennewart		
C	8	V	215–245	31	Ankunft der Heere in Oransche	63	3
	9		246–277	32	Bankett der Heerführer		
	10	(⁺VI)	278–313	36	Rennew. u. Gyb., Fürstenrat	84	4
	11	VII	314–361	48	Aufmarsch der Heere		
D	12	VIII	362–402	41	2. Schlacht	84	4
	13	IX	403–445	43	Willehalms Sieg		
	14		446–466	21	Wh.s Klage um Rennewart	21	1

Der Aufbau des ‚Willehalm'

Mit diesem Teil aus drei Initial-Abschnitten scheint das Ende mit ebenfalls drei solchen Abschnitten zu korrespondieren. Auch hier finden sich 105 Dreißiger, und diese sind mit 84:21 wie 4:1 in die zweite Schlacht und Willehalms Sieg gegenüber Willehalms Klage um Rennewart unterteilt[21]. Dieses Ergebnis beruht allerdings auf der Voraussetzung, daß dieser vierte Hauptteil mit der Schlacht beginnt und daß der ‚Wh.' (oder dieser Teil) mit 466,30 endet. Ich habe also davon abgesehen, daß der Text am Ende um die acht Verse 467,1–8 länger ist. Wolfram schloß mitten in einem Dreißiger mit dem Abschied Willehalms von Matribleiz. Möglicherweise sind auch noch 15 weitere Verse von Wolfram, die die beiden

---

dürfte dabei auch der geringe Umfang von 35 Dreißigern für ein Buch ein Argument gewesen sein. Auf jeden Fall halte ich diese Entscheidung Lachmanns für falsch.

[21] Auch Lachmanns Buch IX scheint zu Unrecht direkt nach der 2. Schlacht zu beginnen, vgl. Anm. 20.

Handschriften G und V darüber hinaus überliefern[22]. Wie auch immer: diese „überschüssigen" Verse sind im Zusammenhang mit der Frage zu sehen, ob Wolfram den ‚Wh.' fertiggestellt hat oder nicht. Ich muß darauf zurückkommen.

Es scheint aber nicht nur zwischen den Hauptteilen 1 und 4 eine solche Korrespondenz im Umfang gegeben zu sein, vielmehr gilt dies auch für den dritten Hauptteil mit der Vorbereitung der zweiten Schlacht. Dieser Teil setzt sich aus zwei Komplexen zusammen, deren erster mit den Initialabschnitten 8 und 9 aus 63 Dreißigern, deren anderer mit den Initialabschnitten 10 und 11 aus 84 Dreißigern besteht. Das ist das Verhältnis 3:4 und verhält sich zu den 105 Dreißigern, die im vierten Hauptteil folgen, wie 3:4:5. Alle Teile des ‚Wh.' mit Ausnahme der Munleun-Episode stehen also zueinander in harmonischen Proportionen, wenn man je zwei oder drei Initialabschnitte zusammennimmt. Sie bestehen aus Vielfachen von 21 Dreißigern, und der erste Hauptteil des ‚Wh.' ist auf der Grundlage von 35 Dreißigern aufgeteilt.

Der Umfang der Munleun-Episode, von Initiale 4 bis 8, fügt sich mit seinen 56 + 53 Dreißigern nicht in diesen Zahlenrahmen. Da ich voraussetze, daß die Teile, die zueinander in harmonischen Proportionen stehen, im Umfang abgeschlossen und endgültig fertiggestellt sind, wäre es ein methodischer Fehler, anzunehmen, der Munleun-Teil hätte vom Autor noch bearbeitet werden sollen, auf daß er z. B. 105 statt 109 Dreißiger umfaßt[23]. Vorläufig scheint es mir das beste, keinerlei Schlüsse aus diesen Zahlen des zweiten Hauptteils zu ziehen, oder anzunehmen, daß der Autor den Gegensatz zwischen der südfranzösischen Welt des Glaubenskampfes, in der Vivianz als Märtyrer starb, in der Willehalm Einsiedler und Heiliger wurde, und der nordfranzösischen höfisch-diesseitigen, unheiligen Welt auf diese Weise unterstreichen wollte.

Die vorgetragenen Proportionen im ‚Wh.' sind unzweifelhaft gegeben und die angenommenen Abschnitte und nur diese sind von alter und glaubwürdiger Überlieferung bezeugt. Hellgardts eingangs zitierte Feststellung, daß bei den von Lachmann behandelten Denkmälern die nötige solide Grundlage in der Überlieferung nirgends gegeben sei, ist für den ‚Wh.' nicht haltbar. Es gibt aber eine Möglichkeit, regelrecht zu messen, ob ein Autor wie Wolfram rein zufällig zu den Proportionen für seinen Text gekommen sein dürfte. Wer Studien zur Benutzung von Zahlen und Proportionen in literarischen Texten liest, stößt immer wieder auf die Bemerkung, ein Ergebnis könne nicht auf Zufall beruhen, ohne daß der

---

[22] Hierzu und zur ganzen Problematik des Schlusses vgl. Ernst-Joachim Schmidt, Stellenkommentar zum neunten Buch des Willehalm Wolframs von Eschenbach, Bayreuth 1979, 574—87 (= B.er Beitr. z. Sprachwiss. 3).

[23] Es ist nicht unmöglich, daß es sich so verhält — wir dürfen dies aber nicht annehmen, es sei denn, es ließen sich überzeugende Argumente ganz anderer Art neu beibringen.

Versuch unternommen wird, diese ganz subjektive (und mir sehr oft auch nicht einleuchtende) Meinung methodisch abzusichern. Was alles zufällig möglich ist, zeigt die Lebenspraxis Tag für Tag. So sollte man fragen, wie groß die Wahrscheinlichkeit ist, daß jemand, der unter 85 Zahlen[24] zu wählen hat, bei 8 Versuchen[25] sechsmal eine aus 7 Zahlen[26] einer besonderen Art trifft. Diese Frage läßt sich mit Hilfe der Binominalverteilung beantworten. Statistiker sehen normalerweise ein Signifikanzniveau von 0,001 als strengen Maßstab an, d. h. jedes Ergebnis unter diesem Wert gilt als solide. In diesem Fall liegt das Ergebnis aber um 10^7 darunter, d. h. die Wahrscheinlichkeit, daß Wolfram unbeabsichtigt nur den Umfang zweier Teile nicht harmonisch proportional zu den übrigen bestimmt hat, ist so überaus klein, daß vernünftige Zweifel an seinem planvollen Handeln bei der Festlegung des Umfangs der Teile nicht möglich sind. Dabei hat die geringe Zufallswahrscheinlichkeit in erster Linie in der großen Zahl aufeinander bezogener Teile ihren Grund, d. h. darin, daß Wolfram immer wieder einen Abschnitt fertigstellte und dabei zu einer aus 105 abgeleiteten Zahl von Dreißigern für den Umfang griff.

Das bisher erzielte Ergebnis erlaubt nun, die Erzähleinheit Dreißiger in einem andern Licht zu sehen. Wolframs Dreißiger sind ja primär nicht Sinneinheiten, und keiner seiner Zeitgenossen hat etwas Vergleichbares benutzt. Wolfram schuf sich ein eigenes, zudem abstraktes Maß, das man beim Vortrag nicht hören kann und das man auch beim Lesen nicht wertschätzen kann, weil es nicht sinntragend ist. Es sieht wie ein reines Ornament aus, wie die schrullige Idee eines Kauzes. Aber es war keine Schrulle, es war für Wolfram vielmehr eine Möglichkeit, seine große Versmenge berechenbar zu machen, einen Text nach Zahl und Proportion abzufassen. Die Rechenfähigkeit war im Mittelalter bekanntlich wenig ausgebildet, und es war opportun, wenn nicht gar notwendig, im Zahlenraum unter 1000 zu verbleiben, wenn man rechnen wollte. Dies war bei einem großen Text erst mit Hilfe einer Einheit Dreißiger möglich.

Bevor ich auf die im ‚Wh.‘ vorliegenden Verhältniszahlen eingehe, seien einige Elemente der beiden spekulativen Zahlenwissenschaften Arithmetica und Musica sowie der Geometria zur Zeit Wolframs besprochen. Musik

---

[24] Der größte angenommene Umfang für einen Abschnitt ist 105, der kleinste 21 Dreißiger. Nimmt man als größten Umfang 84 Dreißiger, ist das Rechenergebnis nur rund dreimal so groß, d. h. ebenfalls überaus klein. Wenn man Siebtel von 105 (30, 45, 60, 75) ebenfalls gelten läßt, obwohl sie im ‚Wh.‘ nicht vorkommen, ist bei einem angenommenen Umfang der Abschnitte zwischen 21 und 84 und 10 Trefferzahlen das genannte Signifikanzniveau auch um 10^6 unterschritten.

[25] Jeder der vier Hauptteile des ‚Wh.‘ ist als zweigeteilt aufgefaßt, d. h. der Munleun-Teil, bei dem sich dies nicht aus den Proportionen ergibt, ist analog und in Übereinstimmung mit Lachmanns Bucheinteilung geteilt worden.

[26] Zu den tatsächlich vorkommenden Zahlen 21, 35, 63, 84, 105 sind alle anderen Zahlen hinzuzuzählen, bei denen sich vergleichbare Proportionen ergeben würden. Dies trifft, wenn man nur Drittel und Fünftel von 105 gelten läßt, nur noch auf 42 als siebte Zahl zu.

wie Arithmetik bauten als Teile der Sieben freien Künste unangefochten auf
Boethius' ‚De arithmetica' und ‚De musica' auf. Von ‚De arithmetica'
sind daher über 200 Handschriften erhalten[27]. Aus diesen Quellen wurde
seit alters die Lehre von den grundlegenden Proportionen verbreitet, auf
denen Harmonie[28] beruht. Die Quarte kann durch Verkürzen einer Saite
im Verhältnis 3:4, die Quinte durch Verkürzen im Verhältnis 1:2 erzeugt
werden (wenn auch aus technischen Gründen nicht genau). In der
Arithmetik war unter anderm das Interesse an den numeri perfecti und an
der Entwicklung der Vielheit aus der Einheit, d. h. an bestimmten arithmetischen Zahlenreihen groß. Vollkommen ist eine Zahl, deren Teiler
addiert wiederum diese Zahl ergeben — im ganzen seinerzeit überschauten
Zahlenraum sind dies laut Boethius (I, 20) nur die vier Zahlen 6, 28, 496
und 8128. Die einfachste Zahlenreihe der genannten Art ist 1, 1 + 1,
1 + 1 + 1 usw., d. h. die Reihe der positiven ganzen Zahlen. Boethius
führte aber im Kap. II, 17 auch z. B. folgende Reihen der „Flächen-
zahlen" vor:

$$1, 1 + 2, 1 + 2 + 3, 1 + 2 + 3 + 4 \ldots \text{ oder } 1, 3, 6, 10 \ldots$$
$$1, 1 + 3, 1 + 3 + 5, 1 + 3 + 5 + 7 \ldots \text{ oder } 1, 4, 9, 16 \ldots$$
$$1, 1 + 4, 1 + 4 + 7, 1 + 4 + 7 + 10 \ldots \text{ oder } 1, 5, 12, 22 \ldots$$

Die erste und einfachste dieser Reihen, die Reihe der Dreieckszahlen, wird
auch zur Deutung literarischer Werke immer wieder herangezogen[29]. Proportionen zwischen einzelnen Gliedern dieser Reihe sind nicht häufig,
was bei der Art ihres Entstehens nicht verwundern kann. Unter den ersten
20 Gliedern dieser Reihe, bis 210, findet sich 15 − 45 − 105 − 120,
10 − 120 − 190 − 210 und 21 − 105 − 210, d. h. die Beziehung zwischen 21, 105 und 210 ist im Rahmen dieser Reihe durchaus ungewöhnlich.

Aus der Geometrie seien zwei Maß-Verhältnisse genannt. Das Verhältnis
des Umkreisradius um ein regelmäßiges Zehneck zur Seitenlänge — in der
Praxis leicht konstruierbar[30] — lieferte den goldenen Schnitt $1 : \frac{1}{2}(\sqrt{5-1})$,

---

[27] Alison White, Boethius in the Medieval Quadrivium, in: Boethius. His Life, Thought
and Influence, hg. v. Margaret Gibson, Oxford 1981, 163 und 190 Anm. 12. Die Boethius-
Texte finden sich in der Pat. lat. 63.

[28] Sehr informativ auch über den musikalischen Aspekt hinaus ist der Artikel Harmonie
von Heinrich Hüschen in der MGG 5 (1956) 1588−1614. Vgl. neben Hellgardts (Anm. 2)
auch v. Simons Buch (Anm. 36).

[29] Vgl. Hellgardt, Problem (Anm. 2) S. 66. So ist z. B. im Goldenen Evangeliar Heinrichs
III. die anscheinend kalkulierte Zahl der Seiten in den Evangelien der beiden Apostel Matthäus
und Johannes 66 und 78, was den Dreieckszahlen über 11 und 12 entspricht; s. dazu den Beitrag Johannes Rathofers in diesem Band.

[30] In einem rechtwinkligen Dreieck mit Kathetenlängen im Verhältnis $1 : \frac{1}{2}$ ist die Hypotenuse $\sqrt{5} : 2$. Trägt man hierauf die kürzere Kathete ab, ergibt sich mit $\frac{1}{2}\sqrt{5} - \frac{1}{2}$ das
gesuchte Maß im Verhältnis zur Kathete mit der Länge 1. So konstruiert ist es weder das
Ergebnis der Teilung einer Strecke noch ein Element aus einer beliebig fortsetzbaren Reihe,
wie sie bei dem dem Goldenen Schnitt zugrunde liegenden Prinzip der stetigen Teilung an sich
gegeben ist.

die Beziehungen zwischen den Seitenlängen im pythagoräischen Dreieck das Verhältnis 3:4:5. Im Gegensatz zu diesem letzteren Verhältnis läßt sich das erstere nicht in ganzen Zahlen ausdrücken. Ihrer geometrischen Natur entsprechend sind sie ja Maßverhältnisse und nicht an Zahlen gebunden. Wie für Pi muß man aber auch hier in der Praxis Merkzahlen für Näherungswerte in Gestalt natürlicher Brüche gehabt haben. Dabei lagen zwei Möglichkeiten nahe: (a) analog zu $\frac{22}{7}$ für Pi ein Bruch aus möglichst kleinen Zahlen wie 5:8 − ein recht ungenauer Wert − oder (b) der Bezug auf eine Rundzahl wie Hundert als Ausgangspunkt. Dies müßte Wolfram bei seinem Hang zu Rundzahlen im ‚P.‘ angesprochen haben. In 62:100 liegt 62 nur wenig über dem Maß des Goldenen Schnitts (ca. 61,8034). Auch wenn Belege fehlen, kann man wohl davon ausgehen, daß um 1200 die Kenntnis vom Goldenen Schnitt als Maßverhältnis, wenn sie existiert hat, für den Praktiker im allgemeinen an eine solche Faustregel gebunden war.

Wenn wir uns nun wieder dem ‚Wh.‘ zuwenden und das soeben Dargelegte mit dem dort erhobenen Befund vergleichen, werden die Proportionen in diesem Werk noch besser verständlich. Proportionen, Harmonie, sind Formgebungsgrundlagen in Musik, Architektur und allen Künsten. Was im Verhältnis 1:2, 2:3, 3:4, 3:4:5 oder nach dem goldenen Schnitt geschaffen ist, ist in den Proportionen vollkommen. Genau solche Beziehungen haben wir aber im ‚Wh.‘ gefunden, aufgebaut auf der Zahl 105 und ihren Dritteln und Fünfteln. Nun ist in der Reihe der Dreieckszahlen 105 wie 21 vertreten, 21 für 6, den numerus perfectus, und 105 für 14, die Zahl der Initialabschnitte des ‚Wh.‘. Das mag Zufall sein, auffällig scheint es mir allemal[31] und eine Möglichkeit, die Verwendung gerade dieser Zahlen zu erklären.

Zu wiederholten Malen ist im Lauf der Untersuchung die Frage von Bedeutung gewesen, ob der ‚Wh.‘ vollendet ist oder nicht. Ich komme nun darauf zurück. Bei der Inhaltsbeschreibung habe ich Gyburcs Bruder Rennewart ausgespart. Rennewart ist ein junger Mann mit Zügen eines Riesen, der in Munleun als Gefangener in der königlichen Küche arbeitet. Er zieht mit Willehalm in den Süden und kämpft ganz unhöfisch wie ein Riese, d. h. mit einer Stange, gegen seine heidnischen Verwandten. Am Ende unseres Texts klagt Willehalm über seinen Tod, weil er in der Schlacht vermißt wird. Es wird daher immer wieder die Frage diskutiert, ob Rennewart wirklich tot ist oder ob er ursprünglich wieder auftauchen sollte. Im französischen chanson-de-geste-Zyklus über Wilhelm von Orange hat ‚Aliscans‘ eine Fortsetzung, in der Rennewart der Held ist.

---

[31] Vgl. auch unten zu 325 als Dreieckszahl von 25 im ‚P.‘. Der Gesamtumfang des ‚Wh.‘, 466 Dreißiger (wenn man von den 8 weiteren Versen absieht!), beruht nicht auf einer Dreieckszahl; an 30. Stelle steht dort 465.

Der formale Aufbau des Texts gibt, wie wir gesehen haben, eine Reihe von Hinweisen zur Frage des Fragment-Charakters:

(1) die zweite Hälfte des ‚Wh.‘ hat 63 : 84 : 105 Dreißiger Umfang,

(2) der erste und der vierte Hauptteil haben den gleichen Umfang von (a) drei Initial-Abschnitten und (b) 105 Dreißigern,

(3) der ganze Text ist durch Initialen im Verhältnis 3 : 4 : 4 : 3 gegliedert,

(4) die Grundzahl für die Dreißiger-Proportionen, 105, ist (a) die Dreieckszahl von 14, der Zahl der Initial-Abschnitte, (b) das Produkt von (1,) 3, 5 und 7.

Eine Entscheidung in dieser Frage lassen diese Hinweise m. E. nicht zu. Die Übereinstimmung beispielsweise zwischen dem ersten und dem vierten Hauptteil könnte gerade darauf beruhen, daß der Autor erkannte, daß er einen wesentlich umfangreicheren Plan mit Rennewart als zweitem Helden nicht würde zu Ende führen können. Er suchte daher einen Abschluß zustande zu bringen, der sich auch in den letzten fertiggestellten Teilen mit dem ursprünglichen Zahlenplan vertrug, und stellte zu diesem Zweck gegen Ende der Arbeit die vorliegende Analogie zum ersten Hauptteil her. Die Aufdeckung dieses formalen Aufbaus ermöglicht aber eine andere Entscheidung, wo man bisher nur Vermutungen anstellen konnte. Sie beweist, daß der Text, den wir haben, keinesfalls ein vorläufiger Kladde-Text ist, daß Wolfram vielmehr Teil für Teil, was den Umfang angeht, planmäßig zu Ende führte − und wohl nicht nur im Umfang, sondern bis ins einzelne.

Gut anderthalb Jahrzehnte vor dem ‚Wh.‘ dürfte Wolfram mit der Abfassung seines ersten epischen Großtexts, des ‚P.‘, begonnen haben. Der ‚P.‘ hat stets im Brennpunkt der altgermanistischen Forschung gestanden, und auch der Aufbau ist vielfach besprochen worden. Die folgende Darstellung gilt im wesentlichen dem Nachweis, daß der im ‚Wh.‘ beobachtete Aufbau nicht eine Eigenart dieses Werkes ist, sondern daß Wolfram im ‚P.‘ bereits in vergleichbarer Weise gearbeitet hat. Auch was ohne den Hintergrund der Verhältnisse im ‚Wh.‘ nur vage Vermutung wäre, kann so den Charakter einer Hypothese mit hohem Wahrscheinlichkeitsgrad beanspruchen.

Der ‚P.‘ ist ein Gralsroman, in dem vieles für die Zeitgenossen literarisch neu war. Drei Aspekte dieser literarischen Neuheit seien zunächst kurz vorgestellt: die außerordentliche Länge, die ungewöhnliche Art zu erzählen und die Form der Erzähleinheiten. Was die Länge betrifft, brauchen wir bloß die Romane Hartmanns von Aue von ungefähr 11 000 (‚Erec‘) und ungefähr 8000 Versen (‚Iwein‘) mit den 25 000 Versen des ‚P.‘ zu vergleichen − oder auch die ‚Eneit‘ Heinrichs von Veldeke mit 13 500 Versen[32]. Analysiert man nun die Art, wie Wolfram erzählte, ist der Grund für diese Länge leicht zu entdecken.

Wolfram erzählte im ‚P.' nicht die Geschichte eines Helden, sondern die Geschichte einer Familie in zwei Generationen. Gahmuret, einer der vorzüglichsten höfischen Ritter, hat zwei Söhne, Feirefiz und Parzival. Feirefiz ist schwarz und weiß, weil seine Mutter schwarz ist, ist zunächst Heide und wird später dennoch der Ahnherr des berühmten und rätselhaften christlichen Reichs des Priesters Johannes in Indien. Der zweite Sohn, nicht der erste, ist die zentrale Figur des Werks. Er wird auf seinem Weg zum Gralskönigtum von uns begleitet. Der lebende König, Parzivals Onkel Amfortas, wartet unter unsäglichen Qualen auf denjenigen, der ihn aus dieser erbärmlichen Lage zwischen Leben und Tod erlöst, indem er nach dem Grund dieser Qualen fragt. Niemand anders als Parzival kann andererseits diese Person sein, und Parzival verzichtet aus falschem Anstand auf die Frage, als er seinem Onkel zum ersten Mal begegnet. Es dauert lange, bis er fähig ist, sich richtig zu verhalten, durch die Frage seinen Onkel zu erlösen und selbst Gralskönig zu werden. Wolfram begann nun nicht dort zu erzählen, wo sein Vorgänger, Chrétien de Troyes, mit seiner Gralserzählung eingesetzt hatte, nämlich mit Parzivals Jugend und seinem Aufbruch in die höfische Welt. Wolfram erzählt zuerst einmal von Parzivals Vater und dessen Liebe zu der heidnischen Mohrenkönigin Belakane und später zu Herzelöude. Dies ist ein in sich geschlossener Erzählteil von zwei Aventiuren Umfang, der analog zur ‚Eneit' Heinrichs von Veldeke erzählt ist, wo Aeneas zuerst die liebeskranke Dido liebte, später Lavinia, durch die er zum Ahnherrn Roms wurde. Für die Haupthandlung knüpfte Wolfram an den Sohn Gahmurets und der Herzelöude, an Parzival, an. Von ihm handelt der größere Teil des Romans, aber Parzival hat sich die Handlung wiederum mit Gawan zu teilen, dem vollkommenen Ritter am Hof des König Artus. Wolfram hat als erster in der deutschen Literatur[33] seinen Helden in dieser Weise über weite Strecken ganz beiseite treten lassen, um Aventiuren eines andern zu berichten, wobei er beide Handlungen sorgfältig durch Zeitangaben und Analogien miteinander verband.

Die Handlung des ‚P.' ist mehrsträngig, der Ort wechselt vielfach, Gahmuret, Parzival, Gawan, Feirefiz sind im Aufbau des Werks von erstrangiger Bedeutung, das Werk ist bei weitem komplexer und länger als der

---

[32] Edward Schröder, Der Prolog der Metamorphosen-Bearbeitung des Albrecht von Halberstadt, in: Nachrichten von der Königl. Ges. d. Wiss. zu Göttingen, philol.-hist. Kl. 1909, 80 hat betont, „daß die Metamorphosenbearbeitung des Albrecht von Halberstadt das umfangreichste Werk der deutschen Litteratur vor der Vollendung von Wolframs Parzival war" – allerdings ist der Umfang nur zu erschließen.

[33] In Wolframs Vorlage, dem unvollendeten Gralsroman Chrétiens, war ein Doppelroman angelegt. Wie der französische Autor ihn durchführen wollte, konnte Wolfram dem Fertiggestellten ebensowenig entnehmen wie wir.

‚Wh.‘, seine Strukturierung durch den Autor umso schwieriger, aber auch umso dringender nötig. Als Strukturebenen kennen wir aus dem ‚Wh.‘ die der Dreißiger, der von goldenen Initialen angezeigten Abschnitte, der Aventiuren und der Aventiurenkomplexe (Haupthandlungsteile). Im ‚P.‘ sind alle Elemente zu finden, allerdings ist ihre spätere Ausprägung offenbar erst im Lauf der Arbeit voll entwickelt worden und daher nicht mit derselben Konsequenz vorhanden. Dies ist für die Analyse des Werks eine schwere Hypothek, vergrößert es doch den Spielraum für Spekulationen in unwillkommener Weise.

Die Ebene der durch kleine Initialen gekennzeichneten Abschnitte war schon Teil des ursprünglichen Konzepts des ‚P.‘, allerdings mit einem grundsätzlichen Unterschied zur späteren Praxis: es handelt sich anfangs um Abschnitte unfester Länge. In den Aventiuren V–XVI, so hat Gesa Bonath festgestellt, werden „Abschnitte, die mehr oder weniger als 30 Verse enthielten, ... grundsätzlich durch benachbarte zu einem Mehrfachen von 30 ergänzt. In der Regel betragen die Abweichungen von der Grundzahl 30 nicht mehr als 4 Verse, es kommen jedoch Abweichungen von 6 Versen oder Lücken (= Abstände von 60 Versen) vor. ... In den Büchern I–IV ist die normale Länge der Abschnitte die gleiche wie in den folgenden, nur sind sie nicht auf eine feste Grundzahl bezogen, d. h. ein 32er-Abschnitt wird nicht grundsätzlich durch einen 28er-Abschnitt ergänzt"[34]. Offenbar erst danach kam Wolfram der Gedanke, aus den im Umfang unfesten Abschnitten eine Einheit, ein Maß zu schmieden, das die Voraussetzung für eine Bestimmung des Umfangs anhand formaler Prinzipien ist. Das schon Fertiggestellte hat Wolfram dem folgenden nur ganz äußerlich angepaßt, indem er den Gesamtumfang der Aventiuren I–IV auf eine durch 30 teilbare Verszahl brachte[35]. Dieses Verfahren, Altes in seinem Recht bestehen zu lassen, wenn man zu neuen Anschauungen kommt und Neues anfügt, ist uns fremd, fürs Mittelalter ja aber charakteristisch[36].

---

[34] Zur Überlieferung des ‚P.‘ haben wir die ebenso scharfsinnige wie gründliche Arbeit von G. Bonath (Anm. 14), hier I, 106. Ihr folgten sehr bald die Arbeit von Schirok (Anm. 8) und Rudolf Anton Hofmeister, Manuscript Evidence in Wolfram's *Parzival*, Urbana/Ill.-Thesis 1971. Die von Bonath I, 106 und 120 geäußerte Vermutung, ein ‚Urparzival‘ könnte in 32ern abgefaßt gewesen sein, hat m. E. nicht viel für sich, s. a. Schirok (Anm. 8) S. 458 f. Zum einen ist die Jeschute-Szene 129,5–138,8 „die einzige Episode, die ... ganz in 32ern abgefaßt ist" (I, 120), zum andern steht dem die oben ausgeführte allgemeine Überlegung zur Entwicklung des Dreißigers als Maß entgegen.

[35] Einzelheiten diskutiert G. Bonath (Anm. 14), I, 94–105. Schirok (Anm. 8) geht in seiner Dissertation über diesen Punkt, an dem sonst auch wohl nicht gezweifelt wird, insofern hinweg, als er damit rechnet, daß Wolfram auch nach Einführung des Dreißigers gegen die Logik dieser Neuerung die Zahl der alten Abschnitte, nicht die Vielfachen von Dreißig als Maß genommen habe (S. 547 ff.).

[36] Ein Beispiel aus der Architektur: „Der Baumeister der Kathedrale von Chartes hat sich bemüht, die Ausmaße der romanischen Kirche beizubehalten und sein Bauwerk den Umrissen

Die Zahl von dreißig Versen als Maß für den Umfang seiner Initial-Abschnitte zu wählen legten Wolfram weder die Tradition noch technische Voraussetzungen nahe, so scheint es. Nun ist aber nachweisbar, daß Wolfram im ‚P.' zur Benutzung von Rundzahlen für den Umfang von Großabschnitten tendierte – ich komme darauf noch zu sprechen. Man wird daher auch hier diese Neigung zur Rundzahl für ausschlaggebend halten dürfen.

Wolframs Bemühungen um eine Maßeinheit sind auch vor dem Hintergrund einer schreibtechnischen Neuerung zu sehen, die im allgemeinen zu wenig beachtet wird. Edward Schröder hat 1909 festgestellt, daß es „aus dem 12. Jh., ja aus der Zeit gegen 1210, wo sich der große Umschlag vollzogen hat, kein sicher datierbares Werk in kurzen Reimpaaren (gibt), für dessen erste Edition die Einrichtung mit abgesetzten Versen wahrscheinlich zu machen wäre. . . . Auch die sämtlichen Werke Hartmanns von Aue sind noch in derartigen Erstlingsausgaben hervorgetreten! . . . Schwierig liegt die Sache bei Wolfram von Eschenbach: für den Willehalm steht eine Editio princeps mit Absetzung der Zeilen fest, bei der Publikation des Parzival aber scheint man von der alten Einrichtung, die für die Separatausgabe der ersten Bücher anzunehmen ist, später zu den abgesetzten Versen in Spalten übergegangen zu sein"[37]. Hieran sind nur geringfügige Abstriche zu machen. Es ist sinnvoller, anzunehmen, daß Wolfram den Übergang zu abgesetzten Versen schon vor der Fertigstellung der Aventiuren V und VI des ‚P.' vollzogen hat, zu der Zeit nämlich, als er die Dreißiger als Maßeinheit ins Auge faßte. Der Wandel hat demnach bei Wolfram vor 1204, nicht erst um 1210 stattgefunden.

Im Zusammenhang mit dem Ende der Aventiure VI, und das ist das Ende des um 1204 abgeschlossenen ersten Teils des ‚P.', hat Wolfram wohl zwei reguläre Dreißiger verfaßt, die im Archetypus und daher in allen Ausgaben vor Aventiure III stehen[38]. Diese sogenannte ‚Selbstverteidigung' (114,5–116,4) dürfte Wolfram vom Ende der Aventiure VI entfernt und dem Original lose beigefügt haben; auf jeden Fall stellt

---

der Fulbertschen Krypta anzupassen, obgleich es sich . . . als äußerst schwierig erwies, den alten Bau mit den neuen gotischen Vorstellungen von der Gestalt einer Kathedrale in Einklang zu bringen": O. v. Simson, Die gotische Kathedrale. Beiträge zu ihrer Entstehung und Bedeutung, Darmstadt 1972² (The Gothic Cathedral. Origin of Gotic Architecture and the Medieval Concept of Order, New York 1956), S. 261.

[37] E. Schröder (Anm. 32) S. 89f.

[38] G. Bonath (Anm. 14) I, 65f. Joachim Heinzle hat ihr in seiner Rezension im Anzeiger f. dt. Altertum 84 (1973) 147 widersprochen. Lachmann (Anm. 16) schrieb S. IX: „Die beiden absätze 114,5–116,4, welche nach der Sangaller handschrift noch zum zweiten buche gehören, habe ich abgesondert, weil es mir deutlich zu sein schien daß sie der dichter erst später hinzugefügt hat . . ." Schirok (Anm. 8) schlägt sie zur II. Aventiure, zur Herzelöude-Handlung (S. 547), was zu rechtfertigen schwerhalten dürfte. Dagegen athetiert er die Dreißiger 336f., also den Schluß der Aventiure VI, die im G-Zweig der Überlieferung fehlen (S. 447–90. 563–68).

sie eine Textpartie am Rande des ‚P.'-Textes dar, die nach dem Abschluß der vierten Aventiure entstanden sein wird.

Die St. Galler Handschrift 857, die den ‚Wh.' enthält, ist auch für den ‚P.' ein Haupttextzeuge (D). Auch hier sind große goldgeschmückte Initialen vorhanden, die zum größten Teil in der übrigen Überlieferung eine Stütze haben. G. Bonath kommt zu dem Ergebnis, daß die folgenden großen Initialen für den Archetypus gesichert oder „fast so sicher" sind: alle Aventiuren-Anfänge außer dem von XIII, außerdem Unterteilungen in den Aventiuren III, V, IX und X[39]. Andererseits führt G. Bonath m. E. überzeugend vor, daß Lachmanns Bucheinteilung Zustimmung verdient, wobei die inhaltlichen Elemente, die ein Buch konstituieren, durchaus unterschiedlich sind[40]. Bis zur Aventiure X enthält „jedes Buch eine in sich abgeschlossene Episode, mit Ausnahme der Bücher III. V. IX, in denen 3 bis 5 Episoden zusammengefaßt werden" (I, 114). Im folgenden (X−XIV) ist „das Gefüge der Handlung" „vielfältiger und komplizierter als in den vorhergehenden Büchern. Anstelle von aneinandergereihten, in sich abgeschlossenen Episoden findet man hier verschiedene Handlungsstränge ineinander verflochten". In der Aventiure XIII „geschieht fast nichts. Gawan ist damit beschäftigt, seine Wunden auszuheilen, und wenn es einen Träger der Handlung gibt, so ist dies der Knappe, der mit einer Botschaft ausgesendet wird, sie bei Artus ausrichtet, mit der Erfolgsmeldung zurückkommt. Am Ende des Buches steht der Aufzug des Artusheeres. Wir haben es also nicht mehr mit Episodenfolgen, sondern mit einer grundsätzlich anderen Art der Handlungsführung als bisher zu tun" (I, 116). Lachmanns Gliederungs „macht ein sehr einleuchtendes Bauprinzip sichtbar: Die Bücher X, XI und XII handeln von den Mühen,

---

[39] G. Bonath (Anm. 14) I, 114f. Schirok (Anm. 8) kommt anhand nicht so klarer Kriterien annähernd zum gleichen Ergebnis, findet aber zusätzlich eine große Initiale bei 138,9 „ausreichend" bezeugt (S. 441, Bonath I, 112). Sie ist für meine Untersuchung ohne Bedeutung und konkurriert mit der bei 129,5 wie die bei 446,1 mit der bei 453,1: Gliederungsfunktion für den Text kann m. E. jeweils nur eine haben. Schirok unterscheidet nicht zwischen Archetypus der Überlieferung und Wolframs Exemplar, wie G. Bonath dies tut. Die von Schirok als „gut bezeugt" bezeichnete große Initiale bei 703,1 hat G. Bonath I, 112 offenbar versehentlich nicht diskutiert: sie hat hier einen Teil der Überlieferung nicht beachtet, vgl. Bonath I, 117 Anm. 20 mit Schirok S. 446 und Hofmeister (Anm. 34) S. 743. Nach G. Bonaths Kriterien ist diese große Initiale wohl als „fast sicher" zu übernehmen. Bumkes Ausführungen (Anm. 12) 1981[5], S. 40f. bleiben hinter den Ergebnissen dieser Arbeiten zurück.

[40] Bumke (Anm. 12) kommt zu dem Schluß, es müsse „offenbleiben, in welche Großabschnitte die Dichtung ursprünglich geteilt war": 1981[5], S. 40. Schirok (Anm. 8) diskutiert Lachmanns Bucheinteilung nicht einmal vor dem Hintergrund der Überlieferung der Großinitialen: „weder die Bucheinteilung noch die regelmäßigen Dreißiger sind in der von Lachmann festgesetzten Form haltbar" (S. 544). Seine „zahlenkompositorische Untersuchung" basiert zwar „auf der Analyse der Handschriftengliederung" (S. 569), nimmt diese aber nicht ernst. So gliedert er 116,5−223,30 in 13 − 13 − 18 − 18 − 44 Abschnitte, während die von ihm anerkannten großen Initialen (s. Anm. 39) zu der Gliederung 13 − 9 − 40 − 44 führen würden, und übergeht die große Initiale bei 553,1 in diesem Zusammenhang ganz (S. 547ff.).

die Gawan an je einem [bzw. einem halben] Tag zu bestehen hat. Auch im
XIII. Buch scheint mir das Band, das die Ereignisse zusammenfaßt, ein
Zeitmaß zu sein" (I, 116f.).

Daß es auch zu den Aventiure-Komplexen des ‚Wh.' im ‚P.' eine Entsprechung gibt, versteht sich bei der Zweisträngigkeit der Haupthandlung
und der Vorschaltung einer zweiteiligen Vorgeschichte von selbst. Der
Wendepunkt der Parzival-Handlung und damit der Angelpunkt des

Hauptteile	Aventiuren	Inhalt	Dreißiger	Anzahl d. Dreißiger	weitere gr. Initialen im At
Vorge- schichte	I	Belacane	*1,1 −58,26*		
	II	Herzelöude	*58,27−114,4*		
Parzival	III	Waldleben, Artus Gurnemanz	**116,5** −179,12		*129,5*
	IV	Condwiramurs	**179,13**−223,30		
	V	Munsalvaesche	*224 −279*	56	*256,1*
	VI	Artus	*280 −337[1]*	58	
Gawan	VII	Obilot	*338 −397*	60	
	VIII	Antikonie	*398 −432*	35	
P.	IX	Trevrizent	*433 −502*	70	*446,1 453,1*
Gawan	X	Orgeluse	*503 −552*	50	*523,1*
	XI	Schastel marveile	*553 −582*	30	
	XII	Orgeluse, Gramoflanz	**583** −626	44	
Schlußteil	XIII	Orgeluse, Artus	*627 −678*	52	
	XIV	Artus, Gramoflanz	*679 −733*	55	**703,1**
	XV	Feirefiz	*734 −786*	53	
	XVI	Munsalvaesche	*787 −827*	40 + 1 (Epilog)	

446,1 gr. Initialen, für den A(rche)t(ypus) gesichert
453,1 gr. Initialen, für den At fast sicher bezeugt

[1] Ursprünglicher Platz der ‚Selbstverteidigung' 114,5−116,4?

Der Aufbau des ‚Parzival'

Gesamtwerks ist zweifellos am Ende der IX. Aventiure gegeben, als Parzival durch den Einsiedler Trevrizent Aufklärung über sich und seine Familie erhalten hat. Die zitierten Ausführungen G. Bonaths lassen allerdings auch erkennen, daß die Aufteilung der Aventiuren XIII—XVI nach dem Helden nicht unproblematisch ist[41]. Zum einen ist Gawan in XIII nicht eigentlich der Held und diese Aventiure deutlich von den Tages-Aventiuren davor unterschieden. Zum andern läßt Wolfram Gawan nicht aus dem Blickfeld verschwinden, als Parzival wieder das Geschehen bestimmt, und mit Parzivals Bruder Feirefiz wird auch noch der Erzählfaden der ersten Aventiure aufgenommen. Die letzten Aventiuren können nicht mehr so strukturiert sein wie die davor, der zweite Gawankomplex geht auf eine andere Art zu Ende, als z. B. der Wechsel vom Parzival-Aventiurekomplex III—VI zum Gawan-Aventiurekomplex VII—VIII vonstatten ging: es folgt ein Schlußteil.

Wenn Wolfram den Dreißiger als Recheneinheit konzipiert hat, muß er bald nach Beginn der Arbeit an der Aventiure V an ein Zählen des Umfangs der einzelnen Großabschnitte, der Aventiuren oder der Aventiurenkomplexe, analog zum ,Wh.' gedacht haben. Die zuvor fertiggestellten Abschnitte können dabei eigentlich nur en bloc, d. h. als 221×30 Verse, in eine solche Rechnung eingegangen sein. Nun ist G. Bonath Wolframs bewußter Rückgriff auf Zahlen und Proportionen in zwei Punkten aufgefallen, beim Gesamtumfang des Werks und beim Umfang einzelner Aventiuren[42]. Läßt man die ,Selbstverteidigung' beiseite[43], so hat der ,P.' nämlich $825 \times 30 = 33 \times 25 \times 30$ Verse Umfang, und die Mehrzahl der Aventiuren V—XVI hat einen Umfang, dessen Dreißigerzahl durch 5 teilbar ist.

Dies ist aber durchaus nicht alles, was sich hier feststellen läßt. Der Gesamtumfang ist nämlich offenbar nicht zufällig auf die beiden Inhaltsteile verteilt: bei Parzivals Fortgang von Trevrizent am Ende der neunten Aventiure ist — ohne die ,Selbstverteidigung' — der 500. Dreißiger gefüllt, d. h. der Gesamttext ist durch den Wendepunkt der Handlung in $20 \times 25 + 13 \times 25$ Dreißiger geteilt. Wenn Wolfram in dieser Weise auf 25 Dreißigern als Maß aufgebaut hat, ist die Zahl von 325 (13×25) Dreißigern des zweiten Teils auffällig, da 325 die Dreieckszahl von 25 ist[44]. Die übliche Aufgliederung des Rests von 325 Dreißigern auf Grund des Inhalts

---

[41] Entsprechend schreibt Bumke (Anm. 12): „Buch X—XIV bringen die Gawanhandlung zum Abschluß. Buch XIV ist zugleich auch ein Parzivalbuch" (1981[5], S. 42).

[42] G. Bonath (Anm. 14) I, 67f. Schirok (Anm. 8) erwähnt diese Beobachtungen G. Bonaths nicht, obwohl er auf die 25 als Gliederungszahl (S. 555. 563) wie auf Rundzahlen (S. 555. 560f.) Wert legt.

[43] Das scheint mir zwar begründbar und sinnvoll, erhält seine Rechtfertigung aber doch nur vom Ergebnis her, also im Zirkelschluß.

[44] Schirok (Anm. 8) S. 563. Dies hätte seine Entsprechung in 105 als der Dreieckszahl von 14, der Zahl der Initialabschnitte im ,Wh.'.

mit einem Einschnitt nach Aventiure XIII läßt sich nicht mehr als proportioniert interpretieren. Auffälligerweise ergibt sich aber eine bekannte Proportion, wenn man Gawans drei Tagesabenteuer (X−XII) dem Rest mit seiner „grundsätzlich anderen Art der Handlungsführung" (G. Bonath) gegenüber stellt, nämlich eine Gliederung nach dem Goldenen Schnitt. Wolfram konnte, wie oben angemerkt, wohl auf Grund einer Faustregel zur Aufteilung (X−XII): (XIII−XVI) kommen, indem er das Verhältnis 62:100 verdoppelte: 124:200. Entweder hat er, wenn er dies getan hat, den Epilog-Dreißiger nicht eingerechnet oder dieser ist gerade hinzugekommen, um dem Goldenen Schnitt genauer zu entsprechen[45]. Die Merkmale dieser Gliederung wären also: Goldener Schnitt, Rundzahl 200 plus Epilog für den größeren Teil (wobei zu berücksichtigen ist, daß Wolfram im ‚P.' unbestreitbar eine Neigung zu Rundzahlen zeigt) und inhaltlich die Scheidung der drei Tagesabenteuer Gawans vom Rest. Auch wenn das folgende wie die Verhältnisse im ‚Wh.' als Hintergrund diese Aufgliederung sicherlich stützen, bleibt, daß sie allenfalls plausibel, aber nicht eigentlich nachgewiesen ist[46].

Ganz ohne Wenn und Aber im Archetypus bereits vorhanden sind dagegen die schon von G. Bonath gesehenen Rundzahlen im Umfang der Aventiuren. Allerdings ist es sinnvoll, nur die Zehner-Vielfachen zu betrachten und die von G. Bonath mitberücksichtigten ungeraden Fünfer-Vielfachen beiseite zu lassen. Wolfram hat nicht nur bei 5 von 12 Aventiuren (V−XVI) ein Zehner-Vielfaches als Umfang gewählt, sondern dabei noch zweierlei hineingelegt. Zum einen sind alle fünf denkbaren Zehner-Vielfachen 30, 40, 50, 60, 70 je einmal vertreten[47], zum andern folgen die Zahlen 70 − 50 − 30 aufeinander. Daß dies nicht auf Zufall beruht, wie

---

[45] 324 zu 200,243 zu 123,757 (Differenz zum Ist-Wert 0,243),
325 zu 200,861 zu 124,139 (Differenz zum Ist-Wert 0,139).

[46] Eine andere Rechnung, die mit der obigen konkurriert und deren Ergebnis noch anziehender sein mag, läßt sich aufstellen, wenn G. Bonath mit einer Vermutung Recht haben sollte. Die große Initiale am Anfang von Aventiure XIII ist „sehr unsicher" bezeugt (G. Bonath (Anm. 14) I, 113), und 267, der erste Dreißiger dieser Aventiure, „steht in direktem Bezug zum Schluß des vorhergehenden Buches" (I, 117). Andererseits entspricht der nächste Einsatz 628,1 f. *Gâwân nâch arbeite pflac slâfens den mitten tac* „dem Beginn der Bücher XI (*Grôz müede im zôch diu ougen zuo: sus slief er unze des morgens fruo*) und XII (Ende Buch XI: *Gâwân sich leite slâfen nider.* − Anfang Buch XII: *Swer im nu ruowe naeme*)" (I, 117). G. Bonath vermutet daher zurückhaltend, ob nicht der Beginn der Aventiure XIII erst bei 628,1 liege. In diesem Falle wäre der ‚P.' insgesamt im Verhältnis 500:125:200 Dreißiger oder 20:5:8 aufgeteilt, wobei 5:8 auch einfache und recht ungenaue Näherungsformel für den Goldenen Schnitt ist. Diese Möglichkeit zeichnet sich durch die Reduktion der Hauptproportionen des ‚P.' auf Vielfache von 25 aus, sie baut aber auf einer Konjektur auf, die sicherlich nicht überall auf Zustimmung stoßen wird − und mit der ich meinen oben beschrittenen Weg, die überlieferten Initialen zugrundezulegen, verlassen habe.

[47] Bei der Komposition von 12 Aventiuren im Umfang zwischen 30 und 70 Dreißigern 5mal je eins der 5 Zehnervielfachen 30, 40 . . . 70 zufällig zu erreichen, ist unwahrscheinlich; das Signifikanz-Niveau 0,001 wird um mehr als das Hundertfache unterschritten $(0,0009 \cdot 10^{-2})$.

man zunächst vermuten sollte, ergibt sich aus einer weiteren Besonderheit der Überlieferung. Wie G. Bonath dargelegt hat, sind die Aventiuren IX und X durch große Initialen untergliedert. Die für den Archetypus sichere Initiale bei 446,1 scheint keine gliedernde Funktion zu haben, die andern beiden teilen die Aventiuren aber in ganz auffälliger Weise:

$$IX\ 70 = 20 + 50$$
$$X\ 50 = 20 + 30$$
$$XI\ 30$$

Im Zusammenhang mit den übrigen Zehner-Vielfachen kann man dieses (außer durch die Ausschaltung der Initiale, die der Archetypus bei 446,1 hat) ohne Manipulation aus der Überlieferung abgelesene Ergebnis wohl unangreifbar nennen[48].

Damit wären wir am Ende dieser Untersuchung von Wolframs großen epischen Werken angekommen, die ihrer Strukturierung galt. Es hat sich zunächst zeigen lassen, daß Wolfram seine Texte im Gegensatz zu seinen Zeitgenossen auf mehreren Ebenen strukturiert hat. Die Überlieferung des ‚Wh.‘ bietet ein vollständiges Gliederungsinventar, und beim ‚P.‘ stellt die Überlieferung der Form offenbar ebenfalls eine solidere Grundlage dar, als man vermuten könnte. In beiden Werken hat Wolfram anhand von Zahlen und Proportionen den Umfang von Teilen festgelegt. Eine Voraussetzung hierfür hat er zu Beginn der V. Aventiure des ‚P.‘ mit dem Dreißiger-Maß geschaffen. Wolfram hat dies getan, obwohl kein Publikum diese Rundzahlen und Proportionen hören, kein Leser sein ästhetisches Vergnügen durch Zählen der Dreißiger vergrößern konnte. Er hat sich auf diese Weise des Kunstcharakters seiner Werke versichert. Wolfram tat damit, was auch zeitgenössische Architekten taten. „Der gotische Künstler“, schreibt Otto von Simson, hat „seinen geometrischen Kanon . . . nicht aus rein ästhetischen Gründen angewendet, da er ihn auch dort benützte, wo er für den Beobachter unsichtbar blieb. So umschreiben nach Viollet-le-Duc alle Rippen unter dem Gewölbe der Kathedrale von Reims gleichseitige Dreiecke, geometrische Formen, die vermutlich kein Besucher der Kirche wahrnimmt. Sogar solch rein technische Gegebenheiten wie die Stärke einer Wand oder eines Pfeilers wurden nach rechtem

---

Hierbei ist nicht berücksichtigt, daß Wolfram ja nicht nur jeweils eine dieser Zahlen, sondern jede je einmal verwendet.

[48] G. Bonath (Anm. 14) erwähnt außerdem, daß die Gralsepisode in der V. Aventiure 25 Dreißiger umfaßt (I, 68), betrachtet die große Initiale bei 239,1 aber zu Recht als unsicher (I, 112 f.) – die gut bezeugte Initiale steht bei 256,1. So nahe beieinander können nicht beide Gliederungsfunktion haben. Allerdings ist diese Episode gerade durch eine Fülle von Rundzahlen-Nennungen im Text gekennzeichnet: im Saal sind 100 Kronleuchter, 100 Liegestätten, 100 Kissen. 25 Jungfrauen ziehen in den Saal ein usw. – Bei den Aventiuren VIII und IX folgen als Umfang 35 und 70 aufeinander, ohne daß ich aus diesem vereinzelten Auftreten ganzzahliger Verhältnisse Schlüsse ziehen möchte.

Maß bestimmt"[49]. Der größte Fehler bei der Interpretation der Werke Wolframs ist sicherlich, den Autor zu unterschätzen. Er ist immer wieder für Überraschungen gut. Der angeblich so genialisch-sprunghafte ungelehrte Dichter erweist sich als ein überlegter Planer. Dichten setzt planvolles Handeln voraus. Wolframs gelehrter Zeitgenosse Gottfried von Vinsauf hat dies in seiner ‚Poetria nova' so formuliert:

> Circinus interior mentis praecircinet omne
> materiae spatium. Certus praelimitet ordo
> unde praearripiat cursum stylus, aut ubi Gades
> figat. Opus totum prudens in pectoris arcem
> contrahe, sitque prius in pectore quam sit in ore.
> Mentis in arcano cum rem digesserit ordo,
> materiam verbis veniat vestire poesis[50].

Wolfram hat diese Verse sicherlich nicht gekannt, aber er hätte ihnen offenbar zugestimmt.

---

[49] v. Simson (Anm. 36) S. 33.

[50] V. 55−61, zitiert nach Hans Eggers, Symmetrie und Proportion epischen Erzählens. Studien zur Kunstform Hartmanns von Aue, Stuttgart 1956, 96. Zum ‚P.' s. dort S. 89−91, sowie ders., Strukturprobleme mittelalterlicher Epik, dargestellt am Parzival Wolframs von Eschenbach, Euph. 47 (1953) 264−67; ders., Vom Formenbau mittelhochdeutscher Epen, in: Der Deutschunterricht 11 (1959) H. 2, S. 91.

WER WAR LAURA?
VERSUCH EINER IDENTIFIZIERUNG
DER NAMENTLICH BEKANNTEN UNBEKANNTEN
IN PETRARCAS LIEBESDICHTUNG*

von WILHELM PÖTTERS (Würzburg/Köln)

0. Problemstellung und Ziel der Untersuchung; 1. Die Identität Lauras und der Aufbau des Canzoniere: zwei Seiten eines einzigen Problems; 2. Zweigliedriges Paradigma: diametrales und zyklisches Verhältnis in den Strukturen der dichterischen Aussage der Sonette; 3. Poesie und Geometrie: die Kreisform des Sonetts; 4. 7^3 in der zahlenästhetischen Anordnung der kalendarischen Daten der Liebesgeschichte; 5. Der Zyklus als Kreis; 6. Kreis und Kreisberechnung: Petrarca – ein Mathematiker? 7. Der brennende Wissensdurst („desire" ardente della verità) oder die Philosophie.

0. Problemstellung und Ziel der Untersuchung

Der italienische Dichter und Humanist Francesco Petrarca (1304–1374) hat in seinem lyrischen Werk, dem sog. Canzoniere (= Rime)[1], eine Frau verewigt, über deren Identität der Schleier des Geheimnisses liegt. Gleichermaßen ungelöst ist das Problem des inneren Gefüges des vom Autor Rerum vulgarium fragmenta überschriebenen Zyklus aus 366 Gedichten. Für das biographische Rätsel und für die Frage der Struktur des Werkes soll im folgenden anhand von sieben Thesen eine gemeinsame Lösung ausgekundschaftet werden.

* Herzlich danken möchte der Verfasser Herrn stud. phil. K. Kröll, der die graphischen Darstellungen angefertigt hat, und Herrn Dr. C. H. Kann (Mathematisches Institut der Universität zu Köln), mit dem die mathematischen Probleme der folgenden Interpretation ausführlich besprochen werden konnten.
[1] Canzoniere = Rime = Rime sparse = Rerum vulgarium fragmenta. Zitiert wird im folgenden nach Francesco Petrarca, Canzoniere. Testo critico e introduzione di Gianfranco Contini. Annotazioni di Daniele Ponchiroli, Torino 1964.

1. Die Identität Lauras und der Aufbau des Canzoniere: zwei Seiten eines einzigen Problems

1.1. Explizite Angaben des Dichters zur Person der von ihm besungenen Frau

Das Wenige, was wir über eine angeblich reale Donna Petrarcas wissen, steht weitgehend in den Gedichten selbst[2]. Der Dichter nennt in der Sestine CCCXXXII, Vers 50, ihren Namen: Laura, einmal auch verschlüsselt Laureta, im Sonett V. Außerdem teilt er uns mit peinlich genauer Datierung einige Zeitangaben zu seiner Liebesgeschichte mit. Er sei, so heißt es wörtlich im Sonett CCXI, am 6. April 1327 zur 1. Morgenstunde in das Labyrinth der Leidenschaft eingetreten. Genau 21 Jahre, so entnehmen wir dem Sonett CCCLXIV, habe er vergeblich um die Gunst der immer abweisenden, meist verschleierten Angebeteten geworben. Denn wiederum exakt an jenem fatalen Tage des 6. 4. zur 1. Morgenstunde sei Laura im Pestjahr 1348 gestorben (cfr. Sonett CCCXXXVI). Danach habe er noch, wie es im Sonett CCCLXIV heißt, genau 10 weitere Jahre über ihren Tod geweint, also bis zum April des Jahres 1358. Zweifel an der kalendarischen Echtheit dieser Daten der Liebesgeschichte und damit gleicherweise Bedenken, was die historische Realität der geliebten Donna angeht, sind bereits in den dreißiger Jahren des 14. Jh. einem der ersten Leser der petrarcaschen Liebesgedichte, dem Bischof von Lombez (Gaskogne) und Freund des Dichters, Giacomo Colonna, gekommen. In der Tat muß an den genannten Daten sofort befremdlich erscheinen, daß die Geschichte dieser großen Leidenschaft so unvermittelt mit dem Tage des 6. 4. 1358 abbricht. Hat der Dichter etwa seine vielbesungene Donna für den Rest seines Lebens aus dem Gedächtnis verbannt, obwohl er seine Arbeit an den Gedichten des Canzoniere bekanntlich noch jahrelang nach 1358 fortsetzte? Hinzu kommt, daß Petrarca z. B. das erste Datum gegen die kalendarische Wirklichkeit auf den Karfreitag des Jahres 1327 (cfr. III, 1–2) fallen läßt. Dieser aber lag nicht – wie der Autor vorgibt – auf dem „6", sondern auf dem 10. April[3]. Ein Versehen also oder eine bewußte Fälschung, welche die quellengeschichtliche Forschung nicht hat aufklären können. Unsere Beweisführung wird deshalb nur auf eine sichere Quelle

---

[2] Außerdem an einer Stelle der Trionfi (Triumphus mortis I, 133; ed. Apollonio/Ferro, Rime e Trionfi, Brescia 1972, 745) und in einer Notiz Petrarcas auf seinem Vergil-Kodex (cfr. Ernest Hatch Wilkins, Vita del Petrarca e La formazione del Canzoniere, a cura di Remo Ceserani, Milano 1980, 107).

[3] Zur Diskussion der hier skizzierten Fragen cfr. Carlo Calcaterra, Feria sexta aprilis, in C. Calcaterra, Nella selva del Petrarca, Bologna 1942, 209–245; Enrico Carrara, La leggenda di Laura, in E. Carrara, Studi petrarcheschi ed altri scritti, Torino 1959, 77–111; H. Friedrich, Epochen der italienischen Lyrik, Frankfurt 1964, 192 sqq.; Thomas P. Roche jr., The Calendrical Structure of Petrarch's Canzoniere, in Studies in Philology 71 (1974) 152–172.

zurückgreifen: den Text. Anhand einer Analyse der inneren Struktur der Rime soll nachgewiesen werden, daß die vom Autor in seine Dichtung eingewobenen Zahlen, insbesondere die sog. data fatale des 6. April 1. Morgenstunde, nicht Zahlen eines realen Tagebuchkalenders, sondern vielmehr einige grundlegende − dem Leser als Fingerzeige gebotene − numerische Elemente einer zahlenästhetischen Komposition des Gedichtzyklus darstellen.

1.2. Die Komposition des Canzoniere: Architektur eines „aedificium"

Wie im Streit um Realität oder fiktiven Charakter der Person der geliebten Donna nehmen gewisse Widersprüche in zeitgenössischen Bemerkungen zum Werk Kontroversen und Unzulänglichkeiten in der Erforschung des Formproblems vorweg. Einerseits spricht der Dichter abfällig von den „nugellae" und „ineptiae" seiner poetischen Arbeit. Andererseits erwähnt er jedoch in einem Brief an seinen Freund Giovanni Boccaccio, daß er schon in seiner Jugend die „fundamenta" zum „aedificium" gelegt habe, was im Kontext als Anspielung auf die planvolle Komposition seines lyrischen Opus verstanden werden kann[4]. Die Selbsteinschätzung des Dichters als Architekt eines „Gebäudes" verstärkt also die Vermutung, daß der Canzoniere ein „gebautes", und das heißt im Mittelalter: ein vom Gesetz der Zahl ganz und gar durchwaltetes Werk ist.

1.3. Hypothese:
Konvergenz des biographischen und des strukturellen Problems

Die Frage der Identität der namentlich bekannten Unbekannten in Petrarcas Liebesdichtung und das Problem des inneren Gefüges seines Gedichtzyklus berühren in gleicher Weise das Zentrum des künstlerischen Geheimnisses des Werkes: die inhaltlich-formalen Gesetze der Komposition, die Statik des „aedificium".

2. Zweigliedriges Paradigma: diametrales und zyklisches Verhältnis in den Strukturen der dichterischen Aussage der Sonette

Die unter 1.3. formulierte Hypothese wird im folgenden anhand einer textimmanenten Strukturanalyse überprüft. Als linguistischer Teil unserer

---

[4] Die hier gemeinte Stelle befindet sich in Seniles V, 3. Cfr. G. Fracassetti, Lettere senili di F. P., Firenze 1869, I, 278. Zur Einschätzung des Urteils cfr. Friedrich, op. cit., 187, und Fausto Montanari, Studi sul Canzoniere del Petrarca, Roma 1958, 9 sq.

Interpretation soll zunächst eine grammatikalische Typologie der Sonette, der wichtigsten poetischen Bausteine des „aedificium", entworfen werden. Sie beruht auf den im wesentlichen übereinstimmenden Ergebnissen der bisherigen Petrarca-Forschung[5].

Jenseits der stilistischen Eigentümlichkeiten jedes einzelnen Gedichtes können wir feststellen, daß die gedanklich-sprachlichen Strukturen der Sonette des Canzoniere zwei Bautypen erkennen lassen, die man unter dem Stichwort „zweigliedriges Paradigma"[6] zusammenfassen kann. Je nachdem ob das Verhältnis der zwei Elemente des ein zweigliedriges Paradigma konstituierenden Ganzen einer Aussage (Syntagma, Satz, Text) oppositiv oder komplementär angelegt ist, ergibt sich einer der beiden folgenden Typen. Allerdings stellen manche Sonette Petrarcas Mischformen dar, in denen beide Prinzipien kombiniert sind.

2.1. Antithese oder diametrales Verhältnis

Den ersten, allgemein als charakteristisch angesehenen Haupttypus der Petrarca-Sonette bilden jene Gedichte, in denen der Dichter seine Schmerzliebe mit einer auf einem antithetischen – man könnte auch sagen: diametralen – Verhältnis beruhenden zweigliedrigen Aussage ausdrückt. Mit Oxymora, lexikalischen Antithesen und adversativen Satzstrukturen umschreibt Petrarca in immer neuer Variation das „dolce-amaro" (CXVIII, 5), die bittersüße Erfahrung der kontrastierenden Wirkung der unerfüllten Liebe[7].

---

[5] Eine ausführliche Begründung der im folgenden vorgelegten Typologie kann hier nicht geliefert werden. Wichtigste Anregung war H. Friedrichs Dreiteilung der Petrarca-Sonette (aszendent, zyklisch, antithetisch), die sich noch abstrakter auf eine Charakterisierung nach zwei Kriterien („bewegte Identität" und „bewegte Polarität") zurückführen läßt (Friedrich, op. cit., 168 sq.). Weitere Literatur: Montanari, op. cit.; Umberto Bosco, Francesco Petrarca, Bari 1961; Dámaso Alonso, La poesia del Petrarca e il petrarchismo (Mondo estetico della pluralità), in Studi petrarcheschi 7 (1961) 73–120; Natalino Sapegno, Francesco Petrarca, in E. Cecchi/N. Sapegno, Storia della letteratura italiana, vol. II: Il Trecento, Milano 1965; Giorgio Fulco, Lezioni sul Canzoniere, Napoli 1969; Raffaele Amaturo, Petrarca, in R. Amaturo e. a., Il Trecento. Dalla crisi dell'età comunale all'umanesimo, Bari 1971 (= vol. II, 1 di La letteratura italiana. Storia e testi, a. c. di C. Muscetta); Alfred Noyer-Weidner, Lyrik und Logik in Petrarcas Canzoniere. Zur ‚Gedanklichkeit' in gattungsverschiedenen Gedichten: Solo e pensoso und Chiare, fresche e dolci acque, in Sprachen der Lyrik. Fs. für Hugo Friedrich zum 70. Geburtstag, Frankfurt 1975, 630–667; Giulio Herczeg, La struttura della frase nei versi del Petrarca, in Studi petrarcheschi 7 (1976) 169–196; Antje Wolters, Probleme der Beschreibung antithetischer Sprachfiguren. Studien zur Rhetorik in F. Petrarcas Canzoniere, München 1976.

[6] Zum Begriff cfr. J. Lyons, Introduction to Theoretical Linguistics, Cambridge 1968, 73 sqq.; H. Seiler, Das Paradigma in alter und neuer Sicht, in Kratylos 11 (1966) 190–205; H. Weinrich, Das zweigliedrige Paradigma, in id., Sprache in Texten, Stuttgart 1976, 82–84; E. Leisi, Paar und Sprache. Linguistische Aspekte der Zweierbeziehung, Heidelberg 1978.

[7] Besonders sprechende Beispiele: CXVIII, CXXXII, CXLVIII, CLXXVIII, CCCXII.

Als eine Konstante des ganzen Werkes spannt sich so – über verschiedene Stufen hinweg und mit zunehmendem Grad an Explizitheit – ein Bogen vom Oxymoron „dolce nemica", der süßen Feindin als Bezeichnung für die immer abweisende Geliebte, über die lexikalischen Antithesen und adversativen Satzverknüpfungen innerhalb der einzelnen Gedichte sowie über das nicht selten oppositiv angelegte Verhältnis zwischen einzelnen Sonetten[8] hin zur adversativ konzipierten Zweiteilung nach der üblichen Gliederung „Vita e morte di Laura" und schließlich sogar bis zur konträr strukturierten Aussage des ganzen Zyklus, die der Autor selbst im prologartigen Eingangssonett als Weg vom „jugendlichen Irrtum" (giovenile errore) zur „klaren Erkenntnis" der Vanitas mundi zusammenfassend kennzeichnet (. . . conoscer chiaramente/che quanto piace al mondo è breve sogno). Das Werk ist also in seiner Ganzheit von einer Skala unterschiedlich expliziter paradigmatischer Gegensätze durchzogen.

2.2. Komplementäres oder zyklisches Verhältnis

Der zweiten Gruppe entsprechen jene Sonette, deren Gedankenführung und sprachliche Gestaltung eine Lineatur besitzen, die man mit Hugo Friedrich „zyklisch"[9] nennen kann. Hierzu gehören insbesondere Gedichte mit implikativen Satzstrukturen (Konditional-, Kausal- und Konsekutivgefüge) sowie anderen Formen des Ausdrucks eines komplementären Verhältnisses (z. B. Komparativstrukturen)[10].

2.3. Das Bild des Kreises

Diametrale Zweigliedrigkeit also und zyklischer Verlauf: der Kreis als Sinnbild der Verbindung des Polaren, als Synthese des Antithetischen, ist bei vielen Exegeten der Lyrik Petrarcas beliebt[11]. Der ganze Gedichtzyklus läßt sich als poetische Gestaltung der vom symbolischen Kreis eines Lebensjahres (365 + 1 Gedichte) umschlossenen männlich-weiblichen *amore*-Spannung begreifen. Numerische Merkpunkte dieses Breviers einer unerfüllten „Zweier"-Beziehung sind die über das Werk verteilten „anniversari" der data fatale (6.4., ora 1ᵃ), die der Dichter im Verlauf des insgesamt 31 Jahre umfassenden Tagebuchs immer wieder – gleichsam als

---

[8] z. B. CCXXIX und CCXXX.
[9] Friedrich, op. cit., 167 sq.
[10] Beispiele: XVI, XIX, CXLI, CCXXIV, CCXXXIII etc.
[11] Und nicht nur in der Literatur zu Petrarca-Sonetten, sondern auch in der Sonettforschung überhaupt. Z. B. spricht W. Mönch (in Walter Mönch, Das Sonett. Gestalt und Geschichte, Heidelberg 1955) vom „Zirkelschwung" und „Kreislauf der Reime" sowie von der „kreisrunden Geschlossenheit" des Sonetts (ib., 34 und 48).

Buchführung des Selbstfindungsprozesses und der Erkenntnis des Tempus fugit — verzeichnet. Diese penetrant wiederkehrenden numerischen Elemente können bei einem Dichter wie Petrarca nur einer ganz besonderen künstlerischen Absicht entsprungen sein.

Wenn nun die Metapher des Kreises mit den Linien des Durchmessers und des Umfangs nicht nur auf die Beschreibung der inhaltlichen und sprachlichen Strukturen der Lyrik Petrarcas, speziell der Sonette, beschränkt bleiben soll, muß nach einer formalen Eigenart seiner Dichtkunst geforscht werden, die das streng entsprechende Seitenstück zum Kreismodell der expliziten Ebene des Textes darstellen könnte.

3. Poesie und Geometrie: die Kreisform des Sonetts

Die elementaren Formgesetze des Sonetts sind gesichertes Gut der Forschung[12]. Trotzdem soll hier die Grunddefinition überprüft werden, nach der im Italienischen — der Sprache, in der diese Gedichtform geboren ist — das Sonett aus 14 Zeilen zu je 11 Silben (= endecasillabi) besteht.

3.1. *Das Sonett im autographen Codex Vaticanus 3195*

Ein Blick in das handschriftliche Original des Canzoniere[13] zeigt, daß Petrarca — wie andere Dichter seiner Zeit[14] — seine Sonette anders schrieb, und zwar in der Anordnung 7 Doppelzeilen zu je 22 Silben, wie es die folgende Ablichtung des Sonetts CXVIII zeigt.

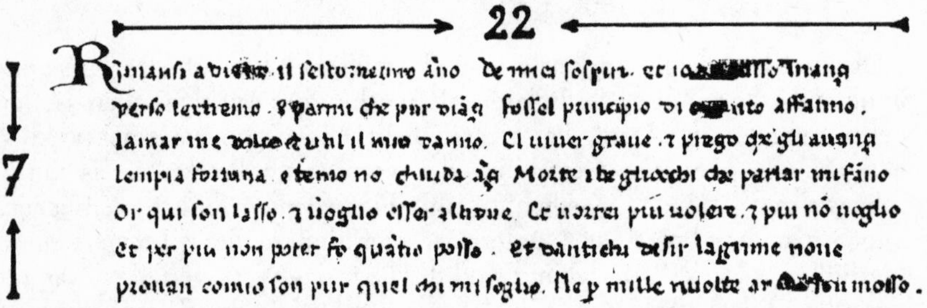

Abbildung 1

---

[12] Außer Mönch op. cit. cfr. Hans-Jürgen Schlütter, Sonett, Stuttgart 1979 (romanistischer Teil von Heinz-Willi Wittschier).

[13] Francisci Petrarche laureati poete Rerum vulgarium fragmenta. L'originale del Canzoniere di Francesco Petrarca. Codice Vaticano Latino 3195. Riprodotto in fototipia, a cura della Biblioteca Vaticana, Milano 1905.

[14] Cfr. L. Biadene, Morfologia del sonetto nei secoli XIII–XIV, Firenze 1977 (anastatischer Nachdruck des im Fasc. 10, vol. IV der Studi di Filologia Romanza, 1888, veröffentlichten Beitrags), 5 sqq.

Diese graphische Darbietung des Sonetts bedeutet nun sicherlich nicht, daß Petrarca nicht die 14 Endecasillabi im Auge gehabt hätte, nennt er doch seine Verskunst „rime", d. h. Verse mit Endreim. Um so mehr dürfen wir in der 7 · 22-Anordnung einen besonderen Grund sehen.

3.2. Die geometrischen Maße des Sonetts

Das im geschriebenen Rechteck gegebene numerische Verhältnis 22 zu 7 deute ich als einen versteckten Hinweis auf einen konkreten geometrischen Kreis mit dem Radius r = 7 und dem halben Umfang $\frac{c}{2}$ = 22.

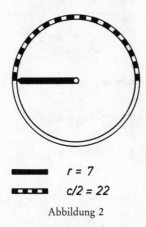

r = 7
c/2 = 22

Abbildung 2

Außerdem ist nun zu bemerken, daß die Basiszahlen des in der 7 · 22-Anordnung geschriebenen Sonetts an Zähler und Nenner des Bruchs $\frac{22}{7}$ erinnern. Das ist der von Archimedes beschriebene, bis auf zwei Stellen nach dem Komma richtige Näherungswert für π ($\frac{22}{7}$ = 3,1428571 gegenüber genauer 3,1415926).

3.3. Der Sonettkreis

Aus den archimedischen Zahlen des Sonetts ergeben sich nun die anderen Abmessungen eines Kreises, den ich wegen seiner völligen Übereinstimmung mit den metrischen Grundzahlen des Sonetts *Sonettkreis* nennen möchte. Es sind dies die Maße, denen kein italienischer Sonettdichter entrinnen kann:
- r = 7 ergibt d = 14 = Zahl der gereimten Verse;
- der Umfang beträgt (nach der Formel c = 2rπ) 14 · $\frac{22}{7}$ = 44, d. h. der Umfang stimmt mit der Silbenzahl eines Quartetts überein, und der halbe Umfang ist identisch mit einer Zeile bei Petrarca;

– die Fläche des Sonettkreises berechnet sich nach der Formel A = r²π, also $7^2 \cdot \frac{22}{7} = 154$, d. h. die Fläche des Sonettkreises entspricht der Summe aller gezählten Silben des (italienischen!) Sonetts: 14 · 11 = 154.

Die errechneten Maße liefern uns die geometrische Figur des dem Sonett entsprechenden Kreises:

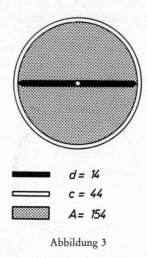

$d = 14$

$c = 44$

$A = 154$

Abbildung 3

3.4. Der geometrische Ursprung des Sonetts

Die ganz besondere Eigenart des Sonettkreises mit r = 7 und $\frac{c}{2} = 22$ besteht darin, daß das Verhältnis von halbem Umfang und Radius eben nicht nur dem Verhältnis nach mit dem archimedischen π-Wert $\frac{22}{7}$ übereinstimmt, sondern darin, daß die Zahlen selbst identisch sind. Die so begründete Übereinstimmung der Kreismaße des Sonetts mit dem archimedischen Kreis kann auf folgende Formel gebracht werden:

$$Sonettkreis = \frac{1/2\,c}{r} = \frac{22}{7} = \pi$$

Aus der Formel läßt sich eine neue Theorie zum eigentlich immer noch ungeklärten Ursprung des Sonetts herleiten[15]. Die mathematische Beweisführung zeigt, daß das Sonett entstanden ist aus der Idee, die klassische Lösung des Mysteriums des Kreises in Dichtung umzusetzen. Das Sonett ist Geometrie in Form von Metrik, sprachlich-rhythmische Konkretisierung der von Archimedes definierten Kreisberechnung. *Das Sonett ist ein Kreis*, und zwar ein Kreis mit den konkreten Maßen $\frac{c}{2} = 22$ und r = 7. Das

---

[15] Cfr. Ernest Hatch Wilkins, The Invention of the Sonnet and Other Studies in Italian Literature, Rom 1959, 11–39; Friedrich, op. cit., 30 sqq.; Schlütter, op. cit., 1 sq. Näheres cfr. W. Pötters, L'origine del sonetto. Una nuova teoria, in Misc. V. Branca (im Druck).

Sonett ist geboren aus dem Geist der Zahl und − was bekannt ist − im Kreis der um Friedrich II. versammelten Dichter-Gelehrten-Beamten am kaiserlichen Hofe in Süditalien und Sizilien[16].

Bei der eminenten Bedeutung der Zahl in der mittelalterlichen Kunst erscheint es ausgeschlossen, daß Petrarca die Konkordanz von *Sonett = Kreis mit r = 7* entgangen sein könnte. Die Wahl des Sonetts liegt sicherlich auch darin begründet, daß der Dichter im geometrischen Sonettkreis der Form den vollendeten Ausdruck der zyklischen bzw. diametralen Lineatur des Inhalts verwirklicht sehen konnte.

Soll nun die These des Sonettkreises nicht lediglich auf einem schönen, aber möglicherweise rein zufälligen Spiel numerischer Übereinstimmungen beschränkt bleiben, wird sie sich als interpretatorischer Schlüssel des ganzen lyrischen Opus zu bewähren haben.

4. 7^3 in der zahlenästhetischen Anordnung der kalendarischen Daten der Liebesgeschichte[17]

Im Gefüge aller Verse und Gedichte ist aber zunächst ein anderes zahlenästhetisches Prinzip zu erkennen. Die kalendarischen Daten der Liebesgeschichte, die sich in den einzelnen sie enthaltenden Gedichten als rationales Element präziser Chronologie durch einen starken Ecart stylistique hervorheben, sind nach einem arithmetischen Gesetz über den Text verteilt: ihre Abstände entsprechen Verssummen, die durch 7^3 bzw. 7^2 teilbar sind. Dieses Prinzip der zahlenästhetischen Anordnung ergibt sich − nach Auszählen aller Verse − aus dem gesonderten Zählen aller Elfsilber und aller Siebensilber, die auf der Ebene der Form die auffälligste zweigliedrige Struktur bilden, und zwar im Canzoniere Petrarcas und in der italienischen Lyrik überhaupt.

4.1. Zahl der Verse

Die Gesamtzahl der Verse des Canzoniere beträgt 7785. Diese Zahl verteilt sich auf die beiden Teile Vita (= I) und Morte (= II) auf 5468 und 2317. Die diese Zahlen voraussetzenden folgenden mathematischen Operationen werden die in der Textüberlieferung nicht immer unumstrittene Zweiteilung der Rime nach dem Sonett CCLXIII als richtig erweisen[18].

---

[16] Ein bekannter Zeitvertreib in diesem Kreis waren mathematische Wettspiele (cfr. Carl B. Boyer, Storia della matematica, Milano 1976, 299).

[17] Zu anderen Aspekten der Daten cfr. Roche, op. cit., und Gianfranco Folena, L'orologio del Petrarca. Estratto da Libri e Documenti, Anno V, N° 3, 1979. Archivio Storico Civico e Biblioteca Trivulziana, Castello Sforzesco, Milano.

[18] Wichtigstes immer wieder angeführtes Gegenargument: erst das Sonett CCLXVII spricht unmißverständlich von einer inzwischen verstorbenen Laura (Oimé il bel viso . . .).

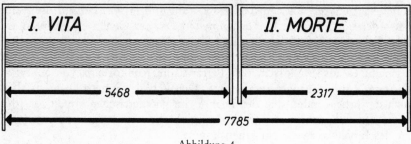

Abbildung 4

4.2. Gesonderte Zählung der Elfsilber und der Siebensilber

Nach Abzug der insgesamt 547 (= I) + 215 (= II) = 762 Siebensilber erhalten wir die Zahl aller Elfsilber, der Bausteine insbesondere der Sonette, nämlich 4921 + 2102 = 7023.

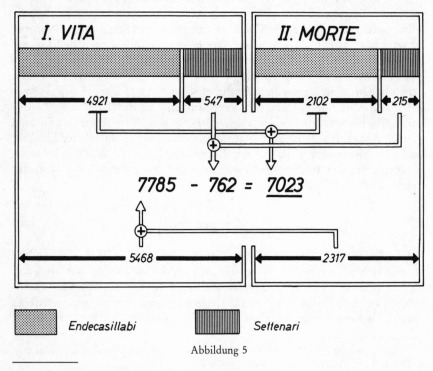

Abbildung 5

Die meisten Herausgeber folgen allerdings der vom Dichter stammenden Einteilung: im Original hat Petrarca nach dem Sonett CCLXIII 7 Seiten blanco gelassen. Der erste der so geteilten zwei Teile hat einen numerisch auffallenden Folienumfang: der letzte Folio trägt — vom Autor selbst paginiert — die Zahl 49 (= 7^2). Angesichts der im folgenden beschriebenen zahlenästhetischen Rolle der Zahl 7 dürfte dies kaum zufällig sein.

4.3. Die Siebenerordnung der „anniversari" der Liebesgeschichte

Das in den drei Summen der Elfsilber andeutungsweise erkennbare Prinzip einer Teilbarkeit durch 7 bestätigt sich in den offenbar genau berechneten Abständen zwischen denjenigen Elfsilbern, in denen der Dichter die kalendarischen Angaben zu seiner Liebesgeschichte macht. Diese expliziten numerischen Markierungen stellen persönliche Anhaltspunkte im fortschreitenden Erkenntnisprozeß vom *errore* zur *verità* dar.

4.3.1. Nehmen wir z. B. den ersten Vers des Sonetts CXVIII (siehe Ablichtung unter 3.1.): Rimansi a dietro il sestodecimo anno. Dieser eindeutig formulierte Hinweis auf den Ablauf des 16. – und somit den Beginn des 17. – Jahres der Leidenschaft ist, fortlaufend durchgezählt, der Vers 2639, nach Abzug der bis zu dieser Stelle vorkommenden 238 Siebensilber aber der 2401. Elfsilber. $2401 = 7^4$ oder – wie wegen der Vergleichbarkeit der folgenden Ergebnisse[19] vorzuziehen ist – $7 \cdot 7^3$.

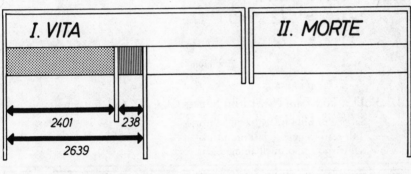

Abbildung 6

4.3.2. Der Mittelpunkt des Liebes-„Labyrinths" findet sich inhaltlich und numerisch im zweiten Terzett des Sonetts CCXI, wo der Augenblick des Verliebens genau bestimmt wird:

> Mille trecento ventisette, a punto
> su l'ora prima, il dí sesto d'aprile
> nel laberinto intrai, né veggio ond'esca.

---

[19] Cfr. auch 5.1.

Der erste Vers dieser überaus exakten Datenangabe ist der 4116. Elfsilber des Canzoniere (vgl. Berechnung in der Skizze). $4116 = 12 \cdot 7^3$, ein offensichtlich markanter Punkt in der numerischen Struktur des Werkes: $12 \cdot 7^3 = 12 \cdot 343 = 3 \cdot 4 \cdot (3 + 4)^3$.

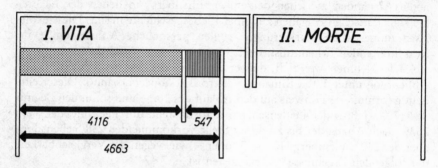

$$4663 - 547 = 4116$$
$$= 12 \cdot 343$$
$$= 12 \cdot 7^3$$

Abbildung 7

4.3.3. Der Tod Lauras wird im Sonett CCCXXXVI mitgeteilt:

Sai che'n mille trecento quarantotto,
il dí sesto d'aprile, in l'ora prima
del corpo uscío quell'anima beata.

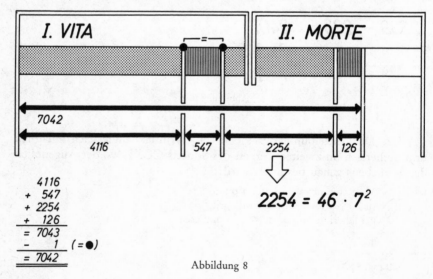

$$
\begin{array}{r}
4116 \\
+ \quad 547 \\
+ \ 2254 \\
+ \quad 126 \\
\hline
= \ 7043 \\
- \qquad 1 \quad (= \bullet) \\
\hline
= \ 7042 \\
\end{array}
$$

$$2254 = 46 \cdot 7^2$$

Abbildung 8

Die Entfernung vom kalendarischen Beginn der Liebe bis zum letzten Vers der Todesnachricht beträgt, nach Abzug der in diesem Teil vorkommenden Siebensilber, 2254 Elfsilber. $2254 = 46 \cdot 7^2$. Dieses Stück des Werkes grenzt sich als besondere Einheit von den durch 7^3 dividierbaren Teilen ab. Auf das neue numerische Element der Zahl 46 müssen wir zurückkommen.

4.3.4. Mittlerweile hat sich durch unsere Zählweise eine Summe von 673 subtrahierten Siebensilbern angesammelt. Zählen wir sie aber zu den 654 Elfsilbern des Endstücks, erhalten wir eine Summe von 1327 Versen. Diese Übereinstimmung mit dem Jahr des Verliebens mag zufällig sein, zumal noch die im Endstück verstreuten 89 Siebensilber als ungeklärter Rest übrigbleiben. Die Summe aller Verse des verbliebenen Schlußteils beträgt mithin $1327 + 89 = 1416$, und zwar Endecasillabi und Settenari zusammen. Die Bedeutung dieser Zahl erschließt sich ebenfalls nicht auf Anhieb. Wir müssen darauf zurückkommen (cfr. 5.5.).

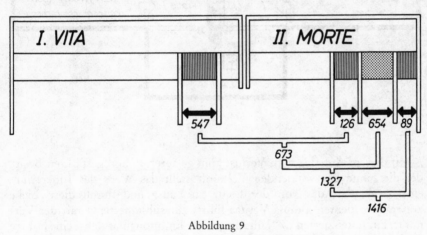

Abbildung 9

4.4. Bedeutung der 7 in der Siebenerordnung der Elfsilber

Die hier angewandte Zählweise bedarf der inhaltlichen Rechtfertigung. Die durch die Subtraktion der Siebensilber ans Licht kommende Siebenerordnung der Elfsilber gehorcht offenbar einem diametralen Prinzip, das dem Merkmal des inhaltlichen Weges vom Irrtum zur Erkenntnis entspricht. Diese Deutung setzt voraus, daß Petrarca der Sieben den geläufigen Symbolwert 7 = „innerer Sitz der Weisheit" (Augustinus[20]) gibt.

---

[20] „sapientiae interior sedes": Augustinus, De libero arbitrio, II, 42 (in Œuvres de Saint-Augustin. VI. Ed. F. J. Thonnard, Paris 1952, 298).

In der antithetischen Strukturierung der dichterischen Aussage entsprechen so einander einerseits die Merkmale „Irrtum" und „Subtraktion der Sieben" als (− ratio) und (− 7) auf der Stufe des Beginns der irdischen Liebe und andererseits die Merkmale (+ ratio) und (+ 7) auf der Stufe der am Ende der Liebesgeschichte gefundenen Wahrheit.

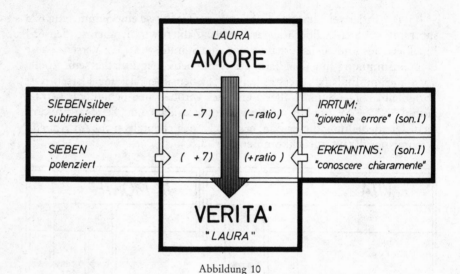

Abbildung 10

Mit diesem Aufstieg vom Verlust zum geläuterten und gestärkten Besitz der die Sinne überwindenden Vernunft stellt das Werk das Itinerarium einer Seele dar, das von der Liebe zu Laura und durch diese Liebe zur transzendenten Donna Veritas führt, zur sublimierten Kraft der Vernunft, zur potenzierten „7", mithin aus der Emotionalität selbst eine höhere Rationalität erwachsen läßt und so die sinnliche Liebe (amor vile) in spirituelle Liebe (amor gentile) verwandelt. Dieses Strukturmodell des Canzoniere kann nur dann Anspruch auf Plausibilität erheben, wenn es gelingt, Lauras Verkörperung des rationalen Prinzips *veritas* aus konkreten Aussagen des Werks heraus zu erklären (cfr. 5.2. und 5.3.).

5. Der Zyklus als Kreis

Zwischen dem Kreis als Formprinzip des Sonetts und der zahlenästhetischen Siebenerordnung gibt es eine kompositorische Verzahnung, die uns eine kreisförmige Konfiguration des ganzen Zyklus erkennen läßt.

5.1. Die architektonische Position des 17. Jahres

Dem Sonett CXVIII, dessen erster Vers als vordere Grenze des 17. Jahres die numerische Position $2401 = 7 \cdot 7^3$ innehat, folgt nach wenigen Kompositionen ein Gedicht, das ähnlich beginnt: Dicesette anni à già rivolto il cielo. Bei fortschreitender Zählung zeigt dieser das Ende des 17. Jahres verkündende Anfangsvers des Sonetts CXXII keine besondere numerische Position. Dagegen trennt ihn vom Schlußvers des 1. Teils des Canzoniere eine Differenz von wiederum exakt $2401 = 7 \cdot 7^3$ Elfsilbern. Mit dieser Zählung einerseits vom Anfang des Werkes bis zum Beginn des 17. Jahres und andererseits vom Ende des 1. Teils an rückwärts bis zum zitierten Endecasillabo, der die hintere Grenze des 17. Jahres bildet, wird das 17. Jahr der Leidenschaft durch symmetrische Gleichheit der den 16 vorhergehenden und der den 4 folgenden Jahren gewidmeten je $7 \cdot 7^3$ ($= 7 \cdot 343$) Elfsilber hervorgehoben.

Das 17. Jahr erstreckt sich vom April 1343 bis zum Osterfest des folgenden Jahres. Die kompositorisch herausgehobene Jahreszahl 1343 (= 17. Jahr der Leidenschaft: $17 = 10 + 7$) ist die Summe aus $1000 + 343 = 10^3 + 7^3$, d. h. die Jahreszahl 1343 enthält als typisches Element (343) die Zahl, die zu ihrer zahlenästhetischen Begrenzung ($343 = 7^3$) im Werk dient.

5.2. Die Position der Canzone CXIX innerhalb des 17. Jahres

Die Zahl der dem 17. Jahr gewidmeten Elfsilber ist $119 = 7 \cdot 17$. Im Mittelpunkt des 17. Jahres steht die Canzone $CXIX = 119 = 7 \cdot 17$. Petrarca schildert hier eine visionäre Begegnung mit Gloria, Fama bzw. Poesia. Diese in ihrer Schönheit die Sonne übertreffende Frau zeigt dem Dichter eine noch schönere Donna, in der die Kommentatoren immer wieder Virtus, Veritas bzw. Philosophia vermutet haben[21]. In seiner lateinischen Schrift Secretum jedenfalls, auf deren Abfassung Petrarca im Commiato der Canzone CXIX verschlüsselt anzuspielen scheint[22], wird die dort ebenfalls im Traum geschaute Lichtgestalt vom Autor selbst Veritas genannt. Die Verse, in denen Gloria, Fama bzw. Poesia ihren Schleier lüftet und dem Dichter das Angesicht ihres zweiten Ichs verspricht, sind die Elfsilber 2440—2478.

Bevor wir nun die inhaltliche und formale Bedeutung dieser wichtigen Textstelle näher beleuchten, sei die auf der Siebenerordnung der Elfsilber und auf der symmetriestiftenden Position des 17. Jahres beruhende Architektur des 1. Teils der Rime in einem Schema zusammenfassend skizziert.

---

[21] Ausführliche Diskussion dieser Frage in der kommentierten Ausgabe von Nicola Zingarelli, Bologna 1964, 698 sqq.

[22] Cfr. CXIX, 106—109: Canzon, chi tua ragion chiamasse oscura, / Di': Non ò cura; perché tosto spero / Ch'altro messaggio il vero / Farà in più chiara voce manifesto.

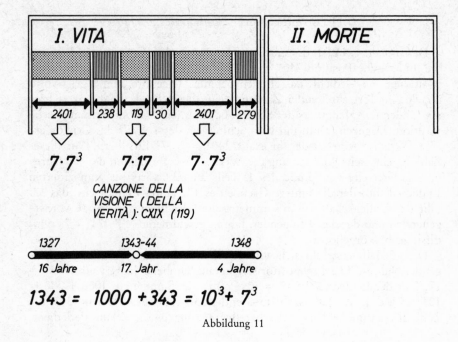

Abbildung 11

5.3. Die zahlenästhetische Stellung der Canzone CXIX
im Gefüge des ganzen Werkes

Am Ende des ersten Teils der Vision, das ist genau der 77. der dem 17. Jahr gewidmeten Elfsilber, tut der Dichter sein brennendes Verlangen nach der Schau der „schöneren Frau" kund:

> . . . ma se de l'esser vostro
> fossi degno udir più, *del desir ardo* (CXIX, 86–87).

Die absolute numerische Position dieses Elfsilbers in der Siebenerordnung der Elfsilber ist $2478 = 2401 + 77 = 7 \cdot 7 \cdot 7 \cdot 7 + 77$.

Mit den Endecasillabi 2479 sqq. wird dem Dichter in seinem Traum ein flüchtiger Blick in die Identität von Fama, Veritas und Laura gewährt. Die ästhetische Sonderstellung dieser den Endpunkt des Weges vom *errore* zur *verità* visionär vorwegnehmenden Verse 2478 und 2479 beruht auf dem skizzierten inhaltlichen sowie auf folgendem formalen Bezug zum ganzen Werk. Aus dem numerischen Verhältnis der Gesamtzahl der Verse des Canzoniere, 7785, zu den beiden – den Übergang vom Diesseits in die Transzendenz und damit die im Jenseits nach dem Schlußwort „pace" erhoffte Vereinigung mit Laura antizipierenden – Versen 2478/9 ergeben sich als Quotienten die beiden Brüche $\frac{7785}{2478}$ und $\frac{7785}{2479}$. Diese beiden Verhältniszahlen stellen die Werte 3,1416464 und 3,1403791 dar. Zwischen den beiden außergewöhnlich exakten Grenzwerten liegt die in der abendländischen Mathematik erst vom 16. Jahrhundert an über die von den Griechen (Archimedes, Heron, Claudius Ptolemäus von Alexandria[23]) her bekannten Werte hinaus noch präziser berechnete Zahl π = 3,1415926 usw.

5.4. Der Kreis des Zyklus (= Makrokreis)

Die Präzision der petrarcaschen Näherungswerte erlaubt es, in den beiden Brüchen aus Gesamtzahl der Verse des Werkes und Kernstelle der Wahrheitsvision ein vom Autor selbst im vorhinein berechnetes Verhältnis von Umfang und Durchmesser eines das ganze „aedificium" umfassenden Universalkreises zu sehen. Dieser stellt in der Makroeinheit der Rime das folgerichtige Gegenstück zum Sonettkreis als ästhetisch-mathematischer Mikroeinheit dar. Der Zyklus ist das, was sein Name etymologisch vorschreibt: ein „cyclos", ein Kreis mit den Maßen c = 7785 und d = 2478.

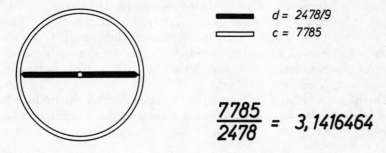

$$d = 2478/9$$
$$c = 7785$$

$$\frac{7785}{2478} = 3,1416464$$

Abbildung 12

Übersehen wir aber nicht die wenn auch nur minimale Ungenauigkeit der rekonstruierten Berechnung des Makrokreises. Da der im Kontrapunkt zum Beginn der Leidenschaft, der „jugendlichen Verirrung", im Vers 2478 geäußerte brennende Wissensdurst die Kreismaße des Gesamtwerkes — sozusagen von der dritten Stelle nach dem Komma an — zu sprengen beginnt, wird die endgültige Schau der Wahrheit zwangsläufig erst nach dem Schlußwort der Rime — „pace", das ist Frieden und Befriedigung der rastlos suchenden Seele — möglich sein. Sie liegt außerhalb der menschlich unvollkommenen Vorstellung vom Kreise.

---

[23] Cfr. infra 6.3.

5.5. *Der Kreis des Zyklus und die* data fatale *des 6.4., 1. Morgenstunde*

3,1416464 – der genauere der beiden π-Werte Petrarcas – zeigt über die Übereinstimmung mit den Maßen des Universalkreises hinaus auffällige Konkordanzen mit dem ominösen Datum der Liebesgeschichte, dem 6. April zur 1. Morgenstunde, und mit der Siebenerordnung der zahlenästhetischen Makrostruktur des Canzoniere.

Die Gesamtzahl der Rime teilt sich, wie wir unter Punkt 4.3. gesehen haben, in drei große Blöcke:

    I. 4116 Elfsilber bis zum Vers, der das Jahr des Verliebens angibt;

    II. $46 \cdot 7^2$ Elfsilber vom Datum der ersten Begegnung, dem Eintreten ins „laberinto", bis zur Todesnachricht;

    III. 1416 Verse als Restteil, der alle gesondert gezählten Siebensilber des Werkes sowie alle Elfsilber von der Todesnachricht bis zum Schlußwort „pace" umfaßt[24].

Die in den Verszahlen der drei Teile in unterschiedlicher Kombination verwendeten drei gleichbleibenden Ziffern 4, 6 und 1 sind die numerischen Elemente der data fatale: aprile (= 4), il dí sesto (= 6), l'ora prima (= 1)[25].

Außerdem setzen sich aus den Zahlen 1, 4 und 6 die Stellen nach dem Komma in Petrarcas π-Wert 3,1416464 zusammen. Die ersten vier Stellen dieser π-Näherung sind sogar in der Abfolge identisch mit der Zahl der 1416 Verse des der Todesnachricht folgenden Schlußteils des Canzoniere. Man könnte hier an eine kompositorische Gestaltung der mathematischen Idee des Restes, des bei der Berechnung von π besonders interessanten Restes nach 3, denken: *3,1416*[26].

Die geheime Siebenerordnung in der linearen Abfolge der Endecasillabi und Settenari, die durch die Daten der Liebesgeschichte begründete Dreiteilung des Werks mit numerisch konkordierenden Versmengen, die per-

---

[24] Die Summe der Verse der drei Blöcke ist $4116 + 46 \cdot 7^2 + 1416 = 7786$. Da der Endecasillabo, der die präzise Angabe des Jahres der ersten Begegnung (1327) enthält, Angelpunkt des ersten und zweiten Teils darstellt und somit bei gesonderter Zählung der Verse der beiden Teile zweimal mitgezählt wird, ist die absolute Summe aller Verse bei durchgehender Zählung $7786 - 1 = 7785$, wie oben unter 4.1. festgestellt.

[25] Die numerische Gleichsetzung des Monats April mit der Zahl 4 setzt voraus, daß Petrarca das Kalenderjahr mit dem Monat Januar anfangen ließ, was wegen der im Mittelalter gebräuchlichen insgesamt sechs Möglichkeiten des kalendarischen Jahresbeginns nicht mit Sicherheit angenommen werden kann, wiewohl vieles dafür spricht, daß Petrarca gerade die auch im Rom des Mittelalters geläufige Art des römischen Kalenders übernommen hat. Im übrigen hat „sich das ganze Mittelalter hindurch trotz der abweichenden offiziellen Schreibungen der Kanzleien der 1. Jan. im bürgerlichen Leben als Jahresbeginn erhalten" (Grotefeld/Ulrich, Taschenbuch der Zeitrechnung des deutschen Mittelalters und der Neuzeit, Hannover 1960, 11).

[26] Bei groben Berechnungen genügt auch heute in der Praxis oft ein π = 3. Cfr. auch Altes Testament, Buch der Könige, VII, 23, wo Maße genannt werden, die von π = 3 ausgehen.

fekte Kreisform der Makrostruktur des Zyklus sowie schließlich die durch den expliziten Zahlenschlüssel 6 − 4 − 1 bestätigte wechselseitige Ergänzung dieser statischen Grunddaten des formalen „aedificium" der Rime sollen wiederum in einem Schema zusammengefaßt werden:

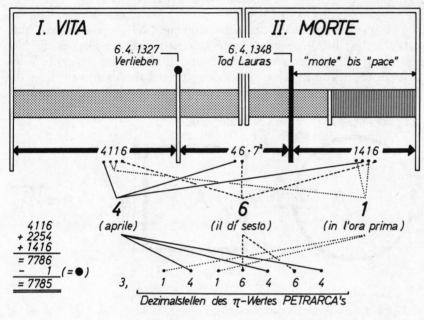

Abbildung 13

5.6. Die Bedeutung der absoluten Silbensummen

Die data fatale aus 4−6−1 findet eine weitere mathematische Deutung im Verhältnis aller Elfsilber zu allen Siebensilbern des Canzoniere, den beiden absoluten Quantitäten des sprachlich-metrischen Materials des dichterischen „aedificium". Das Werk besitzt in toto 82587 Silben, und zwar

$$7023 \cdot 11 = 77253 \text{ und}$$
$$762 \cdot 7 = 5334 \text{ Silben.}$$

Sehen wir nun die beiden Silbensummen der Endecasillabi und der Settenari als Zähler und Nenner eines die beiden metrischen Strukturen in ihrer Relation totaliter repräsentierenden Bruchs (= $\frac{77253}{5334}$), erhalten wir als Verhältniszahl den Quotienten 14,483127. Diese scheinbar willkürliche Zahl ist in Wirklichkeit das Produkt der beiden Faktoren

$$3,1416464 \cdot 4,61 \text{ (genauer 4,6100436),}$$

d. h. Petrarcas π-Wert mal Schlüsseldatum der Liebesgeschichte in der Form April-Komma-sechster-erste Morgenstunde.

5.7. *Quadratur des Kreises*

Es läßt sich mit dem Tag der in der Canzone CXIX geschilderten Vision der Wahrheit die Vermutung weiter erhärten, daß der Dichter die hier rekonstruierten Zahlenverhältnisse bewußt als Maße eines das ganze Werk darstellenden geometrischen Gebäudes geplant hat. Als Beweis diene die Berechnung eines dem Makrokreis in der Fläche entsprechenden Quadrats.

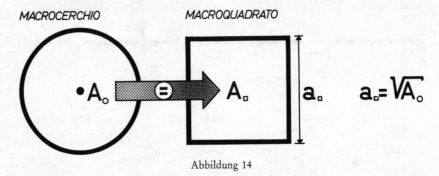

Abbildung 14

Die Fläche des Universalkreises mit $c = 7785$ und $d = 2478$ und somit $r = 1239$ beträgt nach der Formel $A = r^2\pi$, und zwar berechnet mit dem petrarcaschen π-Wert $\frac{7785}{2478}$:

$$A = 1239^2 \cdot \tfrac{7785}{2478}$$
$$A = 4\,822\,807{,}5.$$

Als Seite des der Fläche des Makrokreises entsprechenden Quadrats errechnen wir durch Radizieren

$$a = \sqrt{4\,822\,807{,}5}$$
$$a = 2196{,}0891.$$

Diese scheinbar willkürliche Zahl ist in Wirklichkeit das Produkt der Faktoren

$$6{,}4 \cdot 343 \ (\text{genau } 6{,}4026 \cdot 343).$$

Abermals stimmen die Zahlen unserer mathematischen Rekonstruktion, in diesem Fall die numerische Beschreibung der Quadratur des ästhetischen Makrokreises, mit den Schlüsselzahlen des Werkes überein: mit dem

Datum der Liebesbeziehung, dem 6. April, mit der für die Statik des Gesamtgebäudes zentralen Zahl 343 = 7^3, mit dem aus dem Tagebuch der Liebesgeschichte erschließbaren Datum des Tages der Wahrheitsvision in der Form

6.4. (1)343.

Die Zahlenkombination 6/4/1/343, d. h. data fatale und 7^3, ist das Datum der von Petrarca in der Canzone CXIX (und im Secretum) poetisch geschilderten visionären Begegnung mit der Donna Veritas im 17. Jahr der Leidenschaft. Sie ist zugleich der Schlüssel zum zahlenästhetischen und mathematischen Code des Canzoniere, zur Statik des „aedificium".

Die Austauschbarkeit der Maße des ästhetischen Makrokreises und seines ihm entsprechenden Makroquadrats zeigt, daß Petrarcas poetisch verschlüsselte Mathematik des Kreises gleichzeitig den Versuch einschließt, das mit den Mitteln der euklidischen Geometrie nicht lösbare Problem der Quadratur des Kreises auf rechnerischem Wege anzugehen. Aber der Dichter hat offenbar klar gesehen, daß die Genauigkeit der Berechnung der Kreisquadratur von dem Grad der Näherung an π abhängt. Die absolut exakte Quadratur des Zirkels ist für ihn, wenn wir vom gehaltlichen Kern seiner Liebesdichtung auf eine entsprechende Konzeption der Form rückschließen, wie das „dolce-amaro" einer unerwiderten Liebe: ein schmerzlich erlebtes Oxymoron, ein nur approximativ lösbares Insolubile.

6. Kreis und Kreisberechnung: Petrarca – ein Mathematiker?

Alle bisher beschriebenen Übereinstimmungen einer in der Dichtung der Rime verschlüsselten geheimen Mathematik mit dem explizit vom Autor gelieferten Datum der Liebesgeschichte mögen – so wollen wir einmal allen vorgebrachten Beweisen zum Trotz annehmen – einer Laune des Zufalls entsprungen sein. Gegen diese Position einer radikalen Skepsis gegenüber der numerologischen Forschung lassen sich nun aber zwei weitere Berechnungen ins Feld führen. Sie beruhen auf den vom Dichter selbst im Werk genannten Tempi der Liebesgeschichte, nämlich „21" Jahre Leidenschaft + „10" Jahre Trauer über Lauras Tod = 31 Jahre[27].

Die Jahresangaben zur Gesamtdauer der Liebesgeschichte sind für uns von ganz besonderer Bedeutung. Mit Hilfe dieser festen numerischen Größen können wir nämlich eine innere Systematik erkennen, die alle Einzelteile der hier versuchten Rekonstruktion des zahlenästhetischen Gefüges des Gedichtzyklus in einem gemeinsamen Licht erscheinen läßt.

---

[27] Cfr. CCCLXIV, 1–4: Tennemi Amor *anni ventuno* ardendo, / lieto nel foco, et nel duol pien di speme; / poi che madonna e 'l mio cor seco inseme / saliro al ciel, *dieci altri anni* piangendo.

Dieser geheime architektonische Plan gehorcht seinerseits einem einzigen mathematischen Gedanken, der uns eine – die poetische Ebene transzendierende – wissenschaftliche Dimension der Liebeslyrik Petrarcas offenbart.

Um die Hypothese der mathematischen Bedeutung der beiden Tempi der Liebesgeschichte anhand konkreter Berechnungen zu überprüfen, greifen wir auf unsere beiden wichtigsten Ergebnisse zurück, auf den archimedischen Sonettkreis mit r = 7 und $\pi = \frac{22}{7}$ einerseits und auf den petrarcaschen π-Wert $\frac{7785}{2478} = 3,1416464$ andererseits.

6.1. „Amor hielt mich einundzwanzig Jahre im Liebesbrand gefangen" (CCCLXIV, 1)

Wir tun nun das, was Petrarca vermutlich selbst getan hat: wir vergleichen am einzelnen Sonettkreis den archimedischen Hilfswert $\pi = \frac{22}{7} = 3,1428571$ mit dem in Petrarcas Zyklus verschlüsselten erheblich genaueren Näherungswert $\frac{7785}{2478} = 3,1416464$. Der Unterschied der beiden π-Werte schlägt sich bei der Berechnung des Sonettkreises in einer minimalen Differenz nieder, wie die folgende Berechnung zeigt:

$$\pi = \frac{22}{7} \qquad A = r^2\pi \qquad A = 7^2 \cdot \frac{22}{7} \qquad = 154,00000$$
$$\pi = 3,1416464 \qquad\qquad A = 7^2 \cdot 3,1416464 = 153,94067$$
$$\text{Differenz} = \quad 0,05933$$

Wir wollen nun die an der Fläche des einzelnen Sonettkreises erkannte Auswirkung der verbesserten petrarcaschen π-Näherung auf größere Einheiten des Werkes übertragen, z. B. auf den die 21 Jahre der Leidenschaft betreffenden 1. Teil des Canzoniere. Die sog. Rime in vita enthalten 4921 Elfsilber[28]; das sind – wenn wir den Endecasillabo in seiner primären Funktion als metrischen Baustein des Sonetts sehen – insgesamt $\frac{4921}{14}$ „Sonetteinheiten". Wir multiplizieren nun diese absolute Menge realer und virtueller Sonette des 1. Teils mit dem – für die Kreisfläche einer einzelnen Sonetteinheit ($= \frac{14}{14}$) berechneten – Unterschied der beiden π-Werte. So erhalten wir eine Addition der einzelnen die $\frac{4921}{14}$ Kreisflächen betreffenden Differenzbeträge, die sich auf

$$0,05933 \cdot \tfrac{4921}{14} = 20,854495$$

beläuft.

Das Ergebnis 20,85 erinnert offensichtlich an die 21 Jahre des „Feuers" der Leidenschaft.

---

[28] Cfr. supra 4.2.

Da wir nun aber nicht genau wissen, bis zu welcher Stelle Petrarca seinen π-Wert $\frac{7785}{2478} = 3{,}1416464$ gekannt hat, reduzieren wir diesen Dezimalbruch nach und nach um eine Stelle bis 3,1416. Mit den einzelnen Varianten wiederholen wir die gerade durchgeführte Berechnung der Summe der jeweiligen Auswirkungen des Unterschieds zwischen Archimedes' π und dem Wert Petrarcas. Auch bei diesen modifizierten Berechnungen bleibt indes die Differenz des petrarcaschen π zu Archimedes' Wert $\frac{22}{7}$ so groß, daß die auf die Gesamtzahl der Sonettkreise des 1. Teils der Rime bezogene Summe der einzelnen Abweichungen weiterhin knapp unter oder bereits über 21 liegt. Im einzelnen:

$$20{,}861525 \text{ bei } \pi = 3{,}141646$$
$$20{,}96346 \text{ bei } \pi = 3{,}14164$$
$$21{,}6524 \text{ bei } \pi = 3{,}1416.$$

Die 21 Jahre des Labyrinths der Leidenschaft stellen also eine arithmetische Größe in der verborgenen geometrischen Statik des dichterischen „aedificium" dar. Sie spiegeln in numerischer Form den Versuch des Autors wider, die größere Präzision seiner Kreisberechnung gegenüber dem berühmten Ergebnis des Archimedes rechnerisch zu ermitteln und in die numerische Ästhetik seiner Dichtkunst sowie in seine auf diesem Wege verfolgte geheime Mathematik des Kreises einzubeziehen.

6.2. „Amor hielt mich . . . zehn weitere Jahre in Tränen gefangen" (CCCLXIV, 1 und 4)

Trifft der für die 21 Jahre des Amore ermittelte mathematische Sinn zu, dann müßte auch in den insgesamt 31 Jahren der Liebesgeschichte eine vergleichbare Summe von Fehlerkorrekturen bei der mit verschiedenen π-Werten vorgenommenen Berechnung des Flächeninhalts der insgesamt $\frac{7023}{14}$ Sonetteinheiten[29] des Werkes verborgen sein. Um zu dieser exakten mathematischen Deutung der poetisch verkleideten 31 Jahre zu kommen, wiederholen wir die gerade für die Interpretation der 21 Jahre der Leidenschaft angestellte Berechnung, allerdings in umgekehrter Reihenfolge, da wir jetzt von der festen Größe 31 ausgehen wollen.

Bezogen auf eine einzige Sonetteinheit ergibt sich aus der Summe 31 zunächst eine einzelne Fehlerdifferenz von

$$x \cdot \tfrac{7023}{14} = 31$$
$$x = 31 \cdot \tfrac{14}{7023}$$
$$x = 0{,}0617969.$$

---

[29] Entsprechend den insgesamt 7023 Endecasillabi der Rime (cfr. 4.3.).

Ziehen wir nun diese den Flächeninhalt eines einzelnen Sonettkreises betreffende Fehlerdifferenz von der mit dem archimedischen Hilfswert $\frac{22}{7}$ berechneten Fläche A = 154 ab, erhalten wir einen korrigierten Flächeninhalt von

$$
\begin{array}{r}
154,0000000 \\
-\quad 0,0617969 \\
\hline
153,9382031
\end{array}
$$

Dieser neue Wert der Fläche eines einzelnen Sonettkreises führt uns auf dem Wege der Umstellung der Formel A = r²π zu einer weiteren Bestimmung von π, nämlich

$$A = r^2\pi$$
$$\pi = \frac{A}{r^2}$$
$$\pi = \frac{153,938203}{49}$$
$$\pi = \underline{3,14159598}$$

Dies ist eine bis zur fünften Stelle mit dem korrekten π-Wert übereinstimmende Näherung. Ein präziseres oder auch nur gleich genaues Ergebnis der Kreisberechnung ist in der abendländischen Mathematik erst vom 16. Jh. an überliefert (cfr. infra 6.3.).

Die 31 Jahre der Liebesgeschichte sind also die Summe der einzelnen „erotischen" Schritte der Approximierung an ein immer präziseres π.

Petrarca hat das „aedificium" seiner Liebesgedichte als ein mathematisches System von Kreisen und Kreisberechnungen konzipiert, um sich einer immer genaueren rechnerischen Definition des Mysteriums des Kreises zu nähern. Petrarca hat, was anderen Zeugnissen seiner Zeit zufolge keineswegs Gemeingut damaliger Erkenntnis war[30], die Berechnung des Kreises als ein Approximierungsverfahren erkannt. Dabei hat er sich in seiner poetischen Mathematik des Kreises der Bestimmung des Verhältnisses $\frac{c}{d}$ bis auf einen Abstand von weniger als 0,000004 genähert. Das in mathematischer und mathematikgeschichtlicher Hinsicht bemerkenswerte Ergebnis verlangt nunmehr eine ausführlichere historische Würdigung. Nur so werden sich die herausragende Stellung Petrarcas im zwei Jahrtausende umfassenden Bemühen der Mathematik um eine immer präzisere Berechnung des Kreises und seine mögliche Bedeutung für die Entwicklung des – in seiner poetischen Mathematik offenbar benutzten – Rechnens mit Dezimalzahlen besser ermessen lassen.

---

[30] Näheres im folgenden Abschnitt 6.3.

6.3. Wichtigste Etappen in der Geschichte der Berechnung von π und des Rechnens mit Dezimalzahlen

Im Lichte der Geschichte der Mathematik[31] ergibt sich für die hier vorgelegte Rekonstruktion der petrarcaschen Kreisberechnungen folgendes Bild.

Archimedes, 3. Jh. v. Chr., gilt als der Entdecker des Näherungsverfahrens zur Berechnung von π. Seine mit dem Sechseck, dann 12-Eck und schließlich 96-Eck errechneten Grenzwerte sind $\frac{22}{7}$ (= 3,142857) und $\frac{223}{71}$ (= 3,140845), von denen der Bruch $\frac{22}{7}$ wegen seiner Einfachheit und relativen Genauigkeit in die Geschichte eingehen wird. Nach Archimedes gelingt es Heron und später Claudius Ptolemäus von Alexandria, mit den Brüchen $\frac{211\,875}{67\,441}$ = 3,1416349 bzw. $\frac{377}{120}$ = 3,1416666 die Näherung erheblich zu verbessern. Aus dem gesamten Schrifttum des Abendlandes bis zum Beginn der neuzeitlichen Mathematik im 16. Jh. ist kein genauerer π-Wert bekannt; im Gegenteil, man greift im ganzen Mittelalter immer wieder auf den archimedischen Bruch $\frac{22}{7}$ zurück, z. T. ohne seinen approximativen Charakter zu durchschauen[32].

Nur bei den Chinesen ist ein viel besserer Wert aus dem 5. Jh. bekannt, nämlich der von Tsu Ch'ung-Chih errechnete Bruch $\frac{355}{113}$, der bis zur 6. Stelle (3,1415929 statt 3,1415926) korrekt ist. Inder und Araber rechneten mit Brüchen, die 3,1416 entsprechen. Im Abendland steht also Petrarca mit seiner bis auf 5 Stellen richtigen Näherung einsam in einer uns nur lückenhaft bekannten Überlieferung. Erst ab 2. Hälfte des 16. Jh. gibt es mit François Viète (neun Stellen), Adriaen van Roomen (15 Stellen) und, im Jahre 1610, mit Ludolph van Keulen (35 Stellen) neue entscheidende Schritte in der Berechnung von π. Unter den wenigen Wissenschaftlern der Epoche Petrarcas, die sich mit der Berechnung des Kreises beschäftigt und das Prinzip des Näherungsverfahrens durchschaut haben, ist ein Zeitgenosse des Dichters, der Autor einer 1346 verfaßten Practica geometriae namens Dominicus Parisiensis. Eine wissenschaftliche Beziehung zwischen Petrarca und Dominicus ist m. W. nicht bekannt, erscheint aber denkbar wegen der Paris-Reisen des Dichters.

Historisch ebenfalls problematisch ist die offensichtliche Verwendung von Dezimalzahlen durch Petrarca. Der symbolische Sinn seines π-Wertes 3,1416464, alle seine darauf beruhenden Berechnungen sowie sein Rechnen mit der sog. data fatale in der Form 4,61 und 6,4 lassen indes keinen

---

[31] Der folgende historische Abriß beruht auf Carl B. Boyer, Storia della matematica, Milano 1976, H. Eves, An Introduction to the History of Mathematics, New York 1969, Johannes Tropfke, Geschichte der Elementarmathematik, Leipzig 1921 (I, 136–149: „Dezimalbrüche"; IV, 195–238: „Kreisberechnung").

[32] Zu den wichtigsten Zeugnissen für die Kreisberechnung im Mittelalter (Gerbert, Regimbold von Köln, Franco von Lüttich, Leonardo da Pisa, Dominicus Parisiensis, Nicolaus von Cues) cfr. Tropfke IV, 212 sqq.

anderen Schluß zu als den, daß Petrarca ein dem unsrigen Rechnen mit Dezimalzahlen vergleichbares Verfahren gekannt hat. Zwar gewinnt das Rechnen mit Dezimalzahlen erst vom 16. Jh. an allgemein Anerkennung, aber die Methode als solche war im Abendland mindestens seit dem 12. Jh. bekannt[33].

Aufgrund der mangelhaften Quellenlage und wegen des geheimen Charakters der petrarcaschen Mathematik läßt sich z. Zt. nicht entscheiden, inwieweit die hier rekonstruierten Kreisberechnungen des Dichters und sein Rechnen mit Dezimalzahlen die geniale Leistung eines Einzelgängers darstellen oder ob Petrarca etwa aus orientalischen Quellen oder vielleicht durch die auf seinen ständigen Reisen geknüpften Bekanntschaften wichtige Anregungen erhalten hat.

Zu alledem kommt erschwerend hinzu, daß der in seinen Briefen sehr ausführlich – aber wohl mehr mit künstlerischer Absicht und nicht mit dem Ziel authentischer Konfession – über sein geistiges Leben berichtende Petrarca anscheinend nirgendwo in seinen Schriften seine Beschäftigung mit dem Problem des Kreises erwähnt. Aus seinen Randnotizen in einem in der Pariser Nationalbibliothek aufbewahrten Kodex des Timaios-Kommentars des Chalcidius kann aber andererseits wiederum sein allgemeines Interesse für astronomische und mathematische Fragen geschlossen werden[34].

Die abschließende mathematische und geometriegeschichtliche Würdigung der petrarcaschen Kreisberechnungen bleibt einer Zusammenarbeit von Petrarca-Forschern und Mathematikhistorikern überlassen. Unsere literarhistorische Frage „Wer war Laura?" indes können wir nunmehr zu beantworten wagen.

7. Der brennende Wissensdurst („desire" ardente della verità) oder die Philosophie

7.1. Gemeinsame Erklärung des biographischen Rätsels und des strukturellen Problems

Nach den bekannten Ergebnissen der Petrarca-Forschung ist der Canzoniere auf der expliziten Ebene des Textes, in seiner Materia, die

---

[33] Tropfke I, 137 verweist hier besonders auf das aus dem Arabischen übersetzte sog. Rechenbuch des Johannes von Sevilla (12. Jh.), auf die Demonstratio de minutiis des Jordanus Nemorarius (gest. ca. 1237) sowie auf den aus dem 14. Jh. stammenden, von einem Anonymus verfaßten Algorismus de minutiis, in welchem neben der 60 und der 12 auch die 10 als Grundlage für das Rechnen unter 1 behandelt wird. Für seine Berechnungen stand Petrarca im übrigen der Abacus zur Verfügung.

[34] Es handelt sich um den Codex Latinus 6280 der BN Paris. Aus den von mir überprüften Randnotizen Petrarcas lassen sich jedoch keine konkreten Anhaltspunkte für seine Beschäftigung mit dem Problem des Kreises entnehmen.

Geschichte der Liebe zu einer unerreichbaren Frau, die mit dem Ziel des vom Autor definierten Erkenntnisprozesses, der visionär geschauten transzendenten Donna Veritas, identisch ist.

Nach der hier vorgelegten mathematischen Deutung der Rime ist der Gedichtzyklus auf der impliziten Ebene seiner Forma konzipiert als Darstellung einer geheimen Mathematik, die dem Problem der Kreisberechnung, der unerreichbaren „Wahrheit" der in der Mathematik als „transzendent" charakterisierten Zahl π, gewidmet ist.

Die Idee der Wahrheit verknüpft die beiden Ebenen des Textes. Der Wahrheit in der Gestalt der unerreichbaren Frau und der Wahrheit in der Form der nur approximativ bestimmbaren Größe $\frac{c}{d}$ des Kreises gilt in gleicher Weise der brennende „desire" des Poeta „doctus". Die ideelle Identität der beiden unerreichbaren „Donne" führt uns zur gesuchten gemeinsamen Erklärung des biographischen Rätsels „Wer war Laura?" und des Problems der inneren Struktur des Canzoniere. Die Lösung läßt sich — mit dem Vorbehalt, daß damit die vordergründige, menschliche Dimension der Liebesgeschichte in keiner Weise geschmälert wird — als Formel fassen, nämlich

LAURA = π.

Diese Formel soll im Sinne einer von Dante formulierten Gleichung verstanden werden, nämlich „Filosofia" = „donna di cu' io innamorai appresso lo primo amore"[35]. Laura ist die Verkörperung der Idee der wissenschaftlichen Wahrheit, der Veritas, die der Dichter und Wissenschaftler Petrarca in einem stets vom „Irrtum" und der Verirrung gefährdeten Prozeß der Näherung mit dem ganzen Eros seiner Berufung als Wissenschaftler zu erreichen versuchte. Laura ist die visionär geschaute, aber für den Menschen nicht erreichbare, wie die transzendente Zahl π immer nur unvollkommen bestimmbare absolute Wahrheit. Laura ist die Donna Sapientia, für die das mathematische Wahrheitsproblem π nur eine der denkbaren Erscheinungsformen, allerdings eine besonders sinnfällige, darstellt.

Mit dem Ergebnis LAURA = π sind Inhalt und Form des Canzoniere zu buchstäblicher Einheit zusammengeflossen. Die ideelle Biographie der geliebten Donna bildet die Struktur des Gedichtzyklus und umgekehrt.

7.2. Wertung des Ergebnisses

Die geheime Mathematik des Canzoniere erlaubt es uns, eine einheitliche Antwort, nämlich LAURA = π, auf mehrere grundlegende Fragen zu Inhalt und Form des Werkes zu geben:

---

[35] Dante, Convivio, II, XV, 12 (ed. Busnelli/Valdelli, Firenze 1934/35, I, 238).

1) Wahl des Sonetts aus geometrischen Gründen;
2) zahlenästhetische Ordnung der „anniversari" der Liebesgeschichte in der linearen Abfolge der Verse;
3) inhaltlich-formaler Gleichklang zwischen Erkenntnisprozeß und Siebenerordnung der Elfsilber;
4) der Zyklus als „cyclos";
5) das „dolce-amaro" der Liebe und die Quadratur des Kreises;
6) der anagogische Sinn der sog. data fatale, die kein reales Datum eines wörtlich verstandenen Liebestagebuchs ist, sondern ein vom Autor gelieferter Schlüssel zum geheimen Code seiner poetischen Mathematik;
7) die Frau als Donna Filosofia, die hier als konkretes Problem einer der sieben Artes, der Geometrie, erscheint.

7.3. Ästhetik des Kreises

Den metaphorischen und den geometrischen Kreis hat Petrarca als Sinn- und Abbild der Form-Inhalt-Einheit seiner Liebeslyrik verstanden. Kaum eine andere dichterische Form vereinigt wie das Sonett die diametralen Pole Emotionalität und Rationalität. Das Sonett ist das „reine Ebenmaß der Gegensätze" (A. W. Schlegel[36]). Es gleicht so dem Kreis, der die antithetischen Endpunkte seines Durchmessers auf der Linie des Umfangs wieder vereinigt. Mit dem Kreis als durchgängiger Grundfigur verknüpfen im Canzoniere Oberflächenstruktur der Materia und Tiefenstruktur der Forma die Gegensätze Sinne–Vernunft, Irrtum–Erkenntnis, Amore–Numero, Lyrik und Mathematik, Dichtung und Philosophie zu einer systemhaften Synthese im kleinen und im großen. Diese Versöhnung der paradigmatischen Gegensätze indes – und das liegt zugleich im Geheimnis der Liebe und im Mysterium des Kreises – ist zwar beschreibbar, aber wegen ihres letztlich nur in der Transzendenz erkennbaren Wesens nie absolut exakt definierbar.

Der Kreis ist in der mittelalterlichen Kunst als Zeichen des göttlichen Schöpfungsaktes bekannt[37]. Im Canzoniere haben wir den Kreis als Figur und Idee des künstlerischen „aedificium" identifiziert. Der mittelalterliche Mensch – und in der zahlenästhetischen Anlage seines Werkes gehört Petrarca ganz dem Mittelalter an – versucht, die Gesetze des numerisch bestimmten Ordo auf die Kunst zu übertragen, um ein vollendetes Kunstwerk zu schaffen. In diesem Sinne hat Petrarca den künstlerischen Akt

---

[36] A. W. Schlegel, Das Sonett, in id., Sämtliche Werke, ed. E. Böcking, Leipzig 1846, I, 304.
[37] Eine besonders eindrucksvolle Darstellung Gottes als Architekt, der das kreisrunde Universum mit dem Zirkel abmißt, findet sich in der aus der 1. Hälfte des 13. Jh. stammenden Bible moralisée (Codex Vindobonensis 2554, ed. facsim. Codices selecti, XL, Graz 1973).

selbst, den Kreis der „Kreation", zum Gegenstand seiner poetischen Arbeit gemacht. Indem sein „amore", sein Suchen nach der Lösung des Geheimnisses des Kreises, zugleich eine im Zahlenwerk des „aedificium" verschlüsselte Reflexion über die transzendente Natur des behandelten Problems einschließt, hat die Zahl in der Lyrik Petrarcas eine über die rein zahlenästhetische Funktion hinausgehende wissenschaftliche Dimension gewonnen. Sie ist somit Zeugnis für das, was man aus anderen Anzeichen heraus die „coscienza moderna" Petrarcas genannt hat[38]. Mit der Ästhetik des Kreises steht Petrarca ganz in der Tradition mittelalterlicher Kunsttheorie; mit der Mathematik des Kreises dagegen beweist er seine Zugehörigkeit zur anbrechenden Epoche der Neuzeit.

Der Kreis ist aber nicht nur Sinnbild der Schöpfung, sondern auch Attribut Gottes. Am Ende der Göttlichen Komödie, in den letzten Versen des Paradiso, schildert Dante bekanntlich eine Gottesvision. Die göttliche „imago" erscheint ihm in einem Kreis. Der Dichter äußert den Wunsch, die Vision im einzelnen nachzuzeichnen, muß aber seine Unfähigkeit, das wie im Leuchten eines „fulgore" Gesehene zu beschreiben, sogleich eingestehen. Dante vergleicht sich mit einem Geometer, der vergeblich versucht, den „principio" des Kreises zu bestimmen. Die Beschreibung Gottes ist ebenso unmöglich wie die Definition des Kreises:

> Qual è 'l geometra che tutto s'affige
> per misurar lo cerchio, e non ritrova,
> pensando, quel principio ond'elli indige,
> tal era io a quella vista nova
> (Paradiso, XXXIII, 133–139).

Nach der in diesem Beitrag vorgelegten Deutung des Canzoniere ist Petrarca auf dem Wege einer mit Hilfe der Zahl „verfertigten" Poesie dem von Dante mit Gott verglichenen Geheimnis des Kreises mit wissenschaftlicher Haltung und Absicht nachgegangen. Hat er sich damit vielleicht der Sünde der „superbia" schuldig gemacht? Läßt sich so sein auffälliges Schweigen erklären?

In jedem Fall dürfen wir aber vermuten, daß der in seinen Briefen sonst so freimütige Petrarca unter allen Umständen einen direkten Hinweis auf den geheimen Sinn seines Gedichtzyklus vermeiden wollte, um nicht vor jedem profanen Leser den fiktiven Charakter der geliebten Donna, die mathematische Identität Lauras, offenzulegen. Im übrigen dürfte es seine Absicht gewesen sein, dem sicherlich sehr kleinen Kreis der Initiierten – d. h. den numerologisch und mathematisch versierten Lesern seiner Zeit – die bedeutend geringere Mühe der Rekonstruktion seiner jahrzehntelangen wissenschaftlich-poetischen Bemühungen zu überlassen, und nicht nur die Mühe, sondern auch das ästhetische Vergnügen am Erfolg dieser Mühe.

---

[38] Ugo Dotti, Petrarca e la scoperta della coscienza moderna, Milano 1978.

Hinzu kommt, daß nur die Lektüre des Canzoniere in Form einer getreuen Kopie des autographen Codex Vaticanus 3195 den Leser materialiter in die Lage versetzte, den exakten mathematischen Berechnungen Petrarcas mit Erfolg nachzuspüren. So erhebt sich also wieder die Frage, welche äußeren Umstände oder welche persönlichen Gründe den Autor der Rime dazu veranlaßt haben könnten, einen sicherlich auch von ihm selbst als bedeutend angesehenen Beitrag zum Fortschritt der Wissenschaft in seinem dichterischen Werk derart zu verschlüsseln, daß er der Nachwelt nur mittelbar erhalten bleiben konnte.

Alle diese Überlegungen indes sind möglicherweise spekulativ und recht vordergründig. Was wir trotz aller Fragen und Bedenken festhalten können, ist das durch überprüfbare Berechnungen fundierte mathematische Ergebnis LAURA $= \pi$, das seine ideelle Begründung findet in der auf beiden Seiten der Gleichung ausgedrückten Suche nach der absoluten Wahrheit, dem „desire" della Verità.

Das mittelalterliche Italienisch kennt für LA VERITA' eine synkopierte Parallelform: LA VERTA'[39]. Dieses letzte, geheime Ziel seines Amore, das der Dichter in seinem lateinisch geschriebenen Secretum als Donna Veritas erscheinen läßt, nennt er uns in seinen Rime einmal verschlüsselt im Sonett V: Eine anagrammatische Vertauschung der Silben von LA VERTA' findet sich hier in den drei Silben LAU-RE-TA wieder, in denen die Kommentatoren seit jeher die diminutive Variante von LAURA gesehen haben[40].

Unser in einer Formel zusammengefaßtes Ergebnis können wir nunmehr präzisierend folgendermaßen schreiben:

LAURETA $= \pi =$ LA VERTA'.

---

[39] Im Canzoniere ist nur einmal die Form *veritate* bezeugt (CCLXXII, 6); für *verità* und für *vertà* finden sich keine Belege.

[40] Die anagrammatische Deutung LA VERTA' = LAURETA verdanke ich Henk de Fries (Doorn), der sie während der meinem Vortrag folgenden Diskussion auf der 23. Mediävistentagung in Köln vorgeschlagen hat.

ZAHLENBAU IN SPANISCHER DICHTUNG

von Henk de Vries (Doorn)

Einleitung

Der Zweck dieser Arbeit ist zu zeigen, daß auch in Spanien Dichter versucht haben, ihren Werken eine sinnvolle, von Zahlenverhältnissen und Symbolzahlen bestimmte Form zu geben. Ich behandle hier drei Beispiele aus dem dreizehnten Jahrhundert zum erstenmal, und ziehe zum Vergleich zwei aus der Zeit um 1500 heran, denen ich schon früher Untersuchungen gewidmet habe. Es handelt sich um sehr unterschiedliche Werke: eine Liebesidylle, die in ein Streitgespräch zwischen dem Wein und dem Wasser übergeht; eine Sammlung von Marienlegenden; ein Sternkatalog; ein Leben Christi und eine danteske Reise durch die Jenseitsreiche; und zum Schluß eine humanistische Comedia, die dem Werk Dantes nicht folgt, sondern es persifliert. Bei den verschiedenen Dichtern lassen sich jedoch teilweise die gleichen Bauprinzipien feststellen; um diese dem Leser verständlich zu machen, erkläre ich zunächst einige Begriffe aus der mittelalterlichen Zahlenlehre.

Den uns vertrauten Quadratzahlen stehen öfters Dreieckszahlen gegenüber[1]. Eine Dreieckszahl ist die Summe der natürlichen Zahlen von 1 bis n; für n = 2 zum Beispiel ergibt dies 1 + 2 = 3, eine Zahl, die wie ein aus Pünktchen zusammengesetztes Dreieck (. ˙.) vorgestellt werden kann.

Einige wenige Dreieckszahlen sind „vollkommene Zahlen": die Sechs ist ein numerus perfectus[2], weil sie der Summe ihrer Teiler gleich ist: 1 + 2 + 3 = 6.

Da Schönheit aus der Vollkommenheit der Proportionen erklärt wurde, wundert es nicht, daß häufig einfache Zahlenverhältnisse dem Bauplan eines Gedichts zugrunde liegen. Das einfachste Verhältnis, nämlich 1:1, die aequalitas numerosa, symbolisiert nicht nur Schönheit, sondern auch Gleichwertigkeit und Gerechtigkeit. Die einfachen Verhältnisse bestimmen auch die Harmonie der musikalischen Intervalle; 1:2 ist die Oktave, 2:3 die Quinte, 3:4 die Quarte.

---

[1] Die beiden Kategorien von Zahlen sind miteinander verwandt, weil jede Quadratzahl die Summe zweier Dreieckszahlen ist: 1 + 3 = 4, 3 + 6 = 9, 6 + 10 = 16 usw.

[2] Die nächsten vollkommenen Zahlen sind 28, 496 und 8128, die Dreieckszahlen auf den Basen 7, 31 und 127; die Basen sind immer sogenannte Zahlen von Mersenne.

Das Verhältnis 1:1 wird öfters in Verbindung mit dem Göttlichen Verhältnis angetroffen. Dieses Verhältnis, erst in neuerer Zeit Goldener Schnitt genannt, besteht zwischen den zwei Teilen eines Ganzen, wenn sich der kleinere Teil zum größeren genau so verhält wie der größere Teil zum Ganzen. Es beruht auf der Quadratwurzel der Zahl Fünf[3] und kann darum nur annähernd in ganzen Zahlen ausgedrückt werden. Im Mittelalter, oder schon früher, entdeckte man, daß in einer Zahlenreihe, in der jeder nächste Term die Summe der beiden vorhergehenden Terme ist, das Verhältnis zwischen zwei aufeinanderfolgenden Termen mit dem Fortschreiten der Reihe dem Göttlichen Verhältnis immer näher kommt. Sehr bekannt ist die Zahlenreihe des Fibonacci — mit dem Beinamen „Sohn des Gutmütigen" bezeichnete man den Leonardo von Pisa — die mit den Zahlen 1 und 2 anfängt: 1 2 3 5 8 13 21 34 55 89 144 usw. Zählt man jeweils zwei Terme dieser Reihe zusammen, die zwei Stellen auseinanderliegen, so ergibt sich eine andere Reihe, die mit den Zahlen 1 und 3 anfängt: 1 3 4 7 11 18 29 47 76 123 199 usw. Diese Reihe erreicht dieselbe Annäherung an das Göttliche Verhältnis einen Term später als die erste Reihe. In dieser Hinsicht läßt sich z. B. das Verhältnis 29:47 dem Verhältnis 13:21 gleichsetzen.

Den Zahlen dieser beiden Reihen werden wir in der Folge öfters begegnen, wobei die Zahl 47 gewissermaßen Leitmotiv ist.

Die Razón de amor

Die Razón de amor (um 1205) besteht aus einer Liebesidylle und einem Streitgespräch zwischen dem Wein und dem Wasser[4]. Der Bauplan (s. Schema A) bestätigt die Einheit des Gedichts und die Vollständigkeit des erhaltenen Textes[5].

Die Idylle und zwei der drei einleitenden Stücke werden vom Verhältnis 1:2 bestimmt. Dabei ist nicht nur die Beschreibung des Mädchens mit derjenigen des locus amoenus verbunden (23:46), sondern auch die Erfüllung der Liebe mit der Beschreibung der beiden geheimnisvollen Becher

---

[3] Es ist gleich $(3 - \sqrt{5}):(\sqrt{5} - 1)$ und kann dezimal als $0,61803399:1 = 1:1,61803399$ geschrieben werden.

[4] Hg. unter dem Titel Siesta de abril. (Razón de amor con los denuestos del agua y el vino) in: Crestomatía del español medieval von Ramón Menéndez Pidal (. . .), vol. I, Madrid ²1971, 92—99; ursprünglich von Menéndez Pidal hg. in: RH 13 (1905) 602 ss. Neue, paläographische Ausgabe von G. H. London unter dem Titel The Razón de amor and the Denuestos del agua y el vino. New Readings and Interpretations, in: RPh 19 (1965) 28—47.

[5] Die Verse 155—57 sollten gestrichen werden; an ihre Stelle gehören die Verse 150—52. Vers 191 ist ebenfalls überflüssig: erstens, weil er außer dem Reimschema steht und zweitens, weil er eine Rede des Wassers mit einem verbum dicendi einleitet, was sonst nur bei den Reden des Weines der Fall ist, dort aber ausnahmslos.

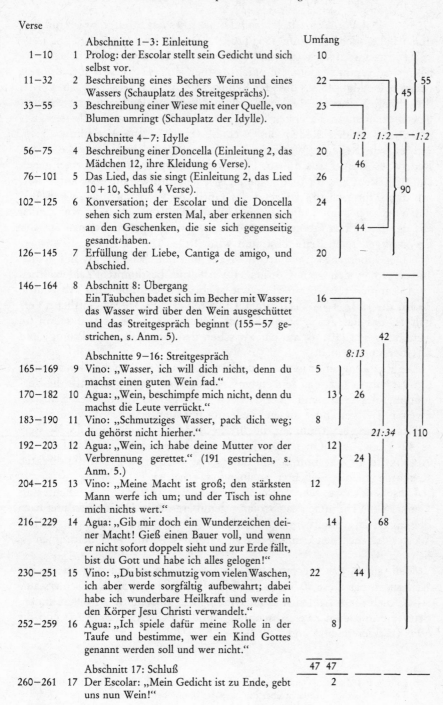

Verse

Abschnitte 1–3: Einleitung   Umfang

1–10   1   Prolog: der Escolar stellt sein Gedicht und sich selbst vor.   10

11–32   2   Beschreibung eines Bechers Weins und eines Wassers (Schauplatz des Streitgesprächs).   22

33–55   3   Beschreibung einer Wiese mit einer Quelle, von Blumen umringt (Schauplatz der Idylle).   23

Abschnitte 4–7: Idylle

56–75   4   Beschreibung einer Doncella (Einleitung 2, das Mädchen 12, ihre Kleidung 6 Verse).   20

76–101   5   Das Lied, das sie singt (Einleitung 2, das Lied 10 + 10, Schluß 4 Verse).   26

102–125   6   Konversation; der Escolar und die Doncella sehen sich zum ersten Mal, aber erkennen sich an den Geschenken, die sie sich gegenseitig gesandt haben.   24

126–145   7   Erfüllung der Liebe, Cantiga de amigo, und Abschied.   20

Abschnitt 8: Übergang

146–164   8   Ein Täubchen badet sich im Becher mit Wasser; das Wasser wird über den Wein ausgeschüttet und das Streitgespräch beginnt (155–57 gestrichen, s. Anm. 5).   16

Abschnitte 9–16: Streitgespräch

165–169   9   Vino: „Wasser, ich will dich nicht, denn du machst einen guten Wein fad."   5

170–182   10   Agua: „Wein, beschimpfe mich nicht, denn du machst die Leute verrückt."   13

183–190   11   Vino: „Schmutziges Wasser, pack dich weg; du gehörst nicht hierher."   8

192–203   12   Agua: „Wein, ich habe deine Mutter vor der Verbrennung gerettet." (191 gestrichen, s. Anm. 5.)   12

204–215   13   Vino: „Meine Macht ist groß; den stärksten Mann werfe ich um; und der Tisch ist ohne mich nichts wert."   12

216–229   14   Agua: „Gib mir doch ein Wunderzeichen deiner Macht! Gieß einen Bauer voll, und wenn er nicht sofort doppelt sieht und zur Erde fällt, bist du Gott und habe ich alles gelogen!"   14

230–251   15   Vino: „Du bist schmutzig vom vielen Waschen, ich aber werde sorgfältig aufbewahrt; dabei habe ich wunderbare Heilkraft und werde in den Körper Jesu Christi verwandelt."   22

252–259   16   Agua: „Ich spiele dafür meine Rolle in der Taufe und bestimme, wer ein Kind Gottes genannt werden soll und wer nicht."   8

Abschnitt 17: Schluß

260–261   17   Der Escolar: „Mein Gedicht ist zu Ende, gebt uns nun Wein!"   2

Schema A. Rekonstruktion des Bauplans der Razón de amor.

(22:44). Das Verhältnis 1:2 verbindet überdies das Streitgespräch mit den drei Stücken der Einleitung (55:110).

Das Streitgespräch wird vom Verhältnis 1:1 und vom Göttlichen Verhältnis bestimmt. Jedem Gesprächspartner sind 47 Verse zugeteilt, von denen beide Male 45 aus direkter Rede bestehen[6]. Das Gespräch läßt sich in drei Etappen einteilen, in denen sich jeweils die beiden Partner das Gleichgewicht halten. In der ersten Etappe, die drei Reden umfaßt, besteht zwischen den beiden Reden des Weines das Göttliche Verhältnis (5:8), während die Rede des Wassers mit 13 Versen gleich lang ist wie die beiden Reden des Weines zusammen. Die zweite Etappe besteht aus zwei gleich langen Reden; und die dritte Etappe ist wiederum wie die erste aufgebaut, mit dem Unterschied, daß jetzt das Göttliche Verhältnis die zwei Reden des Wassers bestimmt und daß der Umfang der drei Teile nicht von Zahlen aus der Reihe des Fibonacci, sondern von verdoppelten Termen aus der davon abgeleiteten Reihe bestimmt wird (8:14:22 = 4:7:11).

Der Übergangsabschnitt (nr. 8 auf unserem Schema) ist mit seinen 16 Versen in den vom Göttlichen Verhältnis bestimmten Zahlenaufbau aufgenommen (16:26 = 8:13), wie auch die Gesamtheit der Abschnitte 8—16, die ja 42 + 68 Verse umfaßt (42:68 = 21:34). Das Göttliche Verhältnis, das das ganze Streitgespräch beherrscht, kündigt sich schon im Verhältnis 5:8 (10:16) an, das zwischen den Abschnitten 1 (Prolog) und 8 (Übergang) besteht.

Die Razón de amor ist somit deutlich als eine Zweieinigkeit konstruiert: das Verhältnis 1:2, das dem ersten Teil zugrunde liegt, verschafft die Verbindung des ersten mit dem zweiten Teil; das Göttliche Verhältnis im zweiten Teil verbindet diesen wiederum mit dem ersten.

Wie schon gesagt, umfaßt die direkte Rede des Weines und des Wassers je 45 Verse, zusammen 90. Da diese Zahl ebenfalls den Umfang der Abschnitte 4—7 bestimmt, soll untersucht werden, wie sich die direkten Reden der beiden Geliebten zueinander verhalten.

Diese sind zwar sehr ungleich verteilt, aber offenbar vom Dichter als Ganzes der Erzählung des Escolar gegenübergestellt. Die Zweiteilung nach diesem Gesichtspunkt ergibt nämlich die Werte 46 und 44, also die gleichen Werte, die auch den Umfang der Abschnitte 4—5 und 6—7 bestimmen (s. Schema B).

Weil jedoch der Escolar selbst der Erzähler ist, ergibt sich ein zweites Kriterium, das diese 90 Verse in 40 der Doncella und 50 des Escolars aufteilt. Auch diese Zahlen sind im Umfang der Abschnitte zurückzufinden, denn die mittleren zwei Abschnitte 5 und 6 haben 50 (26 + 24) und die zwei flankierenden 4 und 7 40 Verse (20 + 20).

---

[6] Die Verse 183 und 204 leiten je eine Rede des Weines ein, die Verse 216—17 beschreiben, wie das Wasser sich fast totlacht über das, was der Wein eben gesagt hat.

Abschnitt Nr.	4	5		6	7			
Direkte Rede der Doncella	−	20	20	12	8	20		⎰40
Direkte Rede des Escolar	−	−		4	2	6	46 ⎱ 6 ⎱ 50
Erzählung (vom Escolar)	20	6	26	8	10	18		44 ⎰

$$20 + 26 = 46 \qquad 24 + 20 = 44$$
$$\text{—} 50 \text{—}$$
$$\text{—} 40 \text{—}$$

Schema B. Umfang der Rollen der Doncella und des Escolar in der Liebesidylle.

Was bedeutet nun diese Zahlenstruktur? Hatten wohl die Kritiker des 19. Jh. recht, als sie an der Verbindung zweier so ungleicher Gattungen Anstoß nahmen: einer idyllischen Liebesszene und eines rohen Streitgesprächs?

Die vom Umfang von jeweils 47 Versen bestimmte Gleichwertigkeit des Wassers und des Weines wird im Dialog, und zwar in den letzten Reden der beiden Gesprächspartner, dadurch erklärt, daß jeder der beiden seine Rolle in einem heiligen Sakrament spielt. Der rohe Ton des Streitgesprächs verhüllt eine himmlische Harmonie.

Die Zahlen 40 und 50, die wir offenbar mit der Doncella, bzw. mit dem Escolar verbinden sollen, symbolisieren aber nicht Ungleichheit, sondern Zusammengehörigkeit: die Zahl 40 „erzeugt" die 50, d. h. die Summe ihrer Teiler ist 50. Dies wurde im Mittelalter als besonders sinnvoll erfahren, weil ja die 40 das Symbol des Fastens und der Enthaltsamkeit und die 50 das Sinnbild der Vergebung der Sünden war[7].

Enthaltsamkeit ist zwar nicht der zentrale Gedanke der Razón de amor, im Gegenteil. Nicht nur bittet der Escolar am Schluß um Wein, sondern es vollzieht sich in der Mitte des Gedichts die Erfüllung der Liebe. Die Struktur des ganzen Werkes weist darauf hin. Die Bitte um Wein kommt im letzten Vers, und das Gedicht besteht nicht nur aus 17, d. h. 16 + 1 Abschnitten, sondern auch aus 257, d. h. $16^2 + 1$ Versen[8]. Der mittelste

---

[7] Cf. die Variante des hl. Augustinus bei Heinz Meyer, Die Zahlenallegorese im Mittelalter, München 1975, p. 165: „Die Vierzig bringt so aus sich die Fünfzig hervor, wie ein gut geführtes irdisches Leben (40) die ewige Ruhe (50) erwirkt."

[8] Auffallend ist, daß Abschnitt 8 aus 16 und Abschnitt 16 aus 8 Versen besteht. Darf man darin einen Hinweis sehen, daß das ganze Gedicht aus $2 \times 8 \times 16 + 1$ Versen besteht? Parallelfälle sind möglicherweise Abschnitt 14 mit 14 Versen und Abschnitt 12, der wie Abschnitt 13 12 Verse hat. Hier haben wir einen besseren Anhalt, denn die zwölf Abschnitte 1−2 und 8−17 haben genau $144 = 12^2$ Verse. Vielleicht wollte der Dichter der Zahl Zwölf, die den katholischen Glauben symbolisiert, die Fünf der Venus gegenüberstellen. Die fünf Abschnitte 3−7 umfassen 113 Verse, doch es ist nicht sicher, daß diese Zahl als Summe der Quadrate von 7 und 8 gemeint ist ($23 + 26 = 49$; $20 + 44 = 64$). Die fünfzehn Abschnitte 3−17 haben $225 = 15^2$ Verse.

Abschnitt (9) ist die erste Rede des Weines, in der er dem Wasser sagt, es habe schlechte Manieren, und seine Gesellschaft ablehnt. Der mittelste Vers (129) kontrastiert inhaltlich mit diesem mittelsten Abschnitt. Das Mädchen preist in ihrem Lied die guten Manieren des Studenten, von denen sie gehört hat, und bringt ihre Sehnsucht nach seiner Gesellschaft zum Ausdruck. Sie liebt ihn, obschon sie ihn noch nie gesehen hat. Gegen die Mitte des Gedichts erkennen sich die zwei an den Geschenken, die sie sich gegenseitig gesandt haben. Dann fährt der Erzähler fort: „Sie nahm sich den Mantel von den Schultern und küßte mich auf Mund und Augen; so grosse Lust hatte sie an mir, dass sie kein Wort zu mir sagen konnte."

Der letzte dieser Verse, „sol fablar non me podía . . ." ist der mittelste Vers der Razón de amor. Das Wort „razón" kann ,Gespräch' bedeuten (und wird zweimal vom Wein in diesem Sinn verwendet), doch in der Mitte dieses Gesprächs wird nicht gesprochen, sondern nur gehandelt! In den nächsten versen singt das Mädchen eine „cantiga de amigo": „Gott der Herr sei gepriesen, daß ich meinen Freund jetzt kenne" – und Leo Spitzer hat darauf hingewiesen, daß das Wort „conocer" ,erkennen' hier im biblischen Sinn gebraucht wird.

Schließlich kann es nicht bedeutungslos sein, daß die Zahl 20 sich so oft in Verbindung mit dem Mädchen findet: ihre Beschreibung in Abschnitt 4, ihr Lied in 5, ihre Worte in 6–7 sind jeweils 20 Verse lang. Wollte der Dichter auf das Alter von 20 Jahren, das ideale Alter für die Liebe[9], hinweisen? Die Erfüllung der Liebe findet in einem Abschnitt von 20 Versen statt.

Obschon ich noch nicht imstande bin, das Verhältnis zwischen der Idylle und dem Streitgespräch zu deuten, glaube ich gezeigt zu haben, daß ein gutes Verständnis des Zahlenbaus für die Interpretation der Razón de amor unentbehrlich ist.

Die Milagros de Nuestra Señora

Gonzalo de Berceo schrieb seine Milagros de Nuestra señora um die Mitte des 13. Jh.[10] in der Cuaderna vía-Form, d. h. in Strophen, die aus vier Alexandrinern bestehen, die alle denselben Reim haben. Den fünfundzwanzig Marienlegenden geht in der Sammlung Berceos ein allegorischer

---

[9] So zum Beispiel in der Historia de la Donzella Teodor, die in einer kritischen Ausgabe von Walter Mettmann vorliegt (Mainz 1962). Auch Melibea, die Geliebte Calistos in La Celestina, ist 20 Jahre alt.

[10] Aus den Strophen 325 und 869 geht hervor, daß er sowohl vor 1246 als nach 1252 schrieb. Kritische Textausgabe von Brian Dutton, London 1971, der auch den lateinischen Prosatext gibt, der Berceos Vorlage am nächsten kommt (die Hs. Thott 128 der königl. Bibl. in Kopenhagen), und die beiden Versionen miteinander vergleicht.

Prolog voraus, der aus 47 Strophen besteht[11]. Dieser Umfang des Prologs ist der Modul, der den ersten Hauptteil des Werkes bestimmt. Wie wir sehen werden, ist die Legendensammlung aus drei Hauptteilen aufgebaut, wobei der Mittelteil von zwei gleich langen Flügeln flankiert wird. Der Beginnflügel setzt sich aus dem Prolog und den ersten vierzehn Legenden zusammen, und letztere sind in drei Gruppen von je 94 (= 2 × 47) Strophen aufgeteilt. Der Prolog und die ersten zwei Gruppen von Legenden schließen jeweils mit einer Abwägung der Vielheit, ja der Unzählbarkeit der Wunder Mariä. Eine solche Abwägung findet sich nicht nur in den Strophen 47, 141 (3 × 47) und 235 (5 × 47), sondern auch in Strophe 100. Auf diese Weise unterstrich der Dichter, daß er den Beginnflügel als ein Dreieck über der Basis Fünf entwarf, das aus dem Prolog und Gruppen von zwei, drei, vier und fünf Legenden besteht (s. Schema C).

In die Mitte der Fünfergruppe, die die Basis des Dreiecks bildet, stellt der Dichter eine Legende (XII) von 25 Strophen, um auf die Gesamtzahl der Legenden seiner Sammlung hinzuweisen. Diesen $25 = 5^2$ Strophen stehen die $16 = 4^2$ der Legende IV gegenüber, denn diese ist die mittlere der drei Legenden, die die mittelste Ebene des Dreiecks bilden, und somit als das Zentrum des ganzen Dreiecks aufzufassen (s. Schema D). Legende IV ist das fünfte Bauelement des Werkes, und gerade in diesem findet sich ein Schlüssel zum Verständnis der Zahl Fünf, die in fünf Strophen (118–122) fünfmal vorkommt. Drei Dinge werden hier mit dieser Zahl verbunden: die fünf Wunden Christi, gleich viele Freuden Mariä und die fünf Sinne des Menschen. Wir sollen, sagt Berceo, Maria an ihre fünf Freuden

Prolog	I	II	III	IV	V	VI	VII	VIII	IX	X	XI	XII	XIII	XIV
47	27	26	15	16	10	18	22	38	16	34	11	25	11	13
	53			41										
		94					94					94 = 2 × 47		

Schema C. Dreiecksstruktur des Beginnflügels der Milagros.

Prolog

I   II

III   IV   V

VI   VII   VIII   IX

X   XI   XII   XIII   XIV

Schema D. Beginnflügel mit Legende IV in der Mitte.

---

[11] Korrekt in der Ausgabe von A. G. Solalinde, Madrid 1922. Dutton irrt sich, wenn er meint, Strophe 47 gehöre schon zur ersten Legende.

erinnern, damit wir durch ihre Fürbitte Vergebung der Sünden erlangen, zu denen uns die fünf Sinne anstiften.

Die Spitze des vom Prolog bestimmten Dreiecks ist der Prolog selber mit seinen 47 Strophen; diese Zahl findet sich aber auch in der Mitte der Basis, weil zwei Legenden mit je 11 Strophen die 25 Strophen der Legende XII flankieren. Zudem sind die Umfänge der Legenden X und XIV von den zwei Zahlen aus der Reihe des Fibonacci bestimmt, deren Summe 47 ist.

Der Prolog beginnt mit der Allegorie an sich, deren Umfang von 15 Strophen, von denen die erste eine captatio benevolentiae enthält, den Umfang des Beginnflügels des ganzen Werkes ankündigt. Der Dichter erzählt, wie er auf einer Pilgerfahrt zu einer grünen Wiese voller Blumen kam, mit klaren Quellen in den vier Ecken, die im Sommer kühles und im Winter warmes Wasser spendeten, wo er sich im Schatten der zahlreichen Obstbäume ausruhte (Strophen 1−5). Die vielen Vögel sangen im Chor, so daß keine irdische Musik damit vergleichbar war (6−10). Die Wiese war immer grün; von den Blumen konnte man pflücken, soviel man wollte, sie wuchsen drei- und vierfach wieder nach; es schien eine Art Paradies zu sein (11−15)[12].

Die Erklärung der Allegorie umfaßt die nächsten 27 Strophen (16−42). Alle Menschen sind in diesem Leben Pilger, die bei der Jungfrau Maria Ruhe finden: sie ist die grüne Wiese (16−20). Die vier klaren Quellen sind die vier Evangelien; der Schatten der Bäume ist die Fürbitte Mariä für die Sünder; die Bäume, die den Schatten werfen, sind die heiligen Wunder Mariä (21−25). Daß die Bäume die Wunder symbolisieren, teilt gerade Strophe 25 mit: dies ist ein Hinweis auf die Gesamtzahl der Legenden. Die Vögel auf den Obstbäumen, die so schön singen, sind Augustin und Gregor und alle diejenigen, die über Maria geschrieben haben und ihr nachgefolgt sind: Propheten, Apostel, Beichtväter, Märtyrer und Jungfrauen (26−30). Die Blumen sind die Ehrennamen Mariä. Siebenundzwanzig Ehrentitel zählt der Dichter auf (31−42), und die Struktur der Aufzählung stellt diese Zahl als das Dreifache der Neun vor[13].

---

[12] Die erste und die dritte der drei Fünfergruppen bestehen aus 1 + 4 bzw. 3 + 2 Strophen, wodurch die Allegorie als ein Dreieck erscheint; in der 10. Strophe sagt der Dichter, er könne nicht ein Zehntel dieser Herrlichkeit beschreiben, und selbst Priore und Äbte könnten das nicht. In Strophe 100 meint er dann, kein Mensch („nul omne") sei imstande, auch nur ein Tausendstel der Wunder Mariä aufzuzählen.

[13] Die Aufzählung ist in drei Serien aufgeteilt, die jeweils mit ein paar Prefigurationen aus dem Alten Testament enden. Jede Serie umfaßt drei Strophen. Die Strophen 31 und 42 sind nämlich Einleitung und Schluß; die 38, zwischen der zweiten und der dritten Serie, spricht von der unendlichen Vielheit der Namen Mariä und ist daher eine unausgesprochene Einladung zum Zählen und ein Hinweis darauf, daß die Zahl der vom Dichter aufgezählten Namen bedeutungsvoll ist. Die erste Serie enthält sieben Mariensymbole (Strophen 32−33) und zwei Prefigurationen (34), die zweite drei symbolische Namen (35 a−c) und vier Prefigurationen (35 d−37) und die dritte acht Symbole (39 a−c) und drei Prefigurationen (39 d−41).

Die Aufzählung der 27 Ehrentitel Mariä schließt die Erklärung ab, die wie gesagt aus 27 Strophen besteht. Die Zahl 27 und deren Dreiteilung bestimmen auch die erste Legende, denn die Erzählung von der Kasel des hl. Ildefons von Toledo (Strophen 48—74) besteht aus drei Phasen von jeweils neun Strophen.

Der Schluß des Prologs umfaßt fünf Strophen (43—47). Hier zählt der Dichter noch einmal die fünf wichtigsten Symbole auf. Die Singvögel, den Schatten der Bäume, die Quellen und die Blumen lasse er nun; jetzt wolle er nur noch auf die Bäume klettern und einige der Wunder Mariä beschreiben. Die glorreiche Jungfrau möge ihn begleiten, damit er imstande sei, dies zu unternehmen und zu vollenden: das werde er für ein von ihr selbst bewirktes Wunder halten. So werden die 25 Marienlegenden vom Wunder ihrer Beschreibung überwölbt: dies ist die Rechtfertigung der Anzahl von 26 Bauelementen, die in der Gesamtstruktur hervortritt. Die Zahlen 25 und 26 bestimmen auch den Bau der zweiten Legende; den drei Phasen dieser Erzählung vom unkeuschen Küster (10 + 10 + 5 Strophen) folgt Strophe 100 (cf. supra und Anm. 12) als eine Art Epilog. Die fünfundzwanzigste und letzte Strophe der Erzählung an sich, die fünfte der dritten Phase (99), hat nicht wie üblich vier, sondern fünf Verse[14].

Die letzte Strophe des Prologs (47) lautet: „En Espanna cobdicio de luego empezar: en Toledo la magna, un famado logar, ca non sé de quál cabo empieze a contar, ca más son que arenas en riba de la mar" — d. h. „In Spanien möchte ich jetzt anfangen, im großen Toledo, einem berühmten Ort, denn sonst wüßte ich nicht wo (wörtlich: an welcher Seite) anfangen zu erzählen (oder: zählen!), denn sie (nämlich die Wunder Mariä) sind zahlreicher als Sand am Meeresufer." Die erste Erzählung beginnt dann mit den Worten: „Im guten Toledo, der königlichen Stadt, die am Tajo liegt, am großen Wasser . . ."

Die Reihenfolge der ersten fünfzehn Erzählungen ist bei Berceo dieselbe wie in der Hs. Thott 128; er folgt einfach seiner lateinischen Vorlage. Die Tatsache, daß die erste Erzählung in Toledo handelt, gewinnt aber bei ihm

---

Insgesamt besteht die Aufzählung aus achtzehn symbolischen Namen und neun Prefigurationen, und die zwei Kategorien von Ehrentitel stehen somit im Verhältnis 2:1 zueinander; im gleichen Verhältnis stehen die sechs Strophen 32—37 mit den ersten zwei Serien zu den drei Strophen 39—41 mit der dritten Serie. Cf. C. Gariano, Análisis estilístico de los „Milagros de Nuestra Señora" de Berceo, Madrid [2]1971, p. 181 s., der 25 Namen findet; sein Irrtum besteht darin, daß er Vers 35 b („ella nos dio el cevo de qui todos comemos") nicht separat rechnet, sondern zum vorangehenden Vers fügt („Ella es dicha fuent de qui todos bevemos"), und in Vers 39 a „uva" ‚Traube' nicht mitzählt, vermutlich, weil es auf „vid" ‚Weinstock' folgt. Ähnlicherweise irrt sich Solalinde (cf. Anm. 11), wenn er die „piértega" usw. (39 d) mit dem „fust de Moÿses" (40 a) gleichstellt.

[14] Sonst hat nur Strophe 866, die letzte der Theophillegende, fünf Verse. Dies ist zugleich die letzte Strophe des Buches. Die Hs. von Ibarreta gibt nämlich die letzten zwei Legenden in umgekehrter Reihenfolge. Mit Recht läßt Dutton die Strophen 867—911 den Strophen 703—866 vorangehen.

eine komplizierte symbolische Bedeutung, auf die er in den Strophen 47 und 48 anspielt. Statt des einfachen „in toletana urbe" spricht dieser Nordspanier vom „guten Toledo, der königlichen Stadt, die am großen Wasser Tajo liegt". Mit den letzten Worten schafft er eine Parallele und einen Gegensatz zu dem „Sand am Meeresufer": Toledo liegt am Wasser, aber nicht am Meer. Der Ausdruck „wie der Sand am Meer" stammt aus dem Buch Genesis (32, 12) und bezieht sich dort auf die Nachkommen Jakobs, wie auch der Begriff „wie der Staub auf der Erde" (28, 14). Vermutlich wollte Berceo indirekt auch auf die Worte hinweisen, die Gott zu Abraham sprach, als er ihm eine Nachkommenschaft so zahlreich wie die Sterne am Himmel verhieß (Gen. 15, 5): „Er führte ihn hinaus und sprach: Sieh doch zum Himmel hinauf, und zähl die Sterne, wenn du sie zählen kannst. Und er sprach zu ihm: So zahlreich werden deine Nachkommen sein"[15]. In der Zeit Berceos blühte in der guten Königsstadt Toledo die Astronomie; unser nächster Abschnitt handelt vom Zählen der Sterne. Nicht umsonst macht Berceo diese Anspielungen in den Strophen 47 und 48, denn diese beiden Zahlen sind Symbole des Sternenhimmels. So erklärt er auf verhüllte Weise seinen Lesern die Bedeutung der Modulzahl 47. Zur gleichen Zeit jedoch erinnert er im Übergang vom Prolog zur ersten Erzählung an die ersten zwei Ehrentitel Mariä: „Stern der Meere" und „der Himmel Königin" (32 b, 33 a).

Mit den Worten, er wisse nicht wo, d. h. an welcher Seite, anfangen zu zählen, weist Berceo auf den symmetrischen Bau seines Werkes hin. Zwischen zwei gleich langen Flügeln befindet sich ein mittlerer Teil, der wiederum symmetrisch aufgebaut ist (s. Schema E). Der mittlere Teil besteht aus 253 Strophen. 253 ist die Dreieckszahl auf der Basis 22. Die erste der sieben Legenden dieses Mittelteils (XV) hat 22 Strophen – und die letzte (XXI) ist das 22. Bauelement.

In der Mitte des Mittelstücks des mittleren Teils ist Legende XIX, „Die wunderbare Entbindung", in der Maria eine schwangere Frau vor dem Ertrinkungstod rettet und darauf als Geburtshelferin auftritt. Die letzten neun Strophen dieser Legende (452–460) stehen genau in der Mitte des

15 Bauelemente	3 Legenden			3 Legenden			1 Legende	4 Legenden
Prolog + I–XIV	XV	XVI	XVII	XVIII	XIX	XX	XXI	XXII–XXV
	22	26	35	18	30	39		
	48			48				
		83			87		83	
329 (7 × 47)				253 (= 11 × 23 = $\therefore$ 22)				329 Strophen

Schema E. Bauliche Symmetrie der Milagros.

---

[15] Die Bibel. Einheitsübersetzung. Freiburg, Basel, Wien 1980.

ganzen Werkes. Strophe 452 berichtet, die Menschen, die von dem Wunder hörten, hätten Gott gelobt; die restlichen acht Strophen geben den Wortlaut dieses Lobliedes. Die mittelste Strophe des ganzen Werkes (456) unterbricht eine Aufzählung dreier Exempla von Menschen, die aus dem Wasser gerettet wurden: Jona, die Kinder Israels im Roten Meer und Petrus. Nach den zwei alttestamentlichen Beispielen fügt Strophe 456 als Kommentar hinzu: „Die köstlichen, vortrefflichen alten Wunder sehen wir heute erneut vor unsern Augen[16]: Herr, deine Freunde finden Furten sogar im Meere, die andern werden auf dem Trocknen ertrunken aufgefunden." In den ersten zwei Versen dieser Strophe denkt Berceo vielleicht auch an seine eigene Sammlung von Marienlegenden, die durch den Gebrauch von Versen und ihre Bauform gegenüber den lateinischen Prosasammlungen eine große Neuerung bedeutet.

Betrachten wir nun die sechs langen und sehr langen Legenden, die auf Legende XIX folgen, so sehen wir, daß Berceo in seiner Strophe 47 nicht nur einen symmetrischen Bau vor Augen hatte, sondern daß die Strophen in seinem Werk auch tatsächlich rückwärts gezählt werden müssen. Diese sechs Legenden — 6 ist die Dreieckszahl auf der Basis 3 — sind, von hinten nach vorne betrachtet, so verteilt wie die ersten fünfzehn Bauelemente von vorne nach hinten (s. Schema F). Die lange Erzählung von Theophil liefert mit ihren 164 = 4 × 41 Strophen den Modul 41, der dann die Zweiergruppe XXIV–XXIII und die Dreiergruppe XXII–XX bestimmt.

Das Verhältnis 4 : 7 : 11 weist auf das Göttliche Verhältnis hin, das zwischen diesen sechs Legenden und den vorhergehenden zwölf besteht (s. Schema G). Dabei ist zu beachten, daß die zwölf vorhergehenden Legenden die kleinere Anzahl Strophen umfassen als die letzten sechs: die achtzehn Legenden sind nach dem Verhältnis 2 : 1 und ihre Strophen nach dem Göttlichen Verhältnis geteilt, aber das Gefälle der beiden Verhältnisse ist gegenläufig[17].

Das Göttliche Verhältnis bestimmt auch die 25 Legenden als Ganzes (s. Schema H). Die Strophenzahlen der Legenden I–XVI und XVII–XXV, 330 und 534, sind das Sechsfache der Zahlen des Fibonacci 55 und 89. Die Unterteilung der 25 = 5^2 Legenden in 16 = 4^2 und 9 = 3^2 kommt mir wie eine Anspielung auf das erste Dreieck des Pythagoras vor, das rechtwinklige Dreieck mit den Katheten 3 und 4, der Hypotenuse 5 und dem Inhalt 6. Letztere Zahl ist, wie gesagt, der Faktor, mit dem die Zahlen

---

[16] „Los antigos miraclos preciosos e onrrados por ojo los veemos agora renovados." Nach dem Exempel des Jona wird schon gesagt: „el miráculo viejo oï es renovado" (454 d).

[17] In der Verhältnisgleichung 279 : 451 = 451 : 730 ist die Zahl 451 der mittlere Term. Vielleicht wollte Berceo die „schöne" oder „goldene" (!) Mitte mit der vollkommenen Zahl Sechs kombinieren. Auch die Tatsache, daß im Spanischen „halb, Hälfte" und „mitten, mittel, Mitte" mit demselben Wort angedeutet werden, kann eine Rolle spielen (sechs ist die Hälfte von zwölf; die sechs Legenden bilden die mittlere Proportionale).

XX	XXI	XXII	XXIII	XXIV	XXV (Theophil)
39	83	42	78	45	164
	164		123 (3 × 41)		4 × 41
				287 (7 × 41)	
		451 (11 × 41)			4:7:11 ←

Schema F. Dreiecksstruktur der letzten sechs Legenden.

VIII–XIX   XX–XXV
12 Legenden   – – 2:1 – –   6 Legenden
279   451
                        730   279:451 = 451:730

Schema G. Stetige Teilung der Legenden VIII–XXV.

I–XVI   XVII–XXV
16 Legenden   9 Legenden
330   – – 55:89 – –   534
                    864 (6 × 144)   330:534 = 534:864

Schema H. Stetige Teilung der fünfundzwanzig Legenden.

Prolog + I–IX   X–XXV
10 Elemente   – – 5:8 – –   16 Legenden
235 (5 × 47)   676 = 26²

Schema J. Umfang der letzten sechzehn Legenden.

Prolog + I–XV   XVI–XXIII   XXIV–XXV
16 Elemente   – – 2:1 – –   8 Legenden   2 Legenden
351   – – 1:1 – –   351 = ∴ 26   209

Schema K. Umfang der ersten sechzehn Bauelemente und der folgenden acht Legenden.

55 und 89 multipliziert sind; und auch die Summe von 55 + 89, das Quadrat von Zwölf, kann mit diesem Dreieck verbunden werden, weil 12 die Summe der drei Seiten ist.

Die Unterteilung der Gesamtheit der 25 = 5^2 Legenden in zwei Quadrate, 16 und 9, gemäß dem Dreieck des Pythagoras, ergibt somit eine stetige Teilung der Strophen. Teilen wir dagegen die 26 Bauelemente gemäß dem Verhältnis 5 : 8 (einem Annäherungswert des Göttlichen Verhältnisses), so finden wir wiederum eine Quadratzahl, 676 = 26^2 (s. Schema J). Die letzten 16 Legenden haben insgesamt 676 = 26^2 Strophen. Hier werden demnach das Quadrat der evangelischen Vier und das der 26, der Zahl der Wunder Mariä, einander gleichgestellt. Die 16 steht auch als 4^2 der Zehn, der Dreieckszahl über der Basis 4, gegenüber.

Ergibt die Rückwärtszählung das Quadrat von 26, so ergibt die Vorwärtszählung vom Anfang bis Legende XXIII zweimal hintereinander die Dreieckszahl auf der Basis 26 (s. Schema K). Bei der Vorwärtszählung verhalten sich die Zahlen der ersten 24 Bauelemente (Prolog und dreiundzwanzig Legenden) wie 2 : 1. Die Dreieckszahl von 26 enthält den Faktor 27, der im Aufbau des Prologs eine so wichtige Rolle spielt (s. oben S. 414 und Anm. 13). Die Gruppe von acht Legenden fängt mit Legende XVI an, die einen Umfang von 26 Strophen hat; die letzte Legende dieser Gruppe (XXIII) hat 78 = 3 × 26 Strophen. Etwas Ähnliches konstatieren wir bei der Rückwärtszählung, die die Quadratzahl 676 = 26^2 ergibt: den letzten 16 Legenden geht die Legende IX mit einem Umfang von 16 Strophen voran.

Es war fromme Bescheidenheit, als Gonzalo de Berceo die Beschreibung der Wunder Mariä ein von ihr selbst bewirktes Wunder nannte. Die Wunder der Struktur seines Werkes stellen die Forschung noch vor viele Aufgaben.

Ich möchte noch einen letzten Anhaltspunkt im Text erwähnen, weil er beweist, daß die Theophillegende ans Ende der Sammlung gehört. Wenn Theophil bereut, seine Seele dem Teufel verkauft zu haben, wendet er sich in einem Gebet an Maria, das er in Strophe 775 beendet. In der folgenden Strophe wird berichtet, das Gebet hätte vierzig Tage und Nächte gedauert, und am vierzigsten Tag sei ihm Maria erschienen. Dies ist eine Schlüsselstelle, denn Strophe 775 ist, wenn die richtige Reihenfolge der letzten zwei Legenden wiederhergestellt ist[18], die 820. des Werkes, und 820 (20 × 41) ist die Dreieckszahl auf der Basis 40. Sie enthält den Faktor 41, der als Modul am Ende des Werkes der 47, die den Anfang bestimmt, gegenübersteht. Nach diesen 820 Strophen folgen bis zum Ende des Werkes noch 91, die Dreieckszahl auf der Basis 13. Die Struktur der Theophillegende gibt demnach an, daß die ganze Sammlung von den Zahlen 40 und 13 bestimmt

---

[18] Cf. Anm. 14.

ist[19]. Mit der Zahl 40 ist wohl die Pönitenz gemeint, zu der Berceo in seinem Schlußwort sein Publikum aufruft (Strophen 861—63, bzw. 906—08). Die Dreizehn symbolisiert Christus und für Berceo vielleicht auch Maria. Deswegen haben die letzten drei Strophen des Werkes zusammen 13 Verse (die letzte hat ja fünf). Sie sind ein Segenswunsch, der mit den folgenden Worten anfängt (Strophe 864, bzw. 909): „Das gebe Jesus Christus und die glorreiche Jungfrau, ohne die nichts Gutes zustande kommt, daß wir dieses leidvolle Leben so führen, daß wir das andre, dauerhafte und leuchtende, gewinnen."

Der Sternkatalog Alfons des Weisen

Dauerhaft und leuchtend erscheinen uns die Sterne. Sind sie nicht ein Abbild des Ewigen? Hat nicht das gerade noch Sichtbare am meisten über das Unsichtbare mitzuteilen? Davon war anscheinend der König von Kastilien und Leon, Alfons der Weise, überzeugt. Sein im Jahre 1276 vollendetes Werk „Die vier Bücher von der achten Sphäre und von ihren 48 Figuren (d. h. Sternbildern) mit deren Sternen"[20] behandelt in den ersten drei Büchern ausführlich die Gestirne des nördlichen Himmels, des Tierkreises und der südlichen Hemisphäre und gibt im vierten Buch eine Zusammenfassung, in der die Zahlen jedoch nicht vollkommen mit denen der drei vorhergehenden Bücher übereinstimmen. Mir scheint, es gibt dafür nur eine einzige Erklärung, nämlich, daß der weise König in der Überzeugung, Gott habe alles mit Maß und Zahl und Gewicht geordnet, in den schönen Zahlen der Sterne das Geheimnis der Schöpfung und der Gottesoffenbarung suchte.

Betrachten wir die Zahlen der Zusammenfassung im vierten Buch. In unserer Tafel (Schema L) stehen ganz links die Zahlen der Sternbilder am nördlichen Himmel (S = Septentrio), am Zodiakus (Z), am südlichen Himmel (M = Meridies) und zusammengezählt am ganzen Firmament (F). Die Sterne der drei Himmelsbereiche sind in der Zusammenfassung in sechs Größenklassen und die Kategorie der „cárdenas" (C) oder Nebulosae eingeteilt. Das ergibt 21 Zahlen, von denen Alfons zehn korrigiert hat („155 = + 4" bedeutet, daß die Zahl 151, die aus den Daten des ersten Buches hervorgeht, um vier vermehrt worden ist, usw.). Die Gesamtzahlen der Sterne sind ganz rechts aufs neue verteilt in solche, die sich innerhalb, und solche, die sich außerhalb der Sternbilder befinden.

---

[19] Inhaltliche Einschnitte teilen die 91 Strophen des Schlusses in 55 (.˙. 10) + 28 (.˙. 7) + 8.

[20] Textausgabe von Manuel Rico y Sinobas, Libros del saber de astronomía del Rey D. Alfonso X de Castilla, Band I, Madrid 1863.

Sternbilder		Sterne, der Größe nach verteilt									
		1.	2.	3.	4.	5.	6.	C	Tot	Int	Ext
21	S	3	16	82	155 = +4	80	26	1	363	330	33
12	Z	5 = −1	5	63 = −1	137 = +1	100 = +1	37 = +1	2	349	289	60
15 (14)	M	7	12	59 = −1	139 = −2	73 = +2	17 = +1	1	308	295	13
48 (47)	F	15	33	204	431	253	80	4	1020	914	106

Schema L. Übersicht des Sternkatalogs von Alfons dem Weisen.

Mit den zehn kleinen Korrekturen brachte der gelehrte König seine Vermutung zum Ausdruck, die „richtige", geheimnis- und bedeutungsvolle Zahl der Sterne sei 1020. Diese Zahl ist das Produkt von 17 und 60, und die Sterne des Tierkreises (Z) sind in $289 = 17^2$ innerhalb und 60 außerhalb der Sternbilder verteilt. Der Quadratzahl 289 steht die Summe der Sterne innerhalb der Sternbilder des nördlichen und des südlichen Himmels mit $330 + 295 = 625 = 25^2$ gegenüber.

Auch die auf die Größe basierte Einteilung ergibt eine schöne Struktur. Für die ersten beiden Größenklassen zusammen gibt die Zusammenfassung die Zahl 48, worin sich mit 84 die Summe der kleinsten Sterne und der „cárdenas" spiegelt. Die mittleren drei Kategorien haben zusammen 888 Sterne, und die Summe der Ziffern dieser drei Zahlen (48, 888 und 84) ist wiederum 48. Auf die Zahl der Sternbilder, 48 oder 47, werde ich später eingehen.

Konstatieren wir bei der Verteilung in externe und interne Sterne eine Gegenüberstellung der Quadratzahlen von 25 und 17, so findet sich etwas Ähnliches bei der anderen Einteilung. Die Sterne dritter bis fünfter Größe des Zodiakus sind zusammen 300, das ist 12×25, denen in diesen drei Kategorien die $588 = 12 \times 49$ Sterne des nördlichen und des südlichen Himmels gegenüberstehen. Hier finden wir also die Quadrate der Fünf und der Sieben nebeneinander.

Diese 588 Sterne des nördlichen und des südlichen Himmels sind besonders schön verteilt; deutlich ist zu sehen, zu welchem Zweck vier der sechs Zahlen korrigiert wurden (s. Schema M). Nicht nur sind nach der Korrektion die Sterne dritter und fünfter Größe zusammen gleich zahlreich wie die der vierten Größe allein, sondern es ergibt sich neben der Dreieckszahl von 17 (Sterne fünfter Größe) die von 29. Dies führt uns zu den 300 Sternen des Zodiakus zurück, denn 300 ist die Dreieckszahl von 24. (Die Basen der drei Dreieckszahlen zusammen verweisen vielleicht verhüllt auf die Gegenüberstellung der Quadrate von Fünf und Sieben zurück, denn die Zahl 24 teilt den Abstand zwischen 17 und 29 in Sieben und Fünf.)

```
S          82 —— 155 ＼    ╱ 80              82 + 73 = 155
(Z)                        ╳                80 + 59 = 139
M          59 —— 139 ╱    ＼ 73
          ‾‾‾        ‾‾‾      ‾‾‾
          141       294      153            153 = 3² · 17 = ∴ 17
                 ╲  294  ╱                  141 + 294 = 435 = ∴ 29
```

Schema M. Die Sterne dritter bis fünfter Größe des nördlichen und des südlichen Himmels.

	2.	3.	4.	5.	6. Größe
S	16	82		80	26
Z			(137)		
M	12	59		73	17
	28	141		153	43

$169 = 13^2$ $196 = 14^2$

Tot. 365
= 5 × 73

365

Schema N. Die Sterne zweiter bis dritter und fünfter bis sechster Größe
des nördlichen und des südlichen Himmels.

	1.	2.	3.	4.	5.	6.	C
S	3						1
Z		5	63	137	100	37	
M	7						1

Tot. 354
= 6 × 59

	1.	2.	3.	4.	5.	6.	C
S		16	82	155	80	26	
Z	5						2
M		12	59	139	73	17	

Tot. 666
= 18 × 37
= ∴ 36

Schema O. Aufteilung des Himmels in 354 + 666 Sterne.

Um die Mitte des Zahlengedichts herum bilden zwei Gruppen von vier symmetrisch plazierten Zahlen die Quadrate von 13 und 14 und damit die Zahl der Tage des Sonnenjahres (s. Schema N). Die Zahl 73, eine der korrigierten Zahlen, die sich in dieser Figur befindet, ist einer der beiden Primfaktoren von 365.

Das ganze Raster der 21 Zahlen der Zusammenfassung kann in zwei symmetrische Figuren zerlegt werden, deren eine die Zahl der Tage des Mondjahres, nämlich 354, ergibt, während die andere 666 Sterne umfaßt (s. Schema O). 666 ist die Dreieckszahl von 36 und bekannt als die Zahl des Tieres in der Offenbarung des Johannes (13, 18). Der Primfaktor 37 der

Zahl 666 befindet sich in der 354-Figur, und umgekehrt befindet sich der Primfaktor 59 der Zahl 354 in der 666-Figur; die beiden Zahlen 37 und 59 gehören zu den zehn korrigierten Zahlen.

Die Zahl der Sternbilder ist 48. Der Titel deutet die beiden Ziffern dieser Zahl und verbindet sie mit dem Werk: „Die vier Bücher der achten Sphäre . . ." Der Text des ersten wie des dritten Buches jedoch spielt verhüllt auf die Primzahl 47 an. Er beschreibt die fünfzehn Sternbilder des südlichen Himmels zwar einzeln, aber weil Centaurus und Lupus zusammengehören, behandelt er ihre Sterne gemeinsam und darum kommt es in den drei Büchern nicht 48, sondern 47 Mal vor, daß eine Gruppe von Sternen der Größe nach verteilt wird.

Über das südliche Doppelsternbild teilt der Text mit, 18 von den 54 Sternen gehörten zum Lupus; es besteht somit das Verhältnis 1:2 zwischen diesen und den 36 Sternen des Centaurus. In den mittleren drei Größen, die in der Zusammenfassung eine so wichtige Rolle spielen, hat das südliche Doppelsternbild 48 Sterne (11 + 15 + 22).

Auch am nördlichen Himmel gibt es zwei zusammengehörige Sternbilder, nämlich, wie sie König Alfons nennt, den Natternjäger und die Natter[21]. Die beiden haben zusammen 47 Sterne, und zwar ausschließlich in den mittleren drei Größen; die Natter hat deren 18 (wie der Lupus) und der Jäger 29, so daß sie zueinander im Göttlichen Verhältnis stehen. Der Größe nach sind die 47 Sterne in 11 + 25 + 11 verteilt (s. Schema P). Die gleiche Verteilung verwendet Berceo in der Mitte der fünf Legenden, die im Beginnflügel seines Werkes die Basis des Dreiecks bilden (s. Schema Q).

	3.	4.	5. Größe
13. Caçador de las culuebras (29 Sterne)	6	14	9
14. Culuebra (18 Sterne)	5	11	2
	11	25	11

Schema P. Aufteilung der 47 Sterne des Ophiuchus und der Serpens in 11 + 25 + 11.

X	XI	XII	XIII	XIV
34	11	25	11	13

Schema Q. Umfang der Legenden X–XIV bei Berceo.

---

[21] „El caçador de las culuebras" und „la culuebra", d. h. Ophiuchus und Serpens. Der Name „Serpiente" deutet bei Alfons den Drachen an, wird aber gelegentlich auch statt „Culuebra" für Serpens gebraucht, so z. B. in der Beschreibung des „Genuflexu" (Hercules). Die von Alfons verwendeten spanischen und lateinischen Namen der Sternbilder sind meistens Übersetzungen aus dem Arabischen.

12. Tenedor de las riendas	13		
─────── (13, 14)			
15. Saeta	5		47 Sterne
16. Aguila	15	34	
17. Delfín	10		
18. Pieça del cauallo	4		

19. Cauallo mayor	20	
20. Mugier encaderada	23	47 Sterne
21. Triángulo	4	

Schema R. Die Zahl 47 als Bauprinzip der Sternbilder Nr. 12 und Nrn. 15—21 des nördlichen Himmels.

Dies ist nicht die einzige Parallele zur Legendensammlung des Berceo. Auch im Sternkatalog wird die Zahl 47 durch eindringliche Wiederholung hervorgehoben. Der Jäger und die Natter sind das 13. und 14. in der Aufzählung der nördlichen Sternbilder; sie werden von Nr. 12 und den Nrn. 15—18 flankiert, die zusammen wiederum 47 Sterne haben, während die drei letzten Sternbilder[22] (Nrn. 19—21) eine dritte Gruppe von 47 Sternen bilden (s. Schema R).

Da die Zahl 47 (der Größe nach in 11 + 25 + 11 verteilt) wie bei Berceo von den Zahlen 13 und 34 flankiert wird, liegt die Vermutung nahe, Berceo habe einen älteren Sternkatalog derselben Tradition gekannt.

Juan de Padilla

Die Zahl 47 war auch am Anfang des 16. Jh. noch ein Symbol des Sternenhimmels. Am Heiligen Abend des Jahres 1500 vollendet der Kartäuser Juan de Padilla sein aus vier „Tafeln" bestehendes Retabel des Lebens Christi. Am Schluß deutet er an, er sei 33 Jahre alt und es zieme ihm jetzt, zu schweigen und nicht mehr zu schreiben als dieses Leben des höchsten Königs. Aber siebzehn Jahre später, als er fünfzig ist, erzählt er, wie der Apostel Paulus ihm befiehlt, die „Zwölf Triumphe der zwölf Apostel"

---

[22] Die Identifikation der Sternbilder ist nicht immer einfach. Woher die Zeichnungen in der Ausgabe von Rico y Sinobas stammen, ist mir nicht deutlich; manche erscheinen spiegelverkehrt. Der „Tenedor de las riendas" ist Auriga, „Saeta" dagegen scheint nicht Sagitta, sondern Vulpecula zu sein, Sagitta und Aquila zusammen bilden „Águila". „Pieça del cauallo" ist Equuleus, „Cauallo mayor" ist Pegasus, die „Mugier encaderada" ist selbstverständlich Andromeda.

zu besingen; sein Versprechen, nicht mehr zu schreiben, bricht er nicht, denn indem er die Strophe des ersten Werkes, die das Versprechen enthält, als 33. Strophe im zweiten Werk zitiert, ist dieses mit 10295 statt 10296 Versen um einen Vers kürzer als das Retabel. Das Leben Christi ist nämlich aus 1289 Strophen von acht Langversen aufgebaut, während die 1144 Strophen der Triumphe, mit Ausnahme der Strophe, die er aus dem Retabel zitiert, neun Langverse haben; dadurch werden die zwei gleich langen Werke von verschiedenen Strophenzahlen bestimmt, welche jedoch ähnlich zusammengesetzt sind, denn die Strophenzahl der Zwölf Triumphe ist 12^2 mehr als tausend und die des Retabels 17^2 mehr als tausend[23].

Die letzten zwei Strophen des Retabels, die das Versprechen, zu schweigen, und ein Akrostichon mit dem Namen des „don Juan de Padilla, monje cartuxo" enthalten, stehen in der Mitte zwischen den beiden Werken. Der Vers „más de la vida del rey soberano" ist der mittelste aller Langverse der beiden Werke und als das Zünglein einer Waage aufzufassen.

Zwischen den beiden Werken besteht nicht nur Gleichgewicht, sondern auch Kongruenz. Das zweite Werk ist eigentlich vierteilig wie das erste, und in beiden besteht zwischen zwei Gruppen von zwei Teilen das gleiche Verhältnis 85 : 58. Die „Tafeln" des Retabels sind kreuzweise gepaart (s. Schema S). Der Umfang der zweiten Tafel enthält den Faktor 59, der vom Dichter als Modul für die beiden Werke verwendet worden ist. Die Zahl 59 symbolisiert für Padilla das Leben Mariä: aus dem Text des Retabels geht hervor, daß Maria 59 Jahre gelebt habe, d. h. fast 60.

Die vier Teile der Triumphe sind nicht kreuzweise, sondern parallel gepaart (s. Schema T). Die Zahl der 354 Strophen des zweiten Teils weist auf das Mondjahr hin; der Mond symbolisiert die Kirche, deren stellvertretendes Haupt, Petrus, im vierten Triumph zusammen mit Paulus besungen wird. Die Zahl der 273 Strophen des dritten Teils spielt auf Numeri 3, 40−51 an, wo berichtet wird, wie Moses die 273 Erstgeborenen unter den Israeliten, welche die Zahl der Leviten überstiegen, auslöste: fünf Schekel erhob er für jeden der überzähligen Israeliten, 1365 Silberschekel betrug das ganze Lösegeld, das er Aaron übergab. Die Zahl 1365 wiederum bestimmt das Retabel, denn den 1289 Strophen in Langversen sind 76 Strophen in Kurzversen beigefügt: jedes Kapitel wird mit einem Gebet in anspruchslosen Achtsilblern abgeschlossen.

---

[23] Die Zwölf Triumphe sind herausgegeben von Enzo Norti Gualdani, Juan de Padilla (el Cartujano), Los doce triunfos de los Apóstoles, tomo II, parte I, Testo, Firenze 1978. R. Foulché-Delbosc übernimmt in seinem Cancionero castellano del siglo XV, Band I, Madrid 1912, die Ausgabe von M. del Riego in Colección de obras poéticas españolas, London 1842. Die beiden Anthologien geben den Text der Triumphe fast vollständig, vom Retabel jedoch nur ein Sechstel. In meiner Dissertation, Materia mirable, Utrecht 1972, habe ich zuviele Hypothesen aufgestellt; für eine bearbeitete Strukturbeschreibung der beiden Werke mit neuen Forschungsergebnissen v. Henk de Vries, Símbolo y estructura en la obra del Cartujano, Anejo núm. 2 de Trayecto, Utrecht 1981.

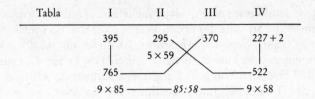

Schema S. Das Verhältnis 85:58 im Retabel.

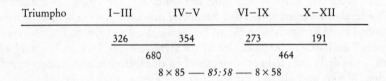

Schema T. Die vier Teile der Zwölf Triumphe und das Verhältnis 85:58.

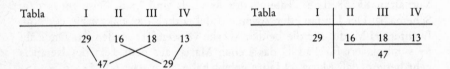

Schema V und W. Das Göttliche Verhältnis zwischen den Büchern des Retabels.

Prolog	14		
1. Kap.	11		
2. Kap.	14	25	51
3. Kap.	12		

Schema X. Umfang des Prologs und der ersten cánticos des ersten Buches des Retabels.

Mit der horizontalen Vierteilung der Triumphe kreuzt sich eine vertikale Einteilung in Textstücke, die den Himmel, die Erde, das Purgatorium und die Hölle beschreiben; aus dieser Kreuzung ergibt sich eine komplizierte Gleichgewichtsstruktur, die 1062 (= 18 × 59 oder 3 × 354) der 1144 Strophen umfaßt[24].

---

[24] V. Símbolo y estructura, o. c., 35–39. Dem Himmel sind 396, der Erde 135, dem Purgatorium 185 und der Hölle 346 Strophen gewidmet; 396 + 135 = 531 = 185 + 346. Dem Himmel stehen die drei anderen Reiche mit einem Gesamtumfang von 666 Strophen gegenüber.

Die ersten drei Teile der Zwölf Triumphe umfassen jeweils fünfzehn Kapitel, der vierte Teil zwölf. Im Retabel hat die zweite Tafel fünfzehn „cánticos" – wie hier die Kapitel heißen – und die vierte zwölf. Die dritte Tafel hat zehn cánticos, denen sieben viel längere „lamentaciones", die das Geschehen am Karfreitag beschreiben, folgen. Die erste Tafel besteht aus 28 cánticos. Da jede Tafel mit einem Prolog beginnt, sind die Kapitelzahlen der vier Bücher 29, 16, 18 und 13, zwischen denen auf zweierlei Weise das Göttliche Verhältnis besteht. In der kreuzweisen Verteilung (s. Schema V), die, wie wir gesehen haben, in den Strophenzahlen das Verhältnis 85 : 58 aufweist, besteht das Göttliche Verhältnis nicht nur zwischen II + IV (29) und I + III (47), sondern auch zwischen III (18) und I (29). Die andere Verteilung (s. Schema W) läßt vermuten, daß in der ersten Tafel eine Deutung der Zahl 29 enthalten ist. Dieses erste Buch beschreibt das Leben Christi bis zu seinem öffentlichen Auftreten. Am Anfang der zweiten Tafel sagt der Dichter, Christus sei „neunundzwanzig heilige Jahre" alt gewesen, als er zur Taufe des Johannes ging.

Im letzten cántico der ersten Tafel wird auf verhüllte Weise die Zahl 29 in zwölf und siebzehn aufgeteilt und letztere Zahl gedeutet. Seit sich der zwölfjährige Jesus im Tempel als Sohn Gottes offenbarte, habe er bis zum Alter von dreißig Jahren (später als 29 präzisiert) kein einziges Wunder getan – dafür gebe es nur apokryphe Quellen –, aber ein großes Wunder sei gewesen, daß er verschwieg, wer er war, nämlich „die Grundursache der Welt und der gute Sohn Gottes". Juan de Padilla folgt somit Christus nach, wenn er zwischen seinen beiden Werken siebzehn Jahre schweigt. Der Ausdruck „der gute Sohn Gottes" scheint darauf hinzuweisen, daß Padilla die Isopsefie des Tetragrammatons jhwh = 17 = tob – Jahweh ist gut – kannte.

Die beiden langen Dichtungen des Kartäusers bilden eigentlich ein einziges Lebenswerk. Beide werden auf gleiche Weise als ein Dreieck vorgestellt, dessen Basis im Falle des Retabels die Zahl 50 und im Falle der Zwölf Triumphe die 47 ist.

Das erste Kapitel des Retabels, der Prolog zur ersten Tafel, zählt 14 Strophen. Die übrigen 1275 = 25 × 51 Strophen entsprechen der Dreieckszahl auf der Basis 50. Der Faktor 51 liegt am Anfang des Werkes und schließt den Faktor 25 ein (s. Schema X). Die Basis befindet sich kurz vor dem Schluß, wo drei cánticos, die zusammen 50 Strophen umfassen, Christi Wiederkehr und das jüngste Gericht beschreiben „und wie diejenigen, die gerettet werden, zum Himmel gehen".

Das erste Kapitel der Zwölf Triumphe besteht aus 16 Strophen. Die restlichen 1128 = 24 × 47 Strophen, die der Dreieckszahl auf der Basis 47 entsprechen, fangen mit zwei Kapiteln von 24 und 23 Strophen an, die zusammen die Basis von 47 Strophen bilden. Am Schluß dieses Textstückes liegt eine Aufzählung von Sternbildern – nicht 47 oder 48, sondern 36, und zwar 18 des nördlichen und nochmals 18 des südlichen Himmels und

des Zodiakus zusammen. Mit diesen Zahlen weist der Dichter wahrschein-
lich auf die bereits erwähnte, 18 × 59 Strophen umfassende Gleichge-
wichtsstruktur hin. Die Aufzählung der Sternbilder unterstreicht, daß der
Dichter, wie er im Prosaprolog sagt, „als ein höheres Fundament seines
Werkes das Gleichnis des Firmaments, d. h. des Sternenhimmels, nimmt".
In den zwölf Tierzeichen besingt er die zwölf Apostel – und 120 andere
Heiligen.

Das Retabel dagegen, dessen vier Bücher laut des Prosaprologs mit
den vier Evangelien übereinstimmen, schließt mit einem Bild des „berühmten Berges" Gibraltar, von wo aus man gegen Norden Europa, gegen
Süden Afrika, gegen Westen den Ozean und gegen Osten das Mittelmeer
und die Balearen sehen kann: die vier Ecken der Erde.

Die Celestina

Von der ersten, kurzen Fassung der Celestina, der Comedia de Calisto
y Melibea, sind drei Drucke erhalten, die innerhalb von drei Jahren erschienen (Burgos 1499 – das Jahr steht nicht ganz fest –, Toledo 1500 und
Sevilla 1501). Der Titel Comedia trügt: es ist eine tragische Liebesgeschichte. Von 1502 an erschien eine erweiterte Fassung, die Tragicomedia
genannt wurde und manchmal den Titel „Comedia oder Tragicomedia"
usw. trug. Der im Prosaprolog nachdrücklich hervorgehobene Zweifel
an der Angemessenheit des Titels spielt gewiß auf eine dritte Möglichkeit
an, die aus einer u. a. von Juan de Mena formulierten Dreiteilung der Stile
hervorgeht: nämlich, daß dieses Drama nicht komisch oder tragisch, sondern satyrisch ist[25]. Juan de Mena ist einer jener Dichter, die Fernando de
Rojas als möglichen Verfasser des ersten Aktes vorschlägt. Er suggeriert
nämlich – ohne es je ausdrücklich zu sagen –, daß er den ersten Akt nicht
selber geschrieben habe. Gerade am Ende des ersten und am Anfang des
zweiten Aktes jedoch legt er jedem der beiden Knechte Calistos die Gegenüberstellung des „Gebenden" und des „Empfangenden" in den Mund:
„dante" – „recibiente". Diese doppelte Anspielung auf Dante Alighieri,
der den ersten Akt unmöglich geschrieben haben kann, beseitigt nicht nur

---

[25] Für diese Dreiteilung der Stile v. F. López Estrada, Introducción a la literatura medieval
española, Madrid ⁴1979, p. 186; sie geht auf Johannes de Garlandia zurück. Die Celestina ist in
vielen modernen Ausgaben vorhanden; empfehlenswert sind diejenigen von H. López Mora-
les (Cupsa, Madrid 1976) und von Dorothy S. Severin (Alianza, Madrid 1969), letztere mit
einer Einleitung von Stephen Gilman. Eine englische Übersetzung gibt J. M. Cohen, The
Spanisch Bawd, Penguin Classics L 142, 1964. An eine Beschreibung der komplizierten
Zahlenallegorie habe ich mich in zwei Aufsätzen herangewagt: La Celestina, sátira encubierta:
el acróstico es una cifra, in: BRAE 4 (1974) 123–152; Sobre el mensaje secreto de Calysto y
Melybea, in: La Celestina y su contorno social, Actas del I Congreso Internacional sobre
La Celestina, Barcelona 1977, 135–151.

jeden Zweifel an Rojas' Urheberschaft des ersten Aktes, sondern charakterisiert das Werk überdies als eine Anticomedia, eine Umkehrung der Divina Commedia. In diesem Sinn sind die Verse zu deuten, die Cervantes dem Quijote vorangehen läßt und in denen er sagt, die Celestina wäre ein göttliches Buch gewesen, wenn sie das Menschliche mehr verhüllt hätte. Auf Rojas spielt Cervantes mit dem Ausdruck an, „der schweigsame Flüchtling" habe „seine ganze Staatsräson in einer Rückzugsbewegung zusammengefaßt". Mit dem Verb „cifrar" ,zusammenfassen' spielt er auf eine „cifra" ,Kode' an, die Rojas seinen Lesern in dem „Rückzug" gegeben hat, nämlich in den 88 akrostischen Versen, die ab Toledo 1500 seine Comedia einleiten, indem sie den Inhalt des Prosabriefes „Der Autor an einen Freund" wiederholen.

Die Celestina ist ein Meisterwerk der Weltliteratur, das sehr modern anmutet; darum fällt es schwer zu glauben, in dem literarischen Kunstwerk liege ein arithmetisches Kunstwerk verborgen. Vermutlich wollte Rojas jedoch seinen Lesern etwas mitteilen, das öffentlich gar nicht ausgesprochen werden konnte. Da er jüdischer Abstammung war, liegt überdies die Vermutung nahe, seine Botschaft hätte mit der Ausweisung der Juden aus Spanien im Jahre 1492 und mit der Verfolgung von Neuchristen durch die Inquisition zu tun. Mit diesem doppelten Boden des Werkes hängt die Spannung im Dialog zusammen, die auch für den „normalen" Leser spürbar ist, und der psychologische Tiefgang, der dazu geführt hat, dieses Drama — es besteht ausschließlich aus Dialog — als den ersten Roman in der spanischen Literatur zu bezeichnen[26].

Das verborgene arithmetische Kunstwerk ist aus drei sich gegenseitig bedingenden Konstruktionen aufgebaut. Die erste besteht aus einer Sammlung von zwölf Zahlen, von denen eine zweimal verwendet wird, die sich in schönen arithmetischen Figuren vereinigen. Die zweite wird von den Namen der dreizehn in der Comedia auftretenden Personen gebildet. Die dritte ist der Kode, der achtzehn Buchstaben — den fünfzehn, aus denen die Namen zusammengestellt sind, und drei zusätzlichen — einen Zahlenwert gibt, und dadurch jedem der dreizehn Namen seine Zahl zuteilt. Als dieses komplizierte Zeichensystem konstruiert war, machte der Dichter den Kode dadurch offenbar, indem er ihn verbarg: der Zahlenwert jedes Buchstabens bestimmte, wie oft er im Akrostichon vorkam. Der Einbau des Kodes in ein Akrostichon sicherte ihn vor einer Zerstörung durch Druckfehler.

In dem im Akrostichon enthaltenen Satz (El bachjler Fernando de Roias acabó la Comedia de Calysto y Melybea e fve nascjdo en la Pvebla de Montalván — ,der Baccalaureus F. d. R. vollendete die CCM und er wurde geboren in P. d. M.') kommt z. B. das A vierzehnmal vor, das E drei-

---

[26] So z. B. A. D. Deyermond, The Middle Ages (= A Literary History of Spain I), London—New York 1971, 170.

zehn. Die Namen der Liebenden werden mit Y geschrieben, dem gramma philosophon, das den Scheideweg zwischen dem Guten und dem Bösen darstellt.

Von den vielen aus den Namenwerten gebildeten Figuren kann ich hier nur die wichtigsten besprechen; andere werde ich nur kurz andeuten. Der Zahlenwert der Hure Elicia (48) ist der Modul einer Figur, in der zwölf Namen mit dem Gesamtwert 576 (= 24² oder 12 × 48) vereinigt sind (s. Schema Y). Die Vermutung liegt darum nahe, daß dieser Name vom Griechischen abzuleiten ist: ἡλικία, ‚Lebensalter‘, auch u. a. ‚heiratsfähiges Alter‘[27]. Die Verteilung der zwölf Personen in vier Reihen von drei Namen erinnert an die Aufstellung der Apostel in manchen Kathedralen.

Crito, der nur einmal spricht, und zwar einen Satz von vier Wörtern, nimmt an dieser Figur nicht teil. In anderen Anordnungen aber spielt er eine Schlüsselrolle. Er erscheint im ersten Akt als sechster auf der Bühne und bringt den Gesamtwert der bis dann Auftretenden auf 284. Auch die fünf höchsten Namenzahlen haben zusammen diesen Wert. Dies sind Schlüssel, die dazu dienen, den Leser eine dritte Gruppe von Namen, ebenfalls mit dem Wert 284, entdecken zu lassen, die einer andern mit dem Wert 220 gegenübersteht. Der symbolische Hintergrund davon ist,

	(a)		(b)		(c)		(d)			
(A)	CALYSTO	42	ELICIA	48	LUCRECIA	55	SEMPRONIO	47	= 192	Kons = 68
(B)	TRISTÁN	34	PLEBERIO	53	MELYBEA	58	PÁRMENO	47	= 192	
(C)	CELESTINA	68	ALISA	43	SOSIA	31	AREÚSA	50	= 192	Kons = 47

| 144 | 144 | 144 | 144 |
| Kons = 58 | | Kons = 42 | |

7	6	8	9	30
7	8	7	7	29
9	5	5	6	25
23	19	20	22	

| 42 | 42 | 84 Buchstaben |

Schema Y. Verteilung der Zahlenwerte von zwölf Namen in vier Dreierreihen und drei Viererreihen. Anzahl der Buchstaben dieser Namen.

---

[27] Cf. W. Pape's Handwörterbuch der griechischen Sprache, s. v. Die zweite der zitierten Bedeutungen paßt gut im Rahmen der Comedia als ironische Persiflage. Die Verwandtschaft mit dem Correlativum ἡλίκος ‚so groß wie‘ macht ἡλικία fast zum Synonym von „Modul“. Auch Bedeutungen wie ‚waffenfähige Mannschaft‘ und ‚Menschengeschlecht‘ sind für die Interpretation der Celestina als Gesellschaftskritik zu beachten.

daß 220 und 284 ein Paar Freundschaftszahlen sind, d. h. jede ist der Summe der aliquoten Teile der andern gleich. In jeder der beiden Gruppen haben die „bösen" Personen zusammen den gleichen Wert (142 im einen Fall und 110 im andern) wie die „guten". Es bilden sich somit zwei Gruppen mit dem gleichen Wert, 252, und es fällt auf, daß in beiden die Summen der Werte der Vokale und der Konsonanten im genauen Verhältnis 2:1 zueinander stehen (s. Schema Z). Die Namen der sechs guten Personen haben zusammen 40 Buchstaben, die Zahl der menschlichen Vollkommenheit; die der fünf bösen 38, Symbol der Krankheit und der Unvollkommenheit.

In diesem Fall stehen Alisa, die Mutter Melibeas, und Areúsa, die Geliebte Pármenos, außerhalb der Figur. Läßt man Crito und Celestina zusammen außer Betracht, so haben von den restlichen elf die sechs Männernamen den gleichen Gesamtwert wie die fünf Frauennamen, nämlich 254. Teilt man die elf auf in Personen, die sterben (vier) und solche, die überleben (sieben), dann besteht zwischen den beiden Gesamtwerten das Göttliche Verhältnis (194:314)[28].

			Vok	Kons					Vok	Kons
6	ELICIA	48		35 + 13		7	MELYBEA	58		43 + 15
9	SEMPRONIO	47	} 142	31 + 16		8	PLEBERIO	53	} 142	37 + 16
7	PÁRMENO	47		34 + 13		5	SOSIA	31		25 + 6
				100 + 42						105 37
9	CELESTINA	68	} 110	44 + 24		8	LUCRECIA	55		34 + 21
7	CALYSTO	42		24 + 18		7	TRISTÁN	34	} 110	18 + 16
						5	CRITO	21		11 + 10
				68 42						63 47
38	Buchstaben			252 = 168 + 84		40	Buchstaben			252 = 168 + 84
				2:1						*2:1*

Schema Z. Verteilung der Zahlenwerte von elf Namen in Gruppen mit den Werten 284 und 220 bzw. zweimal 252. Anzahl der Buchstaben dieser Namen.

---

[28] Das Göttliche Verhältnis verbindet einzelne Namenzahlen miteinander. Crito (21), Tristán (34) und Lucrecia (55) bilden mit drei Zahlen von Fibonacci eine der beiden Gruppen mit dem Wert 110; in der anderen finden wir in Calysto (42) und Celestina (68) die Werte von Crito und Tristán verdoppelt zurück. Auch zwischen Sosia (31) und Areúsa (50) besteht das Göttliche Verhältnis, und es gibt einige Fälle von Personen, die zu einem Paar in diesem Verhältnis stehen, wie Melybea (58) zu den beiden Knechten Calistos (47 + 47 = 94), oder jeder

Crito (= 21) und Celestina (= 68) haben die niedrigste und die höchste Namenzahl. Zusammen haben sie den Wert 89, den auch noch vier andere Paare haben, die alle durch ihren Vokal- und Konsonantenwert miteinander verbunden sind. Diese Konstruktion weist auf das Trio Fortuna, Mundo und Amor hin, das Melibeas Vater Pleberio im epilogartigen letzten Akt anklagt[29]. „Fortuna" ist in Spanien als Euphemismus für die Iniquisition belegt[30], und mit den anderen zwei könnten der Staat und die Kirche gemeint sein.

Die Kupplerin Celestina stellt sicher in dieser Anticomedia allegorisch die Kirche dar, und möglicherweise schließt sich Cervantes bei der Kritik Rojas an, wenn er sagt, Celestina wäre göttlich, wenn sie das Menschliche mehr verhüllte. Crito, ein Kunde der Hure Elicia, den sie eilends in den Schrank mit alten Besen steckt, wenn der eifersüchtige Sempronio kommt, könnte in der umgekehrten Comedia die Güte Gottes darstellen[31] – oder sogar Christus selbst, denn seine Worte „Sorge dich nicht" erinnern an die Bergpredigt.

Was die beiden Knechte betrifft, Sempronio kann man von semper ableiten. Den Namen des anderen deutet Calisto, wenn er sagt (Akt II): „Rufe den Pármeno, und er wird bei mir bleiben" – hier denkt der Autor an gr. παρα-μένω ‚neben Einem bleiben, bei ihm ausharren', auch ‚übrig bleiben, am Leben bleiben'[32]. Auf die Gleichwertigkeit der beiden Knechte deutet Celestina hin, wenn sie sagt (Akt VII): „Ihr beide seid gleich." Nicht nur die Namen der beiden Knechte, auch Durante, der eigentliche Name Dantes, hat den Wert 47 und ist mit dem Verb „durare" zu verbinden.

Dante legt die Handlung seiner Commedia in die drei Tage von Karfreitag bis Ostersonntag des Jahres 1300. Die Struktur der Anticomedia, in

---

dieser beiden (47) zu Crito und Lucrecia (21 + 55 = 76) oder Tristán und Calysto (34 + 42 = 76). Die Fibonacci-Zahlen 89 (v. infra) und 144 (v. supra) spielen eine wichtige Rolle.

[29] Die Vokalwerte von Calysto und Pármeno zusammen (24 + 34) sind dem Zahlenwert des Namens Melybea (58) gleich und ihre Konsonantenwerte (18 + 13) dem Zahlenwert des Namens Sosia (31). In gleicher Weise leiten die Namen von Melybea und Sosia zu Celestina und Crito hin, und diese zu Lucrecia und Tristán. Das Paar Calysto und Sempronio führt unmittelbar zu Lucrecia und Tristán hin. Letztere zwei haben zusammen als Vokalwert 52 und als Konsonantenwert 37. 37 ist der Wert von „Fortuna", während „Mundo" (= 25) und „Amor" (= 27) zusammengezählt 52 ergeben. Dieses Trio weist mit seinem Vokal- und Konsonantenwert (55 bzw. 34) wieder auf Lucrecia bzw. Tristán zurück. Auch steht dem Wert von Mundo (25 = 5^2) die Quadratzahl 64 = 8^2 (= Fortuna 37 + Amor 27) gegenüber. 89 ($5^2 + 8^2$) enthält die Bausteine 5 und 8, aus denen in einer anderen Weise auch 58 aufgebaut ist, die Zahl von Melybea, m. E. die Hauptperson der Tragödie. Die Anzahl der Buchstaben, aus denen die Namen der dreizehn Personen gebildet sind, ist ebenfalls 89.

[30] In einem Brief von Juan Luis Vives von 1525, zitiert von Stephen Gilman, The Spain of Fernando de Rojas, Princeton 1972, p. 174.

[31] Man denke an die griechische Isopsefie θεος = ἀγαθος = ἁγιος = 284; cf. supra.

[32] Cf. Pape, s. v. Letzteres wieder ironisch, denn die beiden Knechte Sempronio und Pármeno sterben.

der einem angeblich älteren ersten Akt fünfzehn weitere Akte hinzugefügt
sind, deutet auf das Jahr 1500 als ideelles Datum hin, und vielleicht auf die
fünfzehn Jahrhunderte Christentum auf dem Fundament des Judentums.
Wenn der Autor im Prosaprolog sagt, das Werk sei in fünfzehn Ferien-
tagen vollendet worden, meint er die Osterferien[33]: eine weitere Parallele
zu Dante. Die Handlung der Anticomedia spielt sich in drei Tagen ab,
führt aber nicht zu einer Himmelfahrt und zu einem Eingehen in die
ewige Glückseligkeit, sondern zum Tod der Liebenden, Calisto und Melibea.

Calisto – κάλλιστος, der Schönste – muß immer fürchten, gesehen
zu werden, und liebt darum die Finsternis. Melibea nennt ihn (Akt XIX
der erweiterten Fassung) „meine leuchtende Sonne" – eine Anspielung
auf die Sonne als Sinnbild Christi wie beim Kartäuser Juan de Padilla. Aber
Calisto stirbt nicht wie Christus um drei Uhr nachmittags, sondern morgens um drei Uhr.

Wie man weiß, enden die drei Cantiche der Divina Commedia mit dem
gleichen Wort, „stelle" ‚Sterne'. Das eigentliche Thema des Werkes wird
im letzten Vers noch einmal kurz zusammengefaßt: „L'amor che muove il
sole e l'altre stelle." Auch die Comedia de Calisto y Melibea scheint von
der Liebe zu handeln. Das wirkliche Thema jedoch wird im zweiten Prosaprolog mit dem Spruch des Herakleitos genannt, daß alles aus Streit entstehe: Omnia secundum litem fiunt. Alles ist umgekehrt in der menschlichen Anticomedia: der Himmel wird zum Dirnenhaus, die Kirche zur
Hexenküche. Celestina, „die Himmlische", ist völlig überzeugt, Melibea
mit der Hilfe des Teufels überredet zu haben, sich mit Calisto einzulassen.

Dieselben Zahlen symbolisieren in dem einen Werk das Göttliche, im
andern das Menschliche. Die letzten Gesänge des Inferno, des Purgatorio
und des Paradiso, die alle mit dem Wort „stelle" enden, zählen bzw.
46, 48 und nochmals 48 Terzinen, zusammen 142, die Zahl, die auch
der Gesamtwert von Sempronio, Pármeno und Elicia ist. Diese drei, deren
Zahlen an den Sternenhimmel erinnern, bilden zusammen eine Dreiergruppe von bösen Personen. Pármeno ist anfangs guten Willens, doch läßt
er sich völlig korrumpieren, im Gegensatz zu Melibea, die sich bis zuletzt
ihrer Schuld bewußt ist. Die Zahl der beiden Knechte, 47, ist wie ein
Sinnbild des Göttlichen Verhältnisses, daß in der Anticomedia zwischen
vier Toten und sieben Überlebenden besteht (s. oben S. 431). Die Göttliche Komödie spielt sogar mit ihrem Gesamtumfang von 4711 Terzinen
auf das Göttliche Verhältnis an.

Doch während Dante sich in der letzten Terzine vorstellt, er werde in die
kosmische Bewegung der Liebe Gottes aufgenommen und erreiche die

---

[33] V. Gilman, o. c. 269–70 und Anm. 2, der bemerkt: „It is curious that a work concerned
in its last act with the finality of death should have been written at precisely this time of year."

höchste Einheit und Glückseligkeit, zeigen die letzten Worte der Anti-comedia, die Pleberio an seine tote Tochter Melibea richtet, wie er von Kummer zerrissen wird: „Warum hast du mich zurückgelassen betrübt und einsam in hac lachrymarum valle?"

CIRCULUS MENSURAT OMNIA

von Joachim Gaus (Köln)

I

Jacob Burckhardt vertrat die Meinung, daß mit der beginnenden Neuzeit die Entdeckung der Welt und des Menschen begonnen habe, die sich in den Kunstzeugnissen ästhetisch veranschauliche. Damit verlegte sich das Interesse der Kunstgeschichte auf die Feststellung der fortgesetzten Entdeckungen immer neuer Aspekte der Realität, die sich in der bildenden Kunst zu zeigen scheint. Weiterhin besteht der Glaube, daß mit Hilfe der Perspektivkonstruktion und der Proportionskunst, denen sich die Künstler seit dem 15. Jahrhundert vermehrt zuwandten, so etwas wie Weltwirklichkeit vorgestellt werden sollte, freilich im reduzierten Sinne einer Beziehung von Gegenstandswelt auf ein sie selbst bedeutendes Bild.

Wenn zum Wesen des Menschen, der nicht über eine gegebene Welt verfügt, sondern diese erst erstellen muß, auch die Betrachtung der natürlichen Vielfalt gehört, zu der er sich in Beziehung setzen will, um das Ideal der Möglichkeiten zu erreichen, so ist anzuerkennen, daß die Kunst der Renaissance Einblicke in solche Betrachtungsweisen eröffnet. Allein der frühneuzeitliche Künstler erkannte in der Veränderlichkeit und Relativität aller wahrnehmbaren Gegenstände einen eigenen Rückstand gegenüber dem Ideal, dem Vollkommenen und seiner Offenbarungsmöglichkeiten. Er bemerkte außerdem die Einschränkung in der Korrespondenz von Naturgesetzen und seinem künstlerischen Schaffen nach diesen Gesetzen, die den Rahmen einer möglichen Subjektivität vorzeichnet und die Zurücknahme des Wahrheitsanspruches bewußt macht.

In dem Bewußtsein, der Veränderlichkeit und Flüchtigkeit der natürlichen Wirklichkeit fortschreitend gestalthafte Formen zu verleihen, konnte der Künstler nur mit Hilfe von Meßverfahren „die Kunst aus der Natur herausreißen", wie es Albrecht Dürer in seinem Ästhetischen Exkurs formulierte[1]. In diesem Sinn muß der vieldeutige Begriff Kunst als Kenntnis von der Vollkommenheit oder Schönheit aufgefaßt werden, als Wissen

---

[1] H. Rupprich, Dürers Schriftlicher Nachlaß, Berlin 1956—1966 (1—3), 3, 295. Vgl. zur Kunsttheorie Dürers E. Panofsky, Dürers Kunsttheorie, vornehmlich in ihrem Verhältnis zur Kunsttheorie der Italiener, Berlin 1915 und J. Bialostocki, Vernunft und Ingenium in Dürers kunsttheoretischem Denken, in: Zeitschr. des Deutschen Vereins f. Kunstwiss. 25 (1971) 107—114.

von der inneren Harmonie, die in den Strukturen der Natur verborgen
ist. Die Entdeckung und Entbergung der Schönheit kann nach Dürer nur
durch einen Geist vollzogen werden, der Talent besitzt, d. h. „obere Ein-
gießungen" berücksichtigt[2]. Ohne sie ist für Dürer keine höchste Erkenntnis des Schönen erreichbar[3]. Die Fähigkeit, Schönheit in ihrer absoluten
Form zu finden, schließt für den Menschen jedoch das Verfahren der
Vergleichung[4] ein. Damit behält die Maßästhetik ihre zentrale Bedeutung in der neuzeitlichen Kunsttheorie, sie vermittelt zwischen dem Wissen um die Beziehungen von Naturwirklichkeit und absoluter Schönheit.

Leon Battista Alberti hat in seinem Lehrbuch zur Baukunst De re
aedificatoria die für die Folgezeit wichtigste Definition der Schönheit gegeben, wenn er schreibt: *pulchritudo esse quendam consensum et conspira-
tionem partium in eo, cuius sunt, ad certum numerum, finitionem col-
locationemque habitam, ita uti concinnitas, hoc est absoluta primariaque
ratio naturae postularit*[5].

Man kann diese Formulierung als selbstverständliche Versicherung begreifen, daß die sichtbare Welt der Dinge, die in quantitativer Größe und in
bestimmbarer Vielheit vorhanden ist, in der Kunst vermittelt wird. Schönheit als innerweltliches Strukturgesetz scheint losgelöst von der Gegen-
wärtigkeit und unumschränkten Möglichkeit des göttlichen Schöpfers
gedacht zu werden. Die ursprünglich theologischen Kategorien der Schönen sind damit unter das Kriterium eines eingeschränkten menschlichen
Weltverhältnisses gestellt, das auch ausschließt, Schönheit als etwas im
göttlichen Weltplan Beschlossenes zu begreifen. So scheint sich das mate-
rielle Substrat der Natur als eine aus sich selbst sinnfreie und damit der
rationalen Verfügung des Menschen freigegebene Potentialität zu zeigen.
Mensura als Verfahren zur Enthüllung von Schönheit konnte so gesehen
zu einem Mittel werden, verschiedene Typen der Dinge vorzustellen,
deren Merkmale den verschiedenen, in der Realität auftretenden Verhält-
nissen entsprechen sollten.

Wenn auch nicht zu bestreiten ist, daß Albertis Kunsttheorie an manchen Stellen unter solchen Voraussetzungen zu begreifen ist, so scheint
es jedoch besonders hinsichtlich des Schönheitsbegriffs nicht angebracht,
Alberti auf einen antiplatonischen Aristotelismus einzuengen[6].

---

[2] H. Rupprich 2, 113. zur Deutung des Begriffs Rupprich 2, 114.

[3] Ähnlich bemerkt Leonardo: „Die Göttlichkeit, die der Wissenschaft des Malers inne-
wohnt, bewirkt, daß sich der Geist emporschwingt . . .", Leonardo, Trattato della Pittura,
ed. H. Ludwig, Wien 1882, deutsche Übers. H. Ludwig, Jena 1925, Nr. 68.

[4] H. Rupprich 3, 294.

[5] L. B. Alberti, De re aedificatoria lib. 9 cap. 5 (Florenz 1485, Nachdruck Alberti Index
4 München 1975, hr. H−K. Lücke) fol. 165 r. Zeile 21−24.

[6] Vgl. W. Tatarkiewicz, History of Aesthetics, Mouton 1974, 3, 89. Das Problem hat G.
Santinello, Leone Battista Alberti Una visione estetica del mondo e della vita, Florenz 1962
richtig gesehen.

Geht man davon aus, daß mensura nicht den Gegenstand voraussetzt, sondern umgekehrt Voraussetzung und Bedingung der Schönheit und Gestalt ist, dann wird Messen ontologisch bedeutsam. Dies bedeutet, daß mensura etwas Seiendes zu einem ihm angemessenen Sein führt. Damit ist etwas über das Verhältnis von Sein und Seiendem ausgesagt, beides soll in einer Angemessenheit stehen. Es ist dabei nicht so, als ob hier zwei Wirklichkeitsebenen einander gegenübertreten, eine reale und eine ideale, dies trifft nicht zu. Schönheit ist bei Alberti eines, *concinnitas* ihre innere Struktur, die in der Angemessenheit der Teile zur Schönheit besteht. *Concinnitas* bezeichnet also das Seiende (*partes*), sofern dieses sein Sein erreicht. Zunächst ist damit ein rein formaler Grundsatz definiert. Das alltägliche Denken versteht den Satz Albertis als eine selbstverständliche Versicherung, daß die Dinge der Natur, die in bestimmter meßbarer Größe und in einer bestimmten Vielzahl vorhanden sind, in der *concinnitas* zusammenhängen. Darüber hinaus aber geht es Alberti um den Versuch einer Gründung von Schönheit als seinsmäßiges Phänomen. Um dies zu verstehen, ist es notwendig zu erklären, was hier mit *numerus, finitio* und *collocatio* gemeint ist.

Numerus als *modus rei* bezeichnet die Bestimmung jedes Teiles, d. h. im *numerus* unterscheidet sich ein Teil gegenüber dem anderen. Damit erlangt jedes Teil seine *forma*, ein Teil wird distinkt von den anderen Teilen. *Numerus* bedingt, daß ein Teil das ist, was es ist, und daß es, da es sich als solches von anderen Teilen absetzt, gezählt werden kann. Damit begründet *numerus* die Art des Seienden und bezeichnet jenen Charakter der Zählbarkeit, der dem Teil deshalb eignet, weil er Wesen hat und ist. So beinhaltet *numerus* den Grund der Schönheit[7].

In diesem Stadium stehen die Teile als Seiendes in einer unwirklichen Zusammenhanglosigkeit, d. h. in einer bloßen *distinctio* des *numerus*. *Finitio* und *collocatio* lösen dieses Nebeneinander und führen die Teile in eine dem Seienden angemessene Ordnung der gegenseitigen Beziehung zu einem Sein hin. Sie bewirken die Hinordnung der Teile auf die eigene Vollendung. Diese Hinordnung übersteigt das Seiende und hebt in sich alle vorhergehende Ordnung auf. *Finitio* stellt zunächst die Beziehung aller Teile in Proportionen her. Sie ist Ordnung der Teile untereinander, garantiert die Hinordnung des Teiles zum anderen. Aus der *finitio* geht die *collocatio* hervor. Sie nimmt das Seiende in seiner Relation in einen Zusammenhang, auf ein Ganzes hin.

In die Zahl gesetzt zu sein, ist die Bedingung, daß die Teile als Seiendes sind. *Finitio* und *collocatio* enthalten die Ausrichtung der Teile zu einer Ordnung, zu einer sinnvollen Vollendung, zur *qualitas*. Die Teile sind also nicht schlechthin, sondern in ihrer Möglichkeit zum Schönen da,

---

[7] Vgl. Augustinus Schönheitsbegriff in: De musica 6, 13 38: „Pulchra numero placent". De lib. arb. 2, 31. De civ. Dei 12, 5.

sie sind gerichtet auf etwas hin. In diese Bewegung aufgenommen zu werden, macht erst das Schönsein der Teile aus. Der Grund dieses Seins ist *concinnitas*, für Alberti oberstes und vollkommenes Naturgesetz, das alles bestimmt (*numerus*), alles formt (*finitio*) und alles ordnet (*collocatio*). Wenn Alberti Schönheit aus Teilen definiert, die durch *numerus = modus* bestimmt sind, deren Entstehung durch *finitio = species* zu einem bestehenden Geformten gemacht wird und dieses Geformte durch *collocatio = ordo* in einen Zusammenklang, d. h. in ein Stadium des in sich Einen gebracht wird, so steht diese Trias in einer Beziehung zu der tradierten Dreiheit *mensura, numerus, pondus,* die aus Sapientia 11, 21 bekannt ist: *Omnia in mensura, et numero, et pondere disposuisti.* Die in diesem Spruch ausgesprochene Grundstruktur des Hervorbringens von Seiendem war für das mittelalterliche Denken Gott. Als apologetisches Diktum der Gottesschöpfung verstanden vesperrte es zunächst jeden Weg des Menschen, durch eigene Hervorbringungen Sein als Schönheit zu erfahren, da das in die Bewegung disponiert sein nichts mit räumlicher Bewegung eines körperlichen Dinges zu tun hat, auch nichts mit seelisch zeitlicher Emotion. Noch im scholastischen System war nur auf Gott der Grundsatz anwendbar, daß der Urheber einer Sache allein der Besitzer ihrer vollkommenen Schönheit sein könne. Dieses Prinzip des *Solus scit, qui fecit* schloß den Menschen als das mit Blick auf sein Tun in die Grenzen der *imitatio naturae* zurückgeworfene Wesen vom Schönheitsbegriff in seiner absoluten Bestimmung aus. Es war im Mittelalter nicht möglich wie in der Antike an die Selbstursprünglichkeit des Seins zu glauben. So wurde mit Konsequenz der Grund alles Schönen aus der immanenten Transzendenz des Menschen in die transzendente Transzendenz Gottes umgedacht. Das bedeutete, daß der Schöpfer und Ordner alles natürlichen selbst außerhalb von jeder Welt anzutreffen und als ein außerhalb der Zeit Wirkender zu denken war. In ihm war eine dem Menschen unerreichbare, weil prinzipiell außerhalb seines Erfahrungsbereiches gelegene und ihm im Leben nicht vergönnte Absolutheit begreiflich. Nach Augustinus ist die *Sapientia divina disponens* „von jener höchsten Wahrheit, die die Zahlen und Harmonie weit kunstvoller (als der irdische Künstler) der gesamten Körperwelt eingegeben hat"[8]. Daraus leitet sich ein zweiter Gedanke des Mittelalters ab, nämlich der, daß die Welt, die sich ausschließlich in bezug auf den Menschen zu erkennen gibt, Gottes Schöpfung und *creatura* ist. In den Zahl- und Seinsgesetzen erblickte Augustinus die

---

[8] Augustinus, De div. quaest. 78. Thierry von Chartres hat diese Frage mehrfach in seinem Tractatus de sex dierum operibus behandelt. Tractatus ed. N. Häring 1969, 245: *Cum autem ex numero sint et pondus et mensura et locus et figura et tempus et motus, et cum omnia quaecumque secundum quantitatem vel qualitatem vel aliquid vel aliquod aliorum habent existere: cum ex numero, inquam omnia praedicta consistant, necesse est ipsam unitatem quae est summa divinitas omnia praedicta eminentia suae naturae transgredi.*

der Schöpfung überall eingeprägte *Vestigia Dei*. Entsprechend Sap. 11, 21 wird das Seiende durch die Bewegung von *mensura* zu *numerus* und zu *pondus* von Gott her und zu Gott zurück charakterisiert. Daß das Seiende so strukturiert ist, klingt in dem Begriff *creatura* an. *Creatura* ist das Seiende, das als Grundbedingung seiner Möglichkeit Gott hat. *Creatura* kann in allem, was an ihr an Schönheit auffällt und aus ihr heraus an Schönheit definiert wird, nur als ein Abglanz, als Offenbarung der Schönheit Gottes aufgefaßt werden.

Schönheit hat in diesem Sinn eine doppelte Bedeutung. Sie besitzt nicht nur den Sinn eines Merkzeichens, sie hat nach Augustinus die gottsuchende Seele des Menschen zum immer Bleibenden zu führen[9]. Ihr kommt gewissermaßen eine anagogische Bedeutung zu. „Versteht sie (die Seele) aber die körperlichen Dinge als bildkräftige Andeutungen und erhebt sich von ihnen zu den geistigen, die in jenen sinnlichen vorgebildet sind, so hat gerade der Übergang für sie etwas Ruhendes, . . . daß sie von der Wallung fortgezogen wird in die Ruhe des Verständnisses"[10]. Schönheit gewährt Ruhe; diesen selbstzwecklichen Sinn der Schönheit erläutert Augustinus am Zustand der Seligen, deren Augen eine erhöhte Sehkraft besitzen, die auch Unkörperliches sehen.

Kehren wir an dieser Stelle zurück zur Ausgangsposition. Schönheit richtet sich in der Kunsttheorie auf eine Gesetzlichkeit der natürlichen Erscheinungen und macht diese zur Voraussetzung ihrer Verwirklichung. Wie das Beispiel Dürers nahelegt, scheint das Problem einer theoretischen Begründung sich auf der Ebene eines reduzierten Anspruches zu bewegen, der die ständige Überholbarkeit seiner Resultate von vornherein einschließt. Gerade in der frühneuzeitlichen Erfahrung der Unerschöpflichkeit der Natur – und zwar nicht nur in der Dimension der Wandelbarkeit und Flüchtigkeit der Gegenstandswelt, sondern sehr viel mehr in der Vermehrung jeder gegenständlichen Erkenntnis als solcher – macht sich das Suchen nach einem Grund als einer wesenhaft auf Transzendenz gerichteten Energie bemerkbar, die aus der Vertrautheit mit dem Unerreichbaren entspringt. Dürers Kupferstich *Melencolia I* von 1514 macht dies in besonders anschaulicher Weise deutlich. Der Künstler stellte eine *Geometria* in Gestalt einer geflügelten Frau dar, die melancholisch geworden ist[11], eine *melancholia artificialis*. Der Zirkel in ihrer Hand ruht, sie schaut nicht gegenstandsbezogen und ist nicht um das richtige und maßgerechte

[9] Augustinus, De vera religione 29, 52.

[10] Augustinus, Ep. 55, 11, 12 vgl. J. Bernhart, Augustinus. Ein Lesebuch aus seinen Werken, München 1922, 102.

[11] Zum Kupferstich allgemein: E. Panofsky u. F. Saxl, Dürers Melencolia I eine Quellen- und Typengeschichtliche Untersuchung, Leipzig–Berlin 1923. E. Panofsky, R. Klibansky u. F. Saxl, Saturn and Melancholy, Studies in the History of Natural Philosophy, Religion and Art, London 1964.

Vorstellen der Gegenstände bemüht. Sie versinkt in tiefes Nachdenken, ihr
Blick ist unbestimmt in die Ferne gerichtet. Sie schaut gewissermaßen
an den Gegenständen vorbei, um ständig bereit zu sein, in das Sein des
Einzelnen vorzugreifen. Nach dem Verborgenen aus eigener schöpferi-
scher Kraft zu fragen, erscheint in diesem Horizont geradezu als Aufgabe und Möglichkeit der *ars*. Einen vergleichbaren Sachverhalt zeigt auch
das Bildnis eines unbekannten Mannes aus dem Umkreis des Gentile Bellini
(um 1500 entstanden, London National Gallery) (s. Tafel XII, Abb. 1).
Der Dargestellte trägt in der linken Hand einen großen Zirkel, während
sein Blick in die Höhe dem von rechts oben einfallenden Licht entgegen
gerichtet ist. Seine Bewegung wird durch das Erheben der rechten Hand
noch unterstützt. Die Suche nach dem Sein, der Schönheit wird in ihrer
Unstillbarkeit und in ihrem Anspruch auf ein Sinnganzes hin der garan-
tierende Faktor und eine spezifische Kraft, die den Aufstieg zu metaphysi-
schen Positionen ermöglicht.

Daß eine solche Interpretation der Bildbeispiele nicht abwegig ist,
können Gedanken über die menschlichen Fähigkeiten belegen, die ein
Freund Albertis, Marsilio Ficino ausführte. Er bezeichnete die menschliche Seele als die Mitte, die gemäß ihrer Substanz an der Ewigkeit und in
ihrem Wirken in der Zeit steht. Damit wird der Mensch selbst als die Mitte
aller Dimensionen zwischen dem göttlichen und dem körperlichen Bereich
begriffen. Er durchmißt mit Hilfe der Sinnlichkeit und Reflexion durch
die der Seele innewohnenden Fähigkeiten (*sensus, imaginatio, phantasia,
intellectus*) die Stufen des Seins und steigt zum begründenden universalen
Prinzip auf[12]. Maß dieses Aufstiegs ist das absolut Eine[13]. Ebensosehr ist
die absolute Schönheit als eine Erscheinungsform des göttlichen Guten
und Einen das wirkende Moment im Aufstieg der Seele[14]. Seit Augustinus
und Plotin, auf die Ficino in seinen Gedanken u. a. zurückgreift, ist dieser
Aufstieg der Seele als eine Abstraktionsbewegung zu verstehen, die sich

---

[12] Zur neoplatonischen Darlegung des platonischen Gedankens von der Seele als Mitte und
als Sitz des Mathematischen, das zwischen dem Intelligiblen und dem Sinnenfälligen vermittelt: J. Trouillard, La méditation de l'âme, in: L'un et l'âme selon Proclos Paris 1972, 27ff.
Vgl. M. Ficino, Theologiae Platonicae de immortalitate animorum libri 18, Angaben nach
der Ausgabe R. Marcel, Marsile Ficin, Theologie Platonicienne (1–3) Paris 1964–1970, 2,
30f. Ficino nimmt fünf voneinander abgegrenzte und aufeinander bezogene Bereiche an, deren
Mitte die Seele einnimmt: Gott-Engel-Seele-Qualität-Körper. Der Mensch ist Bild des
gesamten Universums. Damit schließt Ficino an die Überlieferung an, wenn er von der Seele
meint, sie ahme Gott nach in der Einheit, die Engel in der Geistestätigkeit, die eigene Art in
der Vernunft, die Tiere in der Sinnesempfindung, die Pflanzen in der Ernährungsfähigkeit, die
leblosen Dinge im Sein; die Seele umfängt in gewisser Weise alles; vgl. P. O. Kristeller,
Die Philosophie des Marsilio Ficino, Frankfurt/M. 1972, 88ff.
[13] M. Ficino, De Amore, zit. nach R. Marcel, M. Ficin Commentaire sur le banquet de
Platon, Paris 1956 7, 13 Marcel 257: *rerum omnium terminus et mensura.*
[14] M. Ficino De Amore 6, 17 Marcel 234: *Fons itaque totius pulchritudinis Deus est.*

phasenweise von der vielheitlichen Materialität und von der Vielheit des Geistigen auf eine Einheit zurücknimmt[15].

Wie aber gelangt die Seele des Menschen zu dieser ewigen Einheit. Es muß für sie eine ursprüngliche *pistis*, ein Glaube angenommen werden, aufgrund dessen das Innewerden jener Einheit gelingt. In seinem Traktat über die menschlichen Proportionen schreibt Dürer 1528: „Setze dir niemals in den Kopf, daß du etwas besser machen könntest oder wolltest, als die von Gott erschaffene Natur, der er die Kraft zu ihrem Wirken gegeben hat. Denn dein Vermögen ist kraftlos gegen Gottes Schöpfung. Daraus folget, daß kein Mensch jemals aus seinem Sinn ein schönes Bild machen kann, es sei denn, er habe seinen Geist angefüllt mit vielem Zeichnen und Malen nach der Natur"[16]. Dürer betont, daß allein mit den eigenen Sinnen kein schönes Bild entstehen könne, sondern die Kunst nur über die Sammlung der Sinneneindrücke im Geiste entstehe. Gewissermaßen wird durch das voll gefaßte Gemüt das Singuläre zum Universalen und zwar so, daß der unendlich weit differenzierte Bereich der Sinnenwelt zu einer geistigen Mitte zurückgeführt wird[17]. Mit Hilfe der *scientia* oder der Meßtätigkeit allein zur Erkenntnis des Schönen zu gelangen, bleibt für Dürer letztlich erfolglos. Die Möglichkeit, Schönheit zu erfassen, ergibt sich aus den im Geiste des Künstlers innewohnenden Bildern, die den vielen festgehaltenen und von der Natur abgenommenen Bildern nicht widersprechen müssen, die aber über die Natur auf den Begriff der *pulchritudo absoluta, quae est Deus*[18] gerichtet sind und jene Bilder vervollkommnen, deren Ursprung die Gegenstandswelt darstellen. Ebenso wie einer der Freunde Dürers in bezug auf Plato notiert, daß Gott selbst sich auf die Maßverhältnisse bei der Schöpfung bezogen habe (Willibald Pirckheimer), stützt sich Dürer auf diese Quelle, wenn er in der Einleitung seines Malereitraktates schreibt: „Und will aus Maß, Zahl und Gewicht mein Fürnehmen anfohen". Messen ist „in allen Dingen, sitt-

---

[15] Ficino begreift die Seele als *speculum Dei*, der die Unermeßlichkeit Gottes durch die Kraft seines Geistes wiederzugeben vermag, der denkend über alle zeitlichen und räumlichen Grenzen hinaus in die Unendlichkeit steigt, um sich bis zur unteilbaren, ewigen Natur, zur vollendeten Ganzheit der transfiniten Unendlichkeit emporzuheben. M. Ficino, Opera omnia, Basel 1576 (Nachdruck Turin 1962) 1, 21a, 223a, 685b. Der bei Ficino betonten vollendeten Ganzheit entspricht der platonische Schönheitsbegriff. Schönheit umfaßt, „was immer ist und weder entsteht noch vergeht, weder wächst noch schwindet, das nicht jetzt schön ist, dann aber häßlich, nicht im Vergleich mit dem einen schön, mit dem anderen aber häßlich ist, sondern an und für sich selbst ewig und überall dieselbe Einheit der Gestalt besitzt", Symposion 210Eff. „. . . ein ewig Seiendes, das für sich und mit sich ist und eine einzige Gestalt hat", Symposion 211B.

[16] H. Rupprich 3 295—296.

[17] Meister Eckhart: „Ich alleine bringe alle creaturen uz ir vernunft in mein vernunft daz sie zu mir eine sint", Meister Eckhart, hr. Fr. Pfeiffer, Leipzig 1857, 181.

[18] Nikolaus von Cues, In Die nativitatis Mariae (1456) in Canticum 4, 7 hr. G. Santinello, Padua 1959, 37.

lichen und natürlichen, das Best . . . weliche dann auch bei dem Aller-
höchsten so hoch angesehen ist, daß er alle Geschöpf in Zahl, Gewicht und
Maß geschaffen hab."[19]. Es ist hier nicht notwendig, die theologische
Grundtendenz des Dürerzitates betonen zu wollen. Der Satz zeigt zumindest an, daß Dürer Schönheit als etwas außerhalb von Zeit und Raum Vor-
handenes, als ein transzendentes Phänomen begreift, wenn er an anderer
Stelle Schönheit den „versamlet heymlich schatz des hertzen"[20] nennt, der
im schroffen Gegensatz zur Prozeßhaftigkeit des messenden Vorgehens[21]
und zu den menschlichen Gedankenbildungen steht, durch die man zur
exakten Erkenntnis des sichtbaren Universums gelangt, d. h. der unmittelbar gegenwärtig ist, die Einheit der Gestalt bewahrt, wie es Plato formulierte.

Schon Ficino hebt hervor, daß die Seele eine unbegrenzte Kraft sei,
anders ausgedrückt, sich selbst gegenüber dem Unendlichen ein Maß
anlegt und damit nicht nur jede beliebige Zeit-, Raum- und Bewegungs-
größe, sondern auch die Unendlichkeit selbst mißt. Daraus ergibt sich für
Ficino, daß die Seele zweifellos ihrerseits vollendet ist, „da notwendigerweise das Maß (*mensura*) zum Gemessenen ein Verhältnis hat, während
dem Endlichen zum Unendlichen kein Verhältnis zukommt"[22]. Mit dem
„heymlich schatz des hertzen" umschreibt Dürer in vergleichbarer Weise
den Zusammenstrom der unendlichen Vielfältigkeit sowohl der oberen
geistigen wie der unteren körperlichen Bereiche in der Seele, die als ein
einziger unteilbarer, innerlich lebendiger Mittelpunkt angesehen werden
kann. Diese Mitte vermag die Welt zu verknüpfen[23], sie stiftet *concordantia* oder Harmonie und bildet somit den Grund der Schönheit, sie verursacht auch die kosmologisch und anthropologisch zu fassende Rück-
bewegung des Seienden, zieht an sich und versammelt in sich. Nikolaus
von Cues erblickt in der *consonantia diversorum* den Strand des höchsten
Glücks[24].

---

[19] K. Lange—F. Fuhse hr., Dürers schriftlicher Nachlaß, Halle 1893, 285 9. Jedes
Erkennen von Schönheit bedeutet danach ein Setzen in *proportiones*, d. h. in der Vergleichung
von Bekanntem und Unbekanntem. Ähnlich betont auch Luca Pacioli den Vorrang der
Mathematik vor allen anderen Wissenschaften, indem er auf Sap. 11, 21 verweist. Pacioli,
Divina Proportione, hr. und übers. C. Winterberg (Quellenschriften f. Kunstgesch u. Kunst-
technik des Mittelalters u. der Neuzeit N F 2) Wien 1889, 36.

[20] H. Rupprich 3, 295—196.

[21] „durch Geometria magstu deins werks vil beweyssen, aber nicht alles".

[22] M. Ficino, Theologiae Platonicae 8, 16; vgl. Augustinus, De quantitate animae 5;
Plotin, Enn. V 8, 4 gegen Ende.

[23] Geoffrey von Vinsauf benutzte die Metapher in seinen Betrachtungen über die inventio:
„Laß den Zirkel deines Geistes den gesamten materiellen Bereich umkreisen" Poetria Nova
of Geoffrey of Vinsauf, hr. F. Nims, Toronto 1967, 17.

[24] N. v. Cues, In Die nativitatis, hr. Santinello 1959, 33.

II

In diesen Horizont des durch die Seele in die ursprüngliche Einheit und Schönheit geführten Aufstiegs ist auch das Wesen und die Aufgabe der Kunst eingeschlossen. Sie konnte auf Grund der in ihr realisierten *aequalitas* zum Ansatzpunkt dafür werden, daß die Seele – von einer *species innata* geleitet – aus der unmittelbaren Erfahrung der erscheinenden *aequalitas* auf deren Grund zurückgeht. Hier sei hervorgehoben, daß für Alberti Schönheit nicht in erster Linie eine Bestimmung von Körpern ist, sondern auch der Seele und der Vernunft: *Ut vero de pulchritudine indices non opinio: verum animis innata quaedam ratio efficit . . .*[25]. Das klingt bereits bei Augustinus an, wenn er feststellt: „Du fragst dich, woher das kommt, gehst in dich selbst zurück und erkennst, daß du, was du mit den Körpersinnen anrührst, weder schätzen noch verwerfen könntest, wenn du nicht selbst bestimmte Schönheitsgesetze in dir trügest, mit denen du alles mißt, was du in der Außenwelt an Schönem empfindest"[26]. Nach Augustinus erweist sich der Mensch dadurch einerseits als ein Geschöpf Gottes, andrerseits aber als sein Ebenbild und daher auch als ein Schöpfer. Die endliche Identität mit Gott suggeriert die Formel der Neuzeit: *homo quidam Deus*. Freilich bleibt diese Nobilitierung des Mensch-Seins innerhalb seiner Geschaffenheit; seine schöpferische Aktivität ist gewissermaßen ein Nachzeichnen der göttlichen *pictura*. Damit wiederholt oder vergegenwärtigt das Kunstwerk in wahrnehmbarer Form das Wirken des Intelligiblen im Seienden, die Entfaltung und Erscheinung des Schönen selbst im Bereich des Sinnlichen und Endlichen. Ficino benutzte die bezeichnende Metapher von der erscheinenden Schönheit als Glanz oder Grazie des göttlichen Antlitzes, das in drei Spiegeln leuchtet: *mens, animus, corpus*[27]. Die Kunst kann schließlich einen anagogischen Sinn erlangen, indem sie durch das Schauen des Schönen zur absoluten Schönheit emporführt.

Wenn Alberti bemerkt, „daß die Schönheit eine bestimmte gesetzmäßige Übereinstimmung aller Teile was immer für einer Sache sei, die darin besteht, daß man weder etwas hinzufügen, noch hinwegnehmen oder verändern könnte, ohne sie weniger gefällig zu machen"[28], so verdeutlicht auch er, daß die Schönheit nicht in einer äußerlichen, materiell gedachten *dispositio partium* oder *concinnitas* bestehen kann, also nicht identisch ist mit äußerer Gestalt. Entsprechend sind die drei hervorgehobenen Grundzüge *numerus-finitio-collocatio* (*modus, species, ordo*) sozusagen die nicht-materielle Vorbedingung dafür, daß Schönheit in der Materie gestaltgebend

---

[25] L. B. Alberti, De re aedificatoria lib. 9 cap. 5.

[26] Augustinus, De libr. arb. 2, 42.

[27] M. Ficino, De Amore, Marcel 185.

[28] L. B. Alberti, De re aedificatoria, lib. 6 cap. 2.

erscheint. Diese Gedanken können schließlich auch mit Plotins Äußerung zum inneren Schönwerden des Menschen in Verbindung gebracht werden: „Kehre ein zu dir selbst und sieh dich an, und wenn du siehst, daß du noch nicht schön bist, so tu wie der Bildhauer, der von einer Bildnisbüste, welche schön werden soll, hier etwas fortmeißelt, hier etwas ebnet, dies glättet, das klärt, bis er das schöne Antlitz an der Büste vollbracht hat: so meißle auch du fort, was unnütz und richte, was krumm ist, das Dunkle säubere und mach es hell und laß nicht ab, dein Bildnis zu bauen, bis dir hervorstrahlt der gottförmige Glanz der Tugend, bis du die sophrosyne erblickst, thronend auf ihrem heiligen Sitz"[29].

Wenn bei den Schönheitsbestimmungen der Frühneuzeit aber Sicherheiten gesucht werden, die auf den mathematischen Disziplinen gewonnen werden, so ist damit eine Geschlossenheit des Verhältnisses zwischen der menschlichen Seele als Maß und dem Kunstwerk, d. h. die Bezogenheit der aus dem Menschen hervorgehenden Wirklichkeit auf ihn selbst bedeutet. „Der Mensch geht nicht über sich selbst hinaus, wenn er schöpferisch ist, sondern in der Entfaltung seiner Kraft kommt er zu sich selbst"[30]. Nikolaus von Cues erweitert seinen Gedanken, wenn er die Mathematik als einen im Menschen verankerten Besitz bezeichnet und damit das seinem Geiste angemessene Instrumentarium der Erkenntnis hervorhebt: „Alles Mathematische ist endlich und läßt sich anders gar nicht vorstellen"[31]. „. . . unser Geist, der die Welt des Mathematischen schafft, hat das, was er schaffen kann, wahrer und wirklicher in sich, als es außer ihm ist. So hat der Mensch die bildende Kunst und die Gestaltungen dieser Kunst wahrer in seinem Begriffsvermögen, als sie außerhalb Gestalt bekommen können"[32]. Cusanus hatte damit den platonischen Ideenbegriff relativiert, indem er die auf Zahl- und Maßbedingungen beruhenden Figurationen, die Plato als Formen vollkommener Schönheit angesehen hatte[32], aus dem Bereich der reinen vorgegebenen Ideen ausklammerte. Hier ist zu fragen, ob der Cusaner damit die Autonomie des menschlichen Vermögens gegenüber dem göttlichen Schöpferwillen zur Diskussion stellen wollte. Zumindest wird in seinem Denken die Tendenz deutlich, daß durch die Welt des Mathematischen hindurch das Universum des Absoluten, des Göttlichen

---

[29] Plotin, Enn I 6, 20. Zur Stelle des Durchlichtens des Dunklen vgl. eine Stelle in einem Brief Ficinos an Giovanni Cavalcanti, Opera Omnia, Nachdr. Turin 1962 1, 631: *Pulchritudo corporis non in umbra materiae, sed in luce et gratia formae, non in tenebrosa mole, sed in lucida quaedam proportione, non in pigro ineptoque pondere, sed in convenienti numero et mensura consistit.*

[30] N. v. Cues, De docta ignorantia 1, 12 *Nam cum omnia mathematicalia sunt finita et aliter etiam imaginari nequeant.*

[31] N. v. Cues, De beryllo 32 . . . *quae mathematicalia fabricat, ea quae sui sunt officii verius apud se habere quam sint extra ipsam. Puta homo habet artem mechanicam et figuras artis verius habet in suo mentali conceptu quam ad extra sint figurabilis, ...*

[32] Plato, Timaios 53 E.

und des Schönen in ipso sichtbar, d. h. *symbolice* zugänglich gemacht werde: *ad divina per symbola accedendi nobis via*. Die Mathematik verhilft am ehesten zum Erfassen der Andersartigkeit des Göttlichen[33].

Wenn auf diese vermittelnde Weise die Mathematik und Geometrie kosmologisch und damit ontologisch begründet werden, so konnten sie innerhalb der Kunsttheorie und Kunstpraxis einen appellativen Charakter und eine den Akt des Transzendierens provozierende Funktion besitzen. Dies wird besonders deutlich am Beispiel der Kreisfigur, die in der Kunst der frühen Neuzeit als hervorragende Form gilt. 1548 schuf der Mathematiker, Kartograph und Maler Augustin Hirschvogel ein Selbstbildnis, das er in Kupfer stach[34] (s. Tafel XII, Abb. 2). Der Dargestellte erscheint in Halbfigur hinter einer quadrierten Tischplatte, auf der ein Globus mit daran angelehntem Zirkel zu sehen ist. Daneben liest der Betrachter den Satz: *Circulus mensurat omnia*. Der Globus als Modell der Welt gewinnt in der Betrachtung des Kosmos deshalb an Legitimität, weil in ihm zwar die konstanten Proportionen der essentiellen Bestimmungen, aber nicht die physischen Gegenstände der Welt selbst als Wirklichkeit zutage treten. In ihm ist eine vom natürlichen Vorgegebenen unabhängige Bedeutungsfülle gegenwärtig, die zum Sinnganzen des Kosmos in Beziehung treten kann. Als Ausdruck der Mimesis, der besonderen Selbsttätigkeit und Wirkfähigkeit des Menschen – darin sah bereits Cusanus die gottähnlichste Gabe des schöpferischen Individuums – bringt das Modell etwas zur Darstellung, das auf diese Weise in sinnlicher Fülle gegenwärtig ist: *imago mundi* als Selbstbildnis Gottes[35]. Neben dieser Wertung des Modells enthält es auch eine Art Selbstdarstellung, das Ideal der unendlichen Mannigfaltigkeit

---

[33] N. v. Cues, De docta ignorantia 1, 11: Überschrift „*Quod mathematica nos iuvet plurimum in diversorum divinorum apprehensione?*". Noch ganz im Sinne der symbolischen Theologie des Pseudo-Dionysios fordert Cusanus, man müsse anhand von Musterbildern über das Sinnliche hinaus (*supra omnem capacitatem nostram*) zum Absoluten emporsteigen und jene in transzendenter Weise als sinnbildliche Zeichen (*symbolicos characteres*) für das Mysterium des Absoluten verwenden; vgl. De docta ignorantia 1, 2 und 2, Prolog. Cusanus versucht, die symbolische Methode exakt zu gestalten, indem er mit den Pythagoreern und Platonikern nur rein mathematische Figuren (*mathematicalia signa*), die von der sinnlichen Materie frei sind, als Mittel zur Erforschung des Absoluten zuläßt. Geht die Erforschung von einem Bilde aus, so darf bei diesem, in dessen analoger Übertragung das Unbekannte aufgespürt wird, nichts Zweifelhaftes enthalten sein. Hier beruft sich Cusanus auf *sapientissimi* et *divinissimi doctores*. Daß die Erforschung der *spiritualia per se a nobis in attingibilia* nur symbolisch sein kann, hat seinen Grund darin, daß alles zueinander in einer gewissen uns freilich verborgenen und unfaßbaren Proportion steht, so daß aus allem sich ein Universum aufbaut und alles in einem Größten das Eine selbst ist; vgl. De docta ignorantia 1, 10–12. Cusanus beruft sich außer auf Boethius (De institutione arithmetica 1, 1) auf Pythagoras und Augustinus (De quantitate animae 8–12), der das intellektuelle Sehen, wie es der vermittelnden Rolle der geometrischen Gebilde entspringt, präzisiert hat.

[34] K. Schwarz, Augustin Hirschvogel. Ein deutscher Meister der Renaissance, Berlin 1917, Katalog der Werke, 174, Nr. 40.

[35] N. v. Cues, De visione Dei 25; M. Ficino, De Amore, Marcel 185.

der einzelnen Wege zur Vollkommenheit zurück, d. h. im Globussinnbild veranschaulichen sich die unzähligen, je von einem anderen Punkt aus indefinit anwachsenden Individualitätsebenen[36].

Wendet man sich dem ein Jahr später geschaffenen Selbstbildnis Hirschvogels zu (s. Tafel XIII, Abb. 3), so zeigt sich in der Darstellung ein umgekehrtes Verhältnis von Weltmodell und Mensch. Hirschvogel erscheint sehr klein vor dem großen Bild der Welt. Im Vordergrund steht bildparallel ein Sarkophag, auf dem der Tod als Skelett ruht. Der Dargestellte ist eingebunden zwischen *Vita* und *Mors*. Das Modell der Welt wird überhöht von den sitzenden Personifikationen *Spes* und *Caritas* mit den Beischriften: *Adveniat Regnum tuum und Viat voluntatem tuam*. Ergänzt werden diese Sätze durch zwei weitere Hinweise auf der Sockelplatte des Sarkophages: „Thu des Höchsten seine gepodt" und „So lebestu ewiglich pei Godt". Die Gegenstände in ihrer sinnlichen Erscheinung sind zu besonderen figürlichen Bildungen umgedeutet. Die Kreisform sammelt die einzelnen Elemente, sie steht für die Verbindung von metaphysischer und physischer Ebene, sie bildet nicht das Gegenteil alles Endlichen, sondern steigert sich vom Endlichen zum Unendlichen fort. Diese Vorstellung erinnert an Platos Kosmologie, in der die Welt eine Sphäre genannt wird, die in sich gleichartige, vollendetste aller Figuren, eine „glückselige Gottheit"[37].

Im 15. Jahrhundert war diese Interpretation bekannt, sie verursachte auch die Vorliebe für den Kreis in der Kunsttheorie. Ausgehend von dem Gedanken, daß die Natur nach Vollkommenheit strebt, nennt Alberti unter den idealen Formen als vornehmste den Kreis. „Daß sich die Natur vor allem am Runden erfreut, geht schon aus den Gebilden hervor, die sie selbst zeugt, hervorbringt und schafft. Der Erdball, die Gestirne, die Bäume . . . alles das wollte sie rund haben . . ."[38]. An einer anderen Stelle erweitert er diesen Gedanken mit Blick auf den Menschen. „Die Natur, das ist Gott, vereinigte im Menschen himmlische und göttliche Elemente mit solchen, die ihn zum anmutigsten und edelsten von allen sterblichen Geschöpfen machen"[39]. Mit der Gleichsetzung von Natur und Gott kommt Alberti der platonischen Vorstellung vom Weltganzen als einer sichtbaren Gottheit nahe. Damit wird die Anschauung vom Menschen als Mikrokosmos verbunden, der die Welt complicative in sich enthält. Der Theoretiker bedient sich eines tradierten Bildes, um damit auch die gottähnliche Universalität des Individuums zu veranschaulichen.

---

[36] N. v. Cues, De docta ignorantia 2, 2; De coniecturis 2, 14.
[37] Plato, Timaios 33 B ff. (theòs aisthetós).
[38] L. B. Alberti, De re aedificatoria lib. 7 cap. 4.
[39] L. B. Alberti, I primi tre libri della famiglia, hr. F. C. Pellegrini, Florenz 1911, 236. Vgl. P. H. Michel, La pensée de L. B. Alberti, Paris 1930, 536 ff.

Die Betonung und Hervorhebung der Kreisfigur bei den Renaissancetheoretikern hinsichtlich der Vollkommenheit der Natur findet zunächst eine Begründung bei Vitruv, der sein drittes Buch von De architectura libri decem mit der berühmten Bemerkung über die Proportionen der menschlichen Figur einleitete, die sich in den Proportionen der Kunst und besonders im Tempelbau widerspiegeln sollten. Als Bedingungen der vollkommenen Schönheit und Harmonie des menschlichen Körpers führt er an, daß sich ein wohlgebildeter Mann, *homo bene figuratus* mit ausgestreckten Händen und Füßen in die geometrischen Figuren des Kreises und des Quadrates einfügt[40]. Entsprechend diesen Harmonieprinzipien kann kein Kunstwerk und kein Bauwerk schön sein, „wenn es nicht einem wohlgebildeten Menschen ähnlich ein genau durchgeführtes Gesetz in sich trägt"[41]. Diese einfache Formulierung enthüllte eine grundlegende Wahrheit über den Menschen und über das Universum in ihrer unverbrüchlichen Zusammengehörigkeit. Sie hatte bereits gestalthaften Einfluß auf das mittelalterliche Denken, wenn wir etwa an die Makro-Mikrokosmosvorstellungen und Bilder bei Hugo von St. Victor, Isidor von Sevilla oder Hildegard von Bingen denken[42]. Jedoch bestimmte die vitruvianische Figur die Diskussionen der Renaissancekünstler in einem bis dahin unbekannten Maße. So interpretierte Leonardo den Vitruvtext genauer in seiner Proportionsfigur des *homo ad quadratum* und *homo ad circulum*. Neben Fra Giocondo[43], Cesare Cesarino[44] und Francesco di Giorgio[45] erklärte vor allem Luca Pacioli, ein Freund Leonardos, daß sich im Menschenkörper die beiden Hauptfiguren finden lassen, ohne die kein Kunstwerk gelingen kann. Deshalb seien vom *homo bene figuratus* Vitruvs alle Maße und ihre Bezeichnungen abzuleiten und in ihm alle Zahlenverhältnisse und Maßbezeichnungen zu finden, „durch welche Gott die tiefsten Geheimnisse der Natur enthüllt"[46]. Hier klingt der Glaube an Gott als den einzigen Grund des Naturschönen und der Harmonie an. Wenn

---

[40] Vitruv, De architectura libri decem 3. 1, 1 hr. C. Fensterbusch, Darmstadt 1964, 138.

[41] Vitruv, De architectura libri decem, Fensterbusch 136.

[42] R. Allers, Microcosmus, in: Traditio 2 (1944); E. de Bruyne, Etudes d'esthétique médiévale, Brügge 1946, 2, 275 ff., 350 ff., 361 ff.; G. Perrigo Conger, Theories of Macrocosmus in the history of Philosophy, New York 1922 (Nachdr. 1967). H. Schipperges, Das Bild des Menschen bei Hildegard von Bingen, Beiträge zur philosophischen Anthropologie des 12. Jh., Diss. Bonn 1952. Der Vitruvkanon ist auch im Mittelalter bekannt gewesen. Vgl. den französischen Dialog „Placides et Timeo" (vor 1303): „L'homme est un microcosm. Il est rond comme le monde car il doit avoir autant de hauteur que d'envergure en étendant les bras"; Ch.-V. Langlois, La connaissance de la nature et du monde au moyen âge, Paris 1911, 290. Vgl. auch Guilleaume de Saint-Thierry, De natura corporis et animae, Migne P L 180 708 B.

[43] Fra Giocondo, M. Vitruvius per Jocundum, Venedig 1511, fol. 22 v und r.

[44] C. Cesariano, Di Lucio Vitruvio Pollione de Architectura, Como 1521, fol. 49 und 50.

[45] Fr. di Giorgio, Cod. Ashburniano 361, fol. 12 r., Florenz Bibl. Laurenziana.

[46] L. Pacioli, divina Proportione, hr. C. Winterberg, Wien 1889, 129.

Alberti nicht auf die Vitruvfigur anspielt, so darf dennoch vermutet werden, daß er bei seiner Bestimmung des Menschen von ähnlichen Überlegungen ausgegangen ist. Francesco di Giorgio geht in diesem Zusammenhang einen Schritt weiter, wenn er fragt: *Quod homo imitatur mundum in figura circulari?*[47] (s. Tafel XIII, Abb. 4). Bei ihm wird die Figur nicht nur in seiner kosmischen Deutung gefaßt. Sie erschließt vielmehr durch die sichtbare körperliche Welt (*homo = mundus*) auch die unsichtbaren geistigen Beziehungen zwischen *anima* und *Deus*: *Cum igitur Deus sit intelligibilis sphaera, et mundus hic totum se parebeat in sphaerica figura conspiciendum, homo etiam, qui inter Deum mundumque, hunc medium tenet eadem figura terminare necesse est: et imitari intellectualem illam sphaeram in anima, sensibilem vero in corpore: ut haec praesens pictura docere potest*[48].

Mit Blick auf die genannte Verbindung von *anima* und *Deus* liegt ein Gedanke nahe, den Augustinus ausgesprochen hat: „Denn was an Schönem aus der Seele in die Hand des Künstlers fließt, das kommt von jener Schönheit, die da über unseren Seelen ist"[49]. Und er fährt an anderer Stelle fort: „. . . Du hast den Geist (gegeben), daß er die Kunst erfasse und darin erschaue, was er draußen bilden soll. Du gabst ihm auch einen körperlichen Sinn, mit dem er nun das Bild aus seiner Seele auf den Stoff zu übertragen weiß"[50].

Angesichts der Äußerungen von Francesco di Giorgio ist die Vitruvfigur nicht nur als eine Illustration zu verstehen. Die Kreis- bzw. Quadratfigur ist als Aspekt der Wirkung des Schönen im Seienden zu verstehen. So beruft sich Alberti bei Bauaufgaben, besonders bei Kirchenbauten auf die Kreisfigur oder auf die daraus abgeleiteten Vieleckfiguren, weil sie erhabene Gefühle erwecken und zur Andacht stimmen, das menschliche Herz reinigen und in den Stand der Unschuld versetzen können, der Gott wohlgefällig ist[51]. Der Kreis spiegelt die absolute Schönheit, die in der Natur wirkt. Alberti wünscht die Kirchen so gebaut zu sehen, daß die Eintretenden „sich kaum enthalten können, in Ausrufen zu gestehen, es sei wahrlich ein für Gott würdiger Ort, den sie erblicken". Alberti begreift die geometrische Harmonie des Kirchenbaues nicht antik-heidnisch als kratophantische Erscheinungsform, sondern mit den Augen dessen, dem Harmonie als Natur Gottes zum Schauen und Bewundern gegeben ist. Die Kreisfigur dient ihm dazu, die Gottheit selbst in ihrem Verhältnis zur Welt symbolisch darzustellen. Alle diesem Ideal unterstellte Elemente der Geometrie in der Kunst sollen „reine Philosophie atmen. Der Fußboden

[47] Fr. di Giorgio, De harmonia mundi totius, cantica tria, Venedig 1525.
[48] Fr. die Giorgio, De harmonia mundi Cant. 1, 2, fol. 100v.
[49] Augustinus, Confessiones 10, 34.
[50] Augustinus, Confessiones 11, 5.
[51] L. B. Alberti, De re aedificatoria lib. 7 cap. 3 Anfang.

(der Tempel) soll vor allem Zeichnungen und Figuren zeigen, die auf Musik und Geometrie hinweisen, so daß alles der Bildung des Geistes dient"[52]. Hier tritt der anagogische Sinn der Kunst deutlich zutage. Noch Andrea Palladio hebt im vierten Buch seiner Quattro libri di architettura von 1570 den Kreis hervor, der ihm deshalb so bedeutsam ist, weil sich in ihm nicht nur die *figura del mondo* veranschaulichen läßt, sondern weil die Kreisform im höchsten Grade die Einheit (unità), die unendliche Essenz (infinita essenza), die Gleichmäßigkeit (uniformità) und die Gerechtigkeit Gottes (giustizia) offenbare[53]. Über die kosmologische Bedeutung hinaus lassen sich mit der Kreisform also mystisch-religiöse Vorstellungen verbinden. Sie erhebt nach Alberti die Gläubigen zu Gott und kann deshalb nicht nur räumlich sondern auch geistig erfaßt werden.

III

Für Thomas von Aquin war der vornehmste Effekt, der in die Prinzipien seiner selbst zurückkehrt. *Tunc enim maxime perfectus est, quando in suum redit principium.* Hieraus folgt: *unde et circulus inter omnis figuras et motus circularis inter omnes motus et maxime perfectus, quia in eis ad principium reditur*[54]. In der Kreisfigur erreicht das Wirkende sich selbst, seine Vollendung (*perfectio*). Daraus ist weiter abzuleiten, daß auch die Schönheit im Kreise zur Vollendung gelangt, indem das Wirkende den Effekt auf seinen Zweck hin wirkt, denn der Zweck des Wirkenden ist, im Effekt vermittelt, das Wirkende selbst.

Das so verstandene Symbol des Kreises dient nun bei Nikolaus von Cues dazu, die mystische Erkenntnis Gottes als der „unendlichen Einheit" die alles in sich enthält und alles aus sich entfaltet[55], möglichst einleuchtend zu machen. *Qui (deus) est principium, medium et finis omnium, centrum et circumferentia unverversorum, ut in omnibus ipse tantum quaeratur, quoniam sine eo omnia nihil sunt*[56]. Cusanus bezieht sich bei dieser Formulierung auf den auch an anderer Stelle gebrauchten Satz aus dem pseudohermetischen Liber viginti quatuor philosoporum[57]. Weiter vermerkt Cusanus: *Aliqui qui unitatem infinitam figurare nisi sunt, deum circulum*

---

[52] L. B. Alberti, De re aedificatoria Lib. 7 cap. 10.

[53] A. Palladio, I quattro libri di architettura 1570 lib. 4. A. Blunt, Artistic Theory in Italy 1450–1600, Oxford 1940, 129.

[54] Thomas von Aquin, De veritate catholicae fidei contra gentiles, libri quatuor 2, 46.

[55] N. v. Cues, De docta ignorantia 2, 3: *Deus est omnia complicans in hoc, quod omnia in eo, est omnia explicans in hoc, quod ipse in omnibus.*

[56] N. v. Cues, De docta ignorantia 2, 13.

[57] *Deus est sphaira (intellectualis) infinita, cuius centrum est ubique, circumferentia nusquam*; C. Baeumker, Das pseudohermetische Buch der 24 Meister, Münster 1913, 2. verb. Aufl., in: Studien und Charakteristiken, Münster 1927, 194–214.

dixerunt infinitum. Illi vero qui actualissimam dei existentiam conside-
rarunt, deum quasi sphaeram infinitam affirmarunt[58]. Diese Formel vom
circulus infinitus wird bei Cusanus von der Weltwirklichkeit als *sphaera*
unterschieden, gleichzeitig jedoch wieder auf diese bezogen. *Unde erit*
macchina mundi quasi habens undique centrum et nullibi circumferentiam
quoniam circumferentia et centrum deus est, qui est undique et nullibi[59].
Nam figura mundi contracta est in eius partibus sicut et modus[60]. Daß die
Welt nach Cusanus keine real bezeichnete Mitte besitzt, aber dem Menschen dennoch überall die Illusion des Mittelpunktes gewährt, weil der
Mensch fähig ist *omnia ex se explicare intra regionis suae circulum*[61], diese
Überlegung mag dazu geführt haben, der geometrischen Kreisfigur als
kosmischer Metapher eine neue Aktzentuierung zu geben. Sie gewinnt
Sinnbildlichkeit im Verhältnis zur absoluten Transzendenz. Es bildet sich
nämlich eine Antinomie des *maximum absolute* und des *maximum con-*
tracte heraus. Wenn der Kreis des *maximum contracte* aus der *sphaira*
infinita oder aus dem Kreis mit unendlichem Radius und unendlichem
Mittelpunkt hervorgegangen gedacht wird, so stellt er sich als ein diese
Einheit in aller entfalteten Vielheit bewahrendes Sinngefüge dar. Die innere
Beziehung von *sphaera infinita* und *imago mundi* als *maximum contracte*
veranschaulicht Schedel in seiner 1493 erschienenen Weltchronik auf fol.
V verso in besonderer Weise: der Weltkreis ist in die *sphaera infinita* ein-
beschrieben. Die Kreisfigur kann also kaum den Sinn haben, Einzelaus-
sagen über die Vielfalt der Gegenstände zu machen, sie hat vielmehr
einen Verweisungseffekt auf die infinite *unitas*. Somit ist der Kreis als
pictura mundi nicht als in sich selbst bedeutendes Bild zu verstehen. In
diesem Zusammenhang sind Marsilio Ficinos Gedanken über die Wirkung
oder Bewegung der unendlichen Einheit in der Welt zu nennen. Die infinite *unitas* ist nach Ficino die Ursache für die Geordnetheit des Kosmos.
Gott als *circulus spiritualis* verbindet das Einzelne zu einem Ganzen, deshalb ist der *circulus mundi* umgekehrt auch auf das Ganze und die *unitas*
hin gedacht. Diesen Sachverhalt illustrierten bereits Gottesdarstellungen in
mittelalterlichen Handschriften. So zeigt z. B. die Holkham-Bible auf der
ersten Seite den Schöpfer im Zentrum von Kreisringen zwischen Engeln
und Abyssus, flankiert von Sonne und Mond. Sein Zirkel setzt im Zentrum
des Bildes, mitten in der Figur des Creators an und deutet Gott somit
als Ursprung und Einheit (s. Tafel XIV, Abb. 5). Nach Ficino durchdringt
und beherrscht Gott als der S t r a h l, als der r a d i u s alles (*penetrare per*
omnia). Umgekehrt ist die Welt durch die *diffusio sui ipsius* die *imago* göttlicher Form, die schöne Erscheinung absoluter Schönheit: *Deus omnium*

---

[58] N. v. Cues, De docta ignorantia 1, 12.
[59] N. v. Cues, De docta ignorantia 2, 12.
[60] N. v. Cues, De docta ignorantia 2, 12.
[61] N. v. Cues, De coniecturis 2, 14.

centrum quia unitas simplicissima est actusque purissimus, sese inserit universis[62]. Von diesem In-sich-Sein des Einen gehen Kreise aus, die in je verschiedener Seinsintensität auf den Ausgangspunkt bezogen sind und von ihm bedingt bleiben: *mens, anima, natura, materia*.

Vor dem Hintergrund der Lehre Ficinos von der Selbstentäußerung Gottes auf die Welt und deren Rückbezug auf die göttliche unitas wird der tiefere Sinn der Vitruvfigur in der Renaissancetheorie deutlicher. In dieser Figur geht der Bereich des Intelligiblen und des Sinnlich-Anschaulichen eine Verbindung ein: *visibilis mundi circulus est imago . . . illorum invisibilium circulorum*[63]. Die *commensuratio* oder *dispositio partium* wird in der Gestalt des *homo bene figuratus* nicht äußerlich materiell angesprochen, sie ist nicht identisch mit „äußerer Gestalt"; sie ist vielmehr eine die äußere Gestalt von innen her bestimmende Wesenheit oder Bewegung. Die Erscheinung kann als Glanz des *vultus Dei* begriffen werden.

An dieser Stelle kann ich nicht ausführlich auf das Problem der Gottesebenbildlichkeit eingehen, die in der Bildnismalerei um 1500 häufiger thematisiert wird. Beispielhaft sei das bekannte christomorphe Selbstbildnis Dürers von 1500 hervorgehoben[64] (s. Tafel XV, Abb. 6), das im Modulusverfahren *geometrico more* eine Proportionierung des Kopfes in sechs Teile aufweist, die sich aus der Unterteilung des vertikalen Kreisdurchmessers ergeben. Teilt man den waagerechten Kreisdurchmesser ebenfalls in sechs gleiche Teile und bildet man aus diesen beiden Achsen das den Kreis umschreibende Quadrat, so steht dieses nicht nur in harmonischer Beziehung zum Antlitz des Dargestellten, sondern die Unterteilungen bilden auch nach den Seiten hin zwingende Bildmaße. Außerdem fällt auf, daß der Kopf mit den wallenden Locken ein regelmäßiges Dreieck ausmacht. Zeichnet man dieses ein, so ergibt sich, daß es ein gleichseitiges Dreieck ist, dessen Spitze mit der Mitte des oberen Bildrandes zusammenfällt, und daß die Basis dieses Dreiecks zugleich die Höhe der ganzen Bildtafel im goldenen Schnitt teilt. Man spürt die ordnende Kraft und die Harmonie der Verhältnisse, die dem ganzen Werk eine Erhabenheit verleiht.

Dürers Selbstbildnis erinnert an zahlreiche Christusbilder, die sich durch ihre strikte Frontalität auszeichnen. Die Vera Icon Darstellung aus dem Umkreis des Jan van Eyck — um 1438 entstanden — berührt fast deckungsgleich die Proportionsschemata des Selbstbildnisses Dürers (s. Tafel XV, Abb. 7). Dürer greift mit Sicherheit auf ein tradiertes Formengut zurück.

---

[62] M. Ficino, De Amore 2, 3 Marcel 148.

[63] M. Ficino, De Amore 2, 3 Marcel 148.

[64] München, Alte Pinakothek. F. Winzinger, Albrecht Dürers Münchener Selbstbildnis, in: Zeitschr. f. Kunstwiss. 8 (1954) 43—64. D. Wuttke, Aby Warburgs Methode als Anregung und Aufgabe, Göttingen 1977, in: Gratia. Schriften der Arbeitsstelle für Renaissanceforschung 2, 14—41.

Wie Panofsky bemerkte, wird damit der praktisch angewandten Proportionslehre der Renaissance wieder ein metaphysischer Sinn unterlegt. Man verstand sie nicht nur als eine rationale Grundlage der Schönheit, sondern vielmehr als Ausdruck einer Harmonie zwischen Makrokosmos und Mikrokosmos[65]. In diesem Sinne begreift auch Dürer seine Schöpfergabe als eine „Gottes Wirken entsprechende Fähigkeit", wie er in seinem Lehrbuch der Malerei schreibt. Christus galt seit jeher als verkörpertes Gesetz der Schönheit und nach antiker und christlicher Auffassung verdankt der Künstler sein ingenium göttlicher Begnadung. Christus, in dem sich die göttliche und menschliche Natur unlösbar durchdringen, wird zum erfahrbaren Vermittler zwischen Gott und dem Künstler. Bereits Cusanus hatte von einer *proportio* des Endlichen zum Unendlichen hin gesprochen und Christus als *humana natura* bezeichnet *cum illa sit in se medium alias complicans*[66] und hob weiter hervor, daß *una Christi humanitas in omnibus hominibus* sei[67]. Ficino gab übrigens dieser Christusidee eine Ausformung, durch die sie unmittelbar in die Humanitätsidee überging: *Singuli namque homines sub una idea et in eadem specie sunt unus homo. Ob hanc ut arbitrior rationem sapientes solam illam ex omni virtutum numero hominis ipsius nomine, id est humanitatem appellaverunt, quae omnes homines, quodammodo seu fratres ex uno quodam patre longo ordine natos diligit atque curat*[68].

Angesichts der eindeutigen Bevorzugung des Gedankens, das Schöne sei aliquid *incorporeum*, sei nicht in den Schatten des Materiellen zu finden, bleibt es verwunderlich, daß in der bildenden Kunst seit dem 15. Jahrhundert gerade dem körperlich Schönen, der wirklichkeitsnahen Darstellung des Seienden ein relativ breiter Raum gegeben wird. Es macht sich ein merkwürdiger Zug bemerkbar, der die Körperlichkeit des Darstellungsgegenstandes neu bewertet, freilich ohne diese zu verselbsständigen und ohne den Gedanken zu verdrängen, sie sei Erscheinungsform des absolut Schönen. Zur Veranschaulichung sei exemplarisch die Darstellung der Hei-

---

[65] E. Panofsky, Die Entwicklung der Proportionslehre als Abbild der Stilentwicklung (1921), in: Aufsätze zu Grundfragen der Kunstwissenschaft, hr. H. Oberer u. E. Verheyen, Berlin 1974 (2. Aufl.) 169–204. Schon aus der antiken Tradition ist bekannt, daß neben dem Kreis das gleichseitige Dreieck – in seiner Vollkommenheit – Sinnbild der Gottheit (im Mittelalter dasjenige der Trinität) darstellt; vgl. Reallexikon der Deutschen Kunst 4, col. 406 und Reallexikon für Antike und Christentum 4, col. 310. Die Einbindung des Selbstbildnisses Dürers in das gleichseitige Dreieck bedeutet die Aktivität und das Streben, die difformitas der menschlichen Natur (per conditionem caducam) gleichmäßig in Richtung auf Vollkommenheit der immutabilitas auszuweiten. Dazu die Terminologie bei Hugo von Sankt Victor *homo de hoc statu imperfectionis perveniat ad immutabilitatem et perfectionem . . .*, Adnotationes Elucidatoriae in Pentateuchon 7, Migne P. L. 175, 36.

[66] N. v. Cues, Predigt „Dies sanctificatus", hr. Hoffmann und Klibanski 30.

[67] N. v. Cues, De docta ignorantia 3, 12.

[68] M. Ficino, Epistol. lib. 1 Opera omnia, Nachdr. Turin 1962 1, 635.

ligen Familie von Michelangelo, die sogenannte Doni Madonna von 1503
angeführt. Das Bildformat ist kreisrund. Gemalt ist Christus mit Maria
und Joseph, wie er über die Schulter der zurückgewandten Mutter herun-
tersteigt. Johannes der Täufer erscheint dahinter in einem tiefer gelegenen
Raumabschnitt. Die unbekleideten Gestalten im Hintergrund deuten auf
den heilsgeschichtlichen Zeitraum des Alten Bundes. Vergegenwärtigt wird
der Augenblick der Inkarnation. Gott erscheint in *forma hominis*. Dem
Betrachter wird das Erlebnis redender Kontaktpersonen im Bilde suggeriert. Bildformat und Darstellung sind gewissermaßen inhaltlich aufeinander zu beziehen. Zum besseren Verstehen sei daran erinnert, daß Cusanus die göttliche Trinität konkret geometrisch durch die Teile des Kreises:
Centrum, Diameter und *Circumferentia in circulo* versinnbildlichte[69]. Der
Diameter, der vom Mittelpunkt ausgeht, und die Fläche des Kreises
bestimmt, entspricht nach Cusanus die dem *Principium* wesensgleiche
zweite Person Gottes. In ihm kommt das unsichtbare Prinzip zur Erscheinung, er ist als *explicatio circularis* Gottes zu verstehen[70]. Christus bildet
also nicht allein das Thema, seine Erscheinung im Bilde muß vom Grund
her als eine Ausdrucksform des Göttlichen verstanden werden. Aus der
conspiratio der im Bilde erscheinenden Gestalten untereinander auf einen
Ursprung hin bildet der Kreisumfang die Verknüpfung mit dem Grund.
Die Darstellung der Inkarnation ist die *Eikon* Gottes, d. h. die Gleich-
wesentlichkeit mit dem unsichtbaren Gott, in ihr tritt die *Doxa* Gottes
hervor. Sie wird dem Betrachter unmittelbar anschaulich.

Die Tondoform des Michelangelobildes erscheint kaum als eine zufällige
Bildform. Beachtet werden muß das Verhältnis von Form und *pictura*,
wobei zu berücksichtigen bleibt, daß die Kreisform Zeichenfunktion
besitzt. Es ist demnach eine Aufgabe, das Verhältnis von Zeichen und Bild
richtig zu begreifen. Man kann in der Kunst des 15. Jahrhunderts davon
ausgehen, daß sich allmählich eine Depontenzierung des Zeichens vollzieht
und sich eine immer bildlicher werdende Kunst entwickelt. Dennoch zeigt
besonders die Donimadonna von Michelangelo, daß Kreissymbol und
pictura sich in ihrer gegenseitigen Aussagemöglichkeit verbinden. Die
Christusgestalt muß ganz im Sinne der Andachtspraxis verstanden werden:

---

[69] N. v. Cues, Complementum theologicum 6: „Der Mittelpunkt in der Ewigkeit erzeugt
und entfaltet ewig aus seiner zusammenfaltenden Kraft die erzeugte, an seinem Wesen teil-
habende Linie. Und der Mittelpunkt mit der Linie entfaltet ewig die Verknüpfung (*nexum*)
oder den Umfang . . . Der Mittelpunkt ist der väterliche Ursprung (*principium*) . . . die
Wesenheit (*unitas*). Und die Linie ist wie der Ursprung aus dem Ursprung, also die Gleichheit. Und der Umfang ist wie die Einigung und Verknüpfung“.

[70] N. v. Cues, De docta ignorantia 2, 9: *Et quoniam ipsa est prima explicatio circularis —
mente divina seu ut puncto centrali habente et anima mundi ut circulo centrum explicante —
et complicatio naturalis omnis temporalis ordinis rerum, ideo ipsam propter discretionem et
ordinem numerum moventem dixerunt . . .“.*

Quasi in corde depingitur. Deutlich wird, daß das Kunstwerk der Frühneuzeit Teilhabe durch Anschauung anbieten kann und ein Appell zum
Überstieg in Schönheit und Einheit bleibt[71].

---

[71] Die Bedeutung des Aufstiegs für Michelangelo hat E. Panofsky, The neoplatonic
movement and Michelangelo, in: Studies in Iconology (1939) New York 1962, 171–230,
herausgearbeitet.

MENSURA HOMINIS QUAE EST ANGELI

DIE MASSEINHEIT DES HAUSES GOTTES

von Harald Kümmerling (Köln)

Indem im Konsens des Mittelalters die Kathedrale ein Abbild des Himmels und damit des Hauses Gotts war, hatte sie den Augenzeugenberichten der Seher des Alten und Neuen Testaments Ezechiel und Johannes zu entsprechen. Beiden hatte sich ein Begleiter angeboten, der über ein Maß verfügte, welches die Dimensionen der Himmelsstadt als dessen jeweils ganzzahliges Vielfaches erwies: *et in manu viri calamus mensurae sex cubitorum et palmo; et mensus est latitudinem aedificii calamo uno . . .* (Ez 40, 5); und *et qui loquebatur mecum, habebat mensuram arundineam, ut metiretur civitatem, et portas ejus, et murum . . . et mensus est murum ejus centum quadraginta quatuor cubitorum, mensura hominis, quae est angeli* (Apoc 21, 16−17). Die von Mensch zu Mensch bekanntermaßen vorkommende, von Mensch zu Himmelsboten also zu erwartende unterschiedliche Länge des Ellenbogens wird von Johannes ausdrücklich nicht bestätigt: *mensura hominis, quae est angeli.* Die beiden Engel im Hause des Lot wurden, wie das Verhalten und Vorhaben der Sodomiter beweist, für Menschen gehalten (Gen 19, 8) wie auch der Erzengel Raphael in der Gestalt des Asarja als Reisebegleiter des Tobias (Tob 5, 13). Der Apostel Petrus wurde nach seiner wundersamen Befreiung für seinen Engel gehalten (Act 12, 15), denn an jenem Abend müßte der in das Haus der Maria Einlaß begehrende Mann viel eher des Petrus Engel als etwa Petrus selbst sein. − In diesen genannten Beispielen waren Engel von Menschen nicht zu unterscheiden; auch für ihre Gestalt traf des Johannes Hinweis zu: *mensura hominis, quae est angeli.*

Die Maßeinheit des Himmlischen Jerusalem ist bei Ezechiel wie bei Johannes die Elle, im Falle Ezechiels auch eine bestimmte Ausprägung von deren Vielfachem, nämlich sechs Ellen plus eine Handbreit als Gesamtlänge der Meßrute. Diese letztere Länge als Maßeinheit für Vielfaches im weiteren Verlauf des von Ezechiel geschilderten Meßaktes muß wohl wie deren Teileinheit Elle als eine von der Gestalt des Menschen hergeleitete verstanden werden, denn das Experiment beweist, daß sechs Ellenlängen plus eine Handbreit die Körperlänge eines erwachsenen Mannes ergeben (und zwei Ellenlängen dessen Körperbreite).

Da nach der Vorstellung des Mittelalters während der kanonischen Stundengebete der Chor der Engel oben zusammen mit den Mönchen bzw. Klerikern psallierte, waren die Engel im Hause Gottes anwesend. Ihr Platz war zu Häupten des Gottesvolkes in der Höhe des Gebäudes, wo auf Emporen ihnen geweihte Altäre aufgestellt waren und wo in der gleichen Gebäudezone Darstellungen von Engelchören bildhaft von ihrer Präsenz zeugten. In dieser, den Engeln vorbehaltenen Höhe pflegten zum Innenraum hin durch Arkaden geöffnete Laufgänge durch die Wände derjenigen Gebäudeteile zu führen, die den Mönchen bzw. Klerikern als Ort ihrer Lobgesänge dienten. Im Wechsel mit Sängern in der Höhe des Gebäudes, die den Engelgesang symbolisierten, da sie neben den zum Gebäudeinneren hin gerichteten Engelbildern standen, sangen die um den Altar als den Thron Gottes versammelten Kleriker ihre kanonischen Texte. Ihr Ort war der Chor, derjenige der Engel die Orgel[1].

Das für die Entwicklung der gotischen Baukunst richtungweisende Bauwerk der Kathedrale von Chartres wird sogar zur Gänze in halber Höhe der Innenräume von einem solchen Laufgang (Orgel) umrundet. In dem Transversalschnitt (s. Abb. 1, Tafel XVI) sind mehrere Durchbrüche durch Längs- und Quermauern wie auch durch Stützpfeiler zu erkennen. Die bemerkenswerte Kantenführung der Durchbrüche zeichnet Konturen stehender Menschen nach, den Kopf über abgerundeten Schultern. Diese Durchbrüche nehmen aber nicht nur durch ihre deutlichen Umrisse bezug auf die Menschengestalt, sondern auch durch ihre Maße. Der Durchgang neben dem Scheitelpunkt des Seitenschiffgewölbes ist, wenn wir den oben beigegebenen Maßstab zu Hilfe nehmen, zwei Ellen breit und reichlich sechs Ellen hoch. Mit dieser Höhe scheint der Architekt den Meßstab aus der Vision des Ezechiel zu zitieren, nämlich sechs Ellen und eine Handbreit, die eines Mannes Körpergröße entsprechen. (Die Rißzeichnung von Nef weist in den eingetragenen, hier nicht mehr lesbaren Meßwerten von Mauerabschnitten teils erhebliche Differenzen gegenüber dem beigefügten Maßstab auf. Anlaß und Datum der Rißzeichnung sind nicht bekannt. Die hier beigefügte Fotografie nach einer gerasterten Reproduktion[2] kann die Zeichnung nur sehr schwach wiedergeben, wodurch allerdings die Hinweise auf die ermittelte Maßeinheit besonders deutlich hervortreten.)

Die Höhe des Mauerdurchbruchs durch die Wand zwischen den Räumen oberhalb des Seitenschiffes an der bezeichneten Stelle neben dem Scheitelpunkt des Gewölbes in einen Stechzirkel übernommen erweist sich als die dem Gesamtbau zugrundeliegende Maßeinheit. Die Horizontalen

---

[1] Vgl. H. Kümmerling, Cantantibus Organis. Von Orgelsang und Orgelspiel im Mittelalter, in: FUSA 8/9˙ 1982, 60—78.

[2] aus: O. von Simson, The Gothic cathedral. The origins of Gothic architecture & the medieval concept of order. London 1956, plate 33.

und Vertikalen, des Gebäudes und seiner Teile Breite und Höhe sind offensichtlich mit Hilfe dieses Grundmaßes fixiert worden. Die vollkommenen Zahlen 1, 2, 3 und deren Doppeltes oder Vielfaches bestimmen die Ausmaße des Bauwerks, als sei ihre Vollkommenheit diesem Gebäude einzig angemessen. Die mit ihrer Hilfe herstellbaren Proportionen ergeben die einzig anerkannten musikalischen Harmonien Einklang 1:1, Oktave 1:2, Quinte 2:3, Oktave der Quinte 1:3 z. B. Breite des Innenraumes (von Fensterbahn zu Fensterbahn gemessen) im Verhältnis zur Höhe = 15:15 (1:1), Breite des Seitenschiffes im Verhältnis zu dessen Höhe 3:6 (1:2), Wandhöhe des Hauptschiffes im Verhältnis zur Gesamthöhe 10:15, bzw. des Seitenschiffes 4:6 (2:3).

Der Begleiter Ezechiels hatte aber nicht nur einen Meßstab bei sich, sondern auch ein dünnes Seil aus Flachs, eine Leine: *et funiculus lineus in manu ejus, et calamus mensurae in manu ejus* (Ez 40, 3). Der Prophet teilt über diese Leine nichts weiter mit, nicht deren Länge, nicht den Verwendungszweck, obwohl er sie doch noch vor dem Meßstab erwähnt. Aus der dann folgenden Schilderung kann nicht auf einen bestimmten Meßvorgang geschlossen werden, für den eine Leine notwendig gebraucht würde. Erst als ich auf dem Riß von Chartres mit Stechzirkeln die gekrümmten Linien des Gewölbes nicht messen konnte, erinnerte ich mich des Fadens als Hilfsmittel zur Herstellung einer Ellipse vermittels der Fadenkonstruktion. An zwei − auf den Brennpunkten der Ellipse befestigten − Pflöcken wird ein Faden befestigt, der länger ist als deren Abstand. Ein Farbstift im Winkel des gespannten Fadens um die Pflöcke herumgeführt zeichnet eine Ellipse auf den Untergrund. (Die beiden Einstichpunkte für die Pflöcke sind die Brennpunkte der Ellipse.) Der weiteste Durchmesser stellt sich auf der Hauptachse ein (auf der auch die Brennpunkte liegen), der geringste auf der Nebenachse.

Die Nebenachsen der Ellipsen der Gewölbe in Chartres verlaufen durch den Ansatz der Gewölberippen über den Kapitellen. Vom Schlußstein des Gewölbes bis zum Mittelpunkt der Nebenachse reicht die eine Hälfte der Hauptachse, die dann nach unten hin verdoppelt werden muß. Eine Fadenkonstruktion mit einem Faden von acht Maßeinheiten gemäß der Höhe des genannten Mauerdurchganges an zwei Nadeln befestigt, die auf der Hauptachse je zweieinhalb Maßeinheiten oberhalb und unterhalb der Nebenachse des Hauptschiffes eingestochen sind (also in einer gegenseitigen Distanz von fünf Maßeinheiten), ergibt die elliptische Gewölbekrümmung. Die acht Maßeinheiten der Fadenlänge sind identisch mit der Länge der Hauptachse. Somit kann eine Ellipse durch das Verhältnis von Abstand der Brennpunkte zu Länge der Hauptachse bestimmt werden. Im Falle der vier auf dem Riß von Nef vorkommenden Ellipsen erweist sich die im Bauwerk mitgeteilte und ermittelte Maßeinheit, nämlich die Körpergröße eines Menschen bzw. Engels, als den Bau selbst konstituierend, indem sie nur als Einheit oder als deren Hälfte gebraucht ist. Die vier

Verhältnisse der Gewölbe in Chartres ergeben die musikalischen Intervalle
5:8 = kleine Sexte, 2:3 = Quinte, 3:4 = Quarte und 15:16 (Verdoppe-
lung von 7,5:8) = Halbton, die den Gelehrten während des quadrivialen
Studiums hörbar und einsichtig gemacht worden waren.

Am Beginn des 12. Jahrhunderts hatten in der Schule von Chartres
Thierry und dann sein Bruder Bernhard die Vorarbeiten geleistet für
Alanus de Insulis, welcher der Zeitgenosse jenes Architekten war, der in
den letzten Jahren dieses Jahrhunderts die berühmte Kathedrale von
Chartres errichtete. Über die Rolle der Zahl im Werk des Alanus schreibt
M. Baumgartner: „Alanus preist ihre Macht, ihre verbindende und ord-
nende Kraft. Er rühmt die Erfinder der Zahlen, allen voran Nicomachus
und Pythagoras, als diejenigen, welche die Rätsel der Dinge, ihr Sein, ihren
Wechsel, ihre Ursachen, ihre Bewegung, ihren Zusammenhang durch die
Zahlen zu entschleiern versucht hätten. Die Zahlen sind ihm Prinzip und
Ziel, Urbild und Siegel für die werdende Dinge, und nach ihrem Vorbild
hat die Gottheit, die göttliche Idee, den Dingen ihre Formen und der Welt
ihre Figur eingeprägt. Gleich den Ideen werden sie also zu göttlichen Gedanken und zu Urbildern der geschaffenen Dinge. Sie sind ferner . . .
Ordnung, Gesetz und Zusammenhang stiftende Principien, die Ursachen
und die Samen der Dinge, das Band durch welches alle Ordnung, Gesetzmäßigkeit und Stetigkeit im Wechsel der Erscheinungen bedingt wird. Die
Zahl verknüpft alles, ist Grund für die Einheit des Zusammengesetzten . . .“[3].

Den im Riß von Nef enthaltenen Zahlen, die die Menge der von ihm
gemessenen Zentimeter und Meter bezeichnen, kann diese Rolle nicht
zukommen, weil sich bei diesem Meßverfahren Reihungen von willkürlichen Setzungen ergeben, wie etwa die Folge seiner das Hauptschiff aufsteigend erschließenden Teilmessungen: 9,54 − 5,57 − 0,25 − 0,38 − 3,85
− 0,34 − 1,16 − 2,86 − 9,96. In einer im Anschluß an aufwendig und
genau durchgeführte Messungen in Ebrach hebt Wolfgang Wiemer in
seiner jüngst veröffentlichten Studie[4] die ganzzahligen Maßverhältnisse
hervor, bei denen die Häufung der Proportionen 1:2, 1:3 und 1:4 auf-
falle. An anderer Stelle bedauert er, daß es „noch keine systematischen
Untersuchungen über die Ausführungsgenauigkeit gibt, die man im Mittelalter für Bauten einer bestimmten Epoche und Qualitätsstufe ansetzen
kann.“ Unser Ergebnis aber kann in einem Satz zusammengefaßt werden:
Die Maßeinheit der Kathedrale war anthropomorph.

---

[3] Die Philosophie des Alanus de Insulis im Zusammenhange mit den Anschauungen des
12. Jahrhunderts. Münster 1896 (= Abhandlungen zur Geschichte des Mittelalters II, 4),
75f.
[4] W. Wiemer, Die Geometrie des Ebracher Kirchenplans − Ergebnisse einer Computer-
analyse, in: Kunstchronik 35 (1982) 422−441.

DIE ROLLE DER MENSURA VON MONOCHORD, ORGELPFEIFEN UND GLOCKEN IN DER MITTELALTERLICHEN ARS MUSICA

von Klaus-Jürgen Sachs (Erlangen)

Wilibald Gurlitt prägte 1954 in einem Vortrag vor der Akademie der Wissenschaften und der Literatur zu Mainz die Begriffsbestimmung: „Unter *mensura* versteht die Musiklehre das Prinzip der quantitierenden Zeit-Ordnung in der Musik, ihr quantitatives Ordnungs-Maß: *mensura temporis*. Nach ihr nennt sich alle *gemessene* Musik, besonders die mehrstimmige, aber auch die gemessene einstimmige, *musica mensurabilis (mensurata)*, Mensuralmusik"[1].

Hier also bezog ein führender Musikologe noch vor weniger als drei Jahrzehnten den Begriff *mensura* in der historischen Musiklehre ausschließlich auf das Prinzip der Zeitmessung, somit auf Mensuralmusik und Mensuralnotation. Dies bleibt bemerkenswert, selbst wenn man berücksichtigt, daß Gurlitts Vortrag, betitelt „Form in der Musik als Zeitgestaltung"[2], naheliegenderweise beim Entstehen der Mensuralmusik ansetzte, folglich von der bekannten Definition ausging, mit der Franco (wohl um 1260) *mensura* bestimmte als *habitudo quantitatem, longitudinem et brevitatem cuiuslibet cantus mensurabilis manifestans*[3].

Die Ausschließlichkeit, mit der Gurlitt den Franconischen Mensurbegriff zugrunde legte, ist jedoch symptomatisch dafür, wie wenig seinerzeit und wie spät überhaupt die Musikforschung jenen älteren Begriff von *mensura*, der im folgenden erörtert sei und der in den Traditionen von Mensura monochordi, Mensura fistularum, Mensura cymbalorum greifbar ist, bewußt wahrgenommen und schärfer erfaßt hat — und dies, obwohl charakteristische Zeugnisse dieser Mensurlehre bereits seit Martin Gerberts „Scriptores ecclesiastici de musica sacra potissimum" von 1784, die auch Francos Traktat enthalten, gedruckt vorliegen.

Die Gründe für dieses überraschend späte Eindringen in einen Zentralbereich der mittelalterlichen Musiklehre sind teils in den Texten selbst, teils

---

[1] V. die in Anm. 2 genannte Schrift, 653.

[2] Veröffentlicht in: Abh. der geistes- u. sozialwiss. Klasse, Jg. 1954, Wiesbaden 1955, 651–677.

[3] Jüngste Ausgabe: Franconis de Colonia Ars cantus mensurabilis, ed. G. Reaney u. A. Gilles, o. O. 1974, 25 (= Corpus scriptorum de musica 18); hier die verbesserte Lesart *habitudo quantitativa longitudinem . . .*

in einer sie lange Zeit verkennenden instrumentengeschichtlichen Interpretation zu suchen.

Zu den auffälligsten Kennzeichen der meisten dieser Texte gehören ihre Kürze und Kargheit, ihre inhaltliche Vordergründigkeit und scheinbare Trivialität, die oft exzerptartige oder stereotype Formulierungsweise sowie die recht verstreute, sorglose, zumeist auch anonyme Überlieferung, kurzum: ein wenig attraktiver Habitus der Zeugnisse.

Stößt man beispielsweise im ersten Band von Gerberts Scriptores — übrigens gleich zweimal[4] — auf die unter Nr. 1 wiedergegebene Textpartie, so wird man schwerlich von ihr spontan gefesselt:

Nr. 1 MENSURA MONOCHORDI ET ORGANORUM IN GENERE DIATONICO, IN PRIMO DIAPASON.

c) E habet F & eius octavam, id est, sesquioctavum. D totum E & eius octavum, id est, epogdoum. C totum F & eius tertium, quod est sesquitertium, vel epitrita, id est diatessaron. B totum C & eius octavum, quod est tonus; vel totum E & eius tertium, quod est diatessaron, vel totum F & eius medium, quod est diapente. A totum B & eius octavum, quod est tonus, vel totum D & eius tertium, quod est diatessaron, vel totum E & eius medium, quod est diapente. G habet totum C & eius tertium, quod est diatessaron. G autem, quod est trite synemmenon, habet totum D primi diapason & eius medium, id est, diapente. G. G. A. B. C. D. E. F.

IN SECUNDO DIAPASON MENSURA.

F habet totum G, d) & eius octavum, quod est tonus, vel totum B & eius tertium, quod est diatessaron, vel totum C & eius medium, quod est diapente, vel aliud F duplo, quod est diapason. E to-

Nr. 2 DE CYMBALORUM PONDERIBUS.

Primum quanticumque ponderis. Secundum sesquioctavum primi. Tertium sesquioctavum secundi. Quartum sesquitertium primi. Quintum sesquioctavum quarti. Sextum sesquioctavum quinti. Septimum sesquitertium quarti.

ITEM.

Nr. 3 Prima quantæcumque quantitatis. Secunda sesquioctava primæ. Tertia sesquioctava secundæ. Quarta sesquioctava tertiæ. Quinta sesquitertia secundæ. Sexta sesquioctava quintæ. Septima sesquioctava sextæ. His itaque dispositis in secundo loco una inferenda est, quæ sub sesquitertia fit illi, quæ prius quarta fuit.

Sich den Sachverhalt, nämlich die verschiedenen Meßakte und das Resultat dieser Monochord- und Orgelpfeifenmensur, klarzumachen, kostet eine gewisse Überwindung und führt kaum zu einer unmittelbaren Erhellung. Man erfaßt dabei folgendes: Die Tonbuchstaben repräsentieren Tonhöhen und die ihnen zukommenden Teillängen einer Monochordsaite bzw. einer als Richtschnur dienenden Ausgangs-Pfeifenlänge. Die Maßangaben erfol-

---

[4] Op. cit., 329b (danach zitiert) und 121a. Die Texte Nr. 2 und 3 ibid., 148a, 149a.

gen auf dreierlei Art: durch Addition von Streckenteilen (*E habet F et eius octavam [partem]*), durch Proportionsausdrücke − sei es rein lateinische (*id est sesquioctavum*), sei es der griechischen Geometrie entlehnte (*id est epogdoum*) −, schließlich durch musikalische Intervallbezeichnungen (*id est diatessaron*). Stellt man die in der Textpartie genannten Fakten zusammen − am anschaulichsten in einer graphischen Übersicht wie unter Nr. 4 −, so ergibt sich die stufenweise Herleitung der Töne und proportionalen Saiten- (oder Pfeifen-) Längenmaße einer musikalischen Skala, hier freilich durch Tonbuchstaben signiert, die gegenüber den uns vertrauten um eine Terz differieren:

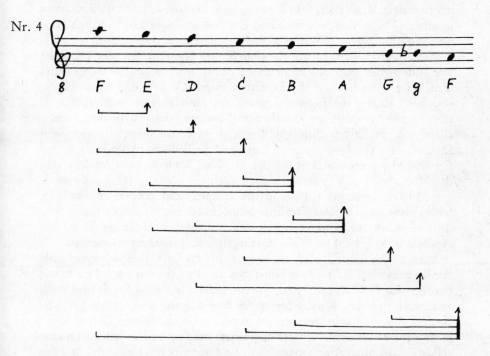

Nr. 4

Diese Skala geht aus von einem Ton *F* mit nicht näher definierter, jedenfalls kürzester Saiten- (oder Pfeifen-) Länge, die zur Gewinnung der Folgestufen proportional verlängert wird. Der Addition von Streckenteilen dienen vier verschiedene Relationen, nämlich *octava* und *tertia pars*, *medium* und *totum*, also die für die Mensurlehre konstitutiven Intervallproportionen der pythagoreischen Tetraktys: 2:1 Oktave, 3:2 Quinte, 4:3 Quarte sowie als Restintervall von Quinte minus Quarte der Ganzton 9:8. Für die Stufen *B*, *A* und (Abschluß-) *F* sind mehrere Herleitungsweisen möglich, die der Text auch nennt (z. B. Stufe *B* als Ganzton von *C*, als Quarte von *E* oder Quinte von *F*); die Resultate dieser Alternativen sind selbstverständlich identisch.

Der Textabschnitt Nr. 1 demonstriert also eine musikalische Skala oder, nimmt man seine Fortsetzung hinzu, das antike Doppeloktavsystem anhand der pythagoreischen Proportionen, verfährt demnach im Prinzip so, wie es aus der Antike und seit der dem Euklid zugeschriebenen Sectio canonis (cap. 19−20) bekannt ist[5], deutet somit in erster Linie auf ein Nachleben antiker Monochordlehre im Mittelalter und zwar in simplifizierter, jedenfalls nicht offenkundig neuer oder origineller Gestalt.

Dieser Eindruck des bloßen Nachlebens einer antiken Tradition in simplifizierter Gestalt läßt sich allerdings schwer vereinbaren mit der relativ großen Zahl von überlieferten Monochordmensurtexten (oder -textversionen) aus dem Mittelalter. Da obsolete, funktionslose Lehrinhalte sich nicht in solcher Dichte der Zeugnisse und Quellen niedergeschlagen haben können, muß ihnen eine durchaus aktuelle Aufgabe zugefallen sein.

Insofern erschien es plausibel, wenn Sigfrid Wantzloeben, der 1911 eine wertvolle Arbeit über das Monochord veröffentlichte[6] und sich darin fürs Mittelalter vor allem auf die Editionen durch Gerbert und E. de Coussemaker[7] stützte, die Eigenbedeutung der mittelalterlichen Monochordlehre in einer verbreiteten praktischen Benutzung des Instruments Monochord sah, das als wichtiges Hilfsmittel im Musikunterricht wie beim Einüben von Gesängen gedient habe und schließlich zu Polychord und Clavichord weiterentwickelt worden sei. Und Wantzloebens Ansicht, daß das Monochord „zu gewissen Zeiten auch die Geltung eines selbständigen Musikinstruments hatte und dementsprechend verwendet wurde"[8], schien nicht nur die mittelalterliche Monochordlehre zu rechtfertigen, sondern überdies von analogen praktischen Aufgaben ähnlicher Texte für *cymbala* (Glöckchen) und *fistulae* (Orgelpfeifen) bestätigt zu werden.

Auch solche Texte finden sich bereits bei Gerbert. Beispielsweise lehrt der Kurztext Nr. 2 dieselben Tonstufen und Proportionen wie Nr. 1, nur bezogen auf Gewichte statt auf Saiten- (oder Pfeifen-) Längen und noch knapper formuliert. Wieder bleibt der Ausgangston unbestimmt (*quanticumque ponderis*), und von ihm aus werden stufenweise zwei Ganztonproportionen, sodann eine Quarte abgeleitet. Fünfter und sechster Ton entstehen − hier ohne Alternativen − als Ganzton der Nachbarstufe, und mit Gewinnung der siebenten Stufe (die in Skizze Nr. 4 der Signatur *G* entspricht) endet die Mensur.

Nimmt man, bei Gerbert eine Seite zuvor, den Text Nr. 3 hinzu, dessen Rubrik *Item* sich auf die vorausgegangene Überschrift *De mensuris Organicarum fistularum* bezieht, so erkennt man nicht nur ein völlig analoges Vorgehen beim Messen der Fistulae, sondern auch einen Fall identi-

[5] Zu dieser Vorgeschichte cf. die in Anm. 14 genannte Schrift, 140−143.
[6] Das Monochord als Instrument und als System, Halle 1911.
[7] Scriptorum de musica medii aevi nova series, 4 Bde, Paris 1864−76.
[8] Op. cit. (Anm. 6), 1.

scher Formulierung von Glocken- und Pfeifenmensur; daß beide hier gleichwohl methodisch differieren (sei es durch korrupte Überlieferung, sei es aufgrund bewußter Umgestaltung), soll in diesem Zusammenhang außer acht bleiben.

Gewiß sind diese drei aus Gerberts Werk vorgelegten Passagen extreme Beispiele für die Kürze, Kargheit und Vordergründigkeit musikalischer Mensurtexte aus dem Mittelalter. Inhaltlich aber geben sie den Kern der Sache vollständig wieder; zugleich machen sie deutlich, wie wenig ansprechend sie auf die Forschung wirken mußten.

Zu diesem Grund für das späte Eindringen der Musikwissenschaft in die Mensurlehre trat die erwähnte primär instrumentengeschichtliche Deutung der Texte. Die Überzeugung, in diesen Traktaten lägen praktische Konstruktionsanweisungen realer Instrumente vor, bildete sich an den Pfeifenmensuren, bestimmte lange Zeit deren Einschätzung und beeinflußte die der Monochord- und Cymbalamensuren. Als folgenschwer erwies sich, daß den Anstoß zur ersten Untersuchung von Mensurae fistularum durch Anselm Schubiger im Jahre 1876[9] ausgerechnet die völlig untypische Quelle Bern (Burgerbibl. B 56) gab, in der tatsächlich — was sonst nahezu nie der Fall ist — Pfeifenmensuren mit einer der höchst seltenen wirklichen Orgelbaubeschreibungen des Mittelalters zusammengestellt sind, nämlich mit den Interpolationen zur Vitruv-Epotome des Cetius Faventinus[10]. Schubigers Auffassung der Pfeifenmensurtexte als „Orgelbautraktate" blieb bis vor 14 Jahren so gut wie unangefochten. Auch das Studium der Mensura fistularum durch den Verf., das zu jener Zeit im Rahmen eines Forschungsauftrages begann, sollte zur Aufhellung des mittelalterlichen Orgelbaus beitragen, wandte sich jedoch bald von der Meinung ab, die Pfeifenmensuren seien für die Orgelbaupraxis bestimmt gewesen. Inzwischen aber hatten Forschungen Joseph Smits van Waesberghes die Kenntnis von Monochord- und Cymbalamensuren beträchtlich erweitert: die Sammeledition der Mensurae cymbalorum von 1951[11] sowie die Text- und Quellenliste der Mensurae monochordi von 1953[12] führten vor Augen, daß beide Traditionen nach Quantität der Zeugnisse, aber auch nach Methoden und Typen des Mensurierens wesentlich reicher überliefert sind, als zuvor ersichtlich war. Für die Pfeifenmensuren nun ergab sich ein ähnliches Bild. Der mittlerweile erschlossene Fundus an Pfeifenmensuren,

---

[9] Zum Orgelbau und Orgelspiel im Mittelalter, in: Musikalische Spicilegien . . ., Berlin 1876, 77–95 (=Publ. älterer praktischer u. theoretischer Musikwerke 5, Jg. 4, Lfg. 2).

[10] Editionen des Traktates in den Vitruv-Ausgaben von V. Rose, Leipzig 1867 (mit H. Müller-Strübing), 285–313, ²Leipzig 1899, 283–304 u. von F. Krohn, Leipzig 1912, 262–283. Zu den Interpolationen cf. die in Anm. 14 genannte Schrift, 252–255, 266–267.

[11] Cymbala (Bells in the Middle Ages), Rom 1951 (= Musicological Studies and Documents 1).

[12] De musico-paedagogico et theoretico Guidone Aretino eiusque vita et moribus, Florenz 1953, 156–185.

der ediert 49 Texte oder Versionen in 179 Einzelaufzeichnungen aus 87 Handschriften umfaßt[13] und seitdem nur noch geringfügig vermehrt werden konnte[14], läßt nun in der Tat zwingende Rückschlüsse auf die Verbreitung und die Bedeutung dieser Lehre, besonders auch auf ihre Position innerhalb der mittelalterlichen Musiktheorie zu und ermöglicht ein differenzierteres Bild von der Genese und der Chronologie des Repertoires.

Zu den Gründen dafür, daß die Mensurlehre so spät erst schärfer erfaßt und der *mensura*-Begriff durch Gurlitt so einseitig temporal verstanden wurde, kommt ein terminologischer Aspekt hinzu. Das Wort *mensura* erscheint, soweit zu erkennen, in der Mensurlehre nie im Gewande eines durch Definition, Erklärung oder Etymologie eingeführten Fachwortes, sondern stets rein vokabular im Sinn von „Maß" oder „Messung". Ein Gegenstück zu den temporalen Mensura-Definitionen Francos und seiner Nachfolger[15] ist trotz der Vielzahl überkommener Mensurtexte unbekannt. Im Repertoire der Pfeifenmensuren, das terminologisch erschlossen vorliegt[16], lassen sich drei Verwendungsnuancen des Wortes *mensura* unterscheiden. Es bezeichnet zuweilen ein beliebiges — freilich präzises — Maß, z.B. das „eines Achtels" (*mensura unius octavi*) oder das des Durchmessers (*mensura diametri*), in der Regel aber das Längenmaß einer bestimmten Pfeife, etwa der „zweiten" innerhalb des Meßverfahrens (*mensura secundae fistulae*). Darüberhinaus aber verstehen die Texte unter *mensura* auch das gesamte Meßverfahren mit allen seinen einzeln erläuterten „Maßnahmen" und, hiermit untrennbar verbunden, dessen Resultat, die so demonstrierte „Maßordnung". Denn es fällt auf, daß in diesem zusammenfassenden Sinn, benutzt vor allem in Überschriften und Incipits, Pluralformen wie im oben erwähnten Titel De mensuris organicarum fistularum höchst selten sind, der Singular hingegen die Regel bildet (z. B. *Tractatulus de mensura fistularum, Antiqua fistularum mensura* u. ä., vgl. auch Text Nr. 1). Nur in diesem Sinn einer umfassenden Maßordnung — als Mensura monochordi, fistularum, cymbalorum — gewinnt das Wort *mensura* in diesen Repertoires eine musiktheoretische Spezialbedeutung, wird es zu einer Art musikalischem Terminus technicus, der in den Quellen des 11. und 12. Jahrhunderts relativ fixiert zu sein scheint, wenngleich auch Titelformulierungen begegnen, die das weithin übliche Wort *mensura* nicht enthalten, doch seinen Sinn beleuchten, indem sie es ersetzen durch *regula* de fistulis, *ordo* fistularum, *ars* ad fistulas organorum metiendas,

---

[13] K.-J. Sachs, Mensura fistularum. Die Mensurierung der Orgelpfeifen im Mittelalter, Teil I: Edition der Texte, Stuttgart 1970.

[14] Vom zuvor genannten Werk Teil II: Studien zur Tradition und Kommentar der Texte, Murrhardt 1980, 372 f.

[15] Z. B. Marchettus von Padua (Gerbert, op. cit. III, 100, 179 a), das Quartum principale (Coussemaker, op. cit. IV, 254 b—255 a) u. Johannes Vetulus de Anagnia (ibid. III, 130 b).

[16] Sachs I (cf. Anm. 13), 150—159.

ratio ad fingendas fistulas[17]. Auch der Sachverhalt dieser terminusartigen Verwendung des Wortes *mensura* offenbarte sich erst angesichts eines systematisch erfaßten und umfangreicheren Textbestandes.

Versucht man nun, im Lichte jener neueren und jüngsten Untersuchungen die Rolle dieser Mensurtexte zu charakterisieren, so ist mit einer Feststellung zu beginnen, die fast selbstverständlich wirkt, doch angesichts der seit Schubiger verbreiteten instrumentenbautechnischen Deutung akzentuiert werden muß:

1. Die Mensurlehre, ausgeprägt in den mittelalterlichen Texten über die *mensura* von Monochord, Pfeifen und Glocken, wurzelt in der boethianischen Redaktion der antiken Musiktheorie, speziell in der pythagoreischen Monochordlehre. Bezogen auf die Mensura monochordi läßt sich diese Feststellung gewiß schon aus Wantzloebens Werk entnehmen; ihre Pointe aber liegt darin, daß die gesamte Mensurlehre als Einheit wie in ihren verschiedenartigen Ausprägungen und Verfahrensweisen auf Boethius basiert.

Unterschiedliches Mensurinstrumentarium begegnet bereits in der Pythagoraslegende, die Boethius[18] nach Nikomachos[19] wiedergibt und bei der das Ausgangsexperiment des Pythagoras bekanntlich an Schmiedehämmern erfolgt. Zielpunkt dieser Legende ist das Dogma einer universalen Gültigkeit und direkten Abbildbarkeit des Zusammenhangs von musikalischem Intervall und zugehörigem pythagoreischen Zahlenverhältnis. Die wiederholt aus Boethius zitierenden Scolica enchiriadis (aus der zweiten Hälfte des 9. Jahrhunderts) behandeln dementsprechend die Mensurlehre stets alternativ und völlig gleich für Saiten (*chordae, fidiculae, nervi*) und Pfeifen (*fistulae*)[20] — ein Verfahren, dem auch Text Nr. 1 folgt.

Ferner gehen methodische Kennzeichen der Mensurlehre unzweifelhaft auf Boethius zurück, so die Herleitung einer Skala durch fortschreitende Teilung der Monochordsaite von beliebiger Ausgangstonhöhe, das Signieren der Tonstufen durch Buchstaben, die Abbildung aller Relationen in einer einzigen Reihe von entsprechend großen ganzen Zahlen, schließlich — wenn auch mehr indirekt — die Möglichkeit, jene Skala als Abwärtsfolge (vom höchsten zum tiefsten Ton) wie (umgekehrt) als Aufwärtsfolge entstehen zu lassen[21].

Der gemeinsame boethianische Ursprung bedingt auch eine gemeinsame Funktion der Mensurlehre: stets haben die Texte zur Aufgabe, die strikte Zahlen- oder Proportionsgebundenheit der musikalischen Intervalle und des aus ihnen gebildeten Tonsystems zu zeigen, somit die Abhängigkeit

---

[17] Sachs II (cf. Anm. 14), 53.
[18] Inst. mus. I, 10—11 (ed. Friedlein, 196—198).
[19] Enchiridion 6, p. 10—13 (ed. Jan, 245—248).
[20] Gerbert, op. cit. I, 195, 204, 205, 209, 211.
[21] Cf. Sachs II, 132—166.

fundamentalster musikalischer Gegebenheiten von einer höheren Ordnung bzw. die Übereinstimmung dieser Ordnung mit jener der Musik
zu erweisen. Dies geschieht, indem die Texte beschreiben, wie sich an den
Mensurinstrumenten – boethianisch ausgedrückt – die Koinzidenz von
sensus (als Gehör-, Gesichts-, Tastsinn) und *ratio* (als Zahlproportion)
demonstrieren lasse – allerdings ist zu ergänzen: vermeintlich.

Denn der Genauigkeitsgrad, mit dem das Beschriebene bei einer Realisierung eintreten kann, ist von Instrument zu Instrument verschieden und
von Zusatzbedingungen abhängig. Beim Monochord gelingt die Abbildung
des Zusammenhangs von Intervall und Proportion weitgehend exakt,
weshalb dieses Gerät zu Recht als Mensurinstrument par excellence gilt.
Bei Pfeifen unterschiedlicher Länge ist jene Koinzidenz nur zu erzielen,
wenn auch alle anderen Maße wie Pfeifenweite, Labium usw. gleichfalls
proportional verändert werden, was aber viele Texte, die ausdrücklich
konstante Weite aller Pfeifen (*aequalis grossitudo omnium*) fordern, gerade
nicht zulassen, so daß hier nur Näherungslösungen möglich sind. Auch
bei Glocken müßten sämtliche Lineardimensionen proportional verändert
werden, so daß die Konstruktion einer Cymbalareihe anhand der Mensurtexte vor besondere Probleme stellt[22]. Angesichts dieser – hier nur skizzierten, physikalisch verwickelten – Sachlage muß man folgern, daß der
Demonstrationszweck der Texte sich oft in der reinen Beschreibung
erschöpfte und nur relativ selten experimentell angegangen wurde; gele-
gentliche Konstruktionsversuche sind freilich aufgrund bestimmter Zusatz-
hinweise unbezweifelbar. Das Problem der Trennung von Theorie und
Empirie in der Mensurlehre gewinnt zentrale Bedeutung durch Ent-
wicklungen, die in den nächsten Feststellungen angesprochen werden.

2. Die Mensurlehre erfuhr seit dem 9. Jahrhundert eine allmähliche
Differenzierung in unterschiedliche Methoden und Typen der Beschreibung (bzw. Realisierung) sowie in die Familien der Mensuren für Monochord, Pfeifen und Glocken. Aus dem 9. und 10. Jahrhundert sind die
Zeugnisse noch recht rar und meist Bestandteil eines umfassenden Musik-
traktats wie der Scolica enchiriadis, Hucbalds De harmonica institutione[23]
und der Epistola de harmonica institutione des Regino von Prüm[24]. Gegen
Ende des 10. Jahrhunderts setzen auch selbständige Mensurtexte ein, deren
Zahl und Überlieferung im 11. Jahrhundert ungemein anwachsen und
deren Vielfalt nun Gruppierungen nach Methoden und Typen – bei Pfeifenmensuren auch eine umrißhafte Chronologie – ermöglicht. In dieser
Phase muß die Mensurlehre ihre höchste Aktualität, Bedeutung und Verbreitung besessen haben. Doch trotz Vielfalt und nun zu verzeichnender
Spuren von Empirie in den Texten blieben deren Grundfunktion und Stel-

---

[22] Ibid., 58–60.
[23] Gerbert, op. cit. I, 103–121.
[24] Ibid., 230–247.

lung innerhalb der Musiklehre gewahrt. Eher vertiefte sich die theoretische Rolle der Mensurlehre, als daß sie sich zugunsten instrumentenbaupraktischer Zwecke wandelte. Hierauf deutet u. a. die folgende Feststellung.

3. Die Mensurfamilien der Monochord-, Pfeifen- und Glockentexte weisen auf einen beabsichtigten Zusammenhang, der sich aus der spätantiken Lehre von der „Divisio instrumentorum" ergibt und dazu benutzt wurde, im Rahmen der Ars musica die schlechthin umfassende Gültigkeit der pythagoreischen Proportionen zu zeigen. Die spätantike Divisio instrumentorum[25] gliedert in die drei Klassen der Saiten-, Blas- und Schlaginstrumente. Boethius und Cassiodor wie ihnen folgende Autoren unterscheiden in Anlehnung an Nikomachos und Porphyrios eine Tonerzeugung durch Spannung oder Berührung (*intentione* oder *tactu*), durch Luftstrom (*spiritu* oder *flatu*) und durch Schlag (*percussione* oder *pulsu*), woraus sich die Klassen der *tensibilia, inflatilia* und *percussionalia* ergeben. Daß sich die Mensurfamilien der Monochord-, Pfeifen- und Glockentexte auf diese traditionelle Dreigliederung des Gesamtinstrumentariums beziehen, zeigt der Eröffnungssatz einer Cymbalamensur[26]:

Omne instrumentum musice, quo communiter utimur, vel fit per tactum ut instrumenta que fiunt per cordas, vel per pulsum ut simbala et huiusmodi, vel per flatum sicut fistule et huiusmodi.

Und eine verbreitete, einflußreiche Pfeifenmensur referiert einleitend die Lehre des Boethius von den *tria genera musicae* (*mundanum, humanum* und *tertium, quod in quibusdam constitutum est instrumentis*)[27] sowie von der Unterteilung des dritten Genus gemäß der Divisio instrumentorum[28]:

Tria genera musicae ab eius studiosis comprehensa esse feruntur, et primum quidem mundanum est, secundum vero humanum, tertium quod in quibusdam constitutum est instrumentis. Hoc vero tertium administratur aut intentione ut nervis aut percussione quadam ut in his, quae in concava quaedam aerea fer⟨i⟩untur atque inde diversi efficiuntur soni, aut spiritu ut ⟨tibiis⟩, organis et in his, quae ad aquam moventur. De administratione intentionis percussionisve non magis dicemus, quoniam de his non est propositum. At vero non est propositum de his instrumentis, quae flatus inspiratione aguntur, pauca tamen secundum scientiae nostrae facultatem scribere conamur.

Da die Familie der Cymbalamensuren erst aus dem 11. Jahrhundert bezeugt ist, also allen Indizien zufolge später einsetzt als die Tradition selbständiger Pfeifenmensuren, scheint der unverkennbare Bezug auf die

---

[25] Cf. E. Hickmann, Musica instrumentalis. Studien zur Klassifikation des Musikinstrumentariums im Mittelalter, Baden-Baden 1971, passim (= Sammlg. musikwissenschaftlicher Abh. 55).

[26] Cf. die in Anm. 11 genannte Edition, 39.

[27] Inst. mus. I, 2 (ed. Friedlein, 187, 189).

[28] Folgendes Zitat nach der wohl ältesten Fassung, ed. Sachs I, 97.

Divisio instrumentorum ein Begleitmoment der erwähnten Phase höchster
Aktualität und Verbreitung der Mensurlehre gewesen zu sein.

4. Der – wie betont wurde – theoretischen Intention der Mensurlehre
stand nicht entgegen, daß in Pfeifenmensuren seit dem späten 10. Jahrhundert auch die physikalisch erklärbare Abweichung zwischen den pythagoreischen Längenverhältnissen und den ihnen zugeordneten Intervallen
berücksichtigt wurde. Offenbar ließ sich, gewiß unter dem Einfluß der
Orgelbaupraxis, jene naive Gleichbehandlung von Saiten und Pfeifen wie in
den Scolica enchiriadis oder in Text Nr. 1 nicht mehr vertreten. Das Verfahren der Mensurtexte, die Proportionen auf eine einzige Maßvariable
eines Tonerzeugers (bei Saiten und Pfeifen: die Länge) anzuwenden und
dem entsprechenden Intervall zuzuordnen, stieß beim tatsächlichen Experiment an Pfeifen zwangsläufig auf die erwähnten Schwierigkeiten, die
bereits Ptolemaios beschrieben hatte, die jedoch Boethius, der auch Ptolemaios benutzte, verschwieg. Denn jene vermeintlich universale und auf
eine Variable beschränkte Darstellbarkeit des Zusammenhangs von Proportion und Intervall, wie sie die Pythagoraslegende suggeriert, ist physikalisch unmöglich. Bei Pfeifen wird das Phänomen der sogenannten Mün-
dungskorrektur wirksam, nämlich einer Differenz zwischen theoretischer
und realer Pfeifenlänge. Doch weder dem Ptolemaios noch den mittelalterlichen Autoren war diese Erkenntnis zugänglich. Für Ptolemaios resul-
tierten alle Abweichungen, die ihm durchaus vertraut waren, aus der
Schwierigkeit, im praktischen Experiment die unkontrollierbaren Fremd-
einflüsse auszuschalten[29]. Die mittelalterlichen Pfeifenmensoren indessen
machten sich die Erfahrung der Orgelbauer zunutze, daß die Tonhöhe auch
von der Pfeifenweite, bei zylindrischen Pfeifen also vom Durchmesser
abhängt, und fanden eine ingeniöse Methode, diesen Zusatzfaktor als
ergänzenden Wert der proportionalen Längenveränderung quasi-pythago-
reisch einzuführen – wohlgemerkt innerhalb einer Mensur, die mit Pfeifen
konstanten Durchmessers rechnet.

Skizze Nr. 5 macht diesen Vorgang deutlich. Die einzelnen Meßakte
einer Mensur (die sich als Auswahl der Möglichkeiten von Nr. 1 = Nr. 4
verstehen läßt) sind hier durch Stufenzahlen schematisch wiedergegeben:
Die Ausgangslänge bei Stufe I ist unbestimmt, beliebig, soll aber – wiederum – den höchsten Skalenton ergeben. Von dieser Länge I aus gewinnt
man den tieferliegenden Ganzton der Proportion 9:8, indem man Länge I
und deren Achtel addiert. Entsprechend schaffen Länge II und deren
Achtel die abermals ganztönig tieferliegende Stufe III. Stufen IV und V
entstehen als Quart- und Quintrelation der Stufe I durch deren jeweilige
Zusatzanteile 1/3 und 1/2. Sinngemäß bilden sich Stufe VI als Ganzton
von V, VII als Quarte von IV, VIII als Oktave von I:

---

[29] Zur gesamten Problematik cf. Sachs II, 65–67, 144–146.

Nr. 5

$$
\begin{aligned}
\mathrm{I} &= \text{beliebig} \\
\mathrm{II} &= \mathrm{I} + \tfrac{1}{8}\,\mathrm{I} + \tfrac{1}{8}\,\mathrm{d} \\
\mathrm{III} &= \mathrm{II} + \tfrac{1}{8}\,\mathrm{II} + \tfrac{1}{8}\,\mathrm{d} \\
\mathrm{IV} &= \mathrm{I} + \tfrac{1}{3}\,\mathrm{I} + \tfrac{1}{3}\,\mathrm{d} \\
\mathrm{V} &= \mathrm{I} + \tfrac{1}{2}\,\mathrm{I} + \tfrac{1}{2}\,\mathrm{d} \\
\mathrm{VI} &= \mathrm{V} + \tfrac{1}{8}\,\mathrm{V} + \tfrac{1}{8}\,\mathrm{d} \\
\mathrm{VII} &= \mathrm{IV} + \tfrac{1}{3}\,\mathrm{IV} + \tfrac{1}{3}\,\mathrm{d} \\
\mathrm{VIII} &= \mathrm{I} + \mathrm{I} + \mathrm{d}
\end{aligned}
$$

Dieses Verfahren der Monochordmessung wird nun in der Pfeifenmensurierung seit dem späten 10. Jahrhundert ergänzt durch völlig analoge Zugabewerte, die dem — für alle Pfeifen gleichen — Durchmesser (= d) entnommen sind, so daß, wie die umrahmte Kolumne der Skizze Nr. 5 zeigt, der Ganzton durch ⅛, die Quarte durch ⅓, die Quinte durch ½ und die Oktave durch 1 als Faktoren für die Zusatzanteile aus Länge und Durchmesser gekennzeichnet sind.

Dieses Pfeifenmensurieren bei Berücksichtigung von Durchmesseranteilen verlieh offenbar der Mensura fistularum besonderes Interesse, weckte die Frage, warum Pfeifen- und Monochordmessung einander nicht völlig entsprächen, und forderte dazu heraus, klarzustellen, daß diese Diskrepanz die universale Geltung der pythagoreischen Proportionen n i c h t prinzipiell beeinträchtige.

Direkte Zeugnisse solcher Diskussionen sind freilich selten, doch gewichtig. Der längste, inhaltlich reichste und für eine Detailinterpretation anspruchsvollste der überkommenen Pfeifenmensurtexte, der übrigens aufgrund etlicher Indizien dem Gerbert von Reims (oder von Aurillac, späterem Papst Silvester II.) zugewiesen werden muß[30], geht von der — wie es heißt — wiederholt und von mehreren gestellten Frage aus, warum die Mensura fistularum der Commensuralitas (dem spezifischen Maßsystem) des Monochords nicht entsprechen könne (*Rogatus a pluribus quam saepe pro captu ingenii demonstrare, quae ratio sit, ut mensura fistularum commensuralitati monochordi nequeat respondere . . .*). Die Antwort erfolgt in einer ausladenden Darstellung des faktischen Mensurenunterschiedes beider anhand von Zahlenreihen, wie sie Boethius verwendete. Eindeutiges, doch unausgesprochenes Ziel dieser Abhandlung aber ist es, die trotz der

---

[30] K.-J. Sachs, Gerbertus cognomento musicus. Zur musikgeschichtlichen Stellung des Gerbert von Reims (nachmaligen Papstes Silvester II.), in: Arch. für Musikwissenschaft 29 (1972), 257–274.

Durchmesserzugaben gewahrte quasi-pythagoreische Regelhaftigkeit der
Mensura fistularum zu zeigen[31].

Auch die ungefähr hundert Jahre jüngere Musica des Aribo, die sich
bereits um eine physikalische Erklärung des Phänomens bemüht, läßt nicht
den geringsten Zweifel an der prinzipiellen Gültigkeit der pythagoreischen
Proportionen für die drei Instrumentenklassen erkennen:

*Arbitror idcirco eodem modo se habere mensuram monochordi cymbalorumque,
quod pulsatio sonum excitat utrimque, tinnitus chordae et cymbali ferit aerem
liberum nullis circumstantiis clausum. Sed distat ab illis mensura fistularum, fortassis
propter aerem in ipsis coarctatum, qui dum se dilatandi libertatem fistulae circumstantiis cohibitus non habeat, quaerit non solum longitudinis, sed etiam grossitudinis
adjectionem. Unde in reperiendo tono non solum prioris fistulae longitudinis, sed
⟨etiam⟩ grossitudinis id est diametri octavam partem assumimus*[32].

Der Passus, dessen Schlußsatz den ersten Meßakt aus Skizze Nr. 5
beschreibt, läßt (im zweimaligen *non solum longitudinis, sed etiam grossitudinis*) erkennen, daß die Identität der Zugabewerte aus Länge und
Durchmesser als wesentliche und gleichsam „pythagoreische" Gesetzmäßigkeit angesehen wird.

Wie sehr die Mensurlehre zur Ars musica, zur Musik-„Theorie",
gehörte und nicht zum Instrumentenbau — der im Rahmen der Artes
mechanicae behandelt wurde und überlieferungsmäßig klar abgesondert
ist —, ergibt sich sowohl aus den umfassenderen Musiktraktaten als auch
aus einigen der isoliert, verstreut aufgezeichneten, vielleicht abgesprengten
Mensurtraktate. In den großen Musiktraktaten wird die Intervall-Lehre,
eines der Fundamente, stets auf die Proportionenlehre bezogen und meist
auch mit einer Mensur, in der Regel für Monochord, verbunden, die das
Tonsystem in seiner zahlhaften Ordnung veranschaulichen soll. Auf dieser
Lehre, zuweilen auch auf einzeln überlieferten Mensuren, bauen sich nicht
selten Erörterungen der Intervall-Species (d. h. der verschiedenen Aus-
füllungsmöglichkeiten von Quart-, Quint- und Oktavräumen) und der
Kirchentonarten auf, so daß die Musik schlechthin, in Traktaten oft repräsentiert durch konkrete (erwähnte oder notierte) Beispiele einstimmiger
Gesänge, als Emanation der zugrunde liegenden zahlhaften Ordnung
erscheint.

Soweit zu erkennen ist, wird diese Ordnung in der Mensurlehre bis Ende
des 10. Jahrhunderts im pythagoreisch-platonischen Sinn als kosmologi-
sches Prinzip aufgefaßt und dargestellt. Eine spezifisch christliche Nuance
gewinnt die in den Mensuren erfaßte Ordnung erst vom 11. Jahrhundert an:
sie wird zum *ordo* der trinitarisch gestalteten Schöpfung Gottes. Bereits

---

[31] Editionen dieses Textes bei Gerbert I, 314a−325b (als Bernelini musica) u. Sachs
I, 59−77; Kommentar bei Sachs II, 171−176, 268−289.

[32] Aribonis de musica, ed. J. Smits van Waesberghe, Rom 1951, 38 (= Corpus scriptorum de musica 2).

die der Divisio intrumentorum entsprechende Dreiheit der Mensurlehre könnte als Triasformel verstanden worden sein, die — wie Josef Rief formulierte — „auf die vestigia trinitatis im Raum des Geschaffenen aufmerksam" macht[33].

Guido von Arezzo freilich verdeckt diese Trias des Instrumentariums, betont aber, daß die Ordnung der Mensurlehre zugleich die Grundlage des Gotteslobes der Kirche sei, wenn er in Versen der Musicae regulae rhythmicae (um 1025) schreibt[34]:

> Nota caute, omnes toni novem fiunt passibus,
> Diatessaron quaternis, sicut supra diximus,
> Diapente semper tribus, Diapason duobus.
> Isto modo monochordum facile est fieri.
> At si cymbala formantur musicorum opere,
> Hae mensurae sunt cavendae maxime in pondere.
> His mensuris comparantur et canora organa,
> Et quaecumque rite fiunt musicorum vascula.
> His mensuris Deo canit tota nunc ecclesia.

Zunächst nennt Guido hier die vier konstitutiven Intervalle und ihre superpartikularen Indizes: Ganzton 9 (Schritte zu 8), Quarte 4 (zu 3), Quinte 3 (zu 2), Oktave 2 (zu 1); sie dienen als Elemente des Monochords, die ebenso bei *cymbala, canora organa* und *musicorum vascula* gültig seien, und zwar bei den Cymbala ausdrücklich „in pondere". Warum Guido außer Monochord, Cymbala und Organa (hier gewiß „die Orgel" als Inbegriff der Fistulae und nicht neutral „Musikinstrument schlechthin"[35]) noch *quaecumque vascula musicorum* („alle möglichen [diskret tonerzeugenden] Gefäße der Musiker") erwähnt, bleibt ebenso offen wie das, was er darunter versteht; Miniaturen bilden gelegentlich Geräte, in der Hand von Musikanten gehalten, ab, die Gabelbecken, Klangplatten und Kastagnetten ähneln, deren Funktion allerdings recht unklar ist[36]. Möglicherweise aber spielt hier in Guidos Text das Bestreben eine Rolle, der Vierzahl konstitutiver Intervalle auch eine Vierzahl von musikalischen Geräten gegenüberzustellen und dadurch zusätzlich eine „Vollständigkeit" beim Erfassen der Erscheinungen zu symbolisieren. Die entscheidende Schlußzeile dieses Abschnitts — mit diesen *mensurae*, nämlich den konstitutiven Intervallen als musikalischer Grundsubstanz, lobsinge nun die ganze Kirche ihrem

---

[33] Der Ordobegriff des jungen Augustinus, Paderborn 1962, 245 (= Abh. zur Moraltheologie 2).

[34] Gerbert II, 27.

[35] Cf. F. Reckow, Artikel Organum (1971), in: Handwörterbuch der musikalischen Terminologie, hg. von H. H. Eggebrecht.

[36] Cf. J. Smits van Waesberghe, Musikerziehung. Lehre und Theorie der Musik im Mittelalter, Leipzig 1969, 156 (= Musikgesch. in Bildern III, 3); neuerdings auch die unten in Anm. 42 genannte Schrift, 42–45.

Gotte — bildet eine Konklusion, der wir in musikalischen Mensurtexten zuvor nicht begegnen.

Trotz der in Guidos Versen erwähnten *vascula* und der Vierzahl der Mensurinstrumente — die sich auch in einem noch zu besprechenden Text findet — tritt die Mensurlehre zur Zeit ihrer dichtesten Tradition, im 11. Jahrhundert, unmißverständlich als Dreiheit der Mensurae monochordi, fistularum und cymbalorum auf. Eine andere, scheinbar vierte Textfamilie, die Mensura organistri — ebenfalls durch Joseph Smits van Waesberghe untersucht[37] —, beansprucht keinen selbständigen Rang: das Organistrum, die Drehleier, ist ein zum mechanischen Streichinstrument umgewandeltes Monochord mit dem Vorzug, jeden Ton beliebig lange, orgelähnlich aushalten zu können, doch mit dem Nachteil, für die Wiedergabe gesanglicher Melodien zu schwerfällig zu sein. Dieses Instrument wie seine Mensuren entstanden erst während der zweiten Hälfte des 11. Jahrhunderts und übten keinen prägenden Einfluß auf die Mensurlehre aus, die in ihrer entscheidenden Phase dreigeteilt war — was zu einer letzten Feststellung führt.

5. Die musikalische Mensurlehre für Saiten, Pfeifen und Glocken deutete nicht nur in ihrer Dreiheit, sondern auch durch die *pondus*-Messung bei den Cymbala auf die Triasformel aus Sap. XI, 21, Gott habe alles nach Maß, Zahl und Gewicht geordnet.

Monochord- und Pfeifenmensuren dokumentieren eine enge und anschauliche Beziehung von *mensura* und *numerus*. Texte wie der erwähnte Traktat des Gerbert von Reims verwenden beide Wörter in eindringlicher Korrespondenz: *ut . . . numeri et mensurae patescant; ut . . . numeri . . . fistularum ostendant mensuras; tam in numeris quam et in mensuris vel monochordi vel fistularum*[38]. Indem nun fast alle Cymbalamensuren[39] die pythagoreischen Proportionen nicht auf bestimmte Längenmaße (mensurae), sondern auf die Wachsgewichte der sogenannten falschen Glocke bezogen (auf die *pondera cerae*), spielte die Mensurlehre für einen mittelalterlichen Traktat-Autor, -Schreiber oder -Leser in wohl unüberhörbarer Weise auf die Triasformel „mensura, numero, pondere" an, „durch die sich der Offenbarungscharakter des Kosmos erschließt"[40]. Da die Tradition der Cymbalamensuren später beginnt als die der Pfeifenmensuren und zuweilen deutlich von dieser abhängt, könnte sie durch das Bestreben ausgelöst worden sein, die Divisio instrumentorum mensurtheoretisch auszuschöpfen. Zu erwägen aber wäre ein noch weitergehender

---

[37] Artikel Organistrum, Symphonia, Drehleier (1972) in: Handwörterbuch der musikalischen Terminologie.

[38] Cf. Sachs I, 60, 69, 72.

[39] Eine Ausnahme liegt vor, wenn die Proportionen auf die Wanddicke (*densitas*) der Glocken angewendet werden, cf. die in Anm. 11 genannte Edition, 39.

[40] E. Hellgardt, Zum Problem symbolbestimmter und formalästhetischer Zahlenkomposition in mittelalterlicher Literatur, München 1973, 201 (= Münchener Texte u. Unters. zur deutschen Literatur des Mittelalters 45).

Gedanke: daß bei Einführung der Cymbalamensuren die *pondus*-Messung gewählt wurde, die instrumentenbautechnisch weder zwingend noch naheliegend ist[41], sondern erhebliche Realisierungsprobleme schafft, könnte rein ideengeschichtlich begründet gewesen sein, nämlich als Aufnahme des letzten Gliedes der biblischen Trias von mensura, numerus, pondus in die Mensurlehre, die zuvor nur *mensura* und *numerus* repräsentierte.

Diese — nicht beweisbare — Möglichkeit wäre jedenfalls weniger überraschend als der tatsächlich unternommene Versuch, den Quadriviumsfächern die Glieder jener Trias thematisch zuzuweisen, dabei die Musica mit dem Begriff *pondus* zu verknüpfen und dies mit der Mensurlehre zu stützen. Solches geschieht in dem jüngst publizierten Text mit dem Incipit Desiderio tuo, fili carissime, den Joseph Smits van Waesberghe edierte, untersuchte und dem Adalboldus von Utrecht zuschrieb (was eine Datierung um 1025 erbrächte)[42]. Dieser Traktat beginnt nach einleitender Epistola mit dem Passus:

Creatrix omnium sapientia creaturas omnes fecit in numero, pondere et mensura. Hoc intelligentes philosophi quattuor artes ordinaverunt: de numeris unam; de ponderibus unam; de mensuris duas. Arithmetica enim docet numerare innumerabilia; geometria et astronomia mensurare immensurabilia. Haec quidem mobilia, illa vero immobilia. Musica vero docet secundum proportionem ponderum comprehendere incomprehensibilia[43].

In dieser Konzeption sind noch Bestandteile der boethianischen Bestimmung der *disciplinae* erkennbar[44]: der Gegensatz *immobilis/mobilis* bei Geometrie und Astronomie, die Umschreibung des boethianischen *ad aliquid* bei der Musica durch *secundum proportionem*. Die Zuordnung von *musica* und *pondus* aber beruht auf Systemzwang, den allerdings der Folgetext zu rechtfertigen versucht. Er geht zunächst auf mensurtheoretische Prinzipien an *chordae, fistulae, cymbala* und — auch hier eine Vierzahl der Instrumente wie die der Quadriviumsfächer — *tabulae* ein und bringt dann eine Mensur völlig singulären Typs, nämlich der Saitenspannungsgewichte (*pondera*) nach dem Vorbild eines angeblichen Experiments aus der Pythagoraslegende, wobei ebenfalls direkte Proportionalität zwischen Intervall und Gewichtsverhältnis behauptet wird, die physikalisch unzutreffend ist. Und diese seltsame *pondus*-Messung an Saiten dient später im Text noch zum Vergleich für den astronomischen *aspectus sextilis*, wird also auf die Musica mundana ausgedehnt. Hier jedenfalls ist eine gewaltsamere Anwendung des Triasbegriffs *pondus* auf die Musik zu konstatieren,

---

[41] Cf. Sachs II, 58—60.

[42] Adalboldi episcopi Ultraiectensis epistola cum tractatu de musica instrumentali humanaque ac mundana, Buren 1981 (= Divitiae musicae artis A. II).

[43] Ibid., 14.

[44] Inst. mus. II, 3 (ed. Friedlein, 228—229).

als sie − der oben angedeuteten Erwägung zufolge − in der Mensura cymbalorum vorläge.

Schließlich begegnen auch eindeutige Anspielungen auf Sap. XI, 21, z. B. wenn Pseudo-Odo (um 1025) im Anschluß an die Monochordlehre äußert, die göttliche Weisheit sei zu preisen, weil sie, wie alles übrige, so auch die *voces hominum* zum Loben nach Zahl und Maß geschaffen habe (*Qua in re divinam sapientiam admirans glorificare poteris, quia sicut omnia reliqua, ita et voces hominum, ut se laudarent in numero et mensura, constituit*[45]). Wie bei Guido wird auch hier die menschliche Stimme in die Gesetzmäßigkeit von Maß und Zahl einbezogen − zweifellos nicht im Blick auf eine gesangstechnisch reine Intonation, sondern als Äußerung des Gesamt- und Idealverständnisses von Musik.

Die skizzierten Befunde deuten darauf hin, daß die unleugbar zentrale Rolle der Mensurlehre innerhalb der Ars musica vom 9. bis 12. Jahrhundert nicht nur mit der Dignität der durch Boethius vermittelten pythagoreischen Proportionen, also einem Erbe der Antike, zusammenhing, sondern, − zumindest seit dem entscheidenden 11. Jahrhundert − auch mit der Überzeugung, diese Proportionen seien Bestandteil des trinitarisch disponierten göttlichen *ordo*.

Es gibt also − um auf Gurlitts Ausgangszitat zurückzukommen − außer und bereits vor der seit Franco entwickelten *mensura temporis* in der mittelalterlichen Musiklehre die intervalltheoretische *mensura* von Monochord, Orgelpfeifen und Glocken. Beide Arten der musikalischen *mensura* aber ergänzen sich und gehören letztlich zusammen, wie es seinen zwingendsten Ausdruck findet in einer Partie aus dem Secundum principale (um 1380), die es der göttlichen Güte zuschreibt, auch die *scientia musicae* nach Gewicht, Zahl und Maß geordnet und dies durch Pythagoras, Boethius und Franco als göttliche Werkzeuge kundgetan zu haben, welche die *certa principia* dieser Ars „fanden":

Antiqua namque instrumenta erant incerta, et multitudo canentium erat caeca, quod nullus hominum differentias vocum ac simphoniae discretionem poterat aliqua argumentatione collegere, nec aliquid certum cognoscere, nisi tantum divina bonitas suo nutu disponeret, qui omnia in pondere, numero et in mensura disposuit. Ita et scientiam istam in ponderibus, in mensuris et in numeris disposuit, et per sua instrumenta nobis patefecit, videlicet per Pictagoram, per Boycium, et per Franconem, qui istius artis certa principia invenerunt[46].

In Anlehnung an die Pythagoraslegende bei Boethius wird hier zunächst die musikalische „Vorzeit" geschildert: das Instrumentarium war „ungenau", die Sängerschar gleichsam „blind", weil niemand die Tonverschie-

---

[45] Gerbert I, 265b−266a.
[46] Coussemaker IV, 206b.

denheiten und die exakten Unterschiede der Konsonanzen durch einen Begründungszusammenhang erfassen und irgendetwas musikalisch „Sicheres" erkennen konnte. Nach dem evidenten Einschnitt (*nisi tantum . . .*) erinnert zwar *suo nutu* noch an Boethius, bei dem Pythagoras *divino nutu* zu jener Schmiede gelangt, doch ist nun die alles nach Maß, Zahl und Gewicht ordnende *divina bonitas* biblischen Verständnisses die schöpferische Instanz auch für die Musik. Pythagoras und Boethius, die eindeutigen Repräsentanten der Mensurlehre, und Franco, der Kronzeuge der Mensuralmusik, „fanden" als göttliche Werkzeuge diesem Text zufolge die *certa principia* der Ars musica — dies kann nur heißen, daß *mensura* im Sinne von Sap. XI, 21 als Prinzip die Tonhöhen wie die Tondauern bestimmt und somit die Musik in ihrer — der Musiklehre seinerzeit zugänglichen — Totalität erfaßt. Musik beruht — nach der Sicht dieses Autors — durch und durch auf *mensura*.

EST MODUS IN REBUS, SUNT CERTI DENIQUE FINES, QUOS ULTRA CITRAQUE NEQUIT CONSISTERE RECTUM (HORAZ, SAT. I, 1, 106)

Einige Bemerkungen[1] zum Symbolcharakter von Maß und Kreis

von GUNTHER G. WOLF (Heidelberg)

I.

Hic est historiarum usus: rerum cognoscere conscientia — dieses Luther-Wort mag auch hier wieder einmal als Leitwort des Erkenntnisinteresses vorangestellt werden: Wenn sich die 23. Kölner Mediävistentagung kürzlich mit dem Thema: *Mensura. Maß, Messen, Maßverhältnisse im Mittelalter* beschäftigte, so ist das vom Blickpunkt obigen Luther-Worts wohl wiederum[2] kein Zufall: Rechte *mâze* — jener mittelalterliche Zentralwert ist gefragt und, indem wir heute an die Grenzen der Machbarkeit und Veränderbarkeit durch Menschen (nicht nur in Ökologie und Begabungstheorie) gekommen scheinen, es wächst das Bedürfnis, frühere Zeiten nach Maß und *mâze* zu befragen[3].

Die verkürzte Mißdeutung[4] des Menschen als Maß aller Dinge, des Menschen, der seinem Leben den Sinn selbst geben kann[5], sein Leben selbst sinnvoll machen kann, schlägt zurück als Pendel zur Frage nach der maßvollen Harmonie, die Gott[6] (oder die Weltvernunft[7] als göttliches Prinzip) den Dingen hineinlegte.

„Es ist ein rechtes Maß in den Dingen, es gibt bestimmte Grenzen, diesseits und jenseits von denen nichts Rechtes bestehen kann." Diese Aussage des Horaz ist im Kontext ethisch gemeint, auf menschliche Verhaltensweise gemünzt. Sie basiert auf der uralten Auffassung, die sich einerseits

---

[1] Diesen Ausführungen liegen Gespräche anläßlich der 23. Kölner Mediävistentagung im September 1982 zugrunde. Die Kürze der bis Redaktionsschluß zur Verfügung stehenden Zeit mag das Skizzenhafte entschuldigen.

[2] Vgl. auch meine Anmerkungen zum 18. (1972) und 20. (1976) Mediävistentag.

[3] Mir scheint, daß das Zeitalter des geradezu irrational vergötterten Rationalismus zu Ende geht. (Vgl. auch „maßlos" als ethische Norm.)

[4] Nicht zu verwechseln mit Vitruvs Lehre oder etwa Augustin, De civitate Dei XXII, 24.

[5] K. Popper, Selbstbefreiung durch das Wissen. (in: Der Sinn der Geschichte. Beck's Schwarze Reihe Bd. 15, 4. Aufl. 1970, 102)

[6] Vgl. Hiob 28, 25 u. 38,5.

[7] Vgl. Heraklit fr. 114.

bei Anaximander und vor allem Heraklit[8] und den Pythagoreern[9], und andererseits im Alten Testament[10] findet, fußend auf noch älteren Traditionen des Erkenntniswertes von Maß und Zahl schon im alten Babylon.

Maß und Zahl sind in Antike und Mittelalter zugleich Seinsprinzip und Erkenntnisprinzip, d. h. Mittel, mit denen der Versuch zur Erkenntnis der göttlichen Schöpfungsharmonie[11] unternommen werden kann. *Est modus in rebus . . .: modus*[12] und *mensura*[13] wohnen den Dingen inne, machen ihre eigentliche Qualität (nicht eben nur Quantität) aus, kraft deren sie so und nicht anders sind, ihren richtigen Stellenwert und Ort im Kosmos[14] haben. Dies ist der tiefere Sinn der Begriffe κόσμος und Ordo, den gerade das Mittelalter als zentralen übernimmt.

Werden *modus/mensura* gestört oder über/unterschritten, so werden die *fines* der göttlichen Ordnung überschritten, ist das rechte Maß gestört und verletzt, die Welt in Unordnung (χάος), sie kann nicht ihrer von Gott gegebenen Bestimmung (rectum) gemäß existieren (nequit consistere).

Das Verlassen oder Verletzen der *goldenen Mitte (aura mediocritas, aequa mens* o. ä.) ist insoweit ein Sakrileg, indem göttliche Ordnung verletzt wird. Eine Fülle von altorientalischen, griechischen, römischen und germanischen Mythen weist darauf hin: immer ist z. B. Hybris-Maßlosigkeit ein Sakrileg, das die göttliche Strafe herausfordert[15], da dieses rechte Maß, die Weltharmonie nicht von Menschen geschaffen, sondern a priori von Gott als Schöpfungsprinzip[16] vorgegeben ist.

Messen als Tun ist daher bis an die Grenzen unserer Neuzeit immer nur der Versuch, vermittels Zahl, Maß, Maßen das (vernünftige) Schöpfungsprinzip zu erkennen und zu enträtseln. Zahlenspekulationen und Zahlenmystik haben von daher ihre Erklärung: Versuche, die Qualität des Seienden durch messen zu erkennen.

Aber dem rechten Maß der Weltharmonie entspricht auch ethisch die Harmonie menschlichen Verhaltens: die goldene Mitte. *Modus* und *men-*

---

[8] fr. 6, 94.

[9] Nach Aristoteles Met. I, 5; II, 5; V, 8; VI, 2; XIII, 1 u. o.

[10] Hiob, l. c.

[11] Vgl. Augustin, de civitate Dei XXII, 24 über den menschlichen Körper als Beispiel; vgl. Anm. 4).

[12] Sehr oft bedeutungsgleich mit *mensura* (vgl. Thesaurus linguae Latinae zu *modus*, Cap. prius: 1252,69—1258,5.

[13] Zur alttestamentlichen angeblichen Wurzel von *mensura*: Lev. 19,35; Hes. 4, 11. 16; 1. Chr. 23, 29; Ez. 4, 11. 16, wo ein Flüssigkeitsmaß gemeint ist. (Vgl. Eucher., instr. 2 p. 159, 7; Hier. in Jes. 3, 6 p. 128 B).

[14] Erstmals scheint λόγος nachweisbar als „rechtes Maßverhältnis" bei Heraklit fr. 6, 94. Für ihn kommt in Maß, Zahl, Harmonie das göttliche Gesetz, das Vernunftprinzip zur Offenbarung. Vgl. auch: Heinz Meyer, Die Zahlenallegorese im Mittelalter (MMS Bd. 25 (1975) und Christel Meier, Gemma spiritalis (MMS Bd. 34/1 – 1977) 498 ff.

[15] Als Beispiel für viele andere: die Hybris der Niobe.

[16] Vgl. Sap. 11, 21: *Omnia in mensura, numero et pondere disposuisti, Domine.*

sura sind zentrale Wertbegriffe. Dies läßt sich auch sprachgeschichtlich nachweisen: aus altindisch *mádhyas* (>* μεθίος) wird vermittels der Wurzel μεθ — sowohl μέσος (τὸ μέσον) wie *medius*, aus dem schon ursprünglich nicht weit entfernten altindischen *mātran* (>* μεθ-τρον) μέτρον, *modus*, *mâze*, *Maß*.

*Mid*gard ist in der germanischen Mythologie der mittlere Bereich, die Welt der Menschen ebenso wie bei den Jainas *Mádhya* loka, die mittlere, dritte Welt der Jagat-triya, in deren kleinstem Teil die Menschen leben. Ich möchte es hier noch offen lassen, welche Wertigkeit in Midgard und Mádhya loka das „*Mittlere*" hat. Der *Mittelweg* hingegen als ethisches Prinzip ist eindeutig und in vielen Kulturen positiv besetzt.

Das uralte, schon um 2300 v. Chr. nachweisbare *TAO* (Weg) ist *Logos, Sinn, Weltgesetz, Vernunft, Gott*; es ist nicht nur Weg des Himmels (Prinzip-Thien TAO), sondern auch rechter Weg des Menschen (ethisches Prinzip-Jên-TAO). Wer „TAO erlangt, TAO hat (tê TAO, yu TAO)" ist ein Heiliger (Schêng Jên)[17].

Die hebräische *tkn-Wurzel* (bemessen)[18] und die aramäische Wurzel *tqn* haben im Niṗʻal die Bedeutung von in *Ordnung* sein.

Bedeutungsnah ist auch die arabische *TRQ-Wurzel* (TaRIQa/TuRQaT), die infolge des (bislang weithin unerforschten) Einflusses des Sufismus auf das Abendland und besonders die Mystik als *rechter Weg (TaRIQa)* große Bedeutung gewann. Der Sufi geht eine *TaRIQa* (Bahn, Lebensregel, Richtung, Strahl, Mittel etc.)[19], oft auch geleitet vom *TaRQ*, dem harmonischen Klang eines Musikinstruments. Dabei läßt der parallele Gebrauch von *TaRQ* und *modus* im Musikbereich aufhorchen.

Von der zentralen Bedeutung der *mâze* im ritterlichen Tugendkatalog (auch nachweislich unter arabisch-sufitischem Einfluß über Spanien, Kreuzzüge etc.) des Mittelalters war schon die Rede. Anstelle vieler Belegstellen eine zentrale: *Aller werdekeit ein füegerinne, daz sît ir zewâre, frouwe Mâze*[20].

Es bleibt also festzuhalten, daß mit den Begriffen *mensura-Maß-modus* im Mittelalter — aber nicht erst seitdem[21], sondern seit ältesten Zeiten — zentrale Begriffe der Metaphysik und der Ethik zur Frage stehen, nicht nur der Physik: nicht der Mensch ist das Maß aller Dinge, sondern Gott. Dieses Maß zu erfassen, zu ermesen[22], heißt für den Menschen, sein eigenes

---

[17] Im Buddhismus wird dies in der „Mittleren Lehre" aufgenommen (vgl. Sannyutta-Nikâya 12, 15). Später bei Nâgârjuna (2. Jhdt. n. Chr.) leicht verändert.

[18] 27 mal im AT; viel häufiger als andre „Maß"-Bezeichnungen.

[19] So Idries Shah, The Sufis (dt. Übers. v. Eggert), Diedrichs 1976, 309.

[20] Walther von der Vogelweide XVI, 1 f.

[21] Verwiesen sei z. B. auf den altindischen Sam (Ausgleich) — a (ewig) — dhi (Erkenntnis/Weisheit) Begriff, der in etwa die „Erleuchtung" kennzeichnet.

[22] Vgl. μεσότης bei Aristoteles.

Maß finden, den rechten Weg gehen[23]. Es ist sein erkenntnisleitendes Interesse des „messens".

II.

Das vollkommenste nulldimensionale geometrische Gebilde ist der *Punkt*; das vollkommenste eindimensionale der *Kreis*; das vollkommenste zweidimensionale die *Kugel*.

Dabei können die Gebilde *Kreis* und *Kugel* als Kurve bzw. Fläche definiert werden, deren je alle Punkte den gleichen Abstand von einem besonderen Punkt, dem *Mittelpunkt* haben. Schon dadurch wird evident, warum für ein theozentrisches Weltbild Punkt, Kreis und Kugel[24] auch symbolisch die vollkommensten[25] Gebilde sein müssen: eben weil sie auf Gott als Mittelpunkt bezogen vorgestellt werden und so zur Erklärung der Weltordnung dienen können.

Ist eine Sache *vollkommen*, so bezeichnet sie der Volksmund auch heute noch als eine *runde* Sache. *Rund* ist das Symbol der Ganzheit und Vollkommenheit[26]. *Circulus mensurat omnia*: Der *Kreis* (κύκλος) und die *Kugel* (σφαῖρα) sind nach C. G. Jung Archetypen der Menschheitsvorstellung[27]. Die vier (oder mit Zwischenfunktionen 8!) Funktionen des Bewußtseins manifestieren sich als vier- (bzw. acht-)geteilter Kreis in religiösen Bildern schon in Felszeichnungen der Megalith-Zeit. Die indisch-tibetanischen Mandalas und besonders die Yantras, die neben dem Kreis auch Quadrat und Dreiecke (meist zwei als männliches und weibliches Symbol) aufweisen, sind beredtes Zeugnis. Zeugnis auch schon für das existenzielle Problem der Verhältnisse der Grundgebilde als Symbole der Ganzheit und der Bewußtseinsfunktionen (auch: vier Himmelsrichtungen, vier Jahreszeiten etc.)[28]. Dabei ist obiter zu bemerken, daß zwei verschränkte Quadrate ein Oktogon, zwei verschränkte Dreiecke meist ein Hexagramm (Davidsstern!) ergeben.

Das *TAO*-Prinzip wurde im alten China als *leerer Kreis*[29] (TAO ○/Wu Ki) dargestellt, geteilt in Hell und Dunkel als TAO ◐ (Thai Ki), durch

---

[23] Vgl. Sir. 30, 33: „Halte Maß in allen Dingen!"

[24] Schon die Pythagoreer nahmen ja die Kreisbewegung der Erde und der Gestirne, später die Kugelgestalt der Erde an. Vgl. auch später in der christlichen Kunst die Pantokrator-Darstellungen mit der Weltkugel und die Bedeutung des Reichsapfels der mittelalterlichen Reichsinsignien.

[25] *Circulus vitiosus* ist daher nicht nur eine logische, sondern auch eine existenzielle Kategorie.

[26] So M. L. von Franz nach: Jaffé, in: C. G. Jung u. a., Der Mensch und seine Symbole (Walter-Verlag Olten 7. Aufl. 1977, 240 ff.).

[27] A. Jaffé, l. c.

[28] Vgl. das existenzielle Problem der Quadratur des Zirkels.

[29] So auch die Bedeutung des altindischen shûnya (= leerer Kreis) Begriffs. Vgl. Pfad zur Erleuchtung. Buddhistische Grundtexte, übers. u. hg. v. H. v. Glasenapp, in: Diederichs Gelbe Reihe 8/1978, 162.

Yin und Yang: Einheit in der Zweiheit, verbunden durch den Lebensodem Khi, Synthese von Satz und Gegensatz in der Ganzheit des *Kreis*-Symbols.

Der *Kreis* mit dem *mundus* (Opfergrube und Welt) als Mittelpunkt ist Grundlage von *Stadt*gründungen[30], wo der conditor urbis in rituellem Kreisumgang[31] um den Mittelpunkt die Stadtgrenzen umschreitet und damit den geheiligten Bezirk[31a] abgrenzt. Dasselbe gilt sinngemäß für den *Tempel*bezirk (τέμενον), den *Gerichts-* und *Kampfplatz*, wo der *Kreis* ebenso magische Schutzfunktion[32] hat wie diese auch in die Phänomene Tafel*runde* und *round* table hineinwirkt[32a].

Der *(runde!) Kreis* ○ ist in der altägyptichen Hieroglypenschrift Piktogramm der *Sonne* und Sinnbild der Endlosigkeit[33] bis hin zur *Seelenwanderung* im Kreislauf der Wiedergeburten (Rad der Wiedergeburten!) (christliches Auferstehungssymbol!).

Der Kreis als *Rad der Wiedergeburt* und *Gesetzes-Rad* (dharma-câkra)[34], als Scheibe wie als Speichenrad findet sich schon auf assyrischen Denkmälern (dort oft mit großen Flügeln), in der indischen Swastika (Hakenkreuz), bei Sonnenkulten in Ägypten und Mittelamerika, bedeutet auf Runenstäben Weihnachten, Wiedergeburt der Sonne, Sonnenwende: *sol invictus* (scil. *victor*)[35].

Der *Heiligenschein*, die „Fortsetzung" des bei Ägyptern, Persern, Juden, Griechen und Römern für göttliche oder heilige Personen üblichen Lichtkreises[36] oder Strahlenkranzes[37] findet seit dem 4. Jahrhundert n. Chr. Einzug in die christliche Kunst als *Glorie* und *Nimbus* (Sonderform: Mandorla), zuerst für die Dreieinigkeit, dann für Maria, die Engel,

---

[30] So Plutarch über die Gründung Roms.

[31] Umkreisen ist eine menschliche Urgebärde mit fast immer rituellem Gehalt. Vgl. auch Buddhas „Umgänge", das Umschreiten der Kaa'ba, Kirch- und Flurumgehungen im Mittelalter und bis heute u. v. a.

[31a] Auch das mystisch-himmlische Jerusalem hat ja diese magische Form.

[32] Vgl. Fausts „Höllenzauber", die mittelalterliche Rechtsfigur des „Umstands". Auch der Ausspruch des Archimedes (gest. 212 v. Chr.) vor seinem Tod: *Noli turbare circulos meos* gewinnt in diesem Zusammenhang an Tiefe und verliert seine „Schrulligkeit".

[32a] Das Wort „einkreisen" hat daher nicht nur eine vordergründig-örtliche Bedeutung, sondern eine hintergründig-magische.

[33] Siehe auch das Symbol der Uräus-Schlange und der Midgard-Schlange.

[34] Vgl. Muṇḍaka Upaniṣhad 2, 26 (câkra-s sprachverwandt mit κύκλος). Zu den Chakras u. a.: H. Johari, Das große Chakra-Buch, 1979, bes. 19 ff. Alle Chakras − mit Ausnahme des untersten (Quadrat)-(sic!) haben als Grundform den Kreis mit je 4, 6, 10, 12, 16, 1000 Lotosblättern, die dem Kreis entspringen.

[35] Dazu die älteren Forschungen vor allem von Usener und passim einschlägig: H. Fichtenau, Arenga, in: MIÖG Ergbd. 18/1957, 35 ff.

[36] Davon die Kränze und Kronen aller Art, bis hin zu den balinesischen Hauskronen (Ziegelkronen), die bekannten europäischen Bügelkronen ähneln.

[37] Vgl. auch das Symbol des sieben (hl. Zahl)-fachen Sonnenkreises, das in der „Zauberflöte" Sarastro als Herrschaftssymbol trägt. Siehe auch die Freiheitsstatue in New York!

Apostel, Heilige[38]. Dabei bleibt als Besonderheit zu erwähnen, daß bei Gottesdarstellungen oft als Symbol seiner Wirksamkeit das Dreieck[39] mit dargestellt wird, während Christusdarstellungen die Kreuz(Rad)-Glorie vorbehalten ist.

Vierspeichiges Rad[40], Kreuzglorie, Radfenster und Rosetten an mittelalterlichen Kirchen — alles das erweist die grundlegende Symbolbedeutung des Kreises.

Für Augustin[41] ist aufgrund von Horaz, Sat. II, 7, 86[41a] der *Kreis das Symbol der Tugend*[42] durch seine *congruentia rationum atque concordantia*.

Der Kreis ist auch das Symbol der Kirche, *praemia mansura quibus iusti merito coronantur in aevo*[42a].

Ist der Kreis Symbol von *Endlosigkeit/Ewigkeit*, so sind es die beiden ineinander verschlungenen Kreise erst recht: Symbol der *Unendlichkeit* in der Mathematik und der (Ewigkeit in der) *Ehe*: die „liegende Acht" (∞). Kein Wunder, daß die „8" zum Symbol der *Auferstehung* wurde, besondere Zahl, bezogen auf Sonntag, Ostern, Pfingsten, Beschneidung und Taufe[43], auch Sinnbild der acht Tugenden[44].

Kein Wunder auch nach alledem, daß eine Fülle von Kultbauten, vor allem auch christliche Kirchen oft *Rund*-Bauten sind. Auch diese Tradition ist alt. Schon in vorbuddhistischer Zeit lassen sich in Indien *mundi*, Erdhügel als Grab- und Opferhügel nachweisen, in Form und Funktion Vorgänger der berühmten halbkugeligen Stupas (mit Umgang[45] zum Umkreisen im Uhrzeigersinn als Zeichen kultischer Verehrung), die später oft geradezu als Symbol Buddhas verstanden wurden. Vorbilder dieser Stupas finden sich auch schon im Zweistromland.

Über die *Rotunda* der Heiligen Grabes-Kirche in Jerusalem[46] werden die *mensuras eiusdem ecclesie et s. sepulcri*[47] vom 5. bis zum 17. Jahrhun-

---

[38] Dabei fällt auf, daß bei orientalischen wie abendländischen Glorien des Mittelalters diese von einem Perlenkranz(?) begrenzt werden.

[39] Die Erforschung und Erkenntnis der Beziehungen zwischen Kreis, Quadrat, Dreieck (Quadratur des Zirkels) ist von daher gesehen sicher nicht nur geometrische Spielerei, sondern ein Versuch, das „Rätsel der Welt" zu lösen. Vgl. Anm. 28.

[40] Das vierspeichige Rad z. B. schon auf syrischen Kirchen des 4. Jahrhunderts.

[41] De quantitate animae, cap. 16.

[41a] Nur der Weise ist wahrhaft frei: *Fortis, et in se ipso totus, teres atque rotundus* (geglättet und rund, so daß nichts haften bleibt, also in sich vollkommen).

[42] Bis hin zum Keuschheitssymbol des Kranzes und des Gürtels.

[42a] MGH SS XV, 1; Migne PL CLXVII c. 590 u. o.

[43] Augustinus, De sermone Domini in monte I, 4. 12.

[44] Candidus, Vita Eigilis MGH SS XV, 1 p. 230/31.

[45] Altindisch: pradaksinā.

[46] Vgl. R. Krautheimer, Introduction to an ‚Iconography of Medieval Architecture', in: Journal of the Warburg and Courtauld Institutes 1942, 1—33.

[47] Vita Meinwerci ep. Patherbr. cap. 209f. (MGH SS XI, 104ff.).

dert überall in Europa kopiert, nicht so sehr exakt als vielmehr typice et figuraliter als Rundkirchen[48]. Das *Oktogon* (s. o.) ist dabei nach Gregor von Nyssa[49] ein *Kreis* mit *acht Ecken*. „It could almost be said that to medieval eyes anything which had more than four sides was approximately a circle" meint Krautheimer[50], auf dessen Ausführungen als grundlegende ich nachdrücklich verweise. Krautheimer leitet die Rundbauweise von Baptisterien und Mausoleen teilweise von römischen Bädern ab, wobei die Rundform der Baptisterien erst nach der Mitte des 4. Jahrhunderts nachweisbar sei und erst im 5. Jahrhundert allgemein wurde.

Zu wenig klar wird dabei, daß mit der allbekannten Übernahme mystischen Gutes aus dem Osten in der christlichen Kirche des 4. und 5. Jahrhunderts (z. B. fallen in diese Zeit ja auch die Anfänge der eigentlichen Heiligenverehrung, der Pantokrator-Darstellungen etc. etc.) sowohl Glorie und Nimbus in die christliche Kunst Eingang fanden wie eben auch Symbol-Bauten, die Kreis und Oktogon in ihrer oben beschriebenen Symbolik aufnahmen: „*8*" ist die Zahl des Heils[51], der Wiedergeburt und Auferstehung, deren Unterpfand im christlichen Glauben ja die Taufe war[52].

Und so schließt sich der Kreis im *circulus mensurat omnia* bis hin zu der weltberühmten Belegstelle, wo Dante die göttliche Vollkommenheit[53] nicht anders als im Gleichnis dreier Kreise darstellen zu können glaubt[54]:

> *Dell' altro lume tre giri*
> *Di tre colori e d'una continenza.*

Es bleibt noch ein Wort zum Sinn und Zweck dieser Ausführungen zu sagen:

Sie können und wollen nicht mehr sein als Anregungen, sich über das Mittelalter und den abendländischen Kulturkreis hinaus mit Begriffen und Symbolen zu beschäftigen, die diese räumlichen und zeitlichen Grenzen[55] ebenfalls transzendieren. Erforschung der und Beschäftigung mit Geschichte

---

[48] Siehe Krautheimer l. c.

[49] Opera VIII, 2.

[50] L. c. 5. 6.

[51] Und des „Einen" (7 + „1"). Vgl. auch die Auffassung vom „ewigen Sabbath" u. a. bei Augustin.

[52] Dazu: Krautheimer, l. c.; passim: R. Staats, Theologie der Reichskrone, in: Monographien zur Gesch. d. Mittelalters hg. von Bosl u. Prinz, Bd. 15/1976, 24 ff., der neben einigem Zutreffenden aber einiges, z. B. die Symbolkraft des Castel del Monte (Oktogonalbau Kaiser Friedrichs II.), völlig verkennt.

[53] Vgl. auch Ps. 84, 12 und Mal. 3, 20.

[54] Paradiso 33, 116 f.

[55] Vgl. Goethe: „Wer sich selbst und andre kennt,
Wird auch hier erkennen:
Orient und Okzident
Sind nicht mehr zu trennen."

können sich heute nicht mehr – unbeschadet aller Kleinarbeit – außerhalb von Menschheitsgeschichte rechtfertigen. D. h. Geschichtswissen-
schaft gewinnt ihre Dignität durch das Erkenntnisinteresse, mehr über uns
als Menschheit zu erfahren.

Zum andern gibt es für Maß und Kreis ein *tertium comparationis*[56]: das
Wissen um die Symbolkraft der „Dinge" als Verweis auf ihre Mitte und
ihren Schöpfer. In einer Zeit des Verlustes von Maß und Mitte, besser:
in einer Zeit, die sich dieses Verlustes schmerzlich bewußt wird, sollen ein
paar Linien historisch-existenzieller Kontinuität angesprochen werden
gleichsam als „Prinzip Hoffnung".

---

[56] Augustinus, De civitate Dei (XXII, 30): „Alle jetzt noch verborgenen harmonischen
Maßverhältnisse . . . werden, ob innerlich oder äußerlich über den ganzen Körper verteilt,
nicht mehr verborgen sein."

NAMENREGISTER

MISCELLANEA MEDIAEVALIA

Veröffentlichungen des Thomas-Instituts der Universität Köln

Universalismus und Partikularismus im Mittelalter

Groß-Oktav. VIII, 320 Seiten, Frontispiz und 2 Bildtafeln.
1968. Ganzleinen DM 96,– (Band 5)

Lex Sacramentum im Mittelalter

Für den Druck besorgt von Rudolf Hoffmann
Groß-Oktav. VIII, 237 Seiten. 1969. Ganzleinen DM 75,– (Band 6)

Methoden in Wissenschaft und Kunst des Mittelalters

Für den Druck besorgt von Rudolf Hoffmann
Groß-Oktav. VIII, 358 Seiten. 1970. Ganzleinen DM 115,– (Band 7)

Der Begriff der repraesentatio im Mittelalter
Stellvertretung, Symbol, Zeichen, Bild

Für den Druck besorgt von Gudrun Vuillemin-Diem
Groß-Oktav. VIII, 390 Seiten, Textabbildungen und 6 Kunstdrucktafeln. 1971.
Ganzleinen DM 141,– (Band 8)

Antiqui und Moderni
Traditionsbewußtsein und Fortschrittsbewußtsein im späten Mittelalter

Für den Druck besorgt von Gudrun Vuillemin-Diem
Groß-Oktav. XVI, 274 Seiten, 2 Abbildungen. 1974. Ganzleinen DM 175,– (Band 9)

Die Auseinandersetzungen an der Pariser Universität im XII. Jahrhundert

Für den Druck besorgt von Gudrun Vuillemin-Diem
Groß-Oktav. VIII, 400 Seiten. 1976. Ganzleinen DM 134,– (Band 10)

Die Mächte des Guten und Bösen
Vorstellungen im XII. und XIII. Jahrhundert über ihr Wirken in der Heilsgeschichte

Für den Druck besorgt von Gudrun Vuillemin-Diem
Groß-Oktav. VIII, 548 Seiten. 1977. Ganzleinen DM 211,– (Band 11)

Preisänderungen vorbehalten

Walter de Gruyter   Berlin · New York

MISCELLANEA MEDIAEVALIA

Veröffentlichungen des Thomas-Instituts der Universität Köln

Soziale Ordnungen im Selbstverständnis des Mittelalters

Herausgegeben von Albert Zimmermann
1. Halbband: Groß-Oktav. X, 335 Seiten, 4 Seiten Tafeln. 1979. Ganzleinen DM 143,−
2. Halbband: Groß-Oktav. VIII, Seiten 337−616, 8 Seiten Tafeln, davon 6 vierfarbig. 1981.
Ganzleinen DM 143,− (Band 12/1−12/2)

Sprache und Erkenntnis im Mittelalter

Akten des VI. Internationalen Kongresses für Mittelalterliche Philosophie
der Société Internationale pour l'étude de la Philosphie Médiévale
29. August bis 3. September 1977 in Bonn

Herausgegeben von Jan P. Beckmann, Ludger Honnefelder, Gabriel Jüssen,
Barbara Münxelhaus, Gangolf Schrimpf, Georg Wieland unter Leitung von Wolfgang Kluxen.
1. Halbband: Groß-Oktav. XVIII, 546 Seiten. 1981. Ganzleinen DM 158,−
2. Halbband: Groß-Oktav. XII, Seiten 547−1112. 1981. Ganzleinen DM 158,−
(Band 13/1−13/2)

Albert der Große
Seine Zeit, sein Werk, seine Wirkung

Herausgegeben von Albert Zimmermann. Für den Druck besorgt von Gudrun Vuillemin-Diem
Groß-Oktav. VIII, 293 Seiten, 8 Tafeln. 1981. Ganzleinen DM 148,− (Band 14)

Studien zur mittelalterlichen Geistesgeschichte und ihre Quellen

Herausgegeben von Albert Zimmermann. Für den Druck besorgt von Gudrun Vuillemin-Diem
Groß-Oktav. VIII, 318 Seiten, 4 Seiten mit Abbildungen.
1982. Ganzleinen DM 158,− (Band 15)

Mensura
Maß, Zahl, Zahlensymbolik im Mittelalter

1. Halbband
Herausgegeben von Albert Zimmermann. Für den Druck besorgt von Gudrun Vuillemin-Diem
Groß-Oktav. XII, 260 Seiten. 1983. Ganzleinen DM 138,− (Band 16/1)

Preisänderungen vorbehalten

Walter de Gruyter Berlin · New York